THE CORPORATE SOCIAL CHALLENGE
Cases and Commentaries

D0107521

The Irwin Series in Management and The
Behavioral Sciences

Consulting Editors
L. L. Cummings and E. Kirby Warren

Advisory Editor
John F. Mee

THE CORPORATE SOCIAL CHALLENGE
Cases and Commentaries

FREDERICK D. STURDIVANT
M. Riklis Professor of Business and Its Environment
The Ohio State University

LARRY M. ROBINSON
Assistant Professor
Georgia State University

HD
60.5
.U5
C688
1981

1981

Revised Edition

Richard D. Irwin, Inc.   Homewood, Illinois   60430

Irwin-Dorsey Limited   Georgetown, Ontario   L7G 4B3

WITHDRAWN

INDIANA UNIVERSITY
SOUTH BEND
SCHURZ LIBRARY

© RICHARD D. IRWIN, INC., 1977 and 1981

All rights reserved. No part of this publication may be
reproduced, stored in a retrieval system, or transmitted,
in any form or by any means, electronic, mechanical,
photocopying, recording, or otherwise, without the prior
written permission of the publisher.

ISBN 0-256-02518-5
Library of Congress Catalog Card No. 80–82449

Printed in the United States of America

1 2 3 4 5 6 7 8 9 0 ML 8 7 6 5 4 3 2 1

*This book is dedicated to the social challenges
we helped create; namely,*

Kaira, Lisha, and Brian

and

Vince, Kristen, Bart, and Nathan

Preface

As was true of its predecessor, this edition of *The Corporate Social Challenge: Cases and Commentaries* was designed to stimulate discussion of some of the most important issues in contemporary society. Business, as one of the most pervasive institutions in the United States, is surrounded by controversies and challenges. If there is to be better understanding of the role of business in society, these controversies and challenges must be the topic of an ongoing dialogue on the college campus as well as beyond.

The organization of the materials in this book is parallel to that of its companion volume, *Business and Society: A Managerial Approach*. The sections contain basically three types of materials. The first type consists of *primary cases* based on original materials provided by the companies as well as access to the individuals involved in the situation described by the case. These cases are written from the vantage point of a *manager* facing an important decision of dealing with some elements of the environment. For maximum effect, therefore; the Mead Corporation (A), Scarbonie, Philips Roxane, Armco, ITT Rayonier, Progressive, and Abbott cases should be discussed from that perspective. Instead of being "outside observers," the participants in these case discussions should identify with the decision maker, analyze his or her company's situation, and recommend a course of action based on that analysis.

The next type of materials consists of *secondary cases* written without the benefit of direct access to internal company data and personnel. Instead, the information was drawn from published sources. While most of these cases may be discussed from a managerial perspective, they also lend themselves to a broader basis for discussion. For example, questions may be raised about the role of government or lower level managers in the fraudulent Equity Funding Corporation, whereas it is unlikely that anyone would want to assume the role of president (unless one wanted to experience, at least vicariously, the sensation of being headed for a federal prison!). In addition to Equity Funding, the J. P. Stevens, American Ship, Farah, GMC Truck and Coach, Three Mile Island, DC-10, Borden, and United Brands cases are based on secondary sources.

Both groups of cases have been thoroughly tested in the classroom and have served as the basis for spirited and thoughtful discussion. We are pleased to have this opportunity to share them with a broader audience.

The third type of materials consists of *commentaries* and *brief articles* on a variety of issues concerning business and its environment. They come from a number of sources and reflect, in some instances, sharply differing points of view. Doubtless some readers will charge ·us with bias in our selection, but in anticipation of that allegation, let us plead that the criteria were provocativeness and relative brevity—to generate dialogue, not to propagandize. There was no attempt to have the commentaries and articles directly parallel the cases in the same section. Indeed, the reader should be warned that "answers" to the cases are not hidden in the subsequent articles. Given the amount of overlap which is bound to exist between such topics, materials from one section may, in fact, be as relevant to subjects contained in another section. Clearly their ordering is less important than their usefulness as discussion vehicles.

A remarkable number of debts are incurred in the process of bringing a book such as this to completion. Perhaps we should first acknowledge the splendid cooperation of the companies involved in the development of the primary cases. Such involvement by a company requires not only time but also a trust in academic integrity and a belief in the value of dialogue. Furthermore, we are heavily indebted to those who conducted research and wrote drafts of the cases. Roy Adler and Claudia Hutchinson deserve particular praise. Others who contributed significantly were Gary Allietta, Rinaldo A. Brusadin, Jerome Cronin, Edith R. Greenwood, Jon A. Moorehead, Robert Peters, Lois Reitzes and Thomas J. Zenisek. Except in two instances, all the cases were prepared under the supervision of the two authors of this volume. We are especially grateful to Robert A. Leone (ITT Rayonier, Inc.) and Michael Lovdal (Mead Corporation) for giving permission for their cases to be used in *The Corporate Social Challenge*.

We also want to acknowledge the assistance of Wilmar F. Bernthal,

University of Colorado and Harvey Nussbaum, Wayne State University for their in-depth review of the book.

Finally, Teresa A. Mobley and Madonna Drees deserve special credit for preparing this manuscript and attending to all the painful details of bringing a book to fruition.

Frederick D. Sturdivant
Larry M. Robinson

Contents

part I

BUSINESS ENVIRONMENT: CHALLENGES TO MANAGEMENT

Business is one of the major institutions in American society. As such it is part of the social, political, and economic structure that defines and helps to shape the nature and character of the nation. No longer shielded by the primacy of property rights and a political philosophy based on laissez-faire, business increasingly finds itself at the vortex of change. Government agencies from the federal to the local level, social activists, concerned consumers, investigative reporters, all play a role in the conduct of business.

Corporate social performance, therefore, has become central to the task of managing a modern business. Management has generally been slow to recognize the centrality of business/society relationships, but external forces have demanded attention. Executives with a broad definition of the role of business in society tend to deal effectively with the demands and expectations of the firm's various stockholders while not sacrificing corporate economic performance.[1]

The period between the late 1960s and early 1980s witnessed rapidly changing expectations in the performance of business and other major institutions. Indeed, public confidence in those institutions declined sharply over that period. As social values changed with respect to the role of women, marriage, corporate accountability, and so forth, the concept of corporate social responsiveness tended to

---

[1] Frederick D. Sturdivant and James L. Ginter, "Corporate Social Responsiveness: Management Attitudes and Economic Performance," *California Management Review*, vol. 19, no. 3 (Spring 1977), pp. 30–39.

supplant the older notion of social responsibility. No longer was simply "not breaking the law" sufficient.

Increasingly, business became a participant in the political arena. Some observers suggested that large corporations, in fact, dominated the political system. Others saw business as but one special interest group contending within a pluralistic process. Whatever the perception of the political power of business, it was clear that the role of the federal government in economic life had expanded dramatically. Federal agencies and regulatory bodies monitored, evaluated, and sometimes controlled management activities.

A less traditional adversary, the media, emerged as a major contender for social influence. Many executives expressed the view that national magazines, newspapers, and especially the television networks were antibusiness. Even those in business who were less suspicious of the press and electronic media often felt that business was not well understood by reporters. Reporting, they felt, too often reflected an ignorance of basic economic facts. Investigative reporters found the traditional private preserves of the corporate world especially alluring during the period of widespread revelations of corporate bribes and payoffs in the wake of Watergate.

The contest between business, the media, government, and other elements of society simply underlines the fact that business is a major institution and is bound to be at the center of social change. The cases and articles in this section provide a rich opportunity to explore a number of these dimensions of business. The J. P. Stevens case has been a major media event and reflects a number of significant social changes within the context of what might appear to be a traditional struggle for collective bargaining. Another secondary case, The American Ship Building Company, concerns an illegal political contribution and its repercussions for the company and the political process. The commentaries in this section raise important questions about government and business as well as the importance of "bigness" and corporate performance.

Case ══════════════════════════════════

J. P. STEVENS & CO., INC.

Whitney J. Stevens walked into the chairman's office of the J. P. Stevens and Company headquarters located in the Stevens Tower. He walked around to the chair behind the desk and sat down. It was January 2, 1980 and he had just become the new company chairman, succeeding James D. Finley. Stevens began working for J. P. Stevens in 1947, as a trainee in one of the Greenville, South Carolina plants. He worked with textile machinery initially and then moved into sales. By 1964 he had been appointed an executive vice president at the New York headquarters and in 1969 was made president when Finley became chairman. The ten years Finley was chairman were the only years in the 166-year history of the company when a Stevens had not headed the firm. Whitney Stevens was now once again moving into an office vacated by Finley.

Stevens swiveled the chair around to the window and looked out at sheets of rain being thrown against the glass by a winter storm and against the few people below, walking down the Avenue of the Americas of New York City. To a degree, thought Stevens, the weather was appropriate since it reflected the conditions surrounding the company lately.

Stevens had inherited, from Finley, a controversial era in the company's labor history. Stevens currently faced a variety of lawsuits dealing with alleged unfair labor practices as a result of the company's resistance to organizational efforts by the Amalgamated Clothing and Textile Workers Union (ACTWU) at its Southern textile mills. The union had chosen Stevens as a test case and the outcome would set the precedent for the existence or continued absence of unions in the industry. As evidence of its determination, the Union had earmarked, beginning in 1976, $1.5 million per year for the next ten years to fight the company.

In addition to labor-management problems, Stevens also had other areas of concern such as rising objections to cotton dust hazards in textile mills, charges of racial discrimination, and charges of intentional mispreparation of tax returns in North Carolina.

Whitney Stevens sat and stared at the rain clouds, reflecting that since 1965 the public perception of his company had changed from one of a quiet textile manufacturer to a company many people currently viewed as a modern-day sweatshop. Stevens put his feet up against the windowsill and thought back through the last 15 years and especially about his former leader, Finley.

CHAIRMAN FINLEY

James D. Finley, chief executive officer of J. P. Stevens from 1969–1979, left his position at the beginning of 1980. Finley had insisted their antiunion stance had not harmed his company in any manner and to the day he left, pursued a strong antiunion line. One acknowledgement he did make of union pressure occurred when he moved the annual meeting from New York to Greenville, South Carolina, in 1978, to avoid the mass demonstrations that had occurred in 1977. Past shareholder meetings witnessed resolutions ranging from investigation of labor policies to demands for accounting of the cost of the company's antiunion stance. All motions to date had been rebuffed by Finley, with the backing of his directors.

A measure of Finley's attitude in directing his company and dealing with its problems may perhaps be best seen in these exchanges with shareholders during the annual meeting. An exchange in 1977:

Finley: This is my meeting, I'm running it.

Shareholder [*politely*]:   By what rules of order do you conduct this meeting, by Robert's Rules of Order?

Finley: No. No rules.

[*Uproar*]

Finley: Now just be quiet and sit down and behave. I can overrule anything. It's the J. P. Stevens rule of order here. That's the way we've been doing it for over 160 years.[1]

In 1978 during a stockholders' meeting, a shareholder told Finley:

The Gallagher President's Report, A Confidential Letter to Chief Executives,

---

[1] Mimi Conway, *Rise Gonna Rise* (Garden City, N.Y.: Anchor Press, 1979), p. 123.

names you, Mr. Finley, as one of the ten worst chief executives for 1977 for "outdated labor practices resulting in contempt of court citation for effort by the National Labor Relations Board to obtain a nationwide injunction against the company, for a union boycott of the company's products."[2]

In 1978, Finley announced he would not be running for reelection to a director seat on Manufacturer Hanover Trust, which held over $1 billion in union deposits. Finley said he would "not go where you're not wanted."[3]

THE COMPANY

J. P. Stevens and Company was a diversified corporation, primarily concentrated in the textile industry in which it was second in sales only to Burlington Industries. In 1978, the company had sales of $1.7 billion and profits of $36 million (see Exhibit 1). Over 44,100 employees worked in the company textile mills located throughout the southeastern states. The majority of plants were located in North and South Carolina.[4]

Stevens textile divisions marketed a wide spectrum of consumer and industrial products. In the apparel area, the firm produced fabrics of wools, cotton and corduroy, and the newer polyester blends. The company was considered to be the industry leader in home furnishings and was currently expanding in this market area. One of the carpet division's lines, Gulistan's Fervor, was recognized as the top-selling item in the industry for the second year in a row in 1978. The company also marketed bedroom fashion lines which included coordinated sheets, bedspreads, comforters, draperies, and dust ruffles. The company's line of designer sheets had been growing in popularity recently. The market for terry cloth products had also been increasing and the Terry, Bath, and Kitchen Products Division were also profitable. Stevens also had an institutional division and a linen supply service which catered to hospitals, motels, and restaurants.

In the industrial products area, Stevens produced items for industries such as synthetics and glass fabrics, which involved specialized lamination and processes, and which were used in air and water pollution control devices. Fiberglass insect screening was recently introduced and was received quite well by home builders. The automotive industry purchased fabrics for headliners, trunk liners, up-

---

[2] Ibid., p. 209.

[3] "A Gathering Momentum against J. P. Stevens," *Business Week* (March 20, 1978), p. 147.

[4] J. P. Stevens Annual Report, 1978, p. 3.

EXHIBIT 1
J. P. Stevens & Co., Inc. and Subsidiary Companies Ten-Year Financial Review

Consolidated Statement of Income for the fiscal year ($ millions)	1978	1977	1976	1975	1974	1973	1972	1971	1970	1969
Net sales	$1,651.4	$1,539.2	$1,421.4	$1,123.0	$1,264.1	$1,114.0	$957.7	$861.1	$892.6	$1,003.0
Less net sales from discontinued operations	—	—	—	—	—	—	10.1	37.9	90.9	96.1
Net sales from continuing operations	1,651.4	1,539.2	1,421.4	1,123.0	1,264.1	1,114.0	947.6	823.2	801.7	906.9
Cost of goods sold	1,472.9	1,369.7	1,250.1	997.6	1,094.1	968.5	848.8	740.5	716.8	791.6
Gross profit on sales	178.5	169.5	171.3	125.4	170.0	145.5	98.8	82.7	84.9	115.3
Selling, general and administrative expenses	93.1	88.8	82.6	71.8	77.9	74.0	61.7	59.9	58.1	58.6
Interest on indebtedness	25.1	19.9	16.9	18.0	19.8	13.2	10.9	10.5	13.3	11.6
Other income	(1.6)	(.7)	(1.9)	(.9)	(1.6)	(.2)	(.3)	(1.8)	(2.1)	(2.0)
	116.6	108.0	97.6	88.9	96.1	87.0	72.3	68.6	69.3	68.2
Income from continuing operations before taxes	61.9	61.5	73.7	36.5	73.9	58.5	26.5	14.1	15.6	47.1
Estimated taxes on income	25.3	26.3	32.6	16.6	34.5	27.7	10.9	7.0	6.6	24.0
Income from continuing operations	36.4	35.2	41.1	19.9	39.4	30.8	15.6	7.1	9.0	23.1
Income (loss) from discontinued operations	—	—	—	—	—	—	(3.0)	(7.7)	(2.7)	3.5
Income (loss) before extraordinary item	36.4	35.2	41.1	19.9	39.4	30.8	12.6	(.6)	6.3	26.6
Extraordinary item	—	—	—	—	—	—	(6.8)	—	—	—
Net income	$ 36.4	$ 35.2	$ 41.1	$ 19.9	$ 39.4	$ 30.8	$ 5.8	$ (.6)	$ 6.3	$ 26.6
Depreciation and amortization charges	$ 44.6	$ 39.5	$ 34.2	$ 32.6	$ 31.8	$ 30.5	$ 29.6	$ 30.9	$ 31.8	$ 31.5
Per Share of Capital Stock ($)										
Income from continuing operations before taxes	$ 4.80	$ 4.78	$ 5.75	$ 2.85	$ 5.77	$ 4.51	$ 1.98	$ 1.04	$ 1.15	$ 3.19
Estimated taxes on income	1.97	2.04	2.54	1.30	2.69	2.13	.82	.52	.48	1.77
Income from continuing operations	2.83	2.74	3.21	1.55	3.08	2.38	1.16	.52	.67	1.72
Income (loss) from discontinued operations	—	—	—	—	—	—	(.22)	(.57)	(.20)	.26
Income (loss) before extraordinary item	2.83	2.74	3.21	1.55	3.08	2.38	.94	(.05)	.47	1.98
Extraordinary item	—	—	—	—	—	—	(.50)	—	—	—
Net income	2.83	2.74	3.21	1.55	3.08	2.38	.44	(.05)	.47	1.98
Net income—fully diluted	2.71	2.61	3.04	1.49	2.92	2.27	.44	(.05)	.47	1.88
Cash dividends	1.09	1.09	1.00	.81¼	1.00	.73¾	.68¼	.88¾	1.09	1.09
Shareowners' equity	37.69	35.96	34.43	32.28	31.54	29.46	27.23	27.32	28.22	28.80

Condensed Consolidated Balance Sheet at the fiscal year end ($ millions)

Cash and marketable securities	$ 13.4	$ 18.5	$ 24.1	$ 17.1	$ 23.1	$ 23.6	$ 28.4	$ 14.7	$ 18.5	$ 15.9
Receivables—net	310.6	281.8	251.1	238.8	246.3	214.4	190.0	173.0	184.3	205.1
Inventories	328.0	311.0	282.5	252.3	251.9	249.2	219.3	218.1	221.1	234.1
Other current assets	5.9	3.6	2.8	1.8	2.6	1.3	4.3	—	—	—
Total current assets	657.9	614.9	560.5	510.0	523.9	488.5	442.0	405.8	423.9	455.1
Total current liabilities	186.5	157.5	165.0	138.6	153.7	169.4	114.7	103.3	99.5	118.8
Working capital	471.4	457.4	395.5	371.4	370.2	319.1	327.3	302.5	324.4	336.3
Fixed assets, at cost	794.2	744.7	703.5	658.2	619.3	583.7	553.9	545.2	525.2	505.9
Accumulated depreciation and amortization	508.5	478.9	453.5	429.5	407.8	386.7	365.2	348.1	330.6	306.9
Net fixed assets	285.7	265.8	250.0	228.7	211.5	197.0	188.7	197.1	194.6	199.0
Other assets and deferred charges	11.5	13.5	14.7	16.8	15.2	14.6	13.6	14.8	8.3	7.8
	768.6	736.7	660.2	616.9	596.9	530.7	529.6	514.4	527.3	543.1
Long-term debt	238.2	244.0	203.4	194.5	187.4	150.0	164.0	143.3	141.9	149.5
Other liabilities and deferred credits	44.0	28.7	14.9	9.3	5.8	3.1	2.2	3.1	4.6	3.8
	282.2	272.7	218.3	203.8	193.2	153.6	166.2	146.4	146.5	153.3
Net assets	$ 486.4	$ 464.0	$ 441.9	$ 413.1	$ 403.7	$ 377.1	$ 363.4	$ 368.0	$ 380.8	$ 389.8
Represented by shareowners' equity:										
Capital stock	$ 90.7	$ 81.2	$ 80.2	$ 79.7	$ 79.7	$ 79.1	$ 87.2	$ 88.6	$ 88.9	$ 89.6
Capital in excess of par value	80.1	73.2	73.3	73.4	73.4	73.4	73.4	73.3	73.2	73.1
Accumulated earnings	315.6	309.6	288.4	260.0	250.6	224.0	202.8	206.1	218.7	227.1
	$ 486.4	$ 464.0	$ 441.9	$ 413.1	$ 403.7	$ 377.1	$ 363.4	$ 368.0	$ 380.8	$ 389.8

holstery, and molded tufted carpeting. The U.S. government had large contracts with J. P. Stevens for uniform materials and other fabrics.

Stevens also had a printing subsidiary group comprised of Foote & Davies, Stevens Graphics, and Mid America Webbpress, which printed a wide range of material including telephone directories, periodicals, direct mail catalogues, and promotional material (see Exhibit 2). While nearly half of Stevens sales were in apparel products, the home furnishings, industrial products, and commercial printing subsidiaries were also important contributors to total sales (see Exhibit 3).

Although the J. P. Stevens Company was well known in the industry, the public, for the most part, was not very familiar with the firm. Stevens did not market its products under its own name, as did Burlington and Farah. Stevens products were distributed under such brand names as J. C. Penney, Utica, and Fruit of the Loom (see Exhibit 4).

LABOR HISTORY OF THE TEXTILE INDUSTRY

In the late 19th century an exodus was begun by textile manufacturers from the Northern states into the Southern region of the United States. The overall reason was lower operating costs due to low level of employment in the South, and later, discouragement of unionization.

The owners of industrial plants found the South's manufacturing environment attractive. The Southern states, ravaged by the Civil War, had to rebuild their industrial base. Heavy equipment had either been turned into useless scrap or had been carried away to the North to pay for "war damages." Southern community leaders, then, were understandably eager to entice heavy industry back into the region to begin a rejuvenation process. Northern manufacturers found the conditions "right," that is, "reasonable" wages and no unions. Thus, a basic and tacit agreement came into being throughout the region which not only discouraged unionization, but encouraged and promoted loyalty to a company that provided jobs. As the 20th century progressed, textile plants, in particular, began to migrate to the rural South. During this period, it was not unusual to see what was referred to as a "company town." In a company town, a manufacturer not only owned the plant, but also the land surrounding it, and all the buildings that comprised the town. The workers rented their homes from the company, were paid in script redeemable at company stores, and sometimes were buried in company owned cemeteries. Even if a plant did not own the real estate, the worker's dependence still existed. Usually, the only work to be had was at the textile mill; if a

EXHIBIT 2
J. P. Stevens Subsidiaries

Stevens has 81 manufacturing plants in the United States. Of this number 35 are located in South Carolina; 26 in North Carolina; 8 in Georgia; 6 in Virginia; and the remaining 6 in Alabama, Connecticut, Massachusetts, Tennessee, and Nebraska. All the plants are owned in fee, with the exception of four plants which are leased.

The principal plants and other materially important physical properties of the company used in manufacturing and/or related operations contain an aggregate of approximately 27,300,000 square feet of floor space. All the plants are well maintained and in good operating condition. The plants, generally, have been operating on a five- to six-day week and on a two- to three-shift basis.

The executive offices and sales headquarters are located in New York City in Stevens Tower, of which Stevens is the principal tenant under a 35-year lease (running from 1970), which may be terminated at the end of 25 years under certain conditions.

Parents and Subsidiaries of Registrant

	Percentage of Voting Securities Owned by Immediate Parent as at October 28, 1978
J. P. Stevens & Co., Inc. (Del.)	
Registrant	Parent
The Black Hawk Corporation (S.C.)	100
Foote & Davies, Inc. (Del.)	100
Foote & Davies Transport Co. (Ga.)	100
Mid-America Webpress, Inc. (Neb.)	100
Inversiones Lerma, S. A. de C.V. (Mexico)	100
Textiles Elasticos United S.A. de C.V. (Mexico)	42.5*
Stevens Beechcraft, Inc. (Del.)	100
Stevens-Bremner (N.Z.) Limited (New Zealand)	50
J. P. Stevens & Co. (Canada), Ltd.	100
J. P. Stevens & Co., Limited (Great Britain)	100
Stevens Elastomeric and Plastic Products Inc. (Del.)	100
Stevens-Genin (France)	100
Stevens Graphics, Inc. (Ga.)	100
Books, Inc. (Ala.)	100
Carolina Ruralist Press, Inc. (N.C.)	100
Florida Printers, Inc. (Fla.)	100
Ruralist Press, Inc. (Ga.)	100
Automated Graphics Unlimited, Inc. (Ga.)	100
Superior Type, Inc. (Ga.)	100
Video Type, Inc. (Ga.)	100
J. P. Stevens International Sales, Inc. (Del.)	100
United Elastic Limited (Canada)	100

In addition to the subsidiaries listed above, there are six inactive subsidiaries having merely nominal capitalization.

* An additional 30 percent of voting securities of this subsidiary is owned by Stevens and 27.5 percent held by a Trustee.

Source: *1978 Annual Report.*

EXHIBIT 3
Total Sales by Product Line (1974-1977)

In years prior to fiscal 1978, the company considered itself, in all material respects, in one line of business. One customer of a subsidiary company accounts for approximately 24 percent of the sales of the commercial printing segment.

The following table shows percentage of total sales for 1977 and prior by product line:

	1977	1976	1975	1974
Apparel..............................	47%	50%	48%	50%
Home furnishings	32	33	34	31
Industrial products	13	13	13	14
Commercial printing	5	2	2	2
Other...............................	3	2	3	3
	100%	100%	100%	100%

Stevens's export sales of products produced in the United States amounted to less than 5 percent of total net sales. In addition, Stevens has modest investments in textile manufacturing plants in Canada, England, and France; and in joint ventures in Mexico and New Zealand.

Source: *1978 Annual Report.*

worker was fired from a plant little recourse remained but to leave the area.

Growth of Unionism

The Industrial Revolution made possible the existence of massive concentrations of economic power wielded by individual owners of industry. After a period of time there came about on the part of the public a growing realization that the lone, individual worker was relatively powerless to exert any influence on his employer to secure equitable working conditions. Thus, as a response to some of the excesses committed by some industrialists against the men, women, and children employed in their plants, public policy, through the legislatures, acted to restore the economic balance of power between the worker and the employer to a more reasonable degree.

Congress enacted a series of labor laws over the years to give workers a degree of economic power to balance that wielded by employers. The intent was to create an "adversarial relationship," constrained by laws to a peaceful bargaining environment, in which dialogue could be conducted. Legislation required that wages, hours, and working conditions be discussed as well as any other topics the two parties could mutually agree upon.

The operative legislation was the National Labor Relations Act (NLRA), also called the Wagner Act, passed in 1935. The Wagner Act guaranteed workers the right to organize, bargain collectively with

EXHIBIT 4
J. P. Stevens Products

J. P. Stevens & Co. is a giant corporation with subsidiaries and associates in Canada, Mexico, France, Belgium, New Zealand and Australia.

J. P. Stevens's subsidiaries in the United States include: Black Hawk Corp. which operates a warehouse in S.C.; Stevens Beechcraft, which services aircraft at the Greenville-Spartanburg, S.C. airport; Southeastern Aviation Inc.; Southeastern Beechcraft, an aircraft distributor; Stevens Grafics Inc., which prints and publishes telephone directories in the southeastern U.S.; Sheffield Industries, a hosiery and leisure slipper manufacturer; J. P. Stevens International Sales Inc.; Control Top Inc.; and Stevens Elastromeric and Plastic Products Inc.

J. P. Stevens markets some of its unfinished products under such names as Wonder-Glass, Astroquartz, Consort, Stevenset, H20, Stevenex, Plus-X, Blen-Tempo, and Allura.

Stevens's finished products are sold as: Stevens Fabrics; Hockanum, Boldenna, Wash Ease, Wool Press, Worumbo, Forstmann, and Andover woolens and worsteds; Appelton flannels and corduroys; Twist Twill, Academy, and Lady Twist Twill cotton work fabrics; Weftamatic, 20 Below, Gesture, Coachman, Lady Consort, Carousel, Stevetex, Windsheer, and Whisper Knit synthetics and blends; Utica, Fine Arts, Beauti-Blend, Mohawk, and Beauticale sheets; Utica, Fine Arts, and Utica/Mohawk blankets; Tastemaker home furnishings, like towels, sheets, and blankets; Simtex tablecloths and table sets; Gulistan, Tastemaker, Contender, and Merryweather carpets; Finesse, Spirit, Fruit of the Loom, Hip-lets, and Big Mama women's hosiery; J. P. Stevens draperies; Kyron interfacings for apparel; and Always in Step women's slippers.

In addition, Stevens manufactures glass fabric insect screening; fabrics for air pollution control; glass fabric for marine insulation and fishing rods; nonwoven backings for handbags, shoes, synthetic leather upholstery, and luggage; synthetic fabrics for soil erosion and flood control; and pharmaceutical stoppers for the health care industry.

Source: J. G. DiNunno, "J. P. Stevens: Anatomy of an Outlaw," *American Federalist*, April 1976, p. 3.

their employers, and if necessary, engage in concerted activity for the purpose of collective bargaining objectives. Section 8 of the NLRA set forth guidelines for unionizing activity and listed prohibited actions, called unfair labor practices, on the part of both union and employer. The employer, for example, could not interfere with, restrain, or coerce employees from joining or leaving a union, or interfere with the formation or administration of a union. Employers were not permitted to discriminate against employees in hiring or firing to encourage or discourage union membership. When deciding whether to accept representation by a union, employees voted in an election administered under very strict conditions by the National Labor Relations Board (NLRB) created by the Act. The employees determined if they wished to be represented by that union when dealing with management. A simple majority vote decided, with votes counted immediately after polls were closed. If a union was defeated, it had to wait one calendar year before another attempt.

Section 8 of the NLRA also contained practices that were prohibited in the period before an election. The courts developed a particular philosophy when deciding violations in this area. If an outright violation of a rule could not be clearly proven, then subjective mental intent might be found to have a psychologically "chilling effect" upon an employee so as to interfere with his or her exercise of free choice and hence destroy the desired "laboratory conditions" of a free election environment. For example, an employer might say to employees at a mass meeting: "Plant X went union last week and shut down. I'm going to be forced to do the same thing if you vote yes tomorrow for the union. Then you will all be out of a job and starving. It's your choice." Such a statement would constitute an unfair labor practice.

THE ISSUE WITH J. P. STEVENS

J. P. Stevens was founded in 1813 in Andover, Massachusetts as a textile manufacturing plant. The company decided shortly after World War II that the South looked more inviting and began to move plants into the Southeast, particularly the Carolinas. The company concentrated most of its plants in these two states which happened to be the least unionized states. In the mid-1970s, North Carolina had 6.8 percent and South Carolina had 8 percent union members in the working population.[5]

In the early 1960s, organized labor decided the last bastion of nonunion companies should fall. This objective arose both from a need to increase membership and from pressure from the unions of the North to bring the Southern workers into the fold, thereby equalizing wage rates and slowing the loss of industries to the South. Burlington Industries, at the time, had a strong reputation as a dedicated antiunion company; Stevens, with a more moderate union posture, was judged to be a better target by union leaders.[6]

The battle between unions and Stevens was joined in 1965 during the first unionizing attempt when a NLRB investigator found Stevens guilty at 21 plants of wholesale violations of the National Labor Relations Act. Since 1965, Stevens was found guilty in 15 separate cases, 8 of which were upheld in federal appeals courts. Three of those cases went to the Supreme Court which rendered decisions against the company in each case. In other instances, the Supreme Court refused

---

[5] "Boycott the Bossman," *Industry Week*, April 30, 1977, p. 99.

[6] "The Battle Heats Up at J. P. Stevens," *Industry Week*, February 28, 1977, p. 104.

to hear Stevens appeals because of lack of merit, thereby affirming appeals courts rulings.[7]

In the period from 1967 through 1979, J. P. Stevens was convicted of numerous violations of Section 8. In many cases, the NLRB returned to federal court to seek contempt judgment after Stevens failed to comply with federal court orders. One appeals court in New York said it could not "view with equanimity the refusal of a large employer to abide by the law of the land and refrain from interfering with the rights of its employees."[8] Another appeals court threatened to jail Stevens officials for refusing to comply with court orders.

In one landmark case making judicial history in labor law, Stevens was found to have engaged in a continuous campaign of vigorous and pervasively illegal resistance marked by threats and actual discharge of employees, plant closings in response to union activism, discharge of employees for testifying before the NLRB, coercive interrogation, surveillance of union members and meetings, restrictions of solicitation by union members, and use of company bulletin boards to post the name of union supporters. J. P. Stevens was found by a federal appeals court to have "so grossly exceeded" the standards of the labor act that "unusual" remedies were required. Normally, a violator was required to post a notice that, in essence, says, "I violated Section 8(a), and I will not do it again." Stevens was required to: (1) post the notice in all plants in North and South Carolina; (2) mail the notice to all employees at home so they could read it in a nonhostile atmosphere so as to more appreciate the impact; (3) convene the employees on company time and have a company officer read it to them (later modified to permit reading by a NLRB official so as not to "unduly humiliate the company"); and (4) give the union access to company premises for one year and use of company bulletin boards where notices are usually posted. Combinations of this ruling were applied not just once, but three times. The fifth Circuit Court of Appeals stated that "never has there been such an example of such classic, albeit crude, unlawful labor practices."[9]

In another case, Stevens was found guilty of wiretapping a union motel room where leaders of a unionization effort were meeting. The company made an out of court settlement for $50,000 prior to trial. A later case dealt with an instance where the company arbitrarily lowered the prevailing wage scale after a pro-union vote.[10]

---

[7] J. G. DiNunno, "J. P. Stevens: Anatomy of an Outlaw," *American Federalist*, April 1976, p. 1.

[8] Ibid., p. 6.

[9] Archibald Cox, *Labor Laws: Cases and Materials.* (Mineola, N.Y.: Foundation Press, Inc., 1977), p. 271.

[10] Ibid., pp. 2 and 6.

Between 1965 and 1976, the company had been required to pay over $1.3 million to 289 workers who were illegally fired by the Stevens company for union activity. Boyd Leedon, a former NLRB chairman, described Stevens as "so out of tune with a humane civilized approach to industrial relations that it should shock even those least sensitive to honor, justice, and decent treatment."[11]

On August 28, 1974, seven Stevens plants in Roanoke Rapids, North Carolina, voted for representation by the Textile Workers Union of America (TWUA). By law, J. P. Stevens was then required to bargain collectively with the union. By the end of 1979, no contract had been signed and a federal appeals court had found five separate counts of "bad faith bargaining" against Stevens, and in one case, directed Stevens to reimburse the union for all past expenses.

OTHER ISSUES

J. P. Stevens's controversies were not limited to the labor relations area. A number of other accusations had been leveled at the company from various sources. In nonunion matters, Stevens entered a plea of "no contest" to government charges in 1973 that it and several other fiberglass manufacturers conspired through secret meetings to fix prices on government contract bids. Stevens paid $260,000 in damages and consented to an injunction prohibiting future practices.[12]

In 1975, a North Carolina tax official charged Stevens had not reported $75 million of taxable inventory in 22 plants going back to 1966. A secret agreement was discovered, going back to 1951, to induce Stevens to locate in certain counties which would allow it to undervalue inventories "in perpetuity." Stevens denied any wrongdoing but began to make some back payments.

Stevens was convicted in several racial discrimination suits. Statistics in one suit indicated over a six-year period salaries for whites averaged about $670 per year more than for blacks. A judge found that there was no evidence that could explain differences due to education, previous experience or length of employment, or other factors.

A procompany organization called J. P. Stevens Employees Education Committee (JPSEEC) opposed union activities. During congressional Labor Management Relations Committee field hearings at Roanoke Rapids on August 9, 1977, a lawyer representing JPSEEC testified. The lawyer was Robert Valois, whose firm had recently successfully blocked a union organizing attempt at another company.

---

[11] Ibid., p. 1.
[12] Ibid., p. 6.

During testimony and questioning, Mr. Valois could not supply any figures relating to a budget, annual costs, how much his firm was paid or who paid them, and where the majority of funds for the JPSEEC committee actually came from.[13]

The committee funds were, however, sufficient to send company employees to the New York headquarters to mount a counter demonstration against the union activists at the 1977 shareholders meeting. The president of the North Carolina AFL-CIO, Wilber Hobby, stated during testimony that one of Mr. Valois's associates used Sen. Jesse Helms's Senate stationery to mail literature for an organization called Americans United Against Control of the Government. It was stated the literature contained a poll "so biased, even I have to answer with a 'yes' because I wouldn't want what he threatened to happen to this company."[14]

The J. P. Stevens Annual Report of 1978 stated that employees were "maintaining their position as among the best paid in the industry. Stevens's hourly paid textile workers earned an average of $4.77 an hour . . . 7.3 percent more than . . . industry averages . . . which was . . . $4.37. Weekly earnings were $204.02 compared to $177.42."[15]

During the company's 1978 annual meeting, an employee responded to such statements, addressing chairman of the board Finley in regard to wages:

> We're off every other weekend. We do fifty-six hours labor for about forty-two hours pay. We work twelve-hour shifts.[16]

Some employees stated that three to five supervisors per plant received very high hourly rates, hence the average figure. According to a survey by University of North Carolina, workers in the state averaged $21 less in wages per week than those engaged in similar jobs in other states, while profits in many North Carolina businesses were higher than in other similar industries in other states. The study concluded that North Carolina ranked last in the nation in hourly industrial wages. New industries paid "prevailing wage rates" instead of the higher out-of-state wages. According to the Textile Workers Union of America, Southern textile workers earned $1.42 per hour less than the average rate of all manufacturing workers.[17]

The textile mill employees received one week of vacation per year

---

[13] Conway, *Rise Gonna Rise*, p. 154.

[14] Ibid., p. 155.

[15] *1978 Annual Report*, p. 11.

[16] Conway, *Rise Gonna Rise*, p. 209.

[17] DiNunno, "J. P. Stevens: Anatomy," pp. 3, 6.

although company policy stated that after five years service workers were entitled to two weeks holiday pay. Employees indicated that the operative word was "entitled" and in reality was ignored. Further, if an employee insisted on the clause he or she would be eventually discharged for various reasons. In a related area, workers often returned from sick leave to find their job taken and no work available, or were given a less desirable job than their former one.[18]

WORKING CONDITIONS

Another area of contention concerned worker health programs. Cotton mill workers suffer from brown lung disease (byssinosis), a respiratory condition similar to black lung in coal miners. The lungs gradually lose their oxygen processing capacity through ingestion of airborne dust which coats the lung walls; the condition can be terminal. One worker had a 40 percent reduction in breathing ability and was discharged by J. P. Stevens for failure to carry out assigned duties. Occupational Safety and Health Administration (OSHA) standards limited dust per cubic meter of air to 1.0 milligram or less in cotton mills. However, studies in textile plants found as much as 2.96 milligrams per cubic meter. It was not uncommon for cotton to pile up to six inches deep on floors with dust so thick in rooms as to create a virtual fog. Stevens, since 1974, had spent over $4.2 million complying with OSHA standards, but stated in the 1978 annual report: "There is a question as to whether the technology exists" to meet the requirements.[19] At the same time, the North Carolina Public Interest Research Group reported a Gaston, North Carolina plant operating with levels of 0.1 to 0.2 milligrams of dust using modern equipment.

Perhaps chairman Finley best summed up his attitude in a statement at the 1976 shareholder meeting: "Byssinosis (brown lung) is something alleged to come from cotton dust. It is a word that's been coined, but has no meaning."[20]

At OSHA hearings, J. Davitt McAteir, an attorney with a public interest law firm, who had investigated black lung in coal miners, reviewed and compared cotton and coal dust standards and then made some direct parallel observations. He stated the procedure proposed by OSHA placing the responsibility

> for monitoring and notifying employees regarding noncompliance in the hands of the employer is the classic case of placing the fox in charge

---

[18] Conway, *Rise Gonna Rise*, p. 39.
[19] *1978 Annual Report*, p. 12.
[20] Conway, *Rise Gonna Rise*, p. 136.

of security at the henhouse. Unless the monitoring program is conducted . . . by the United States . . . the possibility that fraudulent
data will be forthcoming is very real. The hiring of company doctors to
conduct a medical examination is a practice considered even by the coal
industry as Neanderthal. [21]

In June 1976, the unions declared a national boycott of J. P. Stevens
on a scale greater than that ever undertaken by the American labor
movement. The AFL-CIO declared "complete, total, all-out support"
for the effort including financial support. Finley referred to the
boycott as "our cause, our crusade" and stated that the union was
attempting to destroy "management rights."[22] A company spokesman stated that the boycott is "an improper use of the combined
power of many unions."[23]

The union replied the "purpose of the boycott is not to hurt the
workers, but get the company to change its position. It was the company that created the conditions of the boycott by making it impossible for us to get fair elections in the first place."[24] The American
Council of Textile Workers (ACTW) president stated: "Stevens has
got to create an atmosphere in all its plants that if a worker wants a
union, he can join it without any pain or fear. Basically, they've got to
obey the law."[25]

Through 1979, it was difficult to establish how effective the boycott
had been, since J. P. Stevens did not market under its own name. In
addition, only 34 percent of its revenue was derived from consumer
products. At the March 7, 1978, shareholders meeting, Bob Hall,
editor of *Southern Exposure* magazine requested a special report on the
impact of labor management policies on company stock. Hall's statement was printed in the Stevens proxy statement:

> Much evidence indicates that Stevens's stock performance may be af-
> fected by its policies toward labor unions. For example, on August 31,
> 1977, the Second Circuit Court of Appeals opened the way for the
> company to receive stiff fines if it continues violating the labor man-
> agement laws and the Court's orders. The following week, Stevens
> stock fell from 16⅞ to 5⅞ while other textile stocks remained relatively
> unchanged.

In fact, by October 19, J. P. Stevens's stock price was 13 percent

---

[21] Ibid., pp. 66–67.

[22] "The All-Out Campaign against J. P. Stevens," *Business Week*, June 14, 1976,
p. 28.

[23] "A Boycott Battle to Win the South," *Business Week*, December 6, 1976, p. 80.

[24] Ibid.

[25] "A Gathering Momentum," p. 148.

below its low price for 1976. Stevens's stock had performed worse than any other of the leading textile companies. At least one investment consultant attributed the poor performance to Stevens's labor-management problems.[26]

At the meeting, Finley noted first quarter sales in 1978 were $350.3 million up from $334.3 generated in 1977. Profits, however, declined from $7.7 million to $7.1 million. Finley attributed the drop to rising costs and increases in foreign imports.[27]

In 1979, under the leadership of Raymond Rogers, head of ACTW's "corporate campaign," the union used financial pressure to force two directors to resign from Stevens board.

In its boycott efforts, ACTW received endorsement from three Protestant denominations and the National Council of Churches passed out 40,000 preaddressed postcards to mail to Avon and Manufacturers Hanover who were represented on Stevens's board. Other unions indicated they would move over $1 billion in pension funds from Manufacturers Hanover to another bank. As a result of these pressures, the directors of Avon, Manufacturers Hanover, and New York Life resigned from the Stevens board. In the case of New York Life, Rogers organized a slate of candidates to run against the New York Life directors. Under New York law the company would have had to mail out ballots to 6.3 million policyholders and incur the resulting expense. The New York Life director chose instead to quit the Stevens board. Roger's basic intent was to "isolate J. P. Stevens from the mainstream of American business."

Whitney Stevens finished his mental review of recent history and wondered if his great-great grandfather, Captain Nathaniel, the founder of the company, could have even remotely imagined anything like the present size and conditions of the firm. He then recalled something he had told an interviewer from *Fortune* last October when discussing his impending change in duties. Stevens had said his appointment did not really signal a major change in company position and that everyone had become rather "thick-skinned." "The real issue is what do our people in our plants want" he had said. "Our ultimate objection is to the forcing of people into joining a union. Naturally, we'd rather not have a union. We think it is not necessary, not desirable, and certainly not in our employees' interest. This union business is unpleasant and enervating."[28]

However, Stevens mused to himself, that was back in Finley's

---

[26] Conway, *Rise Gonna Rise*, p. 209.

[27] "A Gathering Momentum," p. 147.

[28] "I Couldn't Be Ignored," *Fortune*, October 22, 1979, p. 23.

period. One of the hallmarks of a good leader and manager is to look at all the alternatives open to him, not just those that are personally preferable. He fully intended to act as chairman in the best interests of the shareholders of his company. It was no longer what would Finley do?, but what will Stevens do? It was now time to develop his own perspective on the issues which confronted his company.

Case

THE AMERICAN SHIP BUILDING COMPANY

On August 30, 1974, George M. Steinbrenner, chairman and chief executive officer of The American Ship Building Company, was fined $10,000 by Judge Leroy J. Contie in the Cleveland (Ohio) Federal District Court on felonious charges of illegally contributing to the election campaigns of former President Richard M. Nixon and several members of Congress. In addition, Steinbrenner was fined $5,000 for violation of federal campaign laws, involving participation (in an accessory capacity) after the fact of the violation. The court's actions were taken a week following guilty pleas by American Ship and Steinbrenner to the charges. The company was fined $20,000 for its role in the violations. Although this was the eighth firm and related officer to confess to federal election violations, it was the first case in which Watergate investigators had filed felonious charges.

THE AMERICAN SHIP BUILDING COMPANY

American Ship Building Company was incorporated in 1899; its main lines of business were construction, conversion, and repair of ships; construction of barges; and the supplying of building materials. Divisions of the company included the following: (1) Amship Division: ship building and repair; (2) Tampa Division: ship repair; (3) Nabrico Division: bridge and towboat construction; (4) Building Products Division: metal fabricating and building materials; and (5) Transportation, Cargo, and Material Handling Division.

American Ship was one of the nation's leading independent ship repair, conversion, and construction firms. Historically, the firm had been quite active and successful in the Great Lakes region and had expanded aggressively into the Gulf Coast area through its Tampa Division. In the fall of 1974, discussions were initiated with the Netherlands Antilles island of Curaçao in an attempt to broaden the company's market via joint ventures. By serving governmental agencies as well as the private sector, American Ship played an important role in the delivery of many power-related materials, such as oil and iron ore, to U.S. ports of entry and inland waterways.

Annual sales for the firm had increased from $38 million in 1969 to $95 million in 1973; net income also increased during this period from $1.5 million in 1969 to $4.2 million in 1972—fiscal 1973 net income dropped to $2.3 million, due partly to unrecovered excess costs incurred on a government contract. Part of the firm's success during the 1970s came about as a result of the creation of its Tampa and Nabrico Divisions in 1972 and 1969, respectively. Although revenues generated from federal government contracts did not represent a significant percentage of American Ship's annual totals, a working relationship had been established with federal agencies. One government contract had been initiated in 1965 and another in 1966; both projects, which involved the construction of ships for several agencies, were completed in 1970. In 1974, a project was undertaken with the U.S. Corps of Engineers; the contract called for the repair of government "dredge vessels."[1]

GEORGE M. STEINBRENNER III

Mr. Steinbrenner, despite his relatively young age of 43, had become a significant figure in the shipping industry. After a short career in college football coaching at Northwestern and Purdue universities, Steinbrenner returned to his family's shipping firm, Kinsman Marine Transit Company. In 1968, while serving as Kinsman's president, he became part of a group organized by Roulston and Co., a Cleveland brokerage house, that bought a large block of American Ship Building stock. To avoid a proxy fight within the company, American Ship officials appointed George Steinbrenner chief executive officer. That same year the family's business also became part of American Ship.

Although Mr. Steinbrenner maintained a hectic schedule as top man in the American Ship organization, he was quite active in community affairs. He became involved with the Cleveland Urban Coalition and served as vice chairman of the Greater Cleveland Growth Corporation. In 1968, the Cleveland Press Club named Steinbrenner "Man of the Year" for his civic and philanthropic efforts. Many un-

---

[1] This is a vessel used for scraping the bottom surface of bodies of water.

derprivileged youngsters in the Cleveland area were able to attend college as a result of Mr. Steinbrenner's donation of personal funds. In 1974, he gave $10,000 for the benefit of out-of-work reporters and editors who were on strike against two daily newspapers; the only requirement attached to the funds was that each individual would participate in a lecture series on journalism.

Sports had always been a part of George Steinbrenner's life. He participated in several sports during his high school and college years. After leaving coaching for a career in business, Steinbrenner became involved in several investments in sporting organizations. He took an interest in a local industrial league basketball team, the Cleveland Pipers, that later joined a professional league; through a partnership he bought the team for an undisclosed amount of cash. The team eventually filed bankruptcy with liabilities totalling $125,000. Although Mr. Steinbrenner was not legally obligated for the organization's liabilities, he worked for three years to pay off creditors and investors. In 1972, Steinbrenner joined a group that bought the National Basketball Association's Chicago Bulls, and in 1973 he became major owner and chief executive officer of the New York Yankees.[2] With the Yankees, he often attended important games and other team activities where he entertained prominent guests.[3] Other financial interests in sports included horse racing and breeding; to enhance this interest Mr. Steinbrenner bought 800 acres of land near Ocala, Florida, and built a thoroughbred farm, the Kinsman Stud Farm.

The large financial interests and civic activities also enabled George Steinbrenner to involve himself with many political figures, particularly members of the Democratic Party. In 1969 and 1970, he organized the Democratic Congressional Dinner and was able to raise $803,000 and over $1 million, respectively, for these two events.

Steinbrenner originally became involved with politicians and government representatives in 1968 when he became an executive of American Ship Building. "From the start I knew the secret for American Ship was to get the Great Lakes included in the maritime act—to get the Great Lakes in there so they could get their share of assistance . . . I saw that the whole Great Lakes fleet had to be rebuilt, and the only way this could be done was with help."[4] Coincidentally, Congress had begun considering the amendment of the Merchant

---

[2] In January 1973, a group of businessmen headed by Mr. Steinbrenner purchased the Yankees from the Columbia Broadcasting Company for $10 million.

[3] For the Yankees opening game of the 1974 season, Steinbrenner's guests were Sen. Edward Kennedy (D., Massachusetts) and his son Edward, Jr.

[4] *The Wall Street Journal*, June 25, 1975, p. 16.

Marine Act of 1936 in the same year that Steinbrenner joined American Ship. He then began a three-pronged effort, meeting with politicians and industry officials and lobbying on Capitol Hill. When the act was finally amended, the construction of Great Lakes vessels qualified for tax benefits.

Despite all of his contacts among politicians and governmental agencies, George Steinbrenner discovered that the 1972 presidential campaign would witness an unprecedented amount of pressure on big business to contribute funds to the reelection of the incumbent president, Richard Nixon.

POLITICAL-BUSINESS CLIMATE OF CAMPAIGN 1972

Federal election campaigns were always expensive, and the presidential campaign of 1972 was no exception. This campaign did, however, offer something new for raising campaign funds—the Committee for the Re-Election of the President (CREEP). CREEP was comprised of 500 full-time workers, including 100 volunteers, devoted to the goal of reelecting a president who had become one of the most popular to serve in the White House and was virtually a sure winner for the 1972 election (as per popularity polls and surveys). What made CREEP different from past reelection committees was that it had no formal relationship with the political party of the president, the GOP; instead, it was answerable only to its own leadership. Two members of the CREEP leadership, Maurice Stans and John Mitchell, had served in Nixon's cabinet as secretary of commerce and attorney general, respectively, prior to joining the committee. Another individual who played a leading role in CREEP was President Nixon's personal attorney, Herbert Kalmbach.

By concentrating on wealthy individuals and the business community, CREEP was able to raise an unprecedented $60 million for the 1972 election campaign. There was great emphasis on obtaining most of these funds prior to April 7, 1972, the effective date of the Federal Election Campaign Act of 1971. This new election campaign law required all candidates for federal office to report the name, business address, and occupation of donors who contributed in excess of $100. In effect, the new legislation was designed to require full disclosure of all contributions. Corporate contributions, disallowed even under previous laws, had been overlooked in many earlier campaigns; but it became evident that under the Federal Election Campaign Act of 1971, the guidelines barring corporate contributions would be enforceable.

Although the new legislation did not take effect until April of 1972, corporate contributions prior to this time were eventually investigated, charges were filed, and convictions were handed down against some corporations and/or officers of these firms. Prior to the revelation of American Ship's political contribution, executives of seven major companies admitted to illegal contributions. The companies and the amounts contributed were as follows:

American Airlines	$ 55,000
Ashland Oil	100,000
Gulf Oil	100,000
Goodyear Tire and Rubber	40,000
Minnesota Mining and Manufacturing	30,000
Phillips Petroleum	100,000
Braniff Airways	40,000

The chairman of American Airlines, George Spater, came forward and confessed to authorizing illegal contributions to the Nixon campaign. According to Spater's testimony before the Senate Watergate Committee, American Airlines " . . . was solicited by Herbert W. Kalmbach, who said that we were among those from whom $100,000 was expected."[5] The company then decided to contribute $75,000; of this amount, $20,000 was contributed by company officials and $55,000 was taken from corporate funds. "I knew Mr. Kalmbach to be both the President's personal counsel and counsel for our major competitor [United Airlines],"[6] stated Mr. Spater. He said that many corporations gave funds to the Nixon campaign because they feared government reprisals against them or the advantages that would be gained by competitors. The latter fear was based on statements made by campaign fund-raisers that competitors had already pledged funds. The method used for channeling the funds from American Airlines to CREEP involved a false payment to an agent in Lebanon who then brought the money back to the company in cash; the cash was then forwarded to the committee's headquarters.

Another company which confessed to illegal contributions, Gulf Oil, ordered cash ($100,000) from subsidiaries based in the Bahamas.[7] Ashland Oil entered a nonexistent corporate expenditure on the books of a subsidiary, Gabon Corporation; the funds ($100,000) were then deposited in a Swiss bank account, returned to company headquarters, and finally forwarded to CREEP.[8]

As a result of their illegal contributions, the companies were

---

[5] Michael C. Jensen, "The Corporate Political Squeeze," *The New York Times*, September 16, 1973, pp. F1–F2.

[6] Ibid.

[7] Gulf also made contributions to the campaigns of Sen. Henry Jackson (D., Washington) and Rep. Wilbur Mills (D., Arkansas); both were Democratic hopefuls for their party's nomination.

[8] Ashland also bought a $10,000 ad in the Republican National Convention magazine.

charged with misdemeanor violations. Mr. Spater was not charged with any violation because he was the first to confess; however, officials of Ashland and Gulf were charged with misdemeanors. Each firm was fined $5,000, the maximum penalty for the violation. A vice president of Gulf, Claude C. Wild, Jr., was fined $1,000 for authorizing the company's contribution; chairman Orkin E. Atkins of Ashland was also fined $1,000. The maximum penalty for corporate officials was $1,000 in fines and one year imprisonment.

THE CASE OF AMERICAN SHIP BUILDING

On April 5, 1974, a federal grand jury in Cleveland returned a 15-count criminal indictment against Mr. Steinbrenner and American Ship; the charges stemmed from Watergate investigators' findings that illegal contributions had been made to President Nixon's campaign as well as to various Democratic and Republican congressional campaigns. Committees which received funds from American Ship were as follows:

1. September 1970: $5,000 to a committee supporting the reelection of Rep. Charles A. Mosher (R., Ohio).
2. October 1970: $2,000 to the Democratic Congressional Campaign Committee.
3. October 1970: $500 to the committee for the reelection of Rep. Frank T. Bow (R., Ohio).
4. October 1970: $1,000 to the committee for the reelection of Sen. Vance Hartke (D., Indiana).
5. October 1970 and February 1971: $11,000 to the National Democratic Congressional Dinner.
6. February 1972: $14,000 to the Senate-House Majority (Democratic) Dinner.
7. November 1972: $6,200 to unnamed committees for President Nixon's reelection.
8. April 1972: $25,000 to CREEP.
9. July 1973: $500 to the reelection committee for Sen. Daniel K. Inouye (D., Hawaii).

Two top officials of the firm were also named in the indictment; however, they had been granted immunity from prosecution because of their testimony given before the Senate Watergate Committee. Robert Bartlome, company secretary, and Matthew Clark, company purchasing director, testified before the committee in November of 1973, describing a bogus bonus plan for themselves and six other company employees (see Exhibit 1). Bartlome testified that as early as 1970 plans were formalized for channeling political contributions to

EXHIBIT 1
American Ship Building Employees Who Received Bonus Payments

Name	Title
Robert Bartlome	Secretary
Matthew Clark	Purchasing director
Stanley Lepkowski	Treasurer
Gordon Stafford	Executive vice president
Daniel Kessell	Treasurer for company's fleet of cargo ships
Ian Cushenan	President, transportation, cargo, and material handling
Robert Dibble	Employee
Roy Walker	Employee

both Republican and Democratic interests. He stated that Steinbrenner instructed him to "make a list of loyal employees"[9] who could carry out the necessary instructions that would enable the firm to funnel the contributions; the justification for such action was that Steinbrenner was being pressured for the contributions. The source of this pressure was not mentioned.

The plan devised by Steinbrenner involved the following: (1) each employee on the list was to receive a $5,000 bonus which resulted in an average net amount of $3,700 after taxes; (2) they were then instructed to write two separate checks, in the amounts of $3,000 and $100, from their personal accounts to the designated organization; (3) finally, the remaining $600 was to be returned to the company's petty cash fund.[10]

According to Bartlome, the eight employees received approximately $97,000 during the period 1970–72. Steinbrenner also received a bonus in October 1970 for $75,000.[11] The final bonus for the eight employees was issed on April 6, 1972; on this day, an unnamed corporate vice president was sent to Washington to deliver $100,000 in cash, $75,000 from Steinbrenner's personal funds and $25,000 from the employees, to the CREEP headquarters.[12]

When questioned about the last minute bonuses and their timing, Steinbrenner told Bartlome that the payments needed no elaboration.

---

[9] *The Wall Street Journal,* November 14, 1973, p. 4.

[10] The company's petty cash fund was also used for campaign contributions, according to Bartlome's testimony.

[11] *The New York Times,* November 14, 1973, p. 32.

[12] According to Bartlome, this vice president was not aware of the contents of the delivery package (addressed to Herbert Kalmbach).

Corporate treasurer Stanley Lepkowski questioned Mr. Steinbrenner's actions and was told that " . . . many corporations in the United States do it in this manner."[13] As a result of these final bonuses, Bartlome felt it was necessary to legitimize Steinbrenner's actions in the corporate records. In January of 1973, he composed a memo authorizing the bonuses and backdated the memo one year; the memo was then placed in the company's official records.

In August 1973, Clark, Bartlome, and the six other employees signed sworn affidavits before FBI investigators stating that the bonuses were proper and all contributions were personal in nature. Bartlome said the false information was the result of extensive pressure they had received from Steinbrenner and company general counsel John Melcher.[14]

When the Watergate grand jury subpoenaed the eight employees, they decided to tell the real story behind the bonuses and the company's illegal contributions. As Clark put it, "All I could see was me standing behind bars and [the corporate lawyer] telling me not to worry about it."[15] Upon hearing of the employees' decision to confess, Bartlome said Steinbrenner laid his head on the desk, moaning that he and the company were ruined and mentioned something about jumping off a bridge. He then told Bartlome to "have a good weekend" with his family and handed him an envelope with some cash in it.[16]

George Steinbrenner chose not to testify before the Watergate committee; he told investigators that he would plead the Fifth Amendment. Consequently, it was not until April 5, 1974 that Steinbrenner made a public statement. Through a Cleveland public relations consultant, he said that the Watergate prosecutors offered him the option of pleading guilty to a criminal charge of willful conspiracy to violate election laws, carrying with it a maximum penalty of a $10,000 fine, two years imprisonment, or both. "There was no way I could plead guilty . . . because I just am not guilty of any such violations. I feel it is very important that I state publicly why I have chosen to fight and it is also equally important to ask the public to remember that an indictment is not a conviction."[17]

By August 1974, Steinbrenner agreed to confess on two counts: (1) illegally contributing to election campaigns of Nixon and several

---

[13] *The Wall Street Journal*, November 14, 1973, p. 4.

[14] *The Wall Street Journal*, September 16, 1973, p. 1.

[15] *Newsweek*, November 26, 1973, p. 34.

[16] *The New York Times*, November 14, 1973, p. 32.

[17] *Cleveland Plain Dealer*, April 6, 1974, p. 32.

members of Congress, and (2) participating (in an accessory capacity) after the fact (of illegally contributing to the Nixon campaign).

Despite his confession, George Steinbrenner felt that his actions were the result of extensive pressure from government authorities. American Ship Building was at the time involved in four different actions with the federal government.

> They included a government oceanographic-survey ship called the "Researcher," on which American Ship was negotiating a settlement on a $5.4 million overrun of contract costs; Justice Department antitrust interest in American Ship's acquisition of Great Lakes Towing Co., the largest tugboat company on the Great Lakes; a Labor Department investigation of American Ship's working conditions and safety standards after a fire on a huge iron-ore carrier called the Roger Blough in which four workmen died; and Justice Department objections to American Ship's purchase of Wilson Marine Transit Co., and a shipyard at Erie, Pa., both owned by Litton Industries.[18]

Prior to the solicitations for donations to Nixon's reelection, Steinbrenner apparently felt that American Ship was insulated from such pressures because of his friendship with Thomas Evans, who attended college with him and had also served as a director of American Ship. Evans, a former law partner of Nixon's, was deputy chairman of finance for the presidential campaign, but eventually fell from favor with the reelection committee. However, the numerous actions mounted by federal agencies against his company made it appear that earlier warnings from Steinbrenner's Democratic friends in Washington about Nixon's vindictiveness were well-founded. According to Steinbrenner, he felt that he had no choice but to give CREEP the requested amount of funds.[19]

Governmental action against American Ship and Mr. Steinbrenner was not over, however; they also had violated regulations governing financial reports filed with the Securities and Exchange Commission (SEC).

SEC ACTION AGAINST AMERICAN SHIP AND STEINBRENNER

As a result of the false entries made in the company's financial records for the employee bonuses, in October of 1974 the SEC filed charges against the company: (1) American Ship tried to conceal illegal contributions via ordinary business expenses, and (2) the company failed to disclose to its stockholders that company funds were being used for political contributions and that certain officers who were standing for election as directors were participating in these

---

[18] *The Wall Street Journal*, June 25, 1975, p. 16.
[19] *The Wall Street Journal*, June 25, 1975, p. 16.

activities. In view of the above the SEC recommended that George Steinbrenner be required to refund the company all unauthorized funds used for political purposes, and that a review committee be created, by the company's board of directors, to determine the exact amount that Steinbrenner authorized for political purposes. The company and Steinbrenner agreed to cease the filing of any further false financial reports and agreed to create a review committee which would then report back to the board of directors; however, American Ship and its chairman admitted or denied nothing.

The review committee was comprised of two outside directors (company directors not employed by American Ship), Messrs. James Nederlander and Arnold Sobel, and a nondirector, Mr. Allan Shaw. Mr. Shaw was appointed chairman of the committee.[20]

The review committee's report was completed in May of 1975 and submitted to the firm's board of directors.[21] Of the $97,000 taken from the corporate treasury for political contributions, the committee recommended that George Steinbrenner repay approximately $42,000. In response to the committee's recommendation, Steinbrenner released the following statement:

> . . . I stand ready to reimburse the corporation in line with the committee's recommendations. Right or wrong, the buck stops here. Contributions were made in 1972, we cannot argue that. And while they were made in the full belief that they were legal, I will honor the committee's recommendations and will comply with any action taken by the board with respect to the requirements.[22]

The amount recommended by the committee was linked to the employee bonuses of April 6, 1972. In addition to this liability of $42,000, the committee found only one other irregularity, a $500 contribution to Sen. Daniel Inouye (D., Hawaii), a member of the Senate Watergate Committee. This contribution was traced to the company's petty cash fund.

POST-LITIGATION PERIOD

On February 20, 1975, George Steinbrenner was replaced as chief executive officer by Francis W. Theis. In a quarterly report to stock-

---

[20] Mr. Nederlander, who was president of the Nederlander Theater Corporation, was also Steinbrenner's business partner in several theatrical productions, such as *Applause, Seesaw, Funny Girl, On a Clear Day, George M,* and other theatrical ventures. Mr. Sobel was executive vice president of Material Service Corporation. Mr. Shaw was a former executive vice president of the Cleveland Trust Company, one of American Ship's registrars.

[21] American Ship's board was chaired by Steinbrenner during the review of the committee's recommendations.

[22] *Cleveland Plain Dealer*, May 8, 1975, p. 6–A.

holders, Steinbrenner stated that "The selection of Mr. Theis concludes an intensive search for a new top man qualified to serve as
president and to succeed me in the role of Chief Executive Officer.
Mr. Theis has served as president and chief executive officer of
Hooker Chemical Corporation."[23]

As a result of Mr. Steinbrenner's guilty plea and conviction,
baseball commissioner Bowie Kuhn suspended him from participating in any Yankee activities for a period of two years.[24]

After stepping down as chief executive officer, George Steinbrenner moved his family to Florida and began working out of the company's Tampa office. He then began devoting most of his time to his
interests in horse racing, theatrical ventures, and the Kinsman Marine
Transit fleet of ships (bought back from American Ship along with an
associate). He also returned to fund-raising activities for the Democratic Party. Indeed, at "The 1975 Democratic Congressional Victory
Dinner," Speaker Carl Albert presented Steinbrenner with an en-
graved plaque for his services to the party. The audience of prominent political figures gave the "businessman, sports lover, political
fund-raiser, and felon" a lengthy ovation.[25]

---

[23] American Ship Building Company, *Second Quarter Report to Shareholders*, March
31, 1975.

[24] The commissioner had the authority to take any action he deemed necessary for
the best interests of the sport. In the past, any convicted felon who owned shares in a
professional sports organization was ordered to sell his interest in that organization.

[25] *The Wall Street Journal*, June 25, 1975, p. 1.

Commentaries ════════════════════════════════

1. FTC's Mike Pertschuk Tilts against Congress to Keep Agency Power

Burt Schorr

Washington—It's not quite as historic as Churchill presiding over the dismantling of the British Empire, but tell that to Michael Pertschuk as he paces the floor at predawn hours these days, worrying about how much power his Federal Trade Commission may lose in the weeks ahead.

Thirty-three months ago, when President Carter named him chairman of the Federal Trade Commission, Mr. Pertschuk symbolized the new administration's willingness to put a business gadfly in charge of regulating business. As a Senate staff member, he had a hand in writing laws that helped rejuvenate "the little old lady on Pennsylvania Avenue," as the FTC was once called. Today the 47-year-old Mr. Pertschuk finds himself a different sort of symbol—that of the activist badly out of step in an era of concern about overregulation.

Instead of leading the commission on to new frontiers of consumer protection and trustbusting, he is scrambling to save the FTC from what promises to be the worst setback ever suffered by an independent regulatory agency. Congress appears hellbent on clipping the commission's powers as soon as it gets back to work later this month.

"There seems to be a tide that's sweeping everything before it," Mr. Pertschuk frankly observed the other day as he reviewed the FTC's predicament.

As the legislative showdown approaches, Mr. Pertschuk is seen more often hustling through the gloomy corridors of the FTC headquarters in efforts to keep up staff morale. One staff member, Michael

Source: *The Wall Street Journal*, January 15, 1980, pp. 1 and 16.

Rodemeyer, head of an FTC unit that wrote a proposed rule to protect against abuses by funeral-home operators, was "disappointed and frustrated" by a recent House vote to kill the proposal. But he and his colleagues felt better after the chairman paid them a surprise visit. "He urged us to 'hang in there,' " the young attorney recalls.

LEGISLATIVE DEFENSES

More important, Mr. Pertschuk is striving to strengthen his legislative defenses. He himself has talked with more than 30 senators to explain FTC positions, and his emissaries have sought out chosen lawmakers to fend off legislative threats. The chairman has also been devising new strategies for dealing with Capitol Hill. He is meeting regularly, sometimes daily, with his "5:00 P.M. group," a half-dozen FTC aides and officials, including Albert Kramer, head of consumer protection, and Alfred Dougherty, head of antitrust activities.

One recent concern of the 5:00 P.M. meetings was a suddenly proposed amendment by Sen. Howell Heflin, an Alabama Democrat, that would have significantly reduced the FTC's antitrust authority. Specifically, it would have prevented the FTC from ordering antitrust offenders to sell off assets, unless their cases involved mergers. The proposal threatened to kill five major antitrust cases pending before the commission. Among them: the action against the major oil companies and the one against three breakfast-cereal makers.

In response to a request from the staff of the Senate Commerce Committee, the 5:00 P.M. group put together an FTC briefing team to explain the effects of the amendment on the FTC. It also helped prepare testimony delivered by FTC commissioner Robert Pitofsky against the proposal and recommended witnesses friendly to the agency's position. One of those recommended, John Lewis, president of the National Small Business Association, testified against any weakening of the commission's antitrust powers. To weaken them would let "the law of the jungle . . . prevail in the marketplace, with the bigs devouring the smalls," Mr. Lewis said.

CALLING ON CARTER'S VETO

These arguments, along with office calls on Senators by FTC representatives, probably helped to block the Heflin amendment. "Their concerns certainly helped to shore up some votes," says an aide to Oregon Sen. Robert Packwood, the committee's ranking Republican, who led opposition to the proposal.

Now the Pertschuk team is thinking of how to cool anti-FTC moves on the Senate floor. One possibility already discussed with the White

House is for President Carter to threaten to veto a bill that combines the unwelcome features of pending House and Senate measures restricting the FTC. "A victory may be good politics," says one member of the 5:00 P.M. group. "It would face Congress with the challenge of putting the agency that polices the marketplace out in the streets at a time when voters are worried about business practices adding to inflation."

How well chairman Pertschuk succeeds in this battle—or how badly he fails—is certain to influence the role of the FTC as the government's principal business regulator in the years ahead.

In Mr. Pertschuk's favor is an effervescent, good-humored style that tends to disarm many adversaries. They also acknowledge his sincerity of purpose and devotion to duty. "Even his most persistent critics agree that Mike is determined, bright, dedicated and energetic," says one food-company lobbyist.

Still, the FTC has "gored some influential oxen," observes Calvin Collier, a Ford appointee who preceded Mr. Pertschuk as commission chairman. One of those oxen is the chairman of a major manufacturing company that is contesting FTC antitrust findings. President Carter's appointment of Mr. Pertschuk was a mistake, this executive says; "he's a very bright guy with lousy judgment," the chairman adds.

Critics of Mr. Pertschuk and the commission reel off a number of specific complaints. Among other things, they point to his utterances opposing TV commercials aimed at children. In November 1977, several months before the commission voted to hold hearings on proposals by its staff, for instance, the chairman sent Washington Post writer Colman McCarthy a statement—together with a letter describing the statement as an attempt "to establish underpinnings for a fundamental assault on television advertising directed toward young children." The letter later came to light, and defenders of the commercials felt he had shown clear-cut prejudice on an issue not yet before the commission.

Even though the FTC under Mr. Pertschuk has sought to dilute its pending regulations, its nostrums remain too strong for many businessmen and many lawmakers. They also feel the commission is trying to impose unfair, unnecessary burdens on small business, which is already chafing under government restraints.

Among those unmollified by the FTC's reduction of its original funeral-rule requirements was Republican Rep. Millicent Fenwick. As New Jersey Director of Consumer Protection, Mrs. Fenwick had put through a regulation governing funeral practices. Thus, in the House debate preceding the overwhelming vote against an FTC funeral rule, she could argue—apparently with some persuasiveness—that funeral homes are "small business, local, confined in most cases to one town," and that a federal agency hasn't any place intervening.

Indeed, a number of lawmakers who generally agree with Mr. Pertschuk on consumer-protection issues feel he has failed to adjust to rising congressional irritation with his agency. Democratic Rep. Allan Swift of Washington, for one, cast his vote with the FTC on the funeral rule, but he faults Mr. Pertschuk for lack of political adroitness on that and other issues. "Mike has been painted as a radical interventionist, and unfortunately, he's stuck with that image," says Rep. Swift.

Even the most persuasive FTC chief might encounter resistance in today's pro-business climate on Capitol Hill. At least five Democratic senators, all facing tough reelection battles in 1980, have told the FTC chairman that his agency was doing a needed job but that political problems with businessmen back home "made it hard for them to take a stand" in behalf of the FTC, says a Pertschuk aide.

The first sign of trouble, recalls the FTC chairman, came in 1978 when a House Appropriations subcommittee forbade the agency to use any of its money to promulgate a rule restricting television commercials aimed at children. "I badly misjudged the strength of business and the mood of the subcommittee members," a rueful Mr. Pertschuk concedes today. "They perceived me as arrogant and feisty, and that's the last thing an agency head should be." In those days, says Mr. Pertschuk's artist-wife, Anna Sofaer, "it was a personal blow to Mike that people seemed to have a 'get-Pertschuk' attitude."

The chairman's political standing suffered further from a caustically worded court decision that disqualified him from participation in the children's-TV proceedings. It held that his statements in favor of such a rule showed he had "conclusively prejudged" the matter. (An appeals court overturned that decision, but the FTC chief has chosen to withdraw from the proceeding out of concern that he has become too controversial.

Recently, too, Mr. Pertschuk has been stung by the willingness of some Senate liberals and moderates—once his allies in consumer causes—to back legislation that would reduce the FTC's authority.

The Senate Commerce Committee, once the agency's patron, subsequently voted out a bill to bar FTC rules against "unfair" commercial advertisements, which would kill the children's-TV proceedings. The same measure would block another major FTC proposed rule to ensure fair practices by private groups that set standards for approximately 20,000 consumer products, from computers to nuts and bolts.

Even more restrictions could come on the Senate floor. One particular worry to the FTC: an amendment by Sen. James McClure, an Idaho Republican, that would deprive the agency of authority over physicians, dentists, veterinarians, and lawyers. Its adoption would wipe out an extensive FTC program to cut medical costs by increasing competition among physicians and dentists through advertising and other means.

Some on Capitol Hill believe the FTC's life may be on the line. Even if it isn't, the bills under consideration by Congress are likely "to put a three-to-five-year chill on the commission," a top FTC antitrust official fears.

Thus far, the agency's plight hasn't stirred much public sympathy. Sen. Wendell Ford, chairman of the Senate Consumer Subcommittee, certainly doesn't appear to have been hurt by the decision of the National Consumers League to withdraw an intended consumer award to him because he voted for the pending Senate bill to reduce FTC power. Mail from his Kentucky constituents about the incident has been running 20 to one in his favor, Sen. Ford says. One businessman wrote that it was "the best award you could not receive."

A coalition of consumer organizations here has been seeking to round up grassroots backing for the FTC, but the agency is difficult for most consumers to identify, says Ellen Haas, president of the Consumer Federation of America. "They know about the abuses in the marketplace, and they know that someone in Washington is supposed to protect them. But they don't know who that someone in Washington is."

Perhaps Mr. Pertschuk might do well to take to the TV talk-show circuit to drum up support. He cuts a unique figure in the mostly drab world of federal regulation. Seeing the FTC chairman for the first time, in horn-rimmed glasses, green turtleneck shirt and baggy tweed jacket, one might mistake him for the writer he wanted to be when he was a Yale English major in the 1950s (and before he decided on Yale Law School).

The latent writer in Mr. Pertschuk emerged in 1978 in "A Fable of Regulation: The King's Dilemma," a speech that the FTC chairman wrote and delivered. It was intended as an answer to a Mobil Corp. ad about "King Sam the Avuncular," who cripples innovation and enterprise with "heavy-handed regulation."

Mr. Pertschuk's king decides to dismantle his government to rid his land of "the dread plague of regulation." But his minister warns him that will bring on "dreadful mergers," described as "deadly dragons" that "devour innovative and creative entrepreneurs."

"What do these dreadful mergers look like?" asks the king.

The minister responds: "They are bald, and most hideous of all are the conglomerates: huge, clumsy creatures with greedy eyes and parts that do not fit, a small brain that lacks experience in controlling the limbs. Yet . . . would-be competitors keel over in a dead faint at the sight of their very grossness."

---

2. Abe Lincoln versus Federal Trade Commission

Joseph Furth

It is the year 1864.

A petition for review of Federal Trade Commission cease and desist order has been argued, and just decided by the U.S. Court of Appeals, Seventh Circuit, at Springfield, Illinois.

The petitioner, Mr. Abraham Lincoln, appealed to the court for reversal, but the court ruled that the orders issued by the FTC are affirmed and upheld without modification.

The case came to the Seventh Circuit on petition to review a false representation order issued by the commission, Mark L. Kurkputsch, chairman, relating to improper statements made by Mr. Lincoln to the American public on the date of November 19, 1863, at Gettysburg, Pennsylvania, which invoked wide notoriety under headlines bannered as: **"LINCOLN'S GETTYSBURG ADDRESS"**.

The circuit court held that it had considered the issues with respect to each representation as to whether each was made and whether each was false as charged.

The court found that representations and omissions were false and misleading and constituted unfair and deceptive acts in violation of Sec. 5 and 12 of the FTC Act (15USC Sec 45 and 52).

The court also recognized the fact that Mr. Lincoln was President of the United States at the time such representations were made, albeit the fact of that is not determinative of whether such statements are deceptive and misleading (293 F 3rd at 529).

False Affirmative Representations
Made at Gettysburg, Pa.,
By Abraham Lincoln, Nov. 19, 1863,
PARAGRAPHS ONE THROUGH EIGHT as follows:

Source: *Advertising Age*, December 31, 1979.

1. "Four score and seven years ago" . . . The Court rejects Mr. Lincoln's defense that the facts are accurate, proved, and provable. However, the commission has argued properly that the statement is a classic example of "diminution" and "abnormal overstatement." FTC exhibits (CX-8 and CX-13) indicate convincingly that the public en masse does not have competence to comprehend the exact meaning of "Four Score."

Research reflects that 49.3 percent misconstrue "Four score and seven" as encompassing 47 years, while 48.4 percent are misled in the assumption of the phrase as meaning 407 years, with 2.7 percent "don't knows." The proper rule, therefore, is that if "diminution" can be held to the nondeceptive, hence, legal; "overstatement" or exaggeration is held deceptive and illegal. That is the rule which the law has most wisely adopted (6 TRR, Sec 987, 1862). Judgment affirmed.

2. "Our fathers brought forth on this continent a new nation" . . . The Court is obliged to uphold the FTC complaint that these are vague and frivolous claims of paternity and ancestry. Commission exhibit (CX-52), "Statistics on Family Composition," sustains the findings that 96.3 percent of the forebears of those attending Gettysburg were in other lands of birth at the founding of our "new nation." Thereupon, the court sustains the FTC contention that this is indeed a "skillful, shrewd exercise of innuendo, ambiguity and half-truth which misleads the public," and yet without misstating a fact (US 22, Sup Ct 68, 1847).

3. "Conceived in liberty and dedicated to the proposition that all men are created equal" . . . The rule of obvious falsity is upheld because the petitioner excludes the women and children who comprise the vast majority of the nation's population. If all men are created equal, then women and children are unequal, making exactly opposite determinations. The FTC may attack social-psychological misrepresentation on grounds of "unfairness" rather than, or in addition to, deception (239 NW 2nd, 1839).

4. "Now we are engaged in a great civil war" . . . The deception might be literally and technically true, granted. But FTC precedent makes clear that loose general statements which are commonly known as "puffing," without specific content or reference in enjoinment, are incompatible with facts. Unsubstantiated opinion fact now encroaches on a new area of FTC Regulatory Rule (61 CFR 244, 4 TRR Transfer Binder).

5. "Whether that nation or any nation can long endure" . . . A representation of a state of mind is misrepresentation if the state of mind is otherwise than represented. It is virtually impossible in the view of this Court to designate an honest claim of enduringness as being ordinary and typical to substantially all who have, or will, hear or read this admitted claim (725, 62 NW, 1798).

6. "We are met on a great battlefield of that war, we have come to dedicate a portion of that field" . . . To tell only of a portion, and to tell less than the whole truth is a well known method of deception; and he who deceives by resorting to such method cannot excuse the deception by relying upon the truthfulness per se of the partial truth (328 US 436, 15 Sup. Ct. 758, 1831).

7. "The world will little note nor long remember what we say here" . . . The assumption at law apparently is that the "seller" will just as routinely make statements which "blow down" the object which the "seller" is actually blowing up. No name in law has been given to this process of deflating, but verily it has been given the force of law by a coming concept of Trade Regulatory Law (61 CFR 214, 10 TRR, Sec. 2797, 1863).

8. "We highly resolve . . . that this nation under God shall have a new birth of freedom, and that government of the people, by the people, for the people shall not perish from the earth" . . . The Commission has properly contended that SEC. 15, FTC Act requires affirmative disclosure to reveal facts material with respect to consequences which may result. An erroneous impression that "the government . . . may perish from the earth" is created and the petitioner has gone to broad lengths in promising relief, but deceptive in failing to reveal the presence of the danger.

It is thereby ordered that the Order to Cease and Desist be, and it hereby is, confirmed.

It is further ordered that petitioner Abraham Lincoln, individually, and as an official of the Government of the United States, and his representatives, and members of his administration, directly or by other device shall forthwith cease and desist from representing orally, in writing, or in any manner, directly or by implication further misrepresentations, deceptions, unsubstantiated claims as are embodied in the published instrument designated as the "Gettysburg Address."

We find that the provisions of the order that the FTC recommends are necessary and appropriate to ensure that unfair, false and deceptive speech is ceased.

Petitioner, Mr. Lincoln, contends the order violates rights under the First Amendment, which protects speech. Because the representations herewith cited, subject to the commission's order, were unfair, false and misleading (see part IV, *supra*), it received no protection from the First Amendment.

Mr. Lincoln's appeal is denied in toto.

---

3. Picking Apart the FTC
Arthur E. Rowse and Bob McGrath

A year ago, Congress's main watchdog over regulatory agencies concluded after study that the Federal Trade Commission, the government's principal consumer protection agency, was having "only limited success" in assisting victims of unfair business practices.

The General Accounting Office recommended that legislators boost the agency's authority to police the marketplace and urged the FTC to use the power it has to protect the public more efficiently.

A year later, Congress is picking the FTC apart as if it were a holiday turkey rather than adding meat to its bones. Enjoying the feast immensely—and quietly—are countless business interests which have become targets of FTC actions in recent years.

The latest blow to the agency came November 27 when the House passed an FTC budget authorization bill that would cut off several pending regulations and set up a legislative veto arrangement that would allow either branch of Congress to knock down any FTC action.

It was the first time either branch of Congress had ever voted to block an FTC regulation before it had even been made final.

The most frequent concern expressed by House members was for small business, which was invariably depicted as the victim of costly and unnecessary regulation. In the debate, scarcely a word was said about the effect of FTC restrictions on the buying public.

The antiregulation mood was running even stronger when the Senate Committee on Commerce, Science, and Transportation met

---

Source: *The Sunday Sun*, Baltimore, Md., December 16, 1979, pp. 1 and 3.

November 20 to vote on its FTC budget authorization for the next two years. The committee approved more restrictions on the FTC than the House.

The committee is also considering proposals to cut back the FTC's power to pursue monopolistic practices by breaking up firms that control prices and supplies.

A proposal to restrict FTC power to issue subpoenas (to force disclosure of certain information) is in the bill reported to the full Senate.

If these proposals are passed by both houses, the FTC may have to drop major antitrust cases, including ones against Exxon and other oil firms, ITT-Continental, du Pont, General Motors, Kellogg, General Mills, and General Foods.

Among the people most affected by House and Senate action—if President Carter signs what Congress produces—will be buyers of insurance, cars, cereal, citrus fruits, encyclopedias, and funerals.

Also to be affected would be virtually everybody who buys a trademarked item such as Formica, or a product that must conform to privately set standards, such as lighting, plumbing and construction materials.

If the committee has its way, the FTC would also lose much of its broad power to prevent misleading advertising.

Nearly everything that is advertised comes under the FTC's wings, but few of its cases would be able to get off the ground if Congress follows the Senate committee's recommendation and bans any action against ads on the ground that they are "unfair."

The impetus for this particular attack is the agency's controversial proposals to restrict certain television ads aimed at very young children. The complaint is not that they are untrue, but that they unfairly convince impressionable youngsters to demand sugary items, such as candy and cereal, that have potentially harmful effects on the teeth and diet.

A ban against "unfair" ads would end action involving TV ads of this type. It would also prevent the FTC from acting against ads with unsubstantiated claims, says the FTC.

Congressional critics of the embattled agency contend, however, that action against such ads would still be possible under the agency's authority to take action against false or deceptive ads.

Then, too, there may be a ripple effect that extends beyond the actual curbs imposed on the FTC, especially if the agency takes the blunt messages to heart and draws back from actions that might still be within its power to take.

In the past year, the agency has watered down a number of proposals after reading earlier criticism from Congress.

Among proposed rules that have been cut back or delayed after a wave of complaints from affected businesses have been ones regarding the sale of hearing aids, vocational school courses, and home insulation products.

The agency originally proposed a number of restrictions on claims made for hearing aids in order to prevent misrepresentation. Most of these were dropped in favor of a 30-day trial period; which some large manufacturers already allow.

Original rules on vocational schools would have required disclosure of numerous facts and required students to reaffirm the contract within 14 days before courses could begin. Many of these requirements were dropped, and a ten-day cooling-off period was set, in which a student can drop out and get a prorated refund.

Recently, the agency has postponed to December 31 the effective date for rules requiring manufacturers to include "R" values (the measure of effectiveness) on labels and insulation products.

Even more important to consumers may be actions taken by the full House and by the Senate Commerce Committee to exempt certain industries—certain firms in some cases—from pending FTC actions.

Among these are:

Insurance—By prohibiting the FTC from ever investigating this gigantic industry, Congress will be removing one of the few effective critics of the industry and the way states regulate it.

Since the McCarran-Ferguson Act of 1945, the federal government has been precluded by law from regulating insurance.

But numerous studies, including some done by congressional committees, have concluded that the states are not protecting insurance buyers from deceptive and fraudulent practices costing consumers billions more than necessary each year.

In one year alone, said a recent FTC report on life insurance, buyers lost $1.3 billion they could have earned elsewhere with excess premiums pocketed by the companies.

Another study by the FTC found many elderly people paying through the nose for "Medigap" policies either duplicating each other or providing little protection for the money involved.

These and other studies so enraged the insurance industry that they sought help on Capitol Hill. One senator even suggested that "criminal sanctions" may be necessary to keep the FTC from looking into alleged abuses in insurance.

Automobiles—For five years, the FTC studied the selling of used cars to see what, if anything, could be done to help buyers get what they pay for.

In November 1978, the agency proposed a series of rules designed to provide buyers with more information. Sellers would be required to inspect each car and put either an "OK" or "Not OK" beside each mechanical item on a list. Stickers would also have to disclose warranty terms, safety defects, mileage, what the car was previously used for, and whether it had been totalled in a wreck.

Dealer associations complained that such a sticker would amount to a warranty, which the FTC did not have authority to require. They brought their case to Congress, where they found a friendly reception.

The bill voted by the Senate committee will prevent the FTC from issuing any rules requiring inspection of used cars.

Funerals—The FTC also spent five years investigating the funeral industry, which has been the subject of a series of books and studies alleging widespread abuses and wasteful practices.

One of the most common problems, said the agency staff, was the practice of using package prices rather than itemized prices, thus leaving the buyers often unprepared for the size of the final bill. The FTC proposed that more price information be disclosed.

The agency also proposed that certain practices be changed, including the common one of embalming without permission of relatives or friends of the deceased. Millions of dollars could be saved for consumers, said the agency staff.

Funeral directors fought the FTC all along the way, finally bringing their grievances to Congress. As a result, the FTC pulled back most of its proposed rules, including a ban on package pricing.

Essentially, the rules that are left simply require more disclosure of information. A prominent industry journal concluded that the industry could "live with" the revised rules.

But the funeral industry kept up the fight and succeeded in getting the House to prohibit the FTC from issuing any rules affecting funerals.

Food Prices—Two years ago, the FTC launched an investigation to see what effect, if any, Sunkist Growers, Inc., a large cooperative, was having on prices people pay for citrus fruit in a number of Western states.

According to the agency, Sunkist controls no less than 75 percent of the production of oranges and lemons in the Western states and has used anticompetitive practices to increase that control and set prices.

The FTC has proposed divestiture of some of Sunkist's larger companies in order to bring more price competition.

But Sunkist contends that the FTC has no authority to get into anything having to do with cooperatives because of the Capper-Volstead Act of 1922, which granted agricultural cooperatives immunity from antitrust prosecution. The act is supposed to be administered by the Agricultural Department, but the department has never filed an antitrust case against a cooperative.

Sunkist suggested that the FTC focus instead on the acquisition of food products by large conglomerates. But the agency replied that Sunkist is a large combine itself and that the Capper-Volstead Act was intended to help small farmers, not large organizations. Sunkist sales last year were $513 million.

Rep. Mark Andrews (R., N.D.) won passage of an amendment to the FTC authorization act in the House to block the agency from making an antitrust case against any cooperatives.

Encyclopedias—The FTC has been active in pursuing many alleged abuses in the selling of encyclopedias, particularly the common ploy of posing as interviewers or survey-takers to gain admission into a home.

In a case involving Encyclopedia Britannica, the FTC resolved complaints about misrepresentation by an order requiring, among other things, that company personnel carry a card identifying them as sellers of encyclopedias. The cards must be shown to potential customers at the beginning of the conversation.

The company, however, claims that the FTC requirement that sales personnel identify themselves has put the company at a competitive disadvantage with other companies not so required.

In the Senate committee, Sen. John Warner (R., Va.) won unanimous passage of an amendment requiring the FTC to reopen any final order if an affected company claims that a major change in market conditions has resulted from the order.

Although the rule change is designed to help Encyclopedia Britannica only, it is written broadly enough to be used by many companies to overturn FTC regulations without court review.

Product Standards—Many consumers are required to buy certain products rather than competing ones of equal value or better value because of overly restrictive product standards, according to an FTC study.

Examples cited are requirements for much more electrical lighting than necessary for buildings and requirements for the use of certain kinds of pipe or wiring in new houses and commercial buildings. As much as $3.5 billion in energy waste a year from such standards has been alleged in complaints to the FTC.

The FTC has proposed rules that would require greater consumer representation on standard-setting organizations and would make such groups more responsible for the truthfulness of certifications.

But representation groups, including Underwriters' Laboratories and the American National Standards Institute, succeeded in getting the Senate committee to approve a change in FTC law which would stop the action in its tracks.

The committee voted to prohibit the agency from prescribing "any trade regulation rules with respect to unfair methods of competition."

Although backers of the change said it would affect only the FTC work on standards, the FTC commissioners were not so sure in a letter to the committee urging—unsuccessfully—that it not act on the matter.

General Restrictions—In addition to those specific restrictions are several general ones that are virtually the same in both the House and Senate bills.

They include a requirement that the FTC draw up semi-annual agendas of action for 12 months ahead, plus updates describing the status of pending rules. The FTC would be allowed to propose a rule not on the agenda only if an explanation is given to Congress.

Each item on the agenda would have to include the name, address, and telephone number of the FTC official responsible for responding to any (congressional) inquiries relating to the item.

Whenever the FTC decides on a rulemaking action, it would have to publish a preliminary analysis describing the need for action, any alternatives available and the costs and benefits involved. Deadlines are also set for agency actions.

Semiannual oversight hearings would also be required, thus doubling the usual annual reviews of the agency by appropriate congressional committees.

The Senate bill also would allow winners of court challenges of FTC actions to collect legal fees from the agency. But the bill does not set up extra appropriations for this purpose, so the FTC would have to dip into its operating funds in such cases.

Money for paying expenses for citizen witnesses at agency hearings would also be cut substantially by both bills.

4. Is Bigness Bad for Business?
Ralph Nader and Mark Green

Is bigness badness?

If asked of businessmen about *business,* the answer is reflexively "no." Absolute size is absolutely irrelevant, it is said. Yet when asked of businessmen about *government,* the answer, just as routinely, is "of course." Big government is wasteful, unresponsive, bureaucratically bogged down in red tape. But business advocates can't have it both

Source: *Business and Society Review,* no. 30 (Summer 1979), pp. 20–24.

ways—especially now, as conglomerate mergers grow more frequent and big business grows yet bigger.

Indeed, as one studies the empirical record of our large multinational conglomerates, there are substantial economic and social costs inflicted by their giant size, without offsetting benefits. So let us ask the ritual question once more—and, like the citizen who saw the emperor naked, actually look at the answer rather than assume it. Is bigness badness? Yes, for ten reasons:

1. *Deep pocket:* In the words of economist Corwin Edwards, "The big company can outbid, outspend, or outlose the small one," or as Professor Walter Adams once put it, "Pretending that a firm with ITT's absolute size and aggregate power is a run-of-the-mill newcomer to the grass seed business is not unlike the suggestion that injecting Kareem Abdul Jabbar into a grade school basketball game would have no impact on the . . . probable outcome of the contest." Clorox, for example, was the leading firm in the bleach industry, but when Procter & Gamble acquired it in 1957, the firm became the unassailably dominant leader in the industry. As the Supreme Court said in 1967, smaller competitors and potential competitors, appreciating P&G's financial ability to underwrite huge advertising campaigns or cross-subsidize its subsidiary if necessary, "would become more cautious in competing due to their fear of retaliation by Procter."

2. *Potential competition:* Since LTV, for example, might have entered the steel industry via internal expansion or the acquisition of a small steel firm, there was a loss of potential competition when it took over Jones & Laughlin, the sixth largest steel company. Indeed, the threat of potential entry by a major firm outside an industry can discourage the dominant firms in that industry from raising prices.

3. *Reciprocity:* When subsidiaries within a large conglomerate or between large conglomerates say you-buy-from-me-and-I'll-buy-from-you, competitors can be locked out of markets not because of a superior product, but because of a network of quid pro quos. Cities Service in 1962 was frustrated when it attempted to enter the rubber-oil market, because major tire companies had pervasive reciprocal arrangements with the large petroleum companies. ITT-Sheraton bought Philco-Ford TV sets in exchange for that company's use of Sheraton hotel rooms. "The U.S. economy might end up," *Fortune* magazine once worried, "completely dominated by conglomerates happily trading with each other in a new kind of cartel system."

4. *Mutual forbearance:* In 1923 a duPont executive described his company's policy to Imperial Chemical Industries of Great Britain, number two in the world to duPont. "It is not good business sense to

attempt an expansion in certain directions if such an act is bound to result [in] a boomerang of retaliation." Four decades later, when Continental Foods slashed prices at its Chicago stores, the National Tea Corp., its competitor *and* a buyer of some Continental items, threatened to drop Continental lines from its shelves. Continental then ended its price-cutting campaign. As conglomerate size and diversification increases, argues economist Willard Mueller, who has developed the "mutual forbearance" theory, "the number of contacts shared with competitors, suppliers and customers [increases], thereby increasing the mutual awareness of common interests among firms." As a result, companies pull their punches in the competitive arena.

5. *Diseconomies of size:*   Conglomerate mergers are usually justified by the magic of synergy, that $2 + 2 = 5$. To be sure, economies of scale require that firms be large enough to be efficient. But firms can also be too large to be efficient (or $2 + 2 = 3$). Studies by the Federal Trade Commission and House Antitrust Subcommittee in the late 1960s could not detect any efficiencies as a result of large conglomerate mergers. Which should not be surprising. All chairmen and vice presidents have the same 24-hour day as the rest of us, and if they try to manage 100 subsidiaries rather than two, there will be too little time to make quality judgments about the numerous issues that fly across their desks. And the bigger a firm, the bigger the costs of bureaucracy: excessive paper work; committees reviewing committees; undetected sloth; institutional caution and delay; and Parkinson's law that superiors like to proliferate subordinates. "There is no obvious association between firm size and such dimensions of managerial quality as dynamism, intelligence, awareness, and skill in interpersonal relations," said Frederick Scherer after 86 interviews with business managers. "I am inclined toward the view that the unit costs of management, including the hidden losses due to delayed or faulty decisions and weakened or distorted incentives . . . do tend to rise with the organizational size."

In the ultimate perversion of the marketplace, our dinosaur firms may grow so large that, whatever their inefficiencies, the government cannot afford to let them fail. But if the marketplace is no longer allowed to "penalize" poor managerial decisions, then business has less discipline or incentive to make good decisions and revise bad ones. No wonder, then, that entrepreneurs prefer big to small: It is the ultimate insurance policy. John Cobbs in *Business Week* a few years ago understood this dilemma:

> In the years before World War I, Germany invested so heavily in battleships that, when the war came, it did not dare let them fight. As the U.S. economy slides deeper into recession, the federal government

finds itself in a similar position. The huge U.S. corporations have become such important centers of jobs and incomes that it dare not let one of them shut down or go out of business. It is compelled, therefore, to shape national policy in terms of protecting the great corporations instead of letting the economy make deflationary adjustments.

6. *Innovation:* It is often argued, from an a priori basis, that companies have to be very large in order to afford the risk of large investments in research and development. But facts contradict this abstraction. Having examined many R&D expenditure analyses, Leonard Weiss concluded, "Most studies show that within their range of observation, size adds little to research intensity and may actually detract from it in some industries." Scherer, based on his own compilation of studies correlating firm size and innovation, observed that there were economies of scale for innovation for firms up to 5,000 employees (*Fortune's* 500th firm in 1974 had 6,450 employees), but no advantage beyond that. The famous Jewkes study of invention showed that of 61 basic inventions examined, only 16 resulted from organizational research by large companies. For example, the ballpoint pen was invented by a sculptor, the dial telephone by an undertaker. The firms which introduced stainless steel razor blades (Wilkinson), transistor radios (Sony), photocopying machines (Xerox), and the "instant" photograph (Polaroid) were all small and little known when they made their momentous breakthroughs.

It appears that the best innovation usually emerges from solo inventors or small- and medium-sized firms—not our giant corporations. The latter may be able to *afford* it, but do they *desire* it? If you already dominate an industry, where is the incentive to take a chance on a new and costly approach? We don't associate inventiveness with the centralized planning of socialist economies, even though the planners have substantial R&D resources under their control. The reason is that they, like big businessmen, are not eager to give the green light to new ways which threaten their investment in the old ways.

7. *Jobs and unions:* Conglomerate mergers mean plants are bought, not built. Wealth and jobs are transferred, not created. Antitrust Division chief John Shenefield has estimated that more than one fifth of the growth of large firms has been due to acquisition, not internal growth. Or as Thomas Murphy, the chairman of General Motors, said in 1977, "One reason, in my opinion, that the long-predicted capital spending boom never seems to get off the ground is these acquisitions. Money that would normally go into plant and equipment at this stage of a recovery is being siphoned off by acquisitions."

Workers are also affected, for conglomerate acquisitions upset the power balance between management and labor. Suppose a union represents a small minority of all the workers of a far-flung conglomerate. Then why bother striking the Pittsburgh subsidiary when it accounts for only five percent of company production, and production can simply be transferred to the union-free plant in Spain? This evolution can annul the right to strike, which is labor's only power vis-à-vis management.

8. *Community effect:*   Absentee corporations can have a profound impact on the local communities of companies they purchase. They can decide not merely that a plant is not making money, but that it is not making *as much money* as some other profit center in the worldwide enterprise. Hence an executive in New York City or Brussels might decide to pull the plug on a facility in Youngstown, Ohio, in a way that local ownership would never do.

A study by Jon Udell of the University of Wisconsin indicated that firms acquiring Wisconsin companies tended to use fewer professional services in local communities after a merger. "Most of the acquired firms covered in the survey now use the financial institutions, legal services, and accounting services of parent companies." So after the Chase Manhattan Bank extended a line of credit to Gulf & Western to make acquisitions, G&W reciprocated by moving the acquirees' financial services from local banks to Chase. Following a West German firm's take over of a Detroit chemical company, the late Sen. Philip Hart (D., Mich.) asked, "To what extent will a firm whose headquarters are in another state or another country be disposed to play a significant role on something like the New Detroit Committee?" This erosion of community by absentee business control especially worried former Supreme Court Justice William Douglas. In 1949 he wrote:

> Local leadership is diluted. He who was a leader in the village becomes dependent on outsiders for his action and policy. Clerks responsible to a superior in a distant place take the place of resident proprietors beholden to no one. These are the prices which the nation pays for the almost ceaseless growth in bigness on the part of industry.

9. *Political impact:*   Our democracy assumes, in Judge Learned Hand's phrase, a "multiplicity of tongues" competing in the political

---

Energy Independence for Exxon

With the announcement of first-quarter profits and the onset of the spring gasoline shortage, critics of the oil industry had a field day. President Carter, calling oil profits "enormous," proposed to tax excess profits generated by deregulation—only to be excoriated by Sen. Kennedy, who called the tax a "transparent figleaf" over the vast profits expected from deregulation. In the cynical eyes of many Americans, the major oil companies' concern about the nation's energy problems has extended no farther than the television ads counselling automotive frugality, which first appeared in 1974 and began to reappear this spring. Even if the oil majors have not been directly responsible for shortages, no one doubts that they have greatly profited from them. Under such circumstances, say the cynical, who would expect them to be concerned about energy shortages as long as there is enough gasoline for them to drive to the bank?

But cynicism is an ultimately unsatisfying attitude ("the giddy whirl of a perpetually self-creating disorder," Hegel said) and one to which we are in envy all too prone. A public act that serves to restore our faith demands, therefore, not only our admiration but our gratitude. On May 18 Exxon announced that it had developed a variable-speed electric motor control device which, when fully marketed, could save the United States a million barrels of oil a day. To hasten that happy day for us all, Exxon proposed to spend $1.17 billion to purchase the Reliance Electric Co., which would then produce and market the new device.

But is Exxon primarily concerned with lessening the nation's reliance on oil or its own reliance? The announcement of May 18 was met with widespread expressions of doubt that Exxon's device is substantially different from others that have been available for years, one of which is already marketed by Reliance. Furthermore, Reliance, which last year had profits of $65 million on sales of $966 million, is no longer nearly so concerned with producing electric motors as it once was. Though electric motors accounted for three quarters of Reliance's sales in 1967, they now account for only one tenth. In the interim Reliance has diversified, developing, among other things, an extensive telecommunications business. This is an area in which Exxon has itself been increasingly interested. Its present products include a number of data handling and electronic communication systems. When asked what it intended to do with Reliance's holdings in this area, however, one Exxon official appears to have been surprised. "We just haven't thought about it yet," he said.

—*Unctuous the Cynic*

marketplace. But as large conglomerates grow larger, there are fewer decision-makers deciding who gets business campaign contributions and who doesn't, what advocacy advertisements run, what bills get their decisive support. Montgomery Ward was a strong supporter of a Consumer Protection Agency a few years ago, but it became an inactive supporter after its acquisition by Mobil Oil. Of course, small producers organized into trade groups can have significant political impact, but a giant conglomerate still has privileged political status, as Sen. Philip Hart recognized. "When a major corporation from a state wants to discuss something with its political representatives, you can be sure it will be heard. When that same company operates in 30 states, it will be heard by 30 times as many representatives." A study by political scientists Lester Solomon and John Siegfried in 1975 tried to document this shadowy relationship using the petroleum industry as an example. Their conclusion:

> Particularly striking was (1) the discovery of a negative relationship between firm size and effective corporate income tax rates; (2) empirical evidence systematically linking the relative dominance of large firms in the refining industry in each state to the level of state motor vehicle fuel excise tax rates; and (3) a pattern of regulatory policies with substantial economic payoffs for the industry.

10. Secrecy: Single-line firms have to disclose publicly their profits and losses for their product. But as a conglomerate acquires additional firms, its consolidated income statement describes the firm's overall health but not the profit or loss per product line. So small businesses have to make greater disclosures than their larger, more diversified competitors. And investors and government agencies cannot easily evaluate whether some divisions are earning monopoly returns, or are being subsidized. As conglomerates acquire smaller firms, there is, in an FTC phrase, "information loss."

Some mergers, of course, can lead to genuine economies of scale or can be pro-competitive, as when an outside company acquires a nonleading firm ("toehold acquisition") in an industry in need of competitive stimulation. Too frequently, however, in the words of Henry Simons, a founding father of the Chicago school of economics, the existence of giant conglomerates "is to be explained in terms of opportunities for promotion profits, personal ambitions of industrial and financial Napoleons, and advantages of monopoly power."

Our public policy goal should be to encourage competition. The sentiment and speeches behind the 1890 and 1950 antitrust acts reflect Judge Learned Hand's view that "great industrial consolidations are inherently undesirable, regardless of their economic results." But the language of the law does not reflect this view. It's time to rewrite the law to make it coextensive with the problem.

A two-stage bill could accomplish this goal. First, huge conglomerate mergers—e.g., where each entity had over $100 million in annual sales or assets and the resulting firm was worth more than $2 billion in annual sales or assets—would be flatly prohibited unless the partners could prove that "significant economies of scale" or "significant competitive benefits" would result. Second, no firm with over $500 million in annual sales or assets could acquire any of the four leading firms in concentrated markets, and to the extent that the large firm made any acquisitions it would have to spin off a comparable amount of assets. This approach would leave it to private firms to decide what assets were truly economical to maintain and which to drop. Mergers would be spurred by efficiencies, not the ambitions of "financial Napoleons."

This legislation is socially desirable, economically workable, and politically viable. Indeed, its prospects have never been better. The public is understandably dismayed at the unresponsiveness of big institutions. And for the first time in memory, there is a chairman of the Senate Judiciary Committee, a chairman of the Senate Antitrust Subcommittee, an Attorney General, an Antitrust Division chief, and chairman of the FTC who publicly concurred that unchecked conglomerate mergers are deleterious. At the same time, a renewed merger wave makes reform urgent.

---

5. GM Big Because It's Good: Boss

James Mateja

To critics who charge that General Motors benefits from government regulations at the expense of its competitors because GM can spread the costs over many more cars, GM Chairman Thomas A. Murphy has a one-word reply:

"Hogwash."

To those who say that GM's nearly 60 percent share of the domestic auto market is unhealthy for the industry, Murphy has the same reply.

All that counts, says Murphy, is that GM got big and is getting bigger by playing the game according to the rules but playing it better, and all the rest is, well, hogwash.

"We won't get 100 percent of the market," he says, although he

Source: *Chicago Tribune*, April 29, 1979, pp. 1 and 34. Copyrighted © *Chicago Tribune*. All rights reserved.

hinted in an interview that if every car sold carried a GM label, that would be all right too.

Murphy has heard and read the criticism. He doesn't take kindly to it. True enough, since 1970, GM's share of the market has risen from 46.3 percent to 57.9 percent in 1978, selling 3,924,200 cars in 1970 and 5,385,300 in 1978, an all-time record. But Murphy points out that no one forced 5 million people to buy Chevrolets, Buicks, Pontiacs, Oldsmobiles, and Cadillacs.

The one thing Murphy doesn't talk about is the fact that since he took over as GM chairman the automaker's market share has jumped by 10 percentage points.

GM's assets total $30.5 billion, that's about a billion dollars more than Ford, Chrysler, and American Motors combined. Its wealth doesn't sit well with the competition, especially now that the automakers must spend about $80 billion by 1985 to come out with new, more fuel-efficient cars.

The gripe is that because of its size GM can amortize those costs easily while the others can't.

John Riccardo, Chrysler chairman, points out the difficulty facing the smaller companies.

"The burden of government regulation always falls the heaviest on the smaller companies," Riccardo said.

"If the industry as a whole is feeling the pressure, you can imagine what we at Chrysler are feeling.

"We have always had to overcome the obvious disadvantage of our smaller size. We have always been able to overcome that disadvantage by using our wits, by being flexible and innovative, by picking our spots in the marketplace, and by doing more with less. Government regulation has taken away a great deal of that flexibility.

"It has forced all of us in the industry to do the same research, buy the same tools, perfect the same technology before we put it in the first car. And the bigger companies have more units over which to spread all the costs," Riccardo said.

Lee A. Iacocca, Chrysler president, is a bit more succinct in summing up the size disadvantage.

> "Sure I wish we had the resources of some of our competitors," Iacocca said. "I tell our people, you only get one shot at it. You've got to do it right the first time. We've got a hell of a diesel for example, right now. It's superb. It's our 225 [cubic-inch] dieselized, but they want $220 million here within the company to [go into production]. Well, if I had the resources of some of my major competition, we could just do it. What the hell is another $200 million among friends. We can't do that here. You've got to do it right here one time. We have no slack. When you don't have money running out your ears, you've got to do it right."

Henry Ford II, chairman of Ford Motor Co., is more diplomatic in discussing the effects of GM's size on the competition.

"The big problem for the industry is capital demand in the coming years to meet federal regulations," he said. "Ford, between 1978 and 1985, will spend $20 billion in capital expenditures on tooling and new products to meet federal laws.

"The capital problem is one we all have," he said, but "it certainly is less of a problem for them [GM]."

Ford made clear that his company is not intimidated. "You've got to have competition, the more of it you have the better it is for the consumer. The capital requirements are tremendous, but we at Ford will be able to meet them."

Murphy, in turn, makes clear that if his competitors are looking for sympathy, little or none comes from the 14th-floor executive offices in the GM building in Detroit.

"As long as we obey the laws, we want all the business we can get out there," Murphy insists. To suggest GM's large market share may not sit well with the Federal Trade Commission or the Justice Department only riles Murphy.

"It's like going to a football coach at the start of the season and asking him how he'll do, and he says he'd settle for winning 50 percent of his games. If he plays 14 games, which 7 does he win, which 7 does he lose? If he starts the season losing the first 3 games he's really in trouble."

Along the interstate leading into Detroit Goodyear Tire and Rubber Co. has erected a sign that each few seconds records another industry car sale.

"On January 1 of each year they set that clock back to zero," Murphy says. "We do that, too. We never know how many cars we are going to sell, but I tell our people they better move because we sell cars one at a time."

Any hint that GM's growth will lead to retaliation from the Justice Department irritates Murphy.

"Trust laws were designed to foster competition," Murphy insists. "When a person tells me, 'Hey, friend, if you are too successful, we are going to punish you,' it's a contradiction I can't reconcile myself to. How do you go about only getting X percent of the market," he adds. "I don't know how you'd go about doing that."

Murphy said industry observers who keep close tabs on cars sold and market shares (and each percent gain or loss represents 100,000 cars), should look instead at the numbers of unsold cars and at people who are about to buy.

The GM chairman finds it somewhat amusing that GM is criticized for its size when at one time it, too, had to struggle for survival.

"In the '20s we had 10 percent of the market; Ford had 60 percent," he recalled. "Ford tried to dictate the market: 'This is what I've got in the color I want to give you, and I'm going to tell you what you can buy.'

"The same thing could happen again," he added. "I tell our people you can't get fat and happy, that your press clippings can also be your obituary."

Murphy traces the foundation of GM's surging strength to 1974, when it decided to go ahead with its downsizing program and committed itself to a multibillion dollar program to reshape its cars to make them more fuel-efficient.

"We were averaging 2 m.p.g. less from our fleet of cars than the competition at the time because we had a preponderance of big cars in our fleet," Murphy recalled.

He said his predecessor, Richard Gerstenberg, went before the GM board and convinced it to spend the money to launch the program.

"It meant we had to borrow money and cut our dividend," Murphy said. "Everyone was saying, 'GM is making a mistake, they are abandoning their big cars, and we are going to keep ours and we'll have GM where we want them.'"

In the 1977 model year GM's first down-sized cars appeared. They were roughly 800 to 1,000 pounds lighter and a foot shorter than standard-size cars. Ford Division's general manager, Bennett Bidwell, chided GM saying that at Ford, "We have the last of the whoppers."

But GM cars sold in amazing numbers; the whoppers at Ford and Chrysler sold like day-old burgers. In 1978, in fact, Chrysler simply stopped offering full-sized cars until it could bring out its own downsized models in 1979.

"If we have an advantage today," said Murphy, "it's because back in 1974 we were willing to put our money on the line when people thought the industry was finished after the oil embargo and that we had suffered a mortal blow. We kept our confidence. We were willing to take a risk."

By getting a nearly two-year jump on the competition, GM will have redone every car it offers at least once by 1983 and will have a headstart in front-wheel drive, diesel engines, and turbocharging while the others are still engaged in downsizing.

Thus, the near-term outlook, is for GM, strong as it is, to get stronger. In the 1979 model and calendar year, GM alone among the Big Four is selling ahead of the year-ago pace.

In the 1978 model year the best-selling minicar in the industry was GM's Chevrolet Chevette, best midsize car the Olds Cutlass, full-size car the Chevrolet Impala. Where it came up short was the compact segment, where the Ford Fairmont was dominant.

And what is GM's newest line of cars for 1980? Why, the downsized front-wheel drive compact car line that went on sale April 19. In the first two days GM sold more than 17,000 of those cars and took orders for more than 40,000 others.

Perhaps what GM's competitors should fear the most is Murphy's warning is that no matter how many cars it is selling now, GM isn't satisfied.

"We only have a 25 percent share of the market worldwide," Murphy said. "I'd like to do more."

But he won't sacrifice GM's stronghold in the United States.

"If we compete legally and if because of the value of our products we convince people to buy our cars, well, whatever percent of the market that means we get we are proud of it," he said.

======================================= part II

THE HISTORICAL, IDEOLOGICAL, AND ETHICAL CONTEXT

Most observers support the thesis that business has become the dominant institution in American society. Thus, it is useful to examine the values and beliefs of managers and the ethical basis for business decision-making. This section includes cases and commentaries which treat issues involved in assessing the "rightness" or "wrongness" of specific managerial decisions, viewed from an ethical perspective.

Business leaders are clearly a diverse group, with differing values and beliefs. Nonetheless, it is useful to consider a business ideology, defined by Wayne State University professor Gerald Cavanaugh as ". . . a coherent, systematic, and moving statement of basic values and purpose. It is a constellation of values generally held by a group, and those in that group tend to support one another in that ideology."[1] The ideology of business at the beginning of the 20th century, was, of course, much different from the common views held by executives in the 1980s. The earlier view centered on the preeminence of the stockholders, as highlighted by the quote often attributed to Cornelius Vanderbilt: "The public be damned, I work for my stockholders." The ideology of the time focused on the right of the owner to do with property as he saw fit. The ideology was antiunion and antigovernment. It was believed that the individual, whether business executive or employee, customer or competitor, should be unre-

---

[1] Gerald F. Cavanaugh, *American Business Values in Transition* (Englewood Cliffs, N.J.: Prentice-Hall, 1976), p. 13.

57

strained in freedom to act within the confines of the Constitution as interpreted by the courts.

Ideologies evolve over time as realities force changes in basic beliefs. Thus, by the 1970s, business leaders viewed their role quite differently from their predecessors. Perhaps one of the clearest descriptions of contemporary business ideology has been proposed by the Committee on Economic Development:

> The modern professional manager also regards himself, not as an owner disposing of personal property as he sees fit, but as a trustee balancing the interests of many diverse participants and constituents in the enterprise, whose interests sometimes conflict with those of others. The chief executive of a large corporation has the problem of reconciling the demands of employees for more wages and improved benefit plans, customers for lower prices, government for more taxes, stockholders for higher dividends and greater capital appreciation—all within a framework that will be constructive and acceptable to society.[2]

The so-called managerial ideology described above recognizes the existence of a variety of stakeholders whose self-interest is intertwined with that of the private corporation. The critical task for management is viewed as balancing the needs of all stakeholders.

Business ethics is concerned with the "right" and "wrong" in "good" and "evil" dimensions of business decision-making. It is often difficult to evaluate a given decision as ethical or unethical without details on the motivations and expectations of decision participants. For instance, low expectations followed by low performance does not necessarily represent unethical conduct, as noted by Prof. Robert Bartels, "Simply to make an untrue statement about a product is in itself not unethical, nor to make a shoddy product—that may be bad management, but it is not necessarily unethical."[3] Likewise, a manager who makes a basic moral commitment to do what is right will seldom face charges of unethical behavior.

The cases in this section do not focus on ethical dilemmas, but instead, examine clear instances of fraudulent behavior. Illegal and unethical behavior by the leaders of any institution poses a threat to the very existence of that institution. Therefore, a number of people expressed alarm about the future of the American business system in light of the revelations of corruption and misconduct. For example, Fred T. Allen, chairman and president of Pitney-Bowes, Inc., said to a meeting in Zurich, "I am a troubled man, troubled by the steep de-

---

[2] Committee for Economic Development, *Social Responsibilities of Business Corporations* (New York, 1971), p. 22.

[3] Robert Bartels, "A Model for Ethics in Marketing," *Journal of Marketing,* vol. 31, no. 1 (January 1967), p. 21.

cline in the public's esteem for business and its practitioners. And with the almost daily revelations . . . , the American public's attitude seems likely to turn increasingly sour."[4]

It was not that business had never before experienced public revelations of wrongdoing, but the nation's mood following Watergate seemed especially hostile toward misconduct in any arena. The issue was clearly a source of concern not only for the traditional critics of business, but for its supporters and defenders as well.

The materials in this section thus provide the reader with an opportunity to explore in some depth the evolution and operations of two fraudulent firms. The Four Seasons and Equity Funding cases are then followed by brief commentaries treating business ethics, public attitudes toward business and the profit system, business ideology with respect to imports, and approaches to business corruption.

---

[4] *The Wall Street Journal,* October 17, 1975, p. 14.

Case ═══════════════════════════════════════

EQUITY FUNDING CORPORATION OF AMERICA

Ronald Secrist was worried. Even at the last minute he debated about whether he should go through with his plan. The former administrative officer of Equity Funding Life Insurance Company, a subsidiary of Equity Funding Corporation of America, sat next to the telephone in his empty home. His wife was at work, and their three children had left for school. What about their safety? Shouldn't that concern him more than the shady dealings he knew were going on at Equity Funding? If the people at the company had the power to keep a fraud of such magnitude a secret for so many years, what retribution might await the person who exposed it? There had been rumors of Mafia connections at the company; indeed, one officer had told Secrist that he could get a contract on the life of anyone who talked. What if the authorities didn't believe him? He was still not sure he had enough information to make a case that they would investigate. But this dilemma had been eating away at him for three years. He had felt he would have to say something eventually, but he had to have a job; he had to provide for his family. After all, changing companies four times in the last 12 years did not look good on a resume. So he had gone along with the Equity Funding scheme, all the while plotting ways to expose it. Now that the company had fired him and he had another job, he decided the time was finally at hand. He picked up the receiver and dialed the number of the New York Insurance Department. When that was over, he made another call.

Source: This case drew heavily on Raymond L. Dirks and Leonard Gross, *The Great Wall Street Scandal* (New York: McGraw-Hill Book Co., 1974), for details related to the Equity Funding scandal.

Raymond Dirks, vice president of Delafield Childs, a Wall Street research firm, had found Ron Secrist's story difficult to believe. The New York securities analyst had received a call from Secrist one morning in early March 1973. The man had been fired from his job at Equity Funding Corporation of America, and now he wanted to tell the world that the company was a fraud. An obvious attempt at revenge, it appeared. But there had been rumors about Equity Funding before, and frankly Dirks had never thought much of this "go-go" company himself. The insurance industry, he felt, was generally unethical—and why had Equity Funding prospered during years when so many other insurance companies had gone under? Dirks decided to do some investigating on his own. He talked to present and former employees of Equity Funding, a number of executives of organizations which were clients of his firm, and everyone else he could think of who might have information on Equity Funding. Gradually he developed a picture of what had gone on. Partly because of his efforts, Equity Funding Corporation was exposed as one of the most spectacular frauds in the recent history of American business. On March 27, 1973, the New York Stock Exchange suspended trading in the company's stock, and a full investigation was undertaken.

But during his inquiry into the activities of Equity Funding, Raymond Dirks had gotten himself into serious trouble with the New York Stock Exchange and the Securities and Exchange Commission. In the process of corroborating what he had learned with several of his firm's large institutional clients, Dirks had let them know that something was apparently wrong at Equity Funding. Some of them had sold large blocks of their Equity Funding stock. The institutions and companies which had purchased that stock and had been left holding it when trading was suspended were now suing Dirks for millions of dollars. The Stock Exchange and the SEC accused Dirks of passing inside information to the institutions which "dumped" their stock. Not so, maintained Dirks. The people from whom he had obtained his leads had not been insiders. The insiders had been busy covering everything up. In fact, had he not told his clients and thus caused the stock price to drop suddenly, the scandal might have taken much longer to expose.

THE BEGINNINGS

The company which was to become Equity Funding was established in 1960 as Tongor Corporation, and a year later the name was changed to Equity Funding Corporation of America. One of the company's founders, Gordon McCormick, leading salesman in the United States for the Keystone mutual fund, had an idea for selling a package combining life insurance and mutual funds which he felt would be extremely attractive to buyers of insurance. Equity Funding Corporation was organized to sell McCormick's package, which became known as the "Equity Funding concept." As the program was sold, the customer signed up for both life insurance and mutual fund shares. He first bought a certain number of shares in the mutual fund, and these could then be used as collateral for a loan from Equity Funding Corporation to pay the premium on an insurance policy. Each year for ten years the customer would buy more shares and borrow against them to pay his annual insurance premium. In recent years the purchaser had to pay a minimum of $300 per year for insurance and purchase at least $750 worth of mutual fund shares annually. At the end of ten years, the customer sold enough shares to pay off the loans from Equity Funding. If the mutual funds had performed well during this time, the customer would have enough shares to repay his debt, have a nice profit in excess shares, and own a valuable life insurance policy as well. In addition, if the shares had not depreciated in value, he would have had ten years of free life insurance. The salesman who talked the client into buying the package received a double commission.

This was an ideal time to be in the life insurance business. An average life insurance stock rose 100 percent during 1961[1] and Equity Funding prospered. The major thrust of the company's business was not selling to people who had no life insurance, but rather convincing people who already had policies to cancel them and switch to the insurance-mutual funds combination. Insurance companies called this "twisting," but Equity Funding referred to it as "restructuring."[2] Customers were attracted by the prospect of a considerably higher return on their investments, but, at the same time, the practice did not endear Equity Funding Corporation to the rest of the insurance industry. While twisting was a relatively common practice in the industry, it had never before been used as the basis for a company's existence.

Equity Funding went public in 1964, and it was soon after this event that the fraudulent activities began. Shortly after the company's founding, Gordon McCormick's shares in it had been purchased by his four associates in the venture: Stanley Goldblum, Michael Riordan, Eugene Cuthbertson, and Raymond Platt. Platt died in 1964, and Cuthbertson quit the company the following year, leaving Goldblum and Riordan in control.

Michael Riordan was an outgoing, carousing Irishman whose fa-

---

[1] Raymond L. Dirks and Leonard Gross, *The Great Wall Street Scandal* (New York: McGraw-Hill Book Co., 1974), p. 29.

[2] Dirks and Gross, *The Great Wall Street Scandal*, p. 30.

vorite song was "The Impossible Dream." His father was vice president of Abraham and Strauss and owned a controlling interest in Stern's Department Store. Riordan was a great promoter, was excellent with the sales force, and had a personality that seemed to magnetize people. He was also a heavy drinker and a ladies' man. As chairman of the board of Equity Funding, it was he who thought up new ventures and maintained contact with Wall Street, where he had many close friends. He also provided much of the drive behind the company's sales force.

Stanley Goldblum had worked in a meat-packing plant, rose rapidly to plant supervisor, and then quit to sell insurance. He was variously described by people who knew him as cold, standoffish, authoritarian, arrogant, offensive, untrustworthy, and a loner who had little appreciation for other people's time. One insurance analyst told a *Wall Street Journal* reporter, "If you wanted to describe a man in the insurance business as someone you wouldn't want to do business with, you described him as another Stanley Goldblum."[3] Yet Goldblum's few close friends described him as warm and generous. He made substantial contributions to charity and political campaigns, including over $30,000 worth of Equity Funding stock to the Nixon reelection campaign, and he constantly gave money to his brother and other people out of his own pocket. Goldblum enjoyed high living. An athletic man, he had a $100,000 gym built onto his $300,000 home. He drove two Rolls Royces and a Ferrari, owned a 35-foot racing yacht, and was a knowledgeable art collector. By the early 1970s he was estimated to be worth $30 million. As president of Equity Funding Corporation, Goldblum managed the company and stayed in the background, leaving dealings with the public to Riordan. Ironically, Goldblum was often characterized by acquaintances and employees as straight-laced and puritanical. He became chairman of the National Association of Securities Dealers' business conduct committee during his tenure at Equity Funding. In that capacity he meted our harsh penalties in cases which came before him and was especially concerned with irregularities in the insurance industry. "I was completely taken in by Stanley Goldblum," said Lawrence Williams, vice president for Compliance at Equity Funding and former enforcement officer at the Securities and Exchange Commission. "He [Goldblum] gave the impression that if he caught somebody stealing he wanted him *out.* He seemed so upright."[4]

Stanley Goldblum now appears to have been the major force be-

[3] Hal Lancaster and G. Christian Hill, "Stanley Goldblum Is a Man of Many Facets—But What Are They?" *The Wall Street Journal,* April 27, 1973, p. 17.

[4] Wyndham Robertson, "Those Daring Young Con Men of Equity Funding; The Full Story of an Incredible Fraud," *Fortune,* vol. 88, no. 2 (August 1973), p. 85.

hind the Equity Funding fraud which seemingly stemmed from his obsession with keeping the price of Equity Funding's stock continually on the rise. If the stock price could be kept high, Equity Funding would be able to make acquisitions by trading valuable stock for the assets of other companies. The earnings of the companies thus acquired could be added in with those of the parent company, making Equity Funding appear to be increasing earnings when, in fact, it was losing money. The high stock price was also important in convincing banks to lend money to the company and in order to compensate the company's sales force, which was done largely by giving the salesmen stock options.

THE RISE OF EQUITY FUNDING

Through 1965, Equity Funding Corporation sold insurance and mutual funds as an agent for other companies—principally Pennsylvania Life Insurance Company of Philadelphia and the Keystone mutual funds organization in Boston—and most of its income came from commissions. It did begin to finance some program loans of its own in 1964, however. In 1966, according to a later Equity Funding prospectus, the company sold $226.3 million worth of insurance policies, mostly those of Pennsylvania Life. In addition, while mutual fund sales dropped substantially in that year nationally, Equity Funding reported a 47 percent increase in profits and a 58 percent increase ($6 million) in program loans, $4 million of which it had financed itself.[5] With this kind of rise in the company's earnings, its stock price went steadily upwards.

It was in November of that profitable year that Equity Funding received permission to list its common stock on the American Stock Exchange. In the November/December issue of its publication *American Investor*, the American Stock Exchange noted the following progress being made in its operations:

> *Listing Standards.* Twice since 1962 standards have been raised or supplemented. More important, companies that exceed the higher standards are being attracted to the Exchange. The average newly listed common stock in 1965 represented a company with net tangible assets of more than $6 million (the criterion is $1 million). Similarly, standards for net income, number of shares publicly held, and number of shareholders are being exceeded by wide margins.
>
> Establishment of delisting criteria has resulted in removal of more than 100 issues.[6]

---

[5] Ibid., p. 120.

[6] "Time of Change," *American Investor*, vol. II, no. 10 (November/December 1966), p. 10.

It was also in 1966 that Equity Funding Corporation started its own mutual fund, Equity Growth Fund of America, and the following year it rapidly began to acquire other companies. The year 1967 saw the purchase of Presidential Life Insurance Company of America, a Chicago-based firm. During 1968 and 1969, Equity Funding acquired Bankers National Life Insurance Company of Parsippany, New Jersey; Northern Life Insurance Company of Seattle; a savings and loan association; a mutual funds company; and Investors Planning Corporation, the domestic assets of a Swiss firm called Investors Overseas Services. (Investors Overseas Services was soon to become embroiled in a scandal of its own which involved the transference of millions of dollars of the company's assets to other companies controlled by IOS's chairman of the board Robert Vesco. Also implicated in this far-reaching scheme were the nephew of Richard Nixon, the son of the late Franklin D. Roosevelt, the president of Costa Rica and his son, and a former Cuban foreign minister.)

Equity Funding also entered the oil and gas exploration and cattle breeding businesses. All the while, the corporation's stock continued to soar. By 1969, the stock which had started out at $6.00 a share in 1964 was selling for $80 a share.

But 1969 was a significant year for Equity Funding in other ways. It saw the death of Michael Riordan in a mudslide which engulfed his home, and there were problems with retraining the low-caliber sales force of Investors Planning Corporation and meeting rapidly increasing expenses. Despite these setbacks, Equity Funding reported an earnings increase of nearly 40 percent. Program loans funded by the company had jumped from $19.9 million to $29.5 million.[7] Perhaps the most significant event of all was an agreement entered into by Presidential Life Insurance Company, the Equity Funding subsidiary, with Ranger National Life Insurance Company, whereby Ranger National would reinsure a large amount of Presidential's business. (Presidential also had reinsurance arrangements with other companies.) Reinsuring, a widespread practice in the insurance industry, meant that Ranger National purchased for a substantial sum policies which Presidential sold. Presidential thus acquired needed cash, and Ranger National was promised most of the future premiums from the policies it bought. The details of the deal were described in *Fortune* as follows:

> The new agreement provided that Ranger would take on all of Presidential's business not [re]insured elsewhere in the second half of 1969, and would also get certain other new business through 1973. Over the entire four-and-a-half-year period, Ranger would [re]insure business

---

[7] Robertson, "Those Daring Young Con Men," p. 122.

represented by a maximum of $15 million in first-year premiums. At the end of 1972, Ranger held some $835 million of insurance in force that had been ceded from the Equity Funding subsidiary.

There was one peculiar aspect to the deal. Presidential, whose name was changed to Equity Funding Life Insurance Co. in 1970, *guaranteed* a "persistency rate" of 85 percent in the second year. That is, it guaranteed that policyholders representing 85 percent of the first-year premiums would also pay in the second year—or EFLIC would make up the difference. This unusual provision served as a "kicker" that enticed the [re]insurers to pay more than they normally would have for the business. Under most [re]insurance agreements, the [re]insurer pays around 100 to 120 percent of the first-year premium (which is a bit less than what it would have cost the [re]insurer to write the business itself). But the persistency guarantee assured the [re]insurer of getting back most of its cash outlay by the second year; in addition, the guarantee strongly implied that EFLIC viewed the policyholders as loyal. For these reasons it was able to get 180 percent—and, in some recent agreements, 190 percent.

. . . In practice, this meant that EFLIC would keep the first-year premium and receive an additional 80 percent (or 90 percent) in cash from Ranger. The arrangement naturally did a lot for EFLIC's profits. The costs charged against the [re]insured business in the first year showed up as a little less than the amount of the first-year premium. Hence EFLIC netted a little *more* that the [re]insurance payment. In 1969, thanks to several such [re]insurance agreements, EFLIC contributed significantly to Equity Funding's profits. Altogether, it accounted for about 20 percent of the parent's reported aftertax earnings.[8]

Apparently this arrangement and others like it provided the setting for a major part of the scandal at Equity Funding, which was centered in the Equity Funding Life Insurance Company subsidiary. But the fraud had its beginnings much earlier.

THE FALL

As events have been reconstructed, the fraud at Equity Funding Corporation began with overstatement of assets. While Equity Funding's prospectus of May 25, 1967 indicated that "the greater part" of its $226.3 million worth of life insurance sold in 1966 had been policies of Pennsylvania Life Insurance Company, Pennsylvania Life's own prospectus, dated June 22, 1967, reported that "a total of $58.6 million of face amount of life insurance was sold by Equity Funding agents." No one caught the discrepancy until Alan Abelson

---

[8] Robertson, "Those Daring Young Con Men," p. 122.

of *Barrons* wrote in his "Up and Down Wall Street" column on April 16, 1973:

> Circumstantial evidence . . . indicates that Equity Funding might have been cooking its books a lot earlier than anyone has yet suggested. The possibility was raised to us by a keen-eyed reader with a long memory. And, with the help of our colleague Steve Anreder, we secured a couple of old prospectuses and did a little sleuthing, all of which tends to confirm the suspicion . . . .[9]

Abelson then went on to describe the difference in figures noted above. Apparently earnings were inflated every year after 1966. Of the $6 million in program loans reported sold in 1966, $4 million appear never to have existed. Loans were simply invented and then counted as assets. Nevertheless, in March 1968, Equity Funding's auditors issued an unqualified certification of the company's 1967 financial statement. In later years, the company listed nonexistent bonds and securities as assets and even went so far as to print counterfeit securities. In 1972, the company listed in its year-end statement a purchase of commercial paper worth $8 million. But when investigators later tried to trace the sale, the bank had no record of it. The paper had never existed. By the time the fraud was exposed in April 1973, over $110 million of the assets Equity Funding Corporation claimed to possess were fictitious. Funded loans totaling $62.3 million supposedly made to Equity Funding policyholders simply had never been made. Fictitious bonds amounted to $24.6 million.[10]

In 1970, Equity Funding Life Insurance Company (formerly Presidential Life Insurance Company) began to invent insurance policyholders. Business was slow, and something had to be done to prevent the company from showing a loss, which would have caused the price of Equity Funding Corporation stock to drop. So imaginary policyholders were dreamed up and their policies then reinsured with Ranger National. The cash thus obtained was an excellent boost for profits. But problems arose the following year when 90 percent of the premiums on the reinsured policies had to be turned over to Ranger. To get the money, EFLIC invented still more policies, reinsured *them*, and paid the previous year's premiums with the present year's income. So year by year, the need for more policies mushroomed, until *Fortune* estimated that in the tenth year of the fraudulent operation, Equity Funding would have had to reinsure over $3.7 billion worth of phony insurance policies to pay all the premiums on previous nonexistent policies.[11] In spite of the incredible speed with which the

---

[9] Alan Abelson, "Up and Down Wall Street," *Barrons*, April 16, 1973, p. 1.

[10] Robertson, "Those Daring Young Con Men," p. 84.

[11] Ibid., p. 124.

costs of the fraud mounted, Equity Funding's top officials evidently believed that the phony business could eventually be phased out and the company made completely legitimate.

Nor was financing the only problem with the reinsurance scheme. In order to fool the auditors, EFLIC had to have files on all of its imaginary policyholders, complete with all the information the company would normally obtain on such people noted on the proper forms. Creating these was a time-consuming process, and in addition to hiring clerks who scored particularly low on the company's intelligence test (so they wouldn't wonder why they were forging forms) to perform the tedious work, the executives reportedly had evening "manufacturing parties" at which they gleefully made up names and filled out forms with details on imaginary customers. The invented customers were generally variations of real ones. Information on extant policyholders was altered slightly to form new policies, and these were then scattered throughout various policy number blocks in the computer records to prevent the similarities from being discovered. Ronald Secrist reported receiving letters from the company's internal auditors for Ronald Secret and Ronald Crist which he was expected to sign confirming that those two men had loans from Equity Funding.[12] For the sake of realism, a policyholder had to be "killed off" occasionally. Equity Funding would arrange for the claim to be paid to an employee's address, and apparently this money was sometimes pocketed by the recipient.

In addition, the company's computers had to be programmed in such a way that the auditors could obtain some information—but not too much—on the phony business, identified as "Department 99." The auditors would not check every policy, but would take a sampling of policy files and check the contents with premium receipts and policy reserve information. If files which the auditors requested on imaginary policyholders were incomplete or had not yet been made up, Equity Funding employees would say that these files were temporarily unavailable and then write up the missing documents so that they would be ready the next day. Each insurance policy had a five-digit identification number, but the printout which was given to the auditors contained only the last three digits of that number. In this way, numbers could easily be repeated without causing suspicion. Equity Funding explained the tremendous amount of activity in Department 99 by saying that this represented mail-order sales. It puzzled employees of the computer section that no bills were ever sent to any of the vast number of mail-order customers listed under Department 99.

---

[12] Dirks and Gross, *The Great Wall Street Scandal*, p. 79.

In still another aspect of the scheme, Equity Funding Corporation, which had begun its spectacular rise with an idea for using the same money more than once, put that knack to considerable use transferring funds back and forth from the parent company to its subsidiaries to make it appear that its growing nonexistent assets really were there. *Fortune* described the situation with EFLIC, the site of most of the phony business:

> Beginning in 1970, it appears, the parent would "lend" money to bogus program participants (creating assets for Equity Funding) and credit EFLIC through an intercompany account with similar amounts of money in premium income. EFLIC in turn paid out sales commissions to the various marketing subsidiaries of Equity Funding, and these payments were debited against the intercompany account. The premiums credited to EFLIC exceeded the commissions it paid out, however, so the parent owed money to its life-insurance subsidiary at the end of the year. To clear this account, the parent transferred securities, rather than cash, to the life company. Those securities—in this case $24.6 million in bonds—are the ones that don't exist. [13]

While the policies reinsured in 1969 had apparently been genuine, "by 1972 virtually all the business reinsured—represented by over $7 million in first-year premiums—was phony." [14] EFLIC was now reinsuring policies with Kentucky Central Life, Great Central Life, and Connecticut General Life, as well as Ranger National.

In 1970, Equity Funding applied for permission to list its common stock on the New York Stock Exchange. Permission was granted in October 1970, but the Stock Exchange insisted that Equity Funding enlarge its board of directors and replace its present outside auditor with a larger firm.

Equity Funding Corporation was at that time being audited by the firm of Wolfson, Weiner, Ratoff and Lapin. The man in charge of Equity Funding's daily auditing was an auditor with Wolfson, Weiner named Sol Block. He was not a Certified Public Accountant and had an office on the executive floor of Equity Funding's corporate headquarters. The auditors of Equity Funding's largest subsidiary, Equity Funding Life Insurance Company, were Haskins and Sells. In 1972, after the New York Stock Exchange's decision, Wolfson, Weiner merged with the larger accounting firm of Seidman and Seidman. Seidman and Seidman now became the auditors of the parent corporation as well as the subsidiary, replacing Haskins and Sells at EFLIC. The same individuals who had conducted the Wolfson, Weiner audits now audited Equity Funding for Seidman and Seidman.

---

[13] Robertson, "Those Daring Young Con Men," p. 124.

[14] Ibid.

In further compliance with the Stock Exchange's ruling, four new directors were named to Equity Funding's board in 1972. They were: Fred Levin, executive vice president, Insurance Operations and Marketing, Equity Funding; Gayle Livingston, vice president of the Professional Services and Equipment Group of Litton Industries, Inc.; Samuel B. Lowell, executive vice president, Corporate Operations and Finance, Equity Funding; and Judson Sayre, a retired industrialist who had developed the first automatic home washing machine while at Bendix Corporation and had later been a vice president of Borg-Warner Corporation. Other members of the board included: Yura Arkus-Duntov, executive vice president, Investment Management Operations, Equity Funding; Robert Bowie, director, Institute of International Relations, Harvard University; Herbert Glaser, executive vice president, Real Estate and International Operations, Equity Funding; Stanley Goldblum, president and chairman of the board, Equity Funding; and Nelson Loud, one of the founders of New York Securities Company, a director of several other companies, and a trustee of the Union Dime Savings Bank of New York.

Other parties were keeping their eyes on Equity Funding. During the early 1970s, the company was researched by such prominent brokerage firms as Burnham and Company, Lehman Brothers, Edwards and Hanly, Wertheim and Company, and Adams, Harkness and Hill. The firms' reports ranged from favorable to glowing, and all recommended purchase of Equity Funding's stock. As recently as February 9, 1973, Wertheim and Company reported that Equity Funding was "unlikely to be 'impacted' by [the 'Truth in Insurance' hearings opening in Washington at that time] and that it seemed 'most attractive at about nine times fully diluted earnings.'"[15] A group of institutional analysts chose Equity Funding in 1972 as its favorite stock out of the many finance and financial services securities.[16] In the February 1973, issue of *Institutional Investor,* two of five analysts whose opinions were featured in an article on life insurance companies said that Equity Funding would be one of 1973's star performers.[17] A report was issued by Hayden, Stone, Inc. on March 26, 1973, stating that "several rumors have been circulating which have affected Equity Funding's stock; we have checked these rumors, and there appears to be no substance to them." Hayden, Stone had checked with the insurance departments of Washington, Illinois, and New Jersey (states in which insurance companies owned by Equity Funding were licensed) and "each man told us that he is not conducting an investigation of Equity Funding or any of its subsidiaries,

---

[15] "The Spreading Scandal at Equity Funding," *Business Week,* April 14, 1973, p. 84.
[16] Ibid.
[17] Dirks and Gross, *The Great Wall Street Scandal,* p. 258.

had no present intention of conducting an investigation, and knows of no other insurance department that is conducting such an investigation."[18] A spokesman for Ranger National Life Insurance Company told *Barrons* columnist Alan Abelson that his company had run spot checks on Equity Funding policies and had "never uncovered an instance of fictitious insurance."[19] Indeed, in 1970 the president of Anderson, Clayton, Ranger National's parent company, asked the accounting firm of Peat, Marwick, Mitchell to conduct a special review of EFLIC. The review was begun, and the management of Equity Funding was kept quite busy dreaming up schemes to fool the investigators. But when the men from Peat, Marwick came back for a third visit, they were told that management was simply too busy to provide them with the information they needed. The auditors left and did not return.[20]

On March 6, 1973, Ronald Secrist made his telephone calls to Raymond Dirks and the New York State Insurance Department. Both Dirks and the Insurance Department began investigating. Meanwhile, the Illinois and California insurance departments sent in examiners to conduct a surprise audit of the company. Equity Funding executives tried a lastditch effort to cover up the fraud—including bugging the room in which the examiners were working to find out what they were uncovering—but it was no use. At a board of directors' meeting on April 1, 1973, Stanley Goldblum and two other top executives who had helped him organize the scheme were forced to resign. They protested, asserting that they were entitled to severance and vacation pay, and they offered to run the company as consultants for $200 an hour. Finally, one of the directors ordered them off the premises. The California Insurance Department seized Equity Funding's plush offices on the top floors of 1900 Avenue of the Stars in Century City, changed all the locks on the doors, and installed guards with clubs and pistols to prevent anything from being removed and to keep out the deposed executives.

The company filed for reorganization the following Thursday under Chapter Ten of the Federal Bankruptcy Act. Normally the assets of a bankrupt company would have been sold and the proceeds used to pay its creditors. But under Chapter Ten, Equity Funding could continue to exist. A trustee, Robert Loeffler, formerly a lawyer with Investors Diversified Services, was appointed by the court to take over the company and try to straighten out the mess.

Touche Ross and Company began an audit of Equity Funding to

---

[18] Robert J. Cole, "Anatomy of an Insurance Scandal," *The New York Times,* April 15, 1973, sec. 3, p. 9.

[19] Alan Abelson, "Up and Down Wall Street," *Barrons,* April 2, 1973, p. 25.

[20]Robertson, "Those Daring Young Con Men," pp. 127–28, 132.

find out exactly what was there. Equity Funding Corporation in its 1972 annual report had listed assets of $737.5 million and a net worth of $143.4 million. The audit found the actual assets to be $488.9 million and set the net worth at a *negative* $42 million.[21] The company had never had any genuine profits, and in fact had suffered huge losses each year. The auditors found the accounting at Equity Funding to be "chaotic," and they could not reconstruct an accurate statement of Equity Funding's profits and losses. Millions of dollars of the company's funds could not be found. There was no evidence of embezzlement except of some phony death claims, and it was concluded that the missing money—some $80 million—went to cover the ever-increasing operating costs.

In February 1974, Robert Loeffler, the court-appointed trustee, described the company he was attempting to reorganize as "virtually a fiction concocted by certain members of its management, a fiction enlarged upon year by year, until Equity Funding Corporation of America [was] proclaimed the fastest growing diversified financial company in *Fortune's* list."[22] In November of that year he filed a 239-page report on his findings regarding the fraud with a Los Angeles federal court. In his report, Loeffler characterized the fraud not as the carefully calculated, well-organized scheme some had thought it to be, but rather as a haphazard, frantic series of attempts to cover up each successive fraud with a bigger one, held together by the "lies, audacity, and luck"[23] of Goldblum and his associates.

Loeffler felt that the company could be successfully reorganized, probably as a holding company based upon a couple of its subsidiaries which had been healthy at the time of the collapse. Twenty-two former officers of the company and three auditors had been indicted by federal and state grand juries on charges including conspiracy, mail fraud, stock fraud, filing false bank statements, interstate transportation of counterfeit securities and securities obtained by fraud, falsifying financial statements, and illegal wiretapping. Eighteen of the former officers, including Stanley Goldblum, had so far pleaded guilty, and the trials of others were in progress. As of December 1974, trading had still not been resumed in Equity Funding's stock.

In the meantime, lawsuits totaling in the millions of dollars had been filed against Equity Funding Corporation. It was not known whether the worthless stock now owned by prominent universities

[21] "Criminal Trial in Equity Funding Case Starts Today for Two Former Officers," *The Wall Street Journal*, October 1, 1974, p. 16.

[22] *The Wall Street Journal*, February 22, 1974, p. 6.

[23] William E. Blundell, "Equity Funding Trustee Calls the Fraud Inept, and Assails the Auditors," *The Wall Street Journal*, November 4, 1974, p. 4.

including Princeton, Amherst, Antioch, and Sarah Lawrence, and other institutional investors such as the Ohio State Teachers Retirement System, Salomon Brothers, the Ford Foundation, and the New World Foundation, as well as numerous individuals, would ever regain any value. In addition, those companies which had bought Equity Funding stock in the last frantic days of trading were now suing to force the companies which had sold it—because they knew about the fraud, said the suits—to take back the stock and the losses. It was estimated that these legal actions would take years to complete.

AFTERTHOUGHT

Probably one of the most unusual aspects of the Equity Funding fraud was the fact that it was not a closely guarded secret. It is now believed that over 100 people within the organization were aware of the fraud's existence to some extent. The very nature of the fraud necessitated its rapid expansion and the involvement of more and more people. As the fraudulent activities filtered down from top management to subordinates, it created what trustee Robert Loeffler called "a climate of moral decay."[24] There were numerous cases of individuals' embezzling relatively small amounts of money. Some billed the company for personal expenses; others stole money or checks. When these people were caught, they were not fired but were instead set to work assisting in the fraud. Those who had falsified death claims and pocketed the money now did the same thing for the company. Offenders were even given financial assistance to help them repay what they had taken.

Many employees who were not involved in embezzlement or even directly in the fraud itself nonetheless knew about some aspects of it. Some examples follow.[25]

> Early in 1972, Ron Ronchetti, a specialist in computer systems employed by Equity Funding Life Insurance Company, requested a list of Equity Funding's funded insurance policies to resolve a problem regarding sales commissions. The printout he received listed 18,000 policies; Equity Funding's 1971 annual report had listed 41,121. Shortly thereafter, Ronchetti was fired. He decided not to say anything about his discovery, since his word alone would mean nothing.
>
> Frank Majerus, controller of Equity Funding Life Insurance Company, was ordered by a company official to write up a phony insurance file. Majerus had become increasingly suspicious that something un-

---

[24] Ibid.

[25] For more detailed descriptions of these individuals and situations, see Dirks and Gross, *The Great Wall Street Scandal.*

savory was going on at Equity Funding, and this confirmed his fears. He was so upset that he went to his minister for advice. The minister told him that his first duty was to protect his job for the sake of his family. Still, Majerus was dismayed at the way Equity Funding was being run, and some months later, in October 1971, he resigned. He wanted desperately to tell someone about what he knew, even if it meant implicating himself, but he did not trust the authorities. He was sure he could not convince them to investigate.

Bob Ochoa ran an Equity Funding print shop in Santa Monica. One day Fred Levin, executive vice president for Marketing of Equity Funding, and three other company officials came in to see him. They showed him pictures of securities certificates for a number of leading American companies and asked him to make plates and run copies of them for a presentation they were preparing on retirement programs. The executives insisted on taking everything with them after each evening printing session. Scrap materials had to be put through a paper shredder. Ochoa had done a bit of investing himself. He knew what the securities certificates were, and he was surprised, to say the least. But these men were at the highest levels of the corporation—they must know what they were doing, so why ask questions?

In July 1971, Pat Hopper, administrative officer of Equity Funding Corporation, went to the office of Jim Banks, an attorney and assistant secretary of EFLIC, to OK a letter containing information on Beneficial National Life, a company which underwrote policies for Equity Funding, which had been requested by the New Jersey Insurance Department. Finding the letter to be satisfactory, Hopper told Banks he would send it to the president of Beneficial for his signature. No, Banks told him, he would take care of it. And with that he pulled out a form containing the Beneficial president's signature and traced it onto the letter. Hopper was speechless.

Several months later, Hopper was made vice president for Investments of Bankers National Life Insurance Company, Equity Funding's recently acquired subsidiary in New Jersey. In December 1971, he received a phone call from Lloyd Edens, secretary-treasurer of EFLIC. Edens wanted Hopper to send $3 million from Bankers National to the EFLIC offices in California. Edens would keep it three hours and then return it to Hopper. That way, with the time difference between California and New Jersey, the $3 million would be on the books of both companies at the close of business on December 31. This was the most recent in a series of such requests, all of which Hopper had refused. Arthur Lewis, EFLIC's actuary, informed him that he was costing the company 14 cents a share on its earnings report for the year by his continued refusal to cooperate. Hopper resigned in disgust. He was now convinced that Equity Funding was a fraud, but he knew also that he would say nothing because he had no proof. He was simply relieved to be out of the mess.

Case

FOUR SEASONS NURSING CENTERS OF AMERICA, INC.

In 1973, Jack L. Clark lived in a house which had cost him an estimated $1 million to build. The house resembled a stone fortress on the outside, and the entrance was through ten-foot carved wooden doors. The 20,000 square foot home, which included an all-white living room through which warm water moats flowed, walls of various colors of marble, a reflecting swimming pool with its 4,000 square foot cabana in an inner courtyard, and a large collection of French cut glass and other art objects, had been decorated by Arthur Elrod, one of the most expensive and well-known interior decorators in the United States. It was said that having Elrod decorate a home would cost at least $500,000. In his trophy room, Clark kept the results of his fishing and hunting expeditions, including huge stuffed fish and a number of large African animals—some heads on the wall, and others stuffed in their entirety and standing about the room in different poses—prizes collected on an African safari. Clark could contemplate them all from behind the gigantic yellow marble desk which stood at one end of the room. Three years earlier the company which Clark had founded, Four Seasons Nursing Centers of America, Inc., had declared bankruptcy. The problem was one of liquidity; the company had been nearly out of funds. Clark had resigned his position as president and retired to his sumptuous home.

Source: A series of articles by Rone Tempest which appeared in *The Oklahoma Journal* from February 29 to March 10, 1972, was especially useful in writing this case.

THE BEGINNINGS OF FOUR SEASONS

In 1963, Jack L. Clark was the proprietor of a successful home construction company in Oklahoma City, Oklahoma. He had begun working early as a laborer in the oil fields and had been a milkman, sold building materials for U.S. Gypsum and golf carts for Fairway King, Inc., and then had begun his own company, Fashion Built Homes, Inc. Through his various sales jobs he had gained the reputation of being a "super salesman."

Perhaps Clark's half brother, Tom J. Gray, had this sales ability in mind when he contacted Clark in 1963 about expanding his nursing home business. Gray had operated Gray's Nursing Home, which he had converted from the Hillside Motel in Henrietta, Texas, since 1958. The operation had become quite profitable, and Gray wanted to look into the possibility of building more nursing homes.

Clark and Gray came to the conclusion that there was a definite need for skilled nursing care in the United States. Clark approached Amos D. "Bud" Bouse, another Oklahoma City land developer, with the nursing home idea. Bouse was interested, and the three men set to work to devise the structure of their homes. They came up with what was apparently a revolutionary concept in nursing home design. The homes would be built in an X shape, with four wings extending out from a central area in which two nursing stations were located. This meant that one head nurse could supervise employees and activities in all four wings of the home, whereas in the converted old houses or motels which comprised most of the nursing homes in existence at that time, a head nurse was required for each section of the facility. In Four Seasons Nursing Centers' first annual report, Jack Clark noted that "This design, coupled with our management program, allows Four Seasons to provide more adequate care on a 100-bed facility with 36–44 employees. Facilities of similar size seldom operate efficiently with less than 65. The difference is about $7,000 a month in payroll."[1]

The three men went looking for financing to begin building nursing homes. The nursing home industry did not have a reputation for being highly profitable, but during 1964 and 1965 investors began to take more interest in the field. Financing became easier to get. Clark, Bouse, and Gray built their first home in Odessa, Texas, in 1964.

In 1967, Four Seasons Nursing Centers of America was incorporated in Delaware. Four Seasons issued 300,000 shares of stock and received in return capital stock in 12 other corporations, including nursing homes in a number of cities in the Southwest and several

---

[1] Four Seasons Nursing Centers of America, Inc., 1968 Annual Report.

construction companies owned by Clark and Bouse. After incorpora-
tion, Four Seasons began a period of spectacular growth. In Four
Seasons' 1969 annual report, the company's net income for the year
ending June 30 was reported to be $2,651,000, as compared with 1968
income of $811,000. Operating revenue had increased from $6,577,000
in 1968 to $19,296,000 the following year, and assets had risen from
$7,243,000 to $37,736,000.[2]

HELP FROM UNCLE SAM

The company's growth was largely due to the passage of Medicare
(Title 18, Part A of the Social Security Act) by Congress on July 28,
1965.[3] Medicare covered hospital benefits for the elderly, which went
into effect on July 1, 1966, and provided "extended care" coverage for
those who needed continued care after leaving the hospital. This
second provision became effective January 1, 1967.[4] Since there were
only about 600 hospitals in the entire country which had wards or
wings devoted to convalescent care[5]—a fact which the congressional
proponents of the Medicare bill had overlooked—the Social Security
Administration, which was responsible for administering the program, decided to allow nursing homes to be designated as extended
care facilities, thus making them eligible to receive federal payments.
Through Medicare, persons over 65 could have the first 20 days of
nursing home care paid for entirely by the government. For the next
80 days the government would pay all costs above $5.00 per day. If a
person had to stay longer in a home, he could be classified as medi-
cally indigent—that is, able to meet his other expenses but not his
medical ones—under Title 19 of the Social Security Act, otherwise
known as Medicaid. Medicaid was paid partly by the federal government and partly by the states, usually was coordinated through state
welfare systems, and normally paid the entire cost of nursing home
care. The program was administered by the Medical Services Administration, part of the Department of Health, Education, and Welfare, and thus neither benefits nor standards tended to be coordinated with those of Medicare.

The three founders of Four Seasons saw in the Medicare-Medicaid
welfare program an unusually attractive business opportunity. In
addition, as Jack Clark noted in a speech before the New York Society

---

[2] Four Seasons Nursing Centers of America, Inc., 1969 Annual Report.

[3] Claire Townsend, *Old Age: The Last Segregation* (New York: Grossman Publishers,
1971), p. 38.

[4] Ibid., p. 42.

[5] Ibid., p. 40.

of Security Analysts on July 11, 1969, there was "a shortage in this country of approximately 500,000 skilled beds. The industry is building at the rate of 70,000 beds a year. The over-65 population in America is increasing at the rate of 350,000 per year."[6]

THE METHOD OF OPERATION

With this need for nursing homes in mind, Four Seasons set out to develop a business system which could take maximum advantage of the opportunity. During the first year of the company's existence, the method of operation was to contact a group of physicians in a south-western community of moderate size and attempt to interest them in a limited partnership in a nursing home. The doctors' group, in order to obtain financing to build such a home, would ordinarily have had to put up 25 percent of the amount they wished to borrow. Four Seasons would offer to provide 30 percent of that equity if the doctors could get together the other 70 percent. This meant that, for a $400,000 nursing home, the group of doctors only had to come up with $70,000 instead of $100,000. Four Seasons would build the home and as the general partner would operate the home and be liable for all debts. If the nursing center was a failure, the doctors, with their limited partnership, would lose only the amount they had originally invested, which for a doctor with a large income could simply represent a tax write-off. The doctors would generally refer their patients to the home, which helped to ensure its success.

It was originally felt the doctors would be happy with the nursing homes as sources of revenue and would not interfere with Four Seasons' management of the facilities. This did not prove to be the case, however, and dealing with the doctors' groups became troublesome. This interference, coupled with the company's rapid rate of expansion, caused Four Seasons to look for another sort of buyer for their homes.

The answer to the problem was provided by Four Seasons' investment bankers, Walston and Company, in November 1968. Their idea was to set up Four Seasons Equity Corporation, a company whose purpose would be to search out locations for new nursing centers, buy the centers from Four Seasons of America when they were completed, and pay Four Seasons to manage them. Equity would then get 70 percent of the operating profits.

Walston and Company obtained $19.5 million in financing from ten midwestern insurance companies to set up Four Seasons Equity

---

[6] Rone Tempest, "Nursing Home Empire Began in Texas Motel," *The Oklahoma Journal*, March 2, 1972.

Corporation, and Jack Clark, Amos Bouse, and Tom Gray supplied an additional $3 million. The group of insurance companies was concerned that Equity be separate from Four Seasons. By Securities and Exchange Commission rules, a firm could own no more than 30 per cent of a firm which bought its products and still declare a profit from the sale of those goods. Four Seasons wanted to be able to declare construction profits when they sold nursing homes to Equity. So a corporation called FSN was set up of which Four Seasons owned 30 percent and Equity 70 percent. The profits from nursing home operations in which the two companies participated were placed in this third corporation.

FOUR SEASONS AND THE STOCK MARKET

The first public offering of Four Seasons stock took place on May 9, 1968. Four Seasons issued 300,000 shares of common stock which produced $3 million in capital; in addition, Jack Clark sold 60,000 shares of his own stock in the company for a personal gain of $600,000. This ratio of corporate to executive proceeds for a stock offering was reportedly considered acceptable.

On November 26 of the same year, Four Seasons made a second public stock offering. One hundred thousand shares were sold for the company, resulting in a gain of $5.5 million. Clark, Bouse, Gray, and Montgomery Company, a wholly owned subsidiary of Walston and Company, each sold large blocks of their personal stock totaling 497,800 shares, which brought them profits of $10 million, $6 million, $4 million, and $4 million, respectively.

When Four Seasons made its first public offering in May 1968, its stock was sold for $11 per share. Within four months the price had risen to $42. Before the end of the year Four Seasons stock hit $100 a share. It was split two-for-one and proceeded to rise to $90.75 in 1969. The rapid upward movement of the stock price helped to make Four Seasons a popular "glamour stock," particularly attractive to institutional investors.

In general, nursing home stocks had become extremely popular as the government's increasing interest in the plight of the nation's elderly seemed to ensure the continued profitability of the industry. The number of nursing homes in the United States skyrocketed from 13,000 in 1967 to over 23,000 in 1969.[7] In February 1969, Barrons noted that there were some 50 nursing home corporations "on the market or in registration."[8] A month later, Barrons reported that there were

[7] Townsend, *Old Age: The Last Segregation*, p. 96.
[8] *Barrons*, February 10, 1969, p. 3.

some 74 such corporations.[9] Medicare and Medicaid had been instrumental in transforming a relatively unprofitable, mom-and-pop-style group of small businesses into a giant industry which *Barrons* described early in 1969 as "the hottest investment around today."[10]

THE DECLINE

But the very popularity that the nursing home field enjoyed was one of the factors which helped to bring down Four Seasons. For by 1969, instead of being the only nursing center company listed on a major stock exchange (the American), Four Seasons had a number of major competitors. That year also saw a general slump in stock market activity. Construction costs had nearly doubled during the previous two years. Still another problem was the beginning of a government crackdown on payments to nursing homes. In 1969, the Social Security Administration announced its intention to put a stop to nonmedical payments then being made to nursing homes. Congress too was becoming concerned with the large amounts being spent on the programs and threatened to cut appropriations for Medicaid by $235 million,[11] which caused some states to threaten to stop the matching support they contributed to the Medicaid program. The sizable bureaucracy associated with Medicare and Medicaid made is possible for some nursing homes to charge the government for unperformed services and nonexistent patients, but it also sometimes made it difficult or impossible to obtain payment for actual services.

A last problem facing Four Seasons concerned its accounting practices. Four Seasons had traditionally declared construction profits on partially completed nursing homes. Representatives of the company's auditors, Arthur Andersen and Company, and an architect would go to construction sites and decide what percentage of the project appeared to be completed. Four Seasons would then declare that percentage of the expected construction profits as earnings on its next quarterly report. In 1969, the Securities and Exchange Commission began to put pressure on Four Seasons to stop this practice, and Arthur Andersen converted to a "cost to cost" method of accounting, under which if Four Seasons had incurred two thirds of the estimated costs of building a home, it could count as earnings two thirds of the projected profits from the job.

Another accounting complication involved the company's Four

---

[9] *Barrons,* March 17, 1969, p. 29.

[10] *Barrons,* February 10, 1969, p. 3.

[11] Rone Tempest, "Empire Profits by Selling to Itself," *The Oklahoma Journal,* March 4, 1972.

Seasons Franchise Division, which set up statewide franchises for the parent corporation. Four Seasons Franchise would provide 100 percent of the financing to the company buying one of its nursing homes. The franchisee would make a public stock offering and then take out 25 percent of the proceeds from the sale and return it to Four Seasons Franchise in the form of a franchise fee—which fee Four Seasons would then declare as earnings. In 1969, Arthur Andersen questioned whether this guaranteed financing was anything more than returning the franchise fee to the franchisee—in effect, loaning the buyer all the money it needed to buy Four Seasons' product, which would not be very different from Four Seasons selling nursing homes to itself.

In spite of these difficulties, a remarkable number of people felt Jack Clark could overcome all the problems. Even as the stock market slumped, Clark was busy developing subsidiaries such as Embassy Construction, National Medical Supply Company, Four Seasons United, and Four Seasons Overseas.[12] Clark helped to give the company its glamorous and profitable image with his flamboyant lifestyle and perpetual confident predictions of rapid growth and huge earnings for his company. In a speech before the New York Society of Security Analysts on July 11, 1969, Clark predicted that within six years his company would build the equivalent of 1,000 100-bed nursing centers. Indeed, 70 of those centers would be in operation by the end of 1969.[13] This latter claim was one of the issues brought up by executives of the American Stock Exchange when they called Jack Clark in for a conference on November 3, 1969.

The Exchange was concerned about Four Seasons' practice of declaring 100 percent construction profits on nursing homes of which it was 30 percent owner. In addition, Clark had made some statements in a taped interview regarding $90 million in long-term financing which Four Seasons had obtained, and the Exchange wanted to know the source of that financing. The Exchange was also concerned about the relationship between one of its specialists, Francis R. Santangelo, who was assigned to handle Four Seasons stock, and the Four Seasons' president. That relationship, Clark assured them, was purely social. He and Santangelo had never discussed any detailed matters regarding the stock market. The Exchange was particularly insistent that Four Seasons meet its 7,000-bed prediction by December 31, and that failure to meet that objective be immediately reported to the public.

During that November the price of Four Seasons stock dropped by

---

[12] Rone Tempest, "Glamour Stock Soared on Dreams," *The Oklahoma Journal,* March 3, 1972.

[13] Ibid.

15 points. Nevertheless, on November 30 *The Wall Street Journal* reported:

> Jack Clark, Four Seasons' president, said he expects to report that second quarter net more than tripled year earlier figures. He adds, though, that net might have been even higher had it not been for a company decision to decelerate somewhat expansion of nursing centers and accelerate the entry into combined hospitals, plus child care centers.
>
> Asked whether he was still holding to a statement made in July that Wall Street estimates for the current fiscal year of more than $2.50 a share in earnings on $75 million in revenue were "very reasonable figures," Mr. Clark said: "It's still our intent to come up with earnings of between $2 and $2.50 a share, depending on the number of hospitals and nursing centers that will be started."[14]

Early in 1970, a top executive of Walston and Company, W. W. Greary, began to look into the Four Seasons matter. He found that Four Seasons Equity, which had been founded a year before with $22.5 million, now possessed a total of $800,000 in funds, which was just about enough to purchase two more nursing homes. Walston and Company tried to avert what appeared to be an imminent crisis. A merger between Four Seasons and Four Seasons Equity was suggested, but on close examination it became obvious that they were really one and the same. The two supposedly separate companies were even using interoffice memos for correspondence rather than company letterheads.[15] With the Arthur Andersen decision to alter the way construction profits were being reported, there was no further purpose for the existence of Four Seasons Equity. Mr. Greary recommended that Four Seasons convert its assets into cash by collecting its receivables and by selling all excess land, as well as the company airplane and yacht. Walston and Company soon thereafter informed Four Seasons' management that it would no longer act as their investment banker.

COLLAPSE

Problems now began to descend on Four Seasons in rapid succession. A scandal arose concerning loans which the company had obtained from the state of Ohio in March of 1970. The loans, totaling $4 million, had been made with funds from the State Employees Retirement System of Ohio and the state treasurer's office. This aspect of

---

[14] Rone Tempest, "Exchange Holds Conference with Clark," *The Oklahoma Journal*, March 6, 1972. Copyright 1972 by The Oklahoma Journal Publishing Co.

[15] Tempest, "Glamour Stock Soared on Dreams."

the loan process was perfectly legal, for in 1967 the Ohio legislature had passed bills authorizing the state to invest up to $50 million of its general funds in commercial paper of corporations with prime credit ratings. But two of the four unsecured loans arranged with Four Seasons, as well as some granted to other companies, were for longer periods of time than the 270 days the law permitted. In addition, it became known that companies with loans from the state had paid large finders fees to obtain them. Four Seasons had paid $160,000 to Crofters, Inc., of Columbus, Ohio, a loan-finding firm operated by well-to-do Republicans. Gerald A. Donahue, a partner in Crofters, had held several major political posts in Ohio, including those of state tax commissioner and deputy attorney general, in addition to serving as the chief aid of Sen. William B. Saxbe. Donahue and his two partners in Crofters, Sidney Griffith and Harry Groban, had been paid over $1 million in finders fees for arranging the loans and profit sharing agreements in several housing projects. It was subsequently revealed that the three Crofters' partners had made campaign contributions totaling $33,000 to Republican officeholders.[16]

On April 30, 1970, after disclosure of the Ohio loan scandal, the American Stock Exchange halted trading in Four Seasons stock. The following day, Jack Clark disclosed that Four Seasons had suffered a net loss for the third fiscal quarter. Still optimistic, he announced: "We anticipate earnings for the fiscal year ending June 30 will be comparable with the 80 cents a share earned last year."[17]

But Clark's prediction was not to be. The over-the-counter price of Four Seasons stock continued to plummet, and on May 13 the Securities and Exchange Commission halted all trading in the stock. On May 21, Clark, Bouse, and Gray resigned their positions with Four Seasons, Clark allegedly on his doctor's recommendation, and the other two officials for undisclosed personal reasons. In addition, Gordon H. McCollom, vice president of Walston and Company, resigned from the Four Seasons board of directors.

The president of Four Seasons Franchise, James P. Linn, was named president of the parent corporation. His initial optimism regarding the company's future rapidly faded, and on June 26, 1970, in the Oklahoma City federal court, Four Seasons filed for reorganization under Chapter 10 of the Federal Bankruptcy Act. Inability to raise financing was cited as the reason for filing.

It was later estimated by the court-appointed trustee that Four Seasons' stockholders lost $200 million when the company went

---

[16] *The Columbus Dispatch,* June 27, 1970, p. 14.

[17] Rone Tempest, "Embattled Empire's Dreams Turn to Dust," *The Oklahoma Journal,* March 7, 1972.

bankrupt.[18] Dozens of lawsuits were filed against Four Seasons and Walston and Company. The suits charged that Four Seasons' executives had defrauded the stockholders by issuing false earnings reports and by deliberately making vastly exaggerated forecasts concerning future earnings and the company's plans for development. It was alleged that Four Seasons and Four Seasons Equity were actually one and the same company, so that Four Seasons was in reality selling nursing homes to itself and declaring very substantial earnings in order to create the illusion of a rapidly growing, profitable company and, thus, raise its stock price.

LEGAL ACTIONS

One of the most damaging pieces of evidence was first revealed in a suit filed by a Tennessee stockbroker named Frank Sher. During the trial a document which became known as the "Walston Memorandum" was entered as evidence. The memorandum was alleged to have been written by Four Seasons executives sometime before the company's stock offering in the spring of 1968. It was found openly filed in the company's records after bankruptcy. Some excerpts from the memo follow:

> Let's get Walston's opinion as to when we could sell a sizable portion of our stock, while the stock is at a good price, to guard against having to sell after the public realizes that nursing homes will not meet expectations on earnings.
> Let's get a definite program established with them as to the earliest and subsequent dates when we can dispose of our stock and ensure our personal wealth.[19]

This unusual document led U.S. District Judge Luther Bohanon to make some rather strong statements in open court. On November 2, 1971, at the end of a hearing, he stated:

> The Court now has before it the problem of whether or not Equity . . . and Four Seasons were in effect one and the same. They worked together, a joint adventure, helping one another and helping Jack Clark and his robbers, and that is what they were—nothing short of robbed the American people.
> What happened, in my judgment, has done more to destroy the faith of the American people in the New York Stock Exchange and the American Stock Exchange than any other thing that can happen. There are others, too, but this case within the past two years is the rankest. I

[18] *The New York Times*, December 21, 1972, p. 62.
[19] Rone Tempest, "Who's to Blame in Firm's Fall?" *The Oklahoma Journal*, March 1, 1972. Copyright 1972 by The Oklahoma Journal Publishing Co.

had no idea until the hearing started yesterday of the depth of the evil that was perpetrated upon the American people . . . . It's shameful. It's disgraceful and shameless. This equity company was founded and the court holds and finds, for no other purpose than to augment the income of [Four Seasons Nursing Centers of America] and so that those on the inside would make a killing and that's just what they did.[20]

The first official body to bring action against anyone connected with the Four Seasons fiasco was the American Stock Exchange. The action was brought against Francis R. Santangelo, a member of the Exchange and the specialist in Four Seasons stock. On August 31, 1970, he was fined $10,000 and suspended 14 days by the Exchange for violating its rules in transactions involving the stock of Four Seasons and Walston and Company. The Exchange charged that Mr. Santangelo "engaged in business dealings with officials of a company in whose stock he specialized and . . . maintained close business and social ties with those officials and with an officer of a brokerage firm which acted as underwriter for that company."[21] The Exchange said that Santangelo's activities were "detrimental to the interest and welfare of the exchange."[22]

On November 22, 1971, the American Exchange fined Walston and Company $75,000 and censured the firm for "alleged supervisory failures involving trading in the shares of Four Seasons Nursing Centers of America, Inc."[23] The Exchange also suspended for 30 days two top Walston executives, William D. Fleming, president, and Glenn R. Miller, executive vice president. They were fined $10,000 each and censured. The chairman of the Exchange governing board, Frank C. Graham, Jr., explained the Exchange's action:

> The board determined that Walston and Messrs. Fleming and Miller failed to develop and enforce adequate procedures to prevent unreasonable contacts between the firm's sales personnel and its investment banking clients, and to assure that Walston's sales force didn't violate any duties of the firm. . . . In addition, the board found that Walston and Messrs. Fleming and Miller had failed to take adequate measures to supervise and restrict solicitation by Walston personnel of transactions in the stock of a corporation for which Walston had acted as underwriter and in which Walston and some of its officers held investment positions, thereby failing to avoid conflicts or the appearance of conflicts of the firm's duty of fair dealing.[24]

---

[20] Ibid.

[21] *The Wall Street Journal*, August 31, 1974, p. 4.

[22] Ibid.

[23] *The Wall Street Journal*, November 22, 1971, p. 13.

[24] *The Wall Street Journal*, November 22, 1971, p. 13.

Nevertheless, Walston and Company still maintained that they had done nothing wrong. A company spokesman explained Walston's reaction to the Exchange's ruling:

> While wholly denying any willful violation of law, Walston and Co. elected not to contest the charges to avoid a costly expenditure of time and effort on the part of its personnel. It also agreed to establish additional administrative procedures to further strengthen its existing structure.[25]

After nearly two years of investigation by the Securities and Exchange Commission, the FBI, and the U.S. Postal Service, the *Four Seasons* case was approved for grand jury action by the Department of Justice. On December 20, 1972, federal charges of stock fraud were filed in the Southern District of New York. Eight defendants were named in a 65-count indictment: the three top officials of Four Seasons, two former vice presidents of Walston and Company, and an accountant and two partners of Arthur Andersen and Company. Neither Walston and Company nor Arthur Andersen and Company were named as defendants in the action, however.

The indictment alleged that the defendants had conspired to defraud investors in Four Seasons stock by fraudulently raising the corporation's earnings in order to deceive stock purchasers into paying higher prices. Four Seasons was charged with using phony construction costs, as well as fictitious financial statements, nursing home sales, and franchises, to give an impression of profitability. In addition, the indictment charged Four Seasons with using false financial statements in obtaining the $4 million in loans from the state of Ohio and in selling $15 million in debentures that defrauded investors in Europe.

THE FOUR SEASONS DEFENDANTS

In early June of 1973, Jack Clark pleaded guilty to conspiring to violate federal securities laws. Clark admitted breaking the law by failing to disclose that Four Seasons dominated Four Seasons Equity Corporation by April 1970. Clark insisted that Equity had originally been separate and that Four Seasons had intervened in that company's affairs only when Four Seasons Equity ran into serious money raising problems. He agreed that it then became improper for Four Seasons to continue to declare construction profits from homes it built for Equity. After Clark's plea, the government asked for dismissal of the remaining charges against him.

---

[25] Ibid.

On September 18, 1973, U.S. Judge Thomas P. Griesa sentenced Jack Clark to one year in prison. The sentence was based only on the one charge to which Clark had pleaded guilty, and did not take into consideration the original sweeping indictment made by the government. *The Wall Street Journal* reported that "In passing sentence on Mr. Clark, Judge Griesa said he took into account 'a great deal of' that indicated Four Seasons nursing homes were 'a marked improvement' over traditional facilities for the elderly. Nevertheless, the judge rejected Clark's plea for probation."[26]

On September 23, 1973, before Federal District Judge Luther Eubanks in Oklahoma City, Tom J. Gray pleaded no contest to one count of fraud and agreed to testify for the government against the other defendants being tried. Judge Eubanks was sharply critical of Judge Griesa for the light sentence he had given Jack Clark. Clark could have received five years in prison and a $10,000 fine.

In February of the following year, Gray was sentenced to one year in prison and fined $10,000 for one count of mail fraud. Judge Eubanks stated that Gray's role in the fraud had not been large, but that Gray "benefited and he took his money."[27] This was the heaviest sentence handed down by any court in the entire matter.

An Oklahoma City jury acquitted James P. Linn, former president of Four Seasons Franchise, of all of the nine charges which had been returned against him by a New York grand jury in late 1972.

Amos Bouse was never brought to trial. He was killed in an airplane crash on October 21, 1971, while returning from Dallas, where he had been a guest at a birthday party given for former baseball player Mickey Mantle.

In January 1973, Glenn R. Miller and Gordon H. McCollom, the former president and executive vice president of Walston and Company, pleaded guilty to conspiracy and three counts of fraud. They were fined $40,000 each. A *Wall Street Journal* article noted that Judge Griesa "found their role 'substantially and radically different' from that of inside management at Four Seasons. He considered them 'probably guilty more of errors of omission than anything else' in that they weren't more diligent as directors or in investigating Four Seasons' actual situation."[28] Both men had made a considerable profit by

---

26 *The Wall Street Journal*, September 19, 1973, p. 6.

27 *The Wall Street Journal*, February 22, 1974, p. 4.

28 *The Wall Street Journal*, February 28, 1974, p. 12. The judge might have had in mind the following kind of transaction. In November 1968, Jack Clark, president and chairman of the board, and Amos Bouse, senior vice president and a director of Four Seasons, bought a Falcon fanjet for $1.5 million through a company, Charter Jet, Inc., which the two men had set up with $500 in capital. For the next year, they leased the jet to Four Seasons Nursing Centers of America, Inc., and also used it for their frequent

selling stock either directly or through the Walston and Company subsidiary of Montgomery and Company.

Three Arthur Andersen auditors—Edward J. Bolka, Jimmie E. Madole, and Kenneth J. Wahrman—were charged with securities fraud and mail fraud in the Oklahoma City court. These charges were especially controversial since the criminal prosecution of auditors from a major accounting firm was an almost unheard of event. Lawyers for the three men labeled the charges an attempt by the government to teach the accounting profession an "object lesson." Government prosecutors angrily asserted that their only interest was the specific fraud charges in the *Four Seasons* case.

The Arthur Andersen auditors were charged with certifying Four Seasons financial results which they allegedly knew to be false, and with accepting certain construction costs as genuine when they knew that those costs had never been incurred. The three auditors vigorously denied the charges. They contended that, far from being lenient with Four Seasons, they had objected strongly to a number of the company's accounting practices.

After much deliberation, the federal jury acquitted two of the three defendants of all charges. The jury in the case of Kenneth J. Wahrman became deadlocked, and Judge Eubanks declared a mistrial.

Reaffirming his company's confidence in the three after their trial, John Hennessy, a senior partner of Arthur Andersen, stated that "We believe they were correct in the judgment they exercised at that time [the 1968 and 1969 audits of Four Seasons] and we believe today's [trial] result supports and justifies that conclusion."[29]

FOUR SEASONS REORGANIZATION

On February 11, 1971, Norman Hirschfield, the first trustee appointed by the court for Four Seasons, resigned. Judge Luther Bohanon named as his successor James R. Tolbert III, an Oklahoma City management consultant. In late September of 1971, Mr. Tolbert filed a plan of reorganization for approval by the federal district court in Oklahoma City. The plan provided for the payment, or assumption, of all secured debt and the conversion of unsecured debt into common stock of the reorganized company. A third of the shares in the

---

trips around the country. Four Seasons and its subsidiary, Four Seasons Franchise, paid Charter Jet, Inc., a total of $176,285 to lease the airplane during that time. In December 1969, on a decision of the five-member board of directors, Four Seasons Nursing Centers of America bought the used jet from Charter Jet for $1.5 million. When the reorganized company had to sell the plane in November 1970, they were able to obtain a total of $861,551 for it.

[29] *The Wall Street Journal,* February 8, 1974, p. 19.

new company were to be set aside to apply to claims of persons who had bought Four Seasons stock between May 9, 1968 and June 26, 1970, and had suffered damages from fraudulent representation of the company's condition. The reorganized company was named Anta Corporation.

In July of 1972, Tolbert was named president of Anta Corporation. At that time Judge Bohanon also named eight new directors of the company and ordered that the changeover be completed by September 1, 1972. According to Tolbert, the new corporation would have assets of slightly more than $50 million, and its net worth would amount to $33 million. The new president commented, "It's a very strong company from a balance sheet standpoint. It also will have a good tax position and will be operating at a profit from the very start."[30]

EPILOGUE

On June 21, 1974, Jack Clark was released from prison after serving nine months of his one-year sentence. He had been given 90 days off for good behavior. Clark had been imprisoned in the Safford Federal Correctional Institute at Safford, Arizona, described by *The Daily Oklahoman* as a "minimum security area with no guards."[31] Prisoners at Safford who were well behaved could be granted Sunday passes and weekend furloughs. Clark spent four three-day furloughs with his family during his imprisonment.

In an interview with *The Daily Oklahoman* shortly after his release, Jack Clark continued to maintain that his intentions in founding and operating Four Seasons had been entirely honorable.[32] His unrealistic earnings projections, he claimed, had been the result of being "hounded by brokers" for figures on future earnings and his own naiveté about the ramifications of not meeting those projections.[33]

In July 1974, Clark sold his Oklahoma City mansion for $625,000. He moved with his family to their 1,800 acre cattle ranch near Ada, Oklahoma. Clark expressed the intention to attempt to improve cattle production and marketing methods and to work with youth groups including the Future Farmers of America and the Boy Scouts.

---

[30] *The Wall Street Journal*, July 18, 1972, p. 23.

[31] *The Daily Oklahoman*, June 26, 1974, p. 2.

[32] Ibid.

[33] Ibid.

Commentaries ===

6. Ethics and the Corporation
Irving Kristol

At a time when the reputation of business in general is low, when the standing in popular opinion of the large publicly-owned corporation is even lower, and when there is a keen post-Watergate concern for probity among officials of all organizations, public or private—at such a time one would expect corporate executives to be especially sensitive even to appearances of conflict of interest, or to the mildest deviations from strict standards of fiduciary behavior. Yet this seems not, on the whole, to be the case.

I do not wish to be misunderstood. The majority of corporate executives are certainly honest and honorable men. This, however, is rather like saying that the majority of New York City's police officers are honest and honorable men. Of course they are. But the statement itself implies that a not altogether insignificant minority are less than that, and the presence of such a minority is fairly taken to constitute a rather serious problem. In the case of the corporation, the situation is worsened by the fact that, whereas honest cops will usually express open indignation at corrupt ones, corporate executives almost never criticize other corporate executives, even when these latter are caught *in flagrante delicto.* No one seems to be "read out" of the corporate community—which inevitably leads the outsider to wonder whether this community has any standards of self-government at all.

But to talk in terms of "corruption" is misleading. Problems of corporate ethics only rarely arise out of illegal actions by corporate executives. Such illegal actions are doubtless more frequent than they ought to be, and the response of the business community certainly is far more lethargic than it ought to be, but in the end such illegalities

Source: *The Wall Street Journal,* April 16, 1975, p. 18. Reprinted with permission of Irving Kristol. © Dow Jones & Company, Inc., 1975. All rights reserved.

are quite efficiently disposed of by law enforcement officers. The more common and significant issues in corporate ethics arise from practices which are not illegal, but which seem to reveal a shockingly naive unconcern both for the interests of stockholders and the good opinion of the public. Too many corporate executives seem to be under the illusion that they *are* the corporation. The problem here is rarely one of wicked motives but rather of a bland self-righteousness which does not even perceive an abuse of power for what it is.

GOING PRIVATE

Take, for instance, a rather extreme and somewhat marginal case: the recent efforts of several smaller corporations which, having gone public during the boom years of the 1960s, now wish to "go private." When such a corporation originally went public, the controlling stockholder sold a portion of his shares at a price substantially higher than the present market price. Now, disillusioned by the contemptuous way the stock market treats "his" firm, he uses his power to have the corporation repurchase, *with corporate funds*, that "public" stock. He ends up, if successful, owning the corporation all over again—*and* with a substantial capital gain from the original sale of his stock. However innocent the intentions of the controlling stockholder, the whole operation really amounts to a way for a privately-held corporation to use the mechanism of "going public" in order to trade profitably in its own stock.

Apparently, if incomprehensibly, this procedure is perfectly legal. All right: the law will have its loopholes. But is this way of doing business *ethically acceptable* to the financial and corporate communities? There is no doubt that the public which originally purchased this stock is now under the distinct impression that it has been fleeced. That is certainly undesirable—especially since these stockholders usually own stock in other corporations too, and their indignation is all too likely to spill over and touch all corporations. So why does one observe the boards of directors of the New York and American Stock Exchanges denouncing such a procedure and taking what actions they can to discourage it? Why does one not hear the heads of major Wall Street houses similarly come to the defense of the shareholders? Why don't corporate executives, individually or collectively, put themselves on record? Don't they care?

One supposes they do care—indignant and resentful stockholders are what the financial and business communities least need these days. But apparently they do not regard it as a matter that directly concerns them. Every executive assumes that so long as he personally behaves in a way that is above reproach, he has discharged his moral obligations. This is a fateful error. Precisely because there is never enough individual moral sensitivity to go around, every profession must protect its good name with a measure of collective self-discipline. And it should be clear that if the business community makes so little effort to discipline itself, then the government will step in and do the disciplining for it. That is the least desirable but most predictable outcome.

More directly affecting the large corporations, and therefore with a clear consequence for the good reputation of "big business" generally, is the way in which several firms are fiddling around with stock options for their executives. The officers of a major corporation, for instance, are voting themselves the right to borrow money from the firm so that they will not have to sell out their positions in the company's stock—positions they acquired through stock options financed in turn by bank loans. Because of the decline in the value of a firm's stock, these executives are faced with margin calls from the banks. They stand to lose a lot of money if they cannot answer these calls. So they are transferring these loans to the company, and are justifying this action by the assertion that they will be able to do their job better if they are not distracted by personal financial worries.

It is all very odd, to put it mildly. To begin with, what kind of relief do these executives obtain by virtue of going into debt to "their" corporation rather than to the banks? A debt is a debt, after all. Why should a corporate executive be less "distracted" if he owes money to his employer instead of to a bank or a brokerage house or a personal loan company? If he does achieve greater peace of spirit, it can only be because there exists in the back of his mind the notion that, at some point, the corporation will be a more indulgent creditor. But this in turn raises even more serious questions about the ethical status of this arrangement.

Besides, many of the 40,000 stockholders of this corporation are in, or have been in, exactly the same situation as these executives, and the corporation certainly never did anything to help *them* cope with margin calls. Is it really the company's view that it is wrong for its executives to lose money in the company's stock but a matter of indifference to it if anyone else does? If a company does badly, and its stock falls, are executives a privileged group to be "made whole" through the use of company funds? The company would surely repudiate both of these propositions. Yet its actions in effect assert them.

Or take the case of another large corporation. Its shares, too, have gone way down, thereby making the stock options of its executives worthless. So the company has simply reduced by 50 percent the price at which these options may be exercised. Again, the assumption seems to be that, even though all stockholders are suffering, corporate executives must not lose money in the company's stock—or, in this case, must not fail to make money in the company's stock. But the conventional argument in favor of stock options is that it offers executives an incentive for superior performance. What kind of incentive is it that rewards good and poor performance indifferently?

DISGRUNTLED STOCKHOLDERS

Now, the case of these two corporations has been amply reported in *The Wall Street Journal* and elsewhere. (Since I am interested in making only a general point, there is little to be gained by naming them accusingly.) What I find most interesting is the reaction within the business community to it. Or, to be exact, the absence of any discernible reaction. Why, for example, hasn't one of the prestigious organizations of businessmen thought it proper to suggest a code governing the use and abuse of stock options? It seems to have occurred to no one. Instead, the stock exchanges are mute, the major brokerage houses are mute, the corporate community is mute. Is it surprising, therefore, that there are thousands of stockholders out there whose loyalty to the corporation as an institution has been subverted? And is it surprising that these stockholders should infer from their experiences that more rather than less government regulation of corporations is desirable?

There are just too many other current instances of questionable behavior on the part of corporate executives. For instance, I am struck by the fact that one major company seems to be having considerable difficulty in divesting itself of a large and profitable subsidiary, as required by the Federal Trade Commission. I am willing to think, on general principles, that the FTC is being unreasonable in the conditions it is attaching to the divestiture. But there is an easy way out for the company, one which the FTC could not possibly object to—i.e., spinning off the subsidiary to the company's shareholders. The company has rejected this possibility on the grounds that it is not in the "best interests" of these stockholders.

But why isn't it? It is hard to see why, and I rather imagine that if those shareholders were given the chance to vote on the issue, they might well decide that a spin-off is decidedly in their best interests. They will not, of course, be given any such opportunity. For it is obvious that life would be more interesting—and presumably in the end more profitable—for the company's executives if *they* had $800 million dollars or so to play with, rather than seeing all this money vanish into the pockets of its stockholders. Perhaps these executives will indeed invest this money more wisely than the stockholders could, and to the stockholders' ultimate benefit. But, on the other hand, perhaps not. What does seem clear is that the executives do not even seem to realize that they are involved in a situation that suggests a potential conflict of interests, and that there is an ethical aspect to their decision to which attention should be paid.

THE CORPORATE CLUBHOUSE

And then there are those recurring reports of corporate executives who, having brought their corporations to the brink of ruin, and their stockholders to the brink of despair, "resign" with huge cash benefits. One notes that an executive of such a corporation recently departed with a $2 million cash payment to console him for the loss of his position. Nor is his case so unusual. It is a fact that the corporate community often more nearly resembles a corporate club, in which the genial spirit of "clubbiness" ensures that everyone is adequately provided for. Non-members, of course—stockholders and employes—must learn to cope with the harsh rigors of free enterprise.

It might be said that all this is little more than the froth on the surface of corporate life, of no great significance to the basic economic mission of the corporation, and only remotely relevant to its success in accomplishing that mission. That is true—but somewhat beside the point. The point is that American corporations do have a critical problem with public opinion, and to cope with this problem spend tens of millions of dollars a year on "public relations." Yet a number of these corporations then proceed to behave in such a way as to offend and outrage the corporation's natural constituency: the stockholders. More important, the business community as a whole remains strangely passive and silent before this spectacle. This disquieting silence speaks far more eloquently to the American people than the most elaborate public relations campaign. And it conveys precisely the wrong message.

7. Who Said "Profit"?—Getting Rid of a Dirty Word

Milton Moskowitz

When President Ford played a round of golf last month at Burning Tree, one member of the foursome was his long-time links companion, William G. Whyte, chief Washington lobbyist for the U.S. Steel Corporation. There was probably considerable banter about hooks and slices but one can't help wondering whether Whyte also planted the idea of his present trip in Mr. Ford's mind. Because Whyte is agitated about what he identifies as the "antibusiness bias" of the new Congress. The U.S. Steel lobbyist had just returned from addressing the 18th annual executive symposium held by St. Mary's College at Moraga, California. There he had warned that the business community is "heading into two very difficult years in Washington," and he disclosed that industrial and professional groups are banding together to repel this liberal threat. A move is underway, he said, to unite in a common pro-business cause the following organizations: U.S. Chamber of Commerce, National Association of Manufacturers, Business Roundtable, American Mining Congress, and the American Medical Association. "In unity there is strength," declared Whyte, adding from a rich store of clichés, "the fight is on for the preservation of the American private enterprise system, and this is not the time for the summer soldier or the sunshine patriot." That's certainly appropriate rhetoric for Burning Tree.

Those of us who have covered the financial scene for any period of time (finding our prose tucked away behind the sports pages) are familiar with this old-time religion of business leaders. It has been used to oppose every piece of social legislation ever proposed, whether it be restrictions on child labor, minimum wage laws, social security, a consumer protection agency, or regulations to curb the power of multinationals. The *ad hominem* gambit is always the same: wrap yourself in the free enterprise flag, declaim the evils of big government, and predict the downfall of individual initiative. How many rostrums in hotel banquet rooms have served as anvils for this refrain? Never mind that it has not prevented new social legislation. Never mind that public opinion polls show a declining confidence in business. Never mind that no business leader has ever been able to

Source: *The Nation*, vol. 221, no. 10 (March 15, 1975), pp. 297–99.

reach beyond the rhetoric of an institutional advertisement in *Fortune* to codify these ideas in a coherent, persuasive, rigorous set of precepts. The doctrine of free enterprise works as a knee-jerk reaction to would-be builders of change.

In the past seven years this doctrine has been tempered by the new strain of "corporate social responsibility." Pressed on a number of fronts as, for example, discrimination in hiring, pollution control, and product safety, corporations have responded with various programs—some substantial, some merely token—that have enabled business leaders to dress up the free enterprise straitjacket with the finery of social action. Thus, while Whyte can mount the ramparts to assert that now is the time to defy the very critics who have pressed these issues of social responsibility, his company, U.S. Steel, simultaneously appears in print and on television with its socially conscious advertising theme, "We're involved."

Recently, though, this shadowboxing has developed a new tactic. Business leaders are having a tough time coming to grips with a cardinal construct of the free enterprise theology; that is, profit—what Marx identified as "surplus value." Businessmen have, of course, long argued that the man in the street harbors all kinds of misconceptions about profit. I remember once being at a conference where a corporation president bemoaned the fact that the public seemed to think that companies earned 25 percent on the sales dollar when, in fact, the average is closer to 3 percent. I then asked him what about those companies—IBM, Xerox, Avon Products, for examples—which *did* manage to net 25 percent on the sales dollar, year after year. He looked at me with a startled expression and said, "They do?"

The truth is that in the free enterprise scheme of life there can never be too much profit. Profit is a measure of performance, it's the fat out of which taxes and dividends are paid, it's the base on which stock prices are set—and the game is to come down to the bottom line with as much profit as you can possibly show. And woe betide the manager who makes less money this year than last, or who increases earnings at a rate less precipitous than in previous years. The problem is that other people don't understand this motivating force and when the oil companies produced their recent avalanche of earnings, there were widespread outcries of "obscene" from benighted congressmen, reporters, labor union leaders, Middle East shieks, and ordinary citizens. Economists at Chase Manhattan went to work to show that these profits were needed for reinvestment in energy development, but everyone knows you can't teach economics to the public—and besides, Mobil blew the whole game when it used about $1 billion of its super-profits to buy a controlling interest in Marcor (Montgomery Ward and Container Corp. of America). So what to do?

The answer was so simple, staring the business community in the face, that it's surprising no one thought of it earlier. All that was really needed was to banish the word "profit" from the lexicon of business. Herman L. Weiss, vice chairman of General Electric, was the first to develop this tidy idea. In a talk last May to the New York Chamber of Commerce and Industry, Mr. Weiss noted sadly that "there seems to be a pervasive feeling developing among the general populace of the nation and those in the Congress, that somehow profits, deemed to be unconscionable, are at the root of all evil." He went on:

> I sometimes think it would be well if we could eliminate the word "profits" from our business vocabulary. You know, the way accountants keep books, profits are never considered a cost of doing business. Why shouldn't they be so considered?
>
> Net profits after taxes are usually made up of two things: dividends, which I call the cost of equity; and retained earnings, that part of the revenue reinvested in the enterprise.
>
> I believe dividends or cost of equity to be a cost of doing business just as interest is the cost of borrowing. Retained earnings—or net profit after taxes and dividends or (and I prefer) the revenues reinvested in the enterprise—is a cost of survival.

The vice chairman of GE suggested, accordingly, that corporations alter the way they report their operating results to eliminate this nasty word. For example: for 1973, GE sent me and other business reporters a news release which reported aftertax profits of $585 million on a sales volume of $11.5 billion. That represented a 13 percent increase in sales and a 10 percent increase in profits. Now if Mr. Weiss had been consulted, GE would have reported these results as follows:

> General Electric, in 1973, reinvested a record amount of dollars in its business. The company had total sales of $11.5 billion and it ploughed back $312 million of those revenue dollars into its business, thereby making possible added capacity, productivity advances, more jobs, development of new materials, and exploration of new energy sources.

That kind of reporting makes a lot of sense, Mr. Weiss pointed out, because "it's a lot easier to get mad at an announcement of a 30 percent increase in profits than at 30 or 40 percent increase in the dollars of revenue reinvested in the enterprise to accomplish one or more of the purposes I mentioned." Simple, is it not?

The movement to eliminate "profit" from the business vocabulary enlisted a major ally last month when it was endorsed by Peter F. Drucker. It pays to pay attention when Peter Drucker speaks, and no seer is listened to more attentively by business leaders. Drucker's books are the bibles of corporate management, and businessmen who want the benefit of his expensive counsel must now journey to Southern California, where he teaches at the Claremont Graduate School, part of the Pomona complex. In a *Wall Street Journal* article (February 5) Mr. Drucker carried Weiss's concept much farther.

Businessmen who complain about economic illiteracy "are themselves the worst offenders," he suggested, because "they don't seem to know the first thing about profit and profitability." Then Drucker shot home his message: "For the essential fact about profit is that there is no such thing. There are only costs."

What companies report as "profits," Drucker argued, are really only three different kinds of quantifiable costs. One is the *cost* of the capital they require. Two is the *cost* of the insurance they need to protect them against the risks of uncertainties of economic activity (just as a company spends money on fire insurance, so it must spend money on insurance for "economic, technological and social risks"). Three is the *cost* of "tomorrow's jobs and tomorrow's pensions" (any company that fails to provide for an expansion of jobs and pensions in the future "fails both to cover its own predictable costs and the costs of the economy").

"Businessmen," concluded Drucker, "owe it to themselves and owe it to society to hammer home that there is no such thing as 'profit.' There are only 'costs': costs of doing business and costs of staying in business; costs of labor and raw materials, and costs of capital; costs of today's jobs and costs of tomorrow's jobs and tomorrow's pensions."

There it is, the latest variant of the shell game. *Fortune* and *Forbes* will simply have to revise all those tables wherein they rank companies on "profits." The public is going to feel much better when it realizes that Exxon and IBM have all those costs to bear instead of earnings to trumpet. Since 1932, when Adolph A. Berle, Jr. and Gardiner C. Means published *The Modern Corporation and Private Property,* it has become widely accepted among business scholars that ownership in large corporations is so widely diffused that they are being run, in effect, by their managements, and that these managers need not worry much about who the owners are. What we have done is eliminate any consideration of ownership—there are no owners. Now we have moved another giant step forward. Not only are there no owners—there are no profits. It's beautiful what a little tinkering with the language will do. We can call this the beginning of the "Weiss-Drucker Era." Profits? I don't know what you're talking about.

8. Why Does the Public "Hate" Profits?
Lee Smith

As much of the public sees it, there are three kinds of corporate profits: excessive, windfall, and obscene. As many businessmen see it, the only reason the public feels that way is because it does not understand the modest size and true social function of profits. But would people stop criticizing profits if they were better informed?

Probably not. At least that's what two dozen distinguished economists and business leaders concluded recently when they gathered at Harvard University to discuss the future of the profit system. The two-day conference—held just a few days before the 200th anniversary of the publication of Adam Smith's *The Wealth of Nations*, capitalism's founding document—concluded that hostility toward profits is chronic and that they will continue to be challenged by the public and controlled by government, no matter how well informed people become. Still, the system will survive, at least in some form, because it seems to work better than anything else.

In today's atmosphere, the very word "profit" is sometimes pronounced nervously. Whenever possible, chairman Gabriel Hauge of Manufacturers Hanover Trust Co. uses the word "earnings" because it is less likely to arouse animosity. Massachusetts Institute of Technology economist and Nobel laureate Paul A. Samuelson states the case bluntly: "Profits is today a fighting word."

Ironically, the resentment toward corporate profits seems to be rising in an era when profits are not particularly robust or enviable. True, the dollar amount of earnings has grown considerably over the past 25 years. But their role in the economy has diminished. As a share of the gross national product, aftertax profits declined from almost 9 percent in 1950 to less than 5 percent in 1975. By comparison, wages and other compensation to employees grew from 54 percent to 62 percent. Except for a healthy 15 percent in 1950, aftertax profits as a return on stockholders' equity fluctuated in a trendless range of 9 percent to 13 percent during the same period (see graphs).

The fact that the public believes that profits are as much as six times as great as they really are doesn't really explain the extent of the criticism, suggested Professor Erik Lundberg of the Stockholm School of Economics. "People in Sweden know how large profits are and what they are used for. They are still critical," he explained.

Source: *Dun's Review*, vol. 107, no. 4 (April 1976), pp. 44–45.

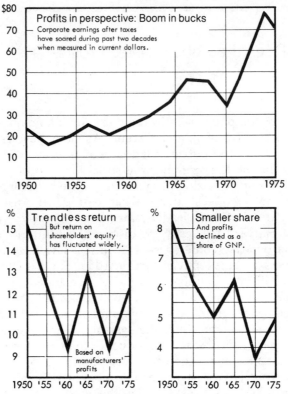

Source: Department of Commerce, Federal Trade Commission.

The Swedes simply do not trust the profit system to function entirely on its own without causing great social damage, he said. With
the expectation of high profits, for example, the Swedish pulp and
paper industry has cut deeply into the country's limited forests.
Similarly, in the United States there is ample evidence—such as half-
finished and empty office buildings—that the profit system is not
always a steady hand unerringly directing scarce resources to their
most productive uses.

Harvard economist Kenneth A. Arrow, a Nobel laureate, dispas-
sionately summed up the public's case against the profit system. Most
of the complaints are as old as the system itself. There has always
been moral indignation against income that is not derived from
"sweat," Arrow maintained. Also, from the very beginning, the
profit system has brought periodic unemployment. "Previous systems had their faults," Arrow said, "but lack of useful work was not
one of them."

Still, none of the participants suggested dismantling the profit system—and they couldn't offer a better substitute even if they were so inclined. If firms do not act to minimize costs and maximize profits, then how are they supposed to behave—for the betterment of mankind? "Think of 14,000 banks trying to act like little Ford Foundations," said Samuelson. "It is hard to give out money on the basis of 'doing good' instead of simply squeezing out a profit." The alternative to the chaotic charity evoked by Samuelson's image of hundreds of thousands of philanthropoids acting independently might be rigid governmental control. That idea seemed to be as unappealing to most of the academics as to the businessmen.

Harvard economist Abram Bergson observed that the centralized Soviet industrial system has been so inefficient that the productivity of Russian workers has been growing at only half the rate of Japanese workers, even though the capital stock per worker has increased at about the same rate in both countries. Although the Soviet leadership has long tried to use a profit system as a means of encouraging managers to innovate, Bergson pointed out, the results have not been very successful.

A Russian plant manager gets a bonus if he meets his production quota and an extra bonus if he improves the system and thereby turns out more than his quota. But if his inventiveness somehow interrupts the production schedule for his industry, he gets no bonus at all. "Most Russian managers seem to choose the quiet life," says Bergson. For the most part, they try to meet their quotas to earn a bonus, but they aren't willing to risk the bonus by trying harder.

In the United States, despite the public complaints about what it perceives to be the high level of profits, there is also a great deal of acceptance of the system itself. Politicians may rail against the earnings of individual firms and industries, but no major political party advocates the elimination of the system. Labor unions in the United States, unlike those in Europe, want more money, not the destruction of the system and the imposition of a new order. Arthur W. Harrigan, executive vice president for finance at International Paper Co., observed that employees grasp the idea that profits are used for expansion and thus create more jobs even though they wildly overestimate the size of corporate earnings.

Henry C. Wallich, a governor of the Federal Reserve Board, maintained that the profit system will make a resurgence in one respect. He argued that, in a sense, top management at many corporations themselves abandoned the profit system in the 1960s by trying to maximize sales and market share instead of pursuing the classic goal of trying to maximize profits. The two objectives are not necessarily identical, he said. But now, he added, there has been a return to the pursuit of profit. "Where there is not enough profit there will be no equity financing," he said simply, "and where there is not enough equity, there will be not much debt money available."

At the same time, Wallich believes that the profit system is losing its influence as the supreme allocator of resources. First came the institutional investors; by trading almost exclusively in the "Nifty Fifty," they drove up the price/earnings ratios of those select corporations and made it relatively easy for them to raise capital, and consequently more difficult for other companies. That process disturbed the natural flow, under which capital is supposed to be directed into the most productive enterprises, not simply the most favored. Now, he said, the government has kept profits low, particularly in the energy industry, with its environmental protection requirements and the retention of price controls and thus diverted investment away from areas that would ordinarily attract it.

There seemed to be a general conviction among the conferees that government interference in the natural workings of the profit system would continue and probably grow, but there was no consensus that all interference is necessarily bad. President Thornton F. Bradshaw of Atlantic Richfield Co. said that government encroachment in areas such as energy is not only inevitable but desirable. The capital demands are simply too great for private enterprise to cope with alone. "We can't spend hundreds of millions of dolars of shareholders' money on solar research," Bradshaw maintained. As Bradshaw sees it, the enlightened businessman will not try to fight government's role in the economy, but rather to shape it. That will mean a diminished future for the profit system, to be sure, but at least a future.

---

9. The Business Cry for More Government Intervention
William Greider

Lately, I keep running into businessmen and corporate managers whose discontents can be summarized in one whining question: Why can't Americans be more like the Japanese?

A few weeks ago, I listened to a steel company executive holding forth on the awesome competitive powers of "Japan Inc."—that government-industry partnership of legend that produces so effectively

Source: *Washington Post*, May 27, 1979, pp. C1 and C5.

and sells so aggressively around the world. Big steel is feeling the pain, and this executive thinks America's only choice is to emulate Japan's success: cartelized planning by government and industry, carving up markets, fixing national goals, wages, whatever.

But what happens to the supposed "free enterprise" that business always extols?

"This would be modified free enteprise," the steel man said, without a trace of irony.

It certainly would. Maybe I am misled by idle cocktail chatter, but my impression is that this idea needs to be watched carefully—and chewed on vigorously by all skeptical small-d democrats. The notion of a unified economic system seems so alluring to a particular kind of business manager, especially those who never read any history. They might start with the Old Testament story of Jacob and Esau.

A few months ago, the chief executive of a major chemical corporation was sermonizing over lunch on "free enterprise," berating a table of journalists for not appreciating the marketplace sufficiently. Someone asked how he would remedy the nation's economic ills. Without missing a step, this business leader also began spelling out a moderate version of "Japan Inc.," a government-business partnership.

Mouths fell open around the table. The man recognized the contradiction—and blushed.

These people would all blush if they recognized the sweet irony of what they are proposing. It is a modern computerized version of FDR's blue eagle—the National Recovery Act, which called for the same sort of cartelized planning in the Depression. These conservative businessmen, without knowing it, are now embracing the old left-liberal idea.

The Supreme Court shot down the NRA eagle as unconstitutional, but in this age of global conglomerate corporations, standing astride national boundaries and doing business in an extraordinary range of products, the idea may have more appeal to that strange conservative mindset that seeks order above all other social values.

If I am right about this (and, as always, I may be wrong), the next decade will produce an upside-down ideological debate on the best economic organization for America. The pro-business conservatives will be leading cheers for vast expansion of government powers. The "reactionaries" will be the new generation of liberals and old-fashioned "free soil" Republicans, people who insist that Americans don't want to be Japanese, that we prefer to remain unruly, disorganized, wildly diverse, and individualistic Americans.

Personally, I suspect a lot of Japanese would rather be Americans too. As their young modern society settles into its extraordinary prosperity, I think we will see more of the unruly individualism that produces so many problems for our government and industry. A decade from now, if not sooner, Japan may be bewailing the "decline in productivity" and denouncing the flakiness of its young people.

In the meantime, however, everyone has to concede that the Japanese have successfully channeled their old military zeal (and fierceness) into the pacific and profitable realms of inventive industrial development. The United States, acting on the highest sense of its own self-interest, encouraged this for 25 years, tolerated Japanese dirty tricks in trading and indulged Japan's new-found devotion to pacificism by providing U.S. defenses, free of charge. That era is over and the Japanese may discover that their "cooperative" economic system is not quite so invincible, once the other trading nations, mainly us, demand that we all play by the same rules.

The United States, for instance, spends billions every year across the far Pacific, defending Japan and its trade routes. Japan, I'm told, profited hugely from our two wars in Asia: Korea and Vietnam. Fine, Japan doesn't want to rearm and we should all cheer that noble commitment. But that shouldn't prevent Japan from paying its full, fair share of the bill. They could send us a check every year (so could Taiwan, Korea, and the Philippines), and it would virtually wipe out the U.S. trade deficit with Japan, $8 billion to $10 billion this year.

I don't think "Japan Inc." will look quite so awesome once this era of adjustment is settled, but the idea does to many U.S. businessmen, especially if their market is getting kicked to pieces by made-in-Japan products. Conservatives in Congress are promoting a new federal department—"the Department of Trade"—which I suspect is a stalking horse for this idea. A new book by a Harvard professor, *Japan as Number One* (Harvard University Press), scolds Americans for not being more all-together like the Japanese.

Ezra Vogel, chairman of Harvard's Council on East Asian Studies, proposes a number of remedies for us, including *"a communitarian vision. In bygone days of more genuinely free enterprise, the model of the independent trader or businessman, like that of the cowboy, was not only appealing but appropriate . . . business leaders now recognize that this model is no longer appropriate in an era in which large organizations confront complex problems, but they nevertheless lament the loss of our individualistic past. Americans tend to think of the organization as an imposition, an outside force, restraining the free individual. Japanese from an early age are taught the values of group life . . . "*

Personally, I prefer to stick with the cowboy.

It feels more American to me, imagining I am a cowboy. Cowboys are what made this country great, also those freewheeling independent traders whom Vogel regards as archaic. I think we should try to keep thinking of ourselves as cowboys, as long as we can. If I have to choose between illusions, I'll take John Wayne and Gary Cooper over Sony and Toyota.

Prof. Vogel has other fix-it ideas for us, including this one: "A small core of permanent high-level bureaucrats. The capacity to provide long-range direction to society requires a continuity of leadership at high levels, a leadership that has the power and responsibility to oversee specific areas of activity, whether in foreign policy, finance, energy, environment, transportation, or regional planning . . . it is not possible to pursue long-term policies when all key personnel change every two to four years."

That's a fancy way of saying that democracy doesn't work. Elected government, subject to the storms and illusions of popular sentiment, can't hack it in the modern age.

The notion that democracy is on its way out must be a favorite at the Harvard lunch tables. It keeps surfacing in different forms from one Harvard professor or another. Henry Kissinger's unspoken premise in diplomacy was that democracy is a long-term loser in the world. Samuel Huntington, the Cold War political scientist, concluded in a nasty little tract on America's domestic ills and unrest that the problem was not bad policies or high crimes and lies from established authority. The problem was "an excess of democracy" among the rabble.

Americans, of course, generally do not buy this. Neither do most elected politicians. America is, after all, too diverse and complex, too grand in size, too wildly open and argumentative, to fit the neat models of national consensus dreamed up at a faculty lunchroom. This is why "Japan Inc." is sure to disappoint its promoters.

I am willing to concede that some sort of increased, more formalized government-business partnership may be an idea of the future, irresistible to those who seek order and stability. But those businessmen are going to be terribly surprised if "Japan Inc." becomes Americanized, for America is not Japan and American politics would likely produce important variations that would horrify the conservatives.

For starters, if huge corporations form working partnerships with our huge government, the rest of us will insist that Ralph Nader be named to the board of directors. Or someone like him. A critic who will ask the nasty questions and scream and holler if the deal doesn't smell right.

Meanwhile, others will propose competing solutions to maintain the political and economic freedoms that are so closely intertwined. One rival proposal is public corporations that compete with the private ones. Paul L. Joffe, a Washington lawyer devoted to the antitrust goals of progressive free enterprise, has written a compelling essay in the *Catholic University Law Review* (Fall 1978) suggesting this future. The goals of antitrust, Joffe suggests, now require creative thinking to counteract the gathering girth of multinational corporations, and one answer may be an array of government-owned corporations, on the rough model of TVA, that will keep the big boys honest. I don't imagine businessmen will like that, but they might bring it on themselves.

Later on, probably, someone will raise a more fundamental question: Who owns these corporations anyway? If we Americans are supposed to follow "a communitarian vision," why shouldn't that vision apply to capital ownership and profits—democratically distributed throughout the land?

I tried to tell this to my friend, the steel man who was pushing "Japan Inc." But it was late at night and we had all had much to drink. He just laughed.

10. More Pressure to Prosecute Executive Crime

For one tense week last September, Francis X. McCormack, senior vice president and general counsel for Atlantic Richfield Co., and 20 other ARCO executives and staffers pored over internal records, insurance documents, Securities and Exchange Commission regulations, and bank reporting rules, trying to decide how to handle a messy situation that could embroil the company in scandal and cost it millions of dollars.

On September 27, after an investigation into some unusual letters of credit that had surfaced at ARCO's Anaconda Co. subsidiary, Charles H. Kraft, a former Anaconda treasurer, had laid out the details of a series of Anaconda-backed loans that he had arranged without authorization for two companies unrelated to Anaconda. The revelation plunged Los Angeles-based ARCO into an agonizing evaluation of its moral and legal obligations regarding the possibly criminal misconduct of one of its executives.

Examples of misconduct on the scale of the ARCO case are hardly commonplace. But when they do occur, the conflicts they threaten between the interests of shareholders, employees, corporate execu-

Source: Reprinted from the December 18, 1978 issue of *Business Week* by special permission, © 1978 by McGraw-Hill, Inc., New York, N.Y. 10020. All rights reserved.

tives, and society at large make them among the toughest problems executives ever face. Yet most corporations have no set policies on how to handle them. Although most companies have long since issued codes of ethics for employees, they possess no comparable guidelines on what to do when the codes are violated. *Business Week* interviews with corporate executives and law enforcement authorities indicate that, in almost all cases, companies deal with each problem on an individual, catch-as-catch-can basis.

THE BEGELMAN AFFAIR

The result has been a dizzying variation from company to company and probably from person to person within companies on how the law is enforced. At ARCO, Kraft was promptly relieved of duty, the SEC and shareholders were quickly informed, and ARCO is currently cooperating with a U.S. Attorney in New York regarding possible criminal prosecution. By contrast, Columbia Pictures Industries Inc. first suspended David Begelman, head of its movie and TV division, in October 1977, after he admitted misusing company funds and fraudulently cashing checks made out to others; reinstated him in December; then responded to public disapproval in February by removing him from the company payroll and giving him a contract as an independent producer. Begelman has been fined $5,000 and put on probation for three years after pleading no contest to charges of grand larceny of $61,000.

But companies may not be able to stick with their ad hoc policies much longer. Pressures are building for the establishment of official, consistent guidelines for handling corporate crime. The pressures are threefold:

1. Growing public awareness of the sheer volume of white-collar crime and its impact on the economy is forcing companies to step up their crime prevention and law enforcement efforts.
2. More and more, corporate executives are being held personally responsible, legally and socially, for misdeeds at all levels of the company.
3. Threats of shareholder and employee lawsuits are making it a matter of self-preservation for companies to follow uniform policies toward criminal infractions within their ranks.

Even Congress has begun to study the subject. Says Steven G. Raikin, counsel to the subcommittee on crime of the House Judiciary Committee, which began hearings on white-collar crime last summer. "We are asking to what extent can large corporations be expected and encouraged to police themselves and to diligently report violations?"

Although solid statistics on the subject are sparse, the most widely quoted figure for the total dollar cost of white-collar crime is the U.S. Chamber of Commerce's estimate of $44 billion a year—more than 10 times the estimated annual cost of street crime. Most experts agree that by far the largest share of these crimes are committed by employees, with the employer as victim. This means that shareholders and customers are bearing the burden of these losses. And yet most law enforcement authorities believe that only a small part of the total losses suffered by companies is ever reported.

"Prosecutors may not prosecute unless the injured party presses charges," says Christopher D. Stone, professor of law at the University of Southern California and author of several works on corporate social responsibility. "If the magnitude [of unreported crime] is as large as I think it is, it becomes a significant social problem. It's one of the major undiscussed problems in business today."

TWO APPROACHES

Most companies take a fairly hard line on crime when it comes to the continued employment of the suspected person. "We have one policy with respect to employees involved in white-collar crime," says the security director of a major office equipment company. "Fire them, regardless of the amount involved." But this is as far as most companies go.

Two things are wrong with this approach, says Los Angeles District Attorney John K. Van de Kamp. "Companies don't recognize that they're putting the culprit back out into the job market, giving him a chance to repeat his behavior with another employer," Van de Kamp says. "Even worse, they are telling their own employees, 'The worst that can happen if you steal from us is that we'll fire you.' "

In some industries, companies have pooled data on people accused of shoplifting or workers' compensation abuse to reduce the likelihood that such employees will be hired elsewhere. But such "blacklists" have inspired lawsuits and have come under fire from the American Civil Liberties Union.

More commonly, employers spread the word about a suspected former employee via the grapevine. "You're not going to make a statement on a recommendation that you don't have full proof of," says James L. Ketelson, chairman of Tenneco Corp. At the same time, notes an oil company executive, "You can damn a guy with faint praise."

Some real problems discourage corporations from pressing charges. Reporting friends and fellow workers to the authorities is socially awkward. "I guess we'd rather take small losses than try to put somebody in jail," says Herbert A. Phillips, vice president and treasurer of Equifax Inc., an Atlanta-based company that investigates private citizens for insurance companies, credit grantors, and potential employers. Phillips knows of only three cases of substantial employee theft, totaling about $65,000, at Equifax. In all three cases, Equifax fired the implicated employee but did not give the evidence to law enforcement authorities for prosecution.

SUITS AND COUNTERSUITS

Even where no paternalistic feelings are involved, it is far easier to fire a suspected employee than to put together a tight legal case against him. "Courts of law require that the defendant be guilty beyond a reasonable doubt," says Walter W. Sapp, Tenneco's senior vice president and chief counsel. "That's a difficult burden. But the corporation doesn't have to establish that degree of proof to fire someone."

Companies also note that they might jeopardize their insurance coverage of the loss if they pressed criminal charges and lost the case. "What it takes to convince us may not convince a jury," says C. Daniel Drake, vice president of the bond department at Insurance Co. of North America, in Philadelphia. "What if we have paid a claim, the company presses charges, and the jury says, 'No, there's room for doubt'? Then, wow . . . "

At that point, the company could face an employee countersuit, Drake suggests. Indeed, even if the company has a hard and fast case against an employee, it may choose not to press charges simply to protect its insurance coverage. "Our bonding company, which makes the decision on whether to press charges, is more interested in restitution," says John C. Malone, president of Tele-Communications Inc., in Denver. "You can't get restitution from someone who is making license plates in the state pen."

A CASE IN POINT

The experience of Lloyd's Electronics Inc., a Compton, California consumer electronics manufacturer, illustrates the dangers companies risk by pressing charges or seeking restitution. Last spring, Lloyd's accountants uncovered $1.1 million in fictitious sales at Products International, a company owned 50 percent by a Lloyd's subsidiary. Bernard R. Lavitch, operating head of Products International, denied responsibility for the erroneous entries. William Friedland, Lloyd's vice chairman, took the case to the Los Angeles police, but came away dissatisfied. "The police wanted to know who was hurt," Friedland says. "They wanted to see blood on the carpet. When there was none, the attitude was, "We'll get around to it eventually.' "

So Lloyd's filed suit against Lavitch, seeking $2.2 million in damages. "We had to disclose the problem, and the suit was a demonstration to our stockholders that we were taking action to protect their interests," Friedland says. Lavitch then countersued both Lloyd's and Friedland in a multimillion dollar suit that sought to implicate Friedland in the manipulation of the figures. "There's a definite danger in a corporation hanging its own wrongdoings on one individual," says Lavitch's lawyer.

For their part, law enforcement authorities charge that companies avoid bringing in cases, because executives fear the publicity and implications of sloppy management such cases produce.

Mitchell S. Cohen, deputy chief of the special prosecutions division of the U.S. Attorney's office in Philadelphia, claims that he often has more trouble getting information out of the companies than out of the accused employees. "I've been lied to, material I've asked for has not been turned over, and I've had to go back a second or third time to get a piece of evidence," he says. "When we subpoena corporate personnel and materials, the attorneys stall, delay, do everything a good defense attorney should do to protract an investigation. But they're not the defendants. I just do not understand why I have to fight the victim as well as the defendant."

Says Denver District Attorney Dale Tooley: "Businesses feel they have no duty to report crime. It's a real problem." Tooley applauds a proposed law to be introduced before the Colorado legislature in January. By requiring the reporting of white collar crime, it would have the double effect of encouraging companies to report crimes and discouraging employees from countersuing, because the company would be protected from civil liability as long as it had a "reasonable basis" for its charge.

In the absence of comprehensive, mandatory reporting legislation, the company's legal responsibility may vary with every case and every state. But whatever the responsibility, Pittsburgh District Attorney Robert E. Colville cautions companies against trying to nail a suspected employee without due regard for his rights to privacy and due process of the law. "Someone who tries to play policeman generally fouls it up pretty badly," he says.

TELL ALL

Some experts even believe that the issues are so complex that a company is better off without a policy. "I don't think it makes sense to try to write a code that would cover every conceivable circumstance," says Donald J. Evans, chairman of the counsel responsibility committee of the American Bar Assn.'s corporate law section.

This same complexity, however, appears to be prompting a growing number of companies to define in advance the roles they will play when confronted with corporate crime. In most cases, they have concluded that, despite the risk of bad publicity, both prudence and morality dictate that they dump all evidence in the laps of law enforcement authorities. At Kemper Insurance Cos., of Chicago, for instance, Vincent L. Inserra, director of internal security, says: "I feel that if anybody is going to decline the responsibility of prosecution, it's going to be the local, state, or federal authorities—not me. I'm not going to be the judge and jury."

part III
MANAGING SOCIAL RESPONSIVENESS

STRATEGIC MANAGEMENT AND SOCIAL RESPONSIVENESS

Since so many corporate policies and practices have intended or unintended social consequences, it is essential that social responsiveness be an integral' part of a company's strategic plan and organizational design. A major test of managerial success is the degree to which a company is compatible with its environment. Since the environment houses, as it were, the economic, social, political, technological threats and opportunities available to a firm, the success of the enterprise is closely linked to its ability to anticipate change and to position itself to be responsive to new environmental forces. To do so, a company needs to know its own nature and purpose (mission), its objectives, and its strategies for achieving those objectives. Even the best of plans are of little value, of course, unless they are effectively implemented. The organization must be structured as well as motivated to facilitate the implementation of the plan.

Once a company has decided that social responsiveness is to be central to its plan, it still faces the challenge of deciding where responsibility for social performance is to be housed in the organization. It may reside with the chief executive officer, staff specialists ("vice president of public affairs") and their departments, or with operating management. Responsibility probably should be shared by all three.

As in any traditional functional area of business, if social responsiveness is to be managed effectively, there must be "a systematic attempt to identify, analyze, measure (if possible), evaluate and

114

monitor the effect of an organization's operations on society. . . ."[1]
Such a method need not be a so-called social audit that was tried by a
number of companies in the 1970s and generally proved unworkable.
There simply needs to be a systematic approach to the assessment of
corporate social performance in selected areas of the company's operations.[2]

Virtually all the cases in this book provide a vehicle for considering
the challenges of managing social responsiveness. The Mead Corporation case is especially valuable in this regard. A primary case prepared under the supervision of Michael Lovdal, Mead Corporation
reviews the relationship of the board and all levels of management
and nonmanagerial employees to the task of social responsiveness. It
is followed by commentaries treating the consequences of disclosing
social performance and the role of the audit committee in these affairs.

---

[1] David H. Blake, William C. Frederick, and Mildred S. Myers, *Social Auditing:
Evaluating the Impact of Corporate Programs* (New York: Praeger Publishers, 1976), p. 3.

[2] See, for example, Frederick D. Sturdivant, *Business & Society: A Managerial Approach*, rev. ed., (Homewood, Ill.: Richard D. Irwin, Inc., 1981), chap. 7.

Case ══════════════════════════════════════

THE MEAD CORPORATION (A)

The Mead Corporation was one of 35 U.S. companies with board-level committees dealing with questions of corporate social responsibility. Mead's Corporate Responsibility Committee (CRC) was unique, however, in that it included company employees along with outside directors as regular members. The Committee had been formed in 1972, at the recommendation of a special board committee and Mead's chairman and chief executive officer, James W. McSwiney. The hope was that by bringing together representatives of two groups—directors and employees—who seldom had an opportunity to share ideas, and by giving them the freedom to choose their own agenda, the flow of "unorthodox" and "unconventional" ideas could be encouraged and stimulated throughout the organization. McSwiney believed that this opening up of communication between the bottom of the organization and the top was essential to Mead's continued health in a society that was demanding that corporations be more responsive to social needs.

In April 1976, Warren Batts, Mead's president and chief operating officer—with the encouragement of McSwiney—was attempting to evaluate the effect of this four-year experiment and to determine whether, at this point, the company would benefit from having management establish more formal links with the Committee. He had just

Source: Copyright © 1977 by the President and Fellows of Harvard College. Reproduced by permission. This case was prepared by Arva R. Clark under the supervision of Michael L. Lovdal.

116

received a paper prepared by an employee member of CRC recommending that Mead establish an ombudsman function with companywide responsibility. In formulating his response to the issues raised in the paper for the next CRC meeting, scheduled for May 27, 1976, Batts was considering whether operating management should become a more active participant in CRC's deliberations.

THE MEAD CORPORATION

The Mead Pulp & Paper Company was founded in Dayton, Ohio in 1846 by Daniel E. Mead and several partners. Mead's grandson, George H. Mead, became president of the corporation in 1910, served as chairman of the board from 1937 to 1948, and was honorary chairman until his death in 1963. Between 1910 and 1963, the Mead Corporation (renamed in 1930) added 37 plants and mills to its two original paper mills in Dayton and Chillicothe, Ohio. Mead's product line, originally limited to magazine paper, expanded under George Mead's leadership to include a wide variety of paper products.

In the 1960s, the company determined to grow and broaden its base, and by 1976, largely as a result of acquisitions, it was producing such products as furniture, school and office products, rubber products, precision castings and coal, as well as pulp and paper.[1] The company owned operating units in 30 states and 23 foreign countries and was one of the ten largest paper manufacturers in the United States.[2] It owned or managed more than 1.5 million acres of timberland in North America. In 1976, forest products (paper, paperboard, packaging, containers, and pulp) accounted for 56 percent of Mead's sales; school, office, and home products, 28 percent; and industrial products (castings, coal, rubber parts, and piping), 13 percent.

Mead's sales reached the $1 billion mark for the first time in 1969, with record net earnings. (See Exhibit 1 for a financial history.) In 1970, however, net earnings dropped substantially because of national declines in the housing market, rising pulp costs, reduced demand for white papers, and strikes at a number of Mead plants. In 1971, earnings showed improvement, but this was followed by a sharp decline in 1972 when wildcat strikes closed plants in Atlanta,

---

[1] Between 1960 and 1974 Mead acquired 40 companies. The largest, in terms of sales volume, were the Woodward Corporation, manufacturers of castings, and coal, rubber, and iron products; Chatfield & Woods, paper merchants; Westab, Inc., producers of educational and consumer products; and Stanley Furniture Company, Inc.

[2] Mead was usually compared with the following companies: Boise-Cascade; Champion; Crown Zellerbach; Georgia Pacific; Great Northern Nekoosa; Hammermill; International Paper; Kimberly Clark; Potlatch; Scott; St. Regis; Union Camp; Westvaro; and Weyerhaeuser.

EXHIBIT 1
Financial History 1970–1976

	1976	1975	1974	1973	1972	1971	1970
Net sales (millions)	$1,599	$1,245	$1,526	$1,299	$1,129	$1,056	$1,038
Net earnings (millions)	$ 89	$ 53	$ 82	$ 49	$ 18	$ 23	$ 20
Return on sales	5.6%	4.2%	5.4%	3.8%	2.3%	2.2%	2.0%
Return on equity.............	14.9%	9.9%	16.2%	10.9%	5.9%	5.2%	4.5%
Per common share							
Net earnings							
(fully diluted)	$ 2.94	$ 1.78	$ 2.72	$ 1.59	$ .57	$ .91	$ .70
Dividends	$ .89	$ .80	$ .60	$ .43	$ .40	$ .67	$ .67
Book value	$24.34	$22.05	$20.80	$17.71	$15.97	$15.86	$15.92
Capital expenditures							
(millions)	$ 76	$ 64	$ 124	$ 77	$ 40	$ 61	$ 44
Total assets							
(millions)	$1,227	$1,091	$1,057	$ 941	$ 862	$ 865	$ 861
Number of employees	26,200	24,000	27,000	32,000	32,000	34,000	34,200
Number of stockholders	29,525	31,197	31,372	32,164	30,119	30,555	30,924

Source: Information supplied by the Mead Corporation.

Georgia and Anniston, Alabama.[3] These were the first major walk-outs the company had experienced since the 1940s.[4]

Mead's sales and earnings reached record highs in 1974. But in the next year earnings were off because of the national recession and because more than 3,000 workers staged walkouts in Escanaba, Michigan (26 weeks) and Chillicothe, Ohio (11 weeks) in response to the company's determination to include Social Security offsets as part of its pension benefits. In addition, Mead's affiliates in British Columbia were closed by industry-wide unrest in Canada. The company recovered rapidly, however, and expected a 76 percent rise in profits for 1976.

THE MEAD ORGANIZATION

In 1976, the Mead Corporation was organized into six operating groups and a corporate staff headed by a group vice president on a peer level with the heads of the operating groups. (See Exhibit 2 for an organization chart.) Originally a paper company with centralized management, Mead began to move towards a decentralized structure during its acquisition program. In 1976, Mead's Paper and Paperboard Groups were made up of the paper and paperboard mills that had previously been the cornerstone of the corporation, and the packaging and container plants that had been acquired and expanded. The four other groups consisted of all the remaining acquisitions.

The expansive phase of Mead's development had been engineered by James W. McSwiney, chairman of the board in 1976, who had joined Mead in 1934 at the age of 18. He had been president and chief executive officer between 1968 and 1971. When he became chairman in 1971, he retained his CEO position, and Paul Allemang (a group vice president since Mead acquired his company in 1966) became president and chief operating officer. Allemang was succeeded in

---

[3] The following description of strike issues appeared in Mead's 1972 Annual Report: "Several hundred employees of Mead Packaging and Containers plants in Atlanta, in response to a local civil rights group that was attempting to organize a citywide minority union, staged a 55-day wildcat strike. Though illegal, it did focus attention on some real problems: minority promotional opportunities, a dust condition, blocked communications. The dust problem was soon dealt with, a representative council formed to survey employee feelings more directly, and a new pre-supervisory training program for blacks and females instituted. A ten-day wildcat strike in Anniston, Alabama, revealed several misunderstandings. New Anniston management has stepped up information-sharing with employees; meetings to answer questions about pensions have proved especially helpful."

[4] Among Mead's 26,200 employees, 16,000 were represented by unions in 1976. The largest (in terms of number of Mead employees represented) were the United Paper Workers International, the Printing Specialists Union, and the United Steel Workers.

EXHIBIT 2
Organization Chart

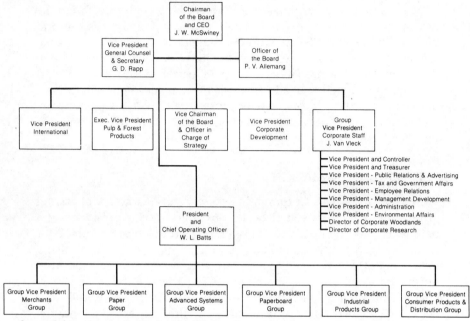

Source: Information supplied by the Mead Corporation.

1973 by Warren Batts, 42, who had joined Mead as a group vice
president in 1971. (Before joining Mead, Batts had been co-founder,
president and CEO of a small hand-tool company.)

Despite its substantial diversity in business, Mead's management
at the corporate level was made up largely of people with back-
grounds in the paper industry until the late 1960s. As new companies
had been acquired, only one, the Stanley Furniture Company, had
brought a "Mead man" into the ranks of its top management. Others,
like the Industrial Products Group (with the former Woodward Corp.
as its core), were run exclusively by the acquired management. A
senior executive commented: "Relations became strained during the
acquisition program, which brought on board a lot of new people and
businesses. The corporate staff was strictly paper-oriented and had
real problems relating to foundries and coal mines."

A manager who had been with Mead since the 1950s described the
paper industry as being high in capital investment, with slow growth
and little chance for marketing innovation. "If you do everything
right and your competitors do everything wrong," he said, "your
market share might change a fraction of one percent." He went on: "It

is not unusual for the average paper manager to ride with his subordinates; he is willing to accept less than perfection. Personal relations always played a major role in the company. The old Mead Paper was almost as much a social organization as a business. When I came with the company, it seemed like a family."

When Batts became president in 1973, the company was examining the fruits of its acquisition phase and beginning to divest itself of 22 operations that did not fit into its long-range plans. In 1975, Batts began the process of integrating Mead's product groups, while strengthening the decentralized management structure. He described Mead's previous structure and its current direction:

> It took time for McSwiney's philosophy of organization and planning to take on meaning. In some groups decentralization was taken to mean that a group vice president was a prince with a moat around his division and his people. You came across his drawbridge at his pleasure.
>
> Now, we have gotten to the point where decentralization means that the group vice presidents are totally responsible for choosing the right people to run their businesses, for seeing problems and opportunities, and for presenting alternatives. But the corporate officers make the final selection among alternatives. We share the responsibility with the group vice presidents for results.

Early in 1974, Batts established the Operating Policy Committee (OPC), which he chaired and which included William Wommack (vice chairman of the board and officer in charge of strategy) and all the group vice presidents. He explained why:

> In order to maximize the results from a decentralized organization there had to be a vehicle for: (1) building common beliefs and goals into the company while recognizing critical differences among units; (2) establishing corporate policies; and (3) strengthening the position of the group vice presidents.
>
> In the past, many people felt—and it was true in some instances—that if someone on the corporate staff had an idea, it was fired right down to the plant managers without the group vice presidents being consulted. Now the OPC serves as a buffer. Sometimes it takes 15 drafts to get an idea in shape. But by the time OPC signs off on it, each group vice president and his people are committed to getting it through the system.

In addition to developing better "top-down" communication, the OPC served as a vehicle for the divisions to exchange ideas. For example, in early 1976 the OPC was considering a program for improving internal communications that had been developed by the Paper Group. This program consisted of employee attitude surveys, management seminars, and management-employee councils. Batts intended that all the group vice presidents would eventually adopt a similar type of communications program, as a result of OPC discussions. Still, he was aware that such adoption would best be voluntary: "Given our organizational philosophy, each group vice president should have final authority in operational matters. I would rather persuade than order them to establish a particular program for internal communications."

The change in the management structure was in some ways a function of the difference in style between McSwiney and Batts in the role of president and chief operating officer. A group vice president made this comparison:

> McSwiney is more likely to say something and then assume it will come out the way he wants it to. He is a powerful man, magnetic, very difficult to say no to, even when you know you should say no. I still have a tendency to think he can't do anything wrong. As CEO, he has the ability to see things that the rest of us, wrapped up in the day-to-day issues, don't think about. He never lets us get too satisfied with ourselves.
>
> When McSwiney was president, he knew all the details and had a compulsion to make all the decisions. Batts likes to know the sequence of steps involved, but he is more willing to give the group vice presidents independence. Still, he is very structured and wants to know how things are likely to turn out.

Since 1971, 5 of 6 group vice presidents and 19 of 24 division presidents had been changed—mostly replaced with people from within the company.

THE MEAD BOARD

During most of the Mead Corp.'s history, many of its directors were members of the Mead family and officers of the corporation. As it acquired new businesses in the 1960s, Mead added top officers of the merged companies to the board. (Exhibit 3 lists the members of the board in 1976.)

In September 1970, James McSwiney became concerned about the board's composition. He was especially interested in achieving a better balance between inside and outside directors. (At that time, Mead's 22-member board included only six directors who were not associated with the Mead family or the company.) With the board's approval, McSwiney appointed a special committee consisting of four outside directors to study the board's functions, size and composition. Alfred W. Jones, who would retire at the end of 1972 after 33 years as a Mead director, was named chairman of the committee. In its final report the "Jones Committee" recommended that:

EXHIBIT 3
Board of Directors (April 1976)

Vernon R. Alden (1965)*
Chairman of the Board
The Boston Company, Inc.
Boston, Mass.
Common shares owned: 600

Ivan Allen, Jr. (1971)
Chairman of the Board
Ivan Allen Company
Atlanta, Ga.
Common shares owned: 200

Warren L. Batts (1973)
President and Chief Operating
Officer
Mead Corporation
Common shares owned: 1100

George B. Beitzel (1973)
Senior Vice President,
International
Business Machines Corporation
Armonk, N.Y.
Common shares owned: 200

William R. Bond (1968)
Chairman of the Board
Cement Asbestos Products
Company
Birmingham, Ala.
Common shares owned: 7500

Newton H. DeBardeleben (1968)
Vice Chairman of the Board
First National Bank
Birmingham, Ala.
Common shares owned: 720

James W. McSwiney (1963)
Chairman of the Board and
Chief Executive Officer
Mead Corporation
Common shares owned: 102,801

H. Talbott Mead (1946)
President
Mead Investment Company
Dayton, Oh.
Common shares owned: 48,244

Nelson S. Mead (1959)
Vice President, International
Mead Corporation
Common shares owned: 28,408

Paul F. Miller, Jr. (1963)
Partner, Miller Anderson &
Sherrerd
(Investment management firm)
Philadelphia, Penn.
Common shares owned: 1000

George H. Sheets (1963)
Executive Vice President
Mead Corporation
Common shares owned: 13,736

William M. Spencer III (1968)
Chairman of the Board
Motion Industries, Inc.
Birmingham, Ala.
Common shares owned: 26,648

Thomas B. Stanley, Jr. (1970)
Investor
Stanleytown, W.V.
Common shares owned: 172,400

C. William Verity (1966)
Chairman of the Board and
Chief Executive Officer
Armco Steel Corporation
Middletown, Oh.
Common shares owned: 2232

John M. Walker, M.D. (1957)
Consultant
White, Weld & Co., Inc.
New York, N.Y.
Common shares owned: 5715

William W. Wommack (1968)
Vice Chairman of the Board and
Officer in
Charge of Strategy
Mead Corporation
Common shares owned: 9404

* Date of appointment to Board.
Source: The Mead Corporation.

> An effective number of directors for a company the size of Mead should
> be between 12 and 15, with inside directors not to exceed one third—
> Outside directors should be chosen for breadth of experience and inter-
> est, and the balance they can bring to the Board's deliberations.

The committee also described the type of person who should be
considered for board membership in the future—namely, heads of
companies similar to Mead in size; owners of large amounts of Mead
stock; one or more people "oriented to minority, ethnic, or other
social concerns," and individuals with the ability to ask critical questions. Finally, the Jones committee analyzed the functions of existing
board committees and recommended that the board establish a "Corporate Responsibility Committee," to provide the company with a
"means of responding to salient social and environmental aspects of
the world."

In keeping with the Jones Committee's recommendations, the
board began to meet six times each year, with meetings averaging
three hours in length. In addition, the executive committee met with
outside directors four times a year. Five other board committees—Finance, Compensation, Audit, Corporate Responsibility, and Corporate Objectives (formed in 1975)—also met periodically throughout
the year. In 1976, outside directors received compensation of $10,000
per year, plus $600 for each executive committee meeting and $400 for
meetings of other board committees.

In 1974, at McSwiney's suggestion, Mead's board appointed
another directors' task force, composed of outside directors and
chaired by Vernon Alden, to reexamine the board and to bring the
original Jones Report up to date. (See Exhibit 4 for excerpts from this
group's report.)

McSwiney often referred to the Mead Corp.'s board as a "working
board." The president of Mead, Warren Batts, offered his perception
of the board:

EXHIBIT 4
Excerpts from Directors' Task Force Report, 1974

**BOARD RESPONSIBILITIES AND EXPECTATIONS
OF MEAD DIRECTORS**

In the legal corporation framework the Mead Board has ultimate *responsibility* for the management of the corporation. The board discharges this responsibility by delegating the executive function to management and by
holding management accountable. In a broad sense, the board holds a *charter
of trust* for the corporation. In this perspective, it stands between the Mead
organization and the outside environment, including shareowners, customers, public, etc.

EXHIBIT 4 *(continued)*

In operational terms, the board reviews and approves or rejects recommendations of Mead management on certain major decisions. . . . Final decisions on such matters as declaration of dividends, mergers, and disposition of principal assets constitute *reserved powers* and require formal action by the board. In addition to these formal actions, directors are expected to counsel management on decisions . . . of major importance . . . such as . . . the charting of business strategy with regard to particular products or markets and major employment fluctuations (growth or curtailment).

One way to sharpen the definition of what the board does might be to distinguish between the board's role and function and the role and function of Mead management. In the functioning of the board organization, directors should review, consider, contribute, formulate, and advise; operating and staff managers should propose, implement, operate, account for and assist . . .

AUDIT AND ACCOUNTABILITY: THE BOARD AGENDA

In the discharge of its duties to audit the operation and to hold management accountable, the Mead board needs access to information. The board's effectiveness is based upon the capability of Mead directors to ask the right questions and their ability to receive prompt and responsive answers. The quality and efficiency of discussions and decisions at Mead board meetings is thus determined by the *quality of information* that the board members receive. It is the responsibility of the chairman of the board to ensure the adequacy of information services to Mead directors. In all cases, board members should have the opportunity (and should take the initiative) to seek information which they need, in addition to regular reports by management. . . .

CORPORATE RESPONSIBILITY

Corporate responsibility is an emergent but not well defined function of corporate boards in their role as trustee, standing between the corporation and society. Corporations in general have not demonstrated a clear sense of how to articulate this function in operational terms (i.e., who in the board should do what, when). Fiscal accounting is precise and financial audits are feasible because measurement standards apply universally across divisional and corporate boundaries. No such universal means of measurement are available for corporate responsibility.

The Mead board has an opportunity to serve in this area, by virtue of the emphasis placed by the chief executive officer, by directors, and by the response throughout the corporation to the establishment and the work to date of the Corporate Responsibility Committee of the board. *We believe and recommend that the board should continue to regard corporate responsibility as one of its major concerns.*

We have a core of outside directors who are truly tough-minded businessmen. They know that the job of a director is basically to protect the shareholder—first, foremost, and always. The board's role is to review and approve corporate objectives and to review management's actions but not to meddle in operations. Among our directors, however, there is a wide spectrum of opinion about the board's role in corporate responsibility. This is the most nebulous area for the board and one that we have to make more concrete.

INITIATION OF THE CORPORATE
RESPONSIBILITY COMMITTEE

In March 1972, the full board of directors accepted the Jones Committee's recommendation to form a Corporate Responsibility Committee. McSwiney described his thinking:

> At the time there were several issues. Blacks were very vocal about the rights of minorities, and equal opportunity for women was also in the spotlight. The term "corporate responsibility" was the new buzz word, and some people thought it was simply a fad. But I took the idea very seriously. I thought a Corporate Responsibility Committee, with both directors and employees as members, could provide a way to send unfiltered information to the top of the organization.
>
> I have a feeling that if you can't stand unfiltered information in an organization, or if you don't get it, you probably are going to make a lot of erroneous assumptions. I saw this committee as a mechanism for encouraging dialogue, and for breaking through the walls that surround managers at the top of the company.

Although he was instrumental in the formation of CRC, McSwiney felt very strongly that he himself should not be a member. He explained why:

> I didn't feel the committee would make a real contribution if the chief executive meddled with it. The resolution of critical or sensitive issues, especially those that involve prestigious positions and talented people, can seldom be achieved by edict. Only when those people who are affected are involved in the process of working out their own solutions is the process likely to become an ongoing part of the system.
>
> A CEO must not become so insecure that he blocks communications—sometimes accurate, sometimes inaccurate, but always believed by those in the system—from reaching the outside directors.

Consistent with this philosophy, McSwiney met with CRC only on two or three occasions after its initiation. However, he and the full board regularly received formal and informal reports from the committee's chairman and secretary on the work and functioning of CRC.

McSwiney chose Gerald D. Rapp, general counsel and vice president for human resources, to chair the committee and he asked three outside directors to serve as members. These four then took responsibility for recruiting three employee members. In their early discussion, the directors mentioned wide outside interests, college background, and youthful thinking as criteria for selection of employee members. One director argued that hourly workers should be represented; another felt that no one should be chosen simply to represent the union point of view. No definite criteria for employee membership emerged from these discussions.

Notices announcing openings for employee membership on CRC were posted at all Mead facilities in the United States. Rapp interviewed every candidate (nearly 100) and his or her supervisor. Next, ten finalists, with their husbands and wives, were invited to meet with the CRC director members in July 1972. On the night they and their spouses arrived for scheduled interviews, finalists were asked to write essays on corporate responsibility and, at dinner, to speak informally about themselves and their goals. One of the finalists described the experience: "It was not enjoyable. You yank someone out of the bottom of the organization and bring him to the Plaza in New York City to meet the directors of the company and it produces some bizarre behavior." Three employees were finally chosen for CRC membership and the committee was introduced to the company in a newsletter. (See Exhibit 5.)

Nine months later, a decision was made to recruit an hourly paid employee for the Committee. Most of the applicants for committee membership were nominated by their supervisors. After employee members narrowed the list of applicants down to ten finalists, all CRC members, in teams of two, conducted interviews and chose two new members: Quepee Gates, a railroad conductor from a Mead facility in Woodward, Alabama; and Warden Seymour, a pipe fitter and union official from a paper mill in Chillicothe.

EARLY COMMITTEE ACTIVITIES

In the summer of 1972, the Corporate Responsibility Committee began to carry out the duties assigned by the full board—duties which represented the CRC's original charter:

Examine and report on the attitudes of all levels of management toward social and environmental responsibilities and concerns.

Examine and recommend specific issues for Board and management consideration and determine their relative priority.

EXHIBIT 5
These Employees and Outside Directors Will Serve on the New Corporate Responsibility Committee

Randy Evans has just been promoted to manager of Customer Service for Mead Paperboard Products' Western Region. He has worked with Mead since 1968.

Annabel Clayton (Mead Packaging) sells convenience packaging to the industrial market in New York. She joined Mead in 1966.

Bobby Bullock started his Mead career in 1962 as an hourly worker at Durham and worked his way up to general foreman of Mead Containers' Spartanburg plant.

G. D. Rapp, Mead's Assistant General Counsel, has been appointed chairman of the new Corporate Responsibility Committee.

W. Walker Lewis, Jr. is General Counsel for Mead. He serves as the Corporate Responsibility Committee's secretary.

Ivan Allen, Jr. is Chairman of the Board of the Ivan Allen Company in Atlanta, which merchandises office supplies and equipment. He served two terms as mayor of Atlanta from 1962 to 1969. He was elected to the Mead board in 1971.

Vernon R. Alden is Chairman of the Board at The Boston Company. He was President of Ohio University from 1962 to 1969, a period characterized by strong student unrest. He has been a Mead director since 1965.

N. H. DeBardeleben is President of the First National Bank of Birmingham. He joined the Mead Board of Directors in 1968.

THREE EMPLOYEES CHOSEN FOR DIRECTORS' COMMITTEE

A three-month search for three employees to fill out the Mead Board of Directors' new Corporate Responsibility Committee has resulted in the selection of a saleswoman, a general foreman, and a customer service manager to serve with three outside directors. The three were chosen from a panel of ten — narrowed down from a field of nearly 80 candidates from all parts of the company — for the contribution each can make to the committee's work.

The board created the committee to help Mead keep abreast of its changing responsibilities — toward the environment, the communities it operates in, its customers and employees — and to see that it is developing sound ways to deal with them. Chairman J. W. McSwiney says that it should "provide a means for unorthodox, unexpected, unconventional — perhaps unwelcome — ideas to emerge and find their way to top level attention."

A small task force is already accumulating fresh data on such topics as Mead woodlands policies, employment practices, and environmental quality programs. The committee expects to draw upon the ideas of all 80 original nominees and welcomes the input of any interested employee. Direct your comments to the committee's chairman, G. D. Rapp, The Mead Corporation, 118 W. First Street, Dayton, Ohio 45402.

HERE ARE THE OTHER FINALISTS WHO VIED FOR COMMITTEE MEMBERSHIP

Grady A. Roberts, Jr. came to Montag in Atlanta in 1971 to help with training for disadvantaged employees. He also works in the Cost Department.

Young Kim, controller for Westab at Sunnyvale, Calif., came to the U.S. for an education and liked it so well he stayed. He joined Mead in 1971.

Ronald Sedenquist, an electrician at Mead Publishing Papers' Escanaba mill, takes an active role in his union. His service began in 1957.

Owen L. Gentry (Board Supply division) is superintendent of the Sylva, N.C. mill. He has been with Mead since 1960.

Mike Noonan, who joined Mead in 1968, is general sales manager for Mead Packaging division in Atlanta.

Howard Hughes is special projects manager with Murray Rubber in Houston, Texas. He came to Mead in 1968.

Lester (Bill) Reed is general manager of Woodward's Chattanooga Coke and Chemical division. He came to Mead in 1966.

Source: The Mead Corporation

Determine and recommend policy related to priority issues.

Project potential new areas of social responsibility and involvement.

Recommend where duties and responsibilities lie throughout the various levels of the company.

To help the committee select its priorities, Rapp, at the direction of the committee, formed a task force to study Mead's performance in pollution control, equal opportunity and land management, and to analyze the attitudes of outside groups (e.g., the National Council of Churches and the Environmental Protection Agency) toward industry. Research assistants to the task force were four recent college graduates who were about to enter graduate school. These researchers gave Mead managers their first inkling of what CRC might be up to. One recalled:

> Their three-month escapade certainly didn't help the credibility of the committee. CRC was brand new from the chairman of the board, so people knew it was important. The next thing they saw were these college kids—"Rapp's Raiders" as they came to be known—marching through their doors, telling them their EEO performance was lousy, their contributions budgets all wrong. And reporting to top management.
>
> One manager got fired. He should have been fired, but there was a direct link between the exposure these kids gave him and his dismissal. He happened to be a highly regarded—incompetent—guy. That he got fired scared a lot of people. Some people quietly let their stomachs churn. Others became outwardly hostile to the committee.

At the conclusion of their studies, the students made several recommendations to CRC. The primary ones were that the company use incentives to reward and punish managers for pollution control and equal opportunity performance and that the company establish a multiple-use strategy for its forests. Within a year, corporate staff reported to CRC that Mead had begun a systematic expansion of hunting, fishing, and hiking rights in its forests, as part of a multiple-use program. By April 1976, however, the company had not formally implemented the researchers' first recommendation.

REACHING THE EMPLOYEES

The employee members of the CRC felt strongly in 1972 that contact with Mead employees was needed to communicate priorities to the committee. To help in this process, Rapp arranged to have Randy Evans released from his regular job and assigned to the human resources staff for three months to coordinate regional meetings. Under

Evans' supervision, 140 employees were chosen, from names submitted by supervisors and general managers, to attend two-day conferences. The conferees included 56 hourly and 84 salaried workers from 48 operating units. Forty-six of the employees were members of minority groups; 38 were women. Evans described the employee meetings:

> Initially, a lot of people were uncertain about the purpose but as things started unfolding on the first evening, they began to see that we were serious. By and large, a feeling of sincerity was communicated, and people said, "Well, if this is real, how can we make it worthwhile?"
>
> The interchange that began happening was just beautiful. One salesman said that salespeople have no job satisfaction. A black hourly worker said: "I'm not concerned with job satisfaction. I don't even know what you're talking about. I've got four children and I'm happy to have a job. And let me tell you what it's like to work in a foundry." This kind of exchange started going on.

Most of the employees who had spent two days discussing what was "right" and what was "wrong" with the Mead Corp. seemed to leave the meetings with good feelings. For many, the opportunity to share information and experiences, at meetings sponsored by the company itself, elicited a positive attitude toward management. One participant wrote to the organizer of a California meeting: "I think we all felt a little proud of Mead and the CRC for this opportunity. We may eventually let a little 'we' creep into our thinking, instead of the ominous 'they.'" In a report prepared for the directors, Evans wrote:

> Employees wanted the existing communications channels to work. They did not want the Corporate Responsibility Committee to do an "end run" around management. Rather, they wanted the CRC to fix the system so that a mutual listening and trust relationship could be developed between the employee and his immediate supervisor.

CRC IN 1973—REPORTING TO MANAGEMENT

Mead's group vice presidents had their first formal contact with CRC early in 1973 at a Hueston Woods, Ohio, retreat, where CRC employee members reported on the 1972 employee meetings. One group VP described the presentation:

> All of us were impressed with the eloquence of the people describing the problems they found in Mead. They were obviously words from the heart. We went down skeptical, but came away really impressed. The issues were pretty clear—better information-sharing and communication and a need to make the system work more effectively.

After the Hueston Woods meeting, the employee members of CRC and a few employees who had attended the 1972 regional conferences met with managers throughout the company. Robert Richards (a manager chosen for CRC membership in 1975) recalled a story he had heard about a 1973 CRC plant visit:

> I heard about the visit from the plant manager. Some CRC people toured his place, a lovely old brick building surrounded by trees. He asked one CRC member how he liked the plant, expecting the usual praise. Instead, the CRC person said: "I don't see any blacks working here. Haven't you hired any?" The manager told him that no blacks lived in that area. In that case, the CRC member said, the manager should be recruiting blacks throughout the state. The manager told me that, in his opinion, CRC was out to manufacture issues where it couldn't find them.

After a year of management meetings, the employee members of CRC expected the organization to respond in some way. But nothing seemed to happen. A senior manager offered this explanation: "After the early meetings, there was an air of endorsement and enthusiasm among the operating managers, but it was not their role to pick up the responsibility for making things happen."

In addition to holding meetings for management and recruiting new committee members in 1973, CRC also heard reports from corporate staff on EEO performance, corporate contributions, programs for employees with drug and alcohol problems, and a placement effort for employees who were laid off when Mead closed a facility in Anniston, Alabama. Exhibits 6 and 7 are examples of the kind of data the Committee received in these reports.

In preparation for the last CRC meeting of 1973, Jerry Rapp, committee secretary, sent several recommendations for the next year's agenda to chairman Vernon Alden:

EXHIBIT 6
Equal Opportunity Percentages, 1974–1976*

Category	April 1, 1976	April 1, 1975	April 1, 1974
Executives, officials and managers	4.2/4.4	3.0/4.0	2.2/3.7
Professionals	15.3/3.6	12.0/3.4	9.9/3.5
Technicians	9.4/7.1	7.0/4.3	6.7/5.5
Sales workers	11.5/4.4	8.1/4.4	5.4/2.9
Office and clerical	75.9/9.8	72.1/9.4	71.0/8.7
Skilled crafts	1.1/12.3	.9/11.8	1.4/11.6
Semi-skilled operatives	14.7/27.7	12.7/26.6	11.8/27.1
Unskilled laborers	29.2/28.9	24.9/27.5	20.8/33.0
Service workers	9.9/37.9	9.6/32.4	8.9/31.1
Total work force	19.6/19.7	18.1/18.6	16.9/20.7

* All females/all minorities (male and female).

EXHIBIT 7
Corporate Gifts, 1969–1975

Year	Net Gifts ($000)	Gifts as Percent of Earnings before Tax	
		Mead	All Industry
1969	$624	1.07%	1.24%
1970	496	1.51	1.08
1971	408	1.06	1.03
1972	440	1.51	.95
1973	453	.90	.86
1974	514	.34	.83
1975	492	.96	n/a

Our basic task now is to see how Mead could institutionalize this process of employee communication. Next, we might consider new major projects that we should undertake ourselves or encourage other Mead people or groups to take on. From the employee meetings, we have identified problems falling into six clusters . . . equal employment opportunity; job satisfaction; communications; the external human environment; the external physical environment; and personal services for employees, such as counseling for retirees, day care centers, clean working conditions . . .

NEW DIRECTORS JOIN CRC

In April 1974, two new director members were appointed. These were C. William Verity, chairman of the board of Armco Steel Company, and George B. Beitzel, senior vice president and director of IBM. (As a means of familiarizing directors with the company, the board rotated membership on CRC.) In the years that followed, members of CRC often referred to this April meeting as a turning point for the committee. It brought two issues into focus: the frustration and disappointment that employee members were experiencing after the intensity of CRC's start-up years, and the difference between director and employee members' perception of the role of CRC within the company.

All the employee members were angry about the corporation's failure to deal with the problems discussed at the employee conferences in 1972 and reported to management in 1973. At the April meeting, they argued that, if it did nothing else, CRC should at least respond to the most widespread complaint voiced at the employee meetings—dirty restroom facilities in plants and mills throughout the company. Both new director members expressed their surprise at the nature of the issue and the manner in which it had been uncovered. One recalled the meeting:

It was hard to get a definition of what the committee was and what it should be doing. At my first meeting, somebody mentioned that the men's rooms were very dirty and said the committee ought to do something about that. I argued that it was not the committee's responsibility. If the company's policy was to keep the men's rooms clean, that was the responsibility of the plant managers.

I didn't think CRC should have been asking employees what was on their minds. That was management's job. I told them that the committee should not be a lightning rod for employee grievances. The only people CRC should be talking to is management, asking them questions about policy.

The employees disagreed. One of the committee members described the April meeting as "the most intense we'd ever had." For all five employee members, it was a disheartening experience. One commented:

Beitzel and Verity came on the committee and pretty much refuted the prior posture of the CRC as a committee that would go out and *do* things. They were most vocal in saying: "This is a committee of the board; you are to ask questions of management and let them respond." They felt actually going into the organization and holding employee meetings was something that management should do, not the members of CRC.

You know, we had put our hearts and souls into this and there were these new members coming in and scaring the hell out of you just by sitting there, and then downgrading everything you'd been doing for the last year and a half.

As a result of this meeting, Jerry Rapp and consultant Constantine Simonides, an MIT vice president, worked together to fashion an agenda for CRC. They spoke with chief executive officers and other top management and staff people from companies all around the country with records of achievement in the area of corporate responsibility. In October 1974, they made a presentation to CRC. Their primary recommendation was that CRC should turn its attention to the world outside Mead and pass the responsibility for employee-oriented programs to management.

Specifically, they recommended that Mead's president and group vice presidents take responsibility for improving communications between managers and employees, that corporate staff plan career development and personal service programs for employees and work more closely with supervisors on equal opportunity planning, and that CRC begin to assess the company's contributions policy and programs for involving Mead employees in the affairs of their communities. Rapp described the meeting: "Our recommendations fell on deaf ears. The employee members were just more interested in internal issues. Our discussion of what other companies were doing, what was going on in the outside world, made no impact at all."

A few weeks before Rapp made this presentation to CRC, employee member Warden Seymour had written a letter to Mead's chairman, expressing his concern about the committee's lack of activity:

> . . . From the time you informed me I had been selected for the committee, I have believed in the good it can do for all the employees and for the corporation. Recently though I have become very discouraged with the lack of activity by the committee. I feel the chairman of the board has a very deep sense of responsibility to all the employees but I feel people under you are reluctant to accept the changes recommended by this body. I feel the only way the committee can survive is with very strong support from you and Mr. Batts . . .

McSwiney responded to Seymour early in November and emphasized his continued support of the committee:

> I also could be discouraged when I think of all the things that have not been accomplished. The existence of the Corporate Responsibility Committee in some ways may aid in raising expectations beyond what can realistically be accomplished; but that is a risk I am willing to live with so long as we can have open dialogue throughout the company about the expectation level and the measures of performance (or lack of performance) about these expectations . . .
>
> During 1975, I would urge you and other committee members to consider contact with fellow employees and others in the context of the committee's responsibility of monitoring progress within the company on the key corporate responsibility issues, with results to be reported to the board and corporate management . . .

In November 1974, the employee members came together to discuss the issues they felt the whole committee should tackle in the coming year. They put together a list of 35 objectives to pursue in 1975 (see Exhibit 8).

NEW EMPLOYEES JOIN CRC

In 1975, three employee members left the committee, and Rapp and Paul Allemang managed the recruitment process for replacements.[5] CRC discussed at great length the problems of recruiting new members because employee members believed that few in the company understood the committee's function. In response to a director's

---

[5] When Paul Allemang stepped down as president, chief operating officer, and director of Mead in 1973, he was appointed to the position of officer of the board. His main responsibility was to help coordinate CRC activities.

EXHIBIT 8
CRC Priorities for 1975 (recommendations from employee members)

1. Examination by board of Mead's policy on involuntary separations, layoffs, terminations and early retirements (equality of treatment with respect to notices and placement and committee audit).
2. Bring together board and employee members of committee.
3. Board examination of Mead's policy and performance regarding corporate contributions.
4. Board examination of Mead's policy regarding educational assistance including leave policy and family assistance.
5. Meetings:
    a. full day.
    b. operating locations.
    c. outside contributors.
    d. times other than board meetings.
    e. six meetings per year.
    f. workshop meetings.
    g. annual meeting with board by full committee with report by employee members.
    h. routine receipt of reports.
    i. outsider take minutes.
6. Audit personal services effort.
7. Inquire, examine, or investigate policy or method of communications to employees, i.e., *Progress Report* (ask Mead people *and* outsiders to review for committee).
8. Board agenda to include CRC report and, perhaps, questions regarding employee concerns.
9. Board examine Mead's policy concerning handicapped people: ex-offenders, physically handicapped, Vietnam veterans, hard-core unemployed, etc.
10. Policy and performance at Mead regarding career planning.
11. Board examine Mead's policy concerning managerial rewards and punishments with respect to EEO performance.
12. Quarterly report to board by management of EEO performance.
13. Board require management to report routinely in advance on actions that impact Mead constituencies—employees, community, suppliers, customers.
14. Individual access to and control of information.
15. Recommend that Mead should have policy with respect to an individual nonunion employee appeals process.
16. Ask for policy on employee recognition.
17. Ask for policy concerning assistance to families of employee who dies.
18. Policy affecting contact with retired employees also disabled.

EXHIBIT 8 *(continued)*

19. Ask for policy on age discrimination.
20. Ask what is company policy regarding minimum physical standards for Mead employee facilities.
21. Policy on CRC membership turnover.
22. Deal with personal problems of members due to CRC service.
23. Decision on staff support to committee.
24. Determine interest, policy, and posture regarding "external" concerns.
25. Decision regarding employee meetings—recommend to management.
26. Examine management efforts to place black males in *top* line positions—what are goals?
27. Company should address attention to determining concerns of middle managers.
28. Company policy regarding response to recent pension legislation.
29. What impact expected from "inflation management" concept and procedures.
30. What attempt and results of management efforts to improve quality of communication between supervisors and subordinates.
31. Connect 1975 CRC agenda with the past two years.
32. Examine the effect of attitude surveys and assessment mechanisms on employees.
33. Board emphasize performance measurement beyond financial results.
34. Ask for Mead's policy on the company's participation in the community.
35. Big external issues—work with other institutions:
    a. ZEG/ZPG impact on Mead.
    b. cooperation vs. competition with respect to unions, competitors, government communication.
    c. conservation.
    d. how people relate to company and what are new ways of relating.
    e. Impact of future technology and discoveries on Mead and its constituencies.

Source: The Mead Corporation

recommendation, Rapp and Allemang prepared a proposal for recruiting new members and discussed it with Warren Batts. They suggested that the group vice presidents select a panel of employees (managers, staff, and hourly workers) to screen candidates from groups other than their own. The candidates so chosen would then be interviewed by all the members of CRC. This would be an annual process.

Batts invited Allemang and Rapp to discuss the proposal at an April 1975 meeting of the group vice presidents. He described what happened at the meeting:

I thought that Paul and Jerry's proposal for getting new members for CRC was sound since it got management involved. So they met with the group vice presidents to discuss the recruitment process. The response from the group vice presidents was not what I expected. They were upset. "We're closing down and selling plants and laying off many in the work force," they said, "and now we're going to have all this song and dance, at great expense." At their insistence, the process of selecting new members was toned down.

In July of 1975, Randy Evans (one of the retiring employee members) made a ten-day trip around the country to interview applicants for CRC, most of whom had been nominated by their supervisors and general managers. Evans chose ten finalists, who were then interviewed by committee members. The four new employee members were: Robert Richards, a marketing manager; Robi Love, coordinator for college employment; David Hubbard, a sales representative in California; and Ister Person, who worked in the order processing department of a paper merchant unit. All four had been nominated for CRC membership; only Person had been unaware of the committee's existence before receiving word of her nomination.

In August 1975, Jerry Rapp sent a memorandum to James McSwiney on the future of CRC. He made four recommendations:

1. Strengthen the leadership and active participation of director members.
2. Balance the employee membership by including middle management and clarify the selection process by involving local operating management.
3. Beef up the staff support to the committee in order to provide more information to members and to communicate the committee's concerns and activities to corporate staff and operating management.
4. Broaden the CRC agenda to include not only employee concerns, but also the concerns of external groups such as customers, shareholders, government agencies, suppliers, and communities in which plants are located.

In October, the new employee members attended an orientation meeting, and in December, their first regular committee meeting. By their second meeting, in February 1976, they were expressing doubts about CRC's ability to get things done. One new member was especially concerned about the employee members' isolation from the directors, and the committee's isolation from the company:

What bothered me from the first was that all the employee members had suggestions for the agenda, issues we felt were important, but we didn't get a chance to discuss them with the directors. We rely on the directors for leadership, and without more direct communication with them, we probably won't have much of an impact on the company. What also bothered me was that we had no formal means of communicating with the organization. We seemed to be operating in a closet.

In a speech delivered at this time, McSwiney offered his views on the committee's progress:

After three years' experience with the Mead Corporate Responsibility Committee, I have found the process in our company both rewarding and frustrating. Things that needed to be said to or about the organization have often been much more effectively stated without my direct participation . . . and this is, of course, a pleasant surprise! When a director, for instance, asks an officer, "Are you humane?", I assure you the penetration and subsequent attitudinal change is much different than if the same question were asked by the CEO . . .

Gaining the understanding and support of middle managers is a crucial step in the effectiveness of a corporate responsibility effort. At Mead, we have not done as well as we would like in this area. We have learned, sometimes painfully, that we must take special care not to threaten middle managers by our anxiety to institute new programs and changes quickly. The understanding and cooperation of middle management is a vital part of making progress in this as well as in any other area that affects operations. We must not allow corporate responsibility to appear as the esoteric mental exercise of top management.

PLANT CLOSING POLICY

At the same time that CRC was recruiting new members in 1975, it was giving its attention to a policy issue that both director and employee members agreed was of major importance to the corporation. This was the company's plant closing policy and the question of management's responsibility to employees who lost their jobs when Mead closed or sold an operating unit. The issue gave the president of the company, Warren Batts, his first direct encounter with the committee.

Following the development and implementation of its strategic plan, between 1973 and 1976, Mead closed 22 of its operating facilities and dropped 8,500 employees from its payroll. The 1973 Annual Report explained;

We made a searching classification of all our businesses in 1971–72. Then we projected each ahead to 1977 and took a look at where they— and the corporation as a whole—would be. That indicated clearly which businesses we should cultivate and which we should move out of to give us the soundest portfolio for the long haul . . .

We've been acting on the analysis, moving out of businesses no longer viable for us and zeroing in on opportunities of special promise . . . To put it simply, we expect to fund businesses with strong growth potential aggressively and to withdraw from those that offer neither growth nor cash.

During CRC's early years, employee and director members occasionally discussed the need to learn whether Mead management had developed a formal companywide policy for dealing with employees affected by plant closings. In December 1974, they raised the issue with Robert Schuldt, vice president of employee development (who was present to report on EEO performance), after employee member Quepee Gates told the committee that he had lost his job in Mead's Woodward, Al foundry that month. Gates was 60 years old and had worked at the foundry for 35 years. What especially troubled him, he said, was that management had notified him at 3:00 P.M., on what he thought was a normal working day, that the plant was closing at the end of the shift.

Two months later, in March 1975, Warren Batts attended a CRC meeting to discuss the company's plant closing policy. Batts reported that a total of 1,825 employees had been laid off in 1974 as a result of 11 plant closings. In most cases, the employees had been notified of the closings from four days to three weeks ahead of time. One hundred and fifty employees had chosen to retire and Mead had helped another 500 to find jobs in other plants or with other companies. The balance chose to remain on unemployment compensation until their eligibility ran out. Batts explained that within the framework of Mead's policy of management decentralization, each division had its own closing policy. This accounted for the disparity in notification dates and severance pay. However, by edict each division followed a standard practice including help from a corporate task force in finding employment for those who wished to work. Progress was monitored by a regular reporting process and managers were rewarded for finding jobs for displaced employees.

In January 1976, Batts reported that a policy statement on plant closings had been officially adopted. One outside director commented: "The one concrete thing CRC did was to get management to put together a policy on how we're going to handle people when we shut down a location. Had the committee not raised the question, we might still not have a policy." CRC members felt that the committee had at last been able to influence the company.

THE OMBUDSMAN ISSUE

In 1976, the employee members of CRC suggested that the committee begin to study Mead's grievance procedures for nonunion employees. Mead had no companywide procedures for handling such problems since the Human Resources staff in each group had this responsibility. Some divisions had set up employee councils that met several times a year to discuss problems directly with management. Others had letter-writing programs, with staff assigned to investigate employees' complaints. One employee member commented on the problem:

> I've worked at a number of locations and know the concerns of white-collar workers and middle managers. They're the unheard segment of the company. They perceive, rightly or wrongly, that the unions have a very effective grievance mechanism and that the top management group takes care of itself but that nobody looks out for them.

Robert Richards, who felt strongly that Mead needed change in this area, volunteered to prepare a paper on an "ombuds function"[6] as a basis for committee discussion at the CRC meeting scheduled for May 27, 1976. In this paper, Richards wrote: "Without a mechanism whereby ideas, complaints, and suggestions are freely discussed, many white collar workers will be functioning in an atmosphere of anxiety, apprehension, and fear." (Excerpts appear in Appendix.)

THE PRESIDENT'S DILEMMA

Warren Batts had had no formal contact with the full CRC until attending the meeting in March 1975 to discuss plant-closing policy. In the years since becoming president, however, he had found that few people understood the reason for the committee's formation and he had heard numerous complaints about its activities:

> There was never any kind of message from the corporate level that explained why directors thought that Mead needed a CRC. Some managers inferred that either the board felt they were not acting in a responsible manner or else someone in the system was chasing the latest corporate fad at their expense.

An operating manager who had been with Mead for 30 years confirmed this view when he summed up his impressions of CRC:

> The general feeling has been that CRC was imposed from the top. It has little or no support or credibility with operating managers. It serves no genuinely constructive purpose. It's a corporate gimmick. The real job of transmitting information, handling two-way communications, and

---

[6] An ombudsman is a person to whom aggrieved parties (e.g., consumers; hospitalized patients; employees) take their complaints. The ombudsman makes an investigation, prepares a report, and attempts to achieve a fair settlement. Traditionally, the ombudsman function was used to protect individuals from abuse by government agencies. The first U.S. corporations to appoint ombudsmen were Xerox Corp., in 1972, and General Electric Company and Boeing Vertel Company, in 1973.

dealing with employee problems should be at the operating level, not the corporate level.

I suppose the intent is to provide the top echelon with grassroots sentiments on what has to be done. But I question whether employee representatives can speak for anyone but themselves. Many things are important at the local level and should be handled locally, not escalated. CRC is kept in place because McSwiney wants it, with the endorsement of the board. But it doesn't enjoy prestige or status with the rest of the company.

A group vice president described his managers' reactions to the committee: "The basic problem is that CRC is seen as a complete bypass of management. Whenever employees can talk directly to directors there is bound to be trouble."

Mead's chairman was aware of the hostility to CRC, but he continued to support it in discussions with board members and management. He made these observations about the company's response to the committee:

There were various types of management reaction to CRC: concern, fear, admiration, pride. But, in general, there was an avoidance of integrating the system into the company. The group vice presidents—their natural inclination reinforced by the negative attitude of some of their managers—constantly sent darts at the people who supported the committee. There were two reasons for this. First, CRC did make some mistakes. It focused solely on employee issues, because this was what mattered to the employee members, as would be expected. But the board and the company had expected the committee to deal with external issues as well. Second, some senior managers wanted to test whether CRC could be eliminated if they criticized it long enough.

I realized from the first that if a new development were to be creative, it was likely to destroy something that already existed. That's the nature of creativity. And if something is destroyed, there is bound to be a certain amount of tension. The main thing is to keep the tension healthy, or at least contained within certain parameters. What has finally happened is that the president of the company has begun to realize that the issues being raised by CRC are real and that all of us are hearing things faster and more directly than we would through the usual channels. He is beginning to see that the full potential for CRC is not being realized because it is outside the system.

I've always believed in the validity of the premise on which CRC was founded, and the whole organization and the board saw that I wanted it to stay. Otherwise, it might have been eliminated. I still think the organization can absorb it. As we move forward, I think CRC will be helpful to Mead, no matter what form it ultimately takes. It could turn out to be a superb thing. The final decision is still out.

Batts, who had to formulate a response to Richards' paper for the next CRC meeting, had a number of questions about the committee and the proposal:

> On the ombudsman question—it's true that there's always been a massive communications gap in companies from the division level down to the foreman level. Where we don't get good marks is with the nonexempt salaried people, the first- and second-level supervisors, and professional staff. But despite our problems, we've found from attitude surveys that Mead always scores higher than average as a good place to work. We have very little turnover at these levels. So we have to be careful about overreacting.
>
> The fact that the CRC has become more and more of a concern to more and more of the operating people is what really bothers me. This is something that has to be wired into the organization; it has to be made into a positive force for the company instead of being a peripheral activity. One of my real questions is: will CRC be a directors' committee, like all other committees of the board, or will it be an employees' grievance committee?

The chairman thought there were two basic questions about the Corporate Responsibility Committee:

> First, how secure must an organization be in order to incorporate such a vehicle into its normal operations? Second, what other alternatives do we have to the "filtering out process" of the pyramid organization?

APPENDIX: EXCERPTS FROM
RICHARDS' BACKGROUND REPORT

WHY THE NEED AT MEAD FOR
AN OMBUDS-TYPE FUNCTION

Without exception, there is a feeling of frustration in all sectors of white collar work force that they are squeezed between the unions and top management. They contend that there is no effective way to bring their complaints, concerns, or frustrations to the decision makers without the fear of possible disciplinary action. Some of the concerns I have heard are as follows:

1. There is no effective mechanism to protect an individual from unjustly being fired.
2. The company takes arbitrary decisions on work hours, retirement, and other fringe benefits without explaining why they made the change, how they arrived at the decision, etc.
3. Bitterness is arising over the differentials in wage/salary policy between union and unrepresented employees. I have had managers with titles such as director, comptroller, and general manager com-

Source: The Mead Corporation.

plain that the differentials, as they have existed over the past few years, have created an almost untenable labor environment. They ask, "Does Mead really believe they are treating our employees fairly? How much longer do they expect the nonrepresented employees to accept merit salary increases substantially below union settlements? We're headed for unionization faster than we think."

In the eyes of many nonrepresented white-collar employees, such problems are being managed through a philosophy of benign neglect. The frustrations being voiced are not from radicals, drug users or troublemakers. They are from some of the outstanding, conservative and loyal members of this company. Without a mechanism whereby ideas, complaints, and suggestions are freely discussed, many white-collar workers will be functioning in an atmosphere of anxiety, apprehension, and fear.

POSSIBLE OPTIONS

While it is not the role of the Corporate Responsibility Committee to develop solutions, I have taken the liberty to scope out some possible options which could be investigated by the directors.

1. Personnel Council—This is a monthly forum where representatives of management and employees sit down to discuss mutual problems and opportunities. This is done on the sectional, departmental, and divisional level, with the main council serving as the top tribunal.
    It is a two-way communication. Employees voice their complaints and suggestions to their elected council representatives who bring them to management's attention at the regular meetings. Management, at the same time, communicates its policies and ideas to employees. Some discussions bear on companywide matters of significance. Others cover irritations that, if allowed to fester, could cause unpleasant consequences.

2. Corporate Ombudsman—This function could entail an individual or a number of individuals who serve as an intermediary between employees and the various departments that frequently make up the corporate staff such as the Benefits Department, Salary Administration, etc.

3. Grievance Committee—It has been suggested that a formal grievance committee be set up. Its function would be a cross between a judge/jury system and an arbitrator. There are several concerns I have with this move. First, this step could lead to very legalistic approaches by some employees and could weaken management's ability to manage properly. Second, it could be too radical a step in solving potential problems that basically arise out of misunderstandings on both sides and therefore might be as productive as desired.

4. The Inspector General—The role of the inspector general within the military is well known by most of us and the use of this concept could have some decided merits. This office could function similar to the way our internal audit department works. It would work with the various divisions, departments and managers to see that the corporate policies, benefits and other services are properly explained and carried out. It would also function somewhat as an intermediary between the employees and the many aspects of the corporation which would affect the employee. This type of function should not impinge upon the managerial prerogatives of management, yet it should help to bring about positive results.

SUMMARY

If the Mead Corp. were to establish a form of ombuds-type function, I believe the following benefits could arise:

1. It would serve as an early warning system (a DEW line) for top management, alerting them of potentially serious problems which might arise.
2. It could alert corporate officials to those areas or individuals whose human skills need improving.
3. Serve as a safety valve on issues that might otherwise create explosive situations.
4. It should help sharpen management to think out decisions affecting people without hindering their ability to manage. The old adage, "It's not what you say but how you say it," applies here.
5. This system should be a preferable alternative to unionization without being viewed as an antiunion movement.

Commentaries ═══════════════════════════════

11. When Businessmen Confess
Their Social Sins

On September 4, Pierre Arnold, managing director of Migros-Genossenschafts-Bund, the giant Swiss food manufacturing and re-tailing cooperative, announced publicly that his company paid women less than men, that many of its jobs were "extremely boring," and that its emissions of noxious nitrous dioxide had risen over a four-year period by 2 percent. Arnold made the admissions, not in response to angry demonstrators or inquiring legislators, but voluntarily in the form of a neatly printed 89-page report. Says Arnold, "It takes courage for an enterprise to point out the difference between its goals and its actual results."

The Migros report is the latest in a series of reports, often called "social balance sheets," that a growing number of European companies—including the German subsidiaries of such multinationals as Rank Xerox, British Petroleum, and Royal Dutch/Shell Group—are presenting to the public. In the United States, where there has been talk of developing similar reports since the early 1970s, corporate executives, government officials, academicians, and accountants are monitoring the European experiments with a mixture of growing interest and concern.

Germany's reports are voluntary and emphasize environment. France passed a law last year that will require large firms to report in 1979 on 1978's employee-company relations. Pressure is building in Britain for mandatory reports. And the United Nations has been pushing for more social accounting data—particularly from multinational corporations (BW—June 26).

The new European reports list both positive and negative effects that companies have on society. Their goal: to defuse potentially

Source: Reprinted from the November 6, 1978 issue of *Business Week* by special permission, © 1978 by McGraw-Hill, Inc., New York, N.Y. 10020. All rights reserved.

damaging criticism and legislation. While some of the reports are little more than colorful public relations brochures, many are becoming increasingly thorough, even venturing into controversial areas.

"A MILESTONE"

The Migros report is the boldest so far. It touches almost all aspects of the co-op's far-flung business operations. It notes prices ("32 percent below" the average of its competitors) as well as labeling practices ("ahead of Swiss legislative requirements"). It discusses work environment and cultural activities. And where sufficient data are not at hand, such as the extent to which Migros is crowding out smaller competitors, the report points the way toward further research. Claims Meinolf Dierkes, director of the government funded Institute for Environment and Society in West Berlin and Migros consultant on the report: "The Migros report is a milestone in social accounting."

Dierkes, 37, is probably Europe's leading theorist and promoter of social accounting. His work as a consultant to such companies as Deutsche Shell is one major reason the social reports in West Germany and Switzerland are widely regarded, along with some in Sweden, as the world's most far-reaching to date.

With the rise of social protest and consumer groups, Dierkes argues that the time when business could "hide behind the walls of political and legislative process" is passing. By forthrightly explaining the impact that companies have on society, by setting public goals, and by gradually moving toward them, he contends, companies can deal directly with their critics and head off simplistic and often harmful legislation. The reports can help companies "redefine the debate in their own terms," he adds.

It was the direct confrontations between companies and protest groups during the early 1970s that have provided the impetus to European social accounting. Recalls Wolf-Rüdiger Ott, who is in charge of social reports for BASF, the German chemical giant: "It was not until Heidi Wieczorek-Zeul [then head of the militant Young Socialists] visited us in 1974 that we started looking at what we were doing."

REPORTS ON BENEFITS

Since then BASF has issued reports listing the sizable retirement, health, and other nonwage benefits that the company provides in an effort to limit union wage and benefit demands. In addition to BASF, some 20 other West German companies publish what they term *Sozialbilanzen*, and Ott claims to know "at least 40" other German

Share of Employees and Stockholders in Net Value Created (sales less depreciation)

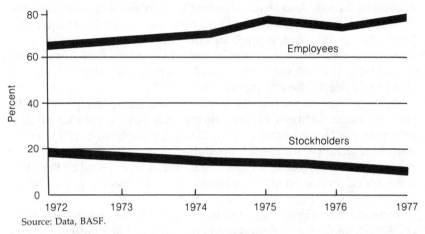

Source: Data, BASF.

companies that have social reports in the works. Dierkes puts the number that are considering such a move at "100 to 150."

Such estimates may be overly enthusiastic. One corporate planner, whose company has quietly rejected the idea of issuing a social report, contends sourly that the whole movement "is the work of professors who have found access to certain companies under attack." In fact, professional accountants have had little to do with the movement, and most of the social reports have emerged from oil and chemical multinationals such as British Petroleum, Shell Oil, Bayer, and BASF, all of which are prime targets for the left.

Other companies that have considered the idea now appear to be growing more hesitant—especially since public sentiment is tilting less against business—because social reports can stir up further public attack. The immediate effect of the Migros report, for example, has been to intensify public comment by critics who dismiss the report as "an alibi." And a scathing attack on the BASF report by leftist BASF worker representatives, although often wildly off the mark, has "clearly" intimidated many companies, according to Hans Wenkebach at Germany's Foundation for Business and Society, a corporate sponsored think tank.

CRITICIZING THE TONE

A more basic objection to the social reports is that even the most serious often shy away from convincing objectivity. The Deutsche Shell report, for example, does not include a section on pollution—

certainly a sensitive issue for a petroleum company. The BASF report excludes the effect of depreciation in its calculation of how total revenues are shared. And that, according to Manfred Reimann, director of the German Chemical Workers' office in BASF'S headquarters town of Ludwigshafen, exaggerates the share going to workers. Critics such as Reimann also object to the "do-gooder" tone of many of the reports. "I don't think they should picture what they have done as a heroic deed," he complains. "It's silly."

Advocates of social reports, however, are surprisingly willing to concede faults in most of the reports that have come out so far. Johannes Welbergen, chairman of Deutsche Shell, says of his company's reluctance to identify pollution sites: "If we deliberately played down a danger that would be harmful, that would be bad. But if the speed limit is 50 miles an hour, I do not think it a good idea to run to the judge every time you do 55."

Instead, Welbergen indicates that Shell will be able to grow increasingly frank over a period of years as the public gradually learns that "a plant is not an ideal piece of equipment." The gradual approach, he says, is also necessary "to gain the support of our own people."

Along with other advocates of social reports, Welbergen contends that the success or failure can only be judged over the long term. "The social balance sheet is only a document," he concludes. But he hopes that it will evolve in thoroughness and believability so that "10 to 20 years hence" it can help counteract pressures that might lead to restrictive legislation.

SOCIAL AUDITING IN THE UNITED STATES GETS A SLOW START

The notion of some kind of "social accounting" or "social audit" for United States companies has been widely discussed since the early 1970s. As a first step, hundreds of large corporations began to devote two or more pages in their annual reports to rather elaborate presentations of what many termed "corporate social responsibility." That initial fad has passed; today most companies simply pay lip service to the idea in several sweeping paragraphs.

A few corporations, however, have expanded their efforts. Norton Co. publishes a special annual report called *Accountability* that chronicles the company's efforts in minority employment, ethics, and energy conservation, in addition to its community activities. And again this year, General Motors Corp. has issued a 60-page *Public Interest Report* in which issues such as safety, customer satisfaction, environment, and South African investments are discussed. Companies such as Atlantic Richfield Co. and Equitable Life Assurance Society also have made strides in the social reporting area. In addition, many of them issue internal reports for use as management tools.

The most ambitious undertaking comes from Bank of America, the chief operating unit of BankAmerica Corp. Two separate committees—one of bank directors and another of bank executives—have developed special public and social policy goals, including regular public reports on the bank's progress.

To date, most U.S. corporate efforts have been largely descriptive. But there have been some moves to put at least tentative numbers on social costs and benefits. After a four-year study, the American Institute of Certified Public Accountants has published some preliminary suggestions on quantification. And Abt Associates Inc., a Massachusetts-based consulting firm, went so far as to make an actual social audit of its operations, complete with an innovative social balance sheet and income statement (BW—Sept. 23, 1972). But when that company's net income fell more than 50 percent last year, its annual social audit was dropped—at a savings of $10,000.

The government, too, has expressed interest in some kind of social accounting. Last year in a speech at Duke University, Commerce Secretary Juanita M. Kreps said that her department intended "to develop and publish a Social Performance Index that will give business a way of appraising the social effects of its business operations." That pronouncement immediately created a storm of protest.

As Kreps acknowledged this year in testimony before a subcommittee of the House Appropriations Committee: "The word 'index' seems to have triggered some psychic alarm system, for it seems to connote a report card of sins and virtues." She asserted that her department "is not intent on ranking or grading companies or creating a new bureaucracy." Rather, Kreps concluded, "it seeks to advance the development of procedures that would enable a corporation to judge its own social performance." And, she added, the use of such a self-measurement system "would be entirely voluntary."

A special Commerce Dept. task force on corporate social performance is hard at work on a report covering what it calls "the state of the art" both in the United States and abroad. It hopes to complete the study by yearend.

"There is no intention of suggesting anything mandatory," says James E. Heard, executive director of the task force. "We simply hope that Commerce can play a role as a catalyst in encouraging corpo-rations to continue developing social accounting reports on their own." Given the varying natures and needs of different companies, he adds, "stan-dardization of such measure-ment and reporting may not be a good idea."

Assessing foreign experi-ments in the field, Heard says: "The state of the art is more advanced in Germany than in the United States, and we have a good deal to learn from them. However, we might not want to do things quite the same way."

12. Fuss at Cal Life Shows Audit Committee Role Is Crucial, Experts Say
Hal Lancaster

LOS ANGELES—On April 12 of last year, members of the audit committee of California Life Corp.'s board learned that the company hadn't filed with the Securities and Exchange Commission its 1978 annual financial report, due 12 days earlier.

The life-insurance holding company was then embroiled with its independent auditors in a bitter accounting dispute—a kind of fight that companies rarely win. Eventually, after the SEC denied a request for extension of the filing deadline, the annual report was filed—in August. By then, the company's directors had ousted its top officers and begun an internal investigation that wouldn't be completed until November.

Moreover, the company eventually reported a disheartening $3.2 million loss for 1978, after publicly predicting shortly before year-end a healthy gain in earnings to $2.6 million from $2.1 million in 1977.

Source: *The Wall Street Journal*, Monday, March 17, 1980 (pp. 1, 29).

The losses continued through 1979, and the SEC, which declines to comment on the case, is said to be still considering action against the company.

TOO LOW A PROFILE?

Where was the audit committee during all this conflict? Apparently, it was largely missing in action. In 1978 and the critical early months of 1979, when the dispute arose, the committee held only two rather perfunctory meetings; at least one other was canceled. It made several recommendations but didn't push aggressively for their adoption. Communication with the auditors was practically nil.

Certainly, the committee had some mitigating problems: a new, inexperienced committee chairman, a chief executive who was hard to deal with, and complex, unanticipated accounting issues. Some people close to the situation contend that the company's problems couldn't have been avoided. They particularly cite the helplessness of any audit committee faced with headstrong management.

However, if Cal Life's audit committee had conformed more closely to the tougher standards that have evolved in recent years for such panels, perhaps the company's difficulties might have surfaced earlier and been handled less disruptively. And in the months after the blowup, Cal Life's audit committee has, in fact, changed significantly. Its membership has been beefed up to five outside directors from three. It has met six times since the May 12 ouster of the prior management and has frequently convened privately with the outside auditors. It has strengthened its role in overseeing internal controls. And it has asked for and receives the same weekly status report on the audit that management gets.

WIDESPREAD TREND

Moreover, a similar change has taken place at many other companies that haven't suffered through the kind of ailments that have afflicted Cal Life. Nowadays, audit committees have teeth. They have benefited from a number of actions that in recent years have broadened their purview beyond the recommendation of auditors and the review of the audit itself.

The SEC, for instance, has frequently entrusted audit committees with investigating and monitoring questionable corporate activities in lieu of a formal inquiry by the commission. And the Foreign Corrupt Practices Act of 1977 forced companies to stiffen internal controls; much of the extra responsibility fell to audit committees.

In addition, in 1977 the New York Stock Exchange required audit committees as a condition for listing. Although the exchange didn't spell out the panels' duties, its 1973 white paper recommended, among other things, that audit committees assess their companies' accounting principles to determine whether they are "unduly conservative or liberal." The American Stock Exchange also has recommended audit committees for its listed companies, a move that many see as a prelude to requiring them.

MORE COMMITTEES

Companies generally have responded. In 1967, for instance, only 19 percent of manufacturing and 31 percent of nonmanufacturing concerns had such committees, according to a survey by the Conference Board. But by 1978, the business-research group found that 97 percent of all companies had them. And the committees were meeting more frequently—about four times a year, compared with only twice as recently as 1972.

Most experts concede, however, that the audit committee's role is still filled with gray areas and is still evolving. How far can or should it go in scrutinizing corporate activities? And is it—as one chief executive warned Conference Board interviewers—gaining too much power?

Such doubts help explain the seemingly passive stance of Cal Life's audit committee. "Who has the supreme wisdom to say he's smarter than the guys who are in there every day?" an audit committee member asks. "Who would have the omnipotence to tell the managers they're incompetent?"

That would have been especially difficult because Cal Life then seemed healthy, with annual profit gains buoying directors' confidence in Harry H. Mitchell, the chairman and chief executive. Mr. Mitchell had rescued the company from an uncertain past and seemed to be leading it into a shining future of growth by acquisition. Besides, the company's chief financial officer, William A. Seymore, was a former member of an accounting team from Deloitte, Haskins & Sells that had audited Cal Life. That background also apparently reassured audit-committee members.

Cal Life's problems were analyzed in a report dated November 7, 1979, and prepared at the request of the audit committee by LaBoeuf, Lamb, Leiby and MacRae, a New York law firm serving as special counsel. According to the report, the company's problems surfaced early in 1979. In an apparent effort to meet its $2.6 million profit projection for 1978, the company's officers labored through 16 trial balances, the report says, while Mr. Mitchell exhorted them to be "creative." Replies Mr. Mitchell now: "Sure, we worked hard to come up with an acceptable profit, but it was all within generally accepted accounting principles."

Finally, a profit figure of nearly $2.6 million was achieved and presented to the auditors on March 23, only eight days before the filing date for the financial statements and more than a month later than the audit schedule had contemplated. Audit committee members didn't know about this delay, however; according to Lowell Clucas, then a member and now chairman of the audit committee, they never received the schedule.

Disagreements developed, principally over the company's attempt to defer what the auditors considered an unusually large amount of so-called indirect costs—including computer time and executive salaries—related to the acquisition of new policies. The auditors were said to lack confidence that the deferred costs could be recovered from future profits. One problem: An alarmingly high percentage of certain life insurance policies were lapsing because premiums weren't being paid.

The audit team said it wouldn't allow much of the deferral. But the company balked; it contended that the auditors were changing the rules after the game was over. And Mr. Mitchell still argues that the high lapse rate was expected and that the policies as a whole were profitable.

The outside directors, disturbed by what one termed a "rambling" document prepared by Mr. Mitchell in defense of his accounting practices, sided with the auditors. They ousted Mr. Mitchell May 12 after a series of secret meetings. Shortly thereafter, most of Mr. Mitchell's management team left, voluntarily and otherwise.

STILL IN THE FRAY

Mr. Mitchell still contends that nothing is fundamentally wrong with the company. He has filed with the SEC a spirited rebuttal to charges made in the special counsel's report to the audit committee. He also has formed a "stockholders' protective committee" that claims to control 27 percent of the common stock; in recently filed proxy material, he says he will seek to regain control of the company through a proxy contest for six of the nine board seats. And he has sued the company in a state court for allegedly breaching his employment contract; the company has countersued and charged him with negligence and breach of fiduciary duty. Several suits also have been filed against the company by stockholders.

Until the April 12 meeting, the debate between the company and the auditors raged on without the knowledge or participation of the audit committee, even though Dean Jones, head of the Deloitte, Haskins and Sells team, "discussed with company officers the need to involve the audit committee in the resolution of the year-end audit" as early as March 24, the special report says. He apparently didn't press the issue until April 11, however.

And even after April 12, the committee remained mostly an observer. At an April 19 board meeting, Mr. Clucas suggested that the group might help resolve the dispute. But Mr. Mitchell vetoed the idea, Mr. Clucas recalls, on the ground that it would show a lack of faith in management.

As late as April 24, the board gave Mr. Mitchell a unanimous vote of confidence. "We were told it was a technical disagreement and could be resolved," recalls Joseph P. Monge, an outside director who subsequently replaced Mr. Mitchell. "We should have gotten a hint, but we didn't. We were lulled into a false sense of security."

So secure did the audit committee feel that it met only twice in 1978: once, in February, to review 1977 financial results, and again, in December, to lay out its operational plan for 1979.

At neither meeting did the committee follow its previous practice of meeting privately with the auditors. At the February meeting, committee members complained that in the prior year the auditors' traditional letter to management on the 1976 audit and the management response didn't get to them until May; this time, they wanted it sooner.

But the complaints weren't followed up. Indeed, the committee was never formally presented during 1978 with the letter on the 1977 audit. That letter was important; it included some much disputed language that the auditors insist should have warned the company about the deferred-costs issue. Mr. Mitchell contends that the letter can't be interpreted in that way.

Also in February, the committee discussed the need for it to monitor internal controls more closely because of the Foreign Corrupt Practices Act. However, it didn't make any recommendations to management.

During this time, management is said to have tried to reassure the committee. In addition, committee members say the independent auditors didn't indicate in conversations that a storm was brewing.

Meanwhile, the newly appointed chairman of the committee, James McMillan, was apparently trying to learn, through reading and seminars, what the committee was supposed to do. Mr. McMillan, president of McDonnell Douglas Finance Corp., hadn't served on such a committee before. Unsure of himself, observers say, he leaned even harder on Mr. Seymore's judgment, which he considered reliable. Since Mr. McMillan resigned from the board last July, he has refused to discuss publicly the events at Cal Life.

In view of Mr. McMillan's inexperience and the apparent disarray of the audit committee, should Deloitte, Haskins and Sells have taken the initiative and brought the problem to the panel, with or without management's knowledge? Such a situation would be "extremely rare," says Haldon G. Robinson, the firm's partner in charge of accounting and auditing services. "I can think of no case where we bypassed management."

UNEASY AUDITORS

Auditors frequently feel that such an action would be a breach of their agreement with management, says Timothy Kennedy, a lawyer who represents Cal Life. But observers note a growing belief that an auditing firm's contract—and primary responsibility—is with the board and shareholders.

"If we couldn't get agreement with management," a partner in a Big Eight accounting firm says, "we'd go right to the board. If we still couldn't, we'd resign. That's an obligation."

Nevertheless, accounting experts contend, the audit committee itself has an obligation to follow audit issues and to seek out the auditor. A Deloitte, Haskins and Sells guidebook even encourages the committees to review "significant audit matters" during an audit.

Directors, however, frequently fear that such assertiveness would upset the genial relationship with management that they find comfortable and necessary to keep the corporate gears well oiled.

"There's a limited amount of time and a lot of ground to cover," Mr. Kennedy contends. "The whole atmosphere and protocol of a board meeting make it difficult to play the role of critic as the SEC envisions." Besides, Mr. Monge says, there is an element of trust among directors, even those on the audit committee. "If management tells you something, you believe it," he says. "Otherwise, you wouldn't be on the board."

Without a full-time staff for audit-committee members, Mr. Monge believes, "it's impossible for an outside director to get into the bowels of the company." Says another Cal Life director: "If we had talked to the auditors two months before, it wouldn't have made any difference. The die was cast; these were all decisions that were made in 1978." In his view, only quarterly audits—prohibitively expensive for a medium-sized company such as Cal Life—would have prevented the problems.

What this shows, Mr. Kennedy concludes is "how easy it is for a conscientious group of outside directors to be soft-soaped by senior management."

Corporate watchdogs insist, however, that diligent members of an audit committee can do the job. "If they're aggressive and take their responsibilities seriously, they can be effective," says D. R. Carmichael, vice president of auditing for the American Institute of Certified Public Accountants. "They don't need to know what's going on in the bowels of the company."

Maybe so, but at least one wary member of the Cal Life audit committee isn't so sure he wants to attempt such a task. "Anyone who assumes an outside directorship these days is taking a substantial risk," he says. "Why you should do it, I don't know."

HUMAN INVESTMENT

It is often said that the most difficult challenges facing managers are "people problems." The importance of employees to organizations is readily apparent. After all, companies are composed of people: people with ambitions, fears, frustrations, grievances, illnesses, economic needs, and so forth. From top to bottom in those companies there is a need to invest in people. The effective manager is always preparing his or her successor. Managers must always seek to allow people to grow and to reach their highest possible level of potential.

Given its critical importance to society as an employer of millions, it is not surprising that business has been under particular pressure to invest well in humans: to make them productive, motivated people who work in a safe environment that is free of racial, sexual, and other forms of improper discrimination. Hence, the treatment of employees is not an "internal" issue. Human investment is as much a social/political issue as ecology or consumerism. As such, management must recognize that corporate social performance is highly influenced by human investment considerations.

The Civil Rights Act of 1964, the Occupational Safety and Health Act of 1970, the Employee Retirement Income Security Act of 1974, and hundreds of other pieces of federal, state, and local legislation have had a profound effect on the employer-employee relationship. The struggle for a better balance between management prerogatives and worker safety and general welfare has been a long one.

The cases in this section provide a sharp contrast in management's attitudes toward workers. Farah Manufacturing Company is a secondary case, prepared from the considerable public record of events related to a prolonged contest between a company which saw itself as a generous, fair, modern, and ethical enterprise and a variety of stakeholders who saw Farah as an oppressive exploiter of its employees. The E. S. Scarbonie Corporation is a primary case, although the identity of the company has been disguised at the request of management. The Scarbonie Company has a detailed system designed to assure employees of fair treatment. The company, nevertheless, encounters difficulties. Employee participation, job safety inspection, and sexual harassment are explored in the commentaries in this section.

Case

FARAH MANUFACTURING COMPANY*

Kenneth Farah walked briskly out to greet the plane taxiing toward the Farah hangar at the El Paso International Airport. Each of the two company jets had been used for some time to shuttle apparel buyers into El Paso for firsthand inspections of Farah's operations and facilities. This series of flights in May 1973 were believed to be the widest use yet made of company aircraft for "customer calls," as opposed to calls by salesmen to the retailers' place of business.

After brief introductions, Mr. Farah led the businessmen through the hangar toward waiting company automobiles. On the way, Mr. Farah stopped to point out the restoration of a silver twin-engine aircraft on one side of the hangar. The plane was an A–20 "Havoc," an American attack bomber which had seen extensive action in the early years of World War II. This particular aircraft had been flown during the war by William F. Farah, Kenneth's father and the president of the Farah Manufacturing Company.

The A–20 was the second such restoration project. The first was a silver B–26, completed in the late 1950s at the cost of several thousand mandays effort. His father had spent many enjoyable hours flying that plane on weekends in the 1960s, when the company was setting annual growth and earnings records. Kenneth now wondered privately if his father would ever be able to fly the A–20.

For the last year, William F. Farah had been the central figure in one of the most controversial and significant labor-media events in

---

* This case is not intended to provide a precise account of the thinking or behavior of the parties involved.

159

the history of the country. The Farah strike, which began May 3, 1972, had not been exceptionally long or violent. A nationwide boycott, which began June 19, 1972, however, was the first time a labor organization had used that tactic to organize a work force. Kenneth's father defiantly resisted unionization.

The publicity surrounding the conflict was destroying the company that William Farah had built. The customer flights were a desperate measure to present Farah's side of the story to its customers.

WILLIAM F. FARAH

William F. ("Willie") Farah was a modern American success story. His father, Mansour Farah, was a Lebanese immigrant who ran a small dry goods company in El Paso and began a small garment manufacturing plant in 1920. When he died in 1937, Willie Farah left college at the age of 18 to help his mother and brother, James, run the company. The company's growth was accelerated by military clothing production during World War II, and in 1947 the company was incorporated.

The corporation went public in 1967, but the Farah family retained control of about 41 percent of the 5.9 million shares of outstanding stock as of 1969. Mr. Farah personally owned about 10 percent of the shares, and controlled another 18 percent as the executor of his brother's estate.[1] James had died at the plant in 1964. As president and chief executive officer of the company, Willie Farah gained a reputation as a tough and stubborn executive. The business in which Farah was engaged made these requisite qualities.

THE APPAREL INDUSTRY

Farah was one of the nation's major producers of men's and boy's casual slacks, shorts, and jackets. Although most manufacturers were, like Farah, specialized in one or two product lines, the clothing industry as a whole was highly competitive because of the ease with which new firms could enter. The 22,000 clothing firms already existing in the industry scrambled after low-profit margins and had a higher rate of business failures than most industries. Because of the high degree of competition, pricing within the industry was very competitive, and the penalty for incorrectly anticipating consumer demand for given styles was severe. By 1970, Farah had established a

---

[1] Deborah DeWitt Malley, "How the Union Beat Willie Farah," *Fortune,* vol. 90, no. 2 (August 1974), p. 165.

prominent place among the many thousands of manufacturers in the industry. The company earned over $8 million that year on about $136 million in sales, and the stock split two-for-one (see Exhibit 1).

The Farah plants of 1970 were not typical trouser manufacturing plants. The industry was highly labor intensive, and limited economies of scale could be achieved with larger sized plants. As a consequence, there were thousands of relatively small, 100 to 200 employee plants, located primarily in the southern United States. The largest volume manufacturer, Levi Strauss & Co., had about 50 such plants located in small towns from Knoxville, Tennessee, to El Paso, Texas, and had contracts with an additional 50 independent producers in the same general area.

Each of these small plants used essentially the same manufacturing procedure. Large cylindrical bales of cloth were received by truck or rail from mills generally located in North Carolina. Higher quality producers checked the "shading" or slight variations in color for the bales, which usually were 48 inches long and often four feet in diameter, weighing 500 to 600 pounds.

Bales which passed the shading test were sent to the "cutting room" to be "spread." Spreading consisted of mounting the bales on a movable carriage which traveled on rails for the length of a "cutting table." The cutting table was often 100 feet long, with longer tables being more efficient. The job of the spreaders was to spread the fabric down smoothly on the table until about 160-ply (or about five to six inches) of fabric had been spread on the table. Spreaders usually walked eight to ten miles a shift.

"Markers" then laid a paper pattern over the fabric. They were judged on how economically they could utilize fabric, in order to minimize "fallout," or waste. Ninety-eight percent usage was a good standard.

"Cutters" then used vibrating electric knives to cut through 160-ply of fabric to make parts for 80 pair of one size pants. Cutting was hard work, and experienced cutters developed extremely strong wrists and biceps.

After the "parts" were cut, they were tied together and the entire "bundle" of parts was placed on a "bundle cart." The bundle cart was then moved to the first "sewing station." A pair of pants required about 50 sewing operations, each accomplished at a separate station. Each station consisted of a seated operator, typically female, and a type of specialized sewing machine. The operator was usually surrounded by partially completed bundles and allowed about six square feet of personal floorspace.

"Bundle boys" moved carts from one operation to the next. At the

EXHIBIT 1   Farah Manufacturing Company Ten-Year Financial Highlights ($000 except per share data)*

	1974	1973	1972	1971	1970	1969	1968	1967	1966	1965
Operating Results										
Net sales	$ 126,447	$ 132,125	$ 155,606	$ 164,570	$ 136,293	$118,250	$92,137	$73,913	$61,346	$48,100
Cost of sales and expenses	129,853	131,821	169,324	151,514	119,031	104,424	79,073	66,142	54,384	43,266
Operating income (loss)	(3,406)	304	(13,718)	13,056	17,262	13,826	13,064	7,770	6,962	4,834
Other income, net	1,016	839	37	313	132	95	107	217	140	50
Interest expense	1,557	1,706	2,462	1,790	1,037	983	476	544	452	228
Earnings (loss) before income taxes and extraordinary credit	(3,947)	(563)	(16,143)	11,579	16,357	12,938	12,695	7,443	6,649	4,655
Income taxes (credits)	(1,907)	(606)	(7,619)	5,550	8,065	6,626	6,428	3,474	3,078	2,176
Earnings (loss) before extraordinary credit	(2,040)	43	(8,524)	6,029	8,291	6,312	6,267	3,969	3,078	2,479
Extraordinary credit	—	—	248	—	—	—	—	—	—	—
Net earnings (loss)	(2,040)	43	(8,276)	6,029	8,291	6,312	6,267	3,969	3,571	2,479
Financial Position										
Current assets	$ 75,079	63,775	73,221	83,325	53,718	$ 47,922	35,297	27,592	19,688	15,019
Property, plant and equipment, net	28,482	27,082	27,549	26,682	21,328	16,702	14,688	11,087	8,439	7,209
Other assets	1,551	497	467	629	1,201	—	—	—	—	—
Total assets	105,112	91,354	101,237	110,636	76,247					
Current liabilities	25,179	9,385	20,075	26,574	16,527	13,736	13,764	6,506	5,763	5,335
Long-term debt	22,954	24,073	23,984	16,892	16,913	16,250	6,650	7,550	7,150	5,250
Other liabilities	3,571	2,448	1,773	1,522	1,227	—	—	—	—	—
Stockholders' equity	53,408	55,448	55,405	65,648	41,508	34,927	29,789	24,391	15,090	11,675
Total liabilities and stockholders' equity	105,112	91,354	101,237	110,636	76,247					
Current ratio	3.0 to 1	6.8 to 1	3.6 to 1	3.1 to 1	3.3 to 1	3.5 to 1	2.6 to 1	4.2 to 1	3.4 to 1	2.8 to 1
Per Share Information†										
Weighted average shares outstanding	5,983,277	5,983,277	5,983,277	5,653,866	5,444,964					
Earnings (loss) per share before extraordinary credit	$ (0.34)	$ 0.01	$ (1.42)	$ 1.07	$ 1.52	$1.16	$1.15	$0.76	$0.76	$0.52
Net earnings (loss) per share	(0.34)	0.01	(1.38)	1.07	1.52	1.16	1.15	0.76	0.76	0.76
Book value per share based on shares outstanding at balance sheet dates	8.93	9.27	9.26	10.97	7.64					
Cash dividends per common share‡	—	—	0.34	0.44	0.40	0.38	0.37	0.29	0.03	0.03

* Years 1970–74 taken from 1974 Annual Report; years 1965–69 taken from 1972 Annual Report.
† Includes the effect of a two-for-one stock split in the form of a 100 percent stock dividend distributed in January 1971 and 5 percent stock dividend distributed in January 1970.
‡ Includes the effect of a two-for-one stock split in the form of a 100 percent stock dividend distributed in January 1971.

end of the 50-operation line, a complete "bundle" of 80 trousers of one size had been produced out of parts which were on the same ply before they were cut.

In order to ensure high productivity, operators were paid on a modified piece rate system. It was not unusual to pay a base minimum wage, with a performance standard that allowed the operator to earn about double the base rate for reaching "standard." An elaborate operator accounting system was developed to record production against standard. To reach standard, many skilled operators performed their tasks literally faster than the eye could follow. Some plants placed spreaders and cutters on incentive, as well.

Industry working conditions were generally not pleasant. Factories were housed in old, low-rent structures. Scrap cloth and lint from operations was ever-present. Operators often "spiked" their fingers with sewing needles, but when manufacturers provided needle-guards they generally found that employees disposed of them because they felt that the guards slowed down production.

The eight Farah plants did not fit this mold.[2] The Farah plants were new and extremely modern. The company noted that "they provide a clean, airy, healthy environment that has a beneficial effect upon the happiness and productivity of all of our people."[3] Leonard Levy, vice president of the Amalgamated Clothing Workers of America concurred that "a cockroach needs a special invitation to get into the place."[4]

Within the industry, Mr. Farah was recognized as a production genius. In 1970, the company reported that "further advances in technology of production were accomplished with the successful, innovative design of new machinery, utilizing advanced electronics and unique mechanisms developed by our own engineers."[5] These advances, however, were not patented because Mr. Farah feared the ideas would be stolen by competitors.[6]

Plant security was extremely strong, but some insiders reported seeing elevated sewing stations that relieved the operator of her typically claustrophobic situation, an overhead system of bundle delivery that eliminated the typical floor congestion of bundle carts, and small packages and bundles being delivered from one end of the plant to another by bundle boys on bicycles. Mr. Farah stated with obvious

[2] Four Farah plants were located in El Paso, including the Gateway plant, which was by far the largest. Two small plants were located in San Antonio, one in Victoria, Texas, and one in Las Cruces, New Mexico.

[3] Farah Manufacturing Company, 1969 Annual Report.

[4] *The New York Times*, September 11, 1972, p. 58.

[5] Farah Manufacturing Company, 1970 Annual Report.

[6] *Fortune*, August 1974, p. 166.

pride that "our people—both production and supervision—are producers without peer. . . . They realize our success as manufacturers and merchandisers is the sole factor that provides them with employment security and opportunities for advancement."[7]

By industry standards, the fringe benefits that Mr. Farah provided his employees were unparalleled. Employees and their families were given free medical, hospital, and dental care, including an annual physical exam and free eyeglasses, if needed. Free bus transportation to and from the plants was provided, as were free coffee and doughnuts during morning and afternoon breaks. Hot lunches on the premises were subsidized. Profit sharing and pension plans were in effect.

Wages were generally on a par with the rest of the industry, but the questions of wages merits the additional perspective gained through the analysis of the unique location of Farah manufacturing facilities.

THE CITY OF EL PASO

The vast majority of Farah employees worked in El Paso, a city almost ideally situated for the manufacturing requirements of men's garments. Located in the westernmost corner of Texas, El Paso was directly across the Rio Grande River from Juarez, Mexico. The combined metropolitan population of the two cities was over 1 million people, with about 360,000 on the El Paso side. About 58 percent of the El Paso population was of Mexican descent,[8] and an estimated 80 percent of the residents were bilingual.

El Paso was not highly industrialized, with primary employment being in government and service industries. The largest component of the city's nonservice economic base was the garment industry, with the four Farah plants, four Levi Strauss plants, a large Billy-the-Kid plant, and 32 smaller firms located in the city. In 1970, Farah was the largest single industrial employer, hiring about 14 percent of the local work force.[9] About 95 percent of Farah's work force was of Mexican ancestry.[10]

The median family income for El Paso in 1970 was $7,792 compared to a national median of $10,474.[11] The cost of living in El Paso, how-

---

[7] Farah Manufacturing Company, 1969 Annual Report.

[8] Jean Caffey Lyles, "The Fight at Farah," The Christian Century, vol. 90, no. 8 (September 26, 1973), p. 935.

[9] The New York Times, September 11, 1972, p. 57.

[10] Rex Hardesty, "Farah: The Union Struggle in the 1970's," American Federationist, vol. 80, no. 6 (June 1973), p. 10.

[11] Ibid.

ever, was extremely low. The low living costs were attributed to the extremely mild weather, the ease of shopping for low-cost goods and services on both sides of the border, and the low wage rates in Mexico. At a time when the U.S. minimum wage was $1.60 per hour, the minimum wage in Mexico was $2.40 per *day*.[12] In 1970, El Paso was the last American city where a family earning $10,000 per year could afford a full-time maid.[13]

The opportunities in El Paso drew many "green card" workers, who were Mexican citizens with permits to work in the United States. While many companies considered this an excellent source of cheap labor, Farah did not. Farah would hire only American citizens, a policy which was later upheld by a federal court decision in 1972.

Unionism in Texas was not strong, chiefly because the closed union shop was illegal. Only 2,200 of El Paso's 20,000 clothing workers were covered by a union contract, and they worked primarily for Billy-the-Kid, which had been unionized since 1944.[14] Late in 1969, the Amalgamated Clothing Workers of America (ACWA) had begun a drive to organize Farah, with some incidents but without significant results.

TROUBLE IN THE EARLY 1970s

In October of 1970, however, the National Labor Relations Board (NLRB) held an election among the cutters and spreaders in the cutting room of the large "Gateway" plant in El Paso. The union won by a vote of 109 to 73, but the company objected that the small group of employees—about seven percent of the plant total—was an "inappropriate unit" for collective bargaining purposes.

In order to go to court with that argument, the company then had to refuse to bargain with the ACWA as a representative of the inappropriate unit. The case was not heard for nearly two years, and during that time, the ACWA used Farah's "refusal to bargain" as a persuasive organizing tool.

At this point, however, ACWA organization attempts were not the key concern of top management. In 1970, knit slacks were introduced for men's casual wear. Farah evaluated the style, but thought that the tendency of knit fabrics to snag would cause disappointment among the customers that tried them. Farah concluded that they would only be accepted for limited use activities, such as golfing. The success of Farah's operation was built on high-speed production, and knits pro-

---

[12] Ibid., p. 12.

[13] *The New York Times*, September 11, 1972, p. 57.

[14] Ibid.

vided an additional problem in this regard. After being spread, knit fabrics would have to be allowed to contract on the cutting table in order for patterns to be cut the right size. Converting to knits would penalize Farah's production more than it would less efficient manufacturers.

For these reasons, Farah did not add knits to its line. By the 1971 spring selling season, the success of knits had become clear. The company, however, had about $27 million in orders for woven fabrics. These orders could have been canceled, thereby passing the loss to Farah suppliers, but Farah considered that this would be an unethical business practice. The result was a $20 million inventory write-down that largely contributed to an $8.2 million loss for 1972. Shares of common stock, which in 1970 had sold at 49½ were by the end of August 1971, selling at 11. It was clear that Farah was no longer a glamour stock.

THE WALKOUT

While Farah executives struggled to return the business to its former position in the industry, Paul Garza, a Farah production worker was fired for lying about an illness in order to be absent from work. Freely admitting his guilt he took several other employees with him to see his supervisor in order to ask for reinstatement. The supervisor told Mr. Garza that the company no longer wanted him and asked the other employees either to return to work or leave the plant. Six mechanics, who had been active in the ACWA organization campaign turned in their tools and left the plant.

The ACWA strengthened its organizing attempts against the company, and the results surprised even the union. By the end of the week, 500 workers had walked off their jobs. Two weeks later, over 2,000 workers had struck.[15] The issues were the workers' rights to provide input to management regarding production quotas, job security, termination policies, and the fundamental right to unionize if desired. About 4,500 workers remained at their jobs.

The union quickly picked up the "Chicano theme" which was already familiar to the public because of Cesar Chavez's farm workers' struggle. Picket signs lettered in Spanish and Farah's close-to-minimum wages made good copy, and Willie Farah's enthusiastic support of traditional American values made him an unusually useful foil for union purposes. An outspoken patriot, he told visitors that:

> It's the worst form of treason for the American businessmen to use foreign labor to the detriment of American labor. Our responsibility is

---

[15] *Fortune*, August 1974, p. 167.

to the American worker. This country gives us everything, and we're gratified to live here.

Everything we buy is American-made. We could go offshore and save thousands of dollars a week. We have only one piece of equipment from overseas—a German cut-off machine. . . . There are two billion foreigners out there willing to work for ten cents an hour. We've got to whip 'em with American know-how and the will to work.[16]

It was said that when Mr. Farah found Japanese-made nails at the site of the construction of his new home, he had a partially completed wall removed and rebuilt with American nails.[17] He was convinced that unionization of a company paying competitive wages and providing model working conditions was morally wrong, and vowed not to capitulate. The union believed that the major issue was the right for employees to unionize, if they so chose.

Mr. Farah's intransigence, the "refusal to bargain," news pictures of the high chain link fences surrounding the plant, and reports of the continued use of guard dogs after the strike began gained little sympathy for the company position. The union additionally claimed the company was guilty of discharging workers for union activities, personal intimidation and coercion, using court orders to bar legal picketing, and obtaining arrest warrants for picketers that were served in the middle of the night. The company charged that workers were beaten by strikers, tires were slashed, and shots were fired through plant windows.[18] No one was seriously hurt by these incidents.

Given the scenario of Chicano strikers and Anglo management in confrontation, the citizens of El Paso remained remarkably unconcerned with the strike. If the company was to be unionized, additional help would need to be enlisted.

THE BOYCOTT

On July 19, 1972, a national boycott of Farah products was called. Organized by the ACWA, the boycott was supported by the AFL–CIO Executive Council and a number of Democratic politicians. Among them were presidential candidate George McGovern, his running mate Sargent Shriver, Sen. Edward Kennedy, Mayor John Lindsey, and Sen. Gaylord Nelson, who headed a National Citizen's Committee for Justice to Farah Workers.

In mid-August, the NLRB held that the firing of Paul Garza—the

---

[16] *The New York Times*, September 11, 1972, p. 58. © 1972 by The New York Times Company. Reprinted by permission.

[17] *American Federationist*, June 1973, p. 7.

[18] *The New York Times*, September 11, 1972, p. 57.

incident causing the initial walkout—had been legal. By this time, however, the issue of the right to organize and the drama of the national boycott had dwarfed all earlier issues.

Getting media play for the nationwide boycott proved to be relatively easy, once the Chicano theme had been established. Mass picketing became a "natural" for TV news coverage, which in turn made it easier to recruit more pickets. Picketing became so intense in the New York area that retailers quit advertising Farah slacks. On December 11, 1972, "Don't Buy Farah Day," 175,000 pickets marched nationwide.[19]

On February 14, 1973, the ACWA placed full-page ads in newspapers in the 13 largest advertising markets to call attention to what it called unfair labor practices at Farah. Included in the ad was a letter "to all Catholic Bishops in the United States" from the Most Reverend Sidney M. Metzger, bishop of El Paso.[20] The letter recommended a boycott of Farah slacks, and was to have a profound effect on the success of the boycott (see Exhibit 2).

The bishop had been involved in labor affairs since 1941,[21] and had tacitly approved of the strike since the beginning. Mr. Farah was not impressed with the bishop's endorsement of the strike, because he thought him ignorant of conditions at the plant. Neither the bishop nor members of his staff had ever been there.[22] Mr. Farah also characterized the bishop as "lolling in wealth" and belonging "to the rotten old bourgeoisie."[23] Bishop Metzger was supported locally in his efforts by Rev. Jesse Munoz, the 32-year-old pastor of El Paso's largest parish. Rev. Munoz was called the "spark" of the strike,[24] and characterized opponents of the strike, such as the editor of the *El Paso Times* and nationally syndicated religious columnist Daniel Poling, as "pimps of the establishment."[25] Munoz believed that "the basic reason [my parishioners] are supporting the strike with such dedication is that they are so determined to change the future of El Paso, mostly for their children, that they will go to any lengths to achieve that goal."[26]

Company advertising director Kenneth Farah responded to the

---

[19] *Fortune*, August 1974, p. 238.

[20] The 70-year-old bishop had been educated at the Gregorian University in Rome and held doctorates in both theology and canon law. A personal friend of Pope John XXIII, he had been bishop of El Paso since 1942.

[21] *American Federationist*, June 1973, p. 5.

[22] *Advertising Age*, March 12, 1973, p. 38.

[23] *The New York Times*, September 11, 1972, p. 57.

[24] *American Federationist*, June 1973, p. 6.

[25] *The Christian Century*, September 26, 1973, p. 936.

[26] *Business Week*, no. 2282 (June 2, 1973), p. 56.

EXHIBIT 2
The "Bishop's Advertisement" Supporting the Boycott From the Bishop of El Paso to the Catholic Bishops of the United States

What follows occurred when a member of the Catholic hierarchy addressed a letter of inquiry to the bishop of El Paso concerning the strike of Mexican-American employees against the Farah Manufacturing Co. The bishop of El Paso addressed his reply to all Catholic bishops in the United States.

1012 North Mesa Street
El Paso, Texas

Your Excellency:

Recently one of our bishops sent me a letter through his diocesan office asking for information concerning the strike at the Farah Manufacturing plant in El Paso. Because of a nationwide boycott of Farah products by the Amalgamated Clothing Workers of America the strike has assumed nationwide importance and its effects are felt in a number of cities throughout the nation. The Bishop's Office wrote that he needed some guidance from people on the scene as to the problems. The following questions were asked in the letter:

1. Do you feel the company is acting in an unjust manner in this strike? Can you point out specific and verified instances of this?
2. Has anyone toured the plants of Farah? What were the conditions?
3. Is the Farah pay scale equitable with other plants in the area? Is the pay adequate to live on?
4. How is this issue defined by the people concerned in regard to the dignity of each party—the strikers and the company?
5. Is the case strong enough that you recommend the Bishop to make a formal request to a retail outlet not to reorder?

My answer to these questions is contained in the following. If you are asked about the merits of the strike I hope this information may be useful.

Yours in Christ,

S. M. Metzger
Bishop of El Paso

Dear Father:

In reply to your letter I must give you pertinent information concerning the Farah situation in El Paso, which is difficult and complicated.

Farah finds it well nigh impossible to be objective and to recognize that the worker has the right to collective bargaining and join a union. The company is convinced that it is doing wonders for the worker and that a union would be detrimental to the worker and to the company. I feel that the company is acting unjustly in denying to the workers the basic right to collective bargaining. We know that these matters are decided by means of federally sponsored representational elections and the Farah Company uses all possible means to block such elections in their plants. Let the workers decide if they

EXHIBIT 2 *(continued)*

want a union or not. If all is so beautiful and ideal as the company publicly proclaims why should they fear an election?

I know that for the past five years complaints were made by Farah workers to their parish priest. This you will understand when you realize that nearly all Farah workers are humble Mexican-Americans who must earn their bread by hard work and who often have a way of coming to their parish priest with personal problems.

There were complaints about the drastic demands for production. This was explained by a worker who has been with the company 14 years. She explains that the great majority of workers make $69.00 per week, which is take-home pay after deducting Social Security, etc. At the present moment her assignment is to sew belts on the finished slacks. The quota amounts to 3,000 belts per day; in an eight-hour work day this means the girls have to sew on 6 belts per minute, and even this would amount to only 2,880 belts per day. The girls say that it is physically possible to sew on only five belts per minute, even with the modern machines they operate. As long as they cannot sew on six belts per minute they cannot get a raise and their wages are frozen at that point. While the quota of 2,760 belts is tolerated the company will dismiss a worker who in their opinion falls too far below 2,760. It has been said that the production demands can be set by the company as high as they want them and they can fire the worker who cannot stand the strain physically. Workers have said that they are treated as production machines and not as human beings. They also said that wages increase only when and if the company wants. Women have also complained that the maternity benefits were far from adequate and that when they returned to work they would lose their position on the pay scale and start as beginners.

It seems to me that there are some flagrant defects in the Farah plants as they are presently operated. Perhaps the most flagrant is that there is no job security; the company can fire anyone anytime and the worker has no appeal. A second very serious defect is that there are no negotiated production standards so that the workers can have a say how much they can produce and are not treated like machines. There should also be negotiated wage increases according to a definite schedule. There should be better maternity insurance and negotiated leaves for illness, etc. and workers should be able to return to their same jobs and same rate of pay.

Farah Company has an impressive list of benefits which look good on paper. At closer scrutiny however, these like the maternity insurance are tokens. I have before me a photocopy of "Your Retirement Benefits" addressed to a worker. It states "This is a total monthly retirement income of $234.50." which looks fine. But $214.50 comes from an estimated amount of Social Security and the monthly retirement check from Farah amounts to $20.00. Nothing is explained about what the actual retirement age is or how many years of work with Farah are required for retirement benefits.

I hope I am not in error when I say that job security for the workers, negotiated production standards, negotiated wage increases according to a definite schedule, adequate maternity insurance and leaves for illness are all in accord with the principles of social justice. All these are lacking in the

EXHIBIT 2 *(continued)*

present Farah Company and these serious defects can be remedied by collective bargaining.

However it should also be noted that without job security and with the high production demands workers live in fear of being dismissed and left without a job if their output falls short of their production quota. Also the company exercises constant supervision to be sure the workers do not complain to others but say the right thing when outsiders visit the plant. This brings me to question whether lower pay than clothing workers are listed under a catch-all listing as "others," although clothing is El Paso's number one industry. In comparison, Chamber of Commerce statistics show that petroleum workers earn an average of $7,500 yearly, metal workers earn $7,200 yearly, food-processing employees average $6,100. The Amalgamated Clothing Workers of America who are seeking a contract with Farah have contracts with three apparel manufacturers in El Paso. These three are Levi Strauss, Hortex Incorporated, and Tex-Togs. Levi Strauss is national but Hortex Incorporated and Tex-Togs are small local companies, much smaller than Farah. Work for which workers at Farah receive $69.00 per week take-home pay, union workers receive $102.00 per week take-home pay, which sounds more like a living wage. If these smaller plants can live with a union contract and prosper why is it so impossible for gigantic Farah to do the same?

When you ask is the annual pay of $3,588.00 at Farah adequate to live on the answer is decidedly "no" in these days of high prices. A single person can get by on this amount but a married person with a family simply cannot adequately support the family with this amount. It about puts bread on the table. Some of our Mexican people have large families and they have serious problems. In terms of social justice $3,588.00 is not an adequate living wage in our day for a family in El Paso.

Farah apparently wasn't aware or didn't want to be aware that resentment was growing. But the fact that today over 3,000 workers are on strike is evidence that both grievances and resentment are real. And by listening to the people over the years one gradually became aware that things at Farah were not actually as they were made to appear.

"Is the case strong enough that you would recommend the bishop to make a formal request to a retail outlet not to reorder?" I answer: Yes, from my knowledge of the case here, I think it is strong enough to recommend to His Excellency that he make a formal request to a retail outlet not to reorder. The strike has assumed national importance and is supported by persons of national prominence. Our own "little people" in El Paso would be crushed if it were not for this national support. His Excellency will of course weigh what I have written and decide what he deems best.

With every good wish and blessing, I am,
Sincerely Yours in Christ,

S. M. Metzger
Bishop of El Paso

EXHIBIT 2 *(continued)*

YOU CAN HELP THE FARAH WORKERS BY NOT BUYING
FARAH SLACKS

U.S. Representative Herman Badillo	Mayor John V. Lindsay
Ramsey Clark, Esq.	Commissioner Bess Myerson, Dept.
Michael Harrington, Author	of Consumer Affairs, The City of
Dorothy Height, President, National	New York
Council of Negro Women	U.S. Representative Ogden Reid
Professor Irving Howe, City	A. Philip Randolph, President,
University of New York	A. Philip Randolph Institute
	Rabbi Henry Siegman

Amalgamated Clothing Workers of America/15 Union Square/
New York, N.Y. 10003

boycott by asserting that in some markets it has "even strengthened our position, because it has focused attention on our products." When asked if Farah would present its case through national advertising he said, "No. We're in the pants business. We're not in the business of arguing."[27] The 1973 advertising budget was approximately double 1972 expenditures, and the customer flights to El Paso had begun.

In late March, the NLRB had censured both Farah and the ACWA for various illegal strike activities. On May 14, the NLRB made the significant ruling that Farah's "refusal to bargain" position that it had assumed since the original cutting room elections of October 1970 was not correct. The NLRB then ordered Farah to bargain. Farah refused in order to take the case to the U.S. Court of Appeals.

Throughout the rest of 1973, a stalemate existed, but media support of the boycott continued. For many church groups, particularly Roman Catholics, the Farah struggle became a moral crusade. Cardinal Mederios of Boston reflected the views of many churchmen when he said "the internal affairs of business become the concern of religious leadership when violations of social justice and human dignity are at stake."[28] *The Christian Century* concluded an article with the hope that "the concern expressed . . . may indicate that at least some of El Paso's upper-middle-class Anglo citizens are beginning to feel uncomfortable living in a city where middle class affluence is built on the poverty of underpaid Chicano workers."[29] The Farah man-

---

[27] *Advertising Age*, March 12, 1973, pp. 38–39.

[28] *Fortune*, August 1974, p. 167.

[29] *The Christian Century*, September 26, 1973, p. 936.

ufacturing company made the annual list of the ten worst performing companies in the social responsiveness area.[30]

Mr. Farah felt that he would only demean the company by replying to what he regarded as extreme propaganda. His nonresponse was used by his opponents as proof of his arrogant and uncaring attitude.

Fiscal year 1973 ended October 31, 1973 with sales of $132 million, down $23 million from the previous year. A negligible profit was shown. The stock price which had been near 50 in 1971 was below 8. In November, Mr. Farah bowed to board of directors' pressure and closed the four small outlying plants. Of the 3,000 employees who had walked out over the previous 18 months, about half remained on strike. The ACWA had spent an estimated $15 million on the strike and boycott.[31]

Very early in 1974, Farah asked the NLRB to hold representation elections in the plants that were still open. The union refused, claiming that a climate of fear prevented the holding of a fair representative election. In actuality, the union had chosen the more time-consuming but less risky course of organizing smaller segments of workers.[32]

In late January, NLRB Judge Walter H. Maloney ruled that the company had pursued "a policy of flouting the NLRB Act and trampling on the rights of its employees as if there was no Act, no Board, and no Ten Commandments."[33] The "Maloney Decision" ruled that all strikers be rehired, that the original six mechanics who walked out be reinstated with back pay plus six percent interest, and that the union be given access to employees. Farah asked for an immediate review of the decision by the NLRB, but its request was refused. The "public relations impact of the decision was devastating" to Farah.[34]

Still, no elections could be held with the litigation pending. The break in the deadlock finally occurred on February 5, when El Paso Mayor Fred Hervey suggested that an informal poll be conducted among current employees, strikers, and those laid off by plant closings. The ACWA would be permitted to campaign and solicit pledge cards from employees in favor of union representation. Both sides agreed.

The result of the poll showed that 62 percent of 7,703 workers supported union representation.[35] As a result, Farah agreed to recognize the union as the bargaining agent for his employees. On Feb-

[30] Milton Moskowitz, "Social Responsibility Portfolio 1973," *Business and Society*, vol. 7, no. 1 (January 15, 1974), p. 1.

[31] *Business Week*, March 2, 1974, p. 25.

[32] *The Christian Century*, p. 935.

[33] *Monthly Labor Review*, vol. 97, no. 4 (April 1974), pp. 73–74.

[34] Farah Manufacturing Company, 1974 Annual Report, p. 5.

[35] *Monthly Labor Review*, p. 73.

ruary 24, 1974, the national boycott was lifted and on March 8, the agreement was ratified. Willie Farah had surrendered.

FINDINGS AFTER THE SETTLEMENT

Although the union had achieved its objectives, two appeals by the company were still pending. The first, decided on March 21, 1974, in the U.S. Court of Appeals, affirmed Farah's position that the initial union election in 1970 among cutting room employees was with an inappropriate unit for collective bargaining purposes. What this meant, from Farah's viewpoint, was that:

> . . . the company was right from the beginning. It was right in October 1970 when it protested that election, in September 1972 when it refused to bargain, and in May 1973 when it refused to obey the NLRB's order that it bargain. And most importantly, the company was wronged by the politicians, prelates and others who unthinkingly parroted Amalgamated's line and solemnly denounced its "refusal to bargain" with the union.[36]

Seven months later, the NLRB review of the "Maloney Decision" also supported the company. The board reversed Judge Maloney's decision regarding the reinstatement of the six mechanics and found merit in the company's contention that Judge Maloney's " . . . numerous characterizations of the employer were unwarranted and injudicious. . . . Accordingly, the board disavows and repudiates the section of the judge's decision entitled 'Farah and the Board: The Past as Prologue' and those comments throughout his decision that intemperately characterized the employer."[37]

---

[36] Farah Manufacturing Company, 1974 Annual Report, p. 5.

[37] *Labor Law Reports*, Case Number 15, 113 (Commerce Clearing House, Inc., 1974).

Case ════════════════════════════════════

THE E. S. SCARBONIE CORPORATION

The E. S. Scarbonie Corporation[1] was a manufacturer of camping equipment (lanterns, tents, and sleeping bags) and garden hand tools headquartered in Minneapolis, Minnesota, with manufacturing facilities located in six of the nation's largest metropolitan areas. Two of these facilities, plants nos. 14 and 16, which produced tents and sleeping bags, were located in the Minneapolis/St. Paul area. In 1972, the company had sales of $78,324,000 and employed some 5,000 people.

On a Wednesday in mid-September 1973, Thomas Walton, vice president of the Camping Equipment Group, Jack Carter, personnel director of the Camping Equipment Group, and William Thompson, personnel director of plants nos. 14 and 16, were gathered in Mr. Walton's office to discuss the recent firing of Alice Reed, a grade-level no. 1 production employee (there were four hourly grade levels, grade no. 1 being the lowest and starting level for all production employees). Miss Reed, who had been fired the previous Wednesday by Joseph Sikes, plant no. 14 superintendent, had called Mr. Walton the following Monday and expressed the opinion that she had been unjustifiably fired and that she wanted to go back to work. (See Exhibit 1 for partial organization chart.)

---

[1] All names, places, and other information that might identify the company have been disguised.

EXHIBIT 1
Partial Organization Chart

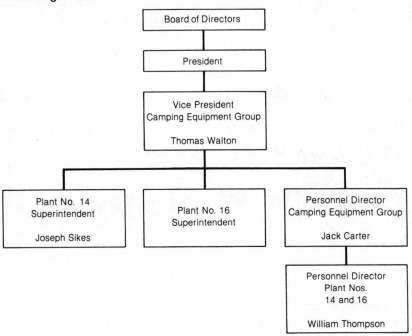

COMPANY BACKGROUND

The E. S. Scarbonie Corporation was founded by its namesake in 1926 as a manufacturer of garden hand tools, and remained as such until Mr. Scarbonie's death in 1960. The company was purchased from Mr. Scarbonie's estate in 1961 by a financier, made its first public stock offering in 1963, and was listed on the New York Stock Exchange in 1971.

The company had grown rapidly since 1962, having made four major acquisitions, and was recognized as a leader in its industry by 1971. The principal outlets for Scarbonie's products were department stores and hardware stores; the company was an important resource for the sporting goods, hardware, and garden departments of major department stores from coast to coast. In addition, sales of the company's products expanded in the early 1970s in the chain garden center store markets. Scarbonie's management attributed the company's growth to its ability to respond to the rapidly growing leisure-time needs of people with quality gardening products. (See Exhibit 2.)

Another foundation for the company's success was believed to be top management's corporate philosophy vis-à-vis employees. Management summarized this philosophy about people as follows:

EXHIBIT 2
E. S. Scarbonie Corporation Financial Statements

Net Sales and Income, * 1963–1972*

Year	Net sales	Net Income after taxes
1963	$13,140,000	$ 332,000
1964	16,158,000	538,000
1965	19,806,000	784,000
1966	25,374,000	930,000
1967	31,876,000	1,372,000
1968	38,808,000	1,626,000
1969	49,334,000	1,400,000
1970	56,328,000	2,170,000
1971	68,246,000	2,548,000
1972	78,324,000	2,900,000

* All figures rounded to the nearest thousand.

Statement of Consolidated Income, 1969–1972

	1972	1971	1970	1969
Net sales.......................	$78,324,602	$68,246,404	$56,328,362	$49,334,734
Cost of sales	51,335,474	43,837,884	36,504,362	32,551,752
Gross profit	26,989,128	24,408,520	19,824,000	16,782,982
Selling, general, and adminis- trative expenses	20,381,546	18,813,200	15,092,236	13,474,626
Operating income	6,607,582	5,595,320	4,731,764	3,308,356
Other deductions, net............	1,098,450	789,014	500,824	619,912
Income before federal income taxes	5,509,132	4,806,306	4,230,940	2,688,444
Federal income taxes	2,610,000	2,258,000	2,060,000	1,288,000
Net income	$ 2,899,132	$ 2,548,306	$ 2,170,940	$ 1,400,444
Per share of common stock (based on the average number of shares outstanding during each year, retroactively adjusted for stock distribution)	$1.60	$1.40	$2.02	$1.44

Consolidated Balance Sheet

	1972	1971	1970	1969
		Assets		
Current assets: .... Cash	$ 2,829,074	$ 1,352,426	$ 2,791,498	$ 1,414,372
Marketable securities, at cost which approximate market	4,587,936	—	—	—
Accounts receivable (less allowances)	9,831,348	7,877,838	6,973,208	6,436,546
Inventories, at lower of cost (first-in, first-out) or market:				
Finished goods	8,815,640	9,908,450	6,245,208	5,272,012
Work in process	776,510	623,650	796,856	825,786
Raw materials	5,489,674	5,532,878	4,786,072	5,663,352
Total inventories.......	$15,081,824	$16,064,978	$11,828,136	$11,761,150

EXHIBIT 2 *(continued)*

	1972	1971	1970	1969
Prepaid expenses and other current assets	487,458	325,450	296,544	395,188
Total current assets	$32,817,640	$25,620,692	$21,889,386	$20,007,256
Property, plant and equipment at cost	$12,174,380	$11,446,646	$ 7,536,904	$ 7,037,392
Less accumulated depreciation and amortization	5,430,494	4,759,888	4,172,190	3,495,958
Net property, plant and equipment	$ 6,743,886	$ 6,686,758	$ 3,364,714	$ 3,541,434
Excess of purchase price over net assets acquired.............	$ 2,576,908	$ 2,582,158	$ 2,377,408	$ 2,377,408
Deferred financing costs	366,304	41,954	—	—
Other assets....................	464,528	376,884	332,834	213,566
Total	$42,968,866	$35,308,446	$27,964,342	$26,139,664

Liabilities and Stockholders' Equity

	1972	1971	1970	1969
Current liabilities:				
Notes payable to banks	$—	$—	$—	$ 4,900,000
Current installments of long-term debt	620,000	638,000	1,228,000	808,508
Accounts payable	3,203,620	3,308,544	2,862,340	3,588,134
Accrued expenses	2,127,740	1,941,586	1,753,992	1,374,042
Federal income taxes	485,048	233,022	1,458,814	760,732
Total current liabilities	$ 6,436,408	$ 6,121,152	$ 7,303,146	$11,431,416
Deferred compensation...........	$ 233,066	$ 190,504	$ 154,982	$ 124,760
Long-term debt, excluding current installments	$14,570,000	10,190,000	4,358,000	3,871,000
Stockholders' equity:				
Preferred stock, without par value. Authorized 250,000 shares; none issued	—	—	—	—
Common stock, $1 par value. Authorized 3,000,000 shares; Issued 1,818,780 shares (excluding 16,000 treasury shares)	3,637,560	2,418,602	2,174,422	1,758,232
Additional capital in excess of par value	10,094,960	11,290,448	7,903,686	3,472,506
Retained earnings	7,996,872	5,097,740	6,070,106	5,481,750
Total stockholders' equity	$21,729,392	$18,806,790	$16,148,214	$10,712,488
Total liabilities and stockholders' equity	$42,968,866	$35,308,446	$27,964,342	$26,139,664

1. The notion of the purely economic man is a myth. People not only want economic rewards, but also want to achieve personal satisfaction through fulfilling work.
2. People want to be associated with a successful and growing company.
3. People want to be active participants in decisions related to their role in the company.

Based upon these assumptions about people Scarbonie's management has committed itself, according to one executive, "to the task of creating an environment within the company that would unleash the hidden potential of the individual, encourage people to utilize their latent capabilities, and motivate people so that they would care enough to share what was within themselves."

During the early 1970s management worked on the introduction and implementation of a team process and a team management system within the company in order to create this environment.

Asking people to participate in decision-making processes that would affect their jobs was the fundamental approach used to create the team approach at Scarbonie. It was believed that helping people to work together at more satisfying jobs would dramatically influence the growth of the company. For example, after management had selected three alternative sites for the construction of the new no. 16 plant (1971), all affected employees were bused to the sites and a vote was taken to select the final location.

The management of Scarbonie believed that its policies would:

1. Lead to a high level of productivity.
2. Improve overall product quality.
3. Lower employee turnover (the turnover rate was down to less than three percent by 1972 compared with an industry rate of five percent).
4. Lessen the threat of unionization.

Management wished to avoid unionization because it was felt that it would increase direct labor costs, thus placing Scarbonie at a competitive disadvantage with respect to foreign price competition. Plant no. 14 represented the company's only experience with an attempted unionization. There had been a strike-force organization attempt in late 1971 which resulted in the rejection of the union in a National Labor Relations Board supervised election.

Although the company was successful in the NLRB election, many of the managers felt that the need for the election was itself a failing of management. And, except for certain difficulties involved in working with a rather aggressive chapter of the NAACP in the Minneapolis area, Scarbonie felt that it was doing an effective job of employee relations. Its minority employment record was one of the best in the area, and its pay scales were somewhat above the market.

THE ALICE REED PROBLEM

One of the company's basic beliefs concerning its employee relations was that it was necessary for each employee to understand as fully as possible what the company expected of him and, in turn, precisely what he could expect of the company. Thus, each new employee received a 22-page employee handbook which contained an explanation of the company's "Point Assignment Procedures (PAP)." The explanation of the system presented most of the circumstances under which an employee could be assigned points for rule violations, placed on probation, and ultimately fired. An excerpt from the handbook covering the PAP system appears in Exhibit 3.

The sequence of events that led to the meeting of Messrs. Walton, Thompson, and Carter in Mr. Walton's office that Wednesday morning in late September 1973 were as follows:

EXHIBIT 3
Statement of Corporate Purpose

Our reasons for existing as a company are the following:

1. To manufacture and sell quality products designed to assure maximum customer satisfaction.
2. To satisfy not only our customers, but also to work to the mutual advantage of suppliers, creditors, distributors, and other groups significantly related to the company.
3. To increase the value of the assets of the company and improve the stockholders' equity and/or return on investment.
4. To create a climate that stimulates, challenges, and channels the human intelligence, ingenuity, and desire of its employees to the fulfillment of the corporate purpose and provide them with a sense of achievement, equitable compensation, plus participation in the results of success.
5. To make a contribution to society by demonstrating how people of all races, creeds, and colors can work together cooperatively to the benefit of each and all.

If we at E. S. Scarbonie Corporation achieve these goals, we will achieve yet another major objective: to contribute significantly to strengthening the economic and social system of our nation.

EXHIBIT 3 *(continued)*

NINE GUIDELINES TO SUCCESSFUL PARTICIPATION

We at Scarbonie believe in people. We believe that our associates are responsible and intelligent adults who want to do the right thing in their work and in their relations with each other. We list the following guidelines and ask that you read them carefully and help us abide by them. They are not intended to be all-inclusive, but they establish the intent of our company's policies.

Guideline 1.   The first element of full participation at Scarbonie is regular work attendance and promptness in reporting to work. Every associate should be at work every working day unless notified not to report. Exceptions will be made for unavoidable and necessary absences. But associates *must* notify their supervisor as soon as possible when they are forced to be absent from work. Any associate who is absent for four consecutive days without notifying his or her supervisor of the reason will be dropped from the payroll.

Guideline 2.   Unethical or immoral behavior is unacceptable. Associates are expected to protect and preserve company property, avoid coming to work under the influence of alcohol or other drugs, and not engage in *any* dishonest act (such as stealing company materials or products or secrets).

Guideline 3.   All of Scarbonie's associates are expected to work safely and to abide by all safety rules. All accidents must be reported to your supervisor immediately.

Guideline 4.   We at Scarbonie do not expect our associates to work every minute of the day, so we provide two break periods and a lunch period. You should work up until the break, lunch, or quitting time—and be back at your work station promptly after the lunch and break periods.

Guideline 5.   We must all be good citizens at Scarbonie. Therefore, fighting, abusive and foul language, sleeping on the job, spitting in unauthorized areas, and such forms of misbehavior must be discouraged.

Guideline 6.   Every organized group must have a leader. Your supervisor is your leader, and his or her instructions and directions must be followed. *You should freely express your opinions or ideas and disagree politely when you believe that you know a better way to do the job.* Common sense and good judgment tell us, however, that refusal to follow instructions and disrespectful language are not in the best interests of either the company or its associates.

Guideline 7.   Out of consideration for his or her associates, good personal hygiene, cleanliness, proper dress, and courteous behavior are expected of every person in our company.

Guideline 8.   Poor work habits, poor housekeeping, careless work, and other signs of lack of job interest and cooperation are harmful to our team spirit, and the job security of all of Scarbonie's people.

Guideline 9.   It is a violation of personal privacy to ask for financial contributions from your associates. The company cannot permit solicitation for any reason whatsoever on company time.

EXHIBIT 3 *(continued)*

YOU, YOUR SUPERVISOR, AND THE GUIDELINES

If you violate one of the guidelines, you should understand that your supervisor has an *obligation* to you and to the company to bring it to your attention. It is his objective to help you *correct* the problem and become a better associate.

Only rarely will such violations lead to termination (failure to observe Guidelines 2, 3, or 6 may, of course, result in immediate discharge). When your Supervisor meets with you he will fill out Form 100 outlining your violation and will assign points. Copies of Form 100 will be given to the Department Head and Plant Manager. Should you disagree with the summary of events or the point assignment, you have five working days in which to discuss this matter with either of those managers. If they feel you should not have been assigned points, the form will be torn up.

The Point Assignment Procedures (PAP) recognize the desire of each of us to prove that we can profit from our mistakes. The entire PAP system is designed to help you be a better associate. We have no desire to be "tough" here at Scarbonie, but we want to be *fair* and the only way to be fair is to see to it that PAP is enforced.

The violation of a guideline will lead to the assignment of points. If your points for a six months' period total 20 or more, you will be asked to meet with the Plant Manager or Department Head. He will discuss the problem, summarize the meeting in a letter (a copy will be sent to you) and you will be placed on 90 days probation unless there are extenuating circumstances.

Normally, this procedure should correct the problem. However, if you should be assigned five or more points during the probationary period, the Plant Manager or Department Manager will call you in again. Together you will decide if it is in the best interests of your associates for you to remain with Scarbonie.

We have provided a "safety valve" system to help you think through this important question. You will be given one full day at your regular wage to stay home and prepare a statement about why you should be allowed to continue with the company. The manager will evaluate your answer and decide if you should be given another chance.

We have worked hard to develop an equitable plan. If you know of ways in which we can improve it, please let us know.

Points for Failure to Observe Guidelines

Guideline number		Points
1.	Late at work station	5
	Tardy	5
	Absenteeism—unexcused and/or excessive	10
	Leaving work station early	5

EXHIBIT 3 *(continued)*

2.	....	25
3.	....	5–25
4.	....	5
5.	....	5–15
6.	....	5–25
7.	....	5
8.	....	5
9.	....	5

Point assignments will run for six months from the date of issue, at the conclusion of which time the points will be voided.

In this way, you may enjoy a completely "clean slate" even after you have received a point assignment by being careful to live up to your responsibilities to yourself, your associates, and your company.

1. On the previous Wednesday morning, Alice Reed called in to her group leader prior to the start of her shift and told her that she had to take her seriously ill boyfriend to the hospital and that she would be in later. However, she never arrived, nor did she call in again that day.

2. The next morning when Alice arrived at her work station, Joseph Sikes, plant no. 14 superintendent, was waiting there to greet her with, "Hey, you don't work here any more; take a seat in the cafeteria and wait for Cindy" (Cindy Mazolotti, the plant personnel secretary; Mr. Thompson was out of town at the time). In the cafeteria Mr. Sikes told Miss Reed that her excuse for not coming to work was not any good and that none of the supervisors wanted her. Miss Reed was very upset and felt that Mr. Sikes had "bad-mouthed" her and left without talking with Cindy Mazolotti.

3. That Friday, Miss Reed called the Camping Equipment Group personnel director, Jack Carter, and said that she wanted both of the payroll checks that she was entitled to right away. Mr. Carter said that he could not do that until the credit union OK'd it early the next week. Mr. Carter heard Alice Reed's boyfriend in the background say that they had to pay her immediately.

4. Early the Next Monday morning, Alice called Mr. Walton and said that she was very dissatisfied with the way she was fired; that after going through her employee handbook she felt that she had not been treated according to the handbook guidelines; and added that she wanted to go back to work. Mr. Walton then called Mr. Carter and Mr. Thompson and told them to meet in his office at 7:30 Wednesday morning with the full story of what had happened.

The following is an excerpted version of the conversation which took place between Walton, Carter, and Thompson on that day.

Thompson: I guess that a summary of Alice's work history is a good place to start. She was with us for six years and was still grade level no. 1. She was never promoted due to a long history of poor ratings and guideline violations. She worked in all five departments under five supervisors over the years, and all their opinions of her were the same. She was lazy, often late or absent with marginally acceptable excuses, slow, and a sloppy worker. At the time of her dismissal, she had 14 points for violations, 5 for Guideline 8 and 9 for violations of Guideline 1. She has always been between 5 and 15 points, never enough to be on probation but a habitual violator. I was in Texas until late that Friday morning and only then found out about Sikes' firing her. We went to lunch together that afternoon, and that's when he told me that he had finally solved one of my problems by firing Alice. He said that she was absent the previous Wednesday and that her excuse was not any good and that was worth ten points, which was enough to fire her; she was a "bad apple" anyway. I told him that that only made 24 points, even if her excuse was not any good. But he had already spread word all over the plant that he had finally gotten rid of "the lazy bitch." We had been thinking of working her out of the system for the past few months anyway, so I think that Joe took advantage of the fact that I was in Texas; but really the only difference is that she was fired sooner rather than later.

Carter: Well, Tom, until you called me on Monday I assumed that this was a normal termination by the standard operating procedure. Alice did call me Friday asking for her checks, but she never said anything to the effect that she was unjustifiably fired. All I ever saw was the usual paperwork as it came in from "14." Anyway, I went out to "14" Monday afternoon and after finding out from Bill the story he had just related to you, I went out on the floor and talked to Alice's supervisor and five or six of the other girls on her line. The consensus was that even though Alice was lazy and sometimes made it hard for them to meet their quota, she "got a raw deal." It was common knowledge out on the floor that Alice was one of Sikes' favorite scapegoats. I think the feeling out there is that Joe just finally found an excuse to get rid of her.

Walton: What about Sikes, Bill? Is he noted for this sort of thing, is this an isolated case, or what?

Thompson: Joe has been with us for seven years. He's been superintendent at "14" for the past three. He has what you might call a "Little Napoleon" complex. He likes and uses his authority a little too much for his own good, as well as for the good of the company. There have been three incidents in which his recommendations for discipline have been refused or reversed and four complaints that he plays favorites or indulges in scapegoating. He once came to me and demanded that a girl be fired because she was "lax" even though she had never been assigned points.

He does not seem to see much value in adhering to the PAP system. Yet, as you both know, "14" is one of our best plants in terms of productivity.

Carter: I had a talk with Sikes yesterday. I asked him why he did not follow proper procedures in firing Alice. He said, "Twenty-four points, 25 points, what is the difference? She was a 'bad apple' and was on the way out anyway." He assumed that Alice would be assigned ten points for an unexcused absence. So I asked him why he felt her excuse was not any good. He said that, ". . . she isn't even married to the bastard she's living with . . . Take him to the doctor, some excuse that is!" I asked him again why he did not comply with the evaluation system as the means of working her out of the company, since the groundwork to do this had already been laid out. He just shook his head and could not answer. I asked him if he realized that tactics like this were just what a union needed to try again to organize "14." Again no reply. He did not seem to understand what I meant when I asked him if he thought it was fair, you know, the way he fired Alice, so I said to him, "Joe, suppose instead of the talk we are having now, I just came up to you today and said, 'Joe, you have stepped out of line once too often. This Alice Reed thing has worked its way up to Mr. Walton and he does not think you handled it properly. So you are fired. Gather up your stuff. We will mail you your checks.' Do you think that would be fair?" He said, "No," and I asked him again if he thought the way he fired Alice was fair. He said, "probably not." I told him that he had better start adhering to procedures and start thinking about the consequences of his actions, because if he were involved in any more incidents, Mr. Walton would really be down on his neck.

Walton: Well, it seems as though there has been a bending of procedure here as well as the possibility of prejudice. Both of which you chose to "let pass," Bill, probably in the belief that nothing would come of it. At any rate, Alice has called me and said that she feels that she was unjustly fired and that she wants to go back to work. What do you think ought to be done about it? Do we tell her, "Sorry, you were fired and that is the end of it"? Do we give her her old job back? Give her a job at "16" [plant no. 16 was located on the other side of the river in St. Paul], or what?

Carter: I think we ought to give her her old job back.

Thompson: You can't be serious, Jack! We already decided to work her out of the company! She is a "bad apple." What do we do, bring her back just to fire her again in three or four months? You know she would never shape up. And what about Joe? We cannot bring her back after he has shot off his mouth all over the plant about how he finally got rid of her.

Carter: The job was unjustifiably taken away from her. She has a right to go back to the exact same job. If it makes Joe look like a fool, too bad. He acted like one anyway. Besides, it would really make it tough for the union organizers.

Thompson: I just cannot see rubbing salt in a healing wound. The negative effects are not and will not be that serious, and we will not make the same mistake again. Besides, how do we know that she would take her old job back?

Carter: If she doesn't want it, we'll offer her a job at "16" at grade level no. 2.

Thompson: "16" is 15 miles away from "14." Alice does not have a car. And what if she does not want that, or anything else, to do with Scarbonie?

Walton: The pressure is on, gentlemen. This is a sensitive matter of employee rights, and it is complicated by the fact that Alice is black.

Commentaries ════════════════════════════════════

13. Volvo's Solution to the Blue-Collar Blues
Pehr Gyllenhammar

In Sweden, as in the United States, yesterday's accepted working conditions are today being rigorously questioned. People in our industries stay shorter and shorter lengths of time at their jobs. Absenteeism is increasing, while the number of people even applying for jobs in industry is decreasing.

There seems to be a correlation between satisfaction and low job turnover. We have noticed that where we have really changed the jobs and the job situation, the rate of turnover has decreased. In our truck plant, the turnover rate has been reduced from about 40 percent to about 10 percent. However, there seems to be less of a correlation between job satisfaction and absenteeism.

We know that many people have left their jobs at Volvo because of various strains imposed by society. Getting to the job often requires long commuting; those living in the big metropolitan areas find it increasingly difficult to make contact with other people; and there are inadequate resources for taking care of children. But we also know that quite a lot of people have been leaving us because they cannot find satisfaction in their jobs.

If Sweden is to enjoy economic growth in the future, we must solve the problem of making people want to work in industry. At Volvo we have given special attention to the question of job satisfaction.

It is our view that industrial work has to be adapted to man and not to the machine. We've acted on this by instituting the following job-enrichment concepts:

Source: Reprinted from *Business and Society Review,* no. 7 (Autumn 1973), pp. 50–53. Copyright 1973, Warren, Gorham, and Lamont, Inc., 210 South Street, Boston, Mass. All rights reserved.

Job rotation.
Management-employee councils.
Small work groups.
Employee-oriented facilities.

SHIFTING JOBS

Many of Volvo's employees participate in job rotation on a volun-tary basis. At our passenger car assembly plant in Gothenburg, for instance, approximately 1,400 of the 7,000 employees are involved. This means that they shift jobs according to a planned program, in which each employee is given both a physical and a psychological change in his job. Thus, not only does he experience a greater variety of tasks than before, but also he gains insight into the work of his coworkers. The job rotation schedule is drawn up by a group of employees led by a foreman.

The need for variety and interest, we believe, is related to a more basic need of employees. Each individual desires, and ought to have, an influence on his own work situation. We have been experimenting with participation in the decision-making process for quite a few years, and the results have been encouraging.

All industrial companies in Sweden with more than 50 employees are required to have work councils, which are mediums "for informa-tion and joint consultation between management and employees through their trade union organizations within the company." These councils work toward greater productivity and greater occupational satisfaction. The way they function in a particular plant may be illus-trated by Volvo's Gothenburg installation. At this plant we have, besides the ordinary local works council, 16 subcouncils, some of them covering manufacturing activities, and others covering staff units and product divisions.

This system of subcouncils and committees makes it possible for the local works council to deal with questions such as production and marketing surveys, investments, and financial reports. We also have a working committee within the local works council comprised of two representatives from management, four from the salaried staff, and three from the hourly wage workers.

At Gothenburg, there are a number of standing worker-manage-ment committees on different subjects, such as improvement propos-als, personnel policies, traffic, health, and safety. The right to arrive at operating decisions, within specified budgets, and to make awards for suggestions, is delegated to some of these committees.

Employee representation—or boards of directors for employees

—is another way in which Swedish workers are encouraged to participate in decision making. The Swedish government recently issued a draft act requiring joint stock companies to conform to legislation as to board representation for employees. Such companies, Volvo among them, now have employee members on their boards. Even before that, however, we were encouraging worker participation on our board. In 1971, Volvo invited its unions to nominate two employee representatives to follow the work of the board in an assistant capacity. One representative of the hourly wage workers and one representative of the salaried workers were selected. After a year's probationary period, all parties agreed to continue the plan, and at the annual meeting of shareholders in 1972 the two representatives were given full membership on the board.

THE TEAM SYSTEM

At the Volvo truck assembly plant in Gothenburg, we have also attempted to promote work satisfaction by introducing a group-oriented kind of job organization based on the team leader system. We began planning this new form in the late 1960s, and have systematically developed it since 1971. The aims of this system are to give the individual a greater say in decisions and to improve the spirited teamwork. At present, there are three to nine men in each leader group at the truck plant.

A vital part of the activities of the team system are the consultations which take place at least once a month to discuss the problems of the group. Participants in this meeting are the team spokesman, another member, a works supervisor, and an industrial engineer. These consultations often result in solutions, such as better tools, that would be impossible to achieve in any other way.

Each team covers a number of employees who have a job in common. The group appoints a team spokesman, who represents the group and keeps in touch with supervisors. This appointment rotates among the members of the group.

Each group is given a certain job to do in a certain amount of time—for example, preassembling brake valves, or drilling side parts of frames—and is paid for the overall result. The work involved is subdivided within the group by the members themselves. The team is responsible—within its phase of production—for the system used, the division of work, and the control procedures.

Introducing the team system meant introducing a new type of leadership. As we discovered, the transition to new ways of thinking about leadership is not easy for everyone. Suddenly we were telling a whole group of people that they were supposed to make their own decisions and influence their own situations. On the other hand, we had a core of foremen and leaders, trained according to the values of the 1950s and 1960s, who had to learn that all their striving to maintain or achieve a position as foreman is not really relevant today. They had to climb down, so to speak, and be part of the group that only yesterday they had led. Both the individual asked to take on new responsibility and the foreman asked to share his with a group have entirely new roles to play.

Since the workers themselves have taken over some of the responsibilities carried earlier by foremen, the latter are now able to undertake new, enlarged tasks involving more responsibility for production planning, and offering more time for personal contact with colleagues. We therefore have intensified our efforts in training and education.

The current and future staff of foremen and production technicians must also meet leadership requirements. This is ensured through continuous training in communication techniques, economy, personnel development, job management, and so forth.

A training section was established in 1969 for the introduction of fitters to work in the truck plant. Employment and introduction activities take about 130 hours and include information on work stations and work safety, together with practical training in special workshops and on the production lines. The training period is spread over the first 16 weeks of employment at Volvo. When a new member joins a group, it is awarded an "instructor's fee" as compensation for the training time required. After six months the employee is eligible for further upgrading.

Difficulties notwithstanding, the surveys we have conducted concerning attitudes of the employees involved in all our job enrichment activities have yielded predominantly positive results. Employees indicate that they are pleased with the greater variation and extent of their jobs, and that they feel a greater sense of teamwork, since they now have a better understanding of each other's work. They take greater satisfaction in their jobs.

CUSTOM-DESIGNED INTERIORS

As we experimented with these new methods of increasing job satisfaction, we realized that often the design of a plant itself can contribute to, or hinder, the implementation of new concepts. It would be better, we reasoned, to consider the needs of the workers first, and then design the plant accordingly. Now we have a chance to try out this theory. Our new thinking in matters concerning the organization of work will be represented in two new plants we are building, one at Kalmar, on the east coast of Sweden, and the other at Skövde, in the middle of the country.

Kalmar

The new car assembly plant at Kalmar will employ about 600 people and will cost approximately $22 million to complete. Production is estimated to begin during the first half of 1974; annual capacity will be 60,000 passenger cars.

The layout of the plant was designed to facilitate the use of work teams. The shape of the building has solved the problem of how to build small workshops into a large plant. The stores of assembly parts will be located in the center of the factory, and the various working teams will be grouped along the outside walls. Each team will have its own entrance, changing room, washroom, and break room.

Different teams will be responsible for different sections of the car, such as the electrical system, steering and controls, or brakes and wheels. Within a team, which will consist of 15 to 25 persons, the members will agree on how the work should be distributed and when and how it should be carried out. The team can vary its rate of work within certain limits; it might agree to work a little faster and then take a break. The members of the team can go to the break room and have a cup of coffee. From this room they can see their work bays so they will know when to return to work.

Assembly work will be organizable in two ways. Under one plan, a team would have stations connected in series, and two or three people at each station would be able to exchange jobs with each other. Workers would follow the body as it moves along the assembly line, and would carry out the jobs at each of the several stations. Under the other system, each working group of two to three persons would do one entire piece of work on each car body, which would remain stationary.

Skovde

The design of our other new facility, an engine plant to be completed at Skovde late this year, also shows the results of our concern for the work environment and job satisfaction. There will be extensively landscaped areas, as well as small annexes for pauses, conversation, and rest. The entire plant will have eye-level windows, which not only give good lighting but also provide contact with the natural surroundings.

Through increased mechanization and automation most of the heavy and monotonous work will be eliminated, so that each individual's job will have more of a supervisory and quality-control nature than previously. The various groups will each be responsible for job tasks such as control, maintenance, material handling, and tool changes. They will also have some responsibility for administrative planning and reporting procedures. As at Kalmar, the new system will provide for change in the work.

A REAWAKENING

Since people have a basic need to work in groups, to feel they belong, and to feel they are appreciated for the job they do, we will in the future—at both our old and our new plants—try to create groups wherever possible. We will endeavor to stimulate cohesion and to introduce more individual control over the work process. We will need to stress that the privilege of increased participation and influence over the work situation must be accompanied by a new sense of responsibility.

Creating job satisfaction does involve taking a risk with production technology. It will also cost the organization money and extra effort. But we hope that through our efforts we will regain our employees' lapsed enthusiasm for their jobs, and thereby lay the foundation for a renaissance in industrial work.

---

14. Job Inspectors Need Warrants, Top Court Rules
Carol H. Falk

WASHINGTON—The Supreme Court held that employers have a constitutional right to bar federal job safety inspectors from their workplaces if the inspectors aren't armed with search warrants.

The ruling appeared to be more a symbolic victory for opponents of

Source: *The Wall Street Journal*, May 24, 1978, pp. 2 and 33.

government regulation than either a crippling defeat for the much maligned Occupational Safety and Health Administration or a strong vindication of individual rights. Its primary effect seemed likely to be an increase in the time and resources the Labor Department agency will have to spend to follow more formal procedures in the future.

Although the court, in its five-to-three decision, said the agency doesn't have the right to make warrantless inspections, it also made warrants easy to get. OSHA can even retain the surprise element of its inspection program by getting warrants from a court in advance without notifying the employer, said Justice Byron White, writing for the majority.

JUSTIFYING A WARRANT

Under the court's ruling, all the inspector would have to show to justify a warrant is that a specific business had been chosen for a spot check on the basis of a general enforcement plan and wasn't being singled out for arbitrary reasons.

Dissenting, Justice John Stevens charged that the majority had misinterpreted the Fourth Amendment, which bars only "unreasonable" searches, and at the same time had weakened the amendment's provision that warrants should be issued only upon a finding of "probable cause." He was joined by Justices Harry Blackmun and William Rehnquist.

Justice William Brennan, who was ill when the case was argued, didn't participate in the decision.

OSHA chief Eula Bingham expressed hope that most businessmen would continue to consent to inspections without warrants. If they do, the agency's work could go on "pretty much as it has," she said at a news conference. OSHA then would have to obtain warrants only in the presumably occasional instances when employers insisted on them.

However, the agency might decide against risking that employers would cover up hazards while the warrant was being obtained. Inspectors then would have to obtain warrants in advance of all inspections, OSHA officials indicated. Mrs. Bingham added that although she didn't have any figures on how much it would cost the agency to comply with the court's decision, "it certainly will cost in terms of paperwork." Labor Department lawyer Benjamin Mintz said the ruling won't affect any citations based on past OSHA inspections for which search warrants weren't obtained. The decision allows a warrantless inspection with employer consent. "We have never forced our way in," he said.

A spokesman for the National Association of Manufacturers said the decision contained "mixed blessings." Forrest Rettgers, executive vice president of the trade group said, "The good news is that OSHA inspectors must be limited to the activity specified in the warrant in order to enter a plant, thus ruling out fishing expeditions. The bad news is that they needn't show probable cause, as in criminal cases, to secure the warrant."

The court's decision doesn't require any changes in the 1970 Job Safety Act itself but only in the way OSHA goes about enforcing it. Although Justice White pronounced the act "unconstitutional insofar as it purports to authorize inspections without warrant or its equivalent," he observed that the act doesn't "forbid the Secretary [of Labor] from proceeding to inspect only by warrant or other process.

The majority also asserted that the ruling doesn't necessarily mean that warrantless search provisions in other regulatory laws also are unconstitutional. The reasonableness of a warrantless search," Justice White said, "will depend upon the specific enforcement needs and privacy guarantees of each statute.

EXCEPTIONS TO REQUIREMENT

He noted that the court has previously approved exceptions to the warrant requirement for certain highly regulated industries, such as liquor and firearms. He added that some other federal inspection laws, covering mine safety and agricultural products, for instance, "already envision resort to federal court enforcement when entry is refused."

Justice Stevens, however, said he thought the decision "renders presumptively invalid" the inspection provisions in those other laws. He argued that the invalidated OSHA inspection program had required a court order when an inspector was denied entry.

OSHA regulations provide that when an employer refuses to permit an inspector on his property, the inspector is to report to his superior who, if necessary, will seek a court order compelling the employer to admit the inspector. OSHA had obtained such an order in the case that reached the Supreme Court, but F. G. Barlow, the Pocatello, Idaho, plumbing, heating and electrical contractor who brought the case, insisted that a search warrant was still required.

Justice White noted that the lower court, which also ruled against OSHA, didn't consider whether the order for inspection that was issued in the Barlow case, "was the functional equivalent of a warrant." He indicated that if such an order were found to satisfy the Fourth Amendment, a challenged inspection could proceed.

RELIANCE ON PAST RULINGS

The majority relied largely on past Supreme Court rulings that warrantless searches are "generally unreasonable" and that this rule applies to businesses as well as homes, and to civil as well as criminal investigations.

Justice White noted that employees aren't being prohibited by the court's ruling from reporting OSHA violations in their own workplace. But he insisted that the owner of a business hadn't "by the necessary utilization of employees in his operation, thrown open the areas where employees alone are permitted to the warrantless scrutiny of government agents."

Justice White added that the court was "unconvinced" that requiring warrants "will impose serious burdens on the inspection system or the courts." He reasoned that "the great majority of businessmen can be expected in normal course to consent to inspection without warrant," though he conceded that, the court's ruling "might itself have an impact on whether owners choose to resist requested searches."

The issuance of a warrant won't depend on "demonstrating probable cause to believe that conditions in violation of OSHA exist on the premises." Justice White emphasized, adding that "probable cause in the criminal law sense" isn't required for purposes of an "administrative search."

THE JUSTICE'S LAMENT

In his dissent, Justice Stevens lamented the relaxed standard for issuing warrants, contending that the framers of the Constitution were more concerned about abuses of the "general warrant" than about warrantless searches. He insisted that if "routine regulatory inspections of commercial premises" are valid, "it is because they comport with the ultimate reasonableness standard of the Fourth Amendment," even though they don't satisfy the usual probable cause standard.

He added that "requiring the inspection warrant . . . adds little in the way of protection to that already provided under the existing enforcement scheme."

The U.S. Chamber of Commerce, which along with the American Conservative Union, supported Mr. Barlow's challenge to the inspections, hailed the court's ruling. Chamber President Richard Lesher said that the business community "should be delighted with this blow for freedom."

Sen. Harrison Williams (D., N.J.), chairman of the Senate Human Resources Committee and a key author of OSHA, said he was "shocked." He added that "Congress will have to ensure that there are ways to provide America's workers with the protections they need and must have to combat the hazards they confront daily in the workplace.

United Auto Workers President Douglas Fraser called the decision "a bad one, considerably weakening a good law." He complained that the ruling "places, property rights of employers above the human rights of workers." Even under the present system, some companies use "subterfuge in efforts to avoid citation," Mr. Fraser charged. "If this occurs with unannounced inspections, in the time it takes the inspector to go from the front office to the plant floor, how often will it occur when employers have prior notice?" he asked.

---

15. Abusing Sex at the Office

It may be as subtle as a leer and a series of off-color jokes, or as direct as grabbing a woman's breast. It can be found in typing pools and factories, Army barracks and legislature suites, city rooms and college lecture halls. It is fundamentally a man's problem, an exercise of power almost analogous to rape, for which women pay with their jobs, and sometimes their health. It's as traditional as underpaying women—and now appears to be just as illegal. Sexual harassment, the boss's dirty little fringe benefit, has been dragged out of the closet.

Authorities can only guess how widespread sexual harassment on the job really is, but the number and nature of reported episodes form an ugly pattern. In Los Angeles, supermarket checker Hallie Edwards walked into a storeroom and found a manager exposing himself and groping for her breasts. After Edwards complained, the chain promoted her boss and transferred her. In Cambridge, Mass., college freshman Helene Sahadi York went to her Harvard professor's office looking for research help. She found an instructor determined to kiss her. In New York, typist Doreen Romano's boss offered her a raise if she would sleep with him. When she refused, he fired her. In each case, the women didn't ignore the incident. Edwards and Romano

---

Source: *Newsweek*, March 10, 1980, pp. 81 and 82. Copyright 1980, by Newsweek, Inc. All rights reserved.

won out-of-court money settlements; York's professor received a university reprimand. "Men are learning that women are not going to take this kind of behavior," says Romano's lawyer, Michael Krinsky.

What women are learning is how to fight back. They've sued, won judicial condemnations of a boys-will-be-boys attitude and convinced at least a few corporations that harassment in the workplace will cost them money. Women have opened counseling centers in major cities and their appearances on television shows in places like Boston and Dallas have prompted enormous viewer response. They've lobbied state legislatures, and they're monitoring federal agencies' threats to lift government contracts from offending companies or, perhaps worse, tie up corporations in protracted equal-employment litigation. "Women are realizing that harassment is a form of discrimination—and it's not O.K.," says San Francisco lawyer Judith Kurtz.

The increase in complaints parallels the upsurge in the number of women working outside the home. "You now have an extraordinary number of women coming into the work force," says Eleanor Holmes Norton, head of the Equal Employment Opportunity Commission. "They are not nearly as inclined to keep these things to themselves these days." Although many have entered the professional ranks, women, as a class, are still largely segregated into "pink collar" jobs—clerks, typists, waitresses—and usually work for a man. Their supervisors often have complete control over raises, promotions and other working conditions, and some treat sexual favors as just another badge of rank. When women reach supervisory level, they sometimes make the same sort of sexual demands on men. "The basic motivation behind it is not sex, it's power," says Georgia State University Prof. Jacqueline Boles, who is preparing a major study on the issue. "Sexual harassment is a lot like rape."

'ATMOSPHERE'

Still, sexual harassment remains difficult to define. Beyond the obvious lewd cases lies an uncharted area. What one woman may dismiss as innocent or manageable flirting may drive another to tranquilizers. In one study, women who felt sexually harassed reported suffering from headaches, nausea, and sleeplessness. "Harassment is not limited to grabbing and pinching," says Karen Sauvigné, program director of Working Women's Institute in New York, which has developed legal strategies for harassment cases. "It's also the atmosphere loaded with sexual innuendoes and jokes." Unsought verbal intimacy, she adds, "makes you feel horrible." For instance, one Atlanta secretary quit her last job after her boss and three other men watched as she locked a long row of filing cabinets and called out, "Isn't she a cutie?" The woman says simply, "They strip you of your dignity."

It is difficult for the law to be clear when the definition of the action remains so elusive. No federal statute specifically bans sexual harassment. Only Wisconsin has identified harassment in its antidiscrimination law; another ten states are considering the matter. So far, enforcement has come mainly from the courts. During the last five years, several federal judges have ruled that if sexual harassment costs women jobs or benefits, it violates Title VII of the 1964 Civil Rights Act, which prohibits sex discrimination in employment. Judges have ordered corporations to pay for lost wages and attorney's fees. "Employers realize that it costs money to allow sexual harassment," says Susan Blumenthal of the National Organization for Women's Legal Defense and Education Fund. "It's affecting them where they're most likely to change."

Even if they have legal recourse, however, victims have serious problems of proof. As in rape cases, women who bring complaints are often taunted with the suggestion that they invited the harassment. In hearings, one person's word against another's may not be enough. Sometimes, written evidence barely suffices. For more than a year, the boss of Cathy Peter, a 37-year-old secretary to a New Jersey school superintendent, repeatedly made passes at her. Because she needed the job, she did not complain. One day, he left a note on her desk describing the attributes of a good secretary. Among them: "neat appearance, slender in body and willing to go to bed with the boss, satisfaction guaranteed." Peter protested to the board of education, which dismissed her charges. Finally, Peter sued. The school board and the superintendent paid her a $14,000 settlement. The superintendent, who resigned after a similar incident with another woman, apologized in writing.

'WAR'

Under any circumstances, bringing a sexual-harassment lawsuit or complaint is emotionally demanding. "A woman has to realize she's declaring war," says Nadine Taub of Rutgers School of Law. Erin Sneed, an attorney for Women for Change, Inc., in Dallas, says, "When a woman comes to me with a good case, my advice is to get another job before you do anything, because you don't want to be blackballed." For Mary K. Heelan, who won a landmark Title VII suit against Johns-Manville, the battle grew very personal. Before the trial, lawyers for her former employer asked her to name all of her previous sexual partners. "It was a ploy to make me think about the awful things they could do to me in court," she says. "It gave me second thoughts."

The psychological drain can be particularly severe in a university. "There needs to be a relationship of trust and even intimacy between student and professor," says attorney Catherine A. MacKinnon, the author of "Sexual Harassment of Working Women" and a teacher at Yale. "Sexual harassment can destroy even the possibility of learning." Affairs between professors and students have long been the subject of campus jokes, but women aren't laughing anymore. Harvard, Yale, and the University of California, Berkeley, are among the institutions where formal charges have been filed. A lawsuit alleging that a Yale political science professor promised an "A" grade in return for sexual intercourse is now pending in federal appeals court.

One result of the new look at sexual harassment is the discovery that women are not the only victims. John[1], 32, married and a father, wanted to enroll in a federally funded training program. A higher-ranking single woman offered to guarantee his admission if he would sleep with her. He did, two or three times, and she provided the promised recommendation. But their relationship had other costs. "She made it very obvious in the office," John says. "She'd come over and say things like, 'I'm looking forward to tonight'." Hal, 31, a married federal bureaucrat, found that his new boss kept inviting him into her office where she would close the door and load the conversation with sexual innuendoes. After two months, she offered to become his sponsor in exchange for sex. "She was so blatant," he says now after transferring to another agency, "I felt like it was a reversal of a '40s movie and I was Betty Grable."

Hollywood's "casting couch" for a long time symbolized the mixture of sex and power in the workplace. Unquestionably, some young women—and men—still try to make their careers with their perfect bodies, and randy producers use professional clout to take advantage of them. "But it's more the exception than the rule now," says Norma Connolly, head of the Women's Committee of the Screen Actors Guild. Hollywood has taken clear steps to curtail sexual harassment. The guild has a watch-dog morals committee and a clause in SAG's industry contract forbids producers to ask actresses to interview in the nude.

No one believes that legalities will eliminate sexual harassment. "To do so places an unfair and totally unrealistic burden on women to come forward in an extremely difficult situation," says the EEOC's Norton. She and others contend that the answer lies in prevention:

---

[1] Men who recount such incidents feel too humiliated and "emasculated" to give their full names for publication.

employers should be educated to treat the workplace as a job and not as a singles bar. To encourage this, the EEOC is preparing guidelines for employers that are expected to parallel rules against racial discrimination. Says Norton, "You can't have one standard for racial epithets and another for sexual."

FAVORS

The Office of Federal Contract Compliance Programs has already circulated for comment its own rules for companies doing business with the government. The regulations would forbid company officials to base any personnel decisions on sexual favors. Firms that violate OFCCP guidelines may be stripped of sizable federal contracts. Many private employers have begun to get the message. Some have incorporated prohibitions against sexual harassment into equal-employment programs and have pledged to deal promptly with grievances. And last December, the federal Office of Personnel Management announced that the government itself would not condone sexual harassment.

For the moment, a woman's best response remains a firm, polite, nonthreatening, "No." That is particularly true for verbal harassment unconnected to professional favor. Even sensitive men, women say, often will engage in this kind of banter unaware that they are offensive. If the man persists, some feminists endorse the actions of a Colorado woman who tired of being patted on her rump. She wheeled around and purposefully grabbed her harasser by his genitals. He didn't bother her anymore.

CONSUMER WELFARE

Although many managers believed consumerism was a minority movement of self-appointed consumer representatives, the movement continued strong through the 1970s and into the 1980s. The Sentry Life Insurance Company national study on consumerism concluded in 1978 that "The consumer movement is here to stay, and in fact, is growing stronger. . . . Leadership groups and consumers alike think that many different industries and services are doing a poor job in serving consumers. . . . The business community is sharply out of step with the American public on consumerism issues."[1] These findings, coming at a time when American businesses were delivering the highest standard of living in the history of mankind, represented a serious indictment. Clearly, the Sentry study suggests that the business/consumer relationship required dramatic improvement in the 1980s in order for business to receive continued support from consumers.

The findings of the Sentry study were extended in 1980 by a review of five research efforts which compared manager's and consumer opinions on consumer issues.[2] The Stanley and Robinson study concluded that:

---

[1] "Consumerism at the Crossroads: A National Opinion Research Survey of Public, Activist, Business and Regulator Attitudes Toward the Consumer Movement," conducted for Sentry Insurance by Louis Harris and Associates, Inc. and the Marketing Science Institute, pp. iv–v (undated).

[2] Thomas J. Stanley and Larry M. Robinson, "Opinions on Consumer Issues: A Review of Recent Studies of Executives and Consumers," *Journal of Consumer Affairs,* Summer 1980, pp. 207–220.

1. The opinion research reviewed suggests significant differences between consumers and business.
2. A large number of consumers disagree with executives about the adequacy of current levels of product quality and safety.
3. Consumer lack of confidence in advertising is widespread and seems to be growing.
4. Executives believe that consumers have adequate levels of product information, while most consumers want more information.
5. There is a wide and increasing difference of opinion between consumers and executives about corporations' concern for consumers.
6. Consumers and executives differ greatly on the need for additional government regulation as a means of solving consumer problems, with consumers preferring more and business people preferring less.
7. Consumer discontent appears to be persisting on many of the dimensions considered.

These conclusions echo earlier findings. For instance, Barksdale and Darden, in the first national study of attitudes about consumerism, concluded that business had a responsibility" . . . to increase the attention given to consumer problems and initiate programs that will improve customer relations. If businessmen do not voluntarily respond to consumer problems and complaints, they may be faced with further government control through legislation."[3]

The business/consumer/government relationship is quite complex, characterized by a great deal of emotion on many issues and generally a paucity of useful research data. The heterogeneity of consumer needs, expectations, and evaluative skills makes it difficult to generalize about consumer problems. Suggested below is one framework for grouping consumer issues.

Perhaps the most visible set of consumer welfare issues concerns the disclosure of information to customers and potential customers. Marketers control product information at three levels: advertising, packaging and labeling, and retail sales effort. There are important consumer welfare issues at each of these points.

1. *Advertising.* Issues related to advertising include false and deceptive advertising, the extent to which advertising influences social values, the aesthetic content of ads, the propriety of advertising directed at children, propriety of advertising by the professions, and appropriate controls on testimonials. The responses to

[3] Hiram C. Barksdale and William R. Darden, "Consumer Attitudes Toward Marketing and Consumerism," *Journal of Marketing*, vol. 35, no. 3 (October 1971), p. 36.

these issues have included attempts at self-regulation and a variety of legislative and regulatory efforts at local, state, and federal levels.

2. *Packaging and labeling.*   Consumers desire point-of-sale information which clearly and quickly provides information important to a purchase decision. One could make a long list of information items that some consumers would need some of the time for some products. Arguments could be made about the costs and benefits associated with each item. The trend in packaging and labeling is toward higher levels of information disclosure. The Truth-in-Packaging Act of 1966 had a major impact by standardizing sizes and language on many labels. However, the act required only voluntary compliance, a feature which prompted Ralph Nader to call it "the most deceptive package of all." Subsequently, other developments to increase disclosure have included: warranty simplification legislation, nutritional labeling, shelf life expiration dating, and improvements in labeling of hazardous substances and flammable clothing.

As just one example of attempts to increase disclosure requirements, the Food and Drug Administration, U.S. Department of Agriculture, and the Federal Trade Commission began, in early 1978, to review the hundreds of regulations which governed the labeling of foods. The results of the hearings, as shown in one of the commentaries, included 30 recommended changes in labeling regulations, all intended to increase levels of information disclosure.

3. *Retail sales effort.*   Information issues at this level include high pressure sales tactics such as bait-and-switch and lo-balling. Also sales tactics directed at vulnerable groups, such as funeral services for the bereaved and burial insurance for the poor, came under intense scrutiny by regulators in the late 1970s.

A second set of consumer welfare issues relate to product design, use, and post-sale service. The issues include the social desirability of products, quality, safety, environmental issues, choice, and adequacy of consumer redress mechanisms.

1. *Social desirability.*   Some group or groups in society may be opposed to a product, often on emotional bases without objective data. For instance, Chelsea, an adult-soft drink introduced by Anheuser-Busch, was condemned by consumer activists as contributing to teenage alcoholism.[4] On the same issue, Malcolm

---

[4] Keith M. Jones, "Chelsea: The Adult Soft Drink: A Case Study of Corporate Social Responsibility," *Journal of Contemporary Business*, vol. 7, no. 4, pp. 69–76.

Hereford's Cows, a line of milk-flavored packaged cocktails introduced by Heublein, Inc., was criticized in the media by Betty Furness and others.[5]

2. *Product quality.*   The reliability,[6] service life, and maintenance needs of a particular product are of some consequence to most consumers. The frequency and severity of product malfunctions can often be a source of considerable consumer frustration. Consumers generally have expectations about useful service life and the costs of maintenance. Issues arise whenever expectations, however unrealistic, are not met.

Product warranties are of special interest to many consumers. The central issue concerns the responsibilities of marketers to consumers with respect to product durability and reliability. Many marketers have simplified warranty language and expanded warranty coverage in conformance to stipulations of the Magnusson-Moss Act of 1975. Still, some marketers were charged with "secret warranties" whereby persistent consumers could get warranty coverage for unexpected product failures beyond the stipulated warranty coverage.[7]

Another set of product quality issues relates to imitation products. Inflation and technology have combined to produce frozen cheese pizzas without cheese, candy bars without chocolate coverings, and lemon meringue pies without lemon or meringue as ingredients. Aside from the question of safety, should there be limits on the amount and types of substitute ingredients permitted in foods?

3. *Product safety.*   The trend in product safety, as in many other issue areas of consumer welfare, has been toward ever higher requirements placed on manufacturers. The Pinto case examined in one of the commentaries focuses on this issue. While everyone is in favor of safe products, the difficult issue involves the trade-off in costs and benefits from increased levels of safety. As one thoughtful analysis has shown, the social costs to insure 100 percent safety may be far more than society is willing to pay.[8]

[5] "Heublein, Inc." in Roy D. Adler, Larry M. Robinson, and Jan E. Carlson, *Marketing and Society: Cases and Commentaries* (Englewood Cliffs, New Jersey: Prentice-Hall, Inc., 1981).

[6] Defined as the probability of the product functioning as intended. Reliability of .99 would indicate that 99 times out of 100, the product would perform correctly.

[7] For an example, see A. I. Schutzer, "My Long Fight to Collect Under VW's 'Secret Warranty,'" *Medical Economics,* June 11, 1979, pp. 133–148 *passim.*

[8] Walter Guzzardi, Jr., "The Mindless Pursuit of Safety," *Fortune,* vol. 99, no. 7 (April 9, 1979), pp. 54–64 *passim.*

4. *Environmental issues.*   Many manmade materials are not found in nature and thus are not fully recyclable according to natural processes. Nonbiodegradable materials include aluminum, mercury, glass, and automobile tires. For instance, aluminum cans and nonreturnable bottles received much attention in the late 1970s and early 1980s because many observers considered the materials to be environmentally harmful. As a second example, fluorocarbon propellants used in many aerosol sprays were found to accumulate in the ozone structure. Accordingly, many marketers faced increasing pressures to replace fluorocarbons with another material which would not harm the environment.[9]

5. *Product choice.*   At a time when the marketplace features more products than ever before, some observers challenge whether consumers have adequate product choice. One of the several issues in the "shared monopoly" antitrust suit against four major cereal manufacturers focused on whether the proliferation of brands produced meaningful product choice alternatives for consumers.

6. *Consumer redress mechanisms.*   There are many consumer grievances. Products do not always function properly and service is often less than adequate. Therefore, many consumer goods companies have attempted to improve customer communications via such mechanisms as hotlines, arbitration, and adaptation of the Scandinavian concept of the ombudsman. These mechanisms have not been totally satisfactory, as an increase in small claims court cases and class action activity attest.

Many companies have recognized the need to improve consumer grievance procedures. During the 1970s, the customer relations function was expanded and elevated by many companies to not only resolve complaints, but to assure representation of consumer welfare interests in corporate decisions which affected customers.

The commentaries at the end of this section present differing views on the role of government in consumer protection. The editorials also suggest that the marketplace is an increasingly complex entity and that "Consumers Aren't All Angels Either." The two cases in this section highlight several of the issues outlined above. Philips Roxane Laboratories, Inc. is a primary case on the issue of antisubstitution

---

[9] For details, see Jeffrey A. Tannenbaum, "The Ozone Issue: Fluorocarbon Battle Expected to Heat Up As the Regulators Move Beyond Aerosols," *The Wall Street Journal,* January 19, 1978, p. 38.

laws in the pharmaceutical industry. The inability of pharmacists, by law, to substitute generic drugs for brand name drugs was viewed by proponents of substitution laws as contrary to the consumer interest. The GMC Truck and Coach Division case considers the issue of school bus safety, including competitive, legal, and school bus operator perspectives.

Case ═══════════════════════════════════════

PHILIPS ROXANE LABORATORIES, INC.

On May 6, 1975, Gerald C. Wojta (pronounced Why-ta), president of Philips Roxane Laboratories, Inc. of Columbus, Ohio, flew to Sacramento, California, to deliver testimony before the California Senate. The speech he gave was similar to one which he had presented before the Michigan Senate in April 1974. In both appearances he spoke in support of the repeal of the state's antisubstitution regulations and in support of pharmacist drug product selection. In giving this testimony he stood almost alone among the drug manufacturers in the United States. The Pharmaceutical Manufacturers Association (PMA), of which Philips Roxane was a member, had come out strongly opposed to the repeal of antisubstitution laws. Mr. Wojta had come under pressure and criticism from other drug manufacturers. He had received several letters and phone calls from other manufacturers who had been unhappy with his stand.

DRUG PRODUCT SELECTION

Drugs had been used for the treatment of disease in man since the beginning of time. The pharmacy profession also dated back to very early times and had generally been responsible for the manufacture of most drugs. The practice of pharmacist-made medications started to decline during the 1920s and 1930s. Drug companies had started to mass-produce pharmaceutical products. As manufacturers extended their distribution and promotion nationwide, the Federal Food and Drug Administration (FDA) began to regulate and set standards for the industry. During the 1930s, the drug manufacturers invested

large sums of money in the research and development of new drugs.
As these products were discovered they were patented, given a brand
name, and then were promoted to the physicians by this brand name.

All drugs had three names which led to a cumbersome nomencla-
ture arrangement. Every drug had a chemical name, like D-threo-(-)-
1-p-nitro-phenyl-2-dichloroacetamido-1, 3-propanediol, which was
assigned by the government and reflected its chemical formula. This
same drug was then given a generic name—in the above example,
chloramphenicol—also by the government. This generic name was
usually the one found in drug studies and textbooks, used in government bids, and was used by the medical schools in their courses
on drugs. This generic name could be used by any manufacturer of
the drug, providing patent laws did not restrict its manufacture to one
source. Where patent laws covered a drug product, usually the company having the rights gave the drug a third, or brand name. For the
above cited drug it was Chloromycetin®. Once a patent had expired
after 17 years, anyone meeting FDA regulations could manufacture
and market the product under the generic name, or give it yet another
different brand name. Because of the laxness in the standards set by
the FDA in the 1940s, which allowed poor manufacturing techniques
to continue, and the unscrupulousness of some pharmacists in using
or making counterfeit products, the drug industry and physicians had
antisubstitution regulations passed in all states.

These regulations held not only that the physician could choose
the drug product needed, a right with which no pharmacist would
argue, but also that he could choose the specific brand or manufacturer. Then the pharmacist could not substitute another brand or
manufacturer without first contacting the physician. If the physician
wrote for the drug by the chemical or generic name, then the pharmacist could use his discretion in selecting the specific brand. With the
enactment of these laws in the 1940s, the brand name-oriented drug
industry was born. The rationale for passing and maintaining the
laws had been the assurance of quality which a brand name denoted.

THE PHARMACY PROFESSION

The profession of pharmacy had been, by and large, silent on the
drug product selection issue until 1971. In 1971, a movement was
started by Dr. William S. Apple, executive director of the American
Pharmaceutical Association (A.Ph.A.) to allow the brand choice to be
reinstated to the pharmacist. The A.Ph.A. was the national association of pharmacists, representing all facets of pharmacy practice. It
had over 48,000 members in the early 1970s and had been the driving

force in most pharmacy legislation actions at the national as well as the state levels. Not all the members had been in support of the association's stand. Notwithstanding some members' apprehensions, the association voiced its opinions. The A.Ph.A. position stated that pharmacists were better trained to make the product selection once the physician had decided on what drug was needed. It stressed the five-year educational requirement for pharmacists which had not existed when the antisubstitution laws had been passed. The point was made that pharmacists in hospitals had been making drug product selections for years without any apparent problems. The position stressed the economic savings to the patient if the selections were made by the pharmacists. Because of the national inflation problem present in the early 1970s, the cost savings argument had been picked up by various activist consumer groups who supported the idea based on its reduction of health care costs. The A.Ph.A. position also anticipated upcoming government regulations which would limit the amount the government would pay for drugs in government-funded programs.

With the exception of support from the consumer groups, the A.Ph.A. found itself alone in its stand. The American Medical Association, the Pharmaceutical Manufacturers Association, and even the National Association of Retail Druggists all responded negatively to the A.Ph.A. stand. By 1974, only two states, Michigan and Kentucky, had repealed the antisubstitution laws. Both had been hotly debated issues and had generated nationwide interest. In 1975, more states started to seek the antisubstitution repeal, and by April, Arkansas and Minnesota had repealed the legislation. Minnesota's bill passed both houses of the legislature without one dissenting vote. By June of 1975, Ohio, Oregon, and California had begun to look into the issue.

THE INDUSTRY

The ethical drug industry supplied a $6.4 billion market in 1974. Ethical drugs were those drugs which were sold only by prescription as opposed to the over-the-counter, or proprietary drugs, which did not need a prescription. Many manufacturers were involved in the production of both classes of drugs. During this period, the ethical drug market was dominated by 26 or so companies which comprised 80–90 percent of the annual sales. The market was not monopolistic, but some senators and economists considered it to be oligopolistic even though there were many large companies. It was estimated that 70 percent of the industry's sales were generated by single-source or patent-protected products. Industry sales had increased by substantial amounts each year since World War II. The industry's profits were the highest of all American industries in 1970 through 1973, and were second only to petroleum in 1974. Exact industry figures were hard to determine because of the diversity of the drug manufacturers and their large numbers.

The Pharmaceutical Manufacturers Association (PMA) was an association of 115 drug manufacturers. It served as an industry spokesman and was considered the lobbying voice of the drug manufacturers. In the mid-1970s several congressional committees began to investigate the drug industry and recommended sweeping changes. The PMA went to the hearings to defend the industry's positions. Senators Edward Kennedy (D., Mass.) and Gaylord Nelson (D., Wis.) conducted separate hearings into the drug industry.

Senator Nelson attacked the industry's high profits. The PMA cited the economic necessity of substantial profits because of the high risks involved in drug research. The PMA also countered the senator by citing the relatively small increase in the consumer price index for drugs. It showed that drug prices had increased only 1.7 percent from 1970 to 1974 as opposed to a 30 percent increase in all health care costs during the same period. The PMA cited this small increase as a sign of the responsiveness of the industry to a need for lower health care costs.

Senator Kennedy focused much of his attention on the drug promotional system which had evolved. The drug industry spent from $500 million to $1 billion in 1974 for the promotion of their products to the prescribers. To this end, there were over 21,000 company salesmen, or detailmen as they were called, calling on the country's prescribers. Senator Kennedy attacked the numbers involved, their apparent lack of standardization, and the uncontrolled use of samples by these detailmen. The PMA countered by endorsing a certification program. The certification program would ensure a minimal level of knowledge and competency among the salesmen, most of whom were not pharmacists. The program would be administered by the colleges of pharmacy under guidelines established by the government. The PMA was not willing to interfere in what each company had decided would be its sampling policy or sales staff size.

One of the biggest problems the industry faced in 1975 was its pricing policies. A Council on Economic Priorities study on antibiotics released in 1975 (Appendix 1) showed the wide discrepancy of prices for one product which had no basis in the economic cost of producing the drug. The study, by comparing several antibiotics, showed that several products were made by one or two manufacturers and marketed by other companies under many names at a wide range of prices. The study also pointed out that a sharp price decline occurred when the patent expired on a product and many suppliers could then enter the market (Appendix 2). PMA answered this survey by citing the differences in manufacturing techniques and the federal price-fixing regulations which had promulgated variances in pricing.

The industry was also under attack for its various pricing schedules. Some companies had as many as 12 different prices for the same product, depending upon who the customer was. In 1974, the Portland Retail Druggists Association (PRDA) brought suit against 12 major manufacturers because of their preferential pricing policies which favored hospitals over retail pharmacies. This purported violation of the Robinson-Patman Act was vigorously denied by the companies and the PMA. The PRDA group obtained a reversal of a lower court ruling against them, and the final outcome of the issue would probably be tied up in the courts for some years. On top of all these problems the industry also had to face the antisubstitution issue.

The PMA position on antisubstitution held that only the physician was in a position to determine what specific drug product should be administered to which patient. It also contended that current FDA regulations were not stringent enough to ensure that all generically alike products were truly alike therapeutically and had the same bioequivalency. Bioequivalency had been a new word developed to describe the ability of a drug, made by two or more manufacturers, to pass from the gastrointestinal tract into the bloodstream and achieve the same blood levels. The bioequivalency of the drug could be altered by the size of the tablet, force used in tablet compression, binders used in making the tablet, tablet coatings, and so forth. The bioequivalency issue had become a major concern because of the PMA. To this latter end, the PMA embarked on a massive physician and pharmacy advertising program to try and get grass roots support for their position (Appendix 3).

There were two other problems which would confront the drug industry if drug product selection were to revert to the pharmacist in all states. Since the 1930s, the drug companies had been directing their selling efforts to the physicians and had virtually neglected the pharmacist. With a change in the practitioner selecting the final dosage form, the drug companies would have to redirect all, or most, of their marketing efforts. Second, many of the patent-protected drugs—as high as 50 percent of them—were to be removed from patent protection by 1980. With this lowering of the single-product market to possibly 30 percent of the total market, as opposed to the 70 percent held in 1975, great uncertainty would be introduced into all the drug companies' projections and plans.

THE COMPANY

Philips Roxane Laboratories was one of 30 different companies of the North American Phillips Corporation. This conglomerate had sales in 1974 of $1.5 billion with net profits of $80 million. It was associated with N. V. Phillips Company of The Netherlands, *who allowed all decisions to be made in the United States*. North American Phillips was very diversified, as reflected by its electrical electronic products (Magnavox), professional equipment (P.M.S.I.), consumer products and services (Norelco), and chemical/pharmaceutical products. Many of the company's products were trademarked, and the company had been active in the support and promotion of branded merchandise.

Philips Roxane Laboratories, Inc., was formed in 1960 when N. A. Phillips purchased the Columbus Pharmacal Company. It was to be the only N. A. Phillips subsidiary in the drug field. Columbus Pharmacal was doing less than $1 million a year in sales and sold primarily to dispensing physicians. Dispensing physicians were doctors who sold drugs to their patients instead of writing prescriptions and having pharmacists fill them. Most pharmacists felt that the physicians should write prescriptions for the medication needs of their patients and were not very favorably disposed toward the companies like Columbus Pharmacal that sold to dispensing physicians. In fact, most pharmacists did not use the products sold by such companies.

Mr. Wojta had been hired as sales manager for the newly renamed drug company. He had a wide and varied background in a retail pharmacy, as a drug salesman, and as the sales manager for Dorsey Laboratories, another drug manufacturer. He became president of Philips Roxane in four years.

As sales manager he had found himself confronted with the following circumstances. His drug company had no patented products; there was a limited research and development department; the firm was virtually unknown in the hospital market and in the retail market. Since it would take years to develop a significant research and development department—at great cost—Mr. Wojta decided to concentrate on the manufacturing of drugs whose patents had expired and to emphasize the hospital market. He felt the hospital market could provide the greatest opportunity for penetration because the hospital pharmacist had greater drug product selection authority than did his retail counterpart. Almost all hospitals had pharmacy and therapeutic committees which determined which drugs would be stocked in the pharmacy. The final drug brand selection was left to the pharmacist. Any physician having staff privileges in the hospital had to sign his approval of accepting whatever brand had been stocked by the pharmacy. Because of the preconsent authority, the pharmacy generally stocked one item of each drug type and this item was usually bought on a bid basis. By directing his sales efforts toward the hospitals, Mr. Wojta felt that he could not only sell his products, but the orders would be larger. Further, he only needed a relatively small sales force.

In the mid-1960s, a new form of drug distribution, called unit dose, came into use. This system was devised to eliminate medication errors in hospitals. Its use soon spread to many large and small hospitals. As nursing homes and extended care facilities began to increase because of Medicare legislation, it was found that these institutions also had a drug distribution problem which unit dose could satisfy. Most could not afford an in-house pharmacist but had to parcel out the pharmacy services to a nearby retail pharmacy or to a hospital, if affiliated. In these extended care facilities there were fewer nurses and other professionals, and closer controls on drugs were mandated.

In a unit dose system, each individual capsule or tablet was packaged and identified. The patients' medication needs were dispensed at the pharmacy, by the day or week depending on the system, and were administered at the institution. Each patient's medication was set up for the time when it was to be given. The person giving the drug had merely to give the medication specified by the pharmacy with each dose of drug identified and packaged. There were fewer chances for error, greater compliance, less nursing time taken, and there were no problems with returns. Unit dose expanded quickly in the late 1960s and most manufacturers started to package individually some of their products. Mr. Wojta saw an opportunity in this area and began offering all the products Philips Roxane produced in unit dose. Philips Roxane was first to offer any liquids in packaging. This action cemented Philips Roxane's position in the institutional market, but it also opened the opportunity for sales to pharmacies which serviced nursing homes. (See Exhibit 1.)

Also, during this time the Philips Roxane research and development staff was able to develop rubeola and rubella vaccine and three other specialty products. They had also begun to work with the National Cancer Institute to develop oral dosage forms of drugs which were being used in cancer treatment.

Philips Roxane employed just over 200 employees by the mid-1970s. It was a nonunion shop and management was very active in its commitment to socially responsive issues. It supported equal opportunity programs for nonwhites and women. It had a 21 percent nonwhite work force which corresponded favorably with the nonwhite population of the city. It also employed almost 50 percent females and had females in management positions. Mr. Wojta was concerned about his employees' welfare and had been described as a shirt-

EXHIBIT 1
Philips Roxane's Channels of Distribution

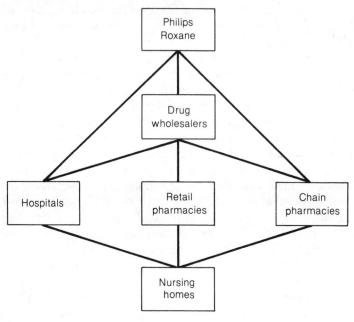

sleeve, grass roots president by one of his employees. Morale and productivity at Philip Roxane were described as exceptionally high.

Sales volume and profits had been on the increase since the very beginning in 1960.[1]

	1960	1965	1970	1974
Net sales, less than	$1,000,000	$2,500,000	$6,000,000	$12,000,000
Net profits, less than	100,000	250,000	280,000	720,000

By 1974, Philips Roxane had begun to saturate the hospital and nursing home market where pharmacists had drug product selection in 40–60 percent of the items. Philips Roxane had approximately 20 detailmen calling on all the major hospitals in the United States. Purchases were made by the hospitals through local wholesalers who stocked Philips Roxane products, or items were purchased directly from Philips Roxane on a bid basis. Therefore, Philips Roxane had been selling directly and through wholesalers. By 1974, the company was also selling some major chains on a direct basis but had no detailmen calling on the general trade. During 1975, the hospital market accounted for about 30 percent of the total drug market.

---

[1] Estimates made by author.

If Philips Roxane, or any other manufacturers of generic drugs, were to make significant inroads into the retail drug market, it would only be after the drug product selection decision had reverted to the pharmacist. By 1974, Mr. Wojta had decided to support the A.Ph.A. stand on antisubstitution repeal. He personally attended pharmaceutical meetings and conventions; he gave generously to the national and state pharmaceutical associations; he increased his journal advertising; and he was soon considered an enlightened pharmaceutical manufacturer by many pharmacists and pharmacy leaders. His company literature stressed: (1) product development; (2) quality assurance; (3) reasonable price; and (4) support of the pharmacist.

Philips Roxane had a very simple marketing approach. The company made all nonpatented drugs for which there was a very sizable market and entered the field with a competitive price (see *Alliance* in Appendix 1). Philips Roxane planned to continue with a research and development function and patent new products as they were developed. However, the largest factor which had evolved was the drug product selection stand. Mr. Wojta had "put his cards on the table" by actively speaking out for pharmacist drug product selection. He wondered if the risk he was assuming was a sound one or if his company would suffer as a result.

APPENDIX 1
Tetracycline Hydrochloride Suppliers (major dosage form 250 mg; package size 1,000 capsules)

Firm name	Brand	Price	Code
American Quinine	—	4.12	t
Sherry	—	7.45	r
Moore Drug Export	—	8.40	r
Interstate	—	8.50	r
Wolins	—	8.67	t
Midway Medical	—	8.95	r
United Research Laboratories	—	9.09	t
Approved Pharmacal	—	9.90	r
Penhurst Pharmacal	—	9.95	r
Arcum	—	10.00	r
Bluco	—	10.50	r
Premo	—	10.66	r
Rondex	—	10.80	t
Zenith	—	11.19	r
ICN	—	11.25	r
Westwood	—	11.50	r

Key: Rank is by price to drug stores.

Code: "r" indicates this is published wholesale price in 1974 *Red Book*, and sales were not significant. "t" indicates average transaction price to drug stores computed by CEP from IMS data, and that average wholesale price is higher. "s" indicates significant sales.

Source: Paul A. Brooke, *Resistant Prices: A Study of Competitive Strains in the Antibiotic Markets* (New York: Council on Economic Priorities, 1975), pp. 73–74.

APPENDIX 1 *(continued)*

Firm name	Brand	Price	Code
Pharmecon	—	11.95	r
Geneva Generics	—	11.95	r
American Laboratories	—	11.95	r
Stayner	—	12.00	r
Bell Pharmacal	—	12.05	r
Columbia Medical	—	12.50	r
Cenci	—	12.75	r
Sheraton	—	12.95	r
Purepac	—	13.00	t
Alliance (Philips Roxane)	—	**13.33**	t
Towne Paulsen	—	13.57	t
Robinson	—	13.60	r
Canfield	—	13.75	r
Richlyn	—	14.00	r
Ulmer	—	14.25	r
Rexall	Rexamycin	14.57	t
Pharmex	—	14.95	r
First Texas	—	16.47	r
Roerig (Pfizer)	Tetracyn	16.87	ts
Rachelle	Tetrachel	17.39	t
Jenkins	—	17.50	r
Barry Martin	—	18.00	r
Bristol	Bristacycline	18.18	ts
McKesson	Kesso-Tetra	18.55	ts
Parke-Davis	Cyclopar	18.75	ts
Sterimco	—	19.00	r
Lannett Co.	—	19.80	r
Barre	—	20.30	r
Bowman	—	21.50	r
Central Pharmacal	Centet-250	22.00	r
Mallinckrodt	QID-Tet	22.00	r
Robins	Robitet	22.40	ts
Squibb	Sumycin	22.70	ts
Upjohn	Panmyclin	23.04	ts
Moore-Kirk	—	23.70	r
Dow	—	24.37	r
Rowell	Ro-cycline	27.00	r
SmithKline	SK-Tetracycline	26.82	ts
Paul Elder	T-250	27.00	r
Lederle	Acromycin V	27.59	ts
Rand	Tetra-MZX	29.90	r
Zemmer	Zemycin	30.00	r
Del Ray	Ala-tet	30.00	t
Coastal Pharmacal	Tetra-co	34.00	t
Winston	Teline	35.00	r
Tracy Pharmacal	—	37.50	r
Amid	Amtet	39.60	r
Metro-Medical	Tet-cy	40.00	r
RPH	Retet	50.00	r

APPENDIX 2
Absolute Published Price Declines (all prices for 250 mg/100 capsules/tablets)

Firm/Brand	Date Introduced	Price								
		1955	1957	1960	1963	1966	1969	1971	1972	1974
Erythromycin										
Abbott/Erythrocin	1954	33.42	30.60	30.60	21.99	21.99	21.99	21.99	21.99	14.99
Upjohn/E-Mycin	1968						21.99	16.49	16.49	13.35
Lilly/Ilotycin	1952	30.60	30.60	30.60	21.99	21.99	21.99	21.99	16.49	14.84
Lowest priced product										5.70
Lilly/Ilosone*	1958			30.60	21.99	21.99	21.99	21.99	21.99	19.80
Tetracycline hydrochloride										
Teteracyn/Roerig	n.a.	30.60	30.60	30.60	26.01	17.60	4.25	4.25	4.25	3.25
Upjohn/Panmycin	1954		35.70	35.70	21.00	17.58	7.89	3.94	3.94	3.94
Bristol/Bristacycline	n.a.			30.60	n.l.	17.74	14.95	4.17	4.17	4.17
Squibb/Sumycin	1957			30.60	22.00	22.57	4.25	4.25	n.l.	3.75
Lederle/Achromycin V	1957			30.60	22.00	17.60	11.22	n.l.	4.50	4.50
Rachelle/Tetrachel	n.a.					6.80	4.20	3.70	3.55	2.85
Lowest priced product										1.90
Pfizer/Terramycin*	1950	30.60	30.60	30.60	22.00	19.80	17.80	17.80	17.80	18.10
Potassium phenoxymethyl penicillin										
Abbott/Composillin VK	1957			28.90	18.42	18.42	8.95	8.95	8.95	8.95
Lilly/V-Cillin-K	1957			30.00†	18.42	14.46	8.95	8.95	8.95	8.95
Lowest priced product										1.85

* Patented products.
† Based on $7.20/24.
n.l. = Not listed in *Red Book*.
n.a. = Not available.

Source: Paul A. Brooke, *Resistant Prices: A Study of Competitive Strains in the Antibiotic Markets* (New York, Council on Economic Priorities, 1975), p. 28.

Bioequivalence

protecting the integrity of your prescription

the weight of scientific opinion:

If the pharmacist substituted a chemically equivalent drug for the one you have specified for your patient—could you be certain of that product's safety and effectiveness simply because the chemical content was the same?

Definitely not, unless bio-equivalence tests and other quality assurance checks had been conducted. The pharmaceutical industry and many scientists have maintained this position for years, but others have questioned it. Now the Office of Technology Assessment of the Congress of the United States has reported on the issue in its Drug Bioequivalence Study.*

Here are a few definitive statements in the O.T.A. report:

"... the problem of bioinequivalency in chemically equivalent products is a real one. Since the studies in which lack of bioequivalence was demonstrated involved marketed products that met current compendial standards, these documented instances constitute unequivocal evidence that neither the present standards for testing the finished product nor the specifications for materials, manufacturing process, and controls are adequate to ensure that ostensibly equivalent drug products are, in fact, equivalent in bioavailability.

"While these therapeutic failures resulting from problems of bioavailability were recognized and well documented, it is entirely possible that other therapeutic failures and/or instances of toxicity that had a similar basis have escaped attention."

The Pharmaceutical Manufacturers Association supports federal legislative amendments that would require manufacturers of duplicate prescription pharmaceutical products, subject to new drug procedures, to document:

(a) chemical equivalence, and

(b) biological equivalence, where bioavailability test methods have been validated as a reliable means of assuring clinical equivalence; or (c) where such validation is not possible, therapeutic equivalence.

In addition, the PMA supports federal legislation that would require certification of all manufacturers of prescription products before they could start in business, annual inspections and certification thereafter, and strict adherence to FDA regulations on good manufacturing practices.

The overall quality of the United States drug supply is excellent. But only a total quality assurance program, envisaged in these and other policy positions adopted by the PMA Board of Directors in 1974, can bring about acceptable levels of performance by all prescription drug manufacturers and thereby assure the integrity of your prescription.

Pharmaceutical Manufacturers
Association
1155 Fifteenth Street, N.W.
Washington, D.C. 20005

*Copies of the complete report on Drug Bioequivalence may be obtained from the Superintendent of Documents, U.S. Government Printing Office, Washington, D.C. 20402.

Case ═══════════════════════════════

GMC TRUCK AND COACH DIVISION

In late 1969, a two-part series of articles appeared in the *Washington Post* concerning one owner's mechanical problems with three new GMC-chassied school buses. Written by Colman McCarthy, a member of the editorial page staff, the articles opened the larger question of school bus safety.

The owner involved was John Donovan, an independent operator in the Washington area, whose drivers transported about 260 children every day to several Washington private schools for an annual fee of about $200 per student. Mr. Donovan claimed to have spent 225 hours trying to resolve what he called unsafe conditions with the buses, and the buses were not yet four months old. Mr. Donovan's problems had started on September 2, 1969, when he and two other drivers picked up the buses in High Point, North Carolina, and were forced to make at least 12 stops for repairs on the way back. Three days later, two of the three buses failed state safety inspections. It was then that Mr. Donovan began keeping a diary of the time spent repairing the buses or taking them to the dealer to be repaired. According to Mr. Donovan, the subsequent three months were the most " . . . frustrating, nightmarish period in my life. Caring for the buses—to keep them safe for the kids who ride them—so dictates my life that nearly everything else is blocked out."[1]

A partial list of the malfunctioning or broken equipment included excessive oil consumption and leakage, gasoline leakage, tires which

---

[1] Colman McCarthy, "Three GMC School Buses and One Man's Ordeal," *The Washington Post*, December 15, 1969, p. A20.

would not hold proper air pressure, loose exhaust hangers, broken motor mounts, burned clutches, and rattling transmissions. Mr. Donovan claimed to have talked with at least five other owners who had similar problems with the same GMC V–6 model bus.

In a summary portion of the first *Washington Post* article, Mr. Donovan was described as being " . . . convinced that General Motors has not been adequately concerned about him or his buses. Nor does the U.S. Government appear to be much concerned about the safety of school children . . . "[2] The second article explained how Mr. Donovan had begun to get action. Assuming that "no major corporation like GMC would knowingly sell unsafe goods to the public," Mr. Donovan was "overwhelmed by not knowing which of the many GMC buttons he should press for relief."[3]

Mr. Donovan finally talked to a newsman who then made several inquiries. Within a day or so, Mr. Donovan received a telephone call from a high GMC official in Pontiac, Michigan, who said that two engineers were being flown in to make things right. That same evening, three local GMC representatives were in Mr. Donovan's apartment discussing his problems with him. Two days later, Kimball Firestone, grandson of the founder of the rubber company, offered to replace all 18 tires on Mr. Donovan's buses.

Virginia Knauer, a presidential assistant for consumer affairs, referred to Mr. Donovan's problems in a Philadelphia speech two weeks later. "If these problems exist on a national basis," she stated, "then there is no question that action should be taken on this matter immediately."[4] The second *Washington Post* article questioned whether other owners of GM products "have to talk to a newsman before action is taken" and concluded with a plea for action regarding school bus safety to "avoid a tragedy before it happens."[5]

The effect of these articles on General Motors and the effectiveness of the corporation's response can best be determined with further background regarding school bus production and safety records.

BACKGROUND ON PRODUCTION

The production of school bus chassis was a miniscule part of General Motors' total domestic business. GM would produce about 4.4 million cars in 1969, and the Truck and Coach Division would pro-

---

[2] Ibid.

[3] Colman McCarthy, "Troubled School Bus Operator Begins to 'Get Action,'" *The Washington Post*, December 22, 1969, p. A16.

[4] Ibid.

[5] Ibid.

duce an additional 834,000 trucks of all types.[6] School bus chassis were only a slightly modified truck chassis, and the 4,000 or so that would become school buses were included in this total.[7]

The entire market for school buses was not large. About 25,000 to 30,000 new buses were purchased every year, usually by school boards who almost always purchased from the lowest bidder. This buying procedure tended to restrict engineering and safety research, as models carrying additional research and development costs would inevitably be higher priced relative to competition. The purchase of school buses was complicated by the fact that the bus bodies were built by independent manufacturers, and the buyer actually bought the bus from distributors for the body maker. Mechanical maintenance was performed by designated dealers for the chassis maker.

There were six major body makers in the United States: Superior (the largest, selling about 8,000 units per year), Wayne, Ward, Carpenter, Bluebird, and Thomas.[8] Most of these manufacturers had plants located in the southern states. Mr. Donovan's buses, for example, were picked up at the Thomas factory in North Carolina. These constructors would place their bodies on whatever chassis the customer specified. The most popular chassis was International Harvester, because it was the cheapest. General Motors' share of the chassis market fluctuated between 12 and 20 percent annually.

BACKGROUND ON SAFETY

The singling out of school buses as unsafe vehicles was puzzling to many industry observers, who knew that about 25 school children had been killed while passengers in school buses in 1969. Compared with an automobile death rate of 2.4 per 100 million miles in 1968, the school bus rate was only 0.06 per 100 million miles, or 40 times safer.[9] If passenger-miles were compared, the difference would be even more dramatic.

There were good reasons why school buses had compiled such an impressive safety record. They were large and very visible to other drivers. They generally operated at much slower speeds than other vehicles at other than peak accident times. They were rarely operated at night. What accidents there were usually were attributed to driver error. School bus drivers worked inconvenient hours at low pay.

---

[6] *Ward's 1971 Automotive Yearbook* (Detroit: Ward's Communications, 1971), pp. 80–81, 84.

[7] *The Wall Street Journal,* December 23, 1969, p. 8.

[8] Estimate based on personal communication with knowledgeable industry sources.

[9] *Iron Age,* vol. 207, no. 18 (May 6, 1971), p. 23.

Occasional outbursts by unruly students made working conditions very unpleasant at times. As a result, it was hard to find experienced drivers, and housewives and juveniles were pressed into service. Some states were so desperate for drivers that a "special license" to operate a school bus was granted to persons who had not qualified for a regular driver's license![10]

The high incidence of driver error meant that no more than about a half-dozen deaths per year could be attributed to mechanical malfunctions. Even minimal safety modifications would raise the cost of new school buses at least five percent.[11] Given an average year's production, the total cost of these improvements would be somewhere around $12 million, and these improvements would protect only those students riding *new* buses. If children's lives could be quantified in dollars and cents, then an average of one life could be saved by the total $12 million annual expenditure.[12]

SAFETY AND MR. DONOVAN'S SPECIFIC PROBLEMS

It was apparent to GM officials that some of the problems reported by Mr. Donovan, such as the alleged 12 stops for repairs he made getting his buses home, were the result of inadequate dealer preparation. Other problems were annoyances that were probably manufacturing shortcomings. None were, in GM's view, safety related. More correctly stated, almost *any* vehicular deficiency could be seen in some context to be safety related. Wind noise, or thinly padded seats, for example, could be seen to contribute to driver fatigue and could therefore be a safety hazard. The safety-relatedness of problems outlined in the initial articles could be placed in perspective as follows:

1. The brake hose which was rubbing the wheel drag line may have been worn through by repeated rubbing, but would *not* have caused the brakes to fail, as alleged. The buses involved had dual brake systems and automatic warning lights to prevent the complete loss of stopping ability.
2. The oil and gas leaks (which were fixed by the dealer a month before the article appeared) were wasteful but not hazardous.
3. The tires which allegedly did not hold their full air pressure were warranted by Firestone, not GM.
4. Exhaust pipe hangers and exhaust fittings in general had been a

---

[10] Floyd Miller, "Bus Crash," *The Reader's Digest,* June 1973, p. 248.

[11] *McCall's,* September 1974, pp. 50–51.

[12] A 5 percent increase in cost would be about $400 per bus. For 30,000 buses per year, the total is $12 million. The average bus life is about six years, so that only about one sixth of the children to be saved would be riding in and protected by new buses.

continuing problem for fleet operators of all types of equipment for decades, because of the extreme vibration to which very long exhaust pipes were subjected.[13] Customer maintenance personnel often rigged their own solutions to this problem. The danger of carbon monoxide poisoning through any exhaust failure was extremely remote.

5.   Clutch wear had historically been extremely sensitive to driver technique. Repeated failure was almost always due to riding or slipping the clutch on a constant basis. Even a severely burned out clutch would not be a safety problem, as it would only preclude the use of full power.

6.   Transmission "rattle" was unpleasant, but bus chassis were built to be simple and rugged, not necessarily smooth and quiet.

Perhaps the most convincing argument regarding the safety-relatedness of these problems was that not one of them was known to have caused an accident or near accident.

ALTERNATIVE RESPONSES

One possible corporate response to the school bus safety issue would be to make no statement and take no special action whatsoever. This would be likely to reinforce the impression of cold, uncaring management at GM that was the theme of the original articles. A second approach would be to take no special action but reply with the type of cost-benefit analysis developed earlier. This plan would open GM to the charge of placing a dollar value on innocent lives. Either of these approaches was especially troublesome, as the children of congressmen and diplomats were among those who rode in Mr. Donovan's buses.

The most aggressive approach would be to recall[14] a number of the 1969 buses in order to inspect and, if necessary, fix the kinds of problems alleged to be occurring. GM had recalled about 10,450, 1967 and 1968 school buses in mid-March in order to replace a rubber seal that would allow brake fluid to leak under unusual braking conditions. Although there had been no deaths or injuries from failure of this part, GM airmailed the parts to all their distributors with instructions that the parts be hand-delivered to dealers.[15] About a

---

[13] *Fleet Owner*, vol. 65, no. 4 (April 1970), p. 187.

[14] A recall involves the identification of a suspected problem common to a specific run of vehicles, and the contacting of the owners of those vehicles to offer inspection and/or repair of the suspected problem at company expense. Most recalls in 1969 were initiated by the manufacturers involved.

[15] *The Wall Street Journal*, March 19, 1969, p. 5.

month later, the same buses were recalled when more than one seal was found to be involved.[16] One drawback of recent recall campaigns was that they were expensive and had been treated in the press not as responsible actions of concerned manufacturers, but as admissions of wrongdoing by the manufacturers.

ACTION TAKEN

On December 22, the second and final article appeared in *The Washington Post*. That same day, Martin Caserio, General Motors vice president and general manager of the Truck and Coach Division, attended a joint press conference in Washington with Joseph Clark, head of the Defects Review Division of the Transportation Department's National Highway Safety Bureau. Mr. Clark said that the bureau had been investigating the complaints for 11 days and would continue the investigations until safety questions were resolved. Mr. Caserio announced that the company was sampling owners of 1969 model buses to determine how widespread the complaints were. He reiterated that GM did not feel that any of the existing defects were safety related, but would recall them for repair if necessary.

Mr. Caserio further disclosed that GM had been inspecting all school buses off its production line for a little more than a year and that dealers also inspected for defects. He then added that, "We think they [the inspections] did work," but if there was correctional work to be done, "we'll step up to our responsibility." Virginia Knauer, President Nixon's Special Assistant for Consumer Affairs, told newsmen that she had been assured by GM President Edward Cole of the company's intention to recall the buses if GM's investigation showed it to be advisable.[17]

In mid-February, the results of the GM survey of 850 of the 4,000 owners of 1969 GM-built chassis were available. Mr. Caserio disclosed in a letter to Virginia Knauer that some of the same problems reported earlier had become apparent, especially those regarding tail pipe hangers, clutch durability, and front brake hoses. He also announced that GM had placed a resident inspector at each plant where bus bodies were mounted on GM chassis.[18] Four days later, GM announced the recall of 4,269, 1968 and 1969 buses for installation of new brake hose retaining springs in order to prevent the possibility of brake line chafing which could result in the loss of hydraulic brake fluid. GM added that it had received no reports of accidents attributa-

---

[16] *The Wall Street Journal*, April 18, 1969, p. 14.
[17] *The Wall Street Journal*, December 23, 1969, p. 8.
[18] *The Wall Street Journal*, February 16, 1970, p. 8.

ble to the problem and that the buses involved had dual brake systems and automatic warning signals to prevent the complete loss of stopping ability if the brake line were worn through.[19]

On July 11, new GM board chairman James Roche talked about corporate communications with consumers:

> We've had warranty policies and believe we've had a pretty responsible record, but like so many other things a better job can always be done. Had we not been able to satisfy our customers reasonably well over the years, in a business such as ours where we depend for a large percentage of our business on repeat customers, we wouldn't be in the position that we're in today. But there are new standards by which people are evaluating products, and it is incumbent on us, if we're going to compete in this business, to meet those expectations.[20]

One month later, GM's third recall of school buses for brake repair since March 1969 was undertaken. More than 10,000 school buses built during 1969 and 1970 were involved. The problem involved the possible distortion of a brake master cylinder reservoir cover by excessive tightening. The defect had been picked up in a manufacturing check, and no accidents or consumer complaints had been involved.[21]

That same month, the National Transportation Safety Board concluded that the construction of school bus bodies encouraged "shearing" in an accident. "Shearing" left knifelike "cookie cutter" edges of sheet metal that contributed to death and injury. The board recommended that manufacturers set rivets closer together, through guidelines specified by the National Education Association.[22]

General Motors agreed to a further recall urged by the Department of Transportation in January 1971. About 9,600, 1967 through 1969 school buses were recalled to modify clutch parts. While disagreeing with a government conclusion that "all parts of the clutch control linkage" were subject to failure, GM said that " . . . we feel it is better to call back the vehicles to modify them to eliminate even the most remote chance of having school children injured in an accident."[23]

In May, about 1,700, 1970 and 1971 V-6 engined school buses were recalled for inspection or replacement of throttle parts. No accidents had been reported due to failure of the part.[24] About 900 rear-engined school buses and 19,000 trucks built in 1960 through 1965 were re-

[19] *The Wall Street Journal,* February 20, 1970, p. 5.
[20] *Business Week,* July 11, 1970, pp. 72–73.
[21] *The Wall Street Journal,* August 11, 1970, p. 7.
[22] *The Wall Street Journal,* August 27, 1970, p. 2.
[23] *The Wall Street Journal,* January 25, 1971, p. 6.
[24] *The Wall Street Journal,* May 17, 1971, p. 4.

called the following month for installation of a clutch and flywheel replacement kit. According to the National Highway Traffic Safety Administration, the recall was voluntary on the part of GM. Observers estimated the cost of the campaign at up to $4 million.[25]

On March 11, 1972, the *Saturday Review* published an expanded version of the John Donovan story written by the original *Washington Post* reporter.[26] The tone of the article, which was subsequently published as part of a book on corporate irresponsibility,[27] was captured in the following paragraph:

> Down the line of corporate responsibility, someone had those thoughts about cheapening the exhausts and mounts, someone seconded those thoughts, and someone else carried them out. Death and injury resulted, and surely GM regrets it. Yet millions of dollars of the $22 billion profit resulted also, and it is not likely that GM has regrets about that.[28]

The article also revealed how some information was gathered from GM officials in interview situations. The three GMC officials who met in Mr. Donovan's apartment, for example, were evidently not aware until the meeting was nearly concluded that Colman McCarthy, who was sitting in on the conversation, was a *Washington Post* reporter.[29] Mr. McCarthy, however, claimed to have clearly stated that he was a *Washington Post* writer immediately upon being introduced. Mrs. Donovan sat in another room during the conversation, making notes in shorthand.[30]

Two weeks after the *Saturday Review* article was published, a train hit a school bus near Nyack, New York, killing five children. Although neither mechanical failure nor a GM chassis was involved, the accident focused attention on school bus safety.

The eighth GM bus recall since early 1969 was announced the following month. The power steering units of 2,500, 1963 through 1965 buses were to be checked for metal cracks.[31]

In the summer of 1972, emphasis on governmental regulation of

---

[25] *The Wall Street Journal*, June 11, 1971, p. 10.

[26] Colman McCarthy, "The Faulty School Buses," *Saturday Review*, March 11, 1972, pp. 50–56.

[27] Robert L. Heilbroner, *In the Name of Profit: Profiles in Corporate Greed* (Garden City, N.Y.: Doubleday & Co., 1972).

[28] Colman McCarthy, "The Faulty School Buses," p. 51. The $22 billion profit figure cited is cumulative profit from 1947 to 1969. According to the 1969 General Motors *Annual Report*, total sales for the year were $24.3 billion and net income was $1.7 billion.

[29] Ibid., p. 55.

[30] Ibid., p. 54.

[31] *The Wall Street Journal*, April 14, 1972, p. 16.

bus safety standards intensified. The Department of Transportation required each state to form an agency for pupil transportation,[32] and issued new safety standards regarding windows and emergency exits to go into effect in September 1973.[33] Senator Jacob Javits (R., N.Y.)[34] and Representative Les Aspin (D., Wis.)[35] introduced bills authorizing the establishment of extended safety requirements.

In September, the National Transportation Safety Board urged that the structural strength of school bus bodies be increased. One analysis indicated that the specifications would require joints five times as strong as those currently used.[36] Earlier that month, General Motors had unveiled a "safety bus" in *Life* magazine. The bus featured a top emergency exit, special padded seats, and a dramatically downsloping hood to aid driver visibility at school bus stops.[37] The Wayne Corporation unveiled the "Lifeguard" bus in April 1973, claiming that it had spent four years and millions of dollars in its development. Special features included five rather than 33 separate outside panels, special seats, larger emergency windows, guardrails, and a larger windshield.[38]

By September 1974, the Wayne bus had been joined on the market by Ward's "Safety Bus," which featured three times the usual number of fastening rivets. Each sold for about 5 percent more than ordinary buses.[39] In addition, instrumented crash test results involving multiple impacts on a Superior bus of standard construction were reported. The $300,000 program undertaken at Superior's expense by an independent testing agency revealed that, after multiple impacts, no penetration into the passenger area, no significant panel separation, and no "cookie cutter" edges were apparent. Seats remained anchored, and no other specific dangers were identified.[40]

NOTE

In June 1976, the base price for a 60-passenger, Superior-bodied, GMC-chassied school bus meeting Ohio state safety standards was

[32] *The Wall Street Journal,* May 10, 1972, p. 12.

[33] *Automotive Industries,* vol. 146, no. 12 (June 15, 1972), p. 86.

[34] *1972 Congressional Quarterly Almanac,* p. 928.

[35] *Automotive Industries,* vol. 147, no. 4 (August 15, 1972), p. 66.

[36] *The Wall Street Journal,* September 25, 1972, p. 28.

[37] *Life,* September 8, 1972, p. 63.

[38] *Fleet Owner,* vol. 68, no. 4 (April 1972), p. 50.

[39] *McCall's,* September 1974, pp. 50–51.

[40] *Automotive Industries,* vol. 151, no. 6 (September 15, 1974), pp. 62–63.

about $12,500. That price did not include heater and defroster, electric signs, or other options. On October 26, 1976, new federal safety standards regarding rupture-proof gasoline tanks, offset seating, emergency side door provisions, and special padded seats were to go into effect. These standards would decrease the capacity of the same basic unit from 60 to 48 passengers and increase the price to about $15,500 per unit.

Commentaries

16. Deregulation Is Another Consumer Fraud
Ralph Nader and Mark Green

A consumer fraud, which in its ultimate impact may trivialize the
deeds of the Robert Vesco's of the world by comparison, is sweeping
the business world. There is a widespread publicity campaign, in
which President Ford seems to be a willing cheerleader, aimed at
confusing wasteful cartel regulation with lifesaving consumer protection regulation.

Directing their broadside indiscriminately at "government regulation," business proponents invariably confuse the two and invariably
conclude that it is consumer regulation which must be curtailed.

Government regulation, to be sure, can inefficiently and irration-
ally worsen inflation.

Rate-setting, entry restrictions, merger permissiveness, technology frustration, political interference, delays, data deprivation, and
incessant business pressure at such agencies as the Civil Aeronautics
Board, Federal Communications Commission, and Interstate Commerce Commission cost consumers between $16 billion and $24 billion annually in waste and overcharges, as we have previously
pointed out.

This is why we wrote seven business trade groups to ask them to
join us in an effort to restore competition and deregulate cartel regulation; only one even replied and none shared our concern for the
regulatory violation of the much-touted free enterprise system.

It is, however, not such cartel regulation but consumer protection
regulation which businessmen today attack—although the distinction
between the two could not be more clear. Cartel regulation replaces
workable competition with government-approved price-fixing (un-

Source: *The New York Times,* June 29, 1975, Sec. 3, p. 14. © 1975 by The New York
Times Company. Reprinted by permission.

less there are bona fide natural monopolies present, economic competition should be allowed to work where it can work). Consumer protection regulation, on the other hand, protects the consumer where the marketplace either cannot or will not.

A traveler can compare the prices of taking a plane or bus between Washington and New York City, and arrive at a choice without the need of a CAB or an ICC. But can consumers smell carbon monoxide seeping into a car, detect that the drug they are giving their children is mutagenic, or taste the cancerous pesticides that went into the production of their food? Or can they refuse to breathe the air pollution given off by local steel mills?

Hence a National Highway Traffic Safety Administration, Food and Drug Administration, and Environmental Protection Agency establish health and safety standards to control such product defects and what economists call "externalities"—cost of production imposed on society but not reflected in product price.

The failure to understand or articulate the distinction between the two types of regulation can perhaps be traced to the fact that cartel regulation is to the profit of producers while consumer regulation benefits consumers.

However adroitly business deregulators drape their arguments in the toga of the public interest, they are engaged in vested-interest advocacy; their line of reasoning is their bottom line. And given the well-documented insensitivity of business to consumer health and safety, their suggestions about consumer regulation are ironic if not presumptuous.

Consider the auto industry. It is perhaps predictable that the companies would blame regulation for problems that are really self-inflicted—the industry's own insistence on large, expensive, fuel-wasting cars invited foreign models to capture a 22 percent share of the market—but the facts do not support their propaganda.

While auto officials fail to emphasize the extent to which regulation can reduce highway casualties and pollution-bred disease, they assert the following: gasoline mileage cannot increase 40 percent over the next four years unless emission and safety standards are relaxed; mandatory five-mile-per-hour frontal crash bumpers add unnecessary weight to the car; $800 to $900 price increases are attributable to "inflation and the large costs of government-mandated equipment."

Yet three government agencies have issued reports documenting that a 40 to 60 percent gain in fuel economy is easily obtainable by 1980 without cutting back on emission and safety standards. Tough bumper standards can save consumers billions of dollars in lower repair costs alone, and need not lead to the 150 pound bumpers with which domestic auto concerns saddle their cars, as foreign manufacturers have proven. Finally, even auto industry price data show the cost of all federal auto regulations for the nine-year period, 1967–1975, to be only $408 per car and, excluding profit, probably near $250.

As Volvo wrote the General Accounting Office last spring, most of the data released by U.S. auto makers on the cost of federal regulation have been biased and "aimed purely at resisting regulation."

Not only should the government maintain vigilant regulation in autos—and drugs too—but, also, regulation should expand into important but neglected areas of consumer health and safety.

For one, a range of carcinogenic toxic substances—trichloroethane, mercury, asbestos, vinyl chloride, and others—has been found in factories and surrounding areas with increased frequency, yet safety testing for these materials often does not occur before sale. Toxic substances legislation is needed to require safety testing and to give the EPA authority to control chemicals if danger is demonstrated.

Then again, the $7 billion cosmetics industry is of increasing concern to toxicologists as its products become more complex. Studies of hexaclorophene in talcum powder, and zirconium in deodorants, are examples of this concern. The Food and Drug Administration has authority to ban such products if it has evidence of their hazards, but usually no one is required to even test these cosmetics, much less produce such evidence.

And there is the fact that a 1972 General Accounting Office study found that about 40 percent of food manufacturing plants were operating under unsanitary conditions—rodent excreta, insect infestation, and pesticides would be found in close proximity to food processing areas. Yet food plants are rarely inspected by the FDA, and inspectors lack access to plant records showing health-related plant problems—limitations which legislation could easily correct.

In conclusion, as the debate over regulation widens, and as we approach President Ford's "regulatory summit" on July 9, it is essential to avoid the conceptual confusion among regulation which should end, regulation which should continue, and new regulation which is needed.

Where the competitive market can provide diverse and competitively priced products—in air and surface transportation rates, for example—deregulation is appropriate.

But where the consumer stands exposed to the kind of technological violence that the marketplace alone cannot contain—sharp protrusions on a dashboard, DDT, radioactive materials, asbestos fibers dumped into our lakes—then government regulation is a humane sine qua non for the public safety.

(If anything, existing regulation must be made more efficient. As of

ten years after the passage of the 1962 drug amendments, the FDA
had taken no action on 2,300 of the 2,800 drugs found to be ineffective
by the National Academy of Sciences.)

In the short run, some product prices may increase slightly to
"internalize" the costs of reduced pollution and hazards; but in the
short and long run, such regulation can save society billions of dollars
in reduced property damage and health costs. Would-be business
deregulators spotlight the former yet ignore the latter.

Thus, the problem with agencies like the NHTSA and EPA is not
that they exist but that they don't perform their missions well
enough. For them to live up to their potential requires the creation of
a consumer protection agency to ensure that existing regulators at
least hear both sides of important business and consumer issues. And
it requires a zealous commitment to principles of fairness and honesty
which benefit not only consumers but also honest business people.

In addition to the obvious need for better appointments, adequate
staffs and streamlined procedures, an agenda for regulatory reform
would include:

Openness of proceedings, avoidance of ex parte contracts at the
commissioner level or the logging of outside contracts.

Citizen standing to file lawsuits, and the provision of attorneys'
fees, when plaintiffs prevail, in order to compel fulfillment of
statutory requirements by ineffective agencies.

Funding systems, such as the $1 million that has been authorized
for the Federal Trade Commission to encourage interested but
impecunious citizens to participate in regulatory activities.

Adequate and innovative sanctions for violation of agency rules or
regulations, and personal sanctions on regulators who themselves demonstrably neglect or flout their statutory obligations.

Strict deadlines, with appropriate penalties, for lawyers and their
respondents who often have an incentive to systematically slow
down proceedings.

Annual reports on the extent of compliance with agency rules by
regulated companies.

The provision of adequate powers—subpoena power—for an
agency to conduct its assigned business.

President Ford, however, neither mentions such an agenda for
consumer regulation nor for that matter, even addresses consumer
groups about their problems. Instead, he tells a business group, in
language far more akin to Herbert Hoover than to his hero Harry
Truman, that regulation is based on "radical social theories that
would collectivize American society and American life."

With such a careless analysis of cartel regulation and consumer protection regulation prevailing in the executive branch, serious and discriminating regulatory reform, if it is to come at all, must be initiated at the other end of Pennsylvania Avenue.

---

17. Consumers Aren't All Angels Either
Rose DeWolf

Oh, I know whose side I'm on . . . I'm a consumer. I bow to no one in my antagonism to useless warranties, fraudulent claims, garbled instructions, hidden flaws, and ridiculous computers which threaten to have me arrested if I don't pay $0.00 right away. If I feel affronted, I can holler for Ralph Nader as loud as anyone.

And yet . . .

Every once in a while, much as I try to fight it, I feel a twinge of sympathy for merchants, manufacturers, and providers of service. Every once in a while, though I feel like a traitor, I want to jump up and say: "You know, consumers can be pretty rotten, too."

Consumers are not all angels. They include in their numbers those who would quite cheerfully cheat, steal, lie, and/or behave with incredible stupidity. There, I've said it and I'm glad.

Take the "switchers," for example. Those are the people who take the price tag from a cheap item and put it on an expensive item before taking the expensive item to the salesclerk. They hope the clerk will be too busy to notice and will sell the goods at a "bargain" price the store hadn't really counted on.

Switchers are everywhere. I once saw this very dignified-looking gentleman craftily switch the lids on a jar of peanuts and a jar of cashews. The prices, you see, were stamped on the lids. The man intended to buy his cashews, quite literally, for "peanuts."

And I have seen a dear little housewife slip a pound of butter into an oleomargarine box, assuming that the check-out clerk would never check. She assumed wrong. All check-out clerks know that trick.

One time I merely mentioned the word "consumer" to a friend of mine who works for a supermarket and the poor guy went bananas. (On special, that week.)

"Consumers!" he wailed. "I'll tell you about consumers. They buy magazines, take them home and read them, then return them for a

---

Source: *DuPont Context*, no. 1 (1973), pp. 9–10. Published by the DuPont Company.

refund claiming their husband bought duplicates . . . they demand to get five cents back on the five-cents-back coupon without buying the product first . . . they finish off bars of candy or bottles of soda while they walk through the store and then don't mention it when it comes time to pay . . . "

Did you know that baby food manufacturers deliberately seal their jars so they'll open with a loud "POP." That, says my friend, is so that a consumer who gets a jar that opens only with a little "poof" knows it has been opened before. Seems some mothers want to taste the food at the store to make sure little junior will like it, but then don't want to buy the jar they tasted.

Do you know why most cereal manufacturers don't give away prizes in the cereal boxes anymore? That's because so many women used to pry open the package, snitch the prize, and leave the unsalable torn box on the shelf. Nowadays, if you want to get that super-spy ring your kid has been crying for, you have to buy the box, clip the coupon, and send 25 cents in coin.

Suburban stores tell of women who "buy" a fancy dress on the Friday just before the Country Club dance and then return it ("I just changed my mind.") on Monday. They get indignant if the clerk says the dress looks as if it had been worn.

There are those who carry on loudly when the billing computer makes a mistake and claims they owe a bill they know they don't owe—but keep awfully quiet when the computer gives them credit they know they don't deserve. That makes it tougher for the store to straighten out the error.

Don't we all know people who brag how they got the "whole car fixed" on the insurance of the guy who merely dented a fender?

My local laundryman claims that if he ever loses a shirt (Heaven forbid), it invariably turns out to be (a) "very expensive, and (b) "just purchased."

"How come I never lose last year's cheap shirt?" he asks. "No. Those are the ones I manage to return. Right?" He is skeptical.

There are, of course, those who cheat the stores even more forthrightly. Shoplifting is at an all-time high. Do you know why manufacturers often pack such little items as batteries, pencils, and razor blades in plastic bubbles attached to huge pieces of cardboard? That's because the cardboard is larger than the average consumer's pocket where many batteries, pencils, and razor blades used to just disappear.

People who deal with consumers sometimes lose patience with them not because the consumers are greedy or dishonest but because they sometimes simply cause problems for themselves.

A local weights and measures inspector told me of pulling a surprise raid on a local butcher shop where the butcher was suspected of resting his elbow on the scale while weighing meat. Did the consumers appreciate the inspector's arrival? They did not.

"They were angry because it was close to dinner time. They started yelling at me," the inspector said. "They said I was holding them up . . . they had to get home to start cooking. They called me a city hall drone. They said I was annoying the butcher who was their friend. Some friend!"

Consumers can be funny. Recently, a spokesman for a national meat canning company told a convention of food editors that consumers persist in sending an open can of meat back to the company to illustrate whatever complaint they're making. The fact is, that after days of travel in the unrefrigerated mail, the product *always* looks awful and smells worse. How can the company possibly tell if the complaint was justified in the first place?

Consumers complain about high food prices and then insist on buying every convenience food on the market. They yell about too loud commercials and then don't buy the products advertised on soft ones.

The government says motorists will be safer if their cars buzz until the safety belts are fastened. But car buyers by the hordes are threatening dealers with mayhem unless the buzzers are unhooked. (The dealers are prohibited by law from complying.)

Consumers are just not always happy with what is being done *for* them. Frankly, I have to admit that *I* was a lot happier before packages of hot dogs had to admit right out in public they they contain ground-up cow's lips. Yechh. Do we have to know *everything?*

I'm not trying to say that the fact that the consumer can be, in his turn, greedy, dishonest, unappreciative, and just plain stupid, in any way excuses commercial interests for being the same. As my mother used to say, "Two wrongs don't make a right."

Still, fair is fair and somebody had to speak out. And now that I have gotten that out of the way, I can get to all these complaint letters I'm preparing for Ralph, and Virginia, and my local office of Consumer Affairs.

18. Saccharin: Now Sweet 'n' Safe?
Matt Clark with Mary Hager

If all the scientific papers, editorials and reports written about saccharin were laid end to end they would reach from Madison Avenue to the Mayo Clinic. Few medical issues have been subjected to so much scrutiny. The controversy began in 1977 when a Canadian study showed that rats fed large amounts of the artificial sweetener got bladder cancer. But a steady stream of subsequent reports questioned whether sacharin poses a serious risk for humans. Last week, two new studies strongly suggest that, for the average user, saccharin is probably safe.

The latest investigations were classic "case control" studies. Dr. Alan S. Morrison and Julie E. Buring of the Harvard School of Public Health compared the dietary habits of 600 patients suffering from cancer of the bladder or urinary tract with nearly as many people without cancer. Drs. Ernst L. Wynder and Steven D. Stellman of the American Health Foundation in New York queried 367 cancer victims and an equal number of healthy controls. By comparing the level of use of artificial sweeteners between cases and controls, the researchers could work out the relative risk, if any, of cancer.

Neither study found a significant relationship between saccharin and cancer. Overall, the Harvard survey found the risk of bladder cancer for sweetener users to be no more than 10 percent higher than for nonusers. Even long-term or heavy consumption of sweeteners showed no "consistent" evidence that sweeteners are carcinogenic. For long-term women users, the risk was slightly higher, but for men it was actually lower. "As a group, users of artificial sweeteners have little or no excess risk of cancer of the lower urinary tract," Morrison and Buring wrote in the New England Journal of Medicine. Wynder and Stellman, reporting in the journal Science, arrived at the same conclusion.

CANCER

Last week's reports are slightly at variance with a large study carried out earlier by the National Cancer Institute. The NCI study, involving 3,000 bladder-cancer patients, showed no overall increased

Source: *Newsweek*, March 17, 1980, p. 102. Copyright 1980, by Newsweek, Inc. All rights reserved.

risk from artificial sweeteners. But it did suggest that people who consume more than four diet drinks per day—or the equivalent of twelve packets of sugar substitute—face a slightly greater chance of getting cancer. Oddly, the NCI study found a slightly increased risk for nonsmoking women, a group that should have a low incidence of bladder cancer. The discrepancies between the NCI and the newer studies, however, might be statistical flukes.

What are diet-conscious Americans supposed to make of the research? "There is no saccharin-induced epidemic of bladder cancer," says Dr. Robert Hoover of NCI. "All this material gives us confidence that there is no need for panic." But Hoover believes saccharin could be a weak carcinogen, whose effects can't be accurately measured by conventional case-control studies. Other researchers point out that artificial sweeteners have been widely used only since the 1960s, perhaps too recently for their cancer-causing potential to register completely. In a New England Journal editorial accompanying the Harvard report, Hoover suggests that a diet drink or two needn't concern the average adult. But he recommends that youngsters and pregnant women avoid artificial sweeteners completely and that heavy use by anyone is ill advised.

Until a truly safe sweetener comes along, saccharin will probably stay on the dinner table. Although the U.S. Food and Drug Administration is compelled to ban any food additive that causes cancer, Congress has stayed the agency's hand by declaring a moratorium. "Now," says Hoover, "saccharin is the only game in town."

---

19. Ford Acquitted in Pinto Trial of Charges of Reckless Homicide in Deaths of 3 Girls
Nick Miller

WINAMAC, Ind.—After more than two months of heated courtroom arguments and nearly four days of jury deliberations, Ford Motor Co. was acquitted of reckless homicide charges in the Pinto trial here.

Jurors decided the No. 2 automaker wasn't criminally liable for the deaths of three Indiana teenage girls whose 1973 Pinto subcompact exploded in flames after it was struck in the rear by a speeding van in

Source: *The Wall Street Journal*, March 14, 1980, p. 5.

August 1978. The legal battle in this tiny farming community received extensive national publicity because both Ford and the prosecution originally billed it as a landmark case that could break new ground in the controversial area of criminal liability for defective products made and sold by any large U.S. corporation.

As the prosecution attempted to present its case, however, a series of rulings by Pulaski Circuit Court Judge Harold Staffeldt severely restricted the scope of the trial and blocked the State of Indiana from introducing the bulk of its evidence and testimony concerning Ford's alleged knowledge about safety hazards in early model Pintos. As a result, the jury never had a chance to consider some of the fundamental legal issues the State of Indiana hoped to raise.

CHIEF PROSECUTOR PLANS TO APPEAL

There's a possibility, though, that the long-awaited verdict won't be the last thing that's heard about the unusual case in the next few months. Michael Cosentino, the chief prosecutor for the State of Indiana, said immediately after the jury's vote for acquittal that he intends to appeal certain of the judge's rulings concerning admissability of evidence and some other technical matters. He wouldn't elaborate on his future strategy.

Despite the verdict, Mr. Cosentino tried to paint the trail as a possible symbolic vindication of the state's arguments about corporate "responsibility." The case may have demonstrated that large corporations "can be brought to trial" for designing dangerous products "and that decisions made in a board room can be (later) scrutinized by a jury," the prosecutor said.

The defense, for its part, maintained that the verdict, which had been expected by most of the attorneys in the case, vindicates more than 1.5 million Pinto models built between 1971 and 1976 that Ford claims have been "maligned" by unfair publicity about fire hazards. Ford's chief defense counsel, former Watergate Prosecutor James F. Neal, said the lengthy, emotional case proved that "if you bring in (corporate officials to testify) and they have a reasonable story to tell, (a jury) will acquit" them.

The trial proved "large corporations can get a fair trial," Mr. Neal asserted.

MARATHON DELIBERATIONS

The seven men and five women on the jury, weary from marathon deliberations that lasted until nearly 3:00 a.m. yesterday and then resumed only seven hours later for another half day, held an unusual news conference in the courtroom after the verdict was announced. After receiving the case Monday afternoon, jurors said they took more than two dozen separate votes before reaching a unanimous verdict.

Arthur Selmer, a 63-year-old retired farmer who served as chairman of the jury, said that during the early voting Monday the panel was divided eight to four in favor of acquittal. By early yesterday morning, however, only one member of the panel, James A. Yurgilas, 32, a mobile home salesman, was holding out for conviction of the auto maker.

Finally, Mr. Yurgilas recalled, he decided to go along with the rest of the panel because "I had to put aside my personal opinion. I couldn't have lived with a hung jury if my being the only dissenter caused it," he said in an interview late yesterday.

In response to questions during the news conference, Mr. Yurgilas conceded he could have "difficulty" living with the final decision, but he didn't go into any details.

RULINGS LIMITED STATE

Ray Schramm, another juror, said he felt the panel "should have been able to see" the evidence the prosecution originally wanted to introduce about how Ford designed and crash tested early model Pintos. The judge's rulings effectively limited the state to the narrow issue of the 1973-model car involved in the crash and only allowed the jury to see about two dozen of the more than 200 documents Mr. Cosentino and his staff of volunteers and law students hoped to use.

In contrast, Ford's defense, which the auto maker says cost at least $1 million and perhaps much more than that, remained almost entirely intact. Unlike the state, Ford was permitted by the judge to introduce films of crash tests on Pintos and several other cars to show how they held up under high-speed crashes.

The automaker also caught the prosecution off guard by presenting two surprise witnesses near the end of the trial who apparently convinced the jury that the Pinto was stopped or traveling very slowly when the accident occurred. Ford's main contention throughout the trial was that other small cars and even full-size cars couldn't have survived the impact of being struck by a 4,000-pound van moving at more than 50 m.p.h. without spilling large amounts of fuel.

The judge said the case "shows corporations can be charged and possibly convicted of crimes. But this wasn't the right case."

The emotion-charged atmosphere on the final day of the trial was reflected in a variety of ways. Neil Graves, the Indiana state trooper who was the first to reach the flaming wreck, started weeping quietly in the courtroom when the verdict was announced.

In Dearborn, Michigan, Ford's directors heard about the jury's final vote in the middle of a meeting and cheered. "Everybody said that's great, good news," according to outgoing chairman Henry Ford II, who attended the meeting.

"We are obviously delighted," said Ford's chairman, Philip Caldwell. "But we are also delighted about the fact that a company that believes its products are right . . . can stand for a principle and have it exonerated by a jury."

Ecology: Energy, Pollution, and Environmental Quality

On March 28, 1979, a nuclear power plant operated by Metropolitan Edison Company at Three Mile Island, Pennsylvania was shut down by the most serious nuclear accident in the history of the commercial nuclear power generation industry. The accident occured even though Met-Ed management team was highly experienced in nuclear power, the technology was well-developed, and the industry was closely regulated by the federal government. The numerous inquiries which followed provided evidence of shortcomings in management, nuclear technology, and government regulations. Much like the first Earth Day, in 1970, the accident put into focus the concerns of many citizens over energy, pollution, and the need to manage environmental quality better. This section examines the challenges to management in minimizing the negative impact of operations on the natural and structural environment.

For private corporations, the energy-related social responsiveness issues in the early 1980s seemed to focus on conservation and use of alternate forms of energy. Increasing reliance on oil as an energy source coupled with dramatic increases in its price led to almost limitless repercussions for companies and consumers alike. Balance of payments problems become chronic, the dollar plunged in value relative to other world currencies, inflation soared, the U.S. military and political position worldwide weakened, and the nation appeared to flounder without a sense of direction with respect to energy policy. In short, the United States was an oil-dependent nation which seemed unwilling to face the harsh reality that the age of petroleum was coming to an end.

241

As energy costs soared, management was faced not only with the need to conserve energy in the production and distribution process, but also government and consumers demanded energy-saving products. Appliance manufacturers were required to provide consumers with "energy efficiency ratings" which estimated annual operating costs. Public utilities found rate increases nearly impossible to obtain at a time when capital requirements were higher than ever before. Manufacturers of products containing petroleum-based components experienced rapid price increases and material shortages became a recurring problem. In short, the notions of conservation and the use of renewable energy resources, or at least more abundant ones, were central to the kind of thinking which was increasingly necessary in dealing with the challenges of business and ecology.

It is a fundamental but often overlooked truism that we are all polluters. Yet clearly much of air, water, solid waste, noise, and aesthetic pollution is directly attributable to business. Perhaps the greatest adverse environmental impact occurs in the production process, particularly in such capital intensive industries as steel, oil, and paper. However, it is important to recognize that pollution occurs at all steps of the production, distribution, and consumption cycle. For instance, at the resource extraction level, oil well leaks and acid drainage from mines can pose major pollution problems. At the other end of the economic cycle, disposal of such items as aluminum cans and mercury batteries also create environmental hazards.

According to the Council for Environmental Quality, in the decade from 1974 to 1983, the United States will spend $217 billion to install and operate pollution control equipment.[1] Fully two thirds of the expenditure will be paid by business. Most of the expense will be for water and air pollution abatement, although solid wastes, noise, thermal pollution, and land reclamation have also become significant issues. Some of the general issues faced by management in complying with ecological imperatives include:

1. *Changing standards.*   Many companies have found satisfactory environmental performance to be a "moving target" because of rapid changes in pollution standards. For instance, in air pollution control, seven federal laws were enacted between 1963 and 1970, while many states and local communities also increased air pollution standards. In some cases, the federal, state, and local standards created nearly impossible situations, such as the paper

---

[1] Gladwin Hill, "The Profits of Ecology: Cleaning the Stable Makes Jobs," *The Nation*, vol. 222, no. 15 (April 17, 1976), pp. 455–58.

mill that required 43 permits from a dozen agencies to expand its largest mill.[2]

2. *Unrealistic standards.* The most frequently cited example of unrealistic standards is the Water Pollution Control Act of 1972, which mandated the use of "best practicable" control technology by 1977, "best available" technology by 1983, and zero level discharge by 1985. The benefits from such rigorous standards may not balance the costs, even if the goals can be achieved. Cost-benefit analysis to support proposed standards is seldom possible because of the difficulty in linking pollutants with adverse effects such as reduced agricultural output. Still, the costs to achieve small increments of improvement in pollution control may not be justified. For instance, to achieve the last 1 percent reduction in pollution may involve spending more than the amount spent to achieve the previous 99 percent reduction.

3. *Inflexible standards.* The extension of demanding pollution control standards to include older production facilities has been of concern to many companies, particularly those in industries featuring high capital costs with long useful life facilities (such as the steel and paper industries). One major issue has been the difficulty of getting variances to continue operations while working out longer range pollution control programs.

The issues cited above are evident in the cases included in this section. Metropolitan Edison Company: Three Mile Island Plant is a secondary case compiled from the massive public record on the nuclear energy controversy and on the details of the worst commercial nuclear accident in the history of the power generation industry. The case is also based on Metropolitan Edison's annual and quarterly reports which indicate that Met-Ed had 20 years of experience with nuclear energy power sources. Armco Steel Corporation: The New Miami Coke Plant is a primary case. The case graphically illustrates the problems faced by a company with a solid, well-earned reputation for social responsiveness as it is confronted with upgrading an older facility into compliance with the Clean Air Act of 1970. Finally, the ITT Rayonier case illustrates the social challenges involved in construction of a production facility in accordance with stringent environmental laws and regulations.

The commentaries provide insight on several dimensions of the business and ecology relationship. For instance, David Brower re-

---

[2] Cited in Robert W. Fri, "Facing up to Pollution Controls," *Harvard Business Review*, vol. 52, no. 2 (March–April 1974), p. 150.

minds readers that "Spaceship Earth" is a closed system which must be carefully regulated by all "operators." The second commentary describes a self-appointed environmental vigilante who called himself "The Fox." This Chicago-area legend focused public attention on businesses which had failed to respond effectively to environmental imperatives. The remaining commentaries focus the debate over nuclear energy. The first comment examines the many positive aspects of nuclear power while the second reading overviews the objections to this energy source along with the impact of those objections on the construction of nuclear power plants.

Case

METROPOLITAN EDISON COMPANY: THREE MILE ISLAND NUCLEAR PLANT

In early July 1979, Mr. William G. Kuhns, chairman of General Public Utilities Corporation, decided to send a letter to the stockholders of his company. He wanted to explain why the Metropolitan Edison Company, the GPU subsidiary which was the major owner and operator of the Three Mile Island Nuclear Station, should not have its operating franchise rescinded. Metropolitan Edison had been criticized for what had been called a "cover-up" during the first hours and days after a nuclear accident at the Three Mile Island near Harrisburg, Pennsylvania which resulted in radiation emissions into the atmosphere. However, a special investigative commission ordered by President Carter concluded that there was no systematic attempt at a "cover-up" by the company. Mr. Kuhns had learned from the incident that for the public to be able to live with nuclear power, the industry must do a better job of increasing their understanding of the facts and terms associated with nuclear technology. He felt that the public must be able to sort, evaluate, and put into perspective the facts about nuclear power.

The Nuclear Regulatory Commission (NRC) would be holding hearings open to the general public at special conferences on the restart of Three Mile Island Unit 1, in the next week in Hershey and Harrisburg, Pennsylvania. In addition to oral comments, written statements could be submitted at any session or mailed to the NRC. Mr. Kuhns wanted to urge his stockholders to make known their feelings concerning the speedy return to service of Unit 1, an action which he felt was not only significant to them and the company, but

245

to the entire country's efforts to cope with its pressing need for energy.

THE INDUSTRY

Nuclear power was introduced into commercial operation in 1957. In 1980; it supplied 14 percent of electricity production and almost 4 percent of total energy consumption nationally. These figures varied however, according to region. In Illinois, for example, nuclear power supplied as much as 50 percent of electricity used.

In 1980, there were 72 nuclear plants operating in the United States. Prior to the Three Mile Island accident, Carter administration energy planners had projected as many as 500 by the year 2,000, producing thus 25 percent of the nation's power. Since the peak year of 1974, however, construction had turned down sharply. One explanation for this was that electric power demand was growing much more slowly than in the 1960s and early 1970s. Another reason was that nuclear construction costs had risen from $100 per kilowatt in the 1960s to $1,000 per kilowatt in the 1970s. Coal-fired plants were less expensive to construct, with costs per kilowatt in the $700–$750 range. General inflation and long delays in getting a plant built were the principal causes of the cost differential. However, the industry contended that nuclear plants already in operation delivered power at a cheaper cost than those fueled by any other method. The Edison Electric Institute, a utility industry association, estimated that atomic plants produced electricity at a cost of $1.71 per kilowatt hour, versus $1.74 to $2.08 for coal-fired plants and $3.96 to $4.54 for plants burning oil.[1]

Even more pressing than the issue of cost, however, was that proven reserves of fossil fuel were rapidly becoming exhausted. According to best estimates, total fossil fuel reserves recoverable at not over twice the 1980 unit cost were likely to run out between the years 2000–2050, if present standards of living and population growth remained constant. Oil and natural gas would disappear first, coal would last longer. Nuclear fuels, while not exactly renewable energy sources, had a tremendous capacity to breed, and moreover, had very high energy output from small quantities of fissionable material. Furthermore, such materials were abundant, placing them in a more favorable category than exhaustible fossil fuels.

Still, the nuclear industry had other limitations, most important of which was the disposal of radioactive wastes. Because of the potential for radioactive discharges, nuclear fuel could not be used directly in

---

[1] "Nuclear Nightmares," *Time*, April 9, 1979, pp. 8–12.

small machines (such as cars, trucks, or tractors) but only in large units to produce electricity or supply heating.

GENERAL PUBLIC UTILITIES CORPORATION

Founded in 1946, General Public Utilities Corporation was an electric utility holding company that provided electricity to some 4 million people living in about half the land area of New Jersey and Pennsylvania. In 1979, it served over 1.5 million customers. More than 31 billion kilowatt-hours of electricity were distributed in 1978. Of this total, 34 percent went to residential customers, 23 percent to commercial accounts, and 37 percent to industry.[2]

The GPU system included three operating companies: Jersey Central Power & Light Company, and in Pennsylvania, Metropolitan Edison Company and Pennsylvania Electric Company. In 1978, the system had total assets of $4.6 billion, making it the nation's 14th largest investor-owned electric utility (See Exhibit 1).

The GPU companies depended primarily on coal and nuclear energy for the generation of electricity. The generation mix in 1978 was 34 percent nuclear, 57 percent coal, and 9 percent oil. The GPU companies were expected by 1985 to have a generation mix of 45 percent nuclear, 47 percent coal, and 8 percent oil, with the addition of a 1,000 megawatt nuclear plant in Forked River, New Jersey.

METROPOLITAN EDISON COMPANY

Metropolitan Edison Company was headquartered in Reading, Pennsylvania, where the company was founded in 1895. Met-Ed served residential, commercial, and industrial customers in southern and eastern sections of Pennsylvania. The company's 2,800 employees operated conventional steam plants at Titus and Portland, Pennsylvania, in addition to a nuclear-powered facility at Three Mile Island (TMI), Pennsylvania. In addition, the company was part-owner, along with Pennsylvania Electric and Jersey Central Power and Light in thirteen other electrical generating plants, using nuclear, coal, and oil fuel. Met-Ed had over 350,000 customers at the end of 1978.

The earnings of Metropolitan Edison had been disappointing in the mid to late 1970s due to several factors. First, the company had spent over $1 billion from 1968 to 1978 on construction of a 1,700 megawatt nuclear generating complex at Three Mile Island. Operating income for 1978 was down over two percent from 1977, due principally to

---

[2] *General Public Utilities Corporation, 1978 Annual Report,* p. 16.

EXHIBIT 1
General Public Utilities Corporation

Company	Revenues ($000)	Total Assets ($000)	Sales Mix			Customers (year-end)	Area Served (sq. mi.)	Peak Load* (mw)	Number of Employees	Fuel Mix		
			Residential	Commercial	Industrial					Coal	Oil	Nuclear
Jersey Central Power & Light	$ 591,294	$1,906,886	41%	27%	29%	677,580	3,300	2,441	3,731	16%	26%	56%
Metropolitan Edison	$ 310,581	$1,239,803	32%	19%	40%	351,554	3,300	1,477	2,784	58%	2%	38%
Pennsylvania Electric	$ 431,753	$1,414,022	29%	21%	43%	501,983	17,600	1,980	4,253	85%	1%	13%
General Public Utilities System	$1,326,644	$4,612,683	34%	23%	37%	1,531,117	24,200	5,898	11,597	57%	9%	34%

*At time of GPU system peak.
Source: General Public Utilities Corporation, *1978 Annual Report*, pp. 16–17.

unrecovered costs related to construction of TMI-2, an 880 megawatt nuclear-powered generating plant which began to produce commercial power on December 30, 1978. Financial statements for 1974–1978 are shown in Exhibits 2 and 3.

Met-Ed had not been able to obtain adequate rate relief to recover increased fuel and operating costs. The company had, since 1974, been in an austerity program, including layoffs, early retirements, and reduced construction expenditures. The outlook for the future, however, was extremely favorable, with TMI-2 coming on line at the beginning of 1979. In fact, president Walter M. Creitz began the president's message in the 1978 report with:

> For Metropolitan Edison Company, 1978 will remain a memorable year, chiefly because of the completion and entry into commercial service of the second Three Mile Island nuclear generating unit. The achievement caps a decade of dedicated effort. It marks the end of a billion-dollar construction project and a significant addition to the generating capabilities of the General Public Utilities corporation of which Metropolitan Edison is a member company.[3]

These words were written on February 21, 1979, barely one month before TMI-2 failed in the most dramatic accident in the history of nuclear-powered generation of electricity.

METROPOLITAN EDISON COMPANY INVOLVEMENT IN NUCLEAR POWER

Ironically, the accident came almost exactly 20 years from the beginning of Met-Ed involvement with nuclear reactors. In December 1958, Met-Ed had joined with other GPU subsidiaries in a 7½-year effort along with Westinghouse Electric Corporation to build and operate a pressurized water-type nuclear reactor at Saxton Station, Pennsylvania. The project was ". . . aimed to give all participants first-hand knowledge of the managerial and technical problems in buying, building, operating and maintaining nuclear plants, as well as affording an experience basis for making decisions when nuclear power technology has developed to a point where nuclear power costs are competitive with costs of power from fossil fuels."[4]

The Saxton Station project received approval from the Atomic Energy Commission in February 1960 and was completed in less than scheduled time at a lower than budgeted cost. The plant produced

---

[3] Ibid., p. 2.

[4] *Metropolitan Edison Company 1958 Annual Report*, p. 6. This section is based wholly on accounts contained in annual reports of the Metropolitan Edison Company from 1958 to 1978.

EXHIBIT 2
METROPOLITAN EDISON COMPANY
Consolidated Statement of Income for the years ended December 31 (in $000)

	1978	1977	1976	1975	1974
Operating revenues	$310,581	$305,223	$264,113	$249,525	$234,238
Operating Expenses:					
Fuel	83,874	76,541	69,392	80,828	78,075
Power purchased and interchanged, net:					
Affiliates	(7,732)	(11,438)	(2,721)	(14,766)	(983)
Others	25,228	23,702	22,431	1,742	18,677
Deferral of energy costs, net	(9,989)	7,132	(12,006)	376	(3,556)
Payroll	33,770	29,635	27,419	25,537	2,617
Other operation and maintenance (excluding payroll)	41,330	33,165	33,771	29,459	24,539
Depreciation	25,485	23,910	22,176	21,198	17,354
Taxes, other than income taxes	25,290	24,176	20,654	20,171	18,218
Totals	217,256	206,823	181,116	164,545	175,941
Operating income before income taxes	93,325	98,400	82,997	84,980	58,297
Income taxes	27,462	31,229	23,962	25,935	12,992
Operating income	65,863	67,171	59,035	59,045	45,305
Other income and deductions:					
Allowance for other funds used during construction	20,882	18,929	17,249	14,138	16,269
Other income, net	78	(1,000)	291	(163)	(210)
Income taxes on other income, net	(29)	226	(213)	22	52
Total other income and deductions	20,931	18,155	17,327	13,997	16,111

Income before interest charges	86,794	85,326	76,362	73,042	61,416
Interest charges:					
Interest on first mortgage bonds	31,961	28,209	26,593	19,513	14,633
Interest on debentures	6,730	6,880	7,004	7,202	7,370
Other interest	3,818	2,397	522	2,562	4,519
Allowance for borrowed funds used during construction—credit (net of tax)	(6,665)	(5,115)	(4,439)	(3,885)	(7,213)
Income taxes attributable to the allowance for borrowed funds	(7,657)	(5,877)	(4,929)	(4,280)	(4,140)
Total interest charges	28,187	26,494	24,751	21,112	15,169
Income before cumulative effect of accounting change	58,607	58,832	51,611	51,930	46,247
Cumulative effect of accounting change					2,437
Net income	58,607	58,832	51,611	51,930	48,684
Preferred stock dividend	10,289	10,289	10,289	10,289	10,289
Earnings available for common stock	$ 48,318	$ 48,543	$ 41,322	$ 41,641	$ 38,395

EXHIBIT 3

METROPOLITAN EDISON COMPANY
Consolidated Balance Sheets
for the year ended December 31
(in $000)

Assets

Utility Plant (at original cost):	1978	1977
In service	$1,257,169	$ 875,685
Less, accumulated depreciation	208,936	188,079
Net	1,048,233	687,698
Construction work in progress	19,670	327,534
Held for future use	12,561	13,151
Totals	1,080,464	1,028,291
Nuclear fuel	64,169	62,477
Less, accumulated amortization	11,052	14,661
Net nuclear fuel	53,117	47,816
Net utility plant	1,133,581	1,076,107
Investments:		
Other physical property, net	171	172
Other, at cost	495	495
Totals	666	667
Current Assets:		
Cash	6,403	4,654
Accounts receivable:		
Affiliates		476
Customers, net	16,958	14,637
Other	18,718	4,260
Inventories, at average cost or less:		
Materials and supplies for construction and operation	10,900	8,828
Fuel	15,267	18,538
Prepayments	568	718
Other	2,742	2,747
Totals	71,556	54,858
Deferred Debits:		
Deferred energy costs	23,221	13,232
Other	10,779	6,659
Totals	34,000	19,891
Total Assets	$1,239,803	$1,151,523

Liabilities and Capital

Long-term debt, capital stock and consolidated surplus:		
First mortgage bonds	$ 462,957	$ 404,499
Debentures	82,700	84,680
Unamortized net discount on long-term debt	(1,636)	(975)
Totals	544,021	488,204
Cumulative preferred stock	139,391	139,391
Premium on cumulative preferred stock	483	483
Less, capital stock expense		26
Totals	139,874	139,848

EXHIBIT 3 *(continued)*

Common stock and consolidated surplus:	1978	1977
Common stock	66,273	66,273
Consolidated capital surplus	280,523	280,523
Consolidated retained earnings	23,019	22,701
Totals	369,815	369,497
Totals	1,053,710	997,549

Current liabilities:		
Debt due within one year	2,102	5,600
Notes payable to banks	35,500	31,250
Accounts payable:		
Affiliates	913	433
Others	17,272	13,846
Customer deposits	571	574
Taxes accrued	6,193	14,759
Interest accrued	11,027	9,341
Other	7,756	6,986
Totals	81,334	82,799

Deferred credits and other liabilities:		
Deferred income taxes	66,643	46,618
Unamortized investment credits......................	33,432	19,971
Other...	4,684	4,586
Totals	104,759	71,175

Commitments and Contingencies		
Total Liabilities and Capital.............................	$1,239,803	$1,151,523

20,000 kilowatts of output for a five-year period, beginning in April 1962. By the end of 1962, Met-Ed announced the project a success, ". . . serving the purpose for which it was conceived, namely: (1) to increase our knowledge about reactor technology; (2) to train personnel in the construction and operation of nuclear reactors; and (3) to provide an experimental reactor operating under actual utility conditions."

The success of the Saxton Station contributed in 1963 to the decision of GPU subsidiary Jersey Central Power and Light to construct the Oyster Creek Station. The 600,000 kilowatt facility was to be built in five years at a cost of $68 million. Met-Ed, which was to participate in the joint venture announced to its shareholders, "This plant will be the first nuclear-fueled generating station in New Jersey and when completed will be the largest privately owned nuclear station in the world."

On March 28, 1967, exactly 12 years to the day prior to the failure of TMI-2, Met-Ed announced to its shareholders that it intended to build a nuclear generating station on Three Mile Island scheduled for an in-service date in 1971. The 840,000 kilowatt plant ". . . is the first atomic plant to be built and owned solely by Met-Ed." Application was made in 1967 to the Atomic Energy Commission and construction was scheduled to begin in 1968.

The Atomic Energy Commission granted a construction permit in May 1968. The company believed it still possible to complete the plant by fall, 1971. In 1969, the completion date was revised to 1972. Also, it was decided in 1969 that a second nuclear unit would be built at Three Mile Island. The second unit, scheduled for completion in 1974 and known as TMI-2, was to be jointly owned by Jersey Central Power and Light and Metropolitan Edison.

In 1970, the completion date for TMI-1 was revised to 1973. Also, it was decided that the Three Mile Island facility would be owned 50 percent by Met-Ed, 25 percent by Jersey Central Power and Light and 25 percent by Pennsylvania Electric. TMI-2 was still scheduled for completion in 1974. Also, in 1970, construction delays and operating problems caused an earnings decline for Metropolitan-Edison, which seriously hampered financing capability in 1971.

By the end of 1971, Met-Ed announced that TMI-1 was 75 percent complete and TMI-2 was nearly 20 percent complete. No completion date was forecast because "the lack of financing capability necessary to fund our vital construction program continues to present a serious problem for the company."

By the end of 1972, TMI-1 was 95 percent complete at a cost estimated at $375 million, and the 880,000 kilowatt TMI-2 was 35 percent complete at an estimated total cost of $465 million. Met-Ed forecast that TMI-1 would be in commercial service by August 1974 and TMI-2 would be operational in spring 1976.

In 1972, the company experienced a change in top management. Frederic Cox, who had been chairman of the board and president of Met-Ed since February 1968, retired at the beginning of 1972. The board elected William G. Kuhns, chairman of the board and Walter M. Creitz as president. Both executives had spent their entire careers with Metropolitan Edison.

Up until 1973, the annual company reports had been 8-page, black and white statements without pictures and one-page narrative coverage about company progress. The 1973 *Annual Report* was strikingly different. The full color 18-page brochure, had an aerial photograph of the Three Mile Island plant on the front and back covers, along with an additional 35 photographs, mostly of company employees and plants. With respect to Three Mile Island, the company announced, "We look forward to 1974 for many reasons; but one of the most exciting is the expected addition of Three Mile Island Nuclear Station Unit No. 1 to the capacity of Met-Ed and the GPU System. It has been a long challenging road and our employees and associates have contributed much to make its production a reality." The total cost of the project was now estimated at $920 million. TMI-1 was scheduled for commercial operation in October 1974; TMI-2 was to be in-service in May 1977.

Unit Number 1 went into commercial operation on Labor Day, September 2, 1974, three years later and at a total cost of $45 million more than originally planned. At the same time, due to a severe cutback in construction caused by financing problems, TMI-2 was delayed to 1978.

Austerity continued for Met-Ed in 1975 due to sharp decreases in industrial demand and unfavorable delays in rate proceedings rulings. However, TMI-1 completed its first full year in operation with an 82 percent overall capacity factor (output divided by maximum rated capacity). The company noted, "This performance is well above average for the industry's experience." Met-Ed still forecast that TMI-2 would go into commercial service in 1978.

In 1976, Met-Ed continued to feel the effects of rising costs in all aspects of doing business. While operating income was substantially the same as in 1975, the rate of return on investment declined from 9.82 percent to 8.73 percent. Met-Ed filed in 1974 for a $70.9 million annual rate increase. The action was ruled on by the Pennsylvania Public Utilities Commission in June 1976. The result was $29.8 million increase per year with the possibility of some retroactive billing. The nuclear plant at Three Mile Island continued its fine operating record, ending the year at a cumulative capacity factor since September 1974 of 71 percent.

In 1977, TMI-1 continued to compile an impressive output record with a capacity factor of 79 percent, more than ten points above the national average for all nuclear plants. Also in 1977 the construction on TMI-2 was completed. The operating license for TMI-2 was received in February 1978. Fuel was loaded and testing began the same month.

On September 19, 1978, TMI-2 was dedicated in an on-site ceremony. John F. O'Leary, deputy secretary of the U.S. Department of Energy was the principal speaker. It was noted at the dedication program that TMI-1 was "one of the top ten performing reactors in the nation. Met-Ed looks to Unit No. 2 for the same reliable, low-cost performance that is so beneficial to our customers." When TMI-2 went into commercial service on December 30, 1978, the future indeed looked bright for Met-Ed.

THE ACCIDENT

The worst accident in the history of commercial nuclear power occurred early on the morning of March 28, 1979, near Harrisburg,

Pennsylvania.[5] At first, it seemed that the crew on duty at the Three Mile Island plant faced only a minor problem when part of the plant's cooling system was inadvertently shutdown. Unit 2's huge turbine, which generated 880 megawatts of electricity had shutdown automatically, as it ought to when the steam that turned it somehow had been cut off. The technicians assumed that the cause would be easy to detect and remedy, but problems and mistakes multiplied quickly. A backup cooling system failed to function because sometime earlier someone had shut, apparently by accident, some key valves. As pressure and temperature began rising in the reactor, a relief valve opened automatically, but failed to close when pressure and temperature were under control. In the ten hours it took to diagnose that problem, thousands of gallons of vital cooling water poured out of the reactor. Further complicating the situation, operators misread conditions inside the reactor and prematurely shut off emergency cooling pumps that had turned on automatically.

For the next several days, radioactive steam and gas seeped sporadically into the atmosphere from the Three Mile Island plant. While engineers struggled to cool the core of the reactor, there was tremendous threat of a "meltdown" in which the core drops into the water coolant at the bottom of its chamber, causing a steam explosion that could rupture the four-foot-thick concrete walls of the containment building; or, the molten core could burn through the even thicker concrete base and deep into the earth. In either case, lethally radioactive gases would be released into the environment. This would be catastrophic, considering that there were nearly 100 tons of deadly radioactive material that made up the core of the large reactor.

Reports differed greatly as to the amount of radiation emitted from the plant. However, the governor of Pennsylvania advised the evacuation of all pregnant women and young children living within five miles of Three Mile Island. Although there was no panic, thousands of residents left the area of their own volition. One woman remarked, "You hear one thing from the utility, one thing from the government, another thing from Harrisburg, and something else from civil defense." The inhabitants of the area, along with the rest of the nation, became confused about the safety of nuclear power.

THE DEBATE

Nuclear stations cost between $500 million and $1 billion to construct. In 1979, there were 72 nuclear generators in commercial operation. In the event of a nuclear shutdown, not only would this huge

---

[5] Details abstracted from "Nuclear Nightmares," *Time*, April 9, 1979, pp. 9–10.

capital investment lie idle, but the cost of power generation of utilities would soar. For instance, Metropolitan Edison was paying $800,000 a day for supplemental power from other utilities, while TMI-1 and TMI-2 were shutdown.[6] According to the Atomic Industrial Forum, without nuclear energy, the United States, in 1978, might have had to burn an additional 470 million barrels of oil to make electricity. This amount of oil could be converted to at least 12 billion gallons of gasoline, a year's supply for 17 million automobiles. If plants under construction in 1979 were allowed to go into operation, the contribution of nuclear power would triple by 1985. The oil burned in one year by a million-kilowatt electric generation plant could be used instead to produce enough gasoline for about 350,000 cars, or enough heating oil for more than 400,000 homes in the northern United States. A nuclear plant such as Three Mile Island could save 10 million barrels of imported oil per year.[7]

A study by the Institute for Energy Analysis of the Oak Ridge Associated Universities estimated the direct annual economic cost of what might be called a modified limited moratorium (no new construction starts after 1980, continued operations of all reactors on line by 1985) as one percent of the GNP. That would be, in 1979 dollars, something like $20 billion a year. In addition to the monetary cost, the industry argued that such a moratorium would increase the principal pollutants from coal plants by 20 percent, and by any of the varying estimates of deaths from coal, that would mean thousands more deaths each year.

A second study on the impact of a nuclear moratorium was conducted by National Economic Research Associates, Inc., a highly respected independent study group. The group studied the cost of several alternatives, any one of which might result from the incident.

It then was forced to make various assumptions, and worked out the results under the different assumptions. In one example, it was assumed that oil prices would continue to rise, that electricity demands would grow at the low end of recent Department of Energy estimates, and that plant modifications required by the Three Mile Island experience would prove relatively inexpensive. Under those assumptions, the group determined the effect of a policy calling for stopping new nuclear power plant construction and decommissioning existing plants by 1985. The results:

1. Impose annual costs on society of $16 billion by 1985 and $22 billion by the year 2000;

---

[6] *General Public Utilities First Quarter and Annual Meeting Report*, 1979.

[7] Atomic Industrial Forum, Inc., *Nuclear Info*, July, 1979, p. 1.

2. Result in an increase in sulfur emissions of 3 to 4 million tons annually—sufficient to wipe out the alleged advantages of the 1977 amendments to the Clean Air Act;
3. Increase oil imports by two million barrels per day by 1985, falling off sharply thereafter as coal is phased in over the longer term; and
4. Increase the number of human fatalities associated with the production and movement of fuel and generation of electricity by 30,000 in the next two decades.

If, in the face of nuclear cutbacks, the industry were unable to bring on line either oil-fueled capacity or coal-fueled capacity, power shortages would result. If all nuclear plants were decommissioned by 1987, and no new capacity beyond current plans were brought on line, then capacity would fall sufficiently short of projected demand so that the resultant cost to the public of power shortages would be $26 billion annually by 1987.

The generation of replacement electricity in the three-state power pool serviced by Three Mile Island (Pennsylvania, Maryland, and New Jersey) would shift sources from 46 percent to 50 percent coal fired. That change, the pronuclear advocates argued, would have inevitable health effects as sulfur dioxide and other pollutants increased in the area. Nuclear power proponents contended that nuclear reactors, routinely operated, were among the most negligible emitters of radiation, and thus the most negligible causes of radiation. Because radiation had been studied longer and more intensively, it was argued, more was known about it than the carcinogens in coal smoke. Thus, it could be measured with great precision and sensitivity.

An Ad Hoc Group made up of technical staff members of the NRC, U.S. Department of Health, Education, and Welfare (HEW), and the U.S. Environmental Protection Administration (EPA) was chosen to assess the health impact on the approximately 2 million offsite residents within 50 miles of the Three Mile Island nuclear station. The study group concluded that the offsite collective dose associated with radioactive material released during the period of March 28 to April 7,• 1979, represented minimal risks. The projected number of excess fatal cancers due to the accident that could occur over the remaining lifetime of the population within 50 miles was approximately one, according to the interagency team's findings. Had the accident not occurred, the number of fatal cancers that would normally be expected in a population of this size over its remaining lifetime was estimated at 325,000. The projected total number of excess health effects, including all cases of cancer (fatal and nonfatal) and genetic ill health to all future generations, was approximately 2.

These figures violently clashed with those of Dr. Helen Caldicott, pediatrician and president of a national organization of doctors opposed to nuclear power, the Physicians for Social Responsibility.

> . . . Out of a predicted 10 million people who would be exposed to radiation, there would be 3,300 prompt fatalities; 45,000 cases of respiratory impairment and burning of the lung; 240,000 cases of thyroid damage; 350,000 cases of temporary sterility in males; 40,000 to 100,000 cases of prolonged or permanent suppression of menstruation in women; 10,000 to 100,000 cases of acute radiation illness. . . . As for babies in utero: 100,000 of them would be exposed. All of them could develop cretinism. There might be 1,500 cases of microcephaly—that is, babies born mentally retarded with abnormally small heads . . . Fifteen years after the event, we could expect 270,000 cases of cancer and 28,800 thyroid tumors and genetic diseases. That all adds up to nearly one million so-called "health effects."[8]

Radiation is invisible, intangible, tasteless, odorless, and silent. It is also measured in unfamiliar units. All of these factors tend to make radiation an object of fear and mystery. Antinuclear spokespersons argued that it would take only one radioactive atom, one cell, and one gene to initiate cancer. One way of evaluating the magnitude of radiation release is to consider the maximum exposure the most exposed member of the public might have gotten. According to the NRC, this amount was 90 millirems, or the equivalent of two chest x-rays. This level of radiation was only slightly less than the difference between the annual natural or background exposure in New Orleans or Denver. The average exposure to persons living within 50 miles of the reactor was 1.75 millirems, or little more than the exposure one gets each year from watching color television.[9]

THE AFTERMATH

President Carter named eleven persons to an independent commission to investigate and explore the Three Mile Island accident. The blue-ribbon commission was headed by John G. Kemeny, president of Dartmouth College, whose early career as a mathematician and philosopher involved research on the Manhattan Project and a stint as an assistant to Albert Einstein. The other appointees included two critics of nuclear power.

In addition to the president's commission, at least seven other separate investigations about or related to the Three Mile Island accident were launched. The NRC conducted its own investigation. On

---

[8] Katie Leishman, "Helen Caldicott: The Voice the Nuclear Industry Fears," *Ms.*, July, 1979, pp. 50–93 *passim*.

[9] Atomic Industrial Forum, Inc., *Nuclear Info*, August, 1979, p. 1.

Capitol Hill, hearings were launched immediately by Sen. Edward M. Kennedy's subcommittee on health and by Sen. Gary Hart's subcommittee on nuclear regulation. Additional hearings were planned by Rep. Morris K. Udall's energy and environment subcommittee, by Rep. Mike McCormack's subcommittee on energy research and production, and by Sen. John Glenn's energy subcommittee of the Government Affairs Committee.

The annual shareholders meeting of General Public Utilities Corp., held on May 25, 1979, served as a forum for discussion of the TMI-2 accident. William G. Kuhns, who had been chairman of the parent corporation since 1975, addressed the shareholders and responded to their questions on the accident. The full text of chairman Kuhn's remarks and the ensuing discussion period follow.

CHAIRMAN'S ADDRESS

At 4:00 A.M. on Wednesday, March 28, TMI-2 was severely damaged in the worst accident in the history of America's nuclear industry.

However, despite all the damage done to the unit, I am grateful that, from all the information available, the accident has not resulted in any injury to the public health.

While we believe that the accident involved a complex interaction of equipment malfunctions, design and instrumentation shortfalls and human response, we do not yet have a full understanding of the exact causes or sequence of events. All of our top priority efforts have been devoted to protecting the health and safety of the public and of our employees. Now, numerous investigations have been initiated and we have pledged our full cooperation and support to them. We are determined to learn as much as we can from this unfortunate accident.

One thing that we already know is that the accident and its aftermath have had a traumatic and profound effect on the local community, on your company and on the industry. We regret this deeply, particularly the impact it has had on the people of the Middletown, Pennsylvania area, who have traditionally strongly supported the TMI project.

I won't go into the details of the accident itself. Instead, Herman Dieckamp, president and chief operating officer, will give an explanation of the accident and TMI's current and future status.

I will not take the time to review GPU's operations in 1978. That information was covered in our Annual Report mailed to you in March. Instead, let's go right into the accident's aftermath and its ramifications for GPU.

Assessing the Impact

Shortly after the accident, as its magnitude became apparent, we began an assessment of its impact on the GPU System and of how best to deal with it.

It still is not possible to determine accurately the ultimate dollar costs.

Aggravating the problem is the unavailability of TMI-1, which was not involved in the accident, but could not go back in service after its fuel reloading because of the activities on site involving TMI-2. We are identifying what must be done to return it to commercial operation.

We also expect that TMI-2 can be restored to service. Experience with the clean up and restoration activities following other nuclear accidents suggests that the problem is technically manageable. But the costs as of now are unknown and the job may take two to four years.

The costs of the accident fall into several broad categories: namely, liability for expenses incurred by others, for example, the expenses of evacuees; physical damage to the facility, interest on money borrowed to cover costs of the accident and other related costs; and the price of replacement energy.

Insurance Coverage

Insurance will cover liability claims up to the legal limit of $560 million. The maximum GPU financial exposure in this area would be $15 million, under provisions of the Price-Anderson Act, which establishes the ground rules for liability in the event of nuclear accidents. The balance would be covered by private and federal insurance programs and assessments on other utility reactor operators.

Insurance will also cover up to $300 million of physical damage to the TMI site. We believe this insurance will pay most of the bill for clean up and repairs, but not for plant improvements or modifications.

Also not covered by insurance will be the interest costs on money we will have to borrow to see us through this emergency. Nor does insurance cover the fixed investment charges associated with TMI-2, estimated at about $8 million per month. We are currently negotiating with a group of banks for a $450 million revolving credit agreement to meet short-term needs. Discussions are in progress concerning the possible issuance of longer-term securities.

The most significant uninsured cost is that of replacement power to make up for the loss of output, about $24 million a month. It will be reduced to $10 million a month when TMI-1 comes back on line. We are aggressively exploring the means of reducing these replacement power costs.

Sharing the Costs

Because of the magnitude of these uninsured costs, we believe they must be shared by GPU's stockholders, customers and employees. Appropriate actions have been taken, and are being planned, to implement this conclusion.

The GPU board of directors, at its April 26 meeting, voted to reduce the quarterly dividend on common stock from 45 cents to 25 cents per share.

We deeply regret the need for this action.

We recognize the importance of our cash dividend policy to our stockholders. Before reaching this decision the board held a number of extensive briefing sessions. All factors bearing on the decision were explored, including recommendations in the many letters and calls we received from shareowners.

The board also suspended the Dividend Reinvestment and Stock Purchase Plan. All funds received since the February 25 payment date will be repaid. It is our intention to reinstate the plan at an appropriate future date.

However, the dividend action does not reflect the full measure of the stockholders' share of the burden. A very significant burden is the decline in the market value of GPU shares since the accident, from just under $18 to less than $10 a share at this point. As of this morning, the shareholders have absorbed a half billion dollar decline in the value of their GPU investment.

Cutting Expenses

The system's directors, officers and other employees are shouldering a share of the burden. A hiring freeze has been imposed, and layoffs are planned, though we hope to minimize them through attrition and incentives to encourage early retirements.

The retainers of the GPU directors have been cut from $7,500 to $6,000 annually and a $100 increase in their $300 meeting fee cancelled. The GPU system officers' scheduled seven percent salary increase has been rescinded, returning them to April 1978 levels, and Herman Dieckamp and I are being rolled back to our April 1977 levels. To date we have avoided cutting the salaries of other employees, as we wish to retain as many of our good people as feasible.

As we announced early in April, the company, as one of many steps to conserve cash resources, suspended all construction projects involving additional generating and transmission facilities. We also have stopped all but the most critical construction programs on existing facilities, and are postponing or reducing non-essential maintenance work.

We have reduced our 1979 construction budget by $125 million and our 1980 construction budget by $225 million. These represent cuts of nearly 30 percent and 45 percent, respectively.

The major generation projects affected are the planned 1,100-megawatt Forked River, New Jersey, nuclear unit, and the Seward-7 coal-fired plant in Western Pennsylvania—both slated for operation in the middle 1980s.

Additionally, we are taking a very close look at operation and maintenance expenses, at all levels throughout the system. To date we have reduced our 1979 budget in those areas by $30 million, a 9 percent cut. We plan to reduce this further.

In addition to reducing officers' salaries and putting a freeze on hiring, we will combine a special early retirement program with a planned reduction of the work force by eliminating about 600 jobs over the next several months. This will reduce payroll costs to a level that will support a minimum construction effort and a reasonable level of service to our customers.

Further, in reducing the work force, employees whose skills and experience could be used to support the recovery operation at TMI will be offered employment there to reduce the cost of outside services over a considerable length of time.

Customers Should Participate

This brings us to our customers. We feel strongly that they also should share the burden. All the economies achieved through the operation of our nuclear plants have been passed on to them. The operation of the TMI-1 Oyster Creek nuclear facilities have already saved customers about $700 million through 1978.

None of these savings have gone to investors in GPU. The customers have been the sole beneficiaries. In light of this, it seems equitable that our customers bear some of the financial risk of nuclear power and share in the burden of the TMI-2 accident.

In proceedings now underway before the New Jersey Board of Public Utilities and the Pennsylvania Public Utility Commission, we will make it clear that the outcome of these proceedings is the key element in determining the future ability of the GPU Companies to serve their customers. We are doing everything possible to provide the agencies with the information they need in reaching their difficult and painful decisions.

The Pennsylvania PUC on April 19 initiated proceedings to determine the appropriate base rate levels for both of our Pennsylvania subsidiaries. Hearings began May 2 and will continue through this month. A decision is anticipated before the end of June. It is *most* important that this schedule be maintained.

Jersey Central Power and Light Company made a rate filing on May 4 with the New Jersey Commission to deal with the impact of the TMI-2 accident on our New Jersey customers. Here, too, we must hope for fast action.

I should add at this point that, at a price, there is adequate capacity in the GPU System and in neighboring, interconnected utilities to meet our near-term customer requirements. However, as we get further into the 1980s, there could be supply problems unless we are able to resume our construction program.

Healing Process Underway

In summary, I can only repeat what I said in my letter to you. Your company has been seriously wounded. But the healing process is underway.

During this period, the GPU stockholders have been an inspiration. There have been many letters and phone calls. We have received many expressions of support, thoughtful suggestions for dealing with the problem, including what dividend action we should take, and come criticisms.

We have received help from many other sources, especially the performance of our own people, which I can only say has been "beyond the call of duty." We are grateful for the assistance of hundreds of experts from other utilities, the nuclear industry, the academic community, and state and federal regulatory agencies.

Commitment Undiminished

Looking to the future, let me emphasize that GPU's commitment to our customers, shareowners and employees continues undiminished.

We are committed to providing our customers with reliable electric service at the lowest cost we can achieve.

We are committed to providing our shareowners with a reasonable return on their investment.

We are committed to providing our employees with the challenge and opportunities of this highly dynamic energy business.

And to fulfill these commitments, GPU is also committed to fostering among its regulators, shareowners, customers and employees a deeper understanding of the necessity for maintaining the financial and operational integrity of General Public Utilities Corporation.

Discussion Period

Following are some of the questions asked, and the answers given, during the meeting's discussion period.

Q. What steps were taken to keep the directors immediately and fully informed after the Three Mile Island Unit-2 accident?

Mr. Kuhns: They received extensive briefings and were kept up to date by telephone calls in the intervals between briefing sessions.

Q. Did the directors discuss management changes at Metropolitan Edison Company in light of the accident?

Mr. Kuhns: At this point, we want to await the outcome of the many investigations now underway and our own review of the events that transpired on March 28 and subsequent events and base any subsequent actions on the evaluation of that information.

Q. Would I be correct to assume that we cannot expect any immediate rate relief, say from the next three to six months, from the regulatory agencies?

Mr. Fred D. Hafer [*vice president-rate case management*]: No, the Pennsylvania Public Utility Commission has indicated that it will close hearings on the cases before them involving Metropolitan Edison Company and Pennsylvania Electric Company by the end of May, so it is reasonable that the PUC would reach a decision during June. Both companies have also asked that the commission take some action in advance of that decision, allowing a higher billing rate beginning in June to start recovering the replacement of energy cost on a more timely basis. [Note: On May 10th, the PUC postponed action on these latter requests.]

In the case of Jersey Central, we filed our case on May 4 and we expect that sometime, perhaps this week, the commission in that state will indicate a time schedule for concluding their proceedings. I think that it is reasonable to expect some action in New Jersey within the next month or two.

Q. Let's presume a negative reaction from the regulatory agencies due to public pressure. What could we shareholders expect on the next dividend date, an increase or a decrease?

Mr. Kuhns. It's really not productive to speculate at this point on what will happen. I think whatever the commissions do would have to be evaluated very carefully and I am not about to suggest what they would have to do to help us accomplish certain things. I think we will have to proceed with the cases and evaluate their reaction and their response and then decide what we have to do at that point.

Q. I think we are all concerned that the dividend may drop again, or be eliminated entirely, and we would like to have some estimate of what the probability of that might be.

Mr. Kuhns: We really can't give it to you at this point, mainly because we don't know. It depends upon what events occur between now and the dividend meeting in July and what we would recommend to the board of directors, or what the board would ultimately do. We really can't predict beyond that.

Q. Assuming you maintain the quarterly dividend of 25 cents for the rest of this year, would you anticipate that a portion of the dividend paid this year would be nontaxable for income tax purposes?

Mr. E. J. Holcombe [GPU comptroller]: I believe that it is quite possible that a portion would be, under the assumptions we've made for planning purposes, but we cannot fix on a definite amount at this point.

Q. I notice that there was some malfunction of equipment, and I would like to know why the manufacturers, namely Babcock and Wilcox, shouldn't be approached to help spare [us] some of the effects of the accident?

Mr. James R. Liberman [GPU's general counsel]: We have sent a letter to B&W and put them on notice that there are indications that certain equipment may have failed to meet the contract requirements and I think that we have reserved any rights that we would have to proceed against B&W.

Several stockholders commented on GPU's public relations efforts at the time of the TMI-2 accident. Mr. Kuhns said that this had been noted by management, and that "we are very serious about examining our posture on public and customer relations, and we recognize the need to improve it."

Q. Why doesn't GPU just dispose of the Met-Ed stock at zero, write it off and get a tax benefit?

Mr. Kuhns: Well, the problem is more than just a Met-Ed problem. It also impacts Jersey Central enormously. We don't feel that walking away from these companies would be doing the best job for the GPU stockholder. We think this is a problem that should be managed, can be managed, and that Met-Ed and Jersey Central and Penelec and the GPU System can recover from this traumatic event and continue to serve the customers and the investors as in the past.

Q. Mr. Creitz [Walter M. Creitz, president of Met-Ed], the newspapers accused you of holding back information that you had. May I have your comment on that please?

Mr. Creitz: It's been our policy and practice to try to tell customers and our neighbors exactly what was going on at all times. And this is exactly what we tried to do. We understood more and more about the extent of the accident as time went on. What we saw as the situation, particularly as it related to the safety and well-being of the people who lived in the area, is the type of information that we tried to provide to the state, to the NRC people there, and to the public. Conditions did change and as this did happen, we attempted to update and relay this to the public.

Q. Can you estimate how long it will be before TMI Unit 1 will be back in operation?

Mr. Dieckamp: If it were simply a matter of restoring the site to a state of normalcy, and of making the technical modifications to the plant that are required of similar plants, we think that could probably be accomplished in three months. There may well be some public hearings and things of that nature before the plant is allowed to go back in operation. So, for planning purposes we are thinking, realistically, the end of the year.

Q. Would someone explain what is being proposed in terms of the early retirement plan as a way of cutting costs?

Mr. Kuhns: The board has approved a program under which employees aged 60 and above with 20 years of service would be eligible for early retirement without any actuarial reduction in their pension because of retiring before age 65.

Q. What is the status of the $450 million revolving credit that the corporation is applying for; I understand it is under negotiation and I just wondered when the outcome might be resolved?

Mr. Verner H. Condon, [*GPU vice president and chief financial officer*]: Our target is prior to the end of this month. And the responses we've had from the banks to date are very supportive.

Q. What would the effect be on the corporation if the PUC were to reinstate the rate increases which were suspended for Met-Ed and Penelec?

Mr. Kuhns: Penelec's share was $25 million and Met-Ed's was $49 million, so that totals $74 million on an annual basis.

Q. This would pretty much solve or help the problem of the $800,000 a day to buy power from other utilities, I take it?

Mr. Kuhns: It would help, but not solve it.

Q. First, I want to thank you for having your meeting in Johnstown, and, since we are here in the coal fields, I was wondering if you could give us some of management's feelings in regard to coal?

Mr. Dieckamp: We certainly hope to generate a significant amount of power in the future from coal. We had planned to build the next coal plant, to be located at Seward, for 1985. In our minds there is no question but that this country's and this region's demands for energy are going to require significant use of coal in the future.

While the full financial impact of the accident was still unknown,

Mr. Kuhns knew that the shutdown was costing about $14 million per month. He believed that TMI-1 could be back in operation in about four months and that TMI-2 could be back in service by 1983 at a cost of about $400 million. However, the Nuclear Regulatory Commission hearings could serve as a formidable obstacle to the restart.

As Mr. Kuhns composed his letter to stockholders, he was aware that antinuclear sentiment was on the rise. In recent months, the nation had witnessed numerous organized protest marches and sit-ins at nuclear facilities. "The China Syndrome," a movie highly critical of nuclear power, was a box office success. A recent best seller by Arthur Hailey, *Overload*, depicted the nuclear industry as poorly managed. Somehow, he must impress upon his shareholders the importance of solid support during the upcoming public hearings.

Case

ARMCO STEEL CORPORATION: THE NEW MIAMI COKE PLANT

While at home in Middletown, Ohio, on the evening of April 27, 1973, John E. Barker, director of Environmental Engineering for Armco Steel Corporation, received the news that his firm had been denied a permit to operate its New Miami coke plant beyond the July 1, 1975 deadline established by the federal Clean Air Act of 1970. The variance request had been denied across the board for 13 steelmaking plants of various manufacturers in the state of Ohio. Mr. John Trapp, the investigator for the Ohio EPA at the New Miami plant in Hamilton, Ohio, noted in his report that the coke ovens were very old and a serious source of air pollution. However, because of Armco's fine previous record at alleviating pollution in its southwestern Ohio plants, he recommended that serious consideration be given to Armco's compliance schedule which would bring the company within the legal limits by late 1977 or early 1978. Mr. Trapp later speculated that the variance request denial had been based on the literal requirements of the law.

THE COMPANY

Armco Steel Corporation mined and processed coal and limestone for the nine steel plants which it operated in the United States and provided diversified products and services worldwide through its various divisions. The company's Metal Products Division had 45 manufacturing plants in the United States and Canada which produced highway, drainage, and construction products, steel buildings, and other industrial products. The Machinery and Equipment Divi-

268

sion was the world's largest supplier of oil and gas well-drilling equipment. Its drilling rigs, pumps, pipe, and other products were used worldwide at both onshore and offshore drilling installations. The International Division was responsible for the export sales of Armco products and steelmaking technology and operated steel manufacturing businesses in 18 countries. HITCO, a wholly owned subsidiary, produced high performance, nonmetallic materials and complex composite products principally for the aerospace and defense industries. Other Armco units conducted insurance, leasing, and financing businesses on a worldwide basis.

Sales for Armco, the third largest producer and profit maker among U.S. steel manufacturers, were $1.9 billion in 1972. Net income totaled $75 million. Income was expected to be over $100 million in 1973 on the strength of almost $2.4 billion in sales.

By 1973, Armco had already spent $125 million on pollution equipment. In Middletown alone the amount was $40 million. Red smoke from the open hearths was a problem in virtually all steel towns; until recently, Middletown was no exception. However, in 1971 the company completed a 21-month project in which $10.5 million was spent on wet scrubbers for the No. 2 open hearth to clean up the smoke and another $1.5 million to then treat the scrub water and remove the solid materials. In the summer of 1969, the company started a new basic oxygen steelmaking complex and installed $5.9 million worth of pollution devices on it and then retired eight old open hearth furnaces which were not equipped with pollution control devices. The new $16 million water treatment plant with a capacity of 144 million gallons per day was larger than the capacity of the water system for the entire city of Cincinnati. The system put the water back in the Miami River cleaner than it came out.

Mr. Barker felt that Armco probably had the best reputation for environmental effort among all steelmakers. A study conducted in 1969 by the Council on Economic Priorities (a private group) on water and air pollution in the steel industry had ranked the company tops among seven companies. Armco gave off only 4.7 pounds of particulate emissions per ton of steel produced, while National Steel, rated the worst, averaged 21 pounds per ton.[1] The CEP study also recognized the efforts of Armco in environmental cleanup, actions such as use of low-polluting electric furnaces, recent rehabilitation of older open hearths, and installation of major water reprocessing facilities. The CEP's estimated cleanup price tag of $2.8 billion for the industry was well below the $3.5 billion estimate of Thomas Barnes at the

---

[1] "Particulate emissions" refer to any liquid or solid particles other than water which are or have been airborne.

Battelle Institute, a research center in Columbus. Barnes headed a group at Battelle which did the estimates for the federal EPA.

THE PROBLEM

Upon arriving at his office in the center of Middletown the next morning, Mr. Barker found a memo from William E. Verity, Jr., chairman of the board of Armco, already on his desk with a copy of EPA denial letter attached (see Appendix 1). The memo requested that Mr. Barker review the company input data for the variance request and be prepared to meet the following week with the corporate comptroller, the production superintendent at Middletown, and Mr. Verity to discuss the company's strategy for the adjudication hearing. At stake was the company's competitive position and its financial condition. The denial of the variance request for the continued operation of the coke batteries at New Miami was, they felt, denying the major pollution abatement efforts made by Armco.

Mr. Barker knew that one of the most important items to be discussed at the meeting would be the disposition of Armco's huge coke ovens and the procurement of ample future supplies of coke for the steel mills.

THE COKING PROCESS

Coke was the result of a process which removed gases and impurities from coal by heating it. "Coking," as the process was called, produced a fuel which burned with a very intense heat and little smoke, making it superior to coal for iron smelting purposes. However, serious pollution problems occurred in the charging (dropping the coal into ovens), pushing (shoving the cooked coke out of the ovens by means of a "pusher" or ram), and quenching (spraying the coke with water to cool it) stages. Fugitive dust[2] escaped during the initial handling of the coal and during the charging operation. Possibly, thought Mr. Barker, modifications could keep the fugitive dust to a minimum in coal handling, and high-pressure steam jets could reduce dust created during charging.

Certain procedures used during the coking process itself led to particulate emissions. A small door had to be opened to admit a bar which leveled the coal in the ovens, and opening this door provided a natural vent from the oven. New oven construction should provide a boot to close the space around the leveling bar when the door was

---

[2] "Fugitive dust" refers to air contaminants emitted from any sources other than a flue or stack.

opened and closed, Mr. Barker noted. Since coke oven gas burned clean, visible emissions during the remainder of the cooking process had to be the result of poor combustion procedures or leaks. Leaks could be repaired but necessitated cooling the ovens, a costly process. Even to cool just one oven, a whole battery had to be shut down, which meant that none of the other ovens could be used. Also, the brick-lined oven walls often collapsed when cooled; considering that some batteries had as many as 100 ovens, shutting down an entire battery to repair only a few ovens could be expensive.

Leaking end doors were also a source of emissions and had to be scraped and cleaned regularly. The jambs also needed to be cleaned periodically. Both operations could be accomplished when oven doors were changed for repair, but maintenance was done by hand. In older 12-foot ovens the practice was relatively easy, but newer 21-foot ovens were considerably harder to clean. When repairing of door knife edges and jambs was not possible, wet clay could be used to seal doors, a method known as luting.

Particulate emissions occasionally occurred during the pushing process because of the thermal draft caused when the doors were opened and the coke was pushed out of the ovens into a quench car. In addition, smoke was sometimes present during pushing due to uncooked or "green" spots in the coke mass. Although coke could not be overcooked, the excess time in the oven necessary to prevent green spots could cause production slowdowns during later stages of the steelmaking process. The cooking time was determined by the width of the oven; the minimum was 16 hours, while 18 to 19 hours were required at times for old batteries.

During the quenching stage, the quench car holding the hot coke was sprayed with water producing a plume of steam which rose in the quench tower. To prevent the steam, containing thermally drafted particulates, phenols, ammonia, and cyanides, from contaminating the ambient air, the quench towers contained baffles, rows of diagonally slanting metal plates on which some of the vapor condensed. It had been suggested to Mr. Barker that more baffles and sprays be added and that the openings of the tower around the quench car be sealed to reduce convection and capture more of the contaminants.

The four batteries at the New Miami plant had been built in the late 1920s. Of the four, one had 7 to 10 years of remaining life, and three had 10 to 12 years. In the environmental engineer's opinion, it was technically and economically unfeasible to reduce substantially the particulate emission of the old single gas main ovens. Additional foremen on each shift to ensure careful operation and maintenance, such as sealing cracks and doors, would help.

As Mr. Barker assessed Armco's position, three facts were

foremost in his mind. First, the very process of exposing superheated material that had a tendency to flake and powder to various temperature changes created thermal drafts that naturally spawned particulate emissions. Second, limited control required major modifications of the existing ovens or construction of entirely new ones. Finally, some new technology was presently available, such as the pipeline charging mentioned in the EPA memo as the "state of the art," but it was expensive and was of marginal value at New Miami; in addition, the planning and installation horizon was so long that the deadline could not be met.

For example, installation of high-pressure charging meant that a second gas main would be needed costing over $40 million, and requiring 24 months to install. Improved quenching operations also meant completely new equipment. As a result, Mr. Barker was in essentially the same position as six months before when Armco asked for a variance from the July 1, 1975 deadline.

THE EPA REGULATORS

The EPA had designated the Butler County area where the New Miami plant was located as priority one in most categories of air pollution and held public hearings to determine the ambient air[3] quality level for the region. The industrial concentration in the Cincinnati corner of the state had eroded the air quality over the years, and the current particulate emission level was over 95 micrograms (μg) per cubic meter for the region. Mr. Barker and several others from the steel industry had been invited to give expert testimony at the hearings.

Although the present level of 95 μg for the region was high, the steel industry felt that with a major modification program at considerable expense the particulate emission standard of 75 μg could be met by 1977 or 1978. Despite the testimony of four or five experts, the proponents of lower standards had prevailed. The ambient air quality standard was set not at 75 μg, but at 60 μg. Mr. Barker firmly believed a standard of 60 μg was technically impossible even with the "state of the art" technology recommended in the EPA denial letter. Indeed, the best rural air in the state of Ohio had an ambient air quality of 45 to 50 μg.

The 60 μg ambient air standard was difficult to judge. Ambient air referred to no specific industry but was a communitywide or regional standard. The particulate regulations applicable to the steel industry came under the general heading "stationary sources." These sources

---

[3] "Ambient air" is the outdoor air that surrounds an entire community or region.

gave off varying degrees of five specific pollutants measured by the Ohio EPA. Likewise, nonstationary sources gave off varying amounts of the same pollutants.[4] Although Armco was the major industrial concern in Middletown, Mr. Barker was not prepared to guess what percentage the company contributed to the overall pollution or just how far the Armco particulate emissions would have to change to bring the community standard to 60 μg. This issue was further clouded by the EPA's inability to control nonstationary polluters such as automobiles.

In addition, the EPA classified the efficiency of most pollution control equipment such as wet scrubbers in terms of particulate matter removed. Low efficiency meant 80 percent removal of particulates; medium, 80 to 95 percent removal; and high, 95 to 99 percent removal. The cost curve for greater efficiency followed a statistical distribution with greater efficiencies being out of the range of economic feasibility.

THE ALTERNATIVES

Later in the week at the meeting with other Armco executives, Mr. Barker explained the alternatives available to the company. First, Armco could take the matter to court and tie the issue up until beyond the 1975 deadline, maybe even beyond 1977 or 1978. Second, the company could shut the coke plant down on July 1, 1975 and go to the open market for its coke needs. Or, third, it could reapply for the variance until such time as coke oven capacity could be modified or new ovens installed in compliance with emission standards. This latter was a doubtful alternative, for it had already been rejected by the EPA and was the sole reason for the meeting.

To Mr. Barker, legal proceedings looked like the easiest and perhaps the least expensive way to delay the closure of the New Miami coke plant. Many steel companies in Ohio had chosen this route and were presently involved in court battles. In Armco's case, Mr. Barker was not sure that 60 μg was a viable ambient air requirement. However, Armco publicly committed itself to pollution abatement in 1966 and willingly quoted this policy to anyone who asked (see Appendix 2 for a complete presentation of the policy). The ideal of socially responsible behavior on which the company had been founded was reaffirmed in writing by the board of directors on December 5, 1969 and distributed in booklet form to all employees. The company had worked hard at curbing air pollution and did not want

---

[4] The federal EPA monitored 5 other pollutants, and a remaining balance of 20 pollutants was not monitored.

to squander a hard-earned reputation in rushing a bad decision in this case.

The second alternative, to shut down the New Miami coke plant on July 1, 1975 and go on the open market for coke, was not without drawbacks. Over 50 percent of the coke ovens in the United States were in the "over 20-year-old" category of the New Miami plant, and many were faced with shutdown. In 1973, very little surplus coke was available in the United States, for nearly all coke was manufactured by steel companies for their own consumption. The maximum available monthly would be 5,000 to 10,000 tons, far short of the 50,000 tons a month needed at Middletown. At best, Armco could spot bid for a limited supply of German coke at approximately two-and-one-half times the U.S. price.[5] Additionally, 70 percent of the energy consumed in the production of iron and steel came from coke and coke oven gas, which was not available commercially, and coke oven by-products. Natural gas and oil were more efficient heat producers but were more expensive and currently not available.

Mr. Barker considered the technical and cost aspects alone to be sufficient arguments against the shutdown. However, the impact on jobs was sure to be on everyone's mind. The 300 employees at the New Miami plant would be immediately laid off. Because 50,000 of the 93,000 tons of coke consumed at Middletown were produced at New Miami, a shutdown would result in a cutback of about 1,000 of the 6,500 Armco jobs in Middletown. The reduction in coke needs would have a domino effect back to the coal fields and forward through the economy. Cold scrap could be used in place of hot metal in open-hearth operations, increasing heat time, and thus fuel consumption, 25 to 30 percent, and reducing production by the same amount. Because all steel companies were currently backordering and operating at capacity, the reduction would hurt such Armco customers as Frigidaire in Dayton and Fisher Body in Hamilton. Unless economic conditions changed drastically, these companies could not secure steel from other sources.

Finally, the company could reapply to the EPA for an operating permit beyond the July 1, 1975 deadline. The decision would require a $150 million capital outlay for a new plant and the best available technology. The plant could be built in Middletown to keep the jobs in Ohio and, if construction were started immediately, could be completed in 33 months, or possibly by the July 1, 1975 deadline. The new installation would be the closed pipeline type with enclosed quench car which could reduce emissions and therefore not jeopardize the

---

[5] No market prices existed on coke, but for comparative purposes Mr. Barker placed a "fictitious" transfer price at somewhat less than $30 per ton.

proposed ambient air quality regulation of 75 μg. However, Mr. Barker was doubtful that the company even then could meet the ambient air standard of 60 μg.

Undertaking the new plant project would mean the cancellation of a newly planned "melt shop" which had been in the works for a number of years. The capital budget had called for the installation of new electric furnace facilities at another plant location as a replacement for a number of open-hearth furnaces. In light of the world competitive situation, it was not likely that the corporate comptroller would give up "his" new furnaces easily. It was common knowledge that the American steel industry had long clung to worn out facilities and was at a competitive disadvantage with the Germans and Japanese who had retooled with the latest equipment after World War II. Further, Mr. Barker knew that to reactivate the old open hearths would require a variance request in the state in which they were located.

APPENDIX 1
EPA Denial Letter

OHIO EPA
Columbus, Ohio

30 April 1973

FROM: The Director of the Ohio EPA, Columbus, Ohio
TO: Director, Armco Steel Corporation, Middletown, Ohio

Dear Mr. Verity:

As you know, the federal Clean Air Act has set ambient air quality standards to be met by July 1, 1975. Coke oven facilities in the state of Ohio have been the subject of extensive hearings for the past six months. Steel manufacturers were asked to submit schedules of compliance. The operators have questioned the availability of technology to bring the coke oven plants into compliance by July 1, 1975.

After extensive study it has been concluded that there is no technical obstacle to compliance with present state and federal regulations.

A sample compliance schedule is enclosed.

[The EPA memo went on to describe the minimum technical modifications which would be necessary in order to bring the existing coke ovens into compliance with EPA regulations.]

At the present time the "state of the art" is the advanced technology of pneumatic or pipeline charging and is far superior to the above modifications. This office is not allowed to stipulate the method used to bring the ovens into compliance and therefore leaves the choice of technology to the company concerned.

APPENDIX 1 *(continued)*

In accordance with the law, thirty days are granted to your company to reply to this letter with a request for an adjudication hearing, should it so desire. If you desire any information or assistance in this regard, please feel free to contact Ms. Mary O'Mally at extension 266–4232 of this office.

Sincerely yours,

William T. Brandon
Director, Ohio EPA

cc: Office of Environmental Affairs
      Ohio Attorney General

OHIO EPA
Compliance Schedule

Battery location:

Plant location:

Milestones:

		Cumulative period (months)
1.	Submit final engineering designs and specifications ..	3
2.	Award contracts for technical modifications	6
3.	Initial on-site construction and modifications	12
4.	Completion on-site construction and modifications ...	22
5.	Achieve final compliance with all applicable State, federal laws, rules, and regulations	26

Start date: May 1, 1973

Special consideration:

A.   Acceptable coke charging methods employed.
B.   No pushing of "green" coke.
C.   Emissions not to exceed opacity[1] regulations.

---

[1] The *Regulations of the Ohio Air Pollution Control Board, Relative to the Control of Sulfur Oxide and Particulate Matter Emissions* (Ohio Department of Health, Columbus, Ohio) defines "opacity" as "a state which renders material partially or wholly impervious to rays of light and causes obstruction of an observer's view."

APPENDIX 2
ARMCO's Pollution Abatement Policy

The pollution of air and water in the United States has resulted from the combined abuses by the general public, municipalities, industries, and other public and private institutions over the past century when the foundation was being laid for our modern industrial economy. To reverse this trend will require both time and the cooperative planned efforts of all segments of our society.

The investment of millions of shareholder dollars in nonproductive facilities must be made in accordance with a carefully planned schedule, over a period of years, so that the financial condition of our company will not be impaired. Any broad-scale, hasty diversion of capital to nonproductive use could adversely affect our entire American economy.

We believe that both legitimate environmental needs and economic feasibility must be taken into account when pollution abatement standards are set. Those who study the massive problem of pollution in the United States realize that pollution abatement facilities are costly and generally nonproductive.

As a corporate citizen, we recognize our responsibility to cooperate fully with private and public agencies in their efforts to protect the nation's water and air resources.

Approved by Board of Directors
February 1966

Case ══════════════════════════════

ITT RAYONIER INC.

ITT Rayonier Inc. specialized in the production of high-quality dissolving sulfite pulps which were sold to domestic and foreign buyers and used in acetate film, cellophane, and rayon yarn.

The ITT Rayonier mill, located at Port Angeles, Washington, was built in 1930 to take advantage of the area's abundant raw materials. In 1977 the forests surrounding Port Angeles continued to be a viable source of pulping materials. In 1977, the mill was the city's largest employer with 300 persons on the payroll. The City of Port Angeles is located west of Puget Sound and north of the Olympic Mountains; it borders on the Strait of Juan de Fuca (see Exhibit 1). Port Angeles is the largest metropolitan area on the Olympic Peninsula with a population of approximately 16,500 people.

The Port Angeles facility averaged approximately 500 tons per day of high-quality, acetate-grade, bleached, dissolving sulfite pulps. The mill operated nine batch digesters and one pulp dryer. The process utilized a chemical recovery plant to burn the spent pulping chemicals called SSL. The thermal energy from this process was supplemented with hog fuel and fuel oil to generate five megawatts of electric power and provide process steam.

SULFITE PROCESS

The process employed by ITT Rayonier is ammonium-based sulfite as shown in Exhibit 2. This process produces a high brightness pulp that can be bleached very easily.

Source: Copyright © 1978 by the President and Fellows of Harvard College. Reproduced by permission. This case was prepared by Bram Johnson under the supervision of Robert A. Leone.

EXHIBIT 1
Map of the Port Angeles Area

In the initial stage, roundwood (logs) are debarked and chipped. Care must be taken to minimize the amount of bark and foreign material entering the raw material stream, since the process does not effectively dissolve noncellulose material. The chips are then mixed with water and pumped into a digester (a large closed vessel). Hot sulfite cooking liquor (sulfurous acid and bisulfite) is then pumped into the digester. The entire batch is subsequently heated under pressure with steam. At the end of the "cook" a valve at the bottom of the digester is opened and the chips are blown out. The violence of the "blow" defibers the soften chips. The digesting process dissolves the lignin, hemicellulose, and resins that bind the cellulose bundles together. The spent cooking liquor (SSL) is drained from the pulp and recovered and burned. The remaining chemicals and dissolved materials are washed from the pulp. The used water then receives primary treatment before it is discharged into the bay.

EXHIBIT 2
Dissolving Sulfite Process

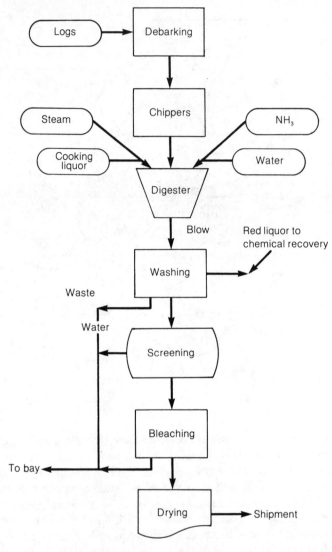

One to six percent of the digester's output is undesirable material, usually knots, bark, dirt, shives, and fiber bundles, which is removed by screening. The pulp yield averages 44 to 46 percent of the chip input, depending on type of raw material. The washed pulp is then bleached, dewatered and packaged for shipment.

POLLUTION CONTROL AT PORT ANGELES

The Port Angeles mill has installed a primary water treatment plant (see Plant Layout, Exhibit 3), an SSL recovery boiler to burn the cooking wastes (recovering heat and chemicals), and a wet scrubber exhaust gas treatment facility. These facilities, including the chemical recovery system, had a capital cost of $38 million. Because of the high

EXHIBIT 3
Port Angeles Plant Layout

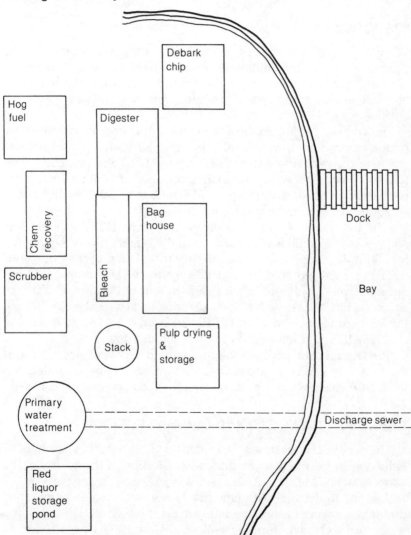

quality of Port Angeles' product, more lignin was removed during the pulping process than for lower grade pulps, producing high BOD (primarily sugars) and pH waste loads.

Seventy percent of the waste load was eliminated through the chemical recovery process, which burns off organic waste. The primary treatment facility removes almost all settleable solids and some of the remaining BOD. The remaining material is discharged through a deep water outfall-diffuser which runs from the mill one and one-half miles into the bay and diffuses into the Strait of Juan de Fuca.

EPA ACTION

Early in 1976, more than four years after they were due, the EPA promulgated effluent limitations for the dissolving sulfite industry. ITT Rayonier and others, immediately challenged these limitations in the Federal Court of Appeals, charging that they violated the Water Quality Act of 1972.

The company argued that treatment would have an *adverse* effect on the environment, as a whole, and that EPA should consider the ability of the receiving waters to absorb the BOD and pH loads. (ITT Rayonier had installed secondary treatment facilities at all other company locations and, to date, spent $250 million on such facilities with an additional $150 million planned.)

EPA on March 4, 1977, issued a notice to ITT Rayonier–Port Angeles that the mill was in violation of the Water Quality Act of 1972 for failure to comply with schedules for installation of pollution control equipment required to meet EPA's effluent limitations. EPA requested that Washington State's Department of Ecology (DOE) take action within 30 days. When the DOE took no action, the U.S. Justice Department filed suit against ITT Rayonier on April 25, 1977, seeking civil penalties and injunctions to force the mill to comply.

The federal court ordered the company to begin construction, and the company had complied although there had yet been no decision in its case challenging the standards on which compliance is based.

SECONDARY TREATMENT AND COMPANY POSITION

The secondary treatment specified by EPA was based on BOD reduction by bacterial action after neutralization of the acidity in the waste water.

After neutralization with lime, the waste water would be pumped into tanks, where bacteria would convert the high BOD wastes into water and CO_2, also forming biological sludge. The expected daily output of sludge from the secondary treatment plant would be up to

4,867 tons. The sludge would be comprised of millions of thick membraned cells that contain about 90 percent water. The sludge would need to be combined with primary sludge and dewatered by chemical or mechanical action before disposal. After this action, the sludge would still contain about 80 percent water. The daily output of this "dewatered" material is estimated at about half an acre foot* or 170 acre feet per year. Since no one to date had developed an economic use for the sludge by-product, there were only two bio-sludge disposal options available. First, the material could be trucked to a land fill site and buried. (As of June, 1977 no suitable site had been located.) Second, the sludge could be incinerated. Since the sludge will not support combustion, ITT Rayonier engineers estimated that incineration would require 1.24 million gallons of oil annually. (See Exhibit 4 for a diagram of the process.)

The capital cost of this secondary treatment facility was estimated at approximately $40 million and would use 8 million watts of additional power, a 66 percent power increase. The plant manager at Port Angeles was uncertain if this additional power could be obtained from the Bonneville Power Authority (BPA). The company noted that if coal were the energy source, 17,000 tons of it would be burned supplying the needed electric power and even though in compliance with EPA's air standard would release 340 tons of air pollutants per year.

The nutrients required annually to support the biological colonies necessary to the treatment were estimated at 280 tons of ammonia (derived from natural gas) and 500 tons of phosphoric acid. Also, 13,440 tons of limestone and 273,000 gallons of oil, to convert the limestone into lime, would be required for sulfite waste neutralization.

ITT Rayonier's management contended that to further clean up Port Angeles' discharge the additional energy required and its resultant pollution would be far more detrimental to the environment than the pollution generated under the mill's current practices.

Further, ITT Rayonier argued before the Washington Pollution Control Hearings Board, and the State Department of Ecology stipulated that:

> Discharge of effluent from Rayonier's Port Angeles mill, after treatment by pollution control facilities in place on February 14, 1976 (i.e., SSL recovery) does not cause violation of water-quality criteria for Class AA (extraordinary) waters nor is there any reason to expect that such discharge will in the future, cause violation of such water-quality criteria.

---

* An acre foot is a unit of volume one acre by one foot deep.

EXHIBIT 4
Diagram of Secondary Sludge Treatment

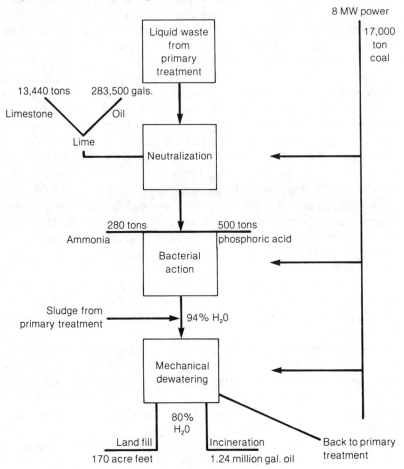

Class AA waters are those that are acceptable for wildlife, fish, shellfish, and recreation. Local plant management estimated that variable costs per ton of pulp would rise $30 if the new treatment plant were in operation. (See Exhibit 5 for a typical sulfite pulp cost per ton breakdown and Exhibit 6 for pulp prices.)

The plant manager said, "Due to the nature of the process and the high quality pulp produced, little can be done to close the process loop. If anything is to be done, it would have to be accomplished at the end of the pipe."

EXHIBIT 5
Estimate of Typical Capital and Operating Costs for the Manufacture of Sulfite Dissolving Pulp

Basis: Process: Bleached magnesium base sulfite; cont. pulping with chemical recovery
         Production: 500 ADT tons/day; 172,500 tons/year

Capital Requirements:	*$ Million*
1. Excluding environmental cost	
Direct manufacturing process	
Total fixed capital	121
Total working capital (3 months delivered cost)	9
	$ 130

Operating costs:	*$/ton*	*$000/year*
Fiber cost	$ 79.8	$13,780
Other raw materials................................	$ 23.0	3,970
Hourly labor	23.1	3,990
Supplies	13.5	2,340
Energy	4.2	720
Factory overhead	8.8	1,530
Capital-related (less capital recovery)	15.5	2,680
Sub-total, factory cost	167.4	29,010
General selling & administration	13.6	2,350
Freight out	31.4	5,430
Total delivered cost, direct mfg.	$212.4	$36,790

Source: Adapted from Arthur D. Little, Inc., *Economic Impacts of Pulp and Paper Industry Compliance with Environmental Regulations*, 1976, Table F19, PPF 35.

EXHIBIT 6
U.S. Dissolving Sulfite Pulp Prices, 1970–1975

Year	*$/ton*
1970	150–157
1971	162–167
1972	162–167
1973	157–162
1974	183–202
1975	335–370

Source: Paper Trade Journals, February 10, 1975, p. 14; January 28, 1974, p. 14; November 11, 1973, p. 29; February 21, 1972, p. 22; February 1, 1971, p. 27; January 26, 1970, p. 56.

Commentaries ══════════════════════════

20. The Third Planet: Operating Instructions
David R. Brower

This planet has been delivered wholly assembled and in perfect
working condition, and is intended for fully automatic and trouble-
free operation in orbit around its star, the sun. However, to insure
proper functioning, all passengers are requested to familiarize themselves fully with the following instructions.

Warning

*Loss or even temporary misplacement of these instructions may result in
calamity. Passengers who must proceed without the benefit of these rules are
likely to cause considerable damage before they can learn the proper operating
procedures for themselves.*

A. COMPONENTS

It is recommended that passengers become completely familiar
with the following planetary components:

1. Air

The air accompanying this planet is not replaceable. Enough has
been supplied to cover the land and the water, but not very deeply. In
fact, if the atmosphere were reduced to the density of water, then it
would be a mere 33 feet deep. In normal use, the air is self-cleaning. It
may be cleaned in part if excessively soiled. The passengers' lungs
will be of help—up to a point. However, they will discover that

---

Source: *The New York Times Magazine,* March 16, 1973, p. 111. © 1973 by The New
York Times Company. Reprinted by permission.

anything they throw, spew, or dump into the air will return to them in due course. Since passengers will need to use the air, on the average, every five seconds, they should treat it accordingly.

2. Water

The water supplied with this planet isn't replaceable either. The operating water supply is very limited: If the earth were the size of an egg, all the water on it would fit in a single drop. The water contains many creatures, almost all of which eat and may be eaten; these creatures may be eaten by human passengers. If disagreeable things are dispersed in the planet's water, however, caution should be observed, since the water creatures concentrate the disagreeable things in their tissues. If human passengers then eat the water creatures, they will add disagreeable things to their diet. In general, passengers are advised not to disdain water, because that is what they mostly are.

3. Land

Although the surface of this planet is varied and seems abundant, only a small amount of land is suited to growing things, and that essential part should not be misused. It is also recommended that no attempt be made to disassemble the surface too deeply inasmuch as the land is supported by a molten and very hot underlayer that will grow little but volcanoes.

4. Life

The above components help make life possible. There is only one life per passenger and it should be treated with dignity. Instructions covering the birth, operation and maintenance, and disposal for each living entity have been thoughtfully provided. These instructions are contained in a complex language, called the DNA code, that is not easily understood. However, this does not matter, as the instructions are fully automatic. Passengers are cautioned, however, that radiation and many dangerous chemicals can damage the instructions severely. If in this way living species are destroyed, or rendered unable to reproduce, the filling of reorders is subject to long delays.

5. Fire

This planet has been designed and fully tested at the factory for totally safe operation with fuel constantly transmitted from a remote source, the sun, provided at absolutely no charge. *The following must be observed with greatest care:* The planet comes with a limited reserve fuel supply, contained in fossil deposits, which should be used only in emergencies. Use of this reserve fuel supply entails hazards, including the release of certain toxic metals, which must be kept out of the air and the food supply of living things. The risk will not be appreciable if the use of the emergency fuel is extended over the operating life of the planet. Rapid use, if sustained only for a brief period, may produce unfortunate results.

B. MAINTENANCE

The kinds of maintenance will depend upon the number and constituency of the passengers. If only a few million human passengers wish to travel at a given time, no maintenance will be required and no reservations will be necessary. The planet is self-maintaining and the external fuel source will provide exactly as much energy as is needed or can be safely used. However, if a very large number of people insist on boarding at one time, serious problems will result, requiring costly solutions.

C. OPERATION

Barring extraordinary circumstances, it is necessary only to observe the mechanism periodically and to report any irregularities to the Smithsonian Institution. However, if, owing to misuse of the planet's mechanism, observations show a substantial change in the predictable patterns of sunrise and sunset, passengers should prepare to leave the vehicle.

D. EMERGENCY REPAIRS

If, through no responsibility of the current passengers, damage to the planet's operating mechanism has been caused by ignorant or careless action of the previous travelers, it is best to request the Manufacturer's assistance (best obtained through prayer).

Final Note

Upon close examination, this planet will be found to consist of complex and fascinating detail in design and structure. Some passengers, upon discovering these details in the past, have attempted to replicate or improve the design and structure, or have even claimed to have invented them. The Manufacturer, having among other things invented the opposable thumb, may be amused by this. It is reliably reported that at this point, however, it appears to the Manufacturer that the full panoply of consequences of this thumb idea of His will not be without an element of unwelcome surprise.

---

21. The Fox: He Stalks the Wild Polluter
J. Madeleine Nash

Aurora is a minor industrial hub some 40 miles west of Chicago. The surrounding area used to be pristine and open, with fields planted in corn or left in wildflowers, but it is now blighted by cheap construction projects and end-to-end shopping centers with huge barren spaces in front. Central Aurora, now decaying, once might have been delightful, for the Fox River flows right through it. But the town chose to turn its back on the river front, and instead of encouraging parks and gardens, watched while local factories poured their effluents into the flowing waters. In March 1969, however, Aurora's wasteland gave birth to a new natural resource: an intrepid environmentalist who called himself—after the beleaguered river he fought for —the Fox.

A graying, middle-aged outdoorsman who answers to the name of Ray, the Fox recently celebrated his fifth "birthday" by walking along Mill Creek, since 1969 the scene of a hotly waged campaign against the Armour-Dial soap company. All in all, the Fox was happy and took time to reflect on his blessings, along with a rare poppy mallow and western cornflower plant he'd just discovered in an undisturbed nook. "I was thinking," said the Fox, "that I should have been done with and over with and gone with for many months. I really didn't think I would survive so long. The only reason I have, I think, is because I have the sympathy of the people."

For a while, the Fox worked alone or with a single close companion. Today, however, his merry band numbers close to 35, and includes school teachers, engineers, factory workers, housewives, and medical doctors. Most of them are well over 30. Like the Fox, they are usually married, with families to protect, and not surprisingly, many are long-time residents of the area. One reason for their involvement

---

Source: Reprinted from *Business and Society Review*, no. 11 (Autumn 1974), pp. 11–13. Copyright 1974 by Warren, Gorham, and Lamont, Inc., 210 South Street, Boston, Mass. All rights reserved.

can be easily gleaned just by sniffing the air. "The next generation," explains the Fox, "is going to look at what we left them. What are we going to tell them—that they can take our dollar bills and stuff them up their noses?"

DIRECT ACTION IS BEST KIND

The Fox began one day five years ago. Here is his account:

> This company had an underground sewer pipe. It's 41⅞ inches in diameter—I know. This company nets $1,000 an hour 365 days a year, and they were using this little stream down here for their own personal sewer. All the governmental bureaucracies had been after them, but it did no good. They had been asked time and again by the sanitation district to put their engineers on the problem, but nothing happened. Finally it got to me. I was walking along this stream and one day I saw all these bluegills. The next day I went back; the stream was full of curds and grease, and the bluegills were all dead. Well, I knew there was this big catch basin, and so on a Sunday night five years ago I gathered up a whole bunch of logs, rocks, bales of straw, even an old mattress I found, and plugged it up. I didn't care if I went to jail or not. I just threw in everything but the kitchen sink—and a month later I threw that in, too. I put up a sign: "Let your engineers go to work on this." Then since I damn well wasn't going to give them my name, I gave them the river's name instead. Because the river couldn't fight for itself, I decided to fight for the river.

Armour-Dial, William F. Jobbins, U.S. Steel, Forty-Eight, Fox Paving Co., Balaban & Katz, U.S. Reduction, Foster Wheeler, and All-Steel are some of the companies which have since felt the Fox's wrath. He has hung accusatory signs on factory walls and overpasses; he has capped chimneys and offensive sewers; he has left dead skunks at the homes of recalcitrant top executives; he has given companies imaginatively packaged deliveries of their own products. In one fabled encounter, the Fox collected a water sample which purportedly came from just outside the sewer outlet of a large aluminum plant in Aurora; he then proceeded to slosh it all over the handsome black slate floor of the company's East Chicago headquarters. The contents: a dead rat, a dead bird, the carcasses of assorted decaying fish. Sighs the Fox, "The little secretary vomited all over the place. She was pregnant, and I felt real bad, so I sent her a dozen roses the next day. When I called to apologize personally, she said, 'The next time you come, the boss's office is to the right.'"

In his five years of action, the Fox claims to have closed down one factory, prompted a number of others to spend money on antipollution devices, and halted the infamous Stratton project which would have plugged the Fox River with a series of locks and dams. Today even long-time adversaries like Armour-Dial pay the Fox his due. "We think the Fox has done a good job in many ways," a spokesman said. "He has called some essential problems to the attention of the public." Of course, the spokesman continued, the Fox has had little influence on Armour-Dial. "We had been working on these problems for a number of years. We already had the money committed—it was all a matter of coming up with the technological know-how."

In the meantime, the Fox has developed some technological know-how of his own. For stuffing sewers, he confides, "Sacrete is awful good. It's even better when you put some oats into your mix. When the oats get wet, they swell up and make a tighter seal." To the delight of his fans, besides consummate technical skill, the Fox has shown a definite talent for prosody, composing limericks against Forty-Eight, and a doggerel rewrite of "Kubla Khan" criticizing U.S. Reduction. One warning, which accompanied a dead skunk, quipped, "You stink up our environment, and nature will stink up yours too." Sometimes the Fox resorts to mime, as in 1972 when he and his followers organized a mass funeral service to bury the scenic beauty of the Fox River. (Shortly afterwards, the Stratton project ground to a halt.) In another escapade, the Fox paid a visit to the famous Picasso statue outside Chicago's towering Civic Center. His purpose was to hang a cartoon protesting Mayor Daley's proposal for an airport on Lake Michigan, but the message also clearly indicted U.S. Steel. "Feel free to use the lake, Dick," said the U.S. Steel figure, pointing to an outhouse. "We always do."

Actually, the Fox explains, this particular excursion was a diversionary tactic designed to draw off the local heat after someone posing as the Fox called up an Aurora factory and threatened to set off a bomb. This brought out the FBI, and for a while all the cops in the area were hot on the Fox's trail. Ever since, the Fox has tuned down his flamboyance and taken a low profile. Today he prefers working with young people to squirming up sewer drains, and his proudest accomplishment is the organization of local Boy Scouts into Fox litter patrols. Still, the Fox obviously enjoys his anonymous notoriety, and in keeping with his position as exalted folk hero, he tells long yarns about all his closest calls. Let's see, there was the time he almost fell through a rotten roof into a sea of molten aluminum . . . the time he was chased through the woods, and almost caught, by a private security guard . . . the time he nearly caught pneumonia after he plugged up a sewer in February. . . . "There was snow on the ground when I crawled up that sewer," Ray chuckles. "And afterwards I stood in the woods stark naked. I had to change my clothes—but boy, it was cold." One thing Ray *doesn't* worry about is the local police force, which he describes as friendly. "When they get a call that the Fox has struck," Ray laughs, "they come out looking for me—with all their sirens screaming, with all their lights lit."

SUPPORT FROM EVERY QUARTER

For a while, there were warrants out for the Fox's arrest, but these all have been withdrawn, and now the Fox has become semirespectable. In Springfield, Illinois, at least one state government official has hung a "Go Fox" sticker on his office door, and a Kane County judge is reputed to have one in his chambers as well. The "litter here" barrels distributed by the Fox Boy Scout troop have become local fixtures, as have the vigilant antilitter patrols. One Aurora resident was abashed to find the candy wrappers and soft drink cans he'd discarded in the woods neatly returned to his front porch. In fact, he was so ashamed he wrote the Fox an apologetic note.

Such power has the Fox's name attained that last year, when a company discharging untreated waste into one of the river's tributary creeks received a similar note, it cleaned up the problem in record time. "There were these periodic accidental spills," Ray remembers. "But our contacts in the plant could let us know exactly when these 'accidental' spills would occur. One day I blew my stack; I was walking alongside the crick and I saw these billions of dead worms floating belly up. So I picked the junk out of the bottom of the crick and after collecting it, there was only one Christian thing to do: give it back to the people who gave it to us. I wrote a note which said, 'Because of your irresponsibility to the environment, you have won free delivery of your product with my signature.'" Six weeks later, smiles the Fox contentedly, the company shaped up.

"There isn't one person among us who's *against* business," protests the Fox. "And we never try to destroy. One rule I always follow is never to jeopardize someone else's life or property. A sticker on a bar of soap doesn't hurt Armour-Dial, really; a skunk doesn't hurt a roof. But it gets the job done. I see a need for a healthy business and a healthy environment together. Any corporation that cannot afford to be environmentally concerned is a marginal operation and should not be around anyway. It's time we started appreciating the beauties of nature as well as the beauties of the buck. Otherwise, we're mighty poor inhabitants of the earth."

Why do businesses balk? The Fox still doesn't understand. One company, he claims, begged off installing an air-pollution control system because of the high estimated cost: $3.9 million. But once its engineers really got going on the problem, they found a mere $125,000 would do the trick. "In other words," laughs the Fox, "they went and applied good old American ingenuity to the problem and found it wasn't that difficult after all. It's funny how, when a little pressure is brought to bear, it suddenly becomes good business judgment to do something about the environment."

The Fox hints mysteriously that another major campaign is in the offing. In fact, he says, he may *never* retire. "The whole existence of the Fox is a tragedy," he sighs. "But a man ought to be able to drink out of a stream when he's thirsty or take his son out fishing."

The Fox, it seems, has his work cut out for him. Only this spring it was announced that fish from the Fox River may be unsafe to eat. They were found to be highly infected with a viral form of cancer, an apparent side effect of living in polluted waters.

---

22. At Least One Section Of the U.S. Is in Love With Nuclear Power
A. Richard Immel

RICHLAND, Wash—Bowing to antinuclear clamor in western Washington, Gov. Dixy Lee Ray recently picked the Hanford Federal Nuclear Reservation in the southeastern quarter of the state as the preferred site for all new nuclear power plants. That brought immediate cheers from the Tri-Cities area abutting the reservation.

Cheers? For nuclear power? That's right. "This is the best site in the country" for nuclear plants, says 69-year-old Glenn Lee, a longtime nuclear-power advocate who publishes the Tri-Cities Herald, the only daily in the area. And there is hardly a soul in Richland, Kennewick or Pasco, the three towns that make up the Tri-Cities, who doesn't agree with him.

This area along the Columbia River is isolated from major population centers, and it has a great deal of talent in nuclear technology. But perhaps its biggest asset as a drawing card for nuclear power is the strong popular support. Such popularity raises the possibility of creating similar pronuclear oases in remote areas of the United States.

Nuclear power may be in big trouble elsewhere, but here the atom is still king. Last year's Three Mile Island accident in Pennsylvania, which shook up the rest of the nation, caused barely a ripple in the Tri-Cities. Local officials still dream of building a vast nuclear-energy

---

Source: *The Wall Street Journal*, Thursday, March 6, 1980, pp. 1 and 34.

park at the Hanford reservation. The park would consist of 20 atomic plants that could power the entire Northwest. Three plants are under construction by a public-power agency, and a consortium of four privately owned utilities recently asked the U.S. government for sites for two more. The community is all for it.

FEW CHEERS FOR NADER

Those who would challenge nuclear power—the Ralph Naders and Jane Fondas—are held in low esteem. When Mr. Nader held an antinuclear rally in Richland last year, he drew a mere 20 supporters of his view, but he also attracted a chanting mob of about a thousand pro-nuclear demonstrators.

If by now you're getting the idea that this is a place apart from the rest of the country, you're right. Welcome to Atomsville, U.S.A.

You can buy groceries at the Atomic Foods Supermarket in Pasco, get a rubdown at the Atomic Health Center in Kennewick and buy your kids "atomic marbles" at the Hanford Science Center in Richland. A local high-school team is nicknamed the Richland Bombers (plutonium for the atomic bomb dropped on Nagasaki was made at Hanford), and the community even has its "atomic man," Harold McCluskey.

In a Hanford accident three-and-one-half years ago, Mr. McCluskey, now 67, suffered the most severe radioactive contamination of any surviving worker in history. A container of radioactive material blew up in his face. At one point his body was so radioactive that medical people attending him had to shield themselves. Today, doc-

tors report, Mr. McCluskey is free of all but 5 percent of the contamination he absorbed. He still isn't well—he has chemical burns, for example, and his nervous system has been affected—but he is well enough to lecture civic groups on the need for improved nuclear safety.

Despite his accident, the retiree remains 100 percent behind nuclear power. "It's the only way out of this crisis," he says, referring to the nation's energy problems. If he were able to, Mr. McCluskey says he would go back to work at Hanford "in a minute."

Politicians here get elected on promises to bring in nuclear waste, not keep it out. Even the local Sierra Club conservationists favor nuclear power. (Most of its members work in the nuclear industry.)

The Tri-Cities is a lonely place for anyone who harbors any antinuclear sentiment. A year and a half ago, Stephen Stalos, a manager of nuclear-waste disposal at the Rockwell Hanford unit of Rockwell International Corp., took a leave of absence to run in the Democratic primary against pronuclear Congressman Mike McCormack. Mr. Stalos ran on a platform of concern about nuclear-waste handling. Although he expected to lose by a two-to-one margin, he hoped his campaign would mark the start of a local dissident movement. He lost by nine to one and later left his job and moved away.

Why is the Tri-Cities so comfortable with nuclear power? "I can tell you in three words: We understand it," says Sam Volpentest. Mr. Volpentest is the 75-year-old cofounder of the Tri-City Nuclear Industrial Council, which promotes the nuclear industry. He says, "We've lived with it and have had no problems for 35 years."

Publisher Lee has devoted the past 20 years to promoting nuclear power. His and his newspaper's views on nuclear power are unequivocal. "It isn't even a calculated risk," he says.

Hanford's nuclear professionals, who recognize risk in everything, wouldn't go quite that far. But they scoff at the blunders of Three Mile Island and say that it couldn't happen here. Keener Earle, a young nuclear engineer, represents the thinking of many of his colleagues who are confident that their education and training give them the ability to handle the nuclear genie safely. "I understand nuclear power," he says. "To me a reactor is simpler than the engine in my car."

Such confidence quickly rubs off. Dean Schau, a state labor-market economist, says he was antinuclear when he came to the Tri-Cities eight months ago, but after talking with Hanford people, he changed his mind. "They aren't afraid of it," he says. "Now they're talking about making a permanent waste-disposal site there. I don't know the technical aspects of it, but they've convinced me they can handle it now and into the future."

Hanford was the site of the nation's first wartime reactor back in 1944 when the federal government selected this isolated place in Washington's desert as the best spot in the nation to make plutonium for the first atomic bombs. Most of the plutonium in the nation's nuclear arsenal was made at Hanford. The government started shutting down the Hanford reactors in the mid-1960s because plenty of plutonium had been stockpiled and a more modern plant had been built in Georgia. Only one of the original nine reactors here is still in operation—the dual-purpose "N" reactor that also produces electrical power for the Washington Public Power Supply System, a statewide agency.

It was when the government started shutting down its Hanford reactors that a handful of local leaders hastily formed the Nuclear Industrial Council to try to keep the surrounding community from dying. Mr. Volpentest recalls the urgency: "At that time Hanford made up 70 percent of the payroll of the area. Take away Hanford and what have we got? Nothing but a big river."

Intense political lobbying, along with some help from Washington's Senators, Democrats Warren Magnuson and Henry Jackson, paid off. The reactor phase-out became the springboard for creation of a dazzling complex of government-sponsored nuclear and other high-technology research and development on and off the reservation.

Billions of federal dollars have poured into the Tri-Cities, and the spigot is still flowing.Current major projects include a nuclear-fuel test facility for breeder-reactor research and work on permanent nuclear-waste-disposal technology. (Hanford already houses, in temporary storage, most of the nation's nuclear waste. Nuclear experts say that the unusual basalt formation beneath the reservation may turn out to be the best place in the United States to permanently store such waste.)

The three nuclear power plants now being built on the reservation are being constructed by the Washington Public Power Supply System. This project, along with the federal work, has made the Tri-Cities one of the fastest-growing communities in the nation. Population has spurted to nearly 130,000. (It was less than 5,000 at the end of World War II.) One of the attractions is high pay. Some Hanford examples: about $16 an hour for carpenters, more than $19 for boilermakers and electricians, and $20 and up for pipe fitters and sheet-metal workers.

Economist Schau says that the number of jobs grew by about seven percent last year, twice the rate of increase for the state as a whole. Because of the nuclear work already begun, he says, this growth "should go on through 1981, regardless of what the national economy does."

The marks of a fast growing, transient population are everywhere: jammed trailer parks, sprawling shopping centers, strings of fast-food restaurants, and roads clogged with traffic at quitting time. "Anyone who has lived here longer than three years is considered an old-timer," says a Kennewick banker.

And there is wide awareness of the source of this prosperity. "Nuclear butters the bread of a lot of people here," Mr. Schau says. Of a work force of 74,000 persons, nearly 20,000 are directly employed by the nuclear industry. The ripple effect is great. "Just about everyone here" depends in some way on nuclear energy for his job, Mr. Schau says. The second largest sector of the labor force is agriculture, which employs a mere 2,000.

While private power companies haven't flocked to this area—they have been reluctant to build plants far away from their customers—that attitude is changing. Puget Sound Power recently announced that it was considering Hanford after running into a buzzsaw of opposition over plans to build a nuclear power plant in the Skagit Valley northeast of Seattle. Warren Ferguson, Puget Sound Power's vice president for energy and construction, says:

"There's no question that in the long term my company and all Northwest utilities will be participating in Hanford's energy center."

---

23. Midwest Nuclear Plant, In the Works 13 Years, Keeps Facing Delays
John R. Emshwiller
and Robert L. Simison

MIDLAND, Mich.—Shock waves from Three Mile Island are still reverberating a year later here, far from the scene of the Pennsylvania nuclear-plant accident.

Effects of the accident probably will continue to be felt by utilities across the nation, especially those involved in the 90 or so nuclear plants currently under construction, as new safety requirements force up their costs and lengthen construction periods. Consumers, in turn, are likely to pay a price in higher costs of products from aspirin to automobiles.

With the Nuclear Regulatory Commission still devising a new set of rules governing nuclear-plant construction, utilities building such

Source: *The Wall Street Journal,* March 4, 1980, pp. 1 and 27.

plants are in a bind. And nowhere is the pinch more obvious than at Consumers Power Co., which supplies much of the power for the factories in Michigan that turn out cars, cornflakes, computers and thousands of other products. General Motors Corp. alone pays the utility about $150 million a year for electricity.

PREVIOUS PROBLEMS

Consumers Power may not be typical of the utilities set back by the Three Mile Island crisis. For one thing, its two-unit nuclear plant near here, which has been in the works for 13 years, faced major problems even before the Pennsylvania accident.

But the extent of Consumers Power's problems became evident recently when the utility raised its cost estimate on the plant project to $3.1 billion, nearly double the earlier estimate of $1.67 billion, and delayed the expected completion three years, to the end of 1984. It blamed the increase largely on reviews and changes it expects to make to meet federal safety requirements flowing from the Three Mile Island accident.

The leap in costs for the Midland plant, it is estimated, could eventually mean a one-third increase in Consumers Power electricity rates.

The problems of Consumers Power aren't unique. Irvin C. Bupp, a Harvard business professor who has worked extensively on nuclear economics, predicts the nuclear-safety furor will add an average of two years to the completion time of each nuclear-plant project. "The nuclear industry is in big trouble," he says.

BIG INVESTMENT

One immediate problem for Consumers Power: whether to press ahead with its troubled plant. Company officials say the chances of abandoning the project are slim. But John Selby, chairman, says an abandonment isn't out of the question. "Right now our investment is $1.3 billion," he says. "We have to decide whether we want to invest another $1.8 billion to make that good." The company is expected to announce plans for the project this week.

Getting the additional money won't be easy. The company expects to have to borrow $3.7 billion in the next five years instead of the $2.4 billion projected before the plant cost estimate was raised. The financial markets may balk at lending that much more to the utility, and Consumers Power's credit rating may ultimately suffer.

Moreover, Consumers Power says, the costs of the Midland project will mean cutting back some other operations, with the risk of creating power shortages in the next few years. But without the Midland plant, the utility warns that more serious shortages may occur later.

"We are in a very serious situation," Mr. Selby says. And Consumers Power's major customers express similar alarm over the delay and the big increase in prospective costs for the Midland plant. The potential consequences are "horrendous," General Motors says. And Charles Drury, chairman of Hayes-Albion Corp., a big auto-industry supplier, says, "A blow like this could cause some hardships down the road."

DOW CHEMICAL'S DILEMMA

For Dow Chemical Co., the hardships may not be far down the road. Dow, potentially the nuclear plant's main customer, has contracts to buy large amounts of electricity and steam for its vast Midland chemical-making complex.

But Dow is concerned that the power supply will be jeopardized by the delay until late 1984 in completing the Consumers Power's plant. Dow's dilemma is whether to wait and hope it doesn't run short, or to line up alternative generating sources and face paying Consumers Power about $430 million for pulling out of its contracts.

Consumers Power and other utilities in similar straits blame the industry's problems largely on the Nuclear Regulatory Commission. The NRC, says Consumers' Mr. Selby, seems ready to "adopt any safety idea that anybody has thought of in the last 20 years."

Actually, except for some changes to deal with the most immediate problems raised by the accident, the NRC hasn't formally adopted anything. It has been trying to put together an "action" plan of new requirements. The latest draft contains some 150 items. They range from such relatively inexpensive ones as improved worker training, to potentially costly design changes aimed at better containment of radiation during major accidents.

The NRC argues that this is complex and time-consuming. But nuclear advocates, besides complaining about the cost of the changes, contend that the NRC's failure to act quickly is itself causing problems.

Niagara Mohawk Power Corp., for instance, recently pushed back by two years the completion date of a nuclear plant it is building in upstate New York. The utility blames the uncertainty surrounding safety rules. "It doesn't make sense to put something in now if you might have to tear it out later," the company says.

While few doubt that Three Mile Island is affecting nuclear projects, some observers say utilities may use the regulatory uncertainties as an excuse to mask other problems. Many nuclear projects had already been set back by lack of money and slower-than-expected growth in demand for electricity, one observer notes, and "a utility may see this as a timely moment to announce a new delay and blame it all on Three Mile Island."

Roger Mattson, a senior NRC official who is leading the agency's effort to devise the "action" plan, thinks the utility industry is "over-reacting" to the safety reviews. He believes the changes being considered can be made with relatively little effect on projects if the effort "is properly managed by the government and industry."

In any case, says Victor Gilinsky, one of the NRC's five commissioners, improved safety is the most important consideration. The costs may be painful, he says, "but it might be the price we have to pay for past neglect."

A "BEST GUESS"

Because the final safety rules aren't yet issued, Consumers Power says it has had to make decisions based on what it anticipates will be necessary. So the increased cost estimate, says Stephen H. Howell, senior vice president for projects engineering and construction, "is our best guess."

The company is scrambling to revise and implement new building plans, an effort complicated by the large amount of work already done. Indeed, to a visitor, the plant looks nearly finished. The two reactors built by Babcock & Wilcox Co. (which, incidentally, supplied the reactor at Three Mile Island) have long been sitting in their 195-foot-high containment buildings.

But lots of work still needs to be done—and in some cases redone. New safety instruments will be installed. Miles of cable are being ripped out and rerouted, and another five million feet will be added. The utility expects to have to replace two multi-million-dollar computers with newer, more powerful models. Before Three Mile Island, the company estimated that 85 percent of the project's engineering work was done; that now has dropped to 59 percent.

Over half the $1.4 billion in additional cost, though, doesn't come from new hardware but from the time needed to get it done, the utility says. It figures about $570 million extra will be needed just to cover interest charges, insurance and taxes during the extended construction period.

TIME IS BIGGEST ENEMY

Indeed, time has probably always been the greatest enemy of the Midland project. When announced in 1967, the 1,361,000-kilowatt facility was supposed to cost about $350 million and be completed by

1975. It was born in an era of little organized opposition to the rapid development of atomic energy. Safety questions now considered important were given little if any attention then.

Unfortunately for Consumers Power, the project has gone on long enough to encounter almost all of the major problems that have beset the nuclear industry. Environmentalists fought it; getting regulatory approvals has taken increasing time and effort and for a while, the company even ran out of money to keep building.

In a vicious circle, each delay opened the project to the next controversy and further setbacks. For instance, part of the redesign going on at Midland is to meet new federal fire-protection criteria derived from a serious fire five years ago at an Alabama nuclear plant.

Though problems at Midland aren't new, the latest are big enough to shake even veteran Consumers Power executives. When the new estimates came in, "I swallowed pretty hard," says Mr. Howell.

IS DOW DECISIVE?

Dow Chemical, with a big stake in the project, also swallowed hard, and then began considering other courses of action. If Dow would pull out of its Consumers Power contracts, some observers doubt the utility could justify completing both nuclear units at Midland.

Dow is already being squeezed by the delays. Its Midland complex currently gets power from two aging plants fired by fossil fuel, and the Environmental Protection Agency recently took the chemical company to court seeking more than $23 million in fines for alleged violations of clean-air laws. Because of the delay in completing the Consumers Power nuclear plant, Dow now says it expects to spend $25 million to keep its powerhouses running in the years ahead. But that effort will only give Dow some breathing room. If it doesn't get power from the new Consumers plant, it will still need to find other sources.

The Michigan Public Service Commission also faces tough decisions. The agency is being urged by opponents of the nuclear plant to disapprove of further financing, but it may not have that power even if it had the inclination. With so much already invested at Midland, PSC Chairman Daniel Demlow says, "There isn't any easy way out."

One customer unperturbed by the Consumers Power setback is Wolverine Electric Cooperative, which intends to stick with its plans to buy 96,000 kilowatts of the nuclear plant's power despite the increased price. "It's just like any other contract," says John Keen, general manager of the cooperative. "We'll pass it on to our customers."

24. HELEN CALDICOTT: The Voice the Nuclear Industry Fears

Katie Leishman

In 1902 Pierre and Marie Curie culminated four years of research in their laboratory shed in Paris: they isolated radium, a shimmering, intensely radioactive element. The young couple's joy was later recounted by their daughter, Eve: "Their two faces turned toward the pale glimmering, the mysterious sources of radiation. . . . Marie was to remember forever this evening of glowworms, this magic."

It is a long line between the glowworms in Madame Curie's laboratory jars and the night lights atop the Three Mile Island nuclear power plant in Middletown, Pennsylvania. But it is a line that pediatrician and nuclear critic Dr. Helen Caldicott can clearly draw.

"The Curies did pioneering research, wonderful work that helped introduce a treatment for cancer. Yet they also, unknowingly, helped create the nuclear problem we have today. Pure science is wonderful. It's in the applied technology that the threat to human life surfaces."

In 1952 Helen Caldicott was a bookish 14-year-old in Melbourne, Australia, when she read Nevil Shute's *On the Beach,* a novel in which humanity is annihilated by a nuclear war. The story haunted her as she grew older and watched the fiction spin into the reality of an international arms race that escalated during the years that she finished her medical studies and got married.

"In 1962, when my husband and I decided to have our first child, I had nightmares thinking that the baby would live to see the horrors that I'd read about as a girl," she recalls.

Caldicott sought more scientific books about nuclear issues after France's 1971 bomb tests in the South Pacific produced high levels of radioactivity in the drinking water of southern Australia. She learned that the carcinogenic and mutagenic substances released by atom bombs were also released in the operation of nuclear power plants. What affected her most was the discovery that children and fetuses were far more vulnerable than adults to radiation dangers.

"I was a pediatrician specializing in cystic fibrosis, the most common of all fatal genetic diseases. I saw my young patients die. I saw other children dying of leukemia and cancer. I realized that these diseases would increase as the radiation in the environment in-

---

Source: *Ms.,* July 1979, pp. 50–93 *passim.*

creased," Caldicott says. "I decided that promoting the elimination of nuclear weapons and power was part of practicing pediatrics and real preventive medicine." By the end of the year, her lectures, editorials, and radio and television appearances had won over 75 percent of Australia's population. Citizens launched a continent-wide boycott of French products that led to a banning of the tests. The young physician's place was established in the international network of antinuclear leaders.

In 1977, Helen Caldicott and her family moved to Boston, where her commitments today include a full-time pediatrics practice at Children's Hospital, international speaking engagements, and the presidency of a national organization of doctors opposed to nuclear power, the Physicians for Social Responsibility. She has also managed to write a book, *Nuclear Madness: What You Can Do!* Little wonder that she moves, walks, and talks like a molecule under pressure.

In a first encounter Caldicott can seem abrupt or inattentive. But just when you've decided that she is perfunctory, she stops mid-sentence and says in her lyrical Australian accent, "It's going to rain so put up your 'brellie. What did you have for breakfast? Eggs? Excellent. That women had violet eyes. So unusual." Then she darts off, humming, checking her watch, and crossing off the next item on her list of things to do.

Before appearing on a local television show, she merely refastens her hair clip and straightens her neckerchief. After the taping she walks—actually, runs—off the set, murmuring, "Sometimes I have so much to say and so little time that everything I say sounds jumbled to me."

It doesn't sound that way to anyone else. "She is probably the most effective antinuclear speaker in the country," says Harvard's Nobel prize-winning biologist, Dr. George Wald. "As a mother and pediatrician, she doesn't hesitate to raise moral questions or display intense emotions about these matters that are life-threatening in the extreme. She has a gift for making the hard scientific facts meaningful to the public."

That gift was especially apparent when she addressed an agitated crowd in a college auditorium in Harrisburg, Pennsylvania, one month after the accident at the nearby Three Mile Island nuclear plant.

"It's an absolute privilege to be here with you," she told her 900 listeners: college students, grandparents with babies in their laps, physicians, families, young couples, and pregnant women.

"My heart was with you last month, because I knew what the consequences would have been if that monster had melted down. My children were in Boston and I was a very worried mother. Boston is a long way from here, but twenty percent of the time, the wind blows from Harrisburg toward Boston—and if there had been a meltdown, Boston would have gone along with Harrisburg."

She paused.

"Of course, eighty percent of the time, the wind blows toward Washington, D.C., which is where the Nuclear Regulatory Commission people live. Which is why they were visibly sweating on national television. They, like me, have read the government's own documents which say what would happen in the event of a meltdown of a thousand megawatt nuclear plant, like the one nearby."

She opened a recent report from the Department of Energy and read aloud:

> Out of a predicted 10 million people who would be exposed to radiation, there would be 3,300 prompt fatalities; 45,000 cases of respiratory impairment and burning of the lung; 240,000 cases of thyroid damage; 350,000 cases of temporary sterility in males; 40,000 to 100,000 cases of prolonged or permanent suppression of menstruation in women; 10,000 to 100,000 cases of acute radiation illness.
>
> As for babies in utero: 100,000 of them would be exposed. All of them could develop cretinism. There might be 1,500 cases of microcephaly—that is, babies born mentally retarded with abnormally small heads.
>
> Fifteen years after the event, we could expect 270,000 cases of cancer and 28,800 thyroid tumors and 5,100 genetic diseases. That all adds up to nearly one million so called health effects.

When she finished reading, the only sound in the room was a baby's crying.

"Did any officials tell you of these figures last month?" she asked the crowd.

"No!" they answered.

"Have they yet told us exactly how much radiation escaped from the plant?"

"No."

"No. In fact, they didn't even measure alpha or beta emission [the most harmful] in the first forty-eight hours after the accident. They said everything was under control. Yet if you read the NRC transcripts, it is clear that those men didn't know what on earth they were doing. And when, by the grace of God, there wasn't a meltdown, those officials say: 'See? We managed. Nuclear power is safe after all.'

"Well, it isn't—and that's what brings me here. Because in my work I see children, as beautiful as yours and mine, die from genetic diseases, from leukemia and cancer—diseases that radiation can induce."

The distress in her voice softened as the parent-turned-professor took her audience—by means of blackboard illustrations and simple explanations—inside a nuclear power plant, an atom, the body, and the womb.

The element critical to the nuclear fuel cycle is uranium. As it decays or fissions in a nuclear reactor, uranium yields 200 fission products, or isotopes; these emit invisible gamma rays and alpha or beta particles. The isotopes may be inhaled; or if they settle on pastures, fields, or rivers, they travel up the food chain and are ultimately ingested by humans.

Isotopes released by a nuclear plant are cesium-135, plutonium, iodine-131, strontium-89 and -90. Once inside the body, these isotopes lodge in different areas or organs, depending on their chemical similarity to the harmless elements that "seek" such regions as the thyroid, reproductive organs, bones, or lungs.

Plutonium is the isotope that most concerns Dr. Caldicott. She says: "Plutonium lodges in the lungs, bones, and gonads. So potent is it that one millionth of a gram is described by most scientists as carcinogenic.

"Imagine: if one pound of plutonium were crushed in bits, and a bit were placed in the lungs of every person on earth, it would kill us all. *One pound.* And yet a one-thousand megawatt nuclear plant produces roughly five hundred pounds of it a year.

"Plutonium contaminates a nuclear plant's waste material, so that it remains radioactive for half a million years. The waste must be stored in isolation. Yet present technology only permits us to store the waste for ten years before it eats through any container and plutonium begins to seep into the air, earth, and water.

"The Department of Energy recently held nationwide hearings to ask us—the public—what they should do with the millions of accumulated gallons of toxic waste. Well, we couldn't tell them. So they reported to the president, saying that they had no solution now, but probably would have one by 1995. That's like me telling a patient with cancer that the prognosis was six months, but I'd probably have a cure in thirty years."

With a few chalk drawings Dr. Caldicott explained what plutonium and other isotopes do inside the body. Radiation produced by radioactive particles breaks through the cell walls, damaging the cell and often the genes in the cell's nucleus. If a sperm or egg cell is struck, the baby may be born with a disease such as diabetes, hemophilia, or cystic fibrosis. Even if the baby manifests no disorders, it will almost always transmit the damaged gene to its offspring; the disease may surface generations later.

Dr. Caldicott used another simple drawing to depict the delayed repercussions if the damaged gene is one that controls the cell's rate of division. "Years later the damaged cell, instead of reproducing normally, manufactures billions of identically damaged cells. That process, called cancer, is most likely to occur when cells are dividing as they do during growth periods. That's why children are ten to twenty times more vulnerable than adults to the effects of radiation—and fetuses most vulnerable of all."

Among the radioactive isotopes which pose the greatest threat to the baby in utero are iodine-131, strontium-89 and -90. Because strontium resembles calcium, it can contaminate mother's milk and lodge in the bones. Radioactive iodine lodges in the fetus's tiny developing thyroid, where, by damaging cells, it may indirectly inhibit the production of hormones that control growth patterns and the development of intelligence and mental function. It also increases the risk of thyroid cancer later in life and hypothyroidism, a condition which, if undetected in the first days after birth, can produce mental retardation or an abnormal sluggishness in speech and movement. Hypothyroidism was observed in babies born to survivors of the Hiroshima bombing.

Of course, the mutagenic effect of high level radiation—like that in Hiroshima—is now commonly recognized. So Dr. Caldicott emphasized studies that demonstrate radiation's harmful effects at much lower exposure levels:

> In 1956 British physician Dr. Alice Stewart released a report on the effects of X rays on babies in utero. It showed that a single X ray to the abdomen of a pregnant women could increase by 40 percent her offspring's chances of developing leukemia. The Stewart study called into question the reliability of "safety" levels of radiation. As Caldicott stresses, "It takes only one radioactive atom, one call, and one gene to initiate the cancer cycle."

> Dr. Joseph L. Lyon of the University of Utah surveyed the counties most affected by the fallout from nuclear tests conducted in Nevada throughout the 1950s and found a doubled incidence of luekemia among children born during the years of testing (1951 through 1958), as compared with those born before and after the testing.

> Radiation physicist Dr. Ernest Sternglass studied the impact of the 1976 Chinese nuclear bomb tests whose radioactive fallout came down in heavy rains over the east coast of the United States. He found that the infant mortality rate in the affected states increased up to 60 percent—in a year when the infant mortality rate nationwide declined by 6.5 percent.

Studies like these had once convinced Helen Caldicott that radioactivity in drinking water was enough to harm her family. But perhaps a study more relevant to the families she addressed in Harrisburg was the one released in 1969 by health physicist Dr. John Gofman. He reported that the normal emissions of a nuclear power plant could, by the year 2000, produce 32,000 excess cancers.

"These plants are dangerous even when they're operating normally," Dr. Caldicott told her audience. "What amazes me is people who say, 'It will take a major accident to make everyone get serious about this problem.' We can't wait for an accident, because it would mean catastrophe the likes of which we've never seen on earth.

"We are at a crossroads in time. What you people in Harrisburg decide to do about that plant could start a chain reaction around the world."

When the lecture was over, the blackboard was covered with a chalky mass of circles, dates, and numbers—and Caldicott was about to miss a plane. But as she hurried out of the auditorium, she stopped to talk with an older woman who had a question.

"Dr. Caldicott, how close to the plant would *you* live and still feel safe?"

Helen Caldicott touched the woman's arm and said softly, "Dear lady, I would move hundreds and hundreds of miles away."

At home in Boston, Caldicott tries to imagine that Harrisburg is millions and millions of miles away—tries to think of anything but nuclear issues. "I can't live with the fears and worry all the time," she says. "I concentrate on the beauty of music, flowers, my children." After scrutinizing Environmental Protection Agency reports for hours, she will lose herself in a mystery novel.

She combines a scientist's healthy pessimism with a child-like faith in people's better instincts. But she is also realistic. A recent trip back home taught her something about human nature. "Australians had forgotten everything we'd accomplished seven years ago. We'd closed the uranium mines. Now they're being reopened on aborigine lands. It seems as if you can never stop stirring the pot, or people stop caring," she says.

Her voice brightens as she describes the beauty of the aborigine territory. "We were there after the rainy season, so the hills were so, so green. The lakes were covered by acres of water lilies. Animals were everywhere—kangaroos, water buffalo, and ibis. Mount Brockman rises above it all, cut by a stream that the aborigines believe is protected by a rainbow snake."

She becomes pensive again and adds with a half-smile: "There's a myth which says that if the rainbow snake is disturbed, it will destroy the world. And now they'll be mining uranium all around this stream. Just what we need—more uranium for more reactors and bombs. Sometimes it seems—"

The phone rings and she runs to answer it. After scribbling a note about the departure time for the plane she's taking for another teach-in, she reappears. The previous conversation is forgotten, and she launches into another topic.

If Helen Caldicott moves quickly, seems preoccupied, or leaves sentences unfinished, it is not just because she has a family to feed, a patient to see, or a plane to catch. It is because she truly believes that time is running out before the promise of the Curies' glowworms is overshadowed by the vengeance of the rainbow snake.

Openness Of The System

One of the major pressures of business in recent years has been the expectation that managers exercise authority and full control over those aspects of their operations which have social consequences. Ironically, the exercise of authority and control can lead to a totalitarian-like atmosphere is an organization. There is a need, therefore, for accountability, but not dictatorial control.

Every major institution faces this dilemma of openness. If business is to be seen as legitimate, people must believe that it is responsive to their needs. That requires some sense of participation in decision making. Participation may come through representation in the corporate governance process; therefore the role of boards of directors in governing companies has emerged as a major issue. The composition, structure, and role of the board is of great importance in determining the appropriate conduct and performance of the corporation.

Another major element of corporate legitimacy is the opportunity for employees to contribute to decision making and to enjoy normal constitutional rights such as free speech, privacy, and due process. The traditional notion that top management exercises the right to control employees and to make all decisions without being questioned has given way to greater concern for human rights.

In short, the corporation cannot be viewed as a secret state protected from societal expectations about freedom. One area of particular significance has been the demand for greater financial disclosure by corporations. Largely as a result of efforts by the Securities and Exchange Commission during the 1970s, many companies were required to provide stockholders with data on sales and earnings by major product line, research and development expenditures, and foreign sales and earnings. The passage of the Foreign Corrupt Practices Act in 1977 required corporations to establish thorough internal control systems to account for the usage of all corporate funds.

Legislation and SEC requirements also tightened executive perquisites. Company cars, company-owned apartments and yachts, country club memberships, and the like had to be reported to shareholders. The pressure for greater openness also resulted in demands on accountants, lawyers, and regular employees to "blow the whistle" when they discover product hazards, fraud, or other forms of improper conduct.

The cases and readings in this section on corporate openness explore a wide range of issues. The section begins with a secondary case, McDonnell-Douglas Company: The DC-10. The case focuses on a product design problem and its implications for management control and disclosure. The Progressive Corporation, a primary case, treats an unusual situation involving a controversial display of art in the corporate headquarters and employee reaction. Borden, Inc.: Columbus Coated Fabrics is a secondary case concerning a series of confrontations between the Columbus Coated Fabrics' employees and management. The numerous articles in this section cover topics central to the openness of the system.

Case

McDONNELL-DOUGLAS CORPORATION: THE DC-10

On the evening of June 12, 1972 American Airlines Flight 96 took off from Detroit Metropolitan Airport with 56 passengers aboard. About five minutes later, the plane had reached 11,500 feet over Windsor, Ontario when suddenly there was a loud bang. Air rushed through the cockpit and the passenger cabin. Part of the rear of the cabin floor collapsed, and dust, ceiling panels, hatch doors, and baggage flew through the air, some of them hitting the passengers. The captain, Bryce McCormick, and his crew were able to regain control of the airplane and fly it back to the Detroit airport for an emergency landing. No one was seriously hurt.[1]

The cause of the near-crash was soon discovered: the rear cargo door had not been completely latched. The switch which turned off the cockpit's warning light had nevertheless been pushed by the mechanism, indicating to the crew that the door was safely closed. In the investigation which began the following morning, the baggage handler who had closed the door, William Eggert, testified that after shutting the cargo door electrically he had attempted to pull down the manual handle, but it would not go down. Unable to see inside the door, and sure that he had followed correct procedure so far, Eggert pulled harder on the handle, using his knee for extra leverage, and the handle went down into the locked position. Noticing that the vent door was still slightly crooked, he lifted the handle and pushed it down again to make sure it was closed. The vent door remained

[1] "No Bomb on Plane; Cargo Door Opened Explosively in Flight," *Los Angeles Times*, June 13, 1972, p. 1.

crooked, but an American Airlines mechanic indicated that this was not an unusual problem with DC-10 vent doors. The investigation showed that the latches had missed going over center by one third of an inch. When Eggert pushed on the exterior handle, one of the bars in the locking pin linkage had broken under the pressure.

Part of the reason the plane had been saved may have been the fact that it carried relatively few passengers (the DC-10 was built to carry 380 people). Under the weight of the full load, more of the floor might have collapsed, and the control cables and hydraulics could have been cut. After the incident, the plane's captain, Bryce McCormick, was asked by McDonnell-Douglas to advise the company as to what action it ought to take. McCormick suggested that they tell all DC-10 pilots what would happen in the event of an explosive decompression and explain the flying techniques he and his crew had used to land the plane safely. The company did not follow his suggestions.

Fifteen days after the Windsor incident, F. D. Applegate, director of product engineering for the Convair Division of General Dynamics Corporation of San Diego, California, wrote a memorandum expressing his frustration with the handling of the DC-10 cargo door problems (see Exhibit 1). He recommended that Convair, a subcontractor on the DC-10 project, contact McDonnell-Douglas "at the highest management level" to convince the company to correct the door design.[2] Applegate's immediate superior, J. B. Hurt, sent the memo to the Convair vice president in charge of the DC-10 project, M. C. Curtis, along with his own comment on it (see Exhibit 2). Hurt indicated that if Convair approached Douglas about the difficulties, they should realize that it would probably mean Convair would have to pay the costs of fixing the faulty door. He referred to the matter as "an interesting legal and moral problem."

THE McDONNELL-DOUGLAS COMPANY

The Davis-Douglas Aircraft Company was founded in 1920 in Long Beach, California by Donald Douglas with $600 of his own capital and $40,000 from a fellow aviation enthusiast, David R. Davis. Douglas, 28, had studied aeronautical engineering at M.I.T. and had worked for an aircraft company, Glenn L. Martin, for five years. The company's name was changed to the Douglas Aircraft Company in 1921, and in 1928 a new company with the same name was organized in Delaware to take over the assets of the California company. Three hundred thousand shares of stock were issued, of which Donald Douglas received 200,000.

---

[2] Paul Eddy, Elaine Potter, and Bruce Page, *Destination Disaster* (New York: Quadrangle/The New York Times Book Co., 1976), p. 185.

EXHIBIT 1
The Applegate Memorandum

27 June 1972
Subject: DC-10 Future Accident Liability.

The potential for long-term Convair liability on the DC-10 has caused me increasing concern for several reasons.

1. The fundamental safety of the cargo door latching system has been progressively degraded since the program began in 1968.
2. The airplane demonstrated an inherent susceptibility to catastrophic failure when exposed to explosive decompression of the cargo compartment in 1970 ground tests.
3. Douglas has taken an increasingly "hard-line" with regards to the relative division of design responsibility between Douglas and Convair during change cost negotiations.
4. The growing "consumerism" environment indicates increasing Convair exposure to accident liability claims in the years ahead.

Let me expand my thoughts in more detail. At the beginning of the DC-10 program it was Douglas' declared intention to design the DC-10 cargo doors and door latch systems much like the DC-8s and -9s. Documentation in April 1968 said that they would be hydraulically operated. In October and November of 1968 they changed to electrical actuation which is fundamentally less positive.

At that time we discussed internally the wisdom of this change and recognized the degradation of safety. However, we also recognized that it was Douglas' prerogative to make such conceptual system design decisions whereas it was our responsibility as a sub-contractor to carry out the detail design within the framework of their decision. It never occurred to us at that point that Douglas would attempt to shift the responsibility for these kinds of conceptual system decisions to Convair as they appear to be now doing in our change negotiations, since we did not then nor at any later date have any voice in such decisions. The lines of authority and responsibility between Douglas and Convair engineering were clearly defined and understood by both of us at that time.

In July 1970 DC-10 Number Two was being pressure-tested in the "hangar" by Douglas, on the second shift, without electrical power in the airplane. This meant that the electrically powered cargo door actuators and latch position warning switches were inoperative. The "green" second shift test crew manually cranked the latching system closed but failed to fully engage the latches on the forward door. They also failed to note that the external latch "lock" position indicator showed that the latches were not fully engaged. Subsequently, when the increasing cabin pressure reached about 3 psi (pounds per square inch) the forward door blew open. The resulting explosive decompression failed the cabin floor downward rendering tail controls, plumbing, wiring, etc. which passed through the floor, inoperative. This inherent

EXHIBIT 1 *(continued)*

failure mode is catastrophic, since it results in the loss of control of the horizontal and vertical tail and the aft center engine. We informally studied and discussed with Douglas alternative corrective actions including blow out panels in the cabin floor which would provide a predictable cabin floor failure mode which would accommodate the "explosive" loss of cargo compartment pressure without loss of tail surface and aft center engine control. It seemed to us then prudent that such a change was indicated since "Murphy's Law" being what it is, cargo doors will come open sometime during the twenty years of use ahead for the DC-10.

Douglas concurrently studied alternative corrective actions, in-house, and made a unilateral decision to incorporate vent doors in the cargo doors. This "band-aid fix" not only failed to correct the inherent DC-10 catastrophic failure mode of cabin floor collapse, but the detail design of the vent door change further degraded the safety of the original door latch system by replacing the direct, short-coupled and stiff latch "lock" indicator system with a complex and relatively flexible linkage. (This change was accomplished entirely by Douglas with the exception of the assistance of one Convair engineer who was sent to Long Beach at their request to help their vent door system design team.)

This progressive degradation of the fundamental safety of the cargo door latch system since 1968 has exposed us to increasing liability claims. On June 12, 1972 in Detroit, the cargo door latch electrical actuator system in DC-10 number 5 failed to fully engage the latches of the left rear cargo door and the complex and relatively flexible latch "lock" system failed to make it impossible to close the vent door. When the door blew open before the DC-10 reached 12,000 feet altitude the cabin floor collapsed disabling most of the control to the tail surfaces and aft center engine. It is only chance that the airplane was not lost. Douglas has again studied alternative corrective actions and appears to be applying more "band-aids." So far they have directed us to install small one-inch diameter, transparent inspection windows through which you can view latch "lock-pin" position, they are revising the rigging instructions to increase "lock-pin" engagement and they plan to reinforce and stiffen the flexible linkage.

It might well be asked why not make the cargo door latch system really "fool-proof" and leave the cabin floor alone. Assuming it is possible to make the latch "fool-proof" this doesn't solve the fundamental deficiency in the airplane. A cargo compartment can experience explosive decompression from a number of causes such as: sabotage, mid-air collision, explosion of combustibles in the compartment and perhaps others, any one of which may result in damage which would not be fatal to the DC-10 were it not for the tendency of the cabin floor to collapse. The responsibility for primary damage from these kinds of causes would clearly not be our responsibility, however, we might very

EXHIBIT 1 *(concluded)*

well be held responsible for the secondary damage, that is the floor collapse which could cause the loss of the aircraft. It might be asked why we did not originally detail design the cabin floor to withstand the loads of cargo compartment explosive decompression or design blow out panels in the cabin floors to fail in a safe and predictable way.

I can only say that our contract with Douglas provided that Douglas would furnish all design criteria and loads (which in fact they did) and that we would design to satisfy these design criteria and loads (which in fact we did). There is nothing in our experience history which would have led us to expect that the DC-10 cabin floor would be inherently susceptible to catastrophic failure when exposed to explosive decompression of the cargo compartment, and I must presume that there is nothing in Douglas's experience history, which would have led them to expect that the airplane would have this inherent characteristic or they would have provided for this in their loads and criteria which they furnished to us.

My only criticism of Douglas in this regard is that once this inherent weakness was demonstrated by the July 1970 test failure, they did not take immediate steps to correct it. It seems to me inevitable that, in the twenty years ahead of us, DC-10 cargo doors will come open and I would expect this to usually result in the loss of the airplane. (Emphasis added.) This fundamental failure mode has been discussed in the past and is being discussed again in the bowels of both the Douglas and Convair organizations. It appears however that Douglas is waiting and hoping for government direction or regulations in the hope of passing costs on to us or their customers.

If you can judge from Douglas's position during ongoing contract change negotiations they may feel that any liability incurred in the meantime for loss of life, property and equipment may be legally passed on to us.

It is recommended that overtures be made at the highest management level to persuade Douglas to immediately make a decision to incorporate changes in the DC-10 which will correct the fundamental cabin floor catastrophic failure mode. Correction will take a good bit of time, hopefully there is time before the National Transportation Safety Board (NTSB) or the FAA ground the airplane which would have disastrous effects upon sales and production both near and long term. This corrective action becomes more expensive than the cost of damages resulting from the loss of one plane load of people.

F. D. Applegate
Director of Product Engineering.

EXHIBIT 2
The Hurt Memorandum

3 July 1972.

From: J. B. Hurt.
Subject: DC-10 Future Accident Liability.

Reference: F. D. Applegate's Memo, same subject, date 27 June 1972.

I do not take issue with the facts or the concern expressed in the referenced memo. However, we should look at the "other side of the coin" in considering the subject. Other considerations include:

1.   We did not take exception to the design philosophy established originally by Douglas and by not taking exception, we, in effect, agreed that a proper and safe philosophy was to incorporate inherent and proper safety and reliability in the cargo doors in lieu of designing the floor structure for decompression or providing pressure relief structure for decompressions or providing pressure relief provisions in the floor. The Reliance clause in our contract obligates us in essence to take exception to design philosophy that we know or feel is incorrect or improper and if we do not express such concern, we have in effect shared with Douglas the responsibility for the design philosophy.

2.   In the opinion of our Engineering and FAA experts, this design philosophy and the cargo door structures and its original latch mechanism design satisfied FAA requirements and therefore the airplane was theoretically safe and certifiable.

3.   In redesigning the cargo door latch mechanism as a result of the first "blowout" experience, Douglas unilaterally considered and rejected the installation of venting provisions in the floor in favor of a "safer" latch mechanism. Convair engineers did discuss the possibility of floor relief provisions with Douglas shortly after the incident, but were told in effect, "We will decide and tell you what changes we feel are necessary and you are to await our directions on redesign." This same attitude is being applied by Douglas today and they are again making unilateral decisions on required corrections as a result of the AAL Detroit incident.

4.   We have been informally advised that while Douglas is making near-term corrections to the door mechanism, they are reconsidering the desirability of following-up with venting provisions in the floor.

I have considered recommending to Douglas Major Subcontracts the serious consideration of floor venting provisions based on the concern aptly described by the reference memo, but have not because:

1.   I am sure Douglas would immediately interpret such recommen-

EXHIBIT 2 *(continued)*

dation as a tacit admission on Convair's part that the original con-
currence by Convair of the design philosophy was in error and that
therefore Convair was liable for all problems and corrections that
have subsequently occurred.

2. Introducing such expression at this time while the negotiations of
SECP 297 and discussion on its contractual justification are being
conducted would introduce confusion and negate any progress that
had been made by Convair in establishing a position on the subject. I
am not sure that discussion on this subject at the "highest management level" recommended by the referenced memo would produce a
different reaction from the one anticipated above. We have an interesting legal and moral problem, and I feel that any direct conversation on this subject with Douglas should be based on the assumption
that as a result Convair may subsequently find itself in a position
where it must assume all or a significant portion of the costs that are
involved.

J. B. Hurt
Program Manager, DC-10 Support Program.

Initially, Douglas built military planes. Its first commercial
airplane, the DC-1, appeared in 1933. The plane's designer, Arthur
Raymond, felt that for Douglas to be a success with commercial aircraft, the company would have to "build comfort and put wings on
it."[3] The DC-1 was quieter and more luxurious than any other planes
built at that time. Its successor, the DC-3, appeared two years later
and proved to be one of the most successful airplanes ever built. Over
10,000 DC-3s were built for use as transport planes during World War
II, and a number of DC-3s were still in service in the 1980s.

Until the mid-1950s, Douglas remained the unchallenged leader in
commercial aviation. However, while Douglas abandoned the idea of
building a pressurized aircraft in 1940, the Boeing Corporation of
Seattle, Washington and the Lockheed Corporation of Burbank,
California continued to work on pressurized planes. In 1940 Boeing
developed the first pressurized passenger airliner, the Model 307
Stratoliner, which carried 33 passengers and travelled at 20,000 feet
(the DC-3 could carry 20 passengers and flew in the comparatively
turbulent air at 11,000 feet). Douglas finally produced a pressurized
airplane, the DC-6, in 1946, but only one year later Boeing entered the
jet era with the XB-47 bomber. The DC-3 remained an extremely

---

[3] Ibid., p. 35.

popular airplane, however. In 1950, two thirds of all the aircraft on scheduled service in the noncommunist countries had been built by Douglas, and in 1955 the figure was 50 percent.[4] It was after the appearance of the Boeing 707 in 1957 that Douglas sales began to fall. In 1956 Douglas sold 106 airplanes; in 1957 it sold 167; in 1958 it still sold more planes than Boeing, Convair, Lockheed, and Fairchild together; but in 1959 the company sold only 22 airplanes, while Boeing sold 73 of its 707s.[5]

In the first generation of commercial jet airliners, there were three classes: long-range, mid-range, and short-range. In the long-range category the competitors were the Boeing 707 and the Douglas DC-8. The 707 was a commercial derivative of a military aircraft—the KC-135—for which the government had paid most of the development costs. The development cost of the DC-8 had been paid by Douglas so the DC-8 always had difficulty being price competitive with the 707. Nevertheless, the DC-8 program was successful. It had a production run of 556, reportedly well above break-even. In the short-range class, the DC-9 was a clear winner over the Boeing 737. However, the Boeing 727 had the crucial mid-range class all to itself and became the biggest money-maker in commercial jet transport history. Douglas' inability to compete with the highly popular 727 contributed to a $75 million loss in 1966, the year in which the company was taken over by the McDonnell Aircraft Company.

The McDonnell Aircraft Company had been founded in St. Louis, Missouri in 1938, nearly 20 years after the Douglas Company. Its founder, James S. McDonnell, was, like Donald Douglas, a graduate of M.I.T. and had spent a number of years working for other aircraft companies. He started his own company with $165,000 in capital and received no orders for the entire first year of the company's existence. In 1939 McDonnell began making parts for military aircraft, and in 1940 the firm received a contract from the U.S. government to research the use of jet propulsion in military airplanes. Beginning in 1946, McDonnell produced an extremely successful line of fighter planes for the military, including the Phantom jets and the Banshee, Voodoo, and Demon fighters which were used extensively during the Korean War. By the mid-1960s McDonnell Aircraft was a very successful and profitable company.

In 1963 James McDonnell bought 200,000 shares of stock in the Douglas Aircraft Company but failed to gain control of the company and subsequently sold the stock. In 1966, however, with Douglas facing bankruptcy, McDonnell was able to present the most attractive

[4] Ibid., p. 41.
[5] Ibid., p. 42.

of several offers to take over the company. Under new McDonnell management, production of the DC-8 and DC-9 airplanes at the Long Beach plant continued, and plans started to be developed for the new DC-10 "airbus." The Douglas plant delivered 195 planes in 1967 and 302 in 1968. Production time was reduced, and Douglas's debts began to be repaid. By July of 1970, *Forbes* could call McDonnell-Douglas "perhaps the healthiest major [airplane manufacturing] company."[6] By 1971, the company ranked 45th on the *Fortune* 500 with sales of $2.1 billion and a net income of $81 million.[7]

THE BUILDING OF THE DC-10

Douglas had begun work on a long-range airliner to carry 400 people in 1965, but when the Boeing 747 was announced in 1966, Douglas decided to slow down its development of the DC-10. The plane was rescheduled to be completed in 1974 or 1975, and Douglas indicated that it hoped waiting would enable the company to build a better airplane. Then in September 1967 Lockheed presented detailed specifications for its L-1011 (later named the TriStar), a wide-bodied, three-engined jumbo jet for short to medium-range travel. Realizing that it was going to lose its opportunity in the wide-bodied jet market to the L-1011 and the 747, McDonnell-Douglas promptly announced two months later that it would produce the DC-10. The development of the DC-10 and the L-1011 progressed at about the same rate.[8]

Then there was the problem of selling the DC-10 to the airlines, which by 1967 flew primarily Boeing jets. Lockheed and McDonnell-Douglas engaged in stiff competition for orders from the major U.S. airlines. Each company tried to present a more favorable package, and concessions were made to the airlines concerning such matters as higher payloads, lower prices, more luxurious interior design, and easier financing.

One concession made by McDonnell-Douglas to American Airlines concerned the cargo doors of the DC-10. McDonnell-Douglas had planned to use a hydraulic system to close the doors—something the company had used before successfully—but American wanted a door closing mechanism with fewer working parts. The airlines' engineers suggested an electrically driven system, and McDonnell-Douglas agreed to the change.

---

[6] *Forbes*, July 1, 1970, p. 31.

[7] "The Fortune Directory of the 500 Largest Industrial Corporations," *Fortune*, vol. 85, no. 5 (May 1972), p. 190.

[8] Douglas J. Ingells, *The McDonnell-Douglas Story* (Fallbrook, Calif.: Aero Publishers, Inc., 1979), ch. 12.

American Airlines agreed to buy the DC-10s for $15.3 million each. Then Lockheed announced a price cut to $14.4 million each for its TriStars, and Eastern Airlines, Trans World Airlines, Delta Airlines, and a British corporation named Air Holdings Ltd. announced that they would buy the TriStar. The remaining major American airline, United, finally chose the DC-10 after Douglas lowered the price by $500,000. Considerable pressure was apparently put on United by the other airlines to buy the TriStar; the argument was that if two airbuses were built, both manufacturers would have difficulty remaining financially healthy. Indeed, had United decided to buy the TriStar, the DC-10 program would have ended; the costs were simply too high to continue developing a plane for which there were few orders. However, one of the reasons United's president George Keck gave for choosing the DC-10 was that he felt it would be bad for the industry if McDonnell-Douglas were forced out of the commercial airplane business.

Development costs for the TriStar and the DC-10 appeared in 1967 to be about $1 billion for each company.[9] Boeing had committed 90 percent of its net worth, $750 million, to the development of the 747. The 747 had been well received as a long-distance aircraft. In order to succeed, the DC-10 the TriStar had to establish that they would be efficient at shorter distances. After the United decision, Lockheed had sold a total of 168 TriStars, and McDonnell-Douglas had sold 86 DC-10s. For both companies to begin to make a profit on these aircraft, however, a total of at least 500 planes would have to be sold. By the mid-1970s, due to the tremendous increase in fuel costs and the fact that air passenger traffic did not increase as had been predicted in the 1960s, it was estimated that it would take 15 to 20 years for the giant airplanes to become profitable.

While the TriStar and the DC-10, as they developed, were roughly equivalent in interior and exterior appearance, there were several major design differences. Large aircraft used hydraulic systems to enable the pilot to operate the controls easily. They employed "redundant" hydraulic systems: that is, while only one system was actually necessary to operate the airplane's controls, one or two parallel systems were installed to enable the plane to function in the event that one or even two of the systems stopped working. The pilot of a smaller jet such as the DC-9 might possibly be strong enough to manipulate the controls of that plane if all three hydraulic systems failed, but this was not the case with the jumbo jets. If their hydraulic systems did not work, the pilot had no way of operating the plane's

---

[9] Ibid., p. 81.

controls. For this reason, both Boeing and Lockheed decided to install four hydraulic systems in the 747 and the TriStar. Indeed, the crash of a 747 in San Francisco in June 1971 was averted by the fourth hydraulic system when the other three were severed during a takeoff mishap. However, McDonnell-Douglas decided to put only three hydraulic systems in the DC-10.

One of the major dangers to any of the wide-bodied jets was "explosive decompression." This problem was associated with the fact that these aircraft, like other jets, flew at 20,000 feet and above, where the atmosphere was extremely thin. Since passengers could not breathe the air at that height, jets that travelled there had to be pressurized—that is, the atmosphere inside the plane had to be similar in pressure and oxygen content to that near the ground. Thus, when a plane reached the higher atmosphere above 11,000 feet, the pressure inside the plane was considerably greater than that outside it. Normally this was no problem, as the aircraft's hull was built to withstand the pressure which in the case of a wide-bodied aircraft was about 20,000 tons, or seven and one half to nine pounds per square inch. But problems arose if a hole developed in the fuselage. This could happen in a number of ways: two airplanes could collide, a bomb might go off in a plane, or a door could come off; in fact, birds had even been known to crash through the pilot's windows. A small hole could be tolerated without difficulty—the air pressure was simply turned up to compensate for the leak. However, if a large hole appeared suddenly in the fuselage, the air inside the plane would rush out at tremendous speed to equalize the pressure inside and outside the plane. This was called "explosive decompression." Internal panels and floors, not as strong as the hull of the airplane, would collapse under the pressure of the escaping air.

A further complication was the fact that the 747, TriStar, and DC-10 all had their vital hydraulic tubes running under the floor of the passenger cabin. Beneath the passenger area was the baggage compartment with its cargo doors. Should one of the cargo doors come off or a bomb of moderate size explode, at least part of the cabin floor would collapse as the air from the passenger cabin above rushed down and out, and some of the hydraulic systems could be severed. In the case of the 747, there were two hydraulic systems on either side of the floor close to the hull wall, and that part of the floor was reinforced by braces. It was unlikely that both sides of the floor would collapse except in the case of a large explosion which, Boeing reasoned, would probably destroy the hull as well. Furthermore, the 747's control cables ran through the plane's ceiling, so that even if only one hydraulic system remained, the plane's controls would function. The TriStar and the DC-10, however, ran both control cables and hydraulic systems under the floor, so that a floor collapse could easily sever all controls and prove disastrous.

An obvious solution to the problem was to make the floors of the widebodied jets strong enough to withstand a sudden depressurization, or to vent them so that air could rush through without crushing the floor. However, the weight of a sufficiently reinforced floor would have meant reducing the number of passengers the jets could carry by about 12, and McDonnell-Douglas felt this would be unacceptable to the airlines. Placing enough vents in the floor to withstand loss of pressure was also a problem. Passengers and luggage could block the vents, and it was questionable whether such a vented floor would be strong enough to support the passengers.

Another way of making the floor collapse unlikely was to make the cargo doors "fail-safe"—that is, to make it impossible for them to come off. The ideal door for this purpose was a "plug" door. This type of door opened into the airplane and was larger than its frame. When closed, the internal pressure pushed the door tighter against its frame, making it impossible for the door to come open. Passenger doors on the wide-bodied jets were of the plug type. There were, however, disadvantages to the plug door: it was heavy, it had to open into the cargo hold, and it had to be very rigid, which meant that it did not bend in response to stress during flight with the rest of the aircraft's frame. Weight had to be kept to a minimum in large aircraft. The airlines wanted to carry as many passengers as possible, and that meant minimizing the weight of parts such as doors. The airlines were also unenthusiastic about doors which opened into the plane and took up valuable cargo space. So a door which opened outward was highly desirable.

The TriStar's solution to the dilemma was a "semi-plug" door which had been used successfully on the Boeing 727. It opened outward from hinges at the top. Along the sides of both door and frame were a series of steel "teeth." When the door was closed (by an electric motor), the teeth of the door passed between those on the frame. Once the door's teeth had passed the ones on the frame, the motor moved the door down several inches until the teeth of the door were directly behind those on the frame. In this position, the door would act as a plug: the pressure inside the door would push it more tightly closed.

The DC-10's cargo door opened outward like those of the 747 and the TriStar. However, it relied on its latching system to hold it in place. It used a series of "over-center" latches, which required a certain amount of pressure to push them down and around a latching bar at the bottom of the door frame. Once past the center of their arc, the latches could not be pushed back except with a pressure equal to that which had pushed them down to begin with. (The principle was similar to that of a light switch.) Thus, the latches could not slip back and open. However, they *had* to move the correct distance around the latching bar in order for the door to stay closed. If they or the motor or the door itself were out of adjustment, it would be possible for the door to appear to be latched when in fact the latches had not gone completely around the bars. Furthermore, the person closing the door had no way of seeing the latching system which was located inside the door. For this reason, it was necessary to have a back-up system to detect whether or not the latches had gone all the way around the latching bars. The DC-10 used a series of locking pins which were supposed to slide into position only after the latches were properly locked. The baggage handler whose job it was to close the door had to press an electric switch which shut the door, then one to latch it. Finally, he manually pushed down a lever to send the locking pins into place. The locking pin mechanism hit a switch as it went down, and this turned off a warning light in the pilot's cabin, indicating that the door was locked. Unfortunately a torque tube in the linkage between the lever which the baggage handler pushed and the locking pins was weak and could be bent rather easily. Thus, the lever could be pushed all the way down even if the latches were not over center and the locking pins could not go all the way down. The light could go off in the cockpit, making the crew think the door was closed. The plane could then take off with an improperly closed door and with a real possibility of explosive decompression.

CONVAIR

Since a vast number of parts were needed for an aircraft such as the DC-10, many of them were made by subcontractors, and one such subcontract went to the Convair Division of General Dynamics Corporation. General Dynamics had experienced serious financial problems in recent years. Indeed, the company's performance in 1971 earned it the dubious distinction of being labeled as one of the ten worst performers on the *Fortune* 500. The St. Louis-based firm had a net income of $22 million in 1971 on sales of $1.9 billion. As the 41st-ranked company on the *Fortune* list in 1970, General Dynamics had also been one of the worst performers with losses of $6.5 million sales of $2.2 billion.[10]

---

[10] "The Fortune Directory of the 500 Largest Industrial Corporations," *Fortune*, vol. 85, no. 5 (May 1972), p. 190 and "The Fortune Directory of the 500 Largest Industrial Corporations," *Fortune*, vol. 83, no. 5 (May 1971), p. 172.

Convair was to do the detail design of the fuselage and doors of the DC-10 according to McDonnell-Douglas specifications. The original contract between McDonnell-Douglas and Convair called for a hydraulic system to close the cargo door latches. The doors were also to have a manual locking system designed so that the handle or latch lever could not be stowed unless the door was properly closed and latched. However, in November 1968 McDonnell-Douglas told Convair that electrical rather than hydraulic actuators were to be used for the door latching system. This, McDonnell-Douglas said, would make each door 28 pounds lighter, and American Airlines had requested the electric system because they felt it would be easier to maintain. The hydraulic system was preferred by the Convair engineers because its fluid maintained a constant pressure on the latches while the door was closed, rather than having its power shut off like an electric current as soon as a switch was released. In addition, in the hydraulic system, unlike the electrical one, the latches could slide back if they were not completely around the latching bars, allowing the door to open as soon as moderate pressure developed inside the aircraft.

In mid-1969, Convair wrote up a "Failure Mode and Effects Analysis" (FMEA) for the DC-10 cargo door to indicate how likely the door was to fail and what the consequences would be. FMEAs would be given to McDonnell-Douglas regarding the safety of all major systems of the plane, and McDonnell-Douglas would likewise send FMEAs to the Federal Aviation Administration in Washington before the plane could be certificated for flight. Convair warned that there were several ways in which the cargo door might not be closed properly and could subsequently come open during flight. It classified this as a "Class 4 hazard," meaning one involving danger to the lives of the passengers and the possible crash of the plane. The FMEA indicated that the warning light in the cockpit might go off because of problems in the circuit regardless of whether the door was closed, and that ground crews could, after visually checking the position of the manually operated door handle, mistakenly think it was in the closed position when it was not. When FMEAs were finally submitted to the Federal Aviation Administration by McDonnell-Douglas, however, they did not discuss the possibility that serious hazards were associated with the cargo doors. General Dynamics was forbidden by its contract with McDonnell-Douglas to discuss any DC-10 problems with the Federal Aviation Administration.

In May 1970 the air conditioning system of "Ship 1," the first DC-10 to be completed, was tested at the Douglas plant in Long Beach. This meant that the plane was pressurized. When the pressure reached about four pounds per square inch, the forward lower cargo door blew out. The escaping air caused part of the passenger cabin floor to collapse. The mishap was blamed on a mechanic who, the company said, closed the door incorrectly. Nevertheless, McDonnell-Douglas decided to modify the cargo door and install a small vent door in it. The purpose of this smaller door was to serve as a check as to whether the cargo door was properly closed. The vent was closed by the handle which pushed down the locking pins. When the handle moved all the way down, the vent door closed. But, as was mentioned earlier, the locking pin linkage could bend and the pins would not go down. The handle, however—and therefore the vent door—could reach their closed position without indicating anything about the condition of the locking mechanism. Boeing had used a similar check on its 747 door (which used a hydraulic system to operate the latches), but their vent doors were closed by the locking pin mechanism and could not close if the pins did not reach their correct position.

An argument between McDonnell-Douglas and Convair ensued over who would pay for the installation of vent doors. McDonnell-Douglas argued that the vent door was a normal design change which Convair should have expected; it was Convair's fault that the floor had collapsed. There was a flaw in the floor design, and Convair had not told McDonnell-Douglas about it as required by their contract. Therefore, Convair should pay for the vent doors. Convair, on the other hand, maintained that the door design was satisfactory, and if Douglas insisted upon modifying it, there were better ways of doing so. Vent doors were installed, but the disagreement over who should pay was not resolved.

Despite the seriousness of the door problem, the DC-10 was completed and certificated as airworthy by the Federal Aviation Administration on July 29, 1971. Shortly thereafter, the planes began to be delivered to their buyers.

THE ROLE OF THE FEDERAL AGENCIES

The Federal Aviation Administration (FAA) was established by an act of Congress in 1958 and was responsible for the regulation of safety standards in American aviation and the promotion of its commercial success. It licensed pilots and airports and operated air traffic control systems. It had to approve each step in the designing and manufacturing of all American aircraft, and it certificated them as "airworthy" when they were completed. It had the power to inspect any aircraft manufacturing plant whenever it chose.

The FAA did not, it claimed, have enough personnel to carry out all the inspections necessary for the certification of an airplane. Therefore, the FAA appointed "Designated Engineering Representatives" (DERs) who were engineers employed by the aircraft manufacturers. It was the responsibility of the DERs to inspect the parts of a plane as they were built and make sure that they complied with FAA regulations. Of the 42,950 inspections conducted on parts of the DC-10 as it was built, about one fourth were done by FAA inspectors, and the remainder were carried out by McDonnell-Douglas engineers in their capacity as DERs.

The National Transportation Safety Board (NTSB) was responsible for the investigation of accidents. However, if its investigation revealed the need for some change in an aircraft or its manner of operation, enforcing the change was the job of the FAA. The FAA had the right to order that the change be made by issuing an Airworthiness Directive, which had the force of a federal law.

In the case of the Windsor incident, the NTSB—after an initial refusal by McDonnell-Douglas to disclose any information on cargo door problems—examined the company's records and found that there had been about 100 reports of problems with the closing of DC-10 cargo doors. The electric actuators sometimes failed to drive the over-center latches all the way around the latching bars. McDonnell-Douglas had first tried lubricating the latching bars. When that did not work, the company sent out a Service Bulletin to all purchasers of DC-10s, recommending that the airlines install heavier gauge wire in the power supply to the actuators to increase their power. The airlines involved (United, American, National, and Continental) had been in the process of making this alteration at the time of the Windsor mishap, but the rewiring had not yet been done on the plane involved in that incident.

The NTSB investigators recommended that it be made "physically impossible" to close the cargo doors improperly. The FAA did not want to ground all the DC-10s, because a large number were involved, and because air traffic during the summer of 1972 was particularly heavy.

The western regional office of the Federal Aviation Administration, headed by Arvin O. Basnight, began drafting the first of a series of Airworthiness Directives which Basnight assumed would be used to enforce modifications to the DC-10 cargo door. The first Airworthiness Directive would make mandatory the rewiring of the doors which had been recommended in the McDonnell-Douglas service bulletin. Subsequently, the installation of a peephole in the doors would be required. The peephole would be one inch square and would be placed over one of the locking pins. This would enable the person closing the door to look in and actually see that one of the pins had moved to its proper position—eliminating the major problem that the baggage handler had no way of seeing whether the door was closed.

But the Airworthiness Directives were never issued. On the morning of June 16, 1972 Mr. Basnight received a telephone call from the president of McDonnell-Douglas' Douglas Division, Jackson McGowen. McGowen told Basnight that he had talked the previous evening with John H. Shaffer, the new administrator of the FAA appointed by president Richard M. Nixon. Shaffer had indicated that since McDonnell-Douglas had been so cooperative with the FAA, there would be no need for the issuance of Airworthiness Directives against the company. Instead, McDonnell-Douglas and the FAA would make a "gentlemen's agreement" that the required work would be done. Basnight and his colleagues in the western division did not feel that such an agreement would be a sufficient remedy, nor that the rewiring would resolve the door closing problem, but their opinion was overruled by the Washington office. Arvin Basnight wrote an account of these events in a "Memorandum to File" dated June 20, 1972, which is reproduced in Exhibit 3.

EXHIBIT 3
The Basnight Memorandum to File

On Friday, 16 June 1972, at 8:50 AM, I received a phone call from Mr. Jack McGowan [sic], president, Douglas Aircraft Company, who indicated that late on Thursday, 15 June, he had received a call from Mr. Shaffer asking what the company had found out about the problem about the cargo door that caused American Airlines to have an explosive decompression.

Mr. McGowan [sic] said he had reviewed with the Administrator the facts developed which included the need to beef up the electrical wiring and related factors that had been developed by the Douglas Company working with FAA.

He indicated that Mr. Shaffer had expressed pleasure in the finding of reasonable corrective actions and had told Mr. McGowan that the corrective measures could be undertaken as a product of a Gentleman's Agreement thereby not requiring the issuance of an FAA Airworthiness Directive.

In light of this data, I consulted with Dick Sliff* as we were already preparing an airworthiness directive and Mr. Sliff advised that several steps seemed advisable to prevent future explosive decompression on the DC-10 cargo doors and the Air Worthiness Directive Board was reviewing what we considered an appropriate airworthiness directive.

Mr. Sliff also indicated that earlier in the week when FAA engineers

* Richard Sliff, then Chief of the Aircraft Engineering Division, Western Region, FAA.

EXHIBIT 3 *(continued)*

contacted the Douglas Company, the company people had not made available any reports indicating problems encountered by the operating airlines with the cargo doors. Mr. Sliff stated that he had raised a fuss because they had not produced the information and on the following day (which was about Wednesday) the company had produced data showing that approximately 100 complaints had been received by the company indicating that the airlines using the DC-10 had noted and reported to the company mechanical problems in locking the bulk cargo doors. Mr. Sliff was disturbed by the company's attitude and felt they had not performed well in that their cooperation with the FAA in considering this data had been unresponsive.

With Mr. Sliff present, I called Mr. Rudolf, FS-1,* and reviewed with him what we were doing, the background data available to me and informed him our Airworthiness Board was in session and asked his guidance as to their continuing this effort. He suggested we continue what we were doing and wanted a copy of our draft airworthiness directive, which Mr. Sliff had already furnished the Washington office by telecopier.

Later in the day, I received a call from Ken Smith, DA-1,† and reviewed basically the same background information, the action of our Airworthiness Board, our judgment as to the appropriateness of issuing an airworthiness directive and was asked by Mr. Smith why our MRRs‡ had not made known the problem of the DC-10 bulk cargo doors so that we were as well informed as to their proper function as the Douglas Company. My response was the reporting system had not disclosed this type of data, the reason for which I would research and advise him.

Mr. Smith queried particularly why the Douglas Company's attitude might be one of not revealing the record of difficulty with the cargo doors to the FAA. Mr. Smith indicated that he concurred with our judgment that an airworthiness directive should be issued and that he would consult with the Administrator.

The Airworthiness Board continued to meet and refine the earlier drafted directive, and I continued to expect some advice from Washington as to a directive being issued. Quite late in the day, having received no advice, we called Mr. Rudolph again and were advised that they had had difficulty locating Mr. Shaffer, but Mr. Smith and Mr. Rudolph together discussed the matter with me. They were planning to have a conference by telephone with the Douglas Company and the three airlines using DC-10 equipment to assure that the objectives for effective operation of the DC-10 cargo doors sought by our proposed draft of an airworthiness directive were accomplished.

Additional time passed and we had no further advice so I again

* James Rudolph, Director of Flight Standards Service, FAA, Washington, D.C.

† Deputy Administrator, FAA, Washington, D.C.

‡ MRR—Mechanical Reliability Reports, regularly sent to the FAA by airlines.

EXHIBIT 3 *(continued)*

called Mr. Rudolph as we had learned through the Douglas Company that the Telecon had taken place and that steps were being taken to accomplish the objective of the proposed airworthiness directive.

Significance of this action includes the fact the drafted airworthiness directive was upgraded by the Airworthiness Directive Board based on data our engineering personnel had worked out with the Douglas Company to add an additional provision that would require drilling the fuselage near the lock bolts on the cargo door to allow a visual inspection of the locking mechanism after the doors were closed.

We so informed Mr. Rudolph at this time and asked him if it would be possible to include this provision in what we then understood to be the message transmitted by the deputy administrator to the Douglas Company and the three airlines involved.

Mr. Rudolph indicated that it was then after office hours in Washington. The message containing basically our draft phraseology had been released by Mr. Smith and since it was over the deputy administrator's signature, Mr. Rudolph could not modify the language and suggested we work the problem on Monday, but indicated he agreed with our proposed amendment.

Early on Monday, 19 June, I received a phone call from Joe Ferrarese, Acting FS-2,* who stated that present with him was Mr. Slaughter, chief, engineering and manufacturing division, FS-100, and that they were calling to advise that the teletype message signed by Mr. Smith and transmitted by Mr. Rudolph relating to the DC-10 cargo doors had been distributed to the three regions where the DC-10s are in primary use and that he was acting on instructions to ask that we destroy all but one copy of this message.

I then told Mr. Ferrarese that I had not seen the message, but would conform with his instruction. Shortly thereafter, the message came in a sealed envelope through our Duty Officer in three copies. I discussed the matter with Messrs. Blanchard and Sliff. We then called Mr. Ferrarese back, told him we had the message, were destroying all but one copy and reviewed with him Mr. Smith's inquiry regarding the MRRs.

I explained I had not engaged in trying to gain Mr. Smith's understanding of the scope of MRRs on Friday, but that I was sure he [Ferrarese] appreciated that the MRRs were designed to cover what was then considered to be significant safety factors involving maintenance and reliability and had not included items such as cargo doors which in earlier forms of aircraft were not judged to be critical to the equipment safety. Therefore, the MRRs available to us could not reasonably be expected to include data in this subject area.

There are other reports called Maintenance Information Summaries which include data of this category in abbreviated form which had surfaced some ten entries indicating such matters as AAL's N105 Trip

* Mr. Rudolph's deputy.

EXHIBIT 3 *(concluded)*

96/11* being delayed 18 minutes at Los Angeles on account of difficulty in locking the bulk cargo door. This data normally is processed with a 30-day time delay and our FAA processes would not normally have surfaced a significant problem with the cargo door from this source of information, but that in retrospect, our personnel concentrating on scanning numerous entries of this nature had disclosed these ten entries.

I gave the original of the message signed by Mr. Smith and transmitted by Mr. Rudolph to Mr. Sliff for his Aircraft Engineering records and destroyed the other two copies in the presence of Messrs. Blanchard and Sliff.

Signed
ARVIN O. BASNIGHT
Director, Western Region

20 June 1972

---

* An American DC-10 flight from Los Angeles to New York, via Chicago.

The FAA sent a request to all the airlines asking that they complete the wiring modifications in the McDonnell-Douglas Service Bulletin and install warning placards telling baggage handlers not to use more than 50 pounds of pressure in closing the cargo doors. McDonnell-Douglas then sent out several additional Service Bulletins. An "Alert" Service Bulletin—meaning that the modification involved safety—asked the airlines to install the peephole, as well as a decal showing what the baggage handler should see if the locking pin was in its proper position. A second, routine Service Bulletin instructed the airlines to place a support plate on the torque tube which was likely to bend if too much pressure was applied in closing the cargo door. This would mean that 440 pounds of pressure would have to be used in closing the door—more than a human being could exert. The locking pins were also to be adjusted so that they would have to travel one quarter of an inch further, which would make it more obvious if the mechanism jammed against latches which were not over center.

Then in February of 1973, after President Nixon had fired John Shaffer and replaced him with Alexander Butterfield, the FAA wrote to all three jumbo jet manufacturers and asked them to reassess their designs in light of the Windsor incident. Specifically, the FAA wanted the manufacturers either to strengthen the floor and add vents to combat the effects of explosive decompression, or reroute the control and hydraulic systems away from the passenger cabin floor. Boeing and Lockheed responded indignantly that their doors were not the same as those of the DC-10, and Boeing pointed out that its control cables did not run under the floor. McDonnell-Douglas maintained that the possibility of a door coming open in flight was "extremely remote."[11] This time, the Washington office of the FAA asked the Western Region office to obtain more information, and the Western Region office responded that:

> We are aware of no subsequent service difficulties [since Windsor] which would constitute a basis for recertification [of the DC-10 floor]. In the light of the above, we feel that an investigation of the detailed nature presented in the memo of 30 May 1973 would be premature.[12]

---

[11] Paul Eddy, Elaine Potter, and Bruce Page, *Destination Disaster*, pp. 162–63.
[12] Ibid., p. 163.

Case ═══

THE PROGRESSIVE CORPORATION

*I encourage dissent. Most people are afraid. The
chief executive has tremendous power. It's a
tremendous responsibility.*
  Peter B. Lewis, November 29, 1974

   Peter B. Lewis, president of The Progressive Corporation, had just
returned from a three-day business trip to Chicago on July 1, 1974.
Among the first things brought to his attention upon his return were
a petition signed by 38 employees and a number of memos protesting
the display of a series of ten 3 × 4 foot pictures of Mao Tse-Tung as
portrayed by the artist Andy Warhol. Mr. Lewis had left the prints on
display in the front entry way of Progressive's main office building in
Mayfield Village, a suburb of Cleveland, Ohio, before leaving for
Chicago. In addition, Mr. Lewis had posted a memo to all employees
explaining the background of the portraits and asking for comments
from the staff. Included with the memo was a personal letter from
John Powers, retired chairman of Prentice-Hall, Inc., to Mr. Lewis
responding to certain concerns Lewis had about the possibility of
displaying the prints. (See Exhibits 1, 2, and 3 for the materials which
were included in the interoffice memorandum.) Mr. Lewis had
purchased the series of prints for his own personal collection, and
they were not the property of the company.

THE COMPANY

   The Progressive Corporation, which became an insurance holding
company in 1965, traced its origins back to 1937. Its largest subsidiary,
Progressive Casualty Insurance Company, was Ohio's leading writer
of substandard automobile insurance (risks canceled or rejected by
other insurance companies). This subsidiary also offered insurance
for motorcycles, commercial vehicles, mobile homes, and other spe-

332

EXHIBIT 1
Inter-Office Memorandum

_____

DATE: JUNE 26, 1974

TO: ALL EMPLOYEES
FROM: PETER B. LEWIS
SUBJECT: MAO TSE-TUNG CONTROVERSY

Someone once told me that art should be defined as "visual provoca-
tion." I think that is right and evidence in the hanging of the Maos
supports that definition.

When I bought these (and I own them personally not the company),
I did so on the advice of Mr. John Powers who is a former chairman of
Prentice-Hall and owner of what is probably the finest collection of
contemporary art in the world. I bought them fundamentally as an
investment. After keeping them in the box for a few weeks, I decided
that maybe they ought to be hung and had a few misgivings, and
therefore, wrote a letter to Mr. Powers.

He responded, and I have attached and underlined the key phrases.

I have not decided that the Maos ought to be hung. I placed them in
the gallery to see what they would look like and gauge the reaction.
Attached also is a letter from Jim Yasinow [Training Director] which
speaks the reaction of many of you I am sure.

I would like to urge that we pursue this controversy for a few more
days, get used to them, look at them. I would like to hear from any of
you who feel like expressing yourselves.

Incidentally, I don't know as much as I ought to about the history of
Mao, but I tend to doubt Jim's statements about him as a murderer.
Anybody who knows something about him is urged to supply the
information.

Peter

pbl;bjp
att.

_____

EXHIBIT 2
Letter from John Powers to Peter B. Lewis

_____

May 17, 1974

Dear Peter:

Your office experience is so identical to mine when I first hung
contemporary art at Prentice-Hall that this letter will try to pack as
many ideas as possible into a few pages. First of all, you must believe
steadfastly in yourself. When six people in a row (people you consider
reasonably intelligent) challenge you, you will inevitably start to doubt
yourself!! Don't let it change your confidence or course of direction. In
time, most of the people who ridicule will start to respond.

EXHIBIT 2 *(continued)*

The artist is a person who sees the world a little bit differently from the rest of the people. He expresses the way he sees it in painting or sculpture or dance or literature or theatre or poetry. Almost without exception, great art was ridiculed by the artists' contemporaries. The first performance of Stravinsky's *Sacre du Printemps* caused a riot. The French Impressionists were called insane by every art critic in France. Teddy Roosevelt called the 1913 Armory Show ridiculous and of no value. But in each case the art changed the world we live in. Mondrian's geometric paintings were called a child's work—but they changed the visual world of today. All modern architecture in any office building reflects Mondrian's way of seeing. Even a Kleenex box is a Mondrial image.

Our visual world today is dominated by imagery from movies and TV. So are communications and politics. The artists of Warhol's age grew up with a TV set at their bedside as infants and in front of them constantly as they grew. To them, and to us, the world today is color and motion. Warhol was fascinated by the changing frames of a movie film but as an artist he could not change frames by flipping his paintings. So he discovered that he could get a change in the "information" a painting (or print) conveyed by making significant (even shocking) color changes. And the subjects he deals with are right out of the news (Liz Taylor, Marilyn Monroe, Jackie Kennedy, car crashes, Elvis Presley) so the big news today for the U.S.A. and for the world is The People's Republic of China, hence Mao.

Mao has many "faces." To the mainland Chinese he is a savior and a demi-God; to the Russians, he is their biggest threat; to Chiang Kai-shek he is a usurper, to North Vietnam an ally, to the U.S.A. a powerful and capable force to be reckoned with, to Japan a neighbor and source of raw material and trade. Now spread out the whole portfolio on the floor and observe the incredible change in each work simply by the change of color. Also consider not only the fact of color, but also the unusual colors Warhol uses—he is also one of our great "colorists" in the tradition of Delacroix or more recently Morris Louis.

Warhol's art either makes you angry or it makes you think—it may do both. But there are few people who, in the presence of a work by Warhol, have a neutral reaction. About all you can say about Andrew Wyeth is "isn't it pretty" which, after all, is a subjective conclusion so it isn't saying anything at all.

Why should a business organization hang a Warhol portfolio of Mao? First it is stimulating—we are always looking for stimulating things for a company. Second, it is controversial and provides a basis for thoughtful discussion (for heaven's sake, nobody has to "like it"— you don't have to like a director's meeting either, but it is a valuable part of a business). Third, it is the art of our time. Whether it is good or bad, evanescent or historical can't be decided by you or me or by those who will object to hanging the portfolio—the perspective of *time* will

EXHIBIT 2 *(concluded)*

test its importance as it must with all art, so don't be backed into a corner of having to prove its merit because you can't. But nobody can prove it is worthless either even tho some people will think they can—those who know least about art being the most certain of their judgment:

"Last of all I turned to the skilled craftsmen . . . I was sure that I would find them full of impressive knowledge. In this I was not disappointed; they understood things which I did not. . . . But, gentlemen, these professional experts . . . on the strength of their technical proficiency they claimed a perfect understanding of every other subject, however important; and I felt that this error more than outweighed their positive wisdom."

Plato, *Socrates' Apology* (Penguin Classic), pp. 51–52

While it takes historical perspective to make a final judgment, there are at times reasons for making a decision today. One such occasion was the compilation of a series of art books on contemporary art. A decision was inevitable on what artists to include and how much space to devote to each one included. A poll of art historians, critics, museum staff and dealers was taken. The results are included with this letter: Warhol received 8 "superlatives" and 2 "excellents" ranking him among the top 14 contemporary American painters and sculptors.

By all means hang the Maos and chin up to the uproar that will follow. You will stimulate some thought and discussion. You are in good company—a set was recently purchased by the president of the world's most important Scientific Book Publishing Co. (Springer Verlag of Heidelberg).

The enclosed list gives you a good guide for further collection of prints. Stick to artists in the upper half of this list—or at least those on the list. (I put Jim Dine in a higher category myself. He makes marvelous prints!! Check PETERSBERG PRESS in New York.)

Buy a set of Campbell's Soup silk screens by Warhol. There are two sets of ten each. They are *very* underpriced today. You will get them at the best price from Ivan Karp at O. K. Harris Gallery, 429 West Broadway (SOHO) New York—call him today (212)777–6868.

Buy a set of new Jasper Johns series just published by GEMINI GEL in L.A. We are just opening ours that arrived today. It is a small edition so it may be sold out at GEMINI still try SID FELSEN (213)651–0513. If he has none, he will tell you where to try at dealers. Johns is one of the greatest printmakers ever.

I hear de Kooning will soon make some lithographs at a new fine art print shop in Bedford, New York. If you have other questions, write and I'll try to help. Regards to you and Toby.

Sincerely,
John

EXHIBIT 3
Memo from Jim Yashinow

June 25, 1974

Peter—

If it is your intent to hang the Mao prints on the walls of this building, I strongly protest, and I am sure there are many others who feel as I
do.

I would no sooner see Mao Tse-Tung on our walls than Lenin, Marx,
Stalin, or Hitler, regardless of the quality of the artwork.

If it is your intent to create controversy, then you have succeeded.
As art, the prints do demonstrate some novel techniques. But the subject matter is in execrable taste.

As a murderer and the world's outstanding proponent of 1984's "Big
Brother is Watching You" philosophy, Mao Tse-Tung is unsurpassed. I
am personally surprised, as well as unhappy that you would want his
likeness hanging in your building.

Jim

---

cial classes of liability and property insurance. The second largest
subsidiary, Progressive American Life Insurance Company, offered
credit-related life and accident and health coverages, while fire and
casualty insurance coverages involving individually tailored forms
and unregulated rates were written by Progressive American Insurance Company. Progressive Premium Budget, Inc., a premium
financing company, provided a time payment program for the premiums written by Progressive Casualty Insurance Company.

The corporation sold its specialty products through independent
insurance agents. Business was solicited by mailings to agents
supplemented by personal visits from salaried and commissioned
field sales people and general agents. This sales effort was directed to
the insurance agent who had only occasional need for specialty
coverage. Progressive had found that such agents were willing to
sacrifice lowest price and/or highest commission for good service on
specialty claims.

For the year ended December 31, 1973, The Progressive Corporation reported total revenues of $37.7 million, an increase of 16.2 per-
cent over the previous year. Net income rose 14 percent for the same
period. The consolidated assets of the firm were $76.5 million, a 14.9
percent increase over the 1972 year end total. In the period 1968–73,
The Progressive Corporation had recorded an annual growth in total
revenues of 25 percent.

Progressive, a firm with approximately 425 employees at the end of

1973, based its operating philosophy on discipline and flexibility, enabling it to react successfully to the constantly changing external environment. The six key elements of the operating philosophy of the company were outlined as follows:

1. Long-range planning, the principal component of which was a current, quantified statement of growth, profit, and diversification goals.
2. Precise one-year plans that took into account current business conditions as well as the long-term goals.
3. A management information system that was sufficiently detailed and timely to identify when and in which areas plans were not being met.
4. A group of well-trained, highly motivated, ingenious, and resilient people who were eager and able to deal with change, viewing it as creating opportunities rather than problems.
5. An organization and a management attitude which encouraged people to maximize their individual contributions.
6. A business philosophy stressing high-quality service.

The two-digit inflation and the economic uncertainty in the United States in 1974 had a negative effect on Progressive's growth and profitability. It was clear that the company's exciting growth record would not be maintained during 1974 and that profits would be down.

THE NEW CORPORATE BUILDING

Because of the company's strong growth in earlier years, in 1970 Progressive had begun looking into finding a new location for its corporate headquarters. The facility then used to house the corporate offices at 3600 Euclid Avenue, Cleveland, Ohio, had been expanded and remodeled 14 times since the company's formation, and it did not appear feasible to make further additions at that location. The need for space had become so critical that the marketing department had been moved into rented office space two blocks from the corporate headquarters.

Coupled with the need for increased office space was the problem of safety. Over the years the community which surrounded the present office building had experienced a sharp increase in crime, leading to some employee concern for their personal safety when going to and coming from the office. This fact appeared to be affecting the company's recruiting effort, as potential new employees were reluctant to work at that location.

In 1972, a 40-acre wooded site in Mayfield Village, an eastern suburb of Cleveland, was purchased. In September 1972, industrial revenue bonds were sold to finance the project, and soon after construction began. The new 74,000-square foot facility was ready for occupancy in March 1974.

The new home office building was set well back from the road and nestled in among large trees. The exterior of the three-story building had a portico effect achieved by white precast concrete columns and arches. The openness of the design was further enhanced by extensive use of bronzed glass walls.

The design criteria for the interior of the building were as follows:

1. Efficient working space.
2. Expansion capabilities.
3. Flexibility of internal areas to accommodate change.
4. Best possible working environment for the employees.

To meet these requirements an open landscape approach was used. Using this concept, large areas in the building were left open and with the use of portable partitions, offices could be created as needed. Often, such partitions were not necessary, as office furnishings (i.e., filing cabinets) could be arranged in a manner which afforded sufficient privacy. The open landscape idea made the work area appear larger, allowed flexibility, and helped to increase communication between workers.

In the center of the building was a circular staircase climbing from the lower level to the top floor. Adjacent to this staircase was an open shaft. Over both the staircase and the shaft was a large skylight which added to the open feeling of the building.

Throughout the new complex there were many large plants and colorful graphics. Prints by name artists were hung throughout the building. On some interior hallways in the lower level, colorful designs had been painted on the walls to brighten the area. Decorative panels needed for acoustics as well as aesthetics were used to divide certain work stations. All in all, Progressive had provided a much superior work environment for its employees, a vast improvement over the old facilities. And it was clear that contemporary art played a central role in the atmosphere of the building.

THE MAO TSE-TUNG CONTROVERSY

Mr. Lewis had become interested in art as an investment vehicle in the early 1970s. In 1973, when the stock market began falling, he had approached the company's board of directors with a proposal to sell $250,000 of the company's existing stock portfolio and invest the funds in art. This idea proved to be too great a departure from conventional investing for the directors, and the proposal was turned down (a rather unusual show of independence by a board given Mr. Lewis's 25 percent stock interest in the company).

However, when the new office building was being finished and decorated, it was decided that $25,000 would be allocated for the purchase of graphic art. The selection of the art was left up to Mr. Lewis and his wife Toby, who had also become very interested in contemporary art. They made six trips to New York and bought 30 pieces of graphic art done by name contemporary artists for the new corporate headquarters.

In April of 1974, Mr. and Mrs. Lewis attended a Young Presidents Organization meeting in Acapulco, Mexico. During the convention, Mr. Lewis attended a seminar on "Art Collecting" given by Mr. John Powers, former chairman of Prentice-Hall and owner of a large collection of contemporary art. In the course of the seminar, Mr. Powers mentioned the quality of craftsmanship displayed in the series of Mao Tse-Tung done by Andy Warhol. The series was a portrait of Mao, face on from the chest up, repeated ten times, each time using a different colored background. The portrait was always done in a black and white newspaper picture look. The background colors ranged from very dark, through pastel shades to bright vibrant colors. Mr. Lewis was familiar with this particular work, as he had been in New York and had seen the original showing of the Mao series. Upon his return from Acapulco, Mr. Lewis, on the recommendation of Mr. Powers, purchased the series for $4,000. Mr. Lewis had the ten prints sent to his office and stored them unframed in a closet.

In June of that year, Mr. Lewis decided to have the pictures framed. He did so and had the art sent back to his office, since he did not have sufficient space in his home to hang the entire series. The pictures were delivered and left propped up against the wall in the front entrance to the building.

The reaction by several of the company's top executives to leaving pictures of Mao on display was immediate. Three of the four men who reported directly to Mr. Lewis asked that the pictures be removed as quickly as possible. Mr. Lewis agreed to do so, but a pressing family matter arose and he was unable to attend to the matter as soon as he had expected. When he returned to the building that night he saw a janitor looking at the graphics. Mr. Lewis asked the man what he thought of the pictures. The janitor replied that he thought they were "fantastic."

By the summer of 1974, there was clearly a need for something "fantastic" to happen at Progressive. Because of declining business conditions, approximately 15 percent of the home office staff had been let go. General morale appeared to be low, as many employees were concerned about job security. Mr. Lewis was keenly aware of

this employee uneasiness and had wanted to do something to allevi-
ate the tension. Mr. Lewis saw the pictures of Mao as an issue which
would distract the employees from their concerns. On June 26th he
posted an interoffice memo (see Exhibits 1, 2, and 3) and left on the
short business trip to Chicago.

EMPLOYEE COMMENTS

Even Mr. Lewis was surprised by the amount of controversy the
graphics stirred up. The following excerpts from some of the memos
he received on the subject reveal the tone of the complaints.

> I cannot appreciate the artistic value of the paintings while in our
> main lobby. The immediate visual image that is portrayed is offensive
> to my personal values as well as my political and religious convictions.
> A visitor to the company is likely to form the same negative impres-
> sion as I did . . .
> Although the collection is your personal property, an onlooker
> would not know this, nor would it matter as they are implied to be part
> of Progressive Ins. Co.
> From a personal standpoint, I would prefer to see an American flag
> as the focal point of the lobby.
>
> > *Will Alt*
> > [Division Manager, Microfilming and Filing]

> I feel that his portraits hanging in our new home office, of which we
> are all very proud, may have an adverse effect on our business relations
> with other companies and agents.
> Cleveland is predominantly an ethnic town, and many of the people
> or their families, have sought refuge in the United States to avoid being
> oppressed by the communistic takeover of their own countries.
> I could well imagine what a veteran of the Vietnam War, or the
> father of a young man killed in such a war, would think of us as a
> business organization if their first impression was a gallery of portraits
> of such a person as this.
>
> > *Betty M. Morgan*
> > [Unit Manager]

> Having spent over one year in Vietnam in a conflict in which the
> enemy of the United States was clearly aided by Mao, I too protest the
> hanging of the portraits.
> Putting the question of the validity of the Vietnam conflict aside,
> thousands of Americans lost their lives in that conflict. I personally
> know that much of the support for North Vietnam came from the
> Chinese Communist nation. Through Mao's aid, many Americans have
> been killed and maimed.
> An advocate of the spread of the Communist way of life, Mao sup-
> ports this doctrine by any means available. I personally have lost sev-

eral close friends in the Vietnam conflict and consider Mao to be an enemy of the American people. For these reasons I, too, protest the hanging of the portraits.

> *Jack Kettler*
> [Manager, Systems and Programming]

. . . hanging this picture is like hanging a picture of Hitler. They are both political figures this world can do without.

> *Steve Hujarski*
> [Systems Analyst]

Support for hanging the portraits of Mao was sparse. However, one employee came out strongly in defense of artistic expression.

> I feel that I am associated with a modern company, in a modern building and the art work should follow the theme. The painting "Whistler's Mother" would be very out of place on the walls of our facility.
>
> Thank God we live in a country where paintings such as the "Warhol Mao Series" can be publicly displayed without fear of reprisal from the government. I sincerely doubt that such a series of Richard Nixon could be displayed in China with the same freedom.
>
> *Ralph A. McMahon*
> [Manager, Claims Training]

The number and tone of the negative memoranda as well as the employee petition left little doubt that the controversy had at least temporarily replaced job security as the prime concern of Progressive's home office personnel. Indeed, the issue had spilled beyond the bounds of the office, as evidenced by the fact that a Cleveland television station had asked permission to send out a camera crew to conduct an interview with Mr. Lewis for the evening newscast. Mr. Lewis was beginning to wonder about the wisdom of following Mr. Powers's advice "to chin up to the uproar . . . ."

Case ══

BORDEN, INC.: COLUMBUS COATED FABRICS

On September 4, 1974, a group of 56 employees of Columbus Coated Fabrics filed suit for $28 million against Eastman Kodak Company, Eastman Chemical Products, Inc., and Borden, Inc., Columbus Coated Fabrics Division of Borden Chemical. The suit was for damages resulting from peripheral neuropathy, a condition believed to be caused by inhaling the fumes of the chemical methyl butyl ketone (MBK). The illness attacked the nerves that control muscles in human limbs, causing weakness, limpness, and lack of coordination. Many important questions about the disease remained unanswered, and a serious aspect of the affliction was the absence of any known medical treatment. Doctors believed the workers with milder cases would recover within months. The prognosis for more serious cases was still in doubt. Whether these workers would recover in a matter of months or years or ever was unknown.

BORDEN, INC.

Borden, Inc., was a multinational firm engaged in the manufacture, processing, and distribution of food, dairy, and chemical products. In 1973, Borden moved its corporate headquarters from New York City to Columbus. For the year ending December 31, 1973, Borden reported $2.5 billion in sales and net income of $73 million (see Exhibit 1).

With nearly 47,000 full-time employees, spread over a wide geographic area, it was Borden's policy that employee relations be governed by practices prevailing in the particular work area and be dealt

342

EXHIBIT 1
Borden, Inc. ($ millions)*

	For the year ended December 31				
	1969	1970	1971	1972	1973
Net sales	$1,918	$1,858	$2,103	$2,149	$2,553
Net income	28	54	61	67	73
Earnings per share	$ .96	$ 1.82	$ 1.99	$ 2.18	$ 2.37

* Financial data from Borden, Inc., *Annual Report*, 1973.

with locally. Approximately 50 percent of Borden's domestic hourly wage employees were covered by collective bargaining agreements which ranged from one to three years. Between 1969 and the fall of 1973, Borden had not experienced a material work stoppage, and, in general, top management considered relations with its employees to be quite satisfactory.

BORDEN CHEMICAL DIVISION

One large component of Borden was its Chemical Division. The year 1973 was a successful one for the Chemical Division, as all-time highs in sales and operating income were recorded for the period. Sales were up 19 percent over the 1972 figures, and operating income advanced 29 percent ahead of 1972 results (see Exhibit 2).

Borden Chemical operated 61 plants in 23 states. The major facility was its petrochemical complex at Geismar, Louisiana, which produced basic materials used in the manufacture of thermoplastic and thermosetting resins, fertilizers, and feed supplements. The outlook for the Chemical Division in 1974 was favorable. Costs were expected to increase substantially, but greater flexibility in pricing was anticipated. Fertilizers and thermoplastics were expected to be the division's principal source of strength.[1]

EXHIBIT 2
Borden Chemical Division ($ millions)*

	1972	1973
Sales	$471.0	$560.0
Percent of total sales	21%	22%
Operating income..................	$ 40.9	$ 52.9
Percent of total income from operations	27%	31%

* Financial data from Borden, Inc., *Annual Report*, 1973.

[1] Borden, Inc., *Annual Report*, 1973, pp. 16–20.

COLUMBUS COATED FABRICS

Columbus Coated Fabrics (CCF) was a relatively minor component of the Chemical Division. CCF's contribution to the total sales of the Chemical Division was below five percent. Contribution to operating income in 1973 was estimated to be somewhat above the percentage contribution to sales. CCF employed approximately 950 people, not including supervisors and office personnel.

The company's main activity was the production and sale of coated wall coverings and upholstery for the automobile industry. Demand for wall coverings had been very favorable over the last few years, and, in order to meet this ever-rising demand, an expansion project was under way in Newark, California. These additional production facilities would increase annual capacity by 15 million yards, approximately 25 percent of total production. CCF's capacity problems were compounded by a three-month curtailment of production at the Columbus plant which began in September 1973. The work stoppage followed discovery of an illness which primarily affected employees in the Columbus plant's printing department.

THE ILLNESS AND INVESTIGATION

Early in 1973, a strange nervous disorder began to affect workers at the CCF plant in Columbus. One of the first and possibly most severe cases was that of Thomas Meade, a 22-year-old machine operator in the print shop. In February, Mr. Meade noticed something unusual happening to his arms and legs. However, his symptoms were vague and unfamiliar, and since his family had a history of arthritis he shrugged off the strange sensations. The symptoms got worse, and by June Mr. Meade needed knee-to-heel braces on his legs in order to walk.[2]

Meanwhile, other men in the print shop began to complain of similar problems. Richard Staneart, another machine operator in the print shop, complained of weakness in his legs in March. After seeing his family doctor who diagnosed flat feet, Mr. Staneart bought a new pair of work shoes and returned to his job. As his condition worsened, Mr. Staneart consulted an orthopedic surgeon who made a tentative diagnosis of peripheral neuropathy. In August, Dr. Mary Gilchrist, a resident in neurology at the Ohio State University Medical School who was treating another CCF worker, confirmed the diagnosis. Chemical poisoning was suspected as the origin of the illness.[3]

---

[2] *The Wall Street Journal*, October 5, 1973, p. 24.

[3] Rachel Scott, *Muscle and Blood* (New York: E. P. Dutton and Co., Inc., 1974), pp. 91–92.

On August 22, 1973, the Ohio State University Hospital reported to the Ohio Department of Health that a worker from the Columbus Coated Fabrics plant had been hospitalized with what appeared to be peripheral neuropathy. Dr. Donald Billmaier of the Ohio Department of Health began an investigation immediately. The state contacted the company and the union officials and began testing the other 950 workers for signs of the illness.

At first it seemed that the problem was confined to the print department. However, further testing revealed that 68 persons in CCF's employ had the illness to some extent. Of those, 38 worked in the print shop and 30 were scattered throughout other departments. Most individuals in the second group had shown symptoms of neuropathy for more than two years, but their medical records attributed its cause to other than occupational circumstances.

The origins of the health problem were not clear. It was known that in mid-1972, CCF had begun experiments with a new chemical in the production process—methyl butyl ketone (MBK). The new chemical had been tested as a replacement for methyl isobutyl ketone (MIBK) which had caused a chemical smog condition and, therefore, did not meet air pollution regulations. The experimental stage with MBK was completed successfully, and it was decided to introduce the new chemical into the process in December 1972. Neither the sister plant in California nor a Toledo-based competitor introduced the chemical.

The chemicals and potential exposures in the print shop had been reasonably well defined. Nevertheless, there was some evidence that the problem might not be localized to the print shop. Corwin Smith, president of Local 487 of the Textile Workers, said, "It was first thought that the solvent (MBK) used in printing might have something to do with it, but after 100 cases were reported, the solvent theory was questioned."[4] Therefore, the conclusion that MBK could have been the cause of the occupational illness was not self-evident. In fact, the *Federal Register*, which listed the official federal standards for industrial air safety, did not list MBK as a potentially hazardous product.[5]

Not knowing the cause of the illness left an environment of uncertainty and fear for both the company and the workers. As late as September 1973, the company's management was unwilling to conclude that the illnesses were related to the work environment. A spokesman for the company stated, "there is no evidence to relate this industrially. We are doing everything we possibly can." He further noted that "Company doctors and insurance investigators

[4] *The Ohio State Daily Lantern,* September 27, 1973, p. 3.

[5] *Federal Register,* vol. 36, no. 105 (May 29, 1971).

have been called in."[6] Union members wanted an immediate shutdown of operations until the plant was properly ventilated and the
sewer system had been overhauled. The local union president said
that the union had "a frustrating time, initially in getting someone to
take action. First we asked the State Health Department to close [the
print shop] down, and they refused. We asked the company, and
they refused. And so, we did it."[7]

On September 7, union members stationed themselves at the gates
and advised workers in the print shop not to report to work. On
September 10, the union (Local 487 of the Textile Workers Union of
America) filed an official complaint with the U.S. District Court in
Columbus against CCF. The complaint stated that 90 percent of the
men in the print department refused to work until the health hazard
had been removed. It also stated that Borden was insisting that the
men return to work or disciplinary action against an unlawful strike
would be taken. It was the position of the union that the company
had breached the labor agreement which contained the provision that
the employees would be provided with a safe place to work. The
union, therefore, requested that the courts declare that their work
stoppage was authorized by the terms of the National Labor Relations
Act. The case was dismissed.

In early September, a "bipartisan" medical committee was formed
to look into the matter and to evaluate the situation at CCF's Columbus plant. A report was to be made to CCF management outlining
possible causes and solutions. The committee consisted of: Dr.
Samuel Epstein, Case Western Reserve, Cleveland, nominated by the
AFL-CIO; Dr. Norman Williams, Jefferson Medical College, Philadelphia, nominated by the Insurance Company of America upon recommendation by Borden, Inc.; and Dr. Donald Billmaier, medical
chief of the Division of Occupational Health of the Ohio Department
of Health.

On September 14, 1973, the committee made known its conclusions. The solvent (MBK) used in the print shop was believed to be
the cause of the illness. It gave off heavy fumes to which the workers
were exposed all day and was the only new addition to the production process over the last few years. Their recommendations, all of
which were implemented by management, were:

1. Switch to a substitute for MBK.
2. Improve ventilation in the work area.
3. Issue respirators to print shop workers.
4. Move lunch areas away from work areas.

---

[6] *The Columbus Evening Dispatch,* September 6, 1973, p. 1.
[7] Rachel Scott, *Muscle and Blood,* p. 92.

In spite of these actions, an atmosphere of fear and distrust persisted.

In mid-October 1973, a federal court hearing was requested in an attempt by the management of CCF to block a state inquiry into the illness which had hit the plant. John Elam, an attorney representing CCF, told federal judge Joseph Kinneary that the hearings by the Industrial Commission of Ohio "would be a kangaroo court." Mr. Elam went on to say, "This is an attempt by a local union president and certain state officials to use the Industrial Commission."[8]

The Industrial Commission said it had arranged the hearings to try and decide whether the plant should be closed and to attempt to determine more fully the cause of the ailment. Attorney Charles Taylor, representing the commission, said about 500 CCF workers had filed claims for workmen's compensation, indicating there was "some medical problem at the plant."[9] Mr. Elam told the federal court the company had made extensive improvements at the plant and there was "no health hazard. . . . " Judge Kinneary issued a preliminary injunction against the Industrial Commission, preventing it from holding the hearings. The Industrial Commission appealed the decision.

Workers returned to their jobs on November 5, after all the medical committee's proposals went into effect. The company position was related by CCF spokesman Maurice O'Reilly. According to Mr. O'Reilly, "Borden picked up the tab for research work and plant improvements." He could not give a definite cost figure since the work was still going on, but he said it was well over $1 million.[10]

Mr. Smith said employees were generally satisfied by the improvements made but went on to say, "there is still an uneasiness since the source of the problem has never been discovered. Everyone is just hopeful the problem is solved." The union president was not satisfied that Borden had done everything it could to clean up the situation. ". . . [W]hen we're dealing with a big company, they only have to do what they want to. I'm sure they only did what they were forced to do," he said.[11] Some of the "forcing" had been an outgrowth of earlier inspections by federal officials. In April and June of 1973, inspectors from the Occupational Safety and Health Administration (OSHA) had found 34 safety and health violations at CCF. Some of these included chemical contaminants in the air. Borden was given until February 1974 to correct them.

Mr. O'Reilly said they were "technical violations" and had been "cleaned up." He defined "technical" as a "dust hazard that could be

[8] *The Ohio State Daily Lantern,* October 19, 1973, p. 3.

[9] Ibid.

[10] *The Ohio State Daily Lantern,* July 15, 1974, p. 3.

[11] *The Columbus Evening Dispatch,* January 14, 1974, p. 1B.

unsafe," but added, "as I recall they were not classified as serious." Mr. O'Reilly went on to say, "if the employees were unsatisfied with working conditions, it's up to the union to include it in contract negotiation."[12]

The union did have considerable leverage since the Columbus CCF plant was completely unionized. Nonexempt employees automatically became union members after a 45-day probation period. Union dues of $3.00 per week were deducted directly from the payroll. The average hourly wage for a CCF employee in 1973 was $4.10, including bonuses and incentives, as compared with an average wage for workers in the Columbus area of $4.69.

CONTRACT NEGOTIATIONS

The existing collective bargaining agreement was due to expire on February 9, 1974. Therefore, Borden, who handled the labor negotiation for CCF, decided to request negotiations on a labor contract renewal in the latter part of November 1973 and suggested an early settlement bonus be granted if settlement was reached by December 18, 1973. Later, this target date was moved back to January 6, 1974, as it became apparent negotiations were bogged down. A statement made by union president Corwin Smith indicated the mood of the negotiations. "The company thinks that since we have been through a long strike this fall, we'll be willing to accept an inadequate contract. They underestimate our people; the workers have a lot of guts."[13]

The union insisted on bargaining on each article, section, and paragraph of the contract. This demand resulted in a long and unproductive series of bargaining sessions. When the company tried to expedite the process by submitting a contract proposal to the union asking for a counterproposal, the union's response was to return again to its line by line, item by item discussion of the existing labor contract. The company repeatedly requested that the union make a counterproposal, but each request met with no response. Finally, Borden requested a caucus and submitted its "final offer." When no response was made by the union, the company left the bargaining table. Company spokesman Joseph Recchi said the union had been made "a very fine offer, the best they've ever had."[14]

The union filed a "refusal to bargain" charge against Borden with the National Labor Relations Board. The NLRB ruled that the company had made "numerous and extensive counterproposals to the

---

[12] *The Ohio State Daily Lantern,* July 15, 1974, p. 3.

[13] *The Ohio State Daily Lantern,* January 23, 1974, p. 3.

[14] *The Columbus Citizen-Journal,* January 25, 1974, p. 5.

union, that the company had made concessions, and that, therefore, there was a valid impasse." The charge against Borden was dismissed.[15]

In late January 1974, the Federal Mediation and Conciliation Service became involved. The two sides, sitting in separate rooms, spoke through a federal mediator, Joseph Santa-Emma, at the Federal Mediation Service Office. The company insisted that the union draw up a counterproposal to the company's final offer. The union said they could not make such a counterproposal until the company responded to a list of union proposals. Glen Wood, a union vice president, said the union's list of proposals included changes in the company's policy concerning vacation, pensions, holidays, and safety control.

On February 5, at a meeting which included the mediator, the union presented its final demands which included a wage increase of $2.10 an hour over the next three years. Company spokesmen reaffirmed that they were not willing to effect significant changes in the contract which would further adversely affect the efficiency of the operation at this plant.

During the week, the company repeatedly requested the union's proposal on health and safety. Finally, the company gave the union a health and safety proposal of its own on Thursday, February 7. The union submitted its counterproposal the next morning. The issue of health and safety was discussed, but no agreement was reached, and the strike began upon the expiration of the contract.

THE STRIKE

Talks between the company and the union broke off on Friday, February 8, 1974, and no further talks were scheduled. However, Mr. Smith said that the union had informed the federal mediator that they were willing to negotiate at any time. Smith said, "union members, who voted 214–14 in favor of the strike, will picket the plant on Grant Avenue around the clock until a settlement is reached."[16] The union offered a health and safety plan "carefully worded as to not infringe on management," Smith said.[17] This plan was rejected. Smith accused the company of "refusing to move on any issue" after negotiations had stalled on February 8.

No further talks were held until early March. At this meeting, striking workers were told the company would begin disassembling

---

[15] Ibid.

[16] *The Ohio State Daily Lantern*, February 11, 1974, p. 3.

[17] Ibid.

plant machinery. This announcement followed Borden's threat to close down the fabrics plant permanently. A union spokesman termed the announcement "another of Borden's attempts to scare the workers."[18]

On March 26, a bomb made of six sticks of dynamite was placed on a windowsill outside the CCF plant office. Damages were estimated at $10,000 and no injuries were reported. Subsequent to the bombing, Borden ran a full-page ad in the *Columbus Evening Dispatch* which union officials described as a cheap attempt to discredit the union.

Columbus Coated Fabrics
NOTICE OF REWARD

At 10:17 P.M. on Tuesday, March 26, an explosion destroyed part of our Columbus Coated Fabrics complex on Grant Avenue. The bomb was made up of six sticks of dynamite. This is particularly tragic since any number of the public passing in the area of the explosion could have been seriously injured or killed. The lives of several members of our supervisory personnel who were acting as fire watchmen at the plant were also endangered. Such acts should be condemned by all responsible company and union officials.

We have not attempted to operate our plant during this strike because we felt violence would occur if we did. Our union employees are fully aware that we have not attempted to operate this plant.

Columbus Coated Fabrics is offering to pay a reward totaling $10,000 to anyone who supplies the information resulting in the arrest and conviction of the person or persons involved in this reprehensible act of violence. The company reserves the right to determine the proper appointment of this reward among those furnishing information should that be required. This offer will remain in effect until further notice.

We will attempt to keep confidential the identity of the person giving the information. Persons having information should call 225–4196 day or night. Police and Security Personnel are not eligible for this reward.

Columbus Coated Fabrics[19]

For the duration of the strike, union members received strike pay which amounted to $22 per week. In addition, those suffering from peripheral neuropathy were to receive additional $79 per week in workmen's compensation benefits. However, Mr. Smith claimed that the company was either stopping payments or making late payments to the afflicted. Under Ohio workmen's compensation laws, Borden was a self-insurer and handled its own compensation because of its large size.

When workmen's compensation cutoffs began, union members

---

[18] *The Ohio State Daily Lantern,* March 6, 1974, p. 3.

[19] *The Columbus Evening Dispatch,* March 31, 1974, p. E–15.

asked State Rep. Mike Stinziano (D., Columbus) to investigate. At a news conference held in early May, Stinziano charged that Borden was not following procedures set up by the Industrial Commission and should therefore be stripped of its self-insured status. "I would pursue this through legislation. The Industrial Commission must make sure workmen's compensation payments do not become a strike-breaking tactic on the part of those companies that elect to be self-insurers," Stinziano added.[20]

As the strike dragged on, some additional members of the Columbus community began taking an active interest. The Justice for Borden Workers Committee was formed in support of the CCF employees and was headed by Fred Gittes, an Ohio State University law student. It was the aim of the committee to make the public more aware of the Borden practices by beginning a boycott of Borden products.

"Borden can't get away with 'no comment' anymore," Gittes said. "That's just not permissible, hence our strategy is to hurt them where they seem most concerned . . . and their concern seems only to be profits. We want to emphasize Borden's profit margin which has increased 30 percent since 1968. We want consumers to know that behind 'Elsie' are a lot of crippled people."[21]

Company spokesman Maurice O'Reilly, when questioned about the boycott, felt it had little effect even in the Columbus area. However, by the middle of May, the company began wooing public opinion. In an effort to explain their side of the story, a full-page ad in the *Columbus Evening Dispatch* read as follows:

WILL THERE BE A VOTE AT COLUMBUS COATED FABRICS?

On January 3, 1974, Columbus Coated Fabrics made an offer to try and settle its contract with Local 487 of the Textile Workers Union of America. The leadership of Local Union 487 did not let its members vote on that offer. Now, after 15 weeks of a strike, and in order to give our employees a chance to have a secret ballot vote, the company has given the union an offer to end the strike.

In addition to increased wages, the package includes many new and important features. One of them is a cost of living provision. Another item relates to severance pay provision of up to $1,000 for those employees who may not be recalled after the strike ends.

Since we have given this proposal in an effort to get our employees a secret ballot vote, we informed the Union Committee that this package will be available for employee acceptance or rejection by secret ballot vote until 1:00 P.M., Wednesday, May 29, 1974.

The company has made a substantial move! We certainly believe that

[20] *The Ohio State Daily Lantern,* May 3, 1974, p. 1.
[21] *The Ohio State Daily Lantern,* April 26, 1974, p. 3.

our employees are entitled to exercise their democratic right on such an important question. It is time they are given the opportunity to accept or reject this package on its merits.

Columbus Coated Fabrics[22]

The strike was finally settled on July 1, 1974, after a five-month work stoppage. With the announcement of the end of the strike, it was stated that by mutual agreement the terms of the contract settlement were not going to be released. Thomas Meade, who by that time was unable to use his hands even for simple tasks such as turning on a lamp and still wore leg braces, was the only CCF worker physically unable to return to work.

---

[22] *The Columbus Evening Dispatch,* May 27, 1974, p. 8.

Commentaries

25. Corporations Should Rally Stockholder Constituency

James J. Kilpatrick

WASHINGTON. This is annual report time for American corporations, and one by one the glossy publications turn up in the mail. Many of them are masterpieces of graphic art, crammed with color photos and peacock pie charts. Some of them will win prizes—but nearly all of them will lose opportunities.

It is a puzzling thing. American corporations have some of the best minds in the nation in their executive offices. They have public relations advisers who are skilled in their arcane art. They have highly paid legislative counsel. Yet these great companies do pathetically little to advance their own interests in one area where something constructive might be accomplished. They rarely seek to rally investors to their cause.

A friend in the pharmaceutical industry recently devoted a few hours to reading the annual reports of the 15 largest pharmaceutical houses in the nation. He was curious to see if these manufacturers made any effort to acquaint their shareholders with the industry's legislative problems. His labors left him depressed.

Only one of the leaders, Squibb, devoted significant space in its annual report to a discussion of what the pharmaceutical industry has to cope with. A couple of others had a phrase here or a sentence there. One of the largest houses, with sales in 1974 of more than $500 million, offered only this lame paragraph:

> In the United States over the past several years, a number of government programs have been proposed to extend a broad range of

Source: *The Washington Star*, May 6, 1975. © 1975 by Washington Star Syndicate, Inc. Reprinted by permission.

health care services to the largest possible group of people. We believe that great care must be exercised in planning the mechanics of these programs to preserve for society the benefits of the nation's flourishing private enterprise in the health care field.

Doesn't that grab you? The author of that tepid mush was talking, in his own feeble way, about a dozen legislative proposals of enormous concern to the pharmaceutical industry. This is an executive who worries constantly about the assaults of Ralph Nader, Common Cause, the Department of Health, Education and Welfare, the Food and Drug Administration, and the senior senator from Massachusetts. But all he could think of to say to his shareholders was that great care must be exercised, etc., etc.

It is incredible. Irving Kristol, one of the country's most brilliant essayists and critics, long ago suggested in *The Wall Street Journal* that corporations seek to develop their own constituency among their stockholders. His point was that the "other side" has plenty of solid constituencies. Organized labor can marshal a million voters overnight. Consumer groups, environmentalists and minorities can apply political pressure in effective ways.

The corporations, for their part, have only their own trade associations. Many of their lobbyists perform effectively. But corporations don't vote. They cannot even lawfully contribute to a congressman's campaign. Where is a constituency to be found?

Three possibilities suggest themselves: customers, employes and stockholders. The customers offer the largest potential, but it is formidably difficult to translate product loyalty into political activism. Not nearly enough is done to inform employes of industry problems and to seek their support: much more could be done in this field.

The shareholders are an untapped political resource. Some 30 million persons own stock in the 4,500 corporations publicly traded. The general custom is to treat them as a meddlesome nuisance. They are not given even the attention that colleges usually give their alumni.

To be sure, as Kristol has pointed out, many of the stockholders are merely speculators as distinguished from investors. They would constitute no permanent constituency. But suppose investors were rewarded every five years by stock bonuses to encourage their continuing interest. Suppose their active political concern were cultivated not only in annual reports but also in regular monthly alumni bulletins. Suppose corporations took the offensive in promoting their cause. Such efforts might not wholly reverse the antibusiness tilt in Congress, but they might improve the balance.

26. A Score Card for Rating Management
Edward McSweeney

One myth about corporate directors is that they select the top man who runs the company. They almost never do. But an even bigger myth is that directors operate a business in the best interests of the owners (stockholders). This is what the law says they should be doing, but the responsibility is so vague, so poorly defined, that directors, particularly those drawn from outside the company, normally don't even try to find out what they should be doing.

If the statutes mean anything, they mean that an outside director should be monitoring top management and scoring it just as carefully as management itself is trying to score its subordinates. Yet in all my years of serving as an outside director on dozens of corporate boards, I have never once heard anyone talk about that task seriously, and never once have I heard any reference to the most critically important aspect of that task: removing a chief executive officer who is falling down on the job.

Why should this be? The answers are known to any experienced director. The outside director is supposed to be independent, but, in fact, he is not much better off than the inside director, whose future depends on compatibility with the chief and who is not about to criticize something the chief has done poorly.

Almost always, the outside director has been selected personally by the chief executive or recommended by a close mutual friend or dominant stockholder. He is chosen on the basis of friendship and loyalty. He becomes a member of a private club. The loyalty of such a group is especially intense when critics question the way the business is being run. Like the old frontiersmen, they wheel their wagons into a circle and prepare to shoot it out.

In most cases, moreover, the outside directors are at the mercy of a top man, who may be the chairman of the board or a dominant stockholder. If he is in the chief executive officer's corner, the outside director will be only as effective as the board chairman wants. If he appears to be a troublemaker, if he is in the wrong camp on an issue, the chairman can find ways to kill him off as a disloyal board member.

Source: *Business Week,* June 8, 1974, pp. 12, 15. Reprinted from the June 8 issue of *Business Week* by special permission. © 1974 by McGraw-Hill, Inc.

THE FRUSTRATIONS

Despite all this, the Penn Central case makes it plain that the Securities and Exchange Commission is going to hold outside directors responsible for monitoring management. Like it or not, they will have to be effective. And I am convinced that the typical outside director will like it very much. I have never talked with any outside director who has given serious thought to the functions, duties, and responsibilities of a director who was not also thoroughly disillusioned and frustrated. This frustration, in my opinion, is largely responsible for the decline in accepting directorships, even more significant than the growing fear among directors of the risk of facing liability suits.

I am not minimizing the liability suits. They are a great nuisance. They have become a way of life for some hungry lawyers and stockholders who, like vultures, swoop down on directors who didn't realize that they were guilty in approving questionable contracts, for example. All of a sudden, a director finds his responsibility driven home by a stockholder suit, and he says, "Holy smoke, how did I get in this spot?"

Sometimes a director goes to jail, but most have some liability insurance. In any case, actual convictions are uncommon. What really scares directors is that the suit will be publicized and, guilty or not, they will become suspect.

The combination of frustration and fear of lawsuits has made it increasingly hard for companies to get qualified outsiders to serve on their boards. Some companies are reverting to the old system of inside boards composed almost entirely of company officers who are completely subservient to the chief executive. Others are selecting their outside directors from the ranks of the lawyers, consultants, and investment bankers, who usually manage to make money out of their directorships. This is unfortunate. It is simply naive to expect an investment banker, who may gain a fat underwriting commission on a new stock issue, to be objective in all instances about the performance of the chief executive and his staff.

I can readily appreciate why many of my colleagues on boards shy away from the task of monitoring top management. But before we outside directors surrender, we ought to at least make a serious effort to be more effective. There is a function for us to perform. We should make a determined, good-faith attempt to perform it.

The basic question, of course, is: How? What means have we for checking on the performance of a chief executive?

THE AUDIT COMMITTEE

One answer has been to set up an audit committee of the board. A good audit committee can eliminate most of those big surprises that pop up when management hasn't let the board know about operating problems until the damage is done. This is certainly a step in the right direction.

A strong chief executive, however, doesn't like even the idea of an audit committee, and he can block its work, slow it down, or minimize its effectiveness in various ways. Most top executives these days know how to take care of themselves, and circumstances force them to concentrate their attention on the short run. They want to see the company's stock rise so that they can cash their stock options and secure their future with a handsome retirement or a consulting contract. This is simply a fact of executive life that an experienced director has to accept. In any case, auditing the company's operations cannot really provide a reliable measure of the chief executive's performance.

That is why, some years ago, I began working on a method for scoring top management on their job performance. Eventually, I wound up with a score card that covers the most significant factors an outside director should try to measure. This scoring system represents my conclusions after many years of studying the functions and responsiblities of top management. It is still experimental, and it will have to be adapted to each individual company. In some cases, it will not be necessary to score all the factors listed. Also, weighting of factors undoubtedly will vary from company to company.

Nevertheless, if outside directors will use even part of such a score card, or make up their own score cards, they should be able to do a far better job than they are now doing—which is practically no job at all so far as monitoring the chief executive goes. If 10 or 12 outside directors pool their score cards, the net judgment is likely to be accurate, regardless of individual variations.

The score card has two parts: general factors and personal factors. In my experience, a chief executive has to be seen from both sides. His performance as shown by financial and operating results must be interpreted in the light of his personal impact on the company and on the world in which it operates.

Most of the items on it lend themselves to an objective, quantitative approach. Directors should be able to compare return on investment and on sales with similar figures for competitive companies. They can often tell whether the corporate image is good or bad by the company's access to the financial community. If they have doubts about organization morale, an employee-attitude survey, designed to protect the identities of the respondents, will provide a better picture than any number of plant visits.

The general score card is reproduced on page 358.

The personal score card necessarily is more subjective, but it is vitally important. It can detect trouble in the making long before anything shows up in the financial and operating statements.

General scoreboard			
	Good	Fair	Poor
Return on stockholders' equity			
Return on sales			
Management of stockholders' assets			
Development of sound organizational structure			
Development of successors			
Development of proprietary products			
Development of organization morale			
Development of corporate image			
Development of growth potential			
Percentage of industry by segments			
Divestments			
Acquisitions			
Application of research and development			
Application of engineering and technology			
International			

I would suggest that the personal scorecard cover these topics and ask these questions:

Corporate citizenship. What does the chief executive give back to the community? Does he overdo it? Does he make a reasonable contribution of time and effort to community and government work without overcommitting himself?

Interlocking directorships. Is he sitting on too many boards to make a real contribution to any of them? Is he risking conflict of interest?

Outside business activities. What percentage of his time should he give to the company that is paying him $100,000 or more?

Health. Is the chief executive watching his physical condition? Is he trying to handle everything himself to the point of exhaustion? Is a periodic medical report available? Is there any question about his use of alcohol?

Builder of human resources.   Is he seriously trying to develop his subordinates as their coach, teacher, and counselor? Or is he aloof, expecting others to perform this task? Does he keep an eye on promising young managers and let them know he is watching them?

Decisiveness.   How does the chief executive meet and solve problems? Does he depend on committees? Postpone action on a problem that might go away? Does he make major decisions arbitrarily—without consulting even the board? Can he live with his decisions? Does he develop tensions and anxiety when things turn out poorly?

Trading in company stock.   Is he behaving like a speculator rather than a manager? Is he asking for trouble with the SEC under the insider trading rules? This is something the board should watch closely.

Outside directors are not used to throwing their weight around. It is small wonder that they are reluctant to assume the critical responsibility of evaluating the chief executive's performance and of removing him if he doesn't measure up.

But the fact remains that the outside directors are the only real safeguard the stockholders have against incompetent management. And I honestly think that nearly all those decent guys serving on boards would very much like to be more effective than they have been. The main trouble is that there has been no procedure for them to follow in monitoring the top man so that they would have solid facts and fair evidence that he is—or is not—doing his job.

That's why I am suggesting a scorecard. It may stir some directors into trying something they should have been doing all along.

---

27. Grumman Panel Finds Payoffs Continued Despite Board's Policy

William M. Carley

In the past three or four years, many corporations have been jolted by disclosures that they were making payoffs on overseas sales, and the companies have gone through further difficulties attempting to put their houses in order. Few, however, have endured the trauma that Grumman Corp. has been going through.

In 1975, with news breaking about investigations of companies for improper payments abroad, Grumman's board adopted its first policy

Source: *The Wall Street Journal,* Wednesday, February 28, 1979, pp. 1 and 25.

prohibiting such payments. Since then, the directors have issued orders in an attempt to put the basic policy into practice.

But many of the company's managers had been involved in payoffs since 1971, and they weren't about to change their ways, according to a special report of the board's audit committee that was filed with the Securities and Exchange Commission. During the past three years, these managers have been ignoring the rules against payoffs, the committee found. When they couldn't ignore the rules, the panel added, they withheld information from the board, circumvented the rules by camouflaging questionable payments, and in one instance defied orders of Grumman's special counsel.

FROM TOP TO BOTTOM

The maneuvers have involved people ranging from salesmen out in the field all the way to the top. According to the report, even John Bierwirth, chairman and chief executive, approved restructuring a transaction in an apparent effort to hide a questionable payment.

Grumman, at least on the issue of such payments, has been a corporation nearly out of control. In the report, completed last month, the audit committee stated:

"Disobedience of the instructions of the board, in some cases clearly willful, was so frequent as to raise serious questions concerning the ability of the board to supervise Grumman's business conduct effectively." At a later point, the committee added, "This company-wide lack of response to the policies and directives of the board created an intolerable situation which cannot be condoned and must not continue."

GETTING TOUGHER

Now the board has gotten tougher. Contracts of several sales consultants involved in payoffs have been terminated, and some sales commissions have been held up. In recent months, a number of Grumman executives have been fired. With something like "trials" of Grumman men under way or about to get under way, more may get the ax. As one insider puts it, "A lot of careers are being smashed."

One career that isn't being smashed is that of Mr. Bierwirth, the chairman and chief executive. The audit committee had some harsh words for Mr. Bierwirth, but earlier this month the board expressed confidence in his "personal and business integrity."

The executives who have been criticized are clearly bitter. Joseph Gavin, the president, whom the report didn't accuse of involvement, takes a different view. He terms it "regrettable that all the people who put men on the moon, built superior aircraft and developed technology for new energy sources must accept this cloud on their company's reputation." But the cloud, he concedes, results "from practices and attitudes so properly criticized in the audit-committee report."

THE GULFSTREAM II

Based in Bethpage, New York, Grumman produces jet fighters for the Navy, fire trucks and buses for municipalities, solar-energy devices and other products. The audit committee's report, however, mainly deals with sales of the Gulfstream II, a small jet used by corporations and foreign governments for their top officials. The Gulfstream II, which sells for about $6 million, was produced and sold by a Grumman subsidiary, Grumman American Aviation Corp. Last September, Grumman Corp. sold the unit to American Jet Industries Inc. In exchange, Grumman received cash and $20.5 million of American Jet preferred stock. It will also get fees for Gulfstreams sold after January 1, 1980—fees that could reach $15 million.

Grumman men—some in Grumman Corp., some in Grumman American and some in Grumman International, another subsidiary—were all involved in selling Gulfstream IIs to foreign governments. In some cases, however, an airplane was sold first to Page Airways Inc., based in Rochester, New York, which generally outfitted the plane with navigation equipment and interior furnishings and which then resold the plane to the final customer.

The SEC is suing Page in federal district court in Rochester, New York, for alleged failure to disclose participation in the payoffs—an allegation Page has strongly denied. Page has also issued a "general denial" of the allegations made against it in the Grumman audit committee's report.

As for Grumman, the SEC brought a civil suit in federal district court in Washington alleging concealment of payoffs. Grumman settled that case without admitting or denying the allegations. The Justice Department filed a criminal suit against Gulfstream American Corp., the renamed American Jet Industries, in federal district court in Washington. That suit also alleged concealment of payoffs. Gulfstream American pleaded guilty and was fined $120,000. Grumman Corp. agreed to pay the fine since it owned about 80 percent of the Gulfstream unit when the violations occurred.

James Bradbury, executive vice president of a unit of Gulfstream American Corp., says that now "under American Jet policies, payoffs simply aren't permitted and aren't authorized, and all personnel have been so advised."

The story of the payoffs, as told by Grumman's audit committee, begins in 1971. According to the committee, starting with "the first sale of a Gulfstream II to a foreign government, the personnel responsible for international Gulfstream II marketing engaged, either directly or indirectly, in activities raising questions as to almost every sale of a Gulfstream II to a foreign government."

It wasn't that the Grumman men initiated payoffs. They were met regularly with requests from local sales agents for "special commissions" that, it was understood, would be passed on to foreign government officials. The requests were hard to turn aside, partly because the Grumman men hadn't had much luck in selling abroad and partly because the special commissions could simply be added to the total price. They would cost Grumman nothing.

A 1971 sales to the government of Cameroun, in Africa, set the "basic pattern" for Grumman salesmen, the audit committee found. Grumman men were happy to pay "special commissions" as long as they could do it through an intermediary, as was done in the Cameroun case. Other questionable deals followed.

But by 1975, the risks were increasing. The Senate Subcommittee on Multinationals was exposing payoffs made by Gulf Oil Corp., Lockheed Corp. and others. And the SEC had begun the drive that was to uncover payments by hundreds of U.S. companies operating abroad.

In October 1975, Grumman's board adopted its first written policy on the subject, prohibiting commissions where illegal under domestic or foreign law. The policy also called for standard forms for sales agent contracts, board approval of the contracts and other procedures.

But while the board was trying to crack down, Grumman's managers were carrying on business as usual, the audit committee said. In August 1975, Grumman agreed to sell two Gulfstream IIs to Saudi Arabia's national airline with $4.2 million in sales commissions, some going to a Saudi sales agent and the balance of $2.5 million going to an American agent who said the money would be channeled to undisclosed third parties. Grumman's top managers became concerned, both about the magnitude of the commissions and about the unidentified third parties.

At this point, according to the audit committee's report, which is vigorously denied by Page Airways, Page's men suggested that the deal be restructured: The planes would be sold to Page, then to Liechtenstein corporation, then to the Saudi airline.

The Page men told Grumman's top managers the Liechtenstein corporation was an established aircraft distribution company; in fact, in had just been set up and served no other purpose in the deal but as a conduit for the $2.5 million, Grumman's audit committee charged.

Restructuring the transaction went on from September through December 1975. Approval of the restructuring was sought by Grumman salesmen from John Carr, Grumman's vice president for administration, and Mr. Bierwirth, the chairman. Even though Grumman's board in October issued its policy banning such payments both executives approved the restructuring, the audit committee said.

Top management's approval of use of the Liechtenstein conduit was a critical action at Grumman. As the audit committee put it in its report:

"Many Grumman sales personnel clearly failed to perceive the 1975 and subsequent directives as mandating a prompt and immediate change in conduct. Apparently contributing to such attitude was the participation of Grumman Corp.'s senior management in the restructuring of (the) Saudi Arabian . . . transaction virtually contemporaneously with the October 1975 directives."

Grumman men then seemed to go on a special-commission spree. They sold a Gulfstream II to Nigerian Airways in 1976 with the understanding that part of the $425,000 commission would be passed on to Nigerian government officials, the audit committee said. The question of whether the 6 percent commission was excessive was brought to Mr. Bierwirth, who decided against trying to cut it. Grumman salesmen also paid commissions on deals in Oman in December 1975 and in Bahrain in 1977 in violation of the Grumman board's policy.

A VENEZUELAN DEAL

Company lawyers trying to enforce the Grumman antipayoff policy got nowhere. In one instance, Grumman's salesmen in 1977 had lined up a sale of a used Gulfstream II to a Venezuelan company, with part of the Venezuelan sale agent's commissions to go to an employe of the purchaser. When a Grumman lawyer found out about that, he said it would violate company policy. The salesmen restructured the deal, arranging to sell the plane to a Panamanian company controlled by the Venezuelan sales agent for resale to the ultimate purchaser, the audit committee reported.

Part of the 1975 policy statement by the Grumman board called for disclosure to a foreign-government purchaser that a sales agent had been retained. In selling Gulfstream IIs, the Grumman American subsidiary ignored this rule, at least until some time last year. On one occasion, in mid-1977, this failure to comply was "in defiance of an express direction" of Grumman's general counsel, Lawrence Pierce, who had learned about the transaction, the audit committee found.

Grumman men also kept directors in the dark. While the Grumman American unit did submit contracts with sales agents to the

board, as required, "information as to the questionable nature of the
various transactions was consistently withheld," the audit committee
found. The committee added: "As late as June 1977, a senior vice
president specifically represented to the board, 'I will state that in the
marketing of the Gulfstream II overseas, we haven't done anything,
that will be embarrassing.'"

In 1977 the Grumman audit committee began its investigation,
hiring Cahill, Gordon & Reindel as outside counsel. The investigation
evidently met with resistance and ridicule. Corwin "Corky" Meyer,
president of the Grumman American subsidiary, according to the
audit committee, "expressed belief that this committee's investigation
was a needless intrusion upon and an interference with Grumman
American's sales activities."

Page Airways, with minor exceptions, refused to cooperate with
the Grumman committee, the panel said. A company that had bought
Gulfstreams and resold them to Saudi Arabia and Morocco gave almost no cooperation, the managing director explaining that he wasn't
interested in becoming involved in "the American investigatory cir-
cus." Foreign sales agents clammed up, and committee representatives trying to interview a Liechtenstein bank officer got a lecture on
bank-secrecy laws instead.

"UNREALISTIC POLICIES"?

Grumman's audit committee concluded that "various (company)
personnel responsible for foreign sales apparently acted in the belief
that Grumman had to be saved from what they perceived to be unrealistic policies and procedures which would put Grumman at a
competitive disadvantage. Even during the committee's investigation, some personnel were still attempting to circumvent the board's
directives and to structure transactions to mask such circumvention."

In the crackdown that has followed, several have lost their jobs,
though Grumman won't say how many. Charles Vogeley, Grumman
American senior vice president for sales, resigned last August. Mr.
Meyer, the president of Grumman American, "abdicated his responsibility" for enforcing Grumman's 1975 antipayoff policy, the audit
committee charged. Mr. Meyer left Grumman early last year, though
for reasons other than the payoff problems.

Those executives who have come under criticism are resentful. Mr.
Vogeley says he was "never given a fair chance" to rebut charges
against him; he declines further comment. Mr. Meyer says there are
"grave inaccuracies in the audit committee report, and had the committee interviewed me directly, I feel we could have set the record
straight."

PAGE'S REPLY

Page Airways is also upset. In a letter to Grumman, a Page attorney blasted the audit committee's report.

Grumman's audit report is filled with "inaccuracies . . . too numerous to reference and explain," the Page attorney wrote. "Your report appears to be a frantic attempt to dignify negative surmise, rumors and gossip, all for the purpose of painting Page in the worst possible light." The attorney added that Page didn't fully cooperate with Grumman's audit committee because it would disclose competitive information and because the investigation wasn't being conducted fairly. He urged the "retraction and correction" of the report.

At Grumman, whether others might be fired isn't known. "I don't want to talk about disciplinary proceedings," Mr. Bierwirth, the Grumman chairman, said in an interview.

The audit committee's criticism of Mr. Bierwirth himself centered on his approval of the Saudi Arabian transaction to include the Liechtenstein company. The deal was altered, the committee said, "specifically because (it was) questionable, and for that very reason the restructuring shouldn't have occurred."

But recently directors gave a vote of confidence not only to Mr. Bierwirth but also to Mr. Gavin, the president, and Mr. Carr, who now is vice chairman.

---

28. Southern Hospitality? As Union Organizers Get to Milledgeville, Ga., The Mayor Holds an Unusual Welcoming Party
Urban C. Lehner

MILLEDGEVILLE, Ga.—Night after night, the workers filed into Mel Tate's room at the Holiday Inn to hear his pitch for the Amalgamated Clothing and Textile Workers Union. Some came apprehensively, aware of local employers' antagonism toward unions. Many worked for J.P. Stevens and Co., which has a history of firing employes who take part in union activities.

The workers had more reason to be apprehensive than they knew. While they were meeting with Mr. Tate and other union organizers in

Source: *The Wall Street Journal*, Friday, February 29, 1980, p. 42.

Room 131, Milledgeville police upstairs in Room 229 were spying on them.

The police in 1976 and 1977 secretly monitored the union meetings, identified those attending and passed on the information to a number of local industrial employers. The police acted on orders from the mayor, with the encouragement of the industrialists and with the alleged cooperation of the motel manager. Disclosures of the spying have added an odd new chapter in the story of the long-continuing struggle between union organizers and industries in the South. And the episode has become a source of embarrassment to a town that was so eager to attract new industry that it may have gone overboard in its efforts to create a favorable climate for business.

A $12 MILLION LAWSUIT

"People here don't like labor unions, but they respect the law," says Milledgeville's current mayor, Dr. Wilbur Baugh. "This isn't the image we'd like our community to project."

Some of the town's policemen, along with the former mayor, the motel manager and some of the industrialists, have told about the spying operation in depositions and affidavits resulting from a $12 million lawsuit filed last year by the textile workers' union and its organizers in federal court in nearby Macon, Georgia. The union, which goes by the acronym ACTWU (pronounced "Act-Two"), hopes the suit will go to trial in April, though a motion to dismiss it is still pending.

The suit charges the officials and the industrialists with illegally conspiring to violate the organizers' right to privacy, freedom of speech and freedom of association. Most of the defendants have settled out of court with the union, leaving Stevens—ACTWU's organizing target all along—as the main combatant. Stevens, a major textile producer, denies any wrongdoing and vows to fight the suit "to the fullest."

The allegations of surveillance and blacklisting have led the National Labor Relations Board to reopen a previously closed case involving Stevens' Milledgeville plant; the NRLB could end up declaring ACTWU the Stevens workers' bargaining agent, even though there hasn't been a representation election.

For Stevens, the Milledgeville episode is just the latest chapter in its 17-year fight to keep labor unions out of its plants. ACTWU, its main adversary, has won a long string of legal victories, including a $50,000 settlement in a previous case involving electronic eavesdropping by two Stevens officials in Wallace, North Carolina. But the union has won representation rights at only 11 of Stevens's 84 plants, and it hasn't succeeded in negotiating a contract at any.

For organized labor, the Milledgeville episode has provided some new ammunition for its claim that local public officials and business leaders sometimes team up to break union-organizing campaigns in the South. "This is not atypical," asserts William Hobgood, assistant U.S. secretary of labor for labor-management relations. He says that companies fighting unions in Southern towns "get all manner of municipal assistance, my investigators tell me."

The notoriety brought by the ACTWU suit has been painful for Milledgeville, a quiet town of 13,000 in central Georgia. Its gracious Greek-revival and Federal-style homes recall the days when Milledgeville was Georgia's state capital, from 1803 to 1868. Later it became known as the home of a state mental asylum. In recent decades, the town has enjoyed an economic boom. A dozen companies built factories on its outskirts during Walter Williams's 18 years as mayor, which ended in 1975.

In the 1975 election, Robert Rice, an affable Texaco distributor, defeated Mr. Williams by forming an alliance with one of the town's most influential black citizens, the Rev. C. Wayman Alston. "Bob Rice didn't beat me; Charlie Alston did," says Mr. Williams. "Charlie delivered the black vote." But it was an alliance that was to lead to Mayor Rice's downfall when it crumbled three years later.

ARRIVAL OF THE UNION MEN

Mr. Rice, like Mr. Williams, was strongly antiunion and considered keeping out unions the key to Milledgeville's success in attracting industry. Mr. Alston, no lover of unions himself, testified that Mr. Rice had a "union phobia." Mr. Rice also remembered that his predecessor, when faced with union drives in the past, had called meetings of civic leaders to urge them to pass the no-union message to workers.

So in August 1976, when J. C. Green, manager of the local Holiday Inn, told the mayor that ACTWU organizers were at work in Milledgeville and staying at the motel, Mr. Rice says in a deposition that he acted quickly. He summoned a number of industry leaders to city hall, informed them of the union threat and outlined his plan.

The police would take down automobile license plate numbers of those attending union meetings, determine the owners of the cars and pass on lists of names to the industry leaders. "Everybody thought it was a good idea," Mayor Rice says in a deposition.

Mr. Rice testified that William Wall, the Stevens plant manager, attended the city-hall meeting as well as a number of subsequent status-report meetings. Mr. Wall denies it. The former mayor's account is supported by other witnesses who attended, including Tom Lahey, an executive with Grumman Aerospace Corp., a Grumman

Corp. subsidiary that makes glass-fiber parts in Milledgeville. Both Grumman Aerospace and Mr. Rice have made cash settlements with the union and have agreed to cooperate with it by turning over documents that may be used in the current case.

Soon the spy machinery was humming smoothly. Detectives William Miller and James Josey, at first accompanied by police chief Charles Osborne, set up their lookout in Room 229 at the Holiday Inn; from the room, they could see both the parking lot and the union organizers' room. They began drawing up lists of license plate numbers. An affidavit given by detective Miller, who since has been killed in an auto accident, indicates he stood watch at the Holiday Inn as often as several nights a week during some stretches of 1976 and 1977. After the lists were typed, Mickie Burrus, the mayor's secretary, would call the industrialists and tell them to pick up the lists. She says in a deposition that she only talked to the top man at each company, including Mr. Wall.

Most of the surveillance occurred at the Holiday Inn, but one episode, described locally as the "pat-down" ruse, took place near the union hall of the one union in town that represents any workers—the Lime, Cement and Gypsum Workers. The ACTWU organizers had borrowed the hall for a meeting, and detectives Miller and Josey were nearby. They sent out a 16-year-old boy on foot as a decoy.

"As he approached the hall, the squad car drew up to him, and Mr. Josey pretended to stop him, pat him down, question him, then place him in the squad car as if he were under arrest. While this diversion was occurring, I observed and dictated into my tape recorder the numbers of license plates of cars outside the union hall," detective Miller said in his affidavit.

Grumman Aerospace in late August of 1976 sent two security officers from its Long Island headquarters to help the police with the spying, according to its managers here. They stayed only a few days, though, after it became clear that few Grumman employes were attending the union meetings. But Stevens's employes were attending them. William Zarkowsky, general manager of Grumman's Milledgeville plant, says in a deposition that Stevens's Mr. Wall told him in September 1976 that "up to 167" of Stevens's 600 employes had attended the meetings, a statistic Mr. Zarkowsky passed on to Grumman higher-ups in a September 16 memo.

Stevens didn't provide the police with investigative help. But several witnesses say that the big textile maker was active otherwise. Mr. Rice in his deposition, recalls a telephone call from Mr. Wall asking the police to keep tabs on a particular union meeting the company had gotten wind of.

AVOIDING CITY HALL

At some point, according to the others' accounts, Stevens became circumspect. Police chief Osborne says he was asked to hand-deliver one of the lists to Mr. Wall at a "secluded area" near the Stevens' plant. Former Mayor Rice testified that Mr. Wall told him that he had been advised it would be in Stevens's best interests for Mr. Wall to "become, you might say, scarce around city hall."

Mr. Rice says he later had lunch with three Stevens officials including Mr. Wall, who thanked him for providing the lists of license numbers and who explained that Stevens lawyers had advised the company it shouldn't participate in the actual surveillance work.

None of this might ever have come out had Mr. Rice stayed on good terms with his political ally, the Rev. C. Wayman Alston, who had attended some of the city-hall meetings and who knew about the surveillance. But Mr. Rice, in the black minister's view, hadn't made good on his promises to put blacks in high city positions. So the two men began to feud.

Finally, in mid-1978, Mr. Rice gave Mr. Alston a $2,700-a-year job as city chaplain—but ordered him to drop his pressure for more jobs for blacks. The minister issued a press release saying Mr. Rice could find himself "another nigger": a few weeks later he disclosed the existence of the union-surveillance scheme to a Macon newspaper, putting union lawyer Jonathan Schiller on the trail.

OUT-OF-COURT SETTLEMENTS

By last April, ACTWU had brought suit against Mayor Rice, Chief Osborne, detective Josey and innkeeper Green. After taking numerous depositions, the union amended its complaint to include a number of industrialists as defendants.

Except for Stevens and its Mr. Wall, the only defendants who haven't settled out of court are Meadows Industries Inc., a carpet-yarn producer, and its executive vice president, Albert Gandy. Mr. Gandy, according to Mr. Rice's deposition, was Stevens's "go-between" with the mayor after Wall had decided to become "scarce" around city hall. Mr. Gandy declines comment.

Mr. Wall, for his part, says he received only one list of license plate numbers and didn't know where that list came from. He says he didn't attend any meetings with Chief Osborne or Mr. Rice at which union surveillance was discussed and wasn't aware of the surveillance. Stevens says it is "confident" that none of its managers "engaged in an unlawful conspiracy."

Since being named a defendant, Stevens has counterattacked. Last fall, it retained former Attorney General Griffin Bell's Atlanta law firm, King & Spaulding, to handle the Milledgeville litigation. Earlier this week, Stevens filed a counterclaim demanding among other things, $100,000 in actual damages and $15 million in punitive damages from the union.

The counterclaim charges the union with abuse of the legal process. It maintains that the original ACTWU suit was a "sham" action brought for the improper purpose of taking depositions to be released publicly as part of a "professional media attack" against Stevens.

A union spokesman says, "We haven't yet seen these (court) papers and don't want to comment until we have seen them."

Stevens also has asked Federal Judge Wilbur Owens to dismiss the suit. The company maintains that the case is a labor dispute within the NLRB's exclusive jurisdiction. Stevens further contends that the union's charges of conspiracy between the company and Milledgeville officials were covered by an earlier, unsuccessful ACTWU suit that made general allegations of Stevens conspiracies. The company's motion to dismiss asserts that even if Stevens had done everything the union says it did, the conduct couldn't have constituted an illegal civil-rights conspiracy.

Whatever the outcome of the lawsuit, the spying incident already has had far-reaching consequences here in Milledgeville. Robert Rice resigned as mayor last summer and moved to Atlanta to begin a new life. He declines to be interviewed, explaining: "I'm not in politics anymore." The Rev. C. Wayman Alston was a loser, too. He was accused of misconduct at the state prison where he served as chaplain.

After investigating 55 days, the state didn't bring charges against Mr. Alston, but he says his effectiveness as a chaplain was destroyed. He retired at age 58. "Whistleblowers always lose," Mr. Alston says.

People in Milledgeville are still debating how much damage has been done to the town's industrial-development dreams. One community leader looks at it from the bright side. Some businesses might be attracted, he thinks, to a place with such an anti-union atmosphere.

But others fear Milledgeville's reputation has been sadly tarnished. "It's unfortunate this had to happen here," says Mayor Baugh. "This is one of the finest little towns in the United States."

29. Complying With the Foreign Corrupt Practices Act
Homer L. Bates and Philip M. J. Reckers

On December 19, 1977, President Carter signed into law the Foreign Corrupt Practices Act of 1977 (FCPA). The Act has far-reaching requirements and a potentially negative impact for the uninformed businessman. While making it a criminal offense for U.S. companies to bribe foreign officials, the Act also establishes demanding internal-control and recordkeeping requirements for *all* publicly held corporations. The new law subjects public companies, their officers, directors, employees, agents, and stockholders to both civil and criminal prosecution for not maintaining an "adequate" internal-control system. Furthermore, the internal-control requirements relate to *all* aspects of the business enterprise, not just foreign bribery.

Recent statements by staff members of the Securities and Exchange Commission (SEC) indicate that the new legislation is viewed as greatly expanding the commission's authority to regulate public companies' internal affairs. The acting chief accountant of the SEC indicated in a recent speech that the SEC is considering requiring a stockholders' report on internal control. The report would take the form of a direct report by the external auditors or a report by management with which the auditor will be "associated."

Two recent lawsuits brought by the SEC attest to its intent to enforce its new internal-control and recordkeeping authority. Both suits allege violations of the accounting-standards provisions of the FCPA, along with violations of SEC reporting and proxy rules. The suit against Aminex Resources Corp. and two of its officers alleges misappropriation of over $1 million of corporate assets. Foreign bribery was not involved in the suit. In the suit against Page Airways Inc. and six of its executives, the SEC charged that illegal foreign payments were made. They were not charged with foreign bribery violations, apparently because the payments took place prior to the December 19, 1977 effective date of the Foreign Corrupt Practices Act. The SEC action, charging that the payments were made without adequate documentation and controls, was based on violations of the accounting-standards provisions of the Act.

This article will describe the major provisions of the FCPA and will

Source: *Business*, July–August, 1979, pp. 35–36.

recommend steps to be taken to comply with the law (see ruled insert on pages 375–77). Both the foreign-corrupt-practices provision and the accounting-standards provision (internal-control requirements) will be addressed.

BACKGROUND

The moving force behind enactment of the Act was the recent disclosures of illegal foreign payments by over 350 U.S. companies to foreign officials and political leaders. The Act attempts to upgrade the ethical behavior of American business and to prevent future corrupt payments. Because external auditors may be unable to detect these payments if they are made from funds maintained outside the firm, Congress included in the legislation requirements for maintaining accurate, fully encompassing books and systems of internal control. This provision was intended to assist in enforcing the legislation.

The SEC has noted that evidence of an illegal payment may point directly to a failure to comply with the internal-control provisions of the Act, and failure to record a transaction correctly or to have appropriate internal controls may provide evidence that one has acted corruptly. Apparently the SEC also plans to relate the accounting-standards provisions of the law to interim financial reporting. For example, a consistent pattern of fourth-quarter adjustments may signal a lack of compliance with the Act.

PROVISIONS OF THE LAW

Foreign Corrupt Practices

The foreign-bribery provisions of the Foreign Corrupt Practices Act cover both publicly held companies (any issuer that has a class of securities registered pursuant to Section 12 of the Securities Exchange Act of 1934 or that is required to file reports under Section 15(d) of that Act) and other "domestic concerns." The Act defines domestic concerns as any individual who is a citizen, national, or resident of the United States or any corporation, partnership, association, joint-stock company, business trust, unincorporated organization, or sole proprietorship whose principal place of business is in the United States or in a territory, possession, or commonwealth of the United States. Although the Act does not mention foreign subsidiaries of U.S. businesses specifically, it appears to include them by prohibiting both direct and indirect payments to foreign officials or political parties.

The Act makes it unlawful to use the mails or any means of interstate commerce to offer, pay, promise to pay, or authorize anything of value to any of the following for corrupt purposes:

1. Any foreign official.
2. Any foreign political party or any official thereof.
3. Any candidate for foreign political office.
4. Any person who knows or has reason to know that all or a portion of anything of value will be offered, given, or promised to any of the foregoing.

The legislation does not stipulate that the illegal action be consummated; an offer is illegal, regardless of whether or not it is accepted. Corrupt purposes are defined as:

> (A) Influencing any act or decision of such foreign official in his official capacity, including a decision to fail to perform his official functions; or
> (B) Inducing such foreign official to use his influence with a foreign government or instrumentality thereof to affect or influence any act or decision of such government or instrumentality,[1]

in order to assist such issuer in obtaining or retaining business for or with, or directing business to, any person.

The legislation does not strictly prohibit political contributions to foreign countries; they are illegal only if meant to obtain business.

The Act does not prohibit so-called "facilitating" or "grease" payments to relatively low-level employees. However, they may be illegal under local law. The Act excludes low-level government employees, whose duties are primarily "ministerial or clerical" from the definition of foreign official. It was argued that grease payments simply expedite a matter toward an eventual act or decision. They are made to secure prompt performance of duties; they are not meant to cause an official to make other than a free-will decision. Legal grease payments include payments to expedite shipments through customs, to secure required permits and licenses, and to obtain adequate police protection.

A company convicted of making illegal payments can be fined up to $1 million; any officer, director, or stockholder acting on behalf of the company who "willfully" violates the illegal-payments provisions of the Act may be fined up to $10,000 and imprisoned up to five years, or both. A violation by an individual must be "willful" to be prosecuted; no such stipulation exists for the company. In order for an employee or agent to be fined and/or imprisoned, the Act provides that the company first must have been found in violation of the Act.

---

[1] *Foreign Corrupt Practices Act of 1977*, sec. 104(a)(1).

This provision was included in the Act to prevent low-level employees or agents from being scapegoats for the company or higher officials.

It appears, however, that individuals who violate the law for their own self-interest may be subject to penalties, regardless of whether or not the company was found to have violated the law. Whether or not an individual's personal actions could subject the company to penalties is questionable. The company's liability may depend on whether or not it had taken adequate steps to monitor its employees' actions. The law prohibits the corporation from either directly or indirectly paying a fine imposed on an individual.

Accounting Standards

The accounting-standards provisions are applicable to any company that has a class of stock registered pursuant to Section 12 of the Securities Exchange Act of 1934 and any company that is required to file reports pursuant to Section 15(d) of that Act. The law amended the SEC Act of 1934 and, therefore, is applicable only to publicly held companies. Although the corrupt-practices provisions are applicable to both publicly held companies and other "domestic concerns," the accounting-standards provisions apply only to the publicly held companies specified previously.

The accounting-standards provisions of the 1977 Foreign Corrupt Practices Act require that registered firms:

(1) Make and keep books, records, and accounts, which in reasonable detail, accurately and fairly reflect the transactions and dispositions of the assets of the issuer . . . , and

(2) Devise and maintain appropriate systems of internal accounting control.

The Act does *not* limit the scope of this requirement to foreign transactions. The requirements relate to all transactions, both domestic and foreign. The "in reasonable detail" qualification was included in the legislation at the suggestion of the American Institute of Certified Public Accountants (AICPA), in order to avoid requiring an unrealistic degree of accuracy and precision. The conference committee stipulated that "in reasonable detail" means that an issuer's books should reflect transactions in conformity with generally accepted accounting principles or other applicable criteria. Accordingly, as expressed in American Institute of Certified Public Accountants Statement on Accounting Standards No. 1 (SAS #1), "reasonable assurance" means that the costs of a particular control should not exceed the benefits to be derived from it and that the evaluation of costs and benefits are subjective.

Preventive Action

Foreign-Bribery Provisions: Because the foreign-bribery provisions of the Corrupt Practices Act apply to *all* U.S. companies, citizens, and residents, and because of the severity of the penalties, it is imperative that strong, effective actions be taken to prevent violations. In this respect, management obviously should seek assistance from its legal counsel and from its independent auditors. In addition, the provisions of the Act should be discussed in detail with the firm's internal audit staff.

A necessary first step in avoiding violations of the FCPA is the implementation of a strict, well-monitored code of conduct for all officers and employees in sensitive positions. Many large corporations have a code of conduct; however, because of the scope of the FCPA, it is incumbent that all companies engaging in foreign trade institute a code of conduct. Those companies that have a code of conduct should review it in light of the FCPA and make changes if necessary; compliance must be monitored regularly.

As part of the monitoring process, all new employees in sensitive positions should be required to read and stipulate, in writing, that they understand the code and agree to abide by it. Any deviation from the code of business conduct should be dealt with harshly. In addition, it is recommended that continuing employees annually represent in writing that they have abided by the code of conduct and that they agree to continue to do so in the future.

Potential illegal indirect payments by agents or intermediaries are extremely difficult to monitor. Because the FCPA makes it illegal to make payments to intermediaries where the company knows, or has reason to know, that all or a portion of the payment will be given as an illegal payment to a foreign governmental or political official, it is important to communicate to intermediaries, as well as to employees, the nature of the Act and the firm's code of conduct. It may be prudent to consider including a clause in all contracts and agreements to the effect that no part of any payment received will be passed on to a foreign governmental or political official. In addition, it would be wise to have annual written statements to the effect that no payments were passed on in the previous year.

Management reliance on external auditors to detect corrupt payments should be limited. Management should realize that the external auditor's concern with illegal payments is restricted to those that may have a *material* effect on the financial statements of the firm; the Corrupt Practices Act prohibits "anything of value" to be paid or offered to foreign officials or political parties. Management should avoid placing too much of a burden on the external auditor. It would be impossible for the independent auditor to detect all potential illegal payments. It would be useful, however, to have the independent auditor include in his report potential areas of concern regarding illegal payments. The audit committee, or the board of directors, then could engage the internal audit staff to investigate further these potential problem areas.

As primary responsibility for compliance with the law rests with the internal audit staff, that staff should undertake a methodical analysis and identification of possible exposures to the illegal-payments penalties of the Act. Steps should be taken to ascertain whether or not manuals and management-authorization polices are up to date in light of the law. Operating practices warrant review, and particular attention should be focused on sensitive areas, such as foreign consultation fees, rebates and refunds, and cash transfers to foreign subsidiaries. Training sessions for the internal audit staff might well be advised, given the new demands placed on them. Responsibility at the highest level of the firm should be established for keeping abreast of future legislative developments and directing corporate response.

Accounting-Standards Provisions: Because of the far-reaching nature, and obvious importance, of the accounting-standards provisions, actions must be taken to assure compliance. All affected personnel must be informed of the accounting-standards provisions of the FCPA. It would be wise to have them represent in writing that they have read, understand, and agree to abide by the provisions. In addition, all current accounting policies and procedures should be reviewed, documented, and communicated to all affected personnel. Besides documenting and communicating the accounting policies and procedures of the firm, it would be prudent to institute a policy in which the accounting and financial staff affirmed, in writing, that they were following the stipulated policies and procedures. As with the code of business conduct, it would be useful to have a policy of annually requiring affected personnel to affirm their understanding of, and compliance with, the firm's accounting policies and procedures. This compliance procedure should be monitored regularly by the internal accounting staff.

It also would be informative for the internal audit staff to flow-chart specific types of transactions to highlight potential problem areas. If the review process indicates any gaps in internal control, changes and/or additions should be made as feasible. In the event that a specific internal-control problem exists, but it is not economically feasible to take any actions (i.e., the estimated costs exceed the estimated benefits), it is incumbent on management to document the problem area, quantify the projected costs and benefits, and bring the matter to the attention of the audit committee or board of directors. The importance of documentation cannot be overemphasized. Given the subjective terminology of the legislation and the emphasis on "willful" violation, it becomes especially important that decisions respecting compliance with the Act be explicit, logically supported, and in writing.

It appears that the SEC would not require adoption of additional internal-control procedures if they were not economically justified to the firm. Documentation of this fact would be an absolute necessity. Management, furthermore, again would be cautioned against placing excessive reliance on the external auditor—in this instance with regard to the evaluation of internal control. The external auditors are concerned primarily with the internal-control system in determining the amount of reliance they can place on the system when performing their audit function. The external auditor, in fact, may not examine certain internal-control procedures if the transactions processed by the system are not material to the financial statements. The independent auditor also may disregard a specific internal-control procedure if more efficient methods of auditing are available. Still, the audit committee of the board of directors should request that the independent auditor report on any questionable internal-control procedures that come to his attention. The responsibility of evaluating the specific policies or procedures belongs to the internal-control staff, which should respond to any and every point raised by the auditor.

The four objectives of the required internal-control systems taken by the legislation from SAS #1 are:

1. Transactions are executed in accordance with management's general or specific authorization;

2. Transactions are recorded as necessary (I) to permit preparation of financial statements in conformity with generally accepted accounting principles or any other criteria applicable to such statements, and (II) to maintain accountability for assets;

3. Access to assets is permitted only in accordance with management's general or specific authorization; and

4. The recorded accountability for assets is compared with the existing assets at reasonable intervals and appropriate action is taken with respect to any differences.[2]

It is obvious that these four objectives are largely subjective and require a high degree of judgment.

Failure to meet the accounting-standards provisions does not give rise to the same penalties as the antibribery provisions. Registrants and individuals with the power to control the direction, management,

---

[2] Ibid., sec. 102(2)(B).

or policies of a registrant, who willfully violate the accounting-standards provisions would be subject to penalties under the SEC Act of 1934. These include a fine of not more than $10,000 and/or imprisonment of not more than five years. In addition, a third party may bring civil litigation against the company for failure to comply with the accounting provisions. (The Act specifically excludes from liability individuals acting in cooperation with the head of any federal department or agency with respect to matters concerned with the national security of the United States, if such cooperation resulted from a specific written directive.)

SUMMARY

From this brief discusison, it is obvious that the 1977 Foreign Corrupt Practices Act is far-reaching and, contrary to its title, it does not apply solely to "foreign corrupt practices." The Act not only includes severe penalties for its violation but also expands the enforcement powers of the SEC. The SEC, furthermore, has taken little time to act; as mentioned previously, two suits already have been brought under the provisions of the Act.

Given the subjective terms in which the legislation is couched, the long-run implications of the record-keeping and internal-control provisions of the law may be even more significant than the current impact. Ultimately, record-keeping and internal-control compliance may come under closer scrutiny on a broader scale. In the not too distant future, SEC regulations may well require external auditors to report on internal controls. The Act opens the door for the SEC to develop specific internal-control standards in the future.

In order to avoid problems associated with violations of the Act, management must take specific action today and monitor closely future legislative and regulatory changes. Today's actions entail communicating the specifics of the Act to the affected parties and gaining written assurances that individuals have read the provisions of the Act and agree to abide by them. A code of business conduct should be instituted and vigorously applied and monitored. The internal-control procedures and policies should be reviewed, documented, communicated, and monitored closely. Any questionable actions should be investigated, and corrective action should be taken and documented.

It is obvious that no firm has the resources or capabilities to assure that all its employees are conducting business within the scope of the Foreign Corrupt Practices Act. It is absolutely necessary, however, that it take all reasonable steps to assure that no obvious violations are occurring, and this requires that the actions of its affected employees be scrutinized and well-documented.

As noted earlier, the FCPA of 1977 may impose a significant negative impact on those businessmen lacking knowledge and understanding of it. With its emphasis on internal controls, however, the Act also may yield some important benefits for those businessmen who seize this opportunity to review their operations in detail.

30. THE CORPORATE LAWYER'S DILEMMA
Stephen Solomon

The corporate bar and the Securities and Exchange Commission— two parties that never back down from a good scrap—have been at odds for several years now over a pair of interrelated questions that could cause an upheaval in the practice of corporate law. The first of these questions is, whom does a corporate lawyer work for: (A) management, (B) the board of directors, or (C) the shareholders? If the answer to the first question is either A or B, a second question arises: when is a lawyer obliged to blow the whistle on his client?

These issues took on new urgency last March when Charles Johnson and William Carter, partners in the prestigious Wall Street firm of Brown, Wood, Ivey, Mitchell & Petty, were suspended from practice before the SEC for failing to require the National Telephone Co. to disclose its true financial condition. It was careening toward bankruptcy, and for several months in 1974–75, during which the company was seeking new capital to keep alive its telephone-leasing business, its press releases, letters to stockholders, and SEC filings were less than candid. Finally, the two lawyers, who had advised the chief executive to make a full disclosure, informed the board of directors, and the chief executive resigned. But an administrative-law judge at the SEC ruled that Johnson and Carter had violated the securities laws by taking part in concealing material facts, and by failing to report to the directors sooner.

The pair can still practice while the case is being adjudicated. It goes next to the full commission. Johnson and Carter vow that if they lose there, they will appeal the verdict through the federal courts. If that happens, most of their colleagues will no doubt be cheering them

Source: *Fortune*, vol. 100, no. 9 (November 5, 1979), pp. 138–40.

on because nothing calls the organized bar to arms quite as stirringly as the prospect of an outsider setting rules on professional conduct.

THE TIES THAT BIND

As for the theoretical questions being raised, lawyers acknowledge that the ultimate authority in a corporation is wielded by the shareholders. But as lawyers see it, this authority is delegated to the board and—within whatever guidelines may have been laid down—by the board to management. So lawyers generally regard management as the party to whom they owe professional loyalty. They also believe that going above the head of the officers, with whom they deal on a regular basis, would drive a wedge of distrust into the relationship and might even result in their dismissal.

Lawyers generally say that, in the absence of clear company guidelines to the contrary, they will appeal to the board only in cases of personal dishonesty—as when the president is emptying the corporate treasury into his pockets—or when the company is pursuing a course that is patently illegal. But attorneys seldom discover personal dishonesty. And managements almost always change course when told that what they plan to do is against the law. More often, the legal questions fall into a gray area, where some defense, however weak, can be made. The National Telephone case involved just such a problem. Management argued that immediate disclosure might be fatal to the company's campaign to corral the additional financing needed for survival. Johnson and Carter disagreed, but they deferred to what seemed to them to be a reasonable business judgment. When the board asked for their opinion, however, they recommended full disclosure.

The National Telephone case is only the tip of the iceberg. What if the board refuses to act, or is itself involved in the illegal activity? Is a lawyer obliged to go to the stockholders, which in effect means sending out the dirty linen for cleaning at the SEC's division of enforcement? In a case arising out of the collapse of National Student Marketing Corp. in 1970, the SEC asserted that lawyers do have such a duty. When the case was finally decided last year, a federal judge disposed of the charges without having to consider this particular point. If the SEC raises the issue again, and its position is upheld by the courts, corporate lawyers, who now tend to act as confidential advisers, would instead be obliged to assume a more independent role, like accountants. Lawyers would have a duty to the investing public as well as to their client.

This strikes a tender nerve with lawyers. They have always considered loyalty to their client to be paramount, though they acknowledge that they have a duty to the legal system as well. Under certain circumstances, for example, a lawyer is authorized to blow the whistle on his client in order to prevent the commission of a crime. All this is governed by several provisions of the bar's Code of Professional Responsibility that are, even for legal writers, an extraordinary achievement in the use of murky cross-references and double negatives. Because the guidelines are so fuzzy, attorneys may be damned if they do and damned if they don't—as a securities lawyer named Stuart C. Goldberg learned. In 1973, Goldberg went to the SEC and blew the whistle on his own law firm and a corporate client, charging that they had omitted material facts in a registration statement. He found himself tangled in years of litigation, accused of negligence and betraying the confidences of a client.

THE LEGAL LIONS ROAR

Faced with these contradictory cases, even Themis might be tempted to tear her blindfold off and look for commonsense solutions. Clearly there are dangers in letting the SEC dictate the rules. If a government agency with prosecutorial authority can punish lawyers who appear before it as adversaries, then it will hold power that it could all too easily abuse.

To fend off the SEC, the lawyers have been trying to write some clearer ground rules themselves. The trouble with this approach is that there is nothing resembling a consensus on these questions within the bar. In fact, there is violent disagreement, as Robert J. Kutak can testify. He is presiding partner of an important and burgeoning firm, Kutak Rock & Huie, which is headquartered in Omaha, and for the past two years he has chaired a special commission of the American Bar Association that is charged with revising the ten-year-old code. The commission produced a working draft that was circulated at a recent A.B.A. meeting in Dallas—and caused a tremendous ruckus. "I was walking into a lion's den with a hunk of red meat," Kutak says, somewhat ruefully.

What awakened the lions were provisions that would greatly expand the circumstances under which lawyers would have to blow the whistle on their clients. As Kutak's draft puts it, a lawyer who discovers that a corporate officer is carrying out an act that is "legally improper and likely to result in significant harm to the organization" is required first to take actions to assure internal review—such as reporting the matter to the board. If the board refuses to act, and the matter appears to be a clear violation of law that is likely to result in "irreparable injury to the organization, or in substantial injury to a person having ownership or membership rights in the organization," the lawyer must take further action, such as notifying the injured person or making a public disclosure. The draft code also requires public disclosure, if necessary, to prevent the commission of any crime that would "seriously endanger the life or safety of a person, result in wrongful destruction of substantial property, or corrupt judicial or governmental procedure."

WHEN IN DOUBT, TELL THE BOARD

One telling question raised by the Kutak code is, what does all this mean? The first layer of the code would probably be reassuring to all those members of corporate boards who wonder now and then about what is *really* going on down in the bowels of the mammoth organization that they are supposed to be governing. The thrust of the draft, simply put, is: when in real doubt, bring it to the board. That is consistent with most state corporation laws, which regard the board as the corporation's governing body, and with the outcome of recent shareholder suits that have greatly widened the liability of directors. A well-informed board, conscious of its own liability, is undoubtedly the most effective brake on corporate misconduct.

The working draft runs into heavier turbulence when it glides from stage one to stage two—where the hired gun must turn on the board itself. Even conservative lawyers would generally agree that there are circumstances in which this must be done. But public disclosure raises practical, legal, and civil-liberties problems that need to be carefully considered. As a practical matter, managers and board members might be reluctant to talk candidly with an attorney who has a hot line to the regulatory authories. Frozen out of sensitive discussions, the lawyer could not do his duty to either his client or society.

"A SYSTEM OF SPIES"

The legal problems are raised by the vagueness of the Kutak commission's present language. "Seriously endanger the life or safety of a person" would obviously cover a spill of nuclear waste, but would it also cover a minor spill of chemicals? As for the threat to civil liberties, Monroe Freedman of Hofstra Law School puts the point succinctly. "Disclosure," he says, "would fundamentally mean a system of government spies and informers."

There is a third body of opinion which holds that the legal ground rules should be drafted by the board. At Connecticut General Insurance Corp., the general counsel has been given written instructions from the president to report either to the board chairman or to the chairman of the audit committee on any outstanding disagreement about a legal matter that could "be important to the welfare of the organization." If the matter can't be resolved, the lawyer has the option of going to the full board. "This makes it clear that reporting to the board is a role the lawyer is expected to perform," says Charles H. Stamm, the general counsel. "It doesn't raise questions of disrespect for the chief executive's judgment."

Mead Corp. has similar instructions for its general counsel. But at Mead, which has an activist board dominated by outsiders, the directors also have their *own* attorney, Albert H. Sealy, who knows the company from more than two decades of work for it as an outside counsel. He attends board meetings and finance and audit committee meetings, and looks at corporate legal problems from the point of view of the directors' liability. General counsel Gerald D. Rapp suggested a separate attorney for the board because he feared that an inside lawyer could get "sucked into helping an executive get a job done. How can he then come to the board and advise it on the merits of the question?"

The board did scuttle part of a management plan last year. With Mead a defendant in several price-fixing cases, the board hired William F. Kenney, a retired general counsel at Shell Oil, to analyze several elements of management's compliance policy. After Kenney identified some problems, the directors amended the plan.

There are several things to be said for the board's taking the lead. It doesn't have to write universal and enduring law, merely a clear set of instructions for its own lawyers, who are presumably eager to comply. It can move more rapidly than the A.B.A.; the Kutak commission won't present its final proposals until 1981, and the debate about them within the bar will go on for years after that. In the meantime, these questions are left in a sort of legal limbo through which the SEC apparently intends to prowl; under the circumstances an inhouse code of conduct seems to be a sensible act of self-protection for both the corporate counsel and the board.

Responsiveness to Social Issues

Perhaps the dominant social issue for business today that does not fit the earlier categories such as human investment, ecology, and openness of the system is the role of American business in foreign countries. Indeed, the disclosure for foreign payoffs and bribes in the mid-1970s moved business center stage for social activists, investigative reporters, and governmental bodies.

Multinational corporations tend to be seen by many as above international law and national loyalties. Often they are seen as separate states—making their own laws, imposing their values on host countries, and exploiting people around the globe. Companies are seen moving manufacturing operations from one country to another in apparent disregard for the economic and social well-being of the communities abandoned. Allegedly devoid of loyalties, they are seen as having little interest in becoming active, participative citizens in the communities where they reside.

This pejorative view is overly simplistic, of course. While certain of the readings in this section identify instances of remarkable callousness on the part of multinational corporations, others suggest sincere efforts of companies to behave responsively and responsibly in the international arena. The Abbott Laboratories: Similac case reveals the complexities of dealing with a controversy surrounding the marketing of a product in less-developed countries even though the product has enjoyed enormous success in advanced economic societies. It is a controversy which is over a decade old and shows little sign of resolution. Unlike the Abbott case, United Brands is derived from secondary sources. It focuses on what may be the most controversial aspect

384

of international business operations; namely, the bribing of host government officials. United Brands is a tragic account of foreign payoffs and their consequences for the company and the personal lives of the managers. The cases and commentaries suggest that doing business across cultural and national boundries multiplies the challenges faced by managers.

Case ═══════════════════════════════════════

ABBOTT LABORATORIES: SIMILAC

On January 3, 1980, David O. Cox, president of the Ross Division of Abbott Laboratories, sat listening to the taped proceedings of a public meeting held on October 8, 1979, the day previous to a World Health Organization (WHO) conference convened in Geneva. This so-called informational meeting was jointly sponsored by two activist organizations—the Interfaith Center on Corporate Responsibility (ICCR) and the Infant Formula Action Committee (INFACT)—who were extremely critical of the marketing practices of the infant formula industry. The "informational meeting" had been widely publicized as a forum for the discussion of the alleged wrongdoings of the infant formula industry with interested parties, the press, and industry representatives invited by the organizers. As Mr. Cox listened to the tapes, he reflected on the basic issues addressed at the WHO conference.

THE BASIC CHARGES

By the end of 1979, a substantial number of charges had been leveled against the use of infant formula in developing countries. Many of them were overlapping or directly related to others, so a clear differentiation between charges could not be made. Perhaps the clearest objections were based on economic and environmental grounds.

Economic objections were given on both the macro and micro levels. It was charged that the nonutilization of breast milk led to economic waste at the macro level. For example, the annual loss of

386

breast milk in Kenya was estimated at $11.5 million. For the developing world as a whole, the cost of wasted human milk was estimated at more than three quarters of a billion dollars. On the micro level, unnecessary usage of formula was seen as a waste of scarce family resources. The cost of sufficient formula to feed a three-month-old child for a day in the United Kingdom was 2 percent of the minimum daily wage, but in India the cost was 23 percent, in Nigeria 30 percent, and in Egypt 41 percent. For older infants, the costs were higher.[1] One way for the mother to lower costs was to dilute the formula, thereby reducing the baby's calorie intake.

Environmental objections hinged on two factors: lack of facilities and usage proliferation. In an environment where a large part of the population lacked fuel for heating, clean water to wash bottles or mix formula, cleaning brushes, spare bottles, or refrigeration in which to store excess formula, the chances of product misuse were very high.[2] Even if promotion was not directed toward that segment, however, critics predicted that product usage would diffuse to the poor. It was alleged that the poor might even consider it more attractive because it would be, in a sense, forbidden. Since the poor could not properly use the product, any sales in developing countries should therefore be prohibited. According to Christian activist Leah Margulies, socially enlightened individuals in developed countries should "help countries decide their real priorities."[3]

The greatest number of specific charges were related to what were seen as predatory advertising practices. The very fact that formula manufacturers worked with native hospital personnel was regarded as a powerful force to legitimize formula in the eyes of mothers. Colorful posters used for decoration in the hospitals, even those that boldly stated that breast milk was best, and the booklets on other aspects of mothercraft that were provided free by formula manufacturers were condemned because they carried pictures of formula products. The traditional Western practice of providing a going-home formula for new mothers was seen as a ploy to cause premature reduced lactation in mothers.

The use of "milk nurses" was especially criticized. Milk nurses were usually trained medical personnel employed by formula manufacturers to teach "mothercraft" techniques such as bathing babies and selecting nutritious foods. In some countries, the only medical guidance for new mothers came from mothercraft personnel because

---

[1] Mike Muller, "The Baby Killer," The War on Want, London, March 1974, p. 7.

[2] See ibid. for a vivid statement in this regard.

[3] Leah Margulies, "Baby Formula Abroad: Exporting Infant Malnutrition," Christianity and Crisis, November 10, 1975, p. 267.

of the shortage of doctors. Milk nurses, however, performed their tasks dressed in uniforms and were alleged to trade on their identification with hospitals to promote formula usage. Two examples supported these allegations: (1) milk nurses had been paid on a sales related (commission) basis by some companies, and (2) retail market share seemed to be remarkably correlated with the number of nurses a company employed. For example, the most extensive mothercraft activities in the Far East took place in the Philippines. Wyeth, Mead Johnson, and Nestlé had an estimated total of 160 mothercraft nurses and a combined market share of 92 percent in 1975. Each mothercraft nurse corresponded to between 0.4 and 0.7 share points for the three companies.

Perhaps the major target for criticism was the use of mass media advertising which, critics believed, led poorly educated mothers to think of formula as a type of wonder drug. Nestlé was especially active in using billboards, idiomatic radio, newspapers, popular magazines, and sound trucks to sell their products. Other companies were less aggressive, but their distributors occasionally placed media advertisements. Abbott Laboratories did no consumer advertising and was particularly adamant in insisting that this type of promotion had no place in the industry.

The critics also saw aggressive sales promotion practices as a fundamental issue. Of special concern was the mass media advertising campaigns undertaken by many of the non-U.S. based producers and some of the Third World distributors of the American formula companies. U.S. infant formula producers were not free of this criticism. For instance, during the "informational meeting," Leah Margulies, an activist member of ICCR, noted the following passage from the Ross Laboratories' training manual for its *domestic* sales force as evidence of what she termed "the misguided behavior of the infant formula industry":

> Hospitals represent one of the most important markets for the sale of infant formula . . . there is a 93 percent brand retention . . . Another point worth remembering is that if nurses are sold and serviced properly they become like extra sales people . . . The salesman should remember to make occasional calls on the second and third shift nurses as well since their influence on mothers is also important.[4]

While not all of the above examples were true as a general rule, responsible industry executives agreed that there were at least some elements of truth in all of the charges.

---

[4] *Infant Formula Sales Training Manual, United States,* Ross Division of Abbott Laboratories, Inc., Undated, p. 30.

INDUSTRY REACTIONS

By early 1975, it had become clear that an industry-wide response was required to combat the charges of industry irresponsibility. Representatives of nine manufacturers, including Abbott, therefore met in Zurich in April of that year for discussions which led to the formation of the International Council of Infant Formula Industries (ICIFI). ICIFI became an official body on September 1, 1975, with the implementation of an official code of conduct governing industry members. The largest members in terms of formula sales were Nestlé Alimentana, Unigate Foods, American Home Products, Glaxo, and Dumex. These corporations held over half of the world market for infant formula. Key factors of the international code were that (1) manufacturers agreed as a matter of policy that breast milk from healthy mothers was best for infants; (2) "milk nurses" or other industry personnel would be paid on a noncommission basis; and (3) formula proportions of powder to water would be standardized among manufacturers in order to decrease the opportunity for incorrect preparation.

Having been a prime mover in the formulation of ICIFI, Abbott Laboratories had an important decision to make regarding acceptance of the code. Abbott's own prototype, International Code of Marketing Ethics (see Exhibit 1), was stronger than the ICIFI code. The ICIFI code did not outlaw direct promotion to the customer and, therefore, in the opinion of Abbott management, did not deal with the central issue. In November 1975, Abbott formally implemented their own code and decided not to join ICIFI. By doing so, Abbott believed it would be free to work for a stronger industry code in general.

Abbott's position then became one of activism. Management made the decision not to keep a low profile, and line managers met a number of times with their chief critics. These meetings required managers to accept the unusual role of being the object of direct criticism, and were taxing both emotionally and in terms of the time away from the operational aspects of the business. However, Abbott's personnel continued to meet with their critics in hopes of resolving the controversy.

Abbott's Ross Laboratories personnel thought their approach to be quite positive. By late 1976, they had set up a "Third World Team" consisting of a coordinator, a nutritionist, a market researcher, and a pediatrician. As of the fall of 1979, this team had grown to a department of approximately 15 people. Along the way, five strategies were identified by Ross for responding to the problems at hand: (1) to create a board of advisors composed of pediatricians and nutritionists who could make and defend policy in the area; (2) to stress the posi-

EXHIBIT 1
Code of Marketing Ethics for Developing Countries With
Reference to Infant Feeding

Because good nutrition is essential to proper health care, we believe super-vision of the infant's diet should be the responsibility of medical and allied personnel whose knowledge of nutritional science and understanding of local needs best qualify them to provide this guidance. We attempt to conduct our business as an adjunct to local health personnel, supporting their efforts through the provision of appropriate health care products and services. We believe that this alliance is especially important in developing countries, where delivery of primary health care to major segments of the population is complicated by unfavorable living conditions. Within this context we are keenly aware of the responsibilities of Abbott Laboratories and Ross Laboratories to make a positive contribution to the health and well-being of infants in developing countries.

In marketing our products in these countries, the management, employees and authorized representatives of Abbott are directed to observe the follow-ing guidelines for ethical behavior:

1. Breast milk of healthy, well-nourished mothers is the best feeding to meet nutritional needs of the infant from birth through four to six months of age, and should continue to be fed thereafter, together with appropriate foods, for as long as possible. Mothers in general—and especially those in the lower income and nonmoney sectors of the economy—should be encouraged to feed their infants at the breast as long as quantity and quality of milk remain adequate.

2. We believe our nutritional products have a valid place in the economy of developing countries, yet we want to restrict their use to feeding infants of relatively affluent parents when breast feeding is not chosen, or to infants of working mothers who cannot breast feed because of separa-tion from their infants, and to infants of mothers who cannot breast feed for any other reason. We recognize that true need for substitute feedings exists in segments of the population not able to purchase them. Gov-ernment sponsored programs or public assistance in some form is the best way to aid mothers who can neither breast feed nor afford a suitable replacement.

3. For those infants who will not or cannot be fed at the breast or who need supplemental nutrition, we offer SIMILAC ® infant formulas, which are patterned as closely after the nutritional qualities of human milk as current knowledge and technology permit. In presenting these products to the medical and allied professions, our goal is to promote awareness and acceptance of physiologic nutrition as the most desirable alternative when breast feeding is not available.

4. We cooperate in every way possible with local health authorities to prevent misuse of our products because of ignorance, poverty, or lack of proper hygienic conditions. We do not encourage use of our products

EXHIBIT 1 *(continued)*

where private purchase would impose a financial hardship on the family, or where inadequate facilities for preparation constitute a hazard to infant health.

5. Our product label carries a statement that breast milk is the preferred feeding for young infants, and emphasizes proper proportions in mixing formula.

6. We work with professional and government agencies, and industry to bring about standardized instructions for mixing all powdered nutritional products, i.e., one scoop (provided in tin of product) of each powder product to a standardized quantity of water, with each scoop individually designed to provide the proper caloric density set by the manufacturer for his product. Such standardization can assist educational efforts of public health personnel to create parental awareness of proper mixing of formula.

7. We believe that promotion of infant feeding products directly to mothers unjustly impels them to make decisions concerning the care and nutrition of their babies for which they lack adequate medical and nutritional knowledge. Therefore, we do not advertise our products through general circulation magazines, directories, newspapers, radio, television, billboards, and other public mass media. In addition, we do not offer special inducements which encourage mothers to use our products independently of professional advice. We terminate a distributorship when it violates these constraints. Further, we believe that no communication to the general public should encroach in any way on the responsibility of health care professionals to provide guidance as their judgment and experience dictate.

8. We direct our resources toward increasing the effectiveness of qualified local health personnel through communications on current health care development and by providing them with service literature for distribution to mothers to (a) promote good nutrition; (b) encourage breast feeding; (c) improve infant and child care; (d) improve sanitation; (e) stress proper preparation of infant formula when recommended by health authorities.

9. We represent accurately the cost of proper infant feeding and use of our products so that professional personnel can better advise mothers according to their economic status.

10. Our advertising is directed to medical and other allied professionals (physicians, midwives, nurses, nutritionists, etc.). It seeks to provide better understanding of the proper role for our products, of their proper preparation, and of our willingness to assist medical personnel in their practice. We attempt to influence use of our products through the presentation of scientific information and the offering of aids to medical practice.

11. Whenever possible, we choose as representatives, experienced, allied medical personnel who understand local needs. They are thoroughly

EXHIBIT 1 *(concluded)*

taught the preference and value of breast feeding, the knowledge and proper application of our products, and the influence of social pressures that can lead to unwise purchases and practices by those who cannot afford to buy infant formula. They are schooled to perform their duties in a professional manner and with integrity. Deception and other unethical practices are expressly forbidden.

12. The activities of our representatives are coordinated with those of medical professionals responsible for infant and mother care. We want them, with the supervision of clinic personnel, to furnish genuine mothercraft outreach services where practical, in support of instructions and counsel received in clinic. Our mothercraft nurses will make home visits only when specifically requested by appropriate authorities.

13. These mothercraft nurses are reimbursed through adequate salary, with monetary incentive given only for true service rendered to the customer and not directly derived from measurement of sales impact. Their functions are to develop product understanding, to render services that facilitate application of our products, and to make available other health care aids, without attempt to incur obligation for services.

14. We want medical and governmental health professionals to advise industry on training its representatives and on establishing the range of mothercraft activities.

15. We recognize the variation that exists between countries as to state of development, economic resources and availability of trained health personnel, and work to assure that our activities in all countries conform to the spirit of this code.

tive accomplishments of Ross Laboratories in peripheral activities such as medical education and solving past nutritional problems; (3) to strengthen further the Abbott Code of Marketing Ethics; (4) to stress the development of a prenatal food for mothers; and (5) to attempt an extensive program of well controlled cross-cultural research.

Although none of these strategies had been fully implemented, Ross nevertheless felt its position was eminently defensible and very proactive. Yet a senior member of the ICCR staff suggested in Geneva that Ross's position had become less responsive during the previous year. In addition, Ross had always believed the U.S market in which they held the largest market share was well served. David Cox was therefore concerned, if not surprised, when he heard Leah Margulies state in Geneva that the ICCR research effort was expanding to the domestic market in the belief that infant formula constituted a health hazard in the less affluent areas of the United States.

BACKGROUND ON ROSS AND ABBOTT

Ross laboratories considered itself to be a collection of evangelists for good health care. The organization was founded in 1903 as the Moores and Ross Milk Company in Columbus, Ohio. By 1924, the company had expanded into a variety of dairy products, but that same year one of the founders, Stanley Ross, met Alfred Bosworth, a famous milk chemist. Bosworth had developed a usable infant formula while working at the Boston Floating Hospital, a pioneering effort at inner city pediatric care. Ross began to produce a formula for Bosworth called "Similac."

In 1928, the profitable ice cream and milk processing operations were sold to the Borden Company. M&R Dietetic Laboratories, the successor company, grew through the depression, won service awards during World War II, and thrived during the baby boom of the 1950s. Iron was added to Similac in 1959, and new plants were opened in the early 1960s, including one in the Netherlands to serve the Common Market. Similac had become the preeminent infant formula in the United States by the mid 1960s.

In 1964, Ross merged with Abbott Laboratories. Like Ross, Abbott had always been concerned with service to the medical profession. Abbott had been founded in 1888 by Wallace Calvin Abbott, a Chicago physician. Frustrated by the erratic availability of quality medication—particularly alkaloidal granules—he proceeded to make and sell his own. By the turn of the century, the Abbott Alkaloid Company consisted of a modern multistory laboratory and manufacturing facility. Through the first half century of the company's existence, it was headed by physicians, and this gave the company a unique orientation. There was extreme emphasis on quality control, advertising was remarkably restrained for the period, and a free medical information service was provided to physicians apart from the drug selling function.

During the first half of the 20th century, Abbott research led to improved products, especially in the field of anesthestics (Butyn, Nembutal, and Pentothol Sodium were created by Abbott scientists), vitamins, and other synthetic chemicals. Later research concentrated on nutritional supplements, of which Sucaryl was probably the best known. In addition, the benefits of Ross' research was extended through the publication of a variety of medical service pieces, a number of which are noted in Exhibit 2.

By 1979, total sales for Abbott Laboratories were approximately $1.7 billion, about 3.7 times the amount recorded in 1971. Net earnings in 1979 were approximately $179.0 million, 7.6 times the total recorded in 1971. About 34 percent of sales were in foreign markets.

EXHIBIT 2
A Partial Listing of Professional Services Sponsored by Ross Laboratories*

1. *Ross Conference on Pediatric Research.*   These conferences, attended by 30 to 40 medical educators, were paid for by Ross and run by prestigious medical schools. The proceedings of a conference typically contained about 15 papers concerned with an important pediatric problem, totalled 90 to 100 pages, and were distributed free to all pediatricians in the United States. At the end of 1976 there had been 68 Ross Conferences.

2. *Ross Conference on Obstetric Research and Ross Roundtable on Critical Approaches to Common Pediatric Problems.*   These conferences, similar in design to those described above, were held less frequently, but each generally contained more papers.

3. *Perinatology, Neonatology, Pediatric Nutrition "Currents"* was an abstracting service published monthly in conjunction with the *Excerpta Medica* and distributed to pediatricians.

4. *Ross Timesaver* was a bimonthly newsletter on current topics. There were actually seven different series under the "Timesaver" name, each published every two months and distributed free to subscribing pediatricians.

5. *Distinguished papers* on children and nutrition was a series of 11 comprehensive papers on classic infant problems, available free upon request.

6. *The Ross Audio Visual Library* contained about two dozen films designed for both professional and lay education and available rent free to physicians.

7. *Ross Laboratories Clinical Education Aids* were a series of pamphlet-slide show packages designed for use in medical schools.

8. *Patient information.*   In addition to the above professional materials, Ross published dozens of pamphlets on the parent-child relationship for the physician to hand out to his patients. These pamphlets were in both Spanish and English, were typically 12 to 20 pages in length, and contained no more than three pages of advertising.

* Unless otherwise noted, topics covered are of general pediatric interest and *not* limited to the topic of infant feeding.

A more detailed breakdown of the financial data is presented in Exhibit 3.

As a division of Abbott Laboratories, Ross continued to concentrate on the production of Similac and other more specialized infant formulas. Ross accounted for about 20 percent of Abbott's total sales and nearly all the parent firm's pediatric sales volume. Most of these sales were in the well-penetrated U.S. market where Similac was the dominant brand. Control of international sales was maintained by Abbott International, the corporate international marketing division. About one fourth of Abbott's pediatric sales were made overseas, but

EXHIBIT 3
Abbott Laboratories Selected Financial Data, 1978 ($ millions)

Year	Sales	Aftertax Earnings	International Sales	Pediatric Sales	International Pediatric Sales
1978	$1445.0	$148.6	$499.1	$ n.r.	n.r.
1977	1245.0	117.8	408.8	n.r.	n.r.
1976	1084.9	92.5	375.9	222.9	$56.4
1975	940.7	70.7	335.4	192.4	47.8*
1974	765.4	55.0	280.1	165.2	37.8
1973	620.4	46.0	219.2	141.0	31.3
1972	521.8	39.4	173.7	124.4	23.7
1971	458.1	23.4	145.9	114.5	18.9
1970	457.5	40.0	128.8	101.3	14.6
1969	403.9	35.2	n.r.	n.r.	n.r.
1968	356.1	32.1	n.r.	n.r.	n.r.
1967	311.1	28.6	n.r.	n.r.	n.r.
1966	275.2	27.5	n.r.	n.r.	n.r.

* The casewriter estimated that less than 25 percent of Abbott's international pediatric sales were of Similac products in developing countries.

n.r. = not reported

this total included both nutritional and pharmaceutical products. Ross Laboratories' records indicated that an estimated 20 percent of their infant formula sales were the result of international transactions. A roster of the major multinational corporations marketing infant formula throughout the world is included as Exhibit 4.

Although the dollar value of the international component of Ross's infant formula sales increased drastically during the 1970s, as a percentage of total sales the volume remained relatively stable. In each year, international infant formula sales represented approximately 20 percent of the total infant formula sales, and even if the international sales had been totally eliminated for each year, Ross's infant formula sales volume would still have increased by approximately 20 percent over each previous year.

However, eliminating the international component of their infant formula sales was not considered a viable alternative by Ross's management. They believed very strongly in the need for infant formula in the Third World. Management believed Ross knew more about infant nutrition than any other company, and that the failure to pass on that knowledge would be ethically unconscionable.

As he reviewed the history of infant feeding practices, David Cox had once summed up Ross's position on the question of infant formula sales to the Third World by stating: "What posture do we take when the child is in the very helpless state of having no breast milk available, and no formula substitute is available?"

EXHIBIT 4
Major Multinational Corporations Marketing Prepared Infant Formula, 1979

Corporation	Subsidiary	Nationality	Major Brand Name	Membership in ICIF?	Estimated Share of World Market*
Nestlé					
Alimentana	—	Swiss	Lactogen (and 26 others)	Yes	35–40
Unigate Foods	Cow and Gate	U.K.	Cow and Gate	Yes	10–15
Glaxo	Ostermilk	U.K.	Ostermilk	Yes	5–10
American					
Home Products	Wyeth	U.S.A.	SMA	Yes	10–15
Mead Johnson	Bristol Myers	U.S.A.	Enfamil	No	10–15
Abbott					
Laboratories	Ross Laboratories	U.S.A.	Similac	No	4–8
Dumex	—	Dutch	Dumex	Yes	5–10

* "World market share" treats total market share outside the United States as 100 percent. These estimates were compiled from secondary sources by the casewriter and are not necessarily reflective of estimates by various corporations.

BACKGROUND ON INFANT NUTRITION

Since the beginning of human existence, babies have been fed what has been called "the original convenience food"—mother's milk. Portable, sanitary, preserved at correct temperatures, nutritious, and possessing yet-unduplicated immunizing agents, human breast milk from healthy mothers has always been universally considered the ideal food for normal infants. Breast feeding has also had some apparent contraceptive aspects and has been economical in terms of total mother-child nutrition as well.

In the event that mothers were unable to feed their own infants, a wet nurse—often a relative—was the traditional answer. Cow's milk and goat's milk were excellent supplements for older children, but poor substitutes as an infant food because of unfavorable nutritional composition and curd tension (a term relating to the strength of protein bonds in the chemistry of milk). The development by Gail Borden of evaporated milk in the late 19th century helped reduce curd tension, but the problems of nutrition and potential milk allergy remained. In the early 1920s, infant formulae were developed in the United States by several companies, including Ross, both from cow's milk and from a variety of vegetable bases. With increasing urbanization and the assumption of more than motherhood roles by many women, the popularity of formula feeding grew. By the late 1950s, about 75 percent of all American babies were fed infant formula at some time during their first year.

As prosperity returned to Europe following World War II, and newly independent Third World nations began their drive toward development, many of the same conditions that had been present in the United States arose internationally. With increasing urbanization, mobility, ability of women to supplement family income, and familiarity with powdered milk through foreign aid programs, infant formula grew in popularity. Those firms that had been selling infant formula internationally expanded their markets.

In the United States, infant formula products had been positioned as a medical specialty requiring the intervention of health care personnel. In developing countries, however, infant formula had been positioned as a food. Promotion, therefore, had been aimed directly at mothers, and it was not unusual to hear a radio jingle or to see a billboard promoting infant formula in developing countries.

Some formula manufacturers worked closely with what local medical personnel there were. Promotion practices included donations or sales at cost to maternity hospitals, sampling of new mothers through "gift packs," and the provision of extensive literature to hospitals regarding proper infant care. The use of milk nurses—women employed by formula manufacturers to educate mothers in all aspects of mothercraft—was generally welcomed in developing countries where medical personnel were in extremely short supply. Many of the medical personnel had been educated in countries where the use of infant formula was widespread.

There was agreement among virtually all informed observers that the extent of breast feeding had declined worldwide concurrent with the introduction of infant formula. It was difficult to generalize from specific studies, however, because of lack of consistent category definitions. A mother who fed formula to her infant ten percent of the time, for example, would be classified as "breast feeding," "formula feeding," or "both," depending on which of three commonly used criteria were employed for a specific study. Furthermore, different studies used varying ages to set the limits of infancy. As might be expected, the percentage of babies fed formula in the first year of life was greater than the percentage fed formula in the first three months.

It was also difficult to ascertain the role that sales promotion played in winning formula converts. Pediatrician Bo Vahlquist, a strong proponent of breast feeding, observed that "a steady decline in breast feeding is taking place also in communist countries where promotion from private industry does not occur."[5]

There was some debate over the length of time that healthy mothers should nurse their children, and when weaning foods should be introduced. Most authorities agreed that four to six months after birth was a reasonable time to begin weaning. A few medical personnel endorsed some native practices of breast feeding for periods of up to several years after birth. Infant formula could be started at any time after birth, but the use of formula tended to be "addictive" in that, when the mother's milk was not used, the supply diminished and more formula was needed to make up for the lack of breast milk.

THE RELATIONSHIP BETWEEN INFANT FORMULA AND INFANT MORTALITY/MORBIDITY

Perhaps ironically, questions about the propriety of using infant formula products in developing countries had arisen at a time when trends in infant mortality have been declining at an impressive rate. (Exhibit 5) This trend reinforced David Cox's belief that the producers of infant formula products had a responsibility to provide their products to meet the "special needs" of many infants. These "special

---

[5] Bo Vahlquist, "Environmental Children's Health," *Clinical Pediatrics*, vol. 15, no. 2 (February 1976), p. 180.

EXHIBIT 5

Trends in Infant Mortality: Selected Developed and Developing Countries

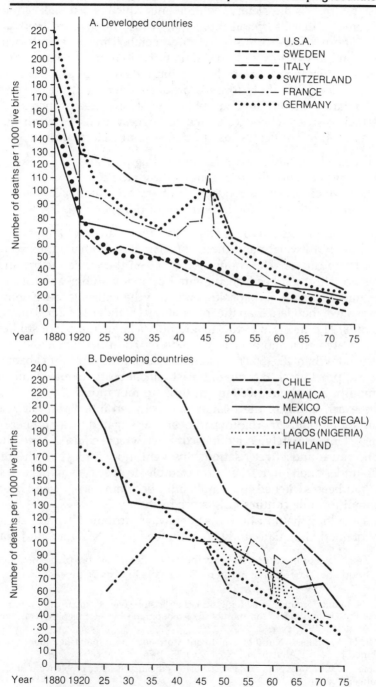

Note: "Infant" is defined as being in the first year of life.

Source: Dr. H. R. Müller, "Nutrition and Infant Mortality," unpublished monograph distributed by Nestlé Alimentana, November 28, 1975, p. 6; data from *Demographic Yearbook*, United Nations.

needs" referred to the dietary requirements which breast milk cannot satisfy due to malabsorption problems, lactose intolerance, milk allergy, inborn errors of carbohydrate metabolism or amino acid metabolism, low birth weight or immaturity, and intestinal resection during early infancy.[6] The feeling of the industry, as expressed by Mr. Cox, was that without formula products the magnitude of Third World infant mortality and morbidity would be greatly increased. Nevertheless, researchers continued to suggest a link between formula use and infant health based upon several factors, including:

1. Low levels of sanitary conditions leading to disease:
2. Shortages of and distance from medical facilities;
3. Shortage of nutritious foods for mothers and infants; and
4. Ignorance regarding the importance of nutritious foods.

These four factors led to several of the direct causes of infant mortality. Low birth weight and the insufficiency of mother's milk were two of these causes. The connection between these two factors and infant mortality had been documented by many studies, and it has been suggested that perhaps 40 percent of the babies in developing countries weighed less than the international standard of 2,500 grams (6 pounds, 11 ounces) at birth.[7] In addition, a large number of studies had indicated that mothers in developing countries often did not secrete more than 400–500 milliliters of milk per day.[8] Normal babies require approximately 500 ml. of breast milk at birth, about 700 ml. at one month, and about 1,000 ml. at three to four months.

The exact nature of the relationship between infant formula use and infant mortality/morbidity had been investigated by a number of studies. Unfortunately, scientific controls which could isolate the specific cause and effect relationships were not employed. The research undertaken often failed, for example, to specify whether a sick baby had been switched to formula after becoming sick or had been fed infant formula continuously since birth.

The resulting malnutrition was not always attributed by mothers to a lack of good food. One study of infant feeding in Nigeria found that

> The cause of malnutrition is attributed to "an inevitable phase in childhood" by 23 percent of mothers, "an act of God" by 56 percent, and "an

---

[6] "The Infant Formula Marketing Practices of Bristol-Myers Company in Countries Outside the United States," an unpublished monograph by the Bristol-Myers Company, August 7, 1975, p. 4.

[7] Dr. H. R. Müller, "Nutrition and Infant Mortality," an unpublished monograph distributed by Nestlé Alimantana, November 28, 1976, p. 6.

[8] Ibid., p. 10. A total of 15 studies establishing the insufficiency problem are cited in Dr. Müller's paper.

evil spirit evoked by wicked people" by 7 percent. Only 20 percent believed that it was due to a lack of good food.[9]

The interactions among maternal ignorance, maternal malnutrition, unsanitary conditions, disease, and medical shortages clearly made the question of infant nutrition in developing countries very complex. Furthermore, the lack of reliable data on virtually all of these variables led to a great deal of speculation and uncertainty. The reason for the general decline in mortality was in itself a topic of speculation.

In spite of the multiple potential interpretations of studies, it was clear that the wider availability of infant formula in developing nations might profoundly modify feeding practices. This prospect attracted the attention of the Protein Advisory Group (P.A.G.) of the United Nations in the early 1970s. At the suggestion of that organization, the World Health Organization (WHO) and UNICEF sponsored a conference on the subject in Bogotá, Colombia in November 1970. The purpose of the conference was to focus discussion on the issue of consumer misuse of foods for infants in developing countries. The conference began with some hostility toward the industry for what was seen as aggressive marketing practices toward those consumers who were almost prevented by lack of education and income from properly using the product. By the end of the conference, some accommodation had been reached between representatives of industry, nutritionists, and government officials.

THE DEVELOPMENT OF INFANT FORMULA FEEDING AS A PUBLIC ISSUE

Although a number of questions had been raised earlier about the product and the marketing practices of the producers, the question of infant formula sales in underdeveloped countries seemed to emerge as a serious public controversy with the Protein Advisory Group conference. This conference was the first forum for the critics and the manufacturers to interact. The publicity generated by the sessions undoubtedly helped propel the issue forward as a matter of public concern.

After the initial conference, the International Pediatrics Association met in Vienna in 1971 to discuss the same issue. Subsequent PAG conferences were then held in Paris in June 1972, in Geneva in De-

---

[9] Olikoye Ransome-Kuti, "Some Cultural and Social Aspects of Infant Feeding in Nigeria," *Modern Problems in Pediatrics*, vol. 15 (1975), p. 123. The percentages did not sum to 100 because of multiple attributions.

cember 1972, and in New York in June of 1973. The tangible outcome of this series of meetings was PAG Statement No. 23, "Promotion of Special Foods (Infant Formula and Processed Protein Foods) for Vulnerable Groups," dated November 1973. The statement contained seven specific recommendations for governments, five for pediatricians, and six for industry (see Exhibit 6).

While the above conference had raised the public's consciousness concerning the sale of infant formula in the Third World, a publication entitled "The Baby Killer" raised the interest in the issue to an emotional pitch. This pamphlet was published in March 1974 by War on Want, a London-based political action group devoted to making poverty a major social issue. "The Baby Killer" accumulated information from personal and published sources to form a powerful indictment of the international infant formula industry. The publication began with the following summary (abridged):

> Third World babies are dying because their mothers bottle feed them with western style infant milk. Many that do not die are drawn into a vicious cycle of malnutrition and disease that will leave them physically and intellectually stunted for life.
>
> The frightening fact is that this suffering is avoidable. The remedy is available to all but a small minority of mothers who cannot breast feed. Because mother's milk is accepted by all to be the best food for any baby under six months old.
>
> Although even the baby food industry agrees that it is correct, more and more Third World mothers are turning to artificial foods during the first few months of their babies' lives. In the squalor and poverty of the new cities of Africa, Asia, and Latin America, the decision is often fatal.
>
> The baby food industry stands accused of promoting their products in communities which cannot use them properly; of using advertising, sales girls dressed up in nurses' uniforms, give away samples and free gimmicks that persuade mothers to give up breast feeding . . .
>
> Where there is no choice but squalor, the choice of an artificial substi-

---

EXHIBIT 6
PAG Statement No. 23 (abridged)

PROMOTION OF SPECIAL FOODS
(INFANT FORMULA AND PROCESSED PROTEIN FOODS)
FOR VULNERABLE GROUPS
18 July 1972, Revised 28 November 1973

Summary

The statement emphasizes the critical importance of breast feeding under the sociocultural and economic conditions that prevail in many developing countries. Infants of more affluent socioeconomic groups in industrialized

EXHIBIT 6 *(continued)*

and developing countries, in the absence of breast feeding, suffer no nutritional disadvantage when fed properly-constituted and hygienically-prepared processed commercial formulas. These infants usually receive sufficient formula and the diet is also supplemented with baby foods. However, the early abandonment of breast feeding by mothers among lower socioeconomic groups can be disastrous to infants, particularly when this occurs without adequate financial resources to purchase sufficient formula and without knowledge of and facilities to follow hygienic practices necessary to feed infants adequately and safely with breast milk replacements. Under such circumstances, and where animal milk and other supplementary protein resources are expensive or in short supply, an important function of the food industry, in close cooperation with governments and physicians, should be the development and marketing of relatively low-cost, nutritionally-equivalent protein foods that can be used to supplement breast feeding.

To assist the various interests concerned with these problems in dealing with them objectively and effectively, the PAG proposes three sets of coherent recommendations: one for governments and United Nations agencies, a second for nutritionists and physicians caring for children, and a third for the food and infant formula industries.

Recommendations to Industry

*1. Food industry leaders should be involved constructively in the solution of the special nutritional problems of vulnerable groups, particularly in developing countries.

*2. The importance of breast feeding should be stressed in employee training and personnel should be instructed to avoid sales and promotional methods that could discourage appropriate breast feeding in any way.

*3. Industry should train its personnel adequately in matters concerning local public health norms, needs and regulations in the implementation of national food and nutrition policies.

4. Industry should recognize and emphasize that the immediate postpartum period and the hospital nursery are not appropriate for any promotion of infant foods directed at other than professional personnel.

*5. To minimize misuse, industry should give special attention to the importance of unambiguous and standard directions for reconstituting formulas from dry or liquid preparations for feeding young infants. The needs of illiterate as well as literate persons should be considered in designing labels. Labels and product literature should foster hygienically-oriented practices such as the use of boiled water and the proper cleaning of utensils.

6. Industry should give active consideration to the development and production of supplementary foods and infant formulas that do not require reconstitution or can be rendered palatable by boiling only.

---

* Recommendations implemented by industry.

tute for breast milk is in reality a choice between health and disease . . .

The results can be seen in clinics and hospitals, the slums and graveyards of the Third World. Children whose bodies have wasted away until all that is left is a big head on top of the shrivelled body of an old man. Children with the obscene bloated belly of kwashiorkor.

Why are mothers abandoning breast feeding in countries where it is part of the culture? Are we helping to promote the trend? What is the responsibility of the baby food industry? What are we doing to prevent avoidable malnutrition?

These questions are being raised by doctors and nutritionists throughout the Third World. War on Want believes that by opening the subject to public debate a solution may be found faster than through silence.[10]

In the months following its publication, dozens of articles paraphrasing portions of "The Baby Killer" appeared in the popular press under such titles as "The Milk of Human Unkindness," "Shrivelled Children, Swollen Profits," and "Formula for Malnutrition." One of the most extreme examples was a German interpretation published in Switzerland by the Third World Action Group entitled "Nestlé's Kills Babies." Because the document allegedly deleted many of the qualifying statements of the original work and singled out Nestlé as the major villian in the controversy, Nestlé promptly sued the organization and its 13 members for libel.

Not all of the publications to appear during this period were solely popular press pieces. Exhibit 6 lists some of the scientific statements made regarding the question of infant formula sales in the Third World. Perhaps the most quoted medical critic of bottle feeding in the less developed parts of the world was Derrick Jelliffe, professor of pediatrics and public health at UCLA. With over 30 years of service in Third World countries and several hundred published articles to his credit, Dr. Jelliffe's views on "commerciogenic malnutrition" became well known. He attributed well-financed, steamroller marketing techniques to the infant formula industry in their attempts to sell what he believed to be totally unaffordable and inappropriate foods for impoverished communities. Dr. Jelliffe believed the industry's claim that they were attempting to take a leadership role in the improvement of child nutrition especially offensive. Not all medical professionals completely agreed with Professor Jelliffe, but he was not alone in his beliefs.

Two very significant works appeared during 1975 which further fueled both the scientific and the emotional criticisms of infant for-

---

[10] Mike Muller, "The Baby Killer," p. 1.

mula. The first was the publication of the "Cornell Report," a monograph written by Ted Greiner, a graduate research associate.[11] Assistance was provided by the aforementioned Dr. Jelliffe; author Robert Choate, whose exposés of the breakfast-cereal industry had been widely read; and nutritionist Michael Latham, whose view that "placing an infant on a bottle might be tantamount to signing the death certificate of the child"[12] was well documented. The monograph reviewed infant food advertising practices back to the 1920s and summarized many of the charges which had been made up till that time.

The second piece was a German film documentary by Peter Kreig entitled *Bottle Babies* which described various marketing practices that allegedly result in the death of many infants. The most powerful scene was of an infant graveyard outside Lusaka, Zambia, where baby bottles and cans of infant formula had been placed by a mother on her child's grave in the belief "that the magic qualities of the formula would carry to the grave and beyond."[13]

During 1976 the infant formula issue received additional publicity from a stockholder suit filed against the Bristol-Myers company. The suit alleged certain untruths were contained in the firm's proxy statements. The complaint regarded Bristol-Myers's claim that they had discontinued advertising in those markets where chronic poverty existed. The legal action was settled out of court where certain modifications of the proxy statements were agreed upon.

The years 1975 and 1976 were also the gestation period of the infant formula division of the ICCR. Leah Margulies stated during the 1979 information day proceeding before the WHO Geneva Conference that the project actually dated from a 1975 Consumer's Union publication, "Hungry for Profits."

The year 1977 saw the birth of a second major critical organization, INFACT. According to Douglas Johnson, head of the INFACT organization, the group began with four local committees in January 1977. What was originally developed as a Minnesota-only organization for the boycott of Nestlé products "quickly became out-of-hand." By January of 1978, Douglas Johnson indicated that 135 local boycott groups existed, while by one year later 400 such groups had been formed.

In 1978, additional publicity was generated by a public hearing

<hr/>

[11] Ted Greiner, "The Promotion of Bottle Feeding by Multinational Corporations: How Advertising and the Health Professions Have Contributed," Cornell University Monograph, 1975.

[12] "Third-World Death Warrant," *The Washington Star*, February 20, 1976.

[13] Quoted in "Bottle Babies," *CNI Weekly Report*, February 20, 1976.

held by the U.S. Senate Health and Science Research Subcommittee. Chaired by Sen. Edward Kennedy, the committee called a number of industry, professional, and critical experts to testify. At one point during the hearings, the president of Nestlé's Brazilian subsidiary was roundly criticized for suggesting that the intent of the critics was the overthrow of the capitalistic system. This statement and the response to it seemed to characterize the emotional nature of the proceedings.

The major infant formula event in 1979 was the Geneva Conference called by WHO and UNICEF. The major purpose of this conference was to bring together all interested parties to discuss once again the appropriateness of the present marketing practices of the infant formula industry in the Third World. The major outcome of the meeting was an agreement that all promotion should be halted in the Third World.

During 1979, "The Baby Killer Scandal" by War on Want was published as well.[14] This sequel to "The Baby Killer" updated the charges made by the earlier work adding additional fuel to the emotional nature of the infant formula question.

The infant formula question also was addressed within the U.S. government by the 96th Congress. During May of 1979, Congressmen Dellums and Miller, both of California, introduced the Infant Nutrition bill of 1979 in the House of Representatives. As reported in the May 16, 1979 issue of the *Congressional Record*, the bill suggested that the increased promotion and availability of infant formula had resulted in a decrease in breast feeding causing escalating infant morbidity and mortality.

In an effort to rectify the problem perceived by the congressmen, the Infant Nutrition bill of 1979 sought to (1) ban all proprietary promotion; (2) require graphic instructions for product use; and (3) require a license to export, sell, or otherwise distribute infant formula in any developing country. To meet the requirements of the proposed legislation, the Federal Trade Commission would also be charged with processing and approving all license applications. In order to have a license approved, the bill would require all companies selling infant formula to submit sufficient data produced through tests or studies to establish that the use of infant formula in each Less Developed Country would not contribute to infant morbidity or mortality among any specific set of consumers. The data presented would have to include, but not be limited to the following:

---

[14] Andy Chetley, *The Baby Killer Scandal*, War on Want, London, 1979.

1. Adequacy and availability of sterilization and refrigeration techniques.
2. Water quality.
3. Epidemiological studies of gastrointestinal, respiratory, nutritional, and dental diseases in infants.
4. Life expectancy and infant mortality rate and causes.
5. Cost of infant formula vis-à-vis family incomes.
6. Literacy levels among target groups of consumers.

Case ===

UNITED BRANDS

Harvey Johnson, vice president in charge of banana operations for United Brands, looked back over the most incredible week of his business career. It was August 1974, and the company had been in the fourth month of the so-called Banana War with several of the Central American republics where United Brands grew its popular "Chiquita Brand" bananas.

The "war" had started when Honduras, the country that supplied about 35 percent of the company's bananas, had instituted a tax of 50 cents on each 40-pound box of bananas. By the beginning of the current month, Panama and Costa Rica had also levied taxes so that the company was currently paying an average of 37 cents a box on all bananas exported from Central America. Clearly, these countries had learned some lessons from the oil-producing countries, and their policies were reflected in higher costs to the company and, ultimately, higher prices to American consumers.

Then, in the early part of the week, Mr. Johnson had been approached in Miami by the Honduran minister of the economy, Abraham Bennaton, who indicated that the tax could be rolled back if the company were willing to make a substantial payment to Honduran officials.[1] Mr. Johnson was stunned. Honduras instigated the tax; a Honduran recision would probably undermind the entire cartel. In cold economic terms, the figure mentioned—$5 million over a period of time—was a bargain. It would save the company about $7.5 million in the first year, and would probably discourage taxes in future years

---

[1] This portrayal is not intended to be a precise reflection of either the thinking or behavior of the parties involved.

408

as well as destroy the current cartel. To Mr. Johnson, the idea of a bribe to influence government policy was unacceptable, but it was clear that Mr. Bennaton's offer would have to be reported to higher management.

Because of the magnitude of the decision involved, Mr. Johnson took the matter up directly with Eli Black, the chief executive officer of United Brands, the following day. Mr. Black rejected the demand, but asked Johnson to report the offer to John Taylor. Mr. Taylor, a United Brands senior vice president, was Mr. Johnson's immediate superior.

Mr. Johnson had reason to feel that he had handled the situation quite well. He had discharged his responsibility to report the offer and the matter was closed. He then thought about how different the outcome was from the probable workings of the old United Fruit Company, the corporation from which United Brands had sprung.

THE UNITED FRUIT COMPANY

The United Fruit Company was incorporated in 1899 and shortly thereafter bought out a number of other fruit companies whose holdings were in Central America. The Central American republics at the time were poor, weak, and governed by a few powerful families whose interest in the general welfare was minimal.

United Fruit entered the Central American countries with offers of capital benefits such as seaports, railroads, utilities, and schools in exchange for the sale or use of government land on which to grow bananas. The governments also received a one-cent-per-bunch export tax. At the time, bananas were considered a luxury fruit in the United States and Europe, because the short six-week life of the fruit after picking meant that shipment delays or inefficiencies would lead to rotten cargo. The company soon established that it was tough enough to fight back with either *la mordita* ("the bribe") or physical force when its marketing timetables were threatened.[2] At the beginning of World War I, the United Fruit Company was the most powerful single force in Central America, and gave the countries the nickname of "banana republics."

After World War I, the nations became very aware of the value of the concessions they had given United Fruit, and some terms were renegotiated. Nevertheless, the governments were deeply in debt and still borrowed money from United Fruit. It was claimed that government appointments were cleared through the company and that unfriendly heads of state could be removed with a phone call

[2] H. J. Maidenberg, "New Rules, Harsh Life in Bananas," *The New York Times*, May 11, 1975, pp. 3-1, 3-9.

from United Fruit.[3] The depression period brought diseases that destroyed many plantations, but United Fruit continued its investments and social services in Central America, and brought in new, spoil-resistant and bruise-resistant varieties of bananas that were easier to harvest.

By the end of World War II, most Latin American workers had become skilled and literate. Many were operators of complex machinery. Some filled managerial positions. The standard of living was relatively high and the "banana republics" bought goods and services on the world market with American currency. Still, there was pressure for local ownership of land and facilities, and for freedom from perceived foreign domination.

In response to this pressure, United Fruit developed an Associate Producer Program in the early 1960s. Company land was turned over to local growers while the company supervised cultivation and purchased bananas from the growers. By the late 1960s, almost half of the bananas were grown under this program, but problems had arisen. Local producers had allowed working, health, and social conditions to deteriorate, unions found organization more difficult with the larger number of owners, and company quality standards were harder to enforce.

By this time, United Fruit had branched out into other types of operations. It acquired some petroleum and natural gas facilities in the 1950s, a Belgian fresh produce distributor in 1962, A&W Drive-Ins of Canada, Ltd. in 1966, and Baskin-Robbins, Inc. in 1967. Still, about 64 percent of corporate sales were from banana operations.

In spite of problems with the Associate Producer Program the company's overall financial position was quite strong, with some $100 million in liquid assets and no debts. While management deliberated over how to solve operational problems on September 24, 1968, they learned that controlling interest in the company had been purchased by Eli M. Black.[4]

ELI BLACK

Eli Black was a 48-year-old former rabbi who had grown up in a poor family on Manhattan's Lower East Side. His family included ten

---

[3] Ibid., p. 3–1.

[4] "Majority" interest in a corporation is 51 percent. "Controlling" interest in a widely held firm is generally regarded as between 5 and 10 percent, since it is nearly impossible to join shareholders together who hold more than these percentages. Eli Black's AMK Corporation had purchased about 9 percent on September 24.

generations of rabbis and scholars, and he was graduated from Yeshiva University in 1940, then served a Long Island congregation for four years.

He left his congregation because he felt his ministry was not fulfilling and that his sermons had little effect on people's lives.[5] He initially joined Lehman Brothers investment house and then American Securities Corporation, where part of his responsibilities involved handling the financing for American Seal-Kap Corporation, a moderate-sized producer of milk bottle caps.

In 1954, Mr. Black became chairman and chief executive officer of American Seal-Kap Corporation. He dropped unprofitable lines, bought out other concerns, employed the corporation's funds to the fullest extent, and in 1965 renamed it AMK Corporation.

In late 1966, AMK acquired one third of John Morrell & Company, a large meat-packer in Chicago which was 20 times AMK's size. This move confirmed Mr. Black's unique ability of "uncovering value on a large scale, getting control of it, and putting it to work uncovering more assets."[6] AMK acquired the rest of John Morrell & Company on the final day of 1967.

The bespectacled Mr. Black was characterized by associates as a reserved, serious, formal man who smiled frequently but seldom laughed. He maintained tight personal control of his businesses and "wasn't comfortable with people who disagreed with his views."[7] He participated in no sports and rarely took nonbusiness vacations.

Mr. Black's hobby *was* his business but he tried to blend it with his strong concern for social causes. His son Leon once said that his father believed that "a man's reach must extend beyond his grasp,"[8] and that he took other people's problems on as if they were his own. He was intimately involved in the economic condition of the state of Israel (as a director for PEC Israel Economics Company) and in the economic condition of the United States. Later he would send a detailed plan for steering the United States through the energy shortage to his friend, Sen. Abraham Ribicoff of Connecticut. He was confident that he could solve social problems because "he was used to being able, by the force of his intellect, to get through problems to solve them."[9]

---

[5] *The Wall Street Journal,* February 14, 1975, p. 15.

[6] "United Fruit's Shotgun Marriage," *Fortune,* vol. 79, no. 4 (April 1969), p. 122.

[7] Mary Bralove, *The Wall Street Journal,* May 7, 1975, p. 26.

[8] *The Wall Street Journal,* February 14, 1975, p. 1.

[9] Ibid., p. 1.

UNITED BRANDS UNDER ELI BLACK

On February 13, 1969, Eli Black became a director of United Fruit and later that year his AMK Corporation acquired a majority interest. In June of 1970, AMK Corporation voted to merge with United Fruit, and United Brands was born.

At about the same time, the corporation began modernizing its more outdated banana installations, and turned some of them over to local management. In 1970, Mr. Black personally negotiated with Cesar Chavez's United Farm Workers Union on behalf of the company's lettuce subsidiary, making United Brands the first and only major lettuce grower to sign with the union until 1975. At the signing of the contract, Mr. Black invited Mr. Chavez to his Rosh Hashanah services where Mr. Chavez read a prayer. A friend of Mr. Black said, "You should have seen it. It was something you could point out to your kids and say—'See, business and social conscience do mix'."[10]

This was only one example of Mr. Black's actions on social responsiveness. A portion of the *1972 Annual Report* of United Brands Company showed the depth of concern the company had developed under Mr. Black.

Every public company has more than one constituency. Its management must answer to the shareholders, but it must also be responsive to the needs of its markets, the aspirations of its employees, and the interests of the general public. The larger the scope of the company, the more numerous those constituencies can become. In the case of an organization with the geographically widespread and varied business interests of United Brands, they can embrace a significant portion of the world.

We have very real responsibilities in each of those areas. They demand more than words; they demand substance. Companies can no longer deal with their responsibilities at the level of appearances only; they can no longer be satisfied with the treatment of effects. We must concern ourselves with causes and United Brands does.

It is because of the successful application of these principles that the *Chicago Daily News* in a story on the company last year reported, "It may well be the most socially conscious American company in the hemisphere." The company's social policies and practices have also led *The New York Times* to report in a recent front page story, "What emerges from talks with labor, management and government is a picture of a company that anticipated the changes that have swept Latin America and has quietly set about adjusting to them."

Judgments like these have been earned. They reflect substantial, long-term commitments which United Brands has made to all of the people to whom the company is responsible. In some instances, this has meant the deliberate evolution away from traditional policies and

---

[10] Ibid., p. 15.

practices. And in others, it has entailed creative vigilance to unexpected needs which the company is equipped to answer.

The most recent example of this kind of responsiveness was provided by the tragedy which took place during Christmas week in Nicaragua. . . . countless thousands of men, women and children were killed. . . . Thousands more were injured and made homeless. It was one of the most destructive earthquakes in Central American history. Within hours, your company—itself no stranger to various kinds of devastation by nature—had begun to respond.

Because one of the first requirements in dealing effectively with disaster is communication, we immediately reopened the Managua office of TRT, United Brands tropical telecommunications subsidiary. TRT remained on the air around the clock for the next several days, providing critical information on the extent of the disaster for the guidance of relief efforts, and informing concerned families and friends of the whereabouts and condition of individuals known to have been in the area at the time of the disaster. During the first frightening hours, TRT provided the only communications link between the stricken city and the outside world.

We offered the full help of our company and its personnel to the Nicaraguan Government and we began to lay out a plan of assistance. On Christmas Day we began the organization of what may be the most comprehensive relief program ever mounted by a private corporation on behalf of the people of another land. NEED, the Nicaraguan Earthquake Emergency Drive, was created by the company and officially registered later that week as a nonprofit corporation and staffed by volunteers from United Brands. . . . Thousands of dollars in contributions poured into NEED from every corner of the country. The advertisements and other announcements pledged that every cent collected will be used to aid the victims of the Managua disaster.

This is only one example of how the company discharges its obligation. The real significance of NEED is the accurate reflection it provides of a far-reaching corporate policy commitment: "to carefully examine all dimensions of our operating practices and management decisions, and to measure them against their potential impact . . . on the environment, on the cultural and social climates in which we operate, on our collective consciences, and on the quality of our lives."[11]

Mr. Black continued to buy and sell major concerns in the 1970s. The company's Guatemala operations were sold to Del Monte in 1972. In 1973, the majority interest in Baskin-Robbins was sold as United Brands began acquiring the Foster Grant Company, a producer of sunglasses and other high-quality plastics.

Banana operations, which in 1972 had contributed about 85 percent to operating income for the corporation, began to falter in 1973 (see financial statements, Exhibits 1, 2, and 3). That year a violent

---

[11] United Brands, *1972 Annual Report*, pp. 38–39.

EXHIBIT 1

United Brands and Subsidiary Companies
Ten-Year Summary of Operations
For Year Ended December 31
($000 except per share amounts)

	1975**†	1974**†	1973*	1972*	1971*	1970‡	1969‡	1968‡	1967‡	1966‡
Net sales	$2,186,525	$2,020,526	$1,841,738	$1,586,747	$1,373,027	$1,447,715	$1,420,270	$815,819	$801,817	$814,811
Operating costs and expenses	2,126,013	2,018,436	1,787,126	1,546,002	1,349,610	1,418,950	—	—	—	—
Operating income	$ 60,512	$ 2,090	$ 54,612	$ 40,745	$ 23,417	$ 28,765	—	—	—	—
Interest and amortization of debt expense	(34,468)	(37,080)	(29,585)	(26,449)	(26,667)	(21,733)	—	—	—	—
Interest income and other income and expenses, net	2,372	2,488	7,952	7,903	6,366	3,752	—	—	—	—
Income (loss) from continuing operations before items shown below	$ 28,416	$ (32,502)	$ 32,979	$ 22,199	$ 3,116	$ 10,784	—	—	—	—
Usual or infrequently occurring items	(1,048)	(26,808)	—	—	—	—	—	—	—	—
Income (loss) from continuing operations before income taxes	$ 27,368	$ (59,310)	$ 32,979	22,199	$ 3,116	$ 10,784	—	—	—	—
Estimated U.S. and foreign income taxes	(17,300)	(12,000)	(15,250)	(12,970)	(7,945)	(6,500)	—	—	—	—
Income (loss) from continued operations	$ 10,068	$ (71,310)	$ 17,729	$ 9,229	$ (4,829)	$ 4,284	$ 24,416	$ 12,090	$ 13,621	$ 8,770
Income from discontinued operations	—	13,768	741	1,508	3,135	—	—	—	—	—
Gains on disposals of discontinued operations	—	10,704	7,238	—	—	—	—	—	—	—
Income (loss) before extraordinary items	$ 10,068	$ (46,838)	$ 25,708	$ 10,737	$ (1,694)	$ (4,284)	—	—	—	—
Extraordinary items	700	3,231	(345)	6,971	(22,318)	(6,408)	—	—	—	—
Net income (loss)	$ 10,768	$ (43,607)	$ 25,363	$ 17,708	$ (24,012)	$ (2,124)	$ 28,660	$ 12,623	$ 16,389	$ 9,190

Average number of primary shares outstanding	10,779	10,775	11,193	11,194	10,779	10,733	—	—	—	—
Primary and fully diluted income (loss) per common share:										
Income (loss) from continuing operations	$ 0.74	$ (6.82)	$ 1.42	$ 0.67	$ (0.65)	$ 0.06	$ 2.07§	$ 1.37§	$ 1.60§	$ 0.94§
Income (loss) from discontinued operations	—	1.28	0.07	0.13	0.29	0.14	—	—	—	—
Gains on disposals of discontinued operations	—	0.99	0.65	—	—	—	—	—	—	—
Income (loss) before extraordinary items	$ 0.74	$ (4.55)	$ 2.14	$ 0.80	$ (0.36)	$ 0.20	$ 2.07§	$ 1.37§	$ 1.60§	$ 0.94§
Extraordinary items	0.06	0.30	(0.03)	0.62	(2.07)	(0.59)	.16	0.07	0.33	0.06
Net income (loss)	$ 0.80	$ (4.25)	$ 2.11	$ 1.42	$ (2.43)	$ (0.39)	$ 2.23	$ 1.44	$ 1.93	$ 1.00
Dividends per common share	0	0	0	0	$ 0.15	$ 0.30	—	—	—	—

* From United Brands, *Annual Report*, 1975.

† The 1974 hurricane loss and 1975 and 1974 gains on bond repurchases were presented as unusual or infrequently occurring items. In accordance with accounting principles applicable for prior years, similar items were presented as extraordinary items.

‡ From United Brands, *Annual Report*, 1971.

§ Fully diluted only given.

EXHIBIT 2

United Brands and Subsidiary Companies
Consolidated Balance Sheet
For Year Ended December 31
($000)

	1975*	1974*	1973†	1972‡	1971§	1970‖	1969#	1968**
ASSETS								
Current assets:								
Cash	$ 31,550	$ 98,976	$ 20,986	$ 18,894	$ 21,514	$ 55,620	$ 37,355	$ 12,725
Marketable securities	30,417	540	20,363	64,225	49,082	35,772	56,148	67,842
Trade receivables, less allowance for doubtful accounts of $5,230 (1974—$4,446)	131,218	125,210	170,135	119,847	92,289	92,322	120,947	45,649
Other receivables	25,225	38,355	—	—	—	—	—	—
Inventories	178,868	176,891	210,689	124,090	115,581	104,773	104,324	25,351
Materials and supplies	—	—	—	25,331	28,441	30,358	28,761	20,288
Prepaid expenses	10,572	9,223	10,876	10,997	11,593	8,546	4,915	3,167
Total current assets	$ 407,850	$ 449,195	$ 433,049	$ 363,384	$ 318,500	$ 327,391	$ 352,450	$ 175,022
Investments and long-term receivables	18,848	32,822	55,072	67,417	44,324	46,398	45,127	9,112
Property, plant and equipment, net	337,306	350,921	403,128	331,018	334,530	362,870	329,410	207,715
Other assets and deferred charges (Note 9)	7,575	10,967	23,016	26,702	36,736	14,675	30,235	49,134
Trademarks	44,931	45,031	47,004	50,249	49,882	46,071	46,174	—
Excess of cost over fair value of net assets acquired	272,190	272,146	276,639	279,069	285,255	282,112	279,508	—
	$1,088,700	$1,161,082	$1,237,908	$1,117,839	$1,069,227	$1,079,517	$1,082,904	$ 440,983

LIABILITIES AND SHAREHOLDERS' EQUITY

	*	†	‡	§	‖	#	**
Current liabilities:							
Notes payable	$ 17,473	$ 62,117	$ 43,419	$ 28,933	$ 48,092	80,703	$ 8,069
Accounts payable	84,792	124,887	87,692	92,806	78,328	72,811	18,776
Accrued liabilities	35,764	—	—	—	—	—	20,600
Long-term debt due within one year	12,057	11,326	14,719	7,656	8,144	5,569	—
U.S. and foreign income taxes	23,037	23,511	22,820	19,874	19,166	24,121	15,808
Deferred U.S. and foreign income taxes	14,145	11,102	10,882	11,436	10,607	15,309	—
Total current liabilities	$ 187,268	$ 232,943	$ 179,532	$ 160,705	$ 164,337	$ 198,513	$ 63,253
Long-term debt	341,583	396,237	402,487	380,280	358,661	320,427	—
Accrued pension and severance liabilities	69,750	54,369	34,596	37,095	34,287	32,524	29,801
Other liabilities and deferred credits	7,784	37,600	7,689	13,158	16,478	18,275	3,278
Total liabilities	$ 606,385	$ 721,149	$ 624,304	$ 591,238	$ 573,763	$ 569,739	$ 96,332
Commitments and contingent liabilities							
Shareholders' equity:							
$3.00 cumulative convertible preferred stock	$ 2,649	$ 2,723	$ 2,738	$ 2,769	$ 2,876	$ 170	$ 3,696††
$1.20 cumulative convertible preferred stock	29,610	29,610	29,610	29,610	29,613	29,524	—
$3.20 cumulative convertible preferred stock	7,357	7,421	7,452	7,452	7,452	276	—
Capital stock, $1 par value	10,782	10,775	10,773	10,781	10,775	21,491	(20,896)‡‡
Warrants and options to purchase capital stock							
Capital surplus	366,498	366,367	366,322	366,303	366,192	365,518	187,876
Income retained in the business	65,419	99,863	76,640	61,074	88,846	96,136	173,975
Total shareholders' equity	$ 482,315	$ 516,759	$ 493,535	$ 477,989	$ 505,754	$ 513,165	$ 344,651
	$1,088,700	$1,237,908	$1,117,839	$1,069,227	$1,079,517	$1,082,904	$ 440,983

* From United Brands, *Annual Report*, 1975.
† From United Brands, *Annual Report*, 1974.
‡ From United Brands, *Annual Report*, 1973.
§ From United Brands, *Annual Report*, 1972.
‖ From United Brands, *Annual Report*, 1971.
From United Brands, *Annual Report*, 1970.
** From United Fruit Company, *Annual Report*, 1969.
†† All preferred stock less cost of reacquisition.
‡‡ Less cost of reacquisition.
§§ Less cost of reacquisition.

EXHIBIT 3

Operations by Product Group
Year Ended December 31
($000)

	1975*	1974*	1973*	1972*	1971*	1970†
Net sales:						
Bananas and related products	$ 657,087	$ 549,440	$ 449,971	$ 450,662	$ 397,551	$ 379,558
Meat-packing and related products	1,329,011	1,288,996	1,258,415	1,012,175	847,056	898,916
Food processing and food services	123,677	103,525	67,624	68,280	74,001	66,555
U.S. agriculture and floriculture	53,205	51,003	48,426	42,461	42,587	29,615
Other	23,545	27,562	17,302	13,169	11,832	8,961
Other	$2,186,525	$2,020,526	$1,841,738	$1,586,747	$1,373,027	$1,383,605
Contribution to Operating Income:						
Bananas and related products	$ 45,396	$ (7,523)	$ 26,323	$ 34,685	$ 11,170	$ 27,441
Meat-packing and related products	11,467	3,765	23,687	6,708	10,417	13,810
Food processing and food services	4,809	1,576	4,900	3,160	275	(1,387)
U.S. agriculture and floriculture	562	2,450	2,011	(2,473)	1,830	(11,028)
Other	3,128	5,349	1,143	1,698	3,223	2,394
Other	65,362	5,617	58,064	43,778	26,915	31,230
Less: Corporate overhead	(4,850)	(3,527)	(3,452)	(3,033)	(3,498)	(3,954)
Operating income	$ 60,512	$ 2,090	$ 54,612	$ 40,745	$ 23,417	$ 27,276

* From 1975 *Annual Report.*
† From 1974 *Annual Report.*

windstorm had hurt production in Honduras, which had provided over one quarter of United Brand's supply. The following year, the company increased its Honduran exports, but competitors also raised shipments to the United States. Their actions resulted in a tremendous oversupply of bananas and a severe depression of prices.

At this time, seven "banana republics" formed a Union of Banana Exporting Countries (UBEC) and presented a plan which called for a tax of $1.00 per 40-pound box of bananas exported. The countries involved claimed that UBEC was necessary to offset increasing fuel costs generated in part by the Organization of Petroleum Exporting Countries (OPEC). The "Banana War" was on.

Honduras enacted a 50-cent tax per 40-pound box in April 1974 which was to begin in June. In August, with a Panamanian tax of $1.00 per box, a Costa Rican tax of 25 cents per box, and the Honduran tax in effect, Mr. Black wrote to shareholders that the company realized the various republics' needs for additional revenue, and said that he intended to negotiate a reasonable formula with the countries involved.

Later that month, United Brands announced it had reached an understanding with the Republic of Honduras for a tax of 25 cents per box with gradual increases beginning in 1975 depending in part on the banana market at the time.[12] In mid-September, Hurricane Fifi struck Honduras, and destroyed about 70 percent of United Brands' plantations there. The $20 million loss suffered by United Brands was greater than the value of corporate net income for the previous four years. The stock price, which a year earlier had been $12 a share, dropped to $4.00. Faced with a third-quarter loss of $40.2 million, Mr. Black began to make arrangements to sell the company's interest in Foster Grant, an acquisition which he had called "the crown jewel of our company."[13]

While heading these negotiations, Mr. Black sent Edward Gelsthorpe to Panama to work out tax and property agreements there. Mr. Gelsthorpe had joined United Brands as senior vice president of marketing in July 1974 and his joining was what Mr. Black called "a major coup." Mr. Gelsthorpe had previously been president of Ocean Spray Cranberries, Hunt-Wesson Foods, and Gillette, all in a period of five years. After a brief period of mutual admiration, the two men began to clash when Mr. Black became deeply involved in financial problems and Mr. Gelsthorpe assumed greater operating control of the company.

---

[12] *The Wall Street Journal,* May 7, 1975, p. 1.

[13] "United Brands Trades More Assets for Cash," *Business Week,* January 13, 1975, p. 35.

As if to widen the split, Mr. Gelsthorpe was based in the old United Fruit home office in Boston, while Mr. Black stayed in the United Brands and original AMK office in New York, close to financial centers. Mr. Gelsthorpe quickly won the loyalty of the Boston group for his take-charge attitude. This group included senior vice presidents John Taylor and Donald Meltzer.[14]

When Mr. Gelsthorpe returned from Panama, he reported the Panama agreement to the board "as a fait accompli."[15] Mr. Black, however, felt that the agreement called for the forced sale to Panama of United Brands' holdings there, and he expressed his disapproval. According to one account, the report at the board meeting was the first Mr. Black had heard about the agreement and he felt as if Mr. Gelsthorpe "had sold the company down the river in order to build up his own reputation."[16] According to Mr. Gelsthorpe, he and Mr. Black were in constant communication through Mr. Meltzer, and both said that Mr. Black had given his approval.

By either account, it was clear that increased internal communications between Mr. Black and his senior vice presidents was in order. The key challenge to Mr. Black, however, remained the financial stabilization of the company in the midst of unprecedented and unforeseeable natural disasters and political events. The resultant crushing work load had allowed little time for the types of social projects, such as the building of a new medical center in Guatemala or the distribution of over 300,000 polio doses in Costa Rica, for which he and United Brands had become well known.

FEBRUARY 1975

With these business problems on his mind, 53-year-old Eli Black read the morning paper on the way to his office on the 44th floor of the Pan American Building in mid-Manhattan. It was Monday, February 3, 1975. The key Watergate defendants had been found guilty of conspiracy to obstruct justice the previous week, and officials at 3M Corporation, Ashland Oil, and Gulf were being indicted for charges stemming from illegal political slush funds.

At 8:20 A.M., Mr. Black locked the doors to his office, smashed an outside window with his attache case, and leaped to the street below. Mr. Black left no word to explain his death. In his briefcase was a note on which he had written "Early retirement—55."

---

[14] *The Wall Street Journal*, May 7, 1975, p. 26.
[15] Ibid.
[16] Ibid.

The Wall Street Journal quoted Samuel Belkin, president of Yeshiva University and a former teacher of Mr. Black's, as saying, "If it were just up to him he would retire, but . . . he thought of his job as a public trust." The *Journal* went on to say that "he had created that role himself by imbuing his job with his own sense of social accountability. In the end, he staggered beneath its weight and found but one possible way to retire—and took it."[17]

UNITED BRANDS AFTER ELI BLACK

The official United Brands statement issued the afternoon of February 3 said that Mr. Black had been under "great strain during the past several weeks because of business pressures. He had been working 16 to 18 hours a day and had become severely depressed because of the tension."[18]

Edward Gelsthorpe, executive vice president expressed his opinion that "the great tragedy of Eli Black's death at this time is that under his leadership the company was on its way to overcoming several crises. We were convinced that the traumatic period was behind us.[19] Knowledgeable sources expected Mr. Gelsthorpe to be named chief executive officer.[20]

Three days after Mr. Black's death, the board met to consider the question of company leadership. A sufficient number of board members knew of the friction between Mr. Black and Mr. Gelsthorpe to block his immediate appointment as president. It was decided that two committees, executive and management, would run the company temporarily and that Dr. J. E. Goldman, a director since 1970 and a group vice president of Xerox would head each. An executive search firm would be hired to help locate a permanent successor. (The composition of the committees and the board before and after Mr. Black's death is shown in Exhibits 4–7).

During the same meeting, Mr. Gelsthorpe and Mr. Taylor explained for the first time to the full board the "Honduras Arrangement." Someone within top management had negotiated the $5 million figure down to $2.5 million, and half that amount had been paid on September 3, 1974, with the rest to follow. The Honduras government had then rolled back the banana tax to 25 cents per box.

The board meeting took place while Price Waterhouse & Co. was

[17] *The Wall Street Journal*, February 14, 1975, p. 15.
[18] Ibid.
[19] Ibid.
[20] Ibid.

EXHIBIT 4

United Brands' Board of Directors as of January 1975

Eli M. Black (elected 1970), 53-year-old president and chairman of the board.

George F. Doriot (elected 1971), 76-year-old former assistant dean of Harvard Business School, founder of American Research and Development Corporation, and a member of several boards.

Robert M. Gallop (elected 1957, from the AMK board), 67-year-old senior vice president and general counsel for United Brands, originally from AMK Corporation.

Donald R. Gant (elected 1972), 47-year-old Harvard MBA, partner in Goldman, Sachs and Co., and member of four other boards.

George P. Gardner, Jr. (elected 1953, United Fruit), 58-year-old senior vice president of Paine, Wessen, Jackson & Curtis, Inc., investment bankers, and a director of the company since its United Fruit days, as well as six others. Asked to resign by Mr. Black in November 1974, he was urged to stay by Mr. Gelsthorpe, and did.

Dr. J. E. Goldman (elected 1970), 54-year-old classmate of Mr. Black at Yeshiva and senior vice president and chief scientist of Xerox Corporation.

Maurice C. Kaplan (elected 1969, AMK), dean of Touro Law School, former assistant director of the SEC, and director of several firms.

Samuel D. Lunt, Sr. (elected 1956, AMK), 70-year-old partner in S. D. Lunt & Co. and director of several firms.

Joseph M. McDaniel (elected 1957, AMK), 73-year-old chairman of The Andrews-Hart Corporation, a financial consulting firm, and director of numerous firms.

Elias Paul (elected 1971), 56-year-old president and chief executive officer of John Morrell & Co. and director of three other firms.

Simon Rifkind (elected 1975), 74-year-old partner in Paul Weiss, Rifkind, Wharton & Garrison and director of several firms.

Norman I. Schafler (elected 1958, AMK), 58-year-old chairman of NRM Corp., Condec Corp., and director of numerous other corporations.

John A. Taylor (elected 1973), senior vice president of United Brands and president of Agrimark Group.

David W. Wallace (elected 1960, AMK), 51-year-old president of Bangor Punta, former executive vice president of AMK Corp., and director of several companies.

Jay Wells (elected 1965, AMK), 59-year-old chairman of the board of Wells National Services Corporation.

EXHIBIT 5
Deletions from and Additions to the Board of Directors of United Brands
January 1975–March 1976

Deletions (dates of service in parentheses):

Eli M. Black (1970–February 1975). Death by apparent suicide.

George F. Doroit (1971–February 1975). Resigned following Mr. Black's death.

Robert M. Gallop (1957–January 1975). An old friend of Mr. Black's from AMK Corporation, he resigned in January 1975 after a heated exchange with Mr. Black in a late December board meeting. He remained as corporate counsel to United Brands.

Maurice C. Kaplan (1969–late 1975). Resigned in late 1975.

Simon H. Rifkind (January 1975–April 1975). Resigned when frustrated in the role of peacemaker between board factions.

John A. Taylor (1973–late 1975). Resigned from the board, but remained senior vice president and president, United Fruit Group.

Additions (dates of election in parentheses);

Norman Alexander (February 1975), 61-year-old president of Sun Chemical Corporation and Ampacet Corporation, a member of several other boards, and an old friend of the Black family.

Wallace Booth (May 1975), 52-year-old president of United Brands.

Max M. Fisher (March 1975), 67-year-old chairman of the board of Sefran Printing Company and member of numerous boards. A major shareholder, he was elected acting chairman of the board in May 1975.

F. Mark Garlinghouse (March 1975), 61-year-old vice president and general counsel for AT&T, chairman of L. F. Garlinghouse Co., and member of several boards.

Edward Gelsthorpe (February 1975; resigned September 5, 1975), 54-year-old executive vice president and chief operating officer of United Brands.

Seymour Milstein (March 1975), private investor and largest single shareholder of United Brands stock.

C. Gilbert Collingwood (late 1975), senior vice president, Finance and Administration for United Brands.

EXHIBIT 6
Executive and Management Committee
after Mr. Black's Death

Executive committee	Management committee
Dr. J. E. Goldman, Chairman	Norman I. Schafler, Chairman
George P. Gardner, Jr.	Norman Alexander
Edward Gelsthorpe	Donald R. Gant
Maurice C. Kaplan	George P. Gardner, Jr.
Elias Paul	Dr. J. E. Goldman
Simon H. Rifkind	David W. Wallace
	Jay Wells

EXHIBIT 7
The Lineup Regarding the New Management Question,
February through May 1975

For Dr. Goldman as Chairman:	For Mr. Alexander as Chairman:
Mr. Wells	Mr. Lunt
Mr. Paul	Mr. Schafler
Mr. Taylor	Mr. Alexander
Dr. Goldman	
New Board Members Pushing for an Outsider (Ultimately Mr. Booth):	Uncommitted Members:
Mr. Fisher	Mr. Gant
Mr. Milstein	Mr. Gardner
	Mr. Garlinghouse
	Mr. Gelsthorpe
	Mr. Kaplan
	Mr. McDaniel
	Mr. Rifkind
	Mr. Wallace

auditing the firm's books, and they were quoted as saying that "the matter came to our attention."[21] Acting on the advice of Price Waterhouse, the board hired counsel. Counsel then brought the matter to the attention of the Securities and Exchange Commission with the request that the matter be kept confidential. It was especially troublesome, however, since the bribe was listed as an expense for tax purposes. It therefore violated both tax laws and the SEC regulations regarding financial disclosure to stockholders.

Before the February meeting, it appeared as if only five men at

---

[21] *The Wall Street Journal*, April 11, 1975, p. 4.

United Brands had known of the payment: Mr. Black; senior vice presidents Taylor, Gelsthorpe, and Meltzer (all based in Boston); and corporate counsel Robert Gallop. If there were a "Boston Plot" against Mr. Black, as some suspected, the Boston group had had heavy ammunition in its arsenal. Messrs. Gelsthorpe and Taylor remained on the board that was attempting to run United Brands by committee.

The committee approach to running United Brands was cumbersome from the beginning. The process of selecting a new chairman was probably best described by *The Wall Street Journal* reporter Mary Bralove:

> There followed a series of acrimonious board meetings. The key controversy was whether to name as United Brands chairman Norman Alexander, chairman of the Sun Chemical Corp. and an old friend of the Black family. "You could hear the shouting out in the hall," a United Brands official says of one of the sessions. At another, Mr. Goldman, who opposed Mr. Alexander, and Norman Schafler, a director who supported him, "nearly came to blows," according to more than one observer.
>
> [Simon Rifkind, a board member who had tried to be a peacemaker, quit last month out of frustration. "I finally couldn't take it," he says.]
>
> By March 10, the board reached a strained compromise. Mr. Schafler became chairman of the management committee while Mr. Goldman remained chairman of the executive committee.
>
> At the next board meeting, that compromise threatened to come apart. At issue, according to sources, was a proposed three-man slate to expand the board. Board member Jay Wells and others opposed the slate because they feared the new members would vote for Mr. Alexander's election as chairman. The board was deadlocked on this issue. Unknown to Mr. Wells however, members who favored the slate had set up an elaborate telephone hookup to another director who had promised to call in from a boat in the Caribbean and vote for the slate. When the call came through, Mr. Wells was furious. In fact, he was so upset that he grabbed the phone and ripped the cord from the wall, thereby effectively ending the meeting.
>
> During this period, the time bomb of public disclosure of the Honduran payoff was ticking in the background. Price Waterhouse had discovered payments of $750,000 that had been made to Italian officials over the last five years. Nobody seemed to know, however, why these payments were made and who authorized them.
>
> Finally, on April 8, *The Wall Street Journal* queried United Brands about payments to a Honduran official, and in response the company publicly admitted the bribes. The secret was out, and everyone scattered to get legal help.[22]

---

[22] *The Wall Street Journal*, May 7, 1975, p. 26.

The company statement had said that the payment to government officials in the Republic of Honduras was authorized by Eli Black and was not accurately reflected on company books and records. The Securities and Exchange Commission then formally accused United Brands of issuing false reports and suspended the trading of United Brands.

General Oswaldo Lopez,[23] president of Honduras, immediately denied the prevalent speculation that he was the official involved. He then met with his cabinet and formed a commission to investigate the allegations. Any Honduran official found to be involved was to be prosecuted to the fullest extent of the law.

The Honduran commission requested all cabinet level ministers to authorize examination of personnel financial records and accounts. All did, except for President Lopez, who was removed as president on April 22 and replaced by the new commander in chief of the armed forces, Colonel Juan Alberto Melgar.

On May 1, Costa Rica announced that it was raising its export tax to $1 per box from 25 cents per box, and was asking other members of UBEC to do the same. On May 5, former President Lopez and his family were preparing for exile in Madrid, although no formal charges had been filed.

On May 7, a *Wall Street Journal* article examining the events leading to Mr. Black's suicide characterized various managers in the Boston office as saying that, since September 1974, Mr. Black had seemed "disoriented," "hooked on drugs," "cracking under the pressure," "not communicating," and "depressed." The same article, however, quoted the response of a long-time friend of Mr. Black: "They [senior Boston office executives] mutinied, and now they have to prove the captain was crazy. It's a chapter right out of *The Caine Mutiny*."[24]

On May 12, United Brands named a new president and chief executive officer. Wallace W. Booth, a 52-year-old senior vice president at Rockwell International, had spent 20 years at Ford Motor Company and had a broad background in financial management and foreign operations. Max M. Fisher, a major shareholder, was named acting chairman of the board.

---

[23] President Lopez was the closest thing to a war hero that the Honduran people had. He had led his troops in the four-day war of 1969 with El Salvador over the outcome of a soccer match. At the end of the fourth day, 2,000 lives had been lost and the El Salvadorians were advancing.

President Lopez originally came to power in a 1963 coup. He was elected in 1965 for a term that lasted through 1971. He returned to power in 1972 in another coup. The week prior to the revelation of the bribe, he had been relieved of his duties of commander in chief of the armed forces in order to concentrate more fully on economic problems.

[24] *The Wall Street Journal*, May 7, 1975, p. 26.

One informed observer commented that:

> Booth will need the help of Gelsthorpe, who was passed over by the
> board in favor of Booth. Booth will have to build loyalty among the
> Boston staff, and he plans to spend some time on Gelsthorpe's turf. The
> ideal combination would be for Gelsthorpe to work in marketing,
> where he has most of his experience, and Booth in operations and
> finance, his strong suit.[25]

May 15 brought the report of the Honduran investigative commission. To the surprise of most observers, it was reported that former
Economic Minister Abraham Bennaton was the official who received
the $1.25 million payment. Bennaton denied his involvement.

The following day, the Honduran commission specified that John
Taylor had paid the bribe money to Bennaton at a meeting on September 3, 1974 in Zurich, Switzerland. Bennaton was formally
charged on May 15. Also May 16, a federal grand jury in Washington
was weighing possible criminal charges against United Brands and its
top executives.

---

[25] "Who Calls the Shots at United Brands?" *Business Week,* May 26, 1975, p. 29.

Note: On September 5, 1975, Edward Gelsthorpe resigned as executive vice president, chief operating officer, and director of United Brands to become president and
chief operating officer of H. P. Hood, Inc., a Boston dairy producer and distributor. The
Hood appointment was the third such executive post he had held in a little over a year,
and the fourth in four years.

Commentaries ══════════════════════════════════

31. The Corporate Crime of the Century
Mark Dowie

Tom Mboya was the hope of the Western world. Bright, energetic, popular, and inclined to be democratic—he was a born leader who, Washington hoped, would rise to power in Kenya and help to keep Africa safe for U.S. commerce. In 1969 he was shot down in the streets of Nairobi. An emergency rescue squad was by his side in minutes. They plugged him into the latest gadget in resuscitative technology—a brand new U.S. export called the Res-Q-Aire. What the rescue team didn't know as they watched Tom Mboya's life slip away was that this marvelous device had been recalled from the American market by the U.S. government because it was found to be totally ineffective. The patient died.

Losing Mboya to the Res-Q-Aire was perhaps a subtle retribution for the United States, for to this day we allow our business leaders to sell, mostly to Third World nations, shiploads of defective medical devices, lethal drugs, known carcinogens, toxic pesticides, contaminated foods, and other products found unfit for American consumption.

Ten years after Mboya's assassination, in fact, Kenya itself remains a major market for unsafe, ineffective, and contaminated American products. At the 1977 meeting of the United Nations Environmental Program, Kenyan minister of water development Dr. D. J. Kiano warned that developing nations would no longer tolerate being used

---

Source: Mother Jones, November 1979, pp. 23–49 passim.

as "dumping grounds for products that have not been adequately tested" and that their people should not be used as "guinea pigs" for chemicals.

The prevailing sentiment in Washington contrasts considerably with Dr. Kiano's. Say the word "dumping" in federal government circles and the predominant response will be "Oh, yes, 'dumping.' Really must be stopped. It's outrageous, not in our economic interests at all . . . unscrupulous bastards. . . . "

Sounds as if we've solved the problem, doesn't it, except what our bureaucrats are talking about, one discovers, is foreign corporations "dumping" low-priced goods on the American market—Japanese cars, Taiwanese televisions, Hong Kong stereos, Australian beef, etc. The export of banned and hazardous products, which *Mother Jones* calls "dumping," is considered business as usual.

As the following articles make painfully clear, dumping is, in fact, big business, as usual. It involves not only manufacturers and retailers, a vast array of export brokers, tramp steamers, black marketeers and go-betweens who traffic an estimated $1.2 billion worth of unsafe goods overseas every year, but also the United States Export-Import Bank, which finances large dumps; the Commerce, State, and Treasury Departments, which have the statutory authority to stop or control dumping, but won't; and a President who, in his quiet way, subverts the efforts of the few progressive members of Congress who seek to pass uniform anti-dumping legislation.

Hard evidence of dumping and its tragic consequences has repeatedly been brought to the attention of federal agencies, the Congress and the White House. Here are some examples:

400 Iraqis died in 1972 and 5,000 were hospitalized after consuming the by-products of 8,000 tons of wheat and barley coated with an organic mercury fungicide, whose use had been banned in the United States.

An undisclosed number of farmers and over 1,000 water buffalos died suddenly in Egypt after being exposed to leptophos, a chemical pesticide which was never registered for domestic use by the Environmental Protection Agency (EPA) but was exported to at least 30 countries.

After the Dalkon Shield intrauterine device killed at least 17 women in the United States, the manufacturer withdrew it from the domestic market. It was sold overseas after the American recall and is still in common use in some countries.

No one knows how many children may develop cancer since several million children's garments treated with a carcinogenic fire retardant called Tris were shipped overseas after being forced off the domestic market by the Consumer Product Safety Commission (CPSC).

Lomotil, an effective anti-diarrhea medicine sold only by prescription in the United States because it is fatal in amounts just slightly over the recommended doses, was sold over the counter in Sudan, in packages proclaiming it was "used by astronauts during Gemini and Apollo space flights" and recommended for use by children as young as 12 months.

Winstrol, a synthetic male hormone, which was found to stunt the growth of American children, is freely available in Brazil, where it is recommended as an appetite stimulant for children.

Depo-Provera, an injectable contraceptive banned for such use in the United States because it caused malignant tumors in beagles and monkeys, is sold by the Upjohn Co. in 70 other countries, where it is widely used in U.S.-sponsored population control programs.

450,000 baby pacifiers of the type that has caused choking deaths have been exported by at least five manufacturers since a ban was proposed by the CPSC. 120,000 teething rings that did not meet recently established CPSC standards were cleared for export and are on sale right now in Australia.

Occasionally, a particularly scandalous dump like one of these will come to the attention of conscientious Americans. Most dumps, however, are performed quietly, the product moving unnoticed in the fast flow of normal trade between nations. And dumping is not limited to chemicals and consumer products. When a firm's production facilities and industrial equipment are condemned by the Occupational Safety and Health Administration, the manufacturer often simply closes up shop and moves the factory to Mexico or Jamaica, where occupational health standards are virtually nonexistent. Even entire technologies are dumped. Nuclear power, which seems certain to receive a "hazardous" classification before long in the United States, is today being dumped on energy-starved nations like the Philippines and India.

We are only beginning to discover how toxic and carcinogenic are some of the chemicals we use, chemicals with the potential to affect the entire global environment and human gene pool. Moreover, the number of other consumer products that maim or kill shows no sign of diminishing. The list of banned and hazardous products is, thus, bound to grow, which *should* make dumping a major international issue for the 1980s.

Early in our investigation, however, we discovered that exposing dumpers was more challenging than we thought it would be. "They're really smugglers," said one of our team in a story meeting. "The only difference between drug smugglers and dumpers is that the products are usually moving in opposite directions."

There is another difference: the government protects dumpers. We talked to countless officials in countless agencies and departments of the government while researching this story—a few of them outspoken opponents of dumping. They would tell us about contaminated foods, baby pacifiers, pesticides, and drugs that were being dumped overseas. They often knew how many of each item were shipped to specific countries, but they would never tell us the brand names, the manufacturers or the names of the export brokers. The answer was always the same. "I'm sorry, that's proprietary information . . . trade secret . . . confidential corporate information." And as we shall see, government protection afforded to dumpers goes way beyond this kind of cover.

Although the bottom line motive is always profit, hazardous products are dumped to solve different problems. For nonmanufacturers—wholesalers, retailers, brokers, importers and exporters—the problem is generally just a matter of inventory. Salvation often comes in the form of a broker, offering to buy the banned goods at a "closeout" price for resale in an unnamed (read, Third World) market.

It's not that simple, however, for manufacturers who have invested capital in tools, dies, assembly plants, personnel, machines and land. When a company like A. H. Robins foresees the withdrawal of a product like the Dalkon Shield intrauterine device, it dumps a million units on foreign countries, voluntarily withdraws the product and closes up shop. The company takes a small loss buying back recalled inventory (which it writes off), and its capital investment is amortized.

CARTER DUMPS DUMPING

It was Tris that brought dumping into the political arena. And the political arena for dumping is Washington. Tris (2,3-dibromopropyl) phosphate is a fire-retardant chemical used to treat synthetic flammable fabrics. In June of 1977, after Tris was found to cause cancer in animals, millions of pairs of infant pajamas and tons of children's sleepwear were suddenly withdrawn from the U.S. market by the CPSC. When some of the manufacturers, stuck with huge repurchased inventories of these carcinogenic garments, threatened to dump them on the overseas markets, the CPSC claimed at first that it had no statutory authority to stop them from doing so. In fact, although the CPSC, the EPA and the FDA together have removed over

500 pesticides, drugs, and consumer products from the American market for health, safety, or environmental reasons, the patchwork of regulations obfuscates what limited power these agencies have to prohibit the export of dangerous products.

When President Carter, who *does* have the authority to stop dumping with a simple executive order, learned of the Tris situation, he authorized the formation of an Interagency Working Group to develop a uniform national policy on dumping. Although such task forces can provide a valuable forum for intra-government communication and often make important policy recommendations, the Interagency Working Group on Hazardous Substances Export Policy (HSEP)—chaired by Carter's special assistant for consumer affairs, Esther Peterson—is, in fact, being used to table the issue until our balance of trade improves. Dumping, you see, is exporting; and although banned and hazardous products represent only about one percent of our total trade, every percent seems to count when we are consistently running a trade deficit of over $25 billion a year.

To determine why the task force report is still nonexistent, we took our investigation to Washington. In a long series of interviews with task force members and White House staff the reason for the delay became clear. The President, intimidated by Congress, is unwilling to take the issue to the Hill, in the face of growing "export fever" and antiregulatory sentiment.

Edward Cohen, staff counsel to both the HSEP task force and the White House Office of Consumer Affairs, asked us to turn off our tape recorder as he explained the dilemma. He also told us he was "one of the good guys in the story." We can't quote what he told us when the recorder was off, but since we don't believe him, it really doesn't matter. Cohen refused to tell us the names of any agency representatives on the task force and throughout our investigation went to elaborate lengths to stop any flow of information to our researchers. When we asked him for innocuous background material on the task force, Cohen exercised "executive privilege" and gave us nothing, forcing us to file Freedom of Information requests with the 16 agencies and departments in the task force. Despite White House efforts to discourage compliance with our requests, we obtained the material from friendly sources in the agencies. More on the contents later.

During the interview, Cohen struggled to remember the correct name of the task force. The records, files and minutes from past meetings were stuffed in a cardboard box under a radiator in his otherwise tidy office. It was clear that dumping and HSEP had slipped a notch or two on the White House agenda. Cohen admitted eventually that it was barely on his own agenda. He persisted, however, in his "good guy" stance.

When we persisted with our investigation, Cohen realized he had a public relations problem on his hands. In fact, when we called the White House to interview Esther Peterson recently, Cohen turned up unexpectedly on the line to tell us he was working on a fourth policy draft for task force review. But when we talked to representatives from all but three of the agencies involved, most barely remembered the task force and felt that the issue was dead. And Cohen recently told Ralph Nader's office that if the fourth draft is not approved, the entire matter will be dropped.

The president can place any product he wants on the commodity control list, which makes exportation of the product absolutely illegal. There are three statutory justifications for placing a commodity on this list: scarcity, national security, and foreign relations.

When Tris-treated clothing was found to be a cancer threat to infants and it became clear that President Carter wasn't going to do anything to stop its export, an alarmed S. John Byington, chairman of the CPSC, wrote in June 1977 to secretary of commerce Juanita Kreps, whose department administers the Commodity Control List. Byington asked her to place the garments on the list, pointing out to her that their export would have "serious implications for foreign policy."

On October 7, nearly four months and, as it turns out, many pajama dumps later, Kreps answered Byington. She had taken the time to consult the state department, which "has advised me that the controls on Tris and Tris-treated garments are not, in the language of the statute, 'necessary to further significantly the foreign policy of the United States to fulfill its international responsibilities'."

Frustrated by months of bureaucratic waffling, the CPSC finally reversed its position on June 14, 1978 by prohibiting the export of Tris-treated sleepwear.

This delay, obfuscation and inactivity are all too typical. Records of Interagency Working Group meetings, which we were able to obtain despite White House efforts to stonewall us, show that commerce and state department representatives are doing everything in their power to prevent the adoption of a uniform policy on dumping.

Although President Carter has mumbled a word or two about the ethics of exporting, he clearly does not consider the use of safe products a human right for non-Americans. In fact, his actions on this matter have pleased the most conservative pro-dumping forces.

On September 26, 1978, the day before the HSEP task force report was due for release, Carter issued a public statement on exports. The

wording of the statement so clearly subverted the intent of any re-
forms the task force might have conceivably proposed that it's little
wonder not a word has been heard from the group since.

NOTIFICATION BEFORE THE DUMP

The liberal compromise on the dumping issue is notification. In-
voking the principles of national sovereignty, self-determination, and
free trade, government officials and legislators have devised a system
whereby foreign governments are notified whenever a product is
banned, deregulated, suspended or cancelled by an American regulatory agency. The notification system is handled by the state department, whose policy statement on the subject reads, in part, "No
country should establish itself as the arbiter of others' health and
safety standards. Individual governments are generally in the best
position to establish standards of public health and safety."

Based on this judgment, an unwieldy and ineffective notification
procedure allegedly places announcements in the hands of the proper
foreign government officials, telling them a certain drug has been
found to be toxic or that babies have strangled in particular brands of
cribs.

The main problem with notification is the logic behind it. Other
governments are generally *not* in a position to establish safety standards, let alone control imports into their countries. In fact, the countries where most of our banned and hazardous products are dumped
lack regulatory agencies, testing laboratories or well-staffed customs
departments. In 1978, Nigeria's Environmental Protection Ministry
was one person. He recently told the U.S. EPA that it didn't matter
whether or not he was notified when a pesticide was suspended;
there was nothing he could do to stop its importation.

When our EPA, FDA, or CPSC finds a product to be hazardous,
they notify our state department as required or as a matter of protocol. State, which we have found to be no opponent of dumping, is
then supposed to send a communiqué to each American embassy
overseas. Each embassy is, in turn, supposed to notify the appropriate foreign officials. However, the Commerce, Consumer, and Monetary Affairs Subcommittee of the House Committee on Government
Operations discovered in hearings held in July of 1978 that the agencies frequently neglected to inform the state department when they
banned a product. For example, the EPA failed to notify State after
suspending such notorious pesticides as kepone, chlordane, and hep-
tachlor. The Government Accounting Office (GAO) also discovered
and testified to the same subcommittee that even when the agencies
did notify State, the communiqués rarely went further than the U.S.

embassies overseas—they almost never reached the foreign officials who might have been able to warn foreign buyers or intercept shipments. One embassy official even admitted to the GAO that he "did not routinely forward notification of chemicals not registered in the host country because it may adversely affect U.S. exporting." The GAO would not tell us the name or location of the official they quoted, but said the sentiment was not unusual.

Some of the foreign officials who have been notified have complained that the communiqués are vague and ambiguous, or else so highly technical that they are incomprehensible.

Of course, even if clear notification about a product were to reach officials in an importing nation, there is nothing to stop the exporters from changing a product's brand name before they ship.

IT'S ALL COMING BACK

Perhaps the only aspect of the whole dumping travesty that has kept the issue alive in Washington is reimportation. Congressmembers and bureaucrats who would otherwise ignore or even encourage dumping become irate upon learning that a hazardous product is being reimported (smuggled) into the United States for sale, or that an imported fruit or vegetable contains residue of a pesticide long-since suspended for American use. Even Esther Peterson, in a memo to the President, expressed concern about reimportation.

Remember, it is perfectly legal to dump hazardous products abroad. There are, however, strict measures to prevent reimportation. The FDA allows manufacturers to export banned drugs and even unapproved new drugs if they are shipped under "an investigational protocol" (for experimentation on other people.) But one of the stipulations for the export of drugs removed from the American marketplace is that they never be offered for domestic sale again.

The CPSC, however, can prohibit the export of goods forced off the American market. It can also stop exports that present "an unreasonable risk to persons in the United States" (through their reimportation, for example), but the CPSC admits that proving unreasonable risk is "very difficult."

HOW TO STOP IT

The White House office of consumer affairs remains confident that a uniform policy on the export of banned and hazardous products will protect foreign consumers. Our investigations, however, indicate that the corporate dumping urge is rooted in a criminal mentality and that dumpers will, as they already have, find new ways to circumvent whatever legal and regulatory barriers stand between their warehouses and profitable markets for their deadly goods.

Global corporations, with their worldwide network of subsidiaries, high technology and marketing systems, far outstrip the puny regulatory efforts of a government that considers corporate crime a minor nuisance at worst. Nothing short of a complete moral transformation of the corporate ethos will stop dumping. Until that unlikely transformation takes place, we recommend the following:

Dumping must be clearly defined by statute, and one term, such as "illegal for export," should be applied to American products found to be too dangerous for use here and, hence, anywhere. We should recognize that there are a few—a very few—products that are unsafe for use in the United States for which the benefits far outweigh the risks in other countries—for example, certain drugs used to treat tropical diseases or pesticides used to kill the malaria-carrying mosquito. In such cases, when the foreign government is appraised of the risk, the products should be cleared for export to that country only.

Dumping should be made a criminal offense.

The government, which already controls exports through the Commodity Control List and the Bureau of Census (where all exports of over $250 are registered), must accept the responsibility of monitoring the outflow of banned and hazardous products. This responsibility should be taken from the Department of Commerce, where it represents an untenable conflict of interest.

Notification of product bans, suspensions, cancellations and withdrawals from registration should be made *directly* by the U.S. regulatory agencies to appropriate foreign officials, in language that can be understood.

The State Department should be relieved of any antidumping responsibility, since it has so deliberately failed to coordinate an effective notification program.

Until all of the above are accomplished, the President should use his powers to stop dumping immediately.

WHAT DUMPING REALLY IS

Executives in major exporting corporations, with the strong support of commerce secretary Juanita Kreps, argue that if the export of banned and hazardous products is prohibited by statute or executive order, foreign buyers will merely turn to European or other suppliers, as they have in the past for weapons and ammunition. Other developed nations do dump; Germany dumps at least as many toxic pesticides as the United States, and no nation on earth can match Switzerland for dumping baby formula. However, the assumption that foreign buyers will import known toxins and recognized lethal products from one country when they can't get them from another is patently ridiculous.

American business leaders, who tout themselves as the most ethical businesspeople in the world, should lead the way in ending dumping worldwide. It's in their best interest to do so, for by dumping toxins on the Third World they are actually poisoning the very markets they seek to develop. Perhaps one day they will even see dumping for what it really is—a subtle genocide.

32. A Boycott Over Infant Formula

From a corporate perspective, it appeared to be wise and even humane to market powdered infant formula in less developed countries, where a large percentage of babies die from malnutrition and disease before they reach the age of five. Yet for the companies involved, that decision has turned into a public relations nightmare.

Church groups advocating breastfeeding have charged that bottle-feeding is contributing to—not alleviating—infant mortality in LDCs, mainly because the formula is often mixed with contaminated water. Using shareholder proposals and a boycott as their major weapons, the church groups have kept pressure on the corporations to change their marketing practices. And this perseverance may be paying off.

The target of the American boycott, Switzerland-based Nestlé Co., has 15 people in the United States working on boycott matters, five of them full time. Nestlé also has engaged the New York public relations firm of Hill & Knowlton Inc. to publicize its story. In recent months, Nestlé has explained its viewpoint in a letter mailed to virtually every U.S. clergyman—numbering about 300,000. The company has stopped sending public relations officials to meetings with the boycotters and now dispatches line and marketing executives.

Nestlé officials deny that the boycott has injured sales, but the adverse publicity has undoubtedly damaged the multinational's corporate image. "My interpretation is that they are feeling the heat of this boycott," says the Reverend J. Bryan Hehir, an associate secretary of the U.S. Catholic Conference.

Source: Reprinted from the April 23, 1979 issue of *Business Week* by special permission. © 1979 by McGraw-Hill, Inc., New York, N.Y. 10020. All rights reserved.

PROPOSALS

Behind the boycott is the Infant Formula Action Coalition (IN-FACT), based in Minneapolis and operating on a yearly budget of $29,000 that is provided by contributions from churches and individuals. Douglas B. Clement, boycott coordinator, says that Nestlé was singled out because it has the largest share (reportedly nearly 50 percent) of the infant formula market worldwide.

Nestlé does not sell infant formula in the United States, but its other products, such as chocolate and instant coffee and tea, are easily recognized by the American consumer. Also, Clement says, the boycott was a response to the difficulty of using legal and shareholder action against a foreign-based company.

At least three of the U.S. corporations that sell infant formula abroad—Bristol-Myers, American Home Products, and Abbott Laboratories—will face shareholder proposals relating to the product this month at their annual meetings. Among other requests, the proposals ask that the companies set up committees to study their marketing of infant formula. In the past, these proposals have been voted down, and Edward C. Baer, a consultant for the Interfaith Center on Corporate Responsibility, a group related to the National Council of Churches, believes that it is unlikely the shareholder proposals will ever pass. "But there is pressure being generated," Baer says. "Companies do not like shareholder resolutions. They go a long way toward trying to convince us to withdraw them."

INFACT and other groups want the companies operating in LDCs to stop promoting the infant formula, to halt the distribution of free samples to mothers, and to end the promotion of the products to health professionals. INFACT maintains that these practices serve to place the infant formula in the hands of the consumers least able to afford them or to use them correctly: illiterate women in rural areas living in housing without running water or electricity. Nursing Sister Margaret Gitau, who works in Kenya, says that the young mothers like the prestige attached to using a bottle from Europe or the United States. But these women are unable to read the instructions and fail to observe even the most basic standards of hygiene, she says. "Water is the major problem," says Gitau. "It must be carried back to the home in cans, so that the bottles are very likely to be contaminated."

'ECONOMIC SUICIDE'

Dr. Roy E. Brown, a nutritionist and pediatrician at New York's Mount Sinai School of Medicine, who spent 10 years working in

THE CHEMICAL THREAT
IN MOTHER'S MILK

While mothers in underdeveloped countries consider powdered milk and bottles a measure of progress, mothers in the U.S. and Europe are returning with increased enthusiasm to breast-feeding. But the federal government and environmental groups are worried that products of the industrialized world—pesticides and chemicals—contaminate mother's milk and may harm infants.

"It's a very significant problem," says Joseph H. Highland, chief scientist for the Environmental Defense Fund (EDF). Of particular concern is the presence of a highly toxic group of chemicals, polychlorinated biphenyls (PCBs), that do not rapidly break down in the environment. These chemicals, as well as pesticides such as DDT, become part of the food chain and accumulate in the body's fat content, especially the tissue in the breast. The chemicals are then easily passed along to a nursing infant.

LOW LEVELS

The Environmental Protection Agency collected samples from more than 1,000 nursing women in 1975 and found that about one third of the milk contained measurable amounts of PCBs. Although the agency did not try to discourage women from breast-feeding, it had enough concern to order three follow-up studies now under way at the National Institute of Environmental Health Sciences (NIEHS).

The levels of the chemicals are low—less than one part per million. But scientists are unsure about the long-term effects of the substances. "PCBs have been found to be toxic at low levels," says Dr. Walter J. Rogan of NIEHS. But he thinks that the amounts currently being detected do not warrant alarm.

The La Leche League, a worldwide organization that promotes breast-feeding, also does not think the problem is severe. However, it has helped line up volunteers to participate in a three-year NIEHS study that will trace the connections between the diet and the milk of nursing mothers.

Some environmentalists are convinced that no more data are needed. And an EDF booklet warns: "Because PCBs cause cancer, they present a risk to the baby, regardless of how small the residue in the milk may seem."

LDCs, says that an infant's system is unable to fight off bacteria from polluted water. The infant may develop gastroenteritis, with vomiting and diarrhea causing severe dehydration and often death, he says.

The companies claim that their promotions are not aimed at poor people in LDCs. "It would be economic suicide to concentrate any sales effort in rural areas, where people can't afford our product," says Henry G. Ciocca, Nestlé's assistant secretary. Ciocca claims that most of Nestlé's powdered milk products are sold in urban areas, where women can afford them and use them properly.

But under pressure from the church groups, Nestlé, Bristol-Myers, AHP, and Abbott have agreed to stop mass-media advertising of their infant formulas in LDCs. Ciocca notes that in the 1950s Nestlé was one of three companies selling infant formula in the LDCs. "Fierce competition developed when the number of companies grew to 17," he says, adding: "I think there were some inappropriate marketing techniques used."

The companies, church groups, and the World Health Organization agree on the desirability of breast-feeding. "Mother's milk is still superior to any infant food product," says Manuel Carballo, a scientist in WHO's unit of maternal and child health. The companies now state prominently in their literature and on packages that breast-feeding is the preferred method of feeding a baby. But the companies believe that their products are valuable as supplemental and weaning foods, while INFACT and WHO officials state that local foods should be developed instead.

WOMEN'S CHOICE

However, the companies say that there is a real need for their products in Third World countries. "Government and medical personnel in these countries tell us that if we [stopped selling infant foods] we would be killing a lot of babies," says Ernest Saunders, Nestlé's vice president for infant nutrition products. And in many of these countries, women are choosing not to breast-feed. "In this society, where the rich don't want to bother with breastfeeding because they have nursemaids and the poor want the status symbol of the fatter baby that formula produces, Nestlé doesn't even have to advertise," says an American nurse in São Paulo, Brazil.

A conference on infant feeding will be held in Geneva in October by WHO and the U.N. Children's Fund. Officials hope that the groups will set guidelines for marketing infant formula that can be followed by all companies operating in LDCs. "To commercially push infant foods as just another product is too dangerous," maintains WHO's Carballo.

33. A Code of Worldwide Business Conduct
Caterpillar Tractor Co.

To Caterpillar People

Large corporations are receiving more and more public scrutiny.

This is understandable. A sizable economic enterprise is a matter of justifiable public interest—sometimes concern—in the community and country where it's located. And when substantial amounts of goods, services and capital flow across national boundaries, the public's interest is, logically, even greater.

Not surprisingly then, growth of multinational corporations has led to increasing public calls for standards, rules, and codes of conduct for such firms.

Three years ago, we concluded it was timely for Caterpillar to set forth *its own beliefs*, based on ethical convictions and international business dating back to the turn of the century.

Experience since then has demonstrated the practical utility of this document—particularly as a means of confirming, for Caterpillar people, the company's operating principles and philosophies.

This revised "Code of Worldwide Business Conduct" is offered under the several headings that follow. Its purpose continues to be to guide us, in a broad and ethical sense, in all aspects of our worldwide business activities.

Of course, this code isn't an attempt to prescribe actions for every business encounter. It *is* an attempt to capture basic, general principles to be observed by Caterpillar people everywhere.

To the extent our actions match these high standards, such can be a source of pride. To the extent they don't (and we're by no means ready to claim perfection), these standards should be a challenge to each of us.

No document issued by

Caterpillar is more important than this one. I trust my successors will cause it to be updated as events may merit. And I also ask that you give these principles your strong support in the way you carry out your daily responsibilities.

Chairman of the Board
Issued October 1, 1974
Revised September 1, 1977

OWNERSHIP AND INVESTMENT

In the case of business investment in any country, the principle of mutual benefit to investor and country should prevail.

We affirm that Caterpillar investment must be compatible with social and economic priorities of host countries, and with local customs, tradition and sovereignty. We intend to conduct our business in a way that will earn acceptance and respect for Caterpillar, and allay concerns—by host country governments—about multinational corporations.

In turn, we are entitled to ask that such countries give consideration to our need for stability, business success, and growth; that they avoid discrimination against multinational corporations; and that they honor their agreements, including those relating to rights and properties of citizens of other nations.

Law and logic support the notion that boards of directors are constituted to represent shareholders, the owners of the enterprise. We have long held the view that Caterpillar board members can best meet their responsibilities of stewardship to shareholders if they are appointed solely by them—and not by governments, labor unions or other non-owner groups.

Board composition and board deliberations should be highly reflective of the public interest. We believe that is a basic, inseparable part of stewardship to shareholders.

We recognize the existence of arguments favoring joint ventures and other forms of local sharing in the ownership of a business enterprise.

Good arguments also exist for full ownership of operations by the parent company: the high degree of control necessary to maintain product uniformity and protect patents and trademarks, and the fact that a single facility's profitability may not be as important (or as attractive to local investors) as its long-term significance to the integrated, corporate whole.

Caterpillar's experience inclines toward the latter view—full ownership—but with the goal of worldwide ownership of the total enterprise being encouraged through listing of parent company stock on many of the world's major stock exchanges.

Since defensible arguments exist on both sides of the issue, we believe there should be freedom and flexibility—for negotiating whatever investment arrangements and corporate forms best suit the long-term interests of the host country and the investing business, in each case.

CORPORATE FACILITIES

Caterpillar facilities are to be located wherever in the world it is most economically advantageous to do so, from a long-term standpoint.

Decisions as to location of facilities will, of course, consider such conventional factors as proximity to sources of supply and sales opportunities, possibilities for volume production and resulting economies of scale, and availability of a trained or trainable work force. Also considered will be political and fiscal stability, demonstrated governmental attitudes, and other factors normally included in defining the local investment or business "climate."

We don't seek special treatment in the sense of extraordinary investment incentives, assurances that competition from new manufacturers in the same area will be limited, or protection against import competition. However, where incentives have been offered to make local investment viable, they should be applied as offered in a timely, equitable manner.

We desire to build functional, safe, attractive facilities to the same high standard worldwide, but with whatever modifications are appropriate to make them harmonious with national modes. They are to be located so as to complement public planning, and be compatible with local environmental considerations.

Facility operations should be planned with the long-term view in mind, in order to minimize the impact of sudden change on the local work force and economy. Other things being equal, preference will be given to local sources of supply.

RELATIONSHIPS WITH EMPLOYEES

We aspire to a single, worldwide standard of fair treatment of employees. Specifically, we intend:

1. To select and place employees on the basis of qualifications for the work to be performed—without discrimination in terms of race, religion, national origin, color, sex, age or handicap unrelated to the task at hand.

2. To protect the health and lives of employees. This includes maintaining a clean, safe work environment free from recognized health hazards.
3. To maintain uniform, reasonable work standards, worldwide, and strive to provide work that challenges the individual—so that he or she may feel a sense of satisfaction resulting from it.
4. To make employment stabilization a major factor in corporate decisions. We shall, among other things, attempt to provide continuous employment, and avoid capricious hiring practices.
5. To compensate people fairly, according to their contributions to the company, within the framework of national and local practices.
6. To foster self-development, and assist employees in improving and broadening their job skills.
7. To promote from within the organization—in the absence of factors that persuasively argue otherwise.
8. To encourage expression by individuals about their work, including ideas for improving the work result.
9. To inform employees about company matters affecting them.
10. To accept without prejudice the decision of employees on matters pertaining to union membership and union representation; and where a group of employees is lawfully represented by a union, to build a company-union relationship based upon mutual respect and trust.
11. To refrain from hiring persons closely related to members of the board of directors, administrative officers and department heads. If other employees' relatives are hired, this must be solely the result of their qualifications for jobs to be filled. No employee is to be placed in the direct line of authority of relatives. We believe that nepotism—or the appearance of nepotism—is neither fair to employees, nor in the long-term interests of the business.

PRODUCT QUALITY

A major Caterpillar objective is to design, manufacture and market products of superior quality. We aim at a level of quality which offers special superiority on demanding applications.

We define quality as the sum of product characteristics and product support which provides optimum return on investment to both the customer and Caterpillar.

Caterpillar products are designed to the same exacting standards, and manufactured to uniformly high levels of quality, throughout the world. Maximum interchangeability of components and parts is maintained—wherever they are manufactured.

We strive to assure users of timely after-sale parts and service availability at fair prices. From our experience, these goals are best achieved through locally based, financially strong, independently owned dealers committed to service. We back availability of parts from dealers with a worldwide network of corporate parts facilities.

We believe pursuit of quality also includes providing products responsive to the need for lower equipment noise levels, compliance with reasonable emissions standards, and safe operating characteristics. We continually monitor the impact of Caterpillar products on the environment—striving to minimize any potentially harmful aspects, and maximize their substantial capability for beneficial contributions.

SHARING OF TECHNOLOGY

Caterpillar takes a worldwide view of technology. We view technology transfer in a broad context—as sharing information, from many varied business functions, aimed at improved company operations everywhere.

We therefore provide design and manufacturing data, and marketing and management know-how, to all Caterpillar facilities, while observing national restrictions on the transfer of information. Managers are encouraged to participate in professional and trade societies. Managers are provided access, on a worldwide basis, to corporate technical competence which is appropriate to their jobs.

We seek the highest level of engineering technology, regardless of origin, applicable to our products and manufacturing processes. We locate engineering facilities in accordance with need, on a global basis. We encourage equitable relationships with inventors, consultants, and research and development laboratories that have technical capabilities with our needs.

We believe the principal threat to future relationships among nations has to do with the widening gap between living standards in industrial and developing countries. Intelligent transfer of technology is a major means by which developing countries can be helped to do what they must ultimately do—help themselves.

However, technology transfer is dependent not only on the ability of people in one nation to offer it, but also in the ability of people in other nations to utilize it. We therefore encourage developing countries to create an environment of law and custom that will maximize such utilization. We support effective industrial property laws, reasonable licensing regulations, and other governmental initiatives which encourage sharing of existing technology with such countries.

Technology is property; it requires time, effort, and money to create, and has value. We believe governments can foster the spread of technology by permitting a reasonable return for its transfer.

FINANCE

The main purpose of money is to facilitate trade. Any company involved in international trade is, therefore, involved in dealing in several of the world's currencies, and in exchanging currencies on the basis of their relative values.

Our policy is to conduct such currency transactions only to the extent they may be necessary to operate the business and protect our interests.

We buy and sell currencies in amounts large enough to cover requirements for the business, and to protect our financial positions in those currencies whose relative values may change in foreign exchange markets. We manage currencies the way we manage materials inventories—attempting to have on hand the right amounts of the various kinds and specifications used in the business. We don't buy unneeded materials or currencies for the purpose of holding them for speculative resale.

INTERCOMPANY PRICING

Our intercompany pricing philosophy is that prices between Caterpillar companies are established at levels equivalent to those which would prevail in arm's length transactions. Frequently, such transactions are between Caterpillar companies in different countries. Caterpillar's intercompany pricing philosophy assures to each country a fair valuation of goods and services transferred—for tariff and income tax purposes.

ACCOUNTING AND FINANCIAL RECORDS

Accounting is called the "universal language" of business. Therefore, those who rely on the company's records—investors, creditors, and other decision makers and interested parties—have a right to information that is timely and true.

The integrity of Caterpillar accounting and financial records is based on validity, accuracy, and completeness of basic information supporting entries to the company's books of account. All employees involved in creating, processing, or recording such information are held responsible for its integrity.

Every accounting or financial entry should reflect exactly that which is described by the supporting information. There must be no concealment of information from (or by) management, or from the company's independent auditors.

Employees who become aware of possible omission, falsification, or inaccuracy of accounting and financial entries, or basic data supporting such entries, are held responsible for reporting such information. These reports are to be made as specified by corporate procedure.

DIFFERING BUSINESS PRACTICES

While there are business differences from country to country that merit preservation, there are others which are sources of continuing dispute and which tend to distort and inhibit—rather than promote—competition. Such differences deserve more discussion and resolution. Among these are varying views regarding competitive practices, boycotts, information disclosure, international mergers, accounting procedures, tax systems, transfer pricing, product labeling, labor standards, repatriation of profit, securities transactions, and industrial property and trademark protection laws. We favor more nearly uniform practices among countries. Where necessary, we favor multilateral action aimed at harmonization of differences of this nature.

COMPETITIVE CONDUCT

Fair competition is fundamental to continuation of the free enterprise system. We support laws prohibiting restraints of trade, unfair practices, or abuse of economic power. And we avoid such practices everywhere—including areas of the world where laws do not prohibit them.

In large companies like Caterpillar, particular care must be exercised to avoid practices which seek to increase sales by any means other than fair merchandising efforts based on quality, design features, productivity, price and product support.

In relationships with competitors, dealers, suppliers, and users, Caterpillar employees are directed to avoid arrangements restricting our ability to compete with others—or the ability of any other business organization to compete freely and fairly with us, and with others.

There must be no arrangements or understandings, with competitors, affecting prices, terms upon which products are sold, or the number and type of products manufactured or sold—or which might be construed as dividing customers or sales territories with a competitor.

Suppliers aren't required to forgo trade with our competitors in order to merit Caterpillar purchases. Caterpillar personnel shall avoid arrangements or understandings prohibiting a supplier from selling products in competition with us, except where: (1) the supplier makes the product with tooling or materials owned by Caterpillar; or (2) the product is one in which the company has a proprietary interest which has been determined to be legally protectable. Such an interest might arise from an important contribution by Caterpillar to the concept, design, or manufacturing process.

No supplier is asked to buy Caterpillar products in order to continue as a supplier. The purchase of supplies and services is determined by evaluations of quality, price, service, and the maintenance of adequate sources of supply—and not by whether the supplier uses Caterpillar products.

Relationships with dealers are established in the Caterpillar dealership agreements. These embody our commitment to fair competitive practices, and reflect customs and laws of various countries where Caterpillar products are sold. Our obligations under these agreements are to be scrupulously observed.

OBSERVANCE OF LOCAL LAWS

A basic requirement levied against any business enterprise is that it know and obey the law. This is rightfully required by those who govern; and it is well understood by business managers.

However, a corporation operating on a global scale will inevitably encounter laws which vary widely from country to country. They may even conflict with each other.

And laws in some countries may encourage or require business practices which—based on experience elsewhere in the world—we believe to be wasteful or unfair. Under such conditions it scarcely seems sufficient for a business manager to merely say: we obey the law, whatever it may be!

We are guided by the belief that the law is not an end but a means to an end—the end presumably being order, justice, and, not infrequently, strengthening of the governmental unit involved. If it is to achieve these ends in changing times and circumstances, law itself cannot be insusceptible to change or free of criticism. The law can benefit from both.

Therefore, in a world characterized by a multiplicity of divergent laws at international, national, state, and local levels, Caterpillar's intentions fall in two parts: (1) to obey the law; and (2) to offer, where appropriate, constructive ideas for change in the law.

BUSINESS ETHICS

The law is a floor. Ethical business conduct should normally exist at a level well above the minimum required by law.

One of a company's most valuable assets is a reputation for integrity. If that be tarnished, customers, investors, and employees will seek affiliation with other, more attractive companies. We intend to hold to a single high standard of integrity everywhere. We will keep our word. We will not promise more than we can reasonably expect to deliver; nor will we make commitments we don't intend to keep.

In our advertising and other public communications, we will avoid not only untruths, but also exaggeration, overstatement, and boastfulness.

Caterpillar employees shall not accept costly entertainment or gifts (excepting mementos and novelties of nominal value) from dealers, suppliers, and others with whom we do business. And we will not tolerate circumstances that produce, or reasonably appear to produce, conflict between personal interests of an employee and interests of the company.

We seek long-lasting relationships—based on integrity—with employees, dealers, customers, suppliers, and all whose activities touch upon our own.

RELATIONSHIPS WITH PUBLIC OFFICIALS

In dealing with public officials, as with private business associates, Caterpillar will utilize only ethical commercial practices. We won't seek to influence sales of our products (or other events impacting on the company) by payments of bribes, kickbacks, or other questionable payments.

Caterpillar employees will take care to avoid involving the company in any such activities engaged in by others. We won't advise or assist any purchaser of Caterpillar products, including dealers, in making or arranging such payments. We will actively discourage dealers from engaging in such practices.

Payments of any size to induce public officials to fail to perform their duties—or to perform them in an incorrect manner—are prohibited. Company employees are also required to make good faith efforts to avoid payment of gratuities or "tips" to certain public officials, even where such practices are customary. Where these payments are as a practical matter unavoidable, they must be limited to customary amounts; and may be made only to facilitate correct performance of the officials' duties.

PUBLIC RESPONSIBILITY

We believe there are three basic categories of possible social impact by business:

1. First is the straightforward pursuit of daily business affairs. This involves the conventional (but often misunderstood) dynamics of

private enterprise: developing desired goods and services, providing jobs and training, investing in manufacturing and technical facilities, dealing with suppliers, paying taxes, attracting customers, earning a profit.

2. The second category has to do with conducting business affairs in a *way* that is socially responsible. It isn't enough to design, manufacture, and sell useful products. A business enterprise should, for example, employ people without discrimination, see to their job safety and the safety of its products, help protect the quality of the environment, and conserve energy and other valuable resources.

3. The third category relates to initiatives beyond our operations, such as helping solve community problems. To the extent our resources permit—and if a host country or community wishes—we will participate selectively in such matters, especially where our facilities are located. Each corporate facility is an integral part of the community in which it operates. Like individuals, it benefits from character building, health, welfare, educational, and cultural activities. And like individuals, it also has citizen responsibilities to support such activities.

All Caterpillar employees are encouraged to take part in public matters of their individual choice. Further, it is recognized that employee participation in political processes—or in organizations that may be termed "controversial"—can be public service of a high order.

But partisan political activity is a matter for individual determination and action. While Caterpillar may support efforts to encourage political contributions by individual employees, the company won't make contributions to political parties and candidates—even where local law may permit such practices.

Where its experience can be helpful, Caterpillar will offer recommendations to governments concerning legislation and regulation being considered. Further, the company will selectively analyze and take public positions on *issues* that have a relationship to operations, when our experience can add to the understanding of such issues.

DISCLOSURE OF INFORMATION

The basic reason for existence of any company is to serve the needs of people. In a free society, institutions flourish and businesses prosper only by customer acceptance of their products and services, and by public acceptance of their conduct.

Therefore, the public is entitled to a reasonable explanation of operations of a business, especially as those operations bear on the public interest. Larger economic size logically begets an increased responsibility for such public communication.

In pursuit of these beliefs, the company will:

1. Respond to reasonable public inquiries—including those from the press and from governments—with answers that are prompt, informative, and courteous.
2. Keep investors and securities trading markets informed about Caterpillar on a timely, impartial basis.

INTERNATIONAL BUSINESS

We believe the pursuit of business excellence and profit—in a climate of fair, free competition—is the best means yet found for efficient development and distribution of goods and services. Further, the international exchange of goods and services promotes human understanding, and thus harmony and peace.

These are not unproven theories. The enormous rise in post-World War II gross national product and living standards in countries participating significantly in international commerce has demonstrated the benefits to such countries. And it has also shown their ability to mutually develop and live by common rules, among them the gradual dismantling of trade barriers.

One of the world's first priorities is to find more effective ways of bringing similar improvement to those developing countries whose participation in the international exchange of goods and services is relatively limited.

As a company that manufactures and distributes on a global scale, Caterpillar recognizes the world is an admixture of differing races, religions, cultures, customs, political philosophies, languages, economic resources, and geography. We respect these differences. Human pluralism can be a strength, not a weakness; no nation has a monopoly on wisdom.

It is not our aim to attempt to remake the world in the image of any one country. Rather, we hope to help improve the quality of life, wherever we do business, by serving as a means of transmission and application of knowledge that has been found useful elsewhere. We intend to learn and benefit from human diversity.

We ask all governments to permit us to compete on equal terms with competitors. This goes beyond the influence a country can exert on our competitiveness within its national boundaries. It also applies to the substantial way a government can control or impact on our business in *other* lands—through domestic taxes and regulations affecting the price of products to be exported, and through "host country" laws affecting our operations outside that country.

We aim to compete successfully in terms of design, manufacture, and sale of our products, not in terms of artificial barriers and incentives.

REPORTING CODE COMPLIANCE

Each officer, subsidiary head, plant or parts department manager, and department head shall prepare a memorandum by the close of each year: (1) affirming a full knowledge and understanding of this code; and (2) reporting any events or activities which might cause an impartial observer to conclude that the code hasn't been fully followed. These reports should be sent directly to the company's General Counsel; General Offices; Peoria, Illinois.

---

34. South Africa and the Foreign Businessman
Stephen Mulholland

Regardless of the path events take in South Africa—that of relatively peaceful evolution along the lines, for example, of a racial partition of the country on internationally acceptable criteria or that of bloody, destructive, and violent revolution—there are risks, as there are always risks, in making investments there.

All investment has within it the element of the wager; even the purchaser of U.S. bonds is wagering that the rate of interest he receives is greater than the rate of inflation that erodes it, not to mention further dilution via the income tax. In the case of South Africa the returns available on investments reflect, as is always the case in these matters, what the market judges the risk to be. Right now, for example, the shares of blue chip companies on the Johannesburg Stock Exchange can be bought on dividend yields in double figures and on price earnings ratios as low as two or three. In addition, prices discount assets heavily while, for the foreign purchaser, the yields are inflated even further, multiples reduced sharply and asset discounts increased through the mechanism of the securities rand. (The rand (R) is the unit of South African currency and it is pegged to the dollar at an official rate of $1.15:R1.00.)

Source: *Across The Board,* June 1978, pp. 4–89 *passim.*

Only foreigners may purchase securities rand and they may be used only to buy securities (both ordinary shares and fixed interest instruments, including government and semi-government stocks) that are listed on the Johannesburg Stock Exchange. Now securities rands, which are, in essence, the proceeds of the sale of assets held in South Africa by nonresidents, can be bought for around 76 cents U.S. (as of April 24), compared with the official rate of $1.15 to the rand. Thus, the foreign buyer of South African shares today benefits not only from the depressed prices ruling on the Johannesburg Stock Exchange due to unfavorable political and social factors, but he or she also benefits from the depressed price of those units of South African currency that are allowed to float freely.

Of course, the user of the securities rand method of purchasing South African shares is making two bets: one of the share (albeit, if he chooses well his yield will provide an ample margin on the downside) and the other on the securities rand, whose value fluctuates in the international money markets as do those of other freely tradable currencies, as Americans have been learning.

I have approached the subject of South Africa, its future, and the role of American business in it from the share market investment aspect because I believe that it is essential for all businessmen to act rationally if they are to survive, prosper, and properly serve their shareholders. And the Johannesburg Stock Exchange is a clear example of how markets adjust to reflect new realities and new expectations. It could well be that those now buying South African industrial and mining shares are on to a good thing and that over time they will do well; or they might be wrong.

It is my belief that the odds favor, although not by a great deal, the possibility of reasonably peaceful development in South Africa, and I employ that description in a relative sense: there's nothing very peaceful about black students engaged in running battles with policemen, but, tragic as South Africa's experiences have been, they are no match for the genocidal atrocities committed in many other nations.

It is not the function of businessmen to conduct the foreign policy of their nations. For better or for worse the politicians and civil servants have that contract. It is my view that the South African policy of the Carter administration is a poor one, not at all well thought out and bearing with it the potential not only for further diminution of America's influence and image in the world but also, as General George S. Brown, chairman of the Joint Chiefs of Staff, put it in his *Military Posture* report for 1978, for "the extension of Soviet influence in Africa." In addition, as I outlined in an article in *The Wall Street Journal* last March, an American policy in southern Africa that fails to consider, and deter, a Russo-Cuban initiative against Rhodesia almost guarantees the entry of South Africa as a powerful combatant in what could develop into a widespread holocaust of death and destruction.

Although, as I have stated, the formation and conduct of foreign policy is clearly not the business of businessmen, it *is* their legitimate concern to try to influence policy if and when they judge that it interferes with their legitimate pursuit of profits and profit opportunities and that such interference is not, in their view, based on interests that are vital to the United States. Morality is not the issue here; in any event, as George Bernard Shaw wrote, the nation which places its morals on the opposite side to its interests is doomed. What American businessmen can and should legitimately concern themselves with is the use of American economic strength (represented by the private sector, the only wealth-producing element in the society) to achieve American foreign policy aims that would appear to them to have little bearing on America's vital interests and, in fact, might well mitigate directly against those interests.

It is perhaps worthwhile repeating here some remarks made by South Africa's leading businessman, Harry F. Oppenheimer—chairman of the Anglo-American and De Beers mining, finance and industrial groups and an implacable opponent of apartheid and its many evils—when he addressed the Foreign Policy Association in New York last October:

> . . . the disagreeable truth [is] that practically no one in South Africa believes that American policy is primarily inspired by an idealistic interest in the welfare of South Africans, black or white.
>
> Particularly in the light of the evolution of the Angolan situation and of what in regard to Rhodesia and Namibia is felt to be an excessive preoccupation with the views of the frontline residents, not all of whom can be regarded as democratic, and their guerrilla protégés, and a tendency to neglect the views and interests of the large proportion of the people who are not in possession of guns, the American attitude toward southern Africa begins to appear to be based neither on the defense of human rights nor on majority rule but on a policy of supporting blacks against whites and armed blacks against unarmed blacks. The practical advantages of such a policy are of course plain to see, but it is perhaps rather difficult to justify it fully in terms of the higher standards of morality that South Africa is being called upon to adopt. In the result, most whites are resentful and frightened by American policy as they understand it and most thinking blacks are, I would say, doubtful and confused.

When America's ambassador to the United Nations describes the Cuban forces in Africa as a stabilizing influence while the chairman of the Joint Chiefs of Staff believes that "Cuban involvement in Africa can be viewed both as a contribution to the extension of Soviet influence in Africa as well as an effort to enhance Cuba's revolutionary credentials," the foreign observer can perhaps be forgiven if he forms the impression that there is a certain lack of coherence in the Carter administration's approach to foreign policy formation in the delicate and explosive African arena. Personally, I would be inclined to treat with greater weight the views of experienced military strategists than those of Ambassador Andrew Young who, with the greatest of respect for his brave and important civil rights achievements, is hardly equipped to jet about the globe conducting an off-the-cuff diplomacy, which recently included the suggestion that the United States would seriously consider arming Marxist Mozambique.

Mr. Carter would do well to recall the problems presidents can invite when they don't keep their executives on a tight leash; although some might call the comparison farfetched, President Truman lived to rue the fact that he allowed Gen. Douglas MacArthur too much leeway and issued to his military subordinate instructions that lacked the precision necessary for skilled crisis management in arenas distant from the White House. It is reasonable for the Russo-Cubans to take at face value the remarks of Ambassador Young; the signals he has been giving out must serve to encourage them in their African incursions. Let us hope and pray that Ambassador Young's indiscretions do not return to haunt him and those in South Africa who will suffer the immediate consequences.

All this, of course, is aimed at making a case for the application of pressure by the American business community against moves to bring additional economic sanctions against South Africa on the ground that, aside from further undesirable interference in the private affairs of business by government, the policy on which such interference is based is bad policy. I do not believe this conflicts with my conviction that the major role of business is to seek to maximize profits within a framework of reasonable law and ethics—it would seem to me to be part of the role of the business community collectively to try to establish, maintain, and improve the climate in which profitable business might be conducted.

Now let us turn to the crisp issue of what business and businessmen with South African interests should do about them. (Insofar as new investment is concerned, let me merely repeat that these should be made on the basis that the return must justify the risk; South Africa is today a high-risk area, although it is arguable that the returns available justify the risk. In addition, of course, businessmen must rationally take into account the potential effects on their existing domestic and foreign activities of overt involvement in South Africa: while I seriously doubt if very many ordinary Americans care much about these matters, there are very real dangers from collective action by groups such as church organizations, trade unions, student groups, and others whose well-intentioned but, in my view, counterproductive activities can and do have adverse effects on particular companies. Even here, however, the effects are not so great as one might believe: I'm sure there are very few car buyers who did not buy a Ford because Henry Ford II has stated emphatically that his organization is staying in South Africa and will, when conditions warrant it, expand the Ford Company's operations there.)

Companies with investments in South Africa (and it is worth bearing in mind that much of these investments derive not from injections of risk capital but from the reinvestment of profits, depreciation and other sources) must decide for themselves, based on the assessment of their executives and advisers, how to proceed in South Africa. The objective of business is not to further the interests of any nation or group of nations but to seek to legitimately maximize profits. If there are more lucrative areas for investment—or areas that, on balance, after the application of sound business criteria—appear more appealing than South Africa, then the businessmen involved have not only no option but, in fact, a duty to shift funds from South Africa.

Recently a number of companies have taken such decisions. Most have, however, either decided to stay on (like Ford and IBM, among many others), to increase their stake, or to enter the South African market for the first time. This, after all, is what business is all about. Businessmen are paid to make rational decisions and execute them. No one can be completely objective, but the collective judgment of the world's business community would seem to indicate that, on balance, South Africa remains a fair risk.

Those who think otherwise may be right; those who stay, expand, or enter anew might be wrong. But surely all this has nothing to do with anyone but the businesses, executives and shareholders concerned, as long as the vital interests of the nation—in this case the United States—are not threatened. I would argue that, in the case of discouraging business with South Africa, it might well be that the vital political interests of Mr. Carter are involved, but certainly not those of the United States.

For those who decide, on strictly business grounds (and there can and should be no other basis for investment), to remain in South Africa it would seem to me to make good business sense for them to do everything in their power within the law to break down the racial barriers in their concerns. Not only will this have beneficial spin-offs in their external public relations but they will discover, as many already have, that the black South African, exposed for so long to the obvious rewards of the free enterprise system but denied its fruits, is an ambitious, keen and loyal employee who will repay many times over any investment in his training and development. By opening up opportunity to a people so long held back, businesses will reap a harvest of increased productivity while at the same time making a vital contribution to the possibility for peaceful accommodation in South Africa, although this last point should not be the basis for an investment or business decision, profitability being the decisive factor.

Good business is good for everyone. As numerous social scientists have observed, it is economic growth and development that break down social stratification and barriers. The force of economic growth is the greatest threat to apartheid; a stagnant economy, its surest guarantee of survival.

And amid all the talk of change, there are those who make what Mr. Oppenheimer has described as "mutually exclusive demands." They call for boycott on the one hand and for the simultaneous economic upliftment of the black South African on the other. Prof. Klaus Knorr of Princeton has studied some 60 attempts over history to apply economic boycotts. The empiric evidence, starting with Napoleon's counterproductive continental blockade of Britain—which laid the foundations of U.S.-British trade—is that the vast majority were dismal failures. Given the ingenuity of man and the fact that there is a price that clears markets, they just don't work and often result in the opposite of what they intended to achieve.

There are, to put it mildly, other opinions on this subject. In a recent article in *Foreign Affairs*, Richard Ullman made a case for an American boycott (combined, preferably, with its Western allies) of Ugandan coffee. Mr. Ullman's argument is persuasive and skillful, and its sting lies in the fact that he sees a coffee boycott—aimed, obviously, at deposing that terrifying man, Idi Amin—as a mere stepping-stone toward the justification of a boycott of South Africa. In a discussion recently at Princeton, Mr. Ullman made it clear that, in his view, the United States, having employed its economic strength against the black tyrant Amin, would have little excuse, in the eyes of Africa and the Third World, not to use it against the white racist John Vorster, prime minister of South Africa.

In other words, Mr. Ullman sees the Pease amendment (which seeks to introduce legislation cutting off all American trade with Uganda) as the deus ex machina of an American boycott of business with South Africa. He writes:

> To take action against Idi Amin while continuing to conduct business as usual with John Vorster would be an affront to the rest of Africa.
> The counters to this argument are not so much logical as political—and avowedly opportunistic. It is undeniably true, given the degree of economic interdependence between South Africa and the West, that

sanctions against Pretoria must be costly if they are to have any chance of effectiveness. *But this, in fact, may be an argument for starting with Uganda.* [My emphasis.] Once Western governments and societies prove willing to apply sanctions against Uganda, at little pain to themselves, it would be politically more difficult for industries and individuals to argue persuasively that comparable measures should not be taken next against South Africa.

There is now, in every Western country, and certainly within the U.S. Congress, a considerable body of opinion that decries what is held to be an international double standard applied to South Africa: those who fulminate at Pretoria's abuses of human rights, it is said, are too often willing to overlook equally grave violations elsewhere, especially in black Africa. A boycott aimed at Uganda would effectively dispose of these allegations of a double standard—and perhaps neutralize those who make them as politically potent opponents of sanctions against South Africa.

Joseph Schumpeter, in his book *Capitalism, Socialism and Democracy*, wrote that the intellectual is he who wields the power of the written and spoken word, and one of the touches that distinguishes him in that he carries no responsibility for the policies he advocates. Such is the case with Mr. Ullman and those who feel as he does. They are sincere and well-intentioned, but, at the same time, naive and shortsighted. How could a boycott, "effective over time" as Mr. Ullman says it would have to be, work against South Africa? By one, and only one, method: the use of military force. The world is too complex to isolate effectively one of its leading traders. (Last year South Africa exported about $10 billion of goods and services; it is one of the world's very few net exporters of food, and contains vast reserves of raw materials vital to the West. In Britain alone, some 70,000 jobs depend directly on trade with South Africa; and, in the 1978 *United States Military Posture*, Gen. Brown states: "Six of the most essential commodities required by modern technological societies are found in southern Africa: chromium, colbalt, industrial diamonds, manganese, platinum group metals, and vanadium. The United States currently depends on this source for a major portion of its industrial requirements.")

The elasticity of demand for its exports is not great, and, while it would no doubt have to accept discounts and pay premiums, its foreign trade would go on even in the face of a compulsory United Nations embargo. To take just one simple example, many South African foreign traders set up European companies which, in turn, handle the financing of their international trade: a bank in Tennessee discounts a bill for a bank in Switzerland or Belgium—the fact that the ultimate client is South African is untraceable.

In an exhaustive study undertaken at the University of the Witwatersrand in Johannesburg, Prof. Arnt Spandau, employing a sophisticated computer model, has calculated that, even taking into account the considerable costs and inconvenience to South Africa of an economic boycott, the country would experience an "exuberant" phase of growth, including massive import substitution projects, in the first five to seven years of such a campaign. After that the situation would, according to his model, deteriorate rapidly, but it is difficult to see how a boycott could be made to work for that length of time without, at the very least, South Africa developing new trading links, increasing its self-sufficiency, and, in any event, effecting internal changes that would, in all likelihood, have come about in any event, which would make her once more an acceptable member of the family of nations.

Crucial to this last suggestion are workable settlements along pro-Western, free enterprise lines in Namibia and Rhodesia. Should peaceful and prosperous multiracial societies develop along such lines on South Africa's borders, their influence for constructive change within South Africa could be immense.

There is enormous potential for a community of nations, aligned with the West and moving away from the racial sicknesses of the past, to develop in southern Africa. What is needed is wise, resourceful, and determined leadership in Western policymaking, and execution to ensure that southern Africa does not fall under the baleful influence of the collectivist forces typified by the Russo-Cuban presence in Africa.

Threats combined with economic blackmail leading inexorably to some sort of military confrontation and a reluctance to employ America's greatest asset—her thrusting, wealth- and job-creating private sector—as a catalyst for change in South Africa are sins that, if persisted in by the Carter Administration, will earn it the censure of history as responsible for what could turn into an unthinkable racial bloodbath.

EPILOGUE: SOCIAL
RESPONSIVENESS AND THE FUTURE

The cases and commentaries reflect not only the past and present of business and its relationships with its environment, but also the future. That is, social and political forces impacting business are nothing new. In a number of the cases it has been seen that issues involving social confrontation and controversy are not easily resolved while a crisis may center on a particular act or event (e.g., the bribe in the United Brands case). Its repercussions may be felt for years. In other instances there is no single event or episode, but rather a process of disagreement by various parties which may make the problem an elusive one (e.g., Abbott Laboratories: Similac). The nature of these conflicts is not likely to change. While feelings may be more intense at one time or another, most of the questions are basic and enduring; and they will tend not to go away.

This is not to suggest by any means that new issues will not emerge. The environment is far too dynamic to support such an assertion. The Viet Nam war is no longer an issue, but the controversy surrounding nuclear power seems to intensify yearly. More subtle but equally significant issues are based in the call for greater accountability and an improved governance process for corporations.

Management really has no choice but to deal with these challenges, whether they be old or new. It requires moving social responsiveness to the core of the definition of what it means to be a successful, enlightened manager.

The book concludes with two significant commentaries. The editorial for the July 1968 issue of *Fortune* may be one of the most provocative calls for reassessment ever issued to American business. The risk

461

of business becoming irrelevant to the primary challenges of our time has not disappeared. Indeed, the title of the concluding article, taken from the 50th anniversary issue of *Business Week,* suggests the topics treated in this book are by no means trivial. The very shape and character of society will depend in large measure on how successful business is in being a dynamic force in responding to changing expectations.

Commentaries ==

35. Business and the Time of Troubles

The Brutal murder of Sen. Robert Kennedy confirms the growing impression that we are in the midst of a Time of Troubles—one of those periods in which the disintegrative forces in society seem at least temporarily more powerful than the integrative. Individuals resort to acts of senseless terror. Groups use force in place of lawful protest to express their grievances. The social system seems unable to cope with the rising wave of disorder. *Society fails to exercise the moral authority to assure compliance with its rules and directives.* It is not enough, at such a time, to deplore the lack of respect for order, or to call for a crackdown on breakers of the peace. The real question, as the president says, is why our society arouses such violent dissent, at just the moment when it is showing a capacity to solve many of the material problems that have afflicted man since the beginning of history. Business not only has an enormous stake in finding the answer to this question—it also, as the most dynamic and powerful element in American society, has the means and the obligation to provide part of the remedy for our current discord.

Robert Kennedy was, of course, first of all a man. He lived a highly individual life. His death is not merely an instance of general social upheaval, but, more immediately, the end of a promising public career and the snuffing out of a brilliant personality. It is perhaps not too late to regret the antagonism that existed between Kennedy and much of business. During his campaign for the Democratic nomination, he was speaking with sensitivity and imagination about the nation's problems, and many of the solutions that he offered were a kind to which business could relate.

In an article on the Democratic presidential race, written by A. James Reichley for this issue and canceled after the assassination, *Fortune* commented:

Source: *Fortune*, vol. 83, no. 1 (July 1968), pp. 57–58. Reprinted by permission.

> Businessmen dislike Kennedy partly because they believe he is immature
> and ignorant of economic realities, but chiefly because they think he does
> not like them. Unlike Humphrey, Kennedy is not the man to disarm his
> critics with friendship and charm . . . Sensing the dislike of
> businessmen, Kennedy tends to reciprocate the feeling, and even to add a
> little bit to prove that he will not be pushed around. All of this has contrib-
> uted to a reputation for radicalism that is largely undeserved. In his in-
> stincts, Kennedy is conservative. His solution to poverty is to find jobs for
> the unemployed in private industry. When he speaks of the need for law
> and order, he is not simply appealing for conservative votes in Indiana and
> Nebraska. (He makes the same speech to Negro audiences.) He views hard
> work, competitive drive, and love of country as absolute moral goods.

Kennedy had many qualities that could have made him the natural
leader of the forces of progressive business. The fact that the two never
got together was the country's loss.

THE DISINTEGRATIVE DENOMINATOR

More, however, than the death of a leader is involved in the assassination of Sen. Kennedy. It is but the most recent in a series of events that
in the space of a few months have shaken American society to its roots.
Consider what has happened: the United States for the first time in its
history has found itself committed to a war to which it can find no
military solution (the uncertain precedent of the War of 1812 has never
clouded the legend of our invincibility); a sizable and vocal body of
American youth have refused to support their country in time of war; a
minority race has demanded immediate end to its inferior status and the
leader of that race has been murdered; dozens of American cities have
been torn by riots, in the course of which it has been the clear though
unannounced policy of government to tolerate looting; the national capital has been occupied by troops and the seat of government protected by
machine guns; a group of political scientists gathering recently at Princeton has felt justified in concluding that for the first time an American
administration has been "toppled" in the European sense; a major
American university has been paralyzed and almost taken over by student radicals and other campuses have been disrupted by riots; various
economic prophets have stated that we are in the most dangerous fiscal
crisis since the early Thirties; and now the brother of our recently assas-
sinated president has been shot down at a climactic moment in his drive
to unseat the ruling powers in his own party.

These events, whether or not they are related, would themselves be
enough to produce a serious social crisis. The fact is that many of them
do seem to be related and to derive from the major disintegrative forces
in our civilization: the decline of conventional religion, the retreat of the

West from world supremacy, the "revolution of rising expectations," the seeming irrelevance of many traditional moral sanctions, the concentration of people in dense urban regions where any sense of community is almost impossible, the development of a technology that seems to substitute its own goals for traditional human goals, the revolution in communications that impairs privacy and prevents detachment, and so forth.

Not all of these developments are necessarily bad—the "revolution of rising expectations," for instance, has led to much real improvement in the material conditions under which people live. But all are disintegrative in that they tend to upset the established order on which our civilization has been based. To the extent that the established order rested on exploitation and injustice, this may ultimately be a good thing—but disorder itself surely must have an immediately destructive effect on human values.

WHERE IS THE ORDERING PRINCIPLE?

It is difficult and probably not productive to try to trace our present disorders to particular causes among the forces of disintegration. The most striking quality about all of them (and the aspect that is most open to practical response) is that they all are instances of a willingness to depart from the established—that is, legal—means of achieving social or personal objectives. Bullets and arson, in other words, have been substituted for elections and debate. While it is true that every society will contain individuals who are prepared to make this choice, no society can survive in a civilized state if it permits resort to violence to become commonplace. At some point—and perhaps at some point very soon—there will develop a public readiness to meet force with naked force, to submit to drastic repression if that is what is needed to restore order. Whether force, unsupported by moral authority, would work is of course questionable. Czarist Russia was not the first autocracy to perish in violent revolution. While force might establish a temporary kind of order, its ultimate effect could be to strengthen the impulse to violence by bottling it up. It would, in any event, destroy or severely curtail many of the cultural values that are the finest achievements of our civilization.

What is needed—desperately—is an ordering principle that will persuade most individuals to identify their objectives with the goals and systems of the society to which they belong. The established authorities in our society have proved woefully inadequate to the task of providing such a principle. In the recent college clashes, the kids had a kind of moral principle—revulsion against all the nation's ethical shortcomings. So did the cops—enforce the law, no matter what the consequences. The university officials in authority had none. They thought in terms of making deals and saving face—of somehow keeping things going and getting back to normalcy. Products of the pragmatic strain in our civilization, they asked only what would work, not what should be done. The essential trouble with pragmatism is that in the long run it doesn't work. Its ultimate value is survival, and human beings, at this stage in development, want more than to survive. This is a truth that Robert Kennedy recognized, and tellingly expressed during the campaign. If his practice did not always live up to his rhetoric, he at least made the generous and idealistic aspects of human nature his political touchstones.

PUTTING VISION INTO PRACTICE

It would be foolish to pretend that businessmen alone can supply the ordering principle or principles that society needs. They have in fact been closely identified with the pragmatic norm—with getting things done, rather than with how and why things are done (and, of course, with the materialism and affluence that the young resent). But they have been quicker than most groups to realize the need for a moral basis for society. When *Fortune* recently asked Henry Ford II why businessmen were becoming involved in finding solutions to the urban crisis, he said, "Because it has to be done." Out of enlightened self-interest? "No, I don't think there's so much of that." Labor has been preoccupied with getting its share of the pie; the politicians have mostly been content to administer the status quo. Many establishment intellectuals have worked so hard at legitimizing pragmatism that they have difficulty recognizing its limitations. The intellectuals of the left either have been tied to a discredited policy of economic centralization and coercion, or have been content to fan the flames of disintegration.

Businessmen—somewhat like the landed aristocracy of 19th-century Britain—have at least been secure enough and sufficiently free from preconceptions to recognize that something is wrong. In addition business *needs* social stability and a high level of moral accountability. Business flourished under the strict ethical standards imposed by the Protestant Reformation. Laissez-faire economics have always been tempered by a Puritan sense of responsibility in the American business tradition. The sweatshops of the 19th century and the shoddy merchandising techniques of the 20th are products of business but so are the Carnegie libraries and the great foundations. This does not mean that business by itself will produce a principle of moral order that will regenerate society. (It obviously does not mean that any principle of order is capable of preventing future assassinations. So long as human existence is imperfect—that is, always—there will be individuals who feel driven to the commission of dreadful acts.) But it does mean that business is prepared to respond to moral challenge, and to provide political support for necessary change. Our future finally is in the hands of politicians, prophets, broad-gauge intellectuals, and perhaps poets. But business, in its broadest sense, offers the techniques and the muscle to put vision into practice.

THE DANGER OF IRRELEVANCE

The Time of Troubles will not end unless and until society again acts as a great magnet to attract the moral energies of its citizens. This will happen, quite simply, when the social system is responsive to the real needs of human nature. At present, society possesses the capacity and even the will to meet most material needs. But our recent experience has shown us—if our training in religion and the humanities did not—that man has many needs that are not specifically material. Can business methods, which have made the United States the most productive society in history, contribute to the fulfillment of these other needs—like personal freedom, sense of community, pride in work, aesthetic pleasure, reunion with nature? If they cannot, business is in danger of becoming irrelevant to the primary challenges of our time.

One thing is certain: if the American system, which at its best relies on personal responsibility as well as on the collective pressures of democracy and the marketplace, fails, there is not much hope for anything that may be put in its place. Old-fashioned elitism has proved too inflexible to accommodate change in even so relatively homogeneous a nation as France. Bureaucratic statism, as represented by the Soviet Union, has long since lost its moral attraction. Talk of a society that will get along without authority is both childish and self-defeating. Anarchy can lead only to rule through force by the very strong. All order, it is true, requires limitation of freedom and results in some degree of injustice, but without order, neither freedom nor justice would be possible.

---

36. The End of the Industrial Society

In retrospect, 1929 was the watershed year of the 20th century: the start of the Great Depression, which swept away all that had gone before and which forever changed the economic face of not only America but the world.

Source: Reprinted from the September 3, 1979 issue of *Business Week*, by special permission, © 1979 by McGraw-Hill, Inc. All rights reserved.

Yet in 1979, only a half-century later—the twinkling of an eye as history goes—the world seems poised to change again. The post-Depression economic mechanisms, which fostered great growth, also set an inflationary fire that no one knows how to put out. Balanced against the government intervention in everyday life that the Depression brought on is a growing demand for less intrusive government. The success of the Organization of Petroleum Exporting Countries has broken up the well-ordered industrial world and forced every nation to fight for its economic life for costly and scarce energy. So the world could change as completely between 1979 and 2029 as it did between 1929 and 1979.

To understand what comes next, it first is necessary to understand what has come before: why the seemingly boundless prosperity of 1929 ended so abruptly and why the Great Depression produced so many profound changes.

It began, of course, with the Crash—Black Tuesday, October 29, 1929, when the U.S. stock market collapsed in the worst market break in history. In dollar terms, the 1973–74 bear market cost investors more money. In percentage terms—and in psychological impact—the 1929 collapse was worse.

By 1932 the index of stock prices had fallen to 30 from its 1929 high of 210; commodity prices, including that of gold, had dropped 40 percent; industrial production had shrunk 50 percent; international trade had slid 30 percent; and the International Labor Organization had estimated that 30 million people were unemployed in the world.

There was no one cause for the Depression. Rather, it was a combination of a lot of things: a grievous miscalculation by U.S. monetary authorities, who eased instead of tightening in 1927, spawning the inflationary bubble that burst in 1929; the spread of political unrest in Europe, which sapped confidence as Nazism became a major political force in Germany; capital shortages in Central Europe left over from the Great War, which dislocated the channels of investment; the inability of the world economic system to absorb shocks and adjust to changes, thanks to the actions of various governments to strengthen commodity cartels and labor unions; technical improvements in agriculture that produced sharply higher yields that caused sharply lower prices for farmers, while the goods they bought were rising in cost; a proliferation of giant frauds in business; a change in attitude that led to heavy borrowing by individuals, corporations, and governments; economic policies that propped up weak businesses instead of allowing them to fail; and finally, after the slowdown started, the imposition of trade barriers to protect domestic manufacturers, which also impeded the flow of goods and capital around the world.

The scenario for the Great Depression ran like this: boom in 1929, financial crisis in 1931, crushing deflation in 1932. The trilogy left a memorable imprint on the minds of peoples of the world, shaping the thinking of individuals, business executives, government bureaucrats, and politicians for the next 50 years. Because of the Depression, governments were induced to intervene actively in economic affairs. That led to a new concept of taxation (to redistribute income by soaking the so-called rich), a new form of regulation (with government ordering how business should operate, allocating scarce resources, and even setting prices), and a new kind of welfare (to pay unemployment insurance, Social Security, pensions, medical and child care expenses).

The stock market crash in 1929 was a traumatic start to a 50-year period that was filled with shocks. Ten years of economic doldrums were followed by ten years of World War II and its aftermath, which produced the cold war's devastating split between East and West blocs.

In 1949 the dolorous pattern changed. Fed by the Marshall Plan, the war-devastated world began to recover. For nearly 25 years the Western world was to enjoy one of the greatest prosperities of all times, lasting until 1974, when OPEC ended the boom by quadrupling the price of oil.

During the 60s, the civil rights movement emerged as a national force in the United States, peacefully at first. Then riots exploded in Newark, Chicago, Watts, New York. Opposition to the Vietnam war produced a counterculture in the United States.

In the 1970s the U.S. turned from a structured, orderly, relatively stable society to one run by power blocs, each with a narrow focus on its own interest, populist in character with an aversion toward the big institutions of business and government, and biased toward egalitarianism. During the 70s the U.S. economy also lost much of its dynamism. Some American companies lost their competitive position in world markets. U.S. economic policy seemed unable to cope with a decline in the growth of productivity, or with raging inflation, horrendous deficits in the balance of payments, a declining dollar, and a clear loss of power in world politics.

From a review of the 50-year period, one startling contrast emerges. That is the difference in the way Americans responded during the first ten years of the half-century compared with the response in the 60s and 70s. In the 30s the public demonstrated exemplary patience despite considerable suffering from abysmal economic conditions. Unemployment, hunger, cold, and death notwithstanding, there were no riots, revolts, or coups d'etat. No such patience was shown in the 60s and 70s. They were a time of riots, civil disobedience, of refusal to serve in the military. Government, instead of being respected, became suspect. Out of Watergate came a disillusionment that has not yet been dispelled.

Through the 50 years of crisis, wars, and drama, the U.S. changed from a simple society—principally exploiting the natural resources of a heavily endowed continent—into a complex urban society whose voice dominated the world for almost half the period. In 1929 its businesses still often reflected the personality of the founding entrepreneurs, whose aim was not only to make money but also to build an empire that would immortalize the founder's name. By 1979 most of these businesses had been acquired and turned into giant impersonal multinationals, run mainly by professional managers whose focus was short term, mainly on earnings per share. Distrust of these corporations coincided with a buildup of environmental and transportation problems that threatened to overwhelm society.

THE FUTURE

Just as 1929 was a watershed year, 1979 is one of transition. By 2029 people will have recognized that today marks the end of the industrial society as we have defined it. The tendency to mass operations, which built the world economy to today's levels, has peaked.

In a new book to be published next year, futurist Alvin Toffler predicts that the industrial society will be replaced by a "Third Wave" in which diversity, not uniformity, will be the key to civilization. The rhythms behind Toffler's Third Wave spring from deep psychological, economic, and technological forces. The businesses that will prosper in the future are those that learn how to customize their products and services—as opposed to standardizing them—at lowest cost, and that can apply the latest technology to the individualization of products and services. To cut costs, the successful producers will use carefully standardized components that fit together in highly customized configurations.

As the industrial society dissipates, so will mass production, mass marketing, the mass media. Toffler, examining what the industrial society was, predicts some of what the next 50 years will bring by looking for exact opposites. The industrial society, he says, was "a civilization based on fossil fuels, on a certain level of technology, on mass transportation, on mass distribution, on the nuclear family, mass education and the corporation, on the mass media, and above all, on the marketplace."

Most of those dependencies will be gone by the year 2029. New industries will spring up. The United States will lose its steel, auto, railroad equipment, machinery, appliance, textile, shoe, and apparel industries to producers in other countries, because American companies are unable or unwilling to compete and because these industries are liquidating themselves in the inflation that has wracked the United States since 1971. Taxes paid on artificial profits produced by increases in the values of inventories, and depreciation insufficient to reproduce the fixed assets, are liquidating corporations in businesses that maintain high inventories and operate lots of plant and equipment.

That does not mean the United States will turn into a society whose people exist by taking in each other's laundry. The old industries will be replaced by at least five others: semiconductors and electronics, information processing, oceanography, industrial applications of space, and molecular biology. What happens in the United States will also evolve in the rest of the industrialized West, because modern communications speed details of such developments around the world.

As mass production wanes and information-processing technology is introduced widely, the factory as we know it will disappear. On assembly lines robots will do much of the work. Many employees will no longer go to a centralized place to perform their jobs; instead, they will work at home. Thus, the United States will see a rise in an electronic version of cottage industries. More people will work in services, too, dealing with people rather than machines.

The return to cottage industries (the production method of 200 years ago) has great implications for society and the way people will live. Employees will have greater control of how they do their jobs. The whole family will be involved in the work—parents, children, and relatives. Sociologists predict that this will strengthen the family unit and reverse the deterioration of family ties that has been under way for nearly 15 years.

But the new cottage industries will also create psychological havoc. Technology will speed job obsolescence. People will have to change careers—not just jobs—three or four times in their lifetimes. By 2029 people will have so many occupational options they will be overwhelmed by the variety, freedom, and opportunity of choice. That could force the government to move in with career-planning programs and tell people what they will do.

One important aspect of the industrial society, according to Toffler, was its separation of the production function from consumption. Factories mass-produced goods that had to be purchased by consumers through the complex of the market with its complicated distribution channels. During the next 50 years, however, Toffler sees a Prosumer emerging, an individual who produces and consumes his own products and services. For example, by calling a computerized information system a person will receive detailed instructions on how to repair the family car and home appliances, cure minor illnesses, or prepare legal documents.

Fifty years from today, people will live 10 to 12 years longer. The standard of living will be much higher. There will be more leisure, more education, and more appreciation of and participation in the arts. The improvement in lifestyle over that of 1979 will be even greater than 1979's improvement over 1929.

But getting to the year 2029 will not be painless. Until at least 2000, the world will be struggling with shortages—shortages of energy, raw materials, and skilled labor. These are the kinds of forces that can lead to war.

The competition for natural resources and markets, combined with growing nationalism, will pit industrialized country against industrialized country, Communist against non-Communist, less developed nations against industrialized countries. The rise of religious nationalism in the Middle East threatens another kind of war. And inside countries there will be increased societal tensions as minorities assert their identities and demand rights to jobs, income, and advancement in society.

John Maynard Keynes emerged as the giant of the past 50 years in economic thought. His greatest insight was that courage was not enough to bring society to full utilization. The great guru of the next 50 years probably has already been born, but has not yet been identified. His contribution will be to devise a way for government to fight inflation while creating a stable environment in which individuals can express themselves, achieve their aspirations, and enjoy the fruits of new technology. That is the challenge of the next 50 years.

Bibliography ═══════════════════════════

Aaker David A., and Day, George S. *Consumerism: Search for the Consumer Interest.* 2d ed. Homewood, Ill.: Richard D. Irwin, 1974.

Abegglen, James C. *Management and the Worker: The Japanese Solution.* Tokyo: Sophia University, 1973.

Abell, Derek F., and Hammond, John S. *Strategic Marketing Planning: Problems and Analytical Approaches.* Englewood Cliffs, N.J.: Prentice-Hall, 1979.

Abrahams, N. M., Atwater, D. C., and Alf, E. F. "Unobtrusive Measurement of Racial Basis in Job-Placement Decisions." *Journal of Applied Psychology,* vol. 62 (1977).

Abt, Clark C. *The Social Audit for Management.* New York: American Management Association, 1977.

Ackerman, Robert W. "How Companies Respond to Social Demands." *Harvard Business Review,* vol. 51, no. 4 (July–August 1973), pp. 88–98.

―――――. *The Social Challenge to Business.* Cambridge, Mass.: Harvard University Press, 1975.

―――――, and Bauer, Raymond A. *Corporate Social Performance: The Modern Dilemma.* Reston, Va.: Reston Publishing Co., 1976.

Adams, Henry. *The Education of Henry Adams.* New York: The Modern Library, 1931.

Adizes, Ichak, and Borgese, Elisabeth Mann, eds. *Self-Management: New Dimensions to Democracy.* Santa Barbara, Calif.: Clio Books, 1975.

Allen, Frederick Lewis. *Only Yesterday: An Informal History of the 1920s.* New York: Harper and Row, Publishers, 1931.

―――――. *The Lords of Creation.* New York: Harper and Row, Publishers, 1935.

―――――. *Since Yesterday: The Nineteen-Thirties in America.* New York: Harper and Row, Publishers, 1940.

————. *The Big Change: America Transforms Itself, 1900–1950.* New York: Harper & Row, Publishers, 1952.

Anderson, Howard J. *Primer of Equal Employment Opportunity.* Washington, D.C.: The Bureau of National Affairs, 1978.

Andreasen, Alan R. *The Disadvantaged Consumer.* New York: The Free Press, 1975.

Andrews, Kenneth R. "Can the Best Corporations Be Made Moral?" *Harvard Business Review,* vol. 51, no. 3 (May–June 1973), pp. 57–64.

Andrews, F. Emerson. *Corporation Giving.* New York: Russell Sage Foundation, 1952.

Anshen, Melvin, ed. *Managing the Socially Responsible Corporation.* New York: The Macmillan Company, 1974.

Anshen, Melvin. *Strategies for Corporate Social Performance.* New York: Macmillan, 1980.

Anthrop, Donald F. *Noise Pollution.* Lexington, Mass.: D. C. Heath & Co., 1973.

Arnold, Thurman W. *The Folklore of Capitalism.* New Haven, Conn.: Yale University Press, 1938.

Aronoff, Craig E., ed. *Business and the Media.* Santa Monica: Calif.: Goodyear Publishing Company, 1979.

Arrow, Kenneth J. *Social Choice and Individual Values.* 2d ed. New Haven: Yale University Press, 1963.

Ball, George W., ed. *Global Companies: The Political Economy of World Business.* Englewood Cliffs, N.J.: Prentice-Hall, 1975.

Barach, Jeffrey. *The Individual, Business & Society.* Englewood Cliffs, N.J.: Prentice-Hall, 1977.

Barber, Richard J. *The American Corporation: Its Power, Its Money, Its Politics.* New York: E. P. Dutton & Co., 1970.

Barci, Oscar T., and Blake, Nelson. *Since 1900.* New York: Macmillan, 1952.

Barnes, Norman Kurt. "Rethinking Corporate Charity." *Fortune,* vol. 90, no. 4 (October 1974), pp. 169–71, 174, 179–80, and 182.

Barnet, Richard J., and Muller, Ronald E. *Global Reach: The Power of the Multinational Corporation.* New York: Simon & Schuster, 1974.

Baron, Robert Alex. *The Tyranny of Noise.* New York: St. Martin's Press, 1970.

Bartels, Robert. *Ethics in Business.* Columbus, Ohio: Bureau of Business Research, College of Commerce and Administration, The Ohio State University, 1963.

Basche, James R., Jr. *Unusual Foreign Payments: A Survey of the Policies and Practices of U.S. Companies.* New York: The Conference Board, 1976.

Bauer, Raymond A., ed. *Social Indicators.* Cambridge, Mass.: The M.I.T. Press, 1967.

————, and Fenn, Dan H., Jr. *The Corporate Social Audit.* New York: Russell Sage Foundation, 1972.

————, and Greyser, Stephen A. *Advertising in America: The Consumer View.* Boston: Harvard University Press, 1968.

————; Pool, Ithiel de Sola; and Dexter, Lewis Anthony. *American Business and Public Policy: The Politics of Foreign Trade.* Chicago: Aldine-Atherton, 1972.

Baumhart, Raymond. *An Honest Profit: What Businessmen Say about Ethics in Business.* New York: Holt, Rinehart & Winston, 1968.

Beard, Miriam. *A History of Business.* 2 vols. Ann Arbor: University of Michigan Press, 1962–63.

Beesley, Michael, and Evans, Tom. *Corporate Social Responsibility.* Totowa, N.J.: Biblio Distribution Centre, 1978.

Bell, Daniel. *The Coming of Post-Industrial Society: A Venture in Social Forecasting.* New York: Basic Books, 1973.

————. "The Revolution of Rising Entitlements." *Fortune,* vol. 91, no. 4 (April 1975), pp. 98–103, 182–85.

————. *The Cultural Contradictions of Capitalism.* New York: Basic Books, 1976.

Bendix, Reinhard. *Work and Authority in Industry: Ideologies of Management in the Course of Industrialization.* New York: John Wiley & Sons, 1956.

Bennis, Warren G.; Benne, Kenneth D; and Chine, Robert, eds. *The Planning of Change.* New York: Holt, Rinehart and Winston, 1969.

Benokraitis, Mijole, and Feagin, Joe R. *Affirmative Action and Equal Opportunity: Action, Inaction, and Reaction.* Boulder, Col.: Westview Press, 1978.

Berg, Ivar. *The Business of America.* New York: Harcourt, Brace & World, 1968.

Berland, Theodore. *The Fight for Quiet.* Englewood Cliffs, N.J.: Prentice-Hall, 1970.

Berle, Adolph A. *The Twentieth Century Capitalist Revolution.* New York: Harcourt, Brace & World, 1954.

————. *Power without Property: A New Development in American Political Economy.* New York: Harcourt, Brace & World, 1959.

————, and Means, Gardiner C. *The Modern Corporation and Private Property.* rev. ed. New York: Harcourt, Brace & World, 1967.

Best, Fred, ed. *The Future of Work.* Englewood Cliffs, N.J.: Prentice-Hall, 1973.

Beveridge, Oscar M. *Financial Public Relations: Tested Techniques for Communicating with Financial Publics.* New York: McGraw-Hill Book Co., 1963.

Bishop, James, Jr., and Hubbard, Henry W. *Let the Seller Beware.* Washington, D.C.: The National Press, 1969.

Bjork, Gordon C. *Private Enterprise and Public Interest.* Englewood Cliffs, N.J.: Prentice-Hall, 1969.

Black, Hillel. *Buy Now, Pay Later.* New York: William Morrow and Co., 1961.

Blair, John M. *The Control of Oil.* New York: Pantheon Books, 1976.

Blake, David H., Frederick, William C.; and Myers, Mildred S. *Social Auditing: Evaluating the Impact of Corporate Programs.* New York: Praeger Publishers, 1976.

————, and Walters, Robert S. *The Politics of Global Economic Relations* Englewood Cliffs, N.J.: Prentice-Hall, 1976.

Blau, Peter M., and Duncan, Otis Dudley. *The American Occupational Structure.* New York: John Wiley and Sons, 1967.

Bliss, Edward, Jr. *In Search of Light: The Broadcasts of Edward R. Murrow, 1938–1961.* New York: Avon Books, 1967.

Blumberg, A. *The Scales of Justice.* Chicago: Aldine Transaction Books, 1970.

Blumberg, Paul. *Industrial Democracy*. London: Constable and Co., 1968.

Blumberg, Philip I. *The Megacorporation in American Society*. Englewood Cliffs, N.J.: Prentice-Hall, 1975.

Boorstin, Daniel J. *The Americans: The Democratic Experience*. New York: Vintage Books, 1974.

Boulding, Kenneth E. "The Economics of the Coming Spaceship Earth." In *Environmental Quality in a Growing Economy*, edited by Henry Jorrett. Baltimore: Johns Hopkins Press for Resources for the Future, 1966.

Boulton, David. *The Grease Machine: The Inside Story of Lockheed's Dollar Diplomacy*. New York: Harper & Row, Publishers, 1978.

Bowerman, Frank R. "Managing Solid Waste Disposal." *California Management Review*, vol. 14, no. 3 (Spring 1972), pp. 104–6.

Bowman, Edward H., and Haire, Mason. "A Strategic Posture Toward Corporate Social Responsibility." *California Management Review*, vol. 14, no. 3 (Spring 1972), pp. 104–6.

Brenner, Steven N., and Molander, Earl A. "Is the Ethics of Business Changing?" *Harvard Business Review* (January–February, 1977).

Briloff, Abraham J. *Unaccountable Accouting: Games Accountants Play*. New York: Harper & Row, Publishers, 1972.

Brown, Courtney C. *Putting the Corporate Board to Work*. New York: Macmillan, 1976.

————. *Beyond the Bottom Line*. New York: Macmillan, 1979.

Brown, William H., III. "Voluntarism and EEOC." *The Conference Board Record*, vol. 10, no. 8 (August 1973), pp. 55–57.

Brownlee, W. Elliot, and Brownlee, Mary M. *Women in the American Economy: A Documentary History, 1675 to 1929*. New Haven, Conn.: Yale University Press, 1976.

Bruyn, Severyn T. *The Social Economy: People Transforming Modern Business*. New York: Ronald Press Co., 1977.

Bunting, John R. *The Hidden Face of Free Enterprise*. New York: McGraw-Hill, 1964.

Bureau of the Census. *Social and Economic Characteristics of the Older Population: 1974*. Current Population Reports, Special Studies Series P–23, no. 57, U.S. Department of Commerce, November 1975.

Bureau of National Affairs, Inc. *The Equal Employment Opportunity Act of 1972*. Washington, D.C., 1973.

Campbell, Robert. *The Golden Years of Broadcasting*. New York: Charles Scribner's Sons, 1976.

Cannon, James S. *Environmental Steel: Pollution in the Iron and Steel Industry*. New York: Praeger Publishers, 1974.

Caplovitz, David. *The Poor Pay More*. New York: The Free Press, 1967.

Carr, Albert Z. "Is Business Bluffing Ethical?" *Harvard Business Review*, vol. 46, no. 1 (January–February 1968), pp. 145–53.

————. "Can an Executive Afford a Conscience?" *Harvard Business Review*, vol. 48, no. 4 (July–August 1970), pp. 58–64.

Carroll, Archie, ed. *Managing Corporate Social Responsibility*. Boston: Little, Brown and Company, 1977.

Carson, Rachel. *Silent Spring*. Boston: Houghton Mifflin Co. 1962.

Catlin, Warren B. *The Labor Problem in the United States and Great Britain.* New York: Harper and Row, Publishers, 1935.

Cavanagh, Gerald F. *American Business Values in Transition.* Englewood Cliffs, N.J.: Prentice-Hall, 1976.

Chafe, William H. *The American Woman: Her Changing Social, Economic, and Political Roles, 1920–1970.* New York: Oxford University Press, 1972.

Chagy, Gideon, ed. *Business in the Arts '70.* New York: Paul J. Eriksson, 1970.

Chamberlain, John. *The Roots of Capitalism.* New York: D. Van Nostrand & Co., 1959.

Chamberlain, Neil W. *Enterprise and Environment: The Firm in Time and Place.* New York: McGraw-Hill Book Co., 1968.

————. *Business and the Cities: A Book of Relevant Readings.* New York: Basic Books, 1970.

————. *The Limits of Corporate Responsibility.* New York: Basic Books, 1973.

————. *The Place of Business in America's Future: A Study in Social Values.* New York: Basic Books, 1973.

Chandler, Alfred D., Jr. *Strategy and Structure. Chapters in the History of the Industrial Enterprise.* Cambridge, Mass.: The M.I.T. Press, 1962.

————. *The Visible Hand: The Managerial Revolution in American Business.* Cambridge, Mass.: The Belknap Press of Harvard University Press, 1977.

Chandler, Marvin. "It's Time to Clean up the Boardroom." *Harvard Business Review,* vol. 53, no. 5 (September–October 1975), pp. 73–82.

Chatov, Robert. *Corporate Financial Reporting: Public or Private Control?* New York: The Free Press, 1975.

Cheit, Earl F., ed. *The Business Establishment.* New York: John Wiley & Sons, 1964.

Christoffel, Tom; Finkelhor, David; and Gilbarg, Dan. *Up Against the American Myth.* New York: Holt, Rinehart and Winston, 1970.

Churchill, Neil C. "Toward a Theory for Social Accounting." *Sloan Management Review,* vol. 15, no. 3 (Spring 1974), pp. 1–17.

Clark, John W. *Religion and the Moral Standards of American Businessmen.* Cincinnati: South-Western Publishing Co., 1966.

Cleary, Edward J. *The ORSANCO Story: Water Quality Management in the Ohio Valley under an Interstate Compact.* Baltimore: The Johns Hopkins Press, 1967.

Clifford, Donald K., Jr. *Managing the Threshhold Company; the Making of Tomorrow's Leaders.* New York: McKinsey & Co., 1973.

Cochran, Thomas C. *Business in American Life: A History.* New York: McGraw-Hill Book Co., 1972.

————, and Miller, William. *The Age of Enterprise: A Social History of Industrial America.* New York: The Macmillan Co., 1942.

Cohen, Sanford. *Labor in the United States.* Columbus, Ohio: Charles E. Merrill Publishing Co., 1975.

Committee for Economic Development. *Social Responsibilities of Business Corporations: A Statement on National Policy by the Research and Policy Committee of the Committee for Economic Development.* New York: Committee for Economic Development, 1971.

_____ . *More Effective Programs for a Cleaner Environment.* New York: 1974.

Commission on Freedom of the Press, The. *A Free and Responsible Press.* Chicago: The University of Chicago Press, 1947.

Commoner, Barry. *The Closing Circle.* New York: Alfred A. Knopf, 1971.

Conference Board, The. *Corporate Organization for Pollution Control.* New York, 1970.

Congressional Quarterly, Inc. *American Work Ethic.* Washington, D.C., 1973.

Cook, Thomas I. *Two Treatises of Government by John Locke.* New York: Hafner Publishing Co., 1947.

Cordiner, Ralph J. *New Frontiers for Professional Managers.* New York: McGraw-Hill Book Co., 1956.

Corson, John J. *Business in the Humane Society.* New York: McGraw-Hill Book Co., 1971.

_____ . "A Corporate Social Audit?" *The Center Magazine,* vol. 5, no. 1 (January–February 1972), pp. 62–65.

_____ , and Steiner, George A. *Measuring Business's Social Performance: The Corporate Social Audit.* New York: Committee for Economic Development, 1974.

Council on Economic Priorities. *Paper Profits: Pollution in the Pulp and Paper Industry.* New York, 1971.

_____ . *The Price of Power: Electric Utilities and the Environment.* New York, 1972.

_____ . *Guide to Corporations: A Social Perspective.* Chicago: The Swallow Press, 1974.

Cox, Edward F.; Fellmeth, Robert C.; and Schulz, John E. *The Nader Report on the FTC.* New York: Richard W. Baron Publishing Co., 1969.

Crew, David F. *Industry and Community.* New York: Columbia University Press, 1979.

Cross, Theodore L. *Black Capitalism: Strategy for Business in the Ghetto.* New York: Atheneum, 1969.

Cunningham, Lynn E., et al. *Strengthening Citizen Access and Governmental Accountability.* Washington, D.C.: Exploratory Project for Economic Alternatives, 1977.

Curtiss, Ellen T., and Untersee, Philip A. *Corporate Responsibilities and Opportunities to 1990.* Lexington, Mass.: Lexington Books, 1979.

Dahl, Robert A. *After the Revolution?* New Haven, Conn: Yale University Press, 1970.

Dale, Ernest. *The Great Organizers.* New York: McGraw-Hill Book Co., 1960.

Dales, J. H. *Pollution, Property, and Prices.* Toronto: University of Toronto Press, 1968.

Dankert, Clyde E.; Mann, Floyd C.; and Northrup, Herbert R., eds. *Hours of Work.* New York: Harper & Row, Publishers, 1965.

Davis, Keith, and Blomstrom, Robert L. *Business and Society: Environment and Responsibility.* 3d ed. New York: McGraw-Hill Book Co., 1975.

DeGeorge, Richard T., and Pichler, Joseph A., eds. *Ethics, Free Enterprise, and Public Policy: Original Essays on Moral Issues in Business.* New York: Oxford University Press, 1978.

Dejon, William L. *Policy Formulation.* New York: CBI Publishers, 1979.

De Schweinitz, Karl, Jr. *Industrialization and Democracy*. Glencoe, Ill.: The Free Press of Glencoe, 1964.

Dewey, John. *Democracy and Education*. New York: Macmillan, 1916.

Dierkes, Mienholf, and Bauer, Raymond A., eds. *Corporate Social Accounting*. New York: Praeger Publishers, 1973.

Dill, William R., ed. *Running the American Corporation*. New York: The American Assembly, Columbia University, 1978.

Dolan, Edwin G. *TANSTAAFL: The Economic Strategy for Environmental Crisis*. New York: Holt, Rinehart & Winston, 1971.

Domhoff, William. *Who Rules America?* Englewood Cliffs, N.J.: Prentice-Hall, 1967.

Donner, Frederick G. *The World-Wide Industrial Enterprise: Its Challenge and Promise*. New York: McGraw-Hill Book Co., 1967.

Douglas, William O. *Democracy and Finance*. New Haven, Conn.: Yale University Press, 1940.

Doz, Yves L., and Prakalad, C. K. "How MNCs Cope with Host Government Intervention." *Harvard Business Review*, vol. 58, no. 2 (March–April 1980).

Drucker, Peter F. *Technology, Management, and Society*. New York: Harper & Row, Publishers, 1970.

————. *The Concept of the Corporation*. rev. ed. New York: John Day Co., 1972.

————. *Management*. New York: Harper and Row, Publishers, 1973.

————. *Management: Tasks, Responsibilities, Practices* New York: Harper & Row, Publishers, 1974.

Durant, Will. *The Reformation: A History of European Civilization from Wyclif to Calvin: 1300–1564*. New York: Simon & Schuster, Inc., 1957.

Edwards, Richard C.; Reich, Michael; and Weisskopf, Thomas E. *The Capitalist System: A Radical Analysis of American Society*. Englewood Cliffs, N.J.: Prentice-Hall, 1972.

Eells, Richard. *Corporation Giving in a Free Society*. New York: Harper and Row, Publishers, 1956.

————. *The Meaning of Modern Business*. New York: Columbia University Press, 1960.

————, and Walton, Clarence. *Conceptual Foundations of Business*. 3d ed. Homewood, Ill.: Richard D. Irwin, 1974.

Ehrlich, Paul R. *The Population Bomb*. New York: Ballantine Books, 1968.

Eichner, Alfred S. *The Emergence of Oligopoly: Sugar Refining as a Case Study*. Baltimore, Md.: The Johns Hopkins Press, 1969.

Eilbirt, Henry, and Parket, I. R. "The Corporate Responsibility Officer: A New Position on the Organization Chart." *Business Horizons*, February 1973.

Elbing, Alvar O.; Gadon, Herman; and Gordon, John R. M. "Flexible Working Hours: It's about Time." *Harvard Business Review*, vol. 52, no. 1 (January–February 1974), pp. 18–28, 33, 154–55.

Elkins, Arthur, and Callaghan, Dennis W. *A Managerial Odyssey: Problems in Business and Its Environment*. Reading, Mass.: Addison-Wesley Publishing Co., 1975.

Emery, Edwin. *The Press and America: An Interpretative History of the Mass Media.* Englewood Cliffs, N.J.: Prentice-Hall, 1972.

Emmet, Boris, and Jeuck, John E. *Catalogues and Counters: Roebuck and Company.* Chicago: The University of Chicago, 1900.

Engler, Robert. *The Brotherhood of Oil: Energy Policy and the Public Interest.* New York: A Mentor Book, 1978.

————. *The Price of Power: Electric Utilities and the Environment.* New York, 1972.

Epstein, Cynthia Fuchs. *Woman's Place: Options and Limits in Professional Careers.* Berkeley: University of California Press, 1970.

Epstein, Edwin M., and Votaw, Dow. *Rationality, Legitimacy, Responsibility: Search for New Directions in Business & Society.* Santa Monica, Calif.: Goodyear Publishing Co., 1978.

Epstein, Edwin M. *The Corporation in American Politics.* Englewood Cliffs, N.J.: Prentice-Hall, 1969.

Etzioni, Amitai. *The Active Society.* New York: The Free Press, 1968.

Ewing, David W. *Freedom inside the Organization: Bringing Civil Liberties to the Workplace.* New York: McGraw-Hill Book Co., 1977.

Farley, Lin. *Sexual Shakedown: The Sexual Harassment of Women on the Job.* New York: McGraw-Hill Book Co., 1978.

Fatemi, Nasrollah, and Williams, Gail W. *Multinational Corporations: The Problems and Prospects.* New York: A. S. Barnes & Co., 1975.

Fellmeth, Robert. *The Interstate Commerce Omission.* New York: Grossman Publishers, 1970.

Fine, Sidney. *Laissez Faire and the General Welfare State.* Ann Arbor: The University of Michigan Press, 1956.

Finn, David. *The Corporate Oligarch.* New York: Simon & Schuster, 1969.

Fisk, George. *Marketing and the Ecological Crisis.* New York: Harper & Row, Publishers, 1974.

Foner, Philip. *Organized Labor and the Black Worker, 1619–1973.* New York: Praeger Publishers, 1974.

Foster, Le Baron R. *Telling a Company's Financial Story.* New York: Financial Executives Research Foundation, Inc., 1964.

Freeman, Roger. *The Growth of American Government.* Stanford: Hoover Institution Press, 1975.

Fremont-Smith, Marion R. *Philanthropy and the Business Corporation.* New York: Russell Sage Foundation, 1972.

Friedman, Milton. *Capitalism and Freedom.* Chicago: The University Press, 1962.

Galbraith, John Kenneth. *The New Industrial State.* 3d ed. Boston: Houghton Mifflin Co., 1970.

————. *Economics and the Public Purpose.* Boston: Houghton Mifflin Co., 1973.

————. "The Defense of the Multinational Company." *Harvard Business Review,* vol. 56, no. 2 (March–April 1978).

Garrett, Thomas M. *Business Ethics.* New York: Appleton-Century-Crofts, 1966.

Gelber, Steven M. *Black Men and Businessmen.* Port Washington, N.Y.; Kennikat Press, 1974.

Gingrich, Arnold, ed. *Business and the Arts: An Answer to Tomorrow.* New York: Paul J. Eriksson, Inc., 1967.

Ginzberg, Eli, ed. *The Negro Challenge to the Business Community.* New York: McGraw-Hill Book Co., 1964.

————, and Yohalem, Alice M. *Corporate Lib: Women's Challenge to Management.* Baltimore: The Johns Hopkins Press, 1973.

Glazer, Nathan. *Affirmative Discrimination: Ethnic Inequality and Public Policy.* New York: Basic Books, Inc., 1975.

Goldman, Marshall I., ed. *Ecology and Economics.* Englewood Cliffs, N.J.: Prentice-Hall, 1972.

————, ed. *Controlling Pollution: The Economics of a Cleaner America.* Englewood Cliffs, N.J.; Prentice-Hall, 1967.

Goldston, Eli. *The Quantification of Concern: Some Aspects of Social Accounting.* Pittsburgh: Carnegie Press, 1971.

Gordon, Francine E., and Strober, Myra H., eds. *Bringing Women into Management.* New York: McGraw-Hill Book Co., 1975.

Gordon, Robert A. *Business Leadership in the Large Corporation.* Berkeley: University of California Press, 1961.

Gras, N. S. B. *Business and Capitalism: An Introduction to Business History.* New York: F. S. Crofts and Co., 1939.

Gray, Irwin, with Bases, Albert L.; Martin, Charles H.; and Sternberg, Alexander. *Product Liability: A Management Response.* New York: AMACOM, 1975.

Green, Mark J. *The Other Government: The Unseen Power of Washington Lawyers.* New York: Grossman Publishers, 1975.

Green, Mark J., ed. *The Monopoly Makers: Ralph Nader's Study Group Report on Regulation and Competition.* New York: Grossman Publishers, 1973.

————; Moore, Beverly C., Jr.; and Wasserstein, Bruce. *The Closed Enterprise System.* New York: Grossman Publishers, 1972.

Greenberg, Edward S. *Serving the Few: Corporate Capitalism and the Bias of Government Policy.* New York: John Wiley & Sons, 1974.

————. *Understanding Modern Government: The Rise and Decline of the American Political Economy.* New York: John Wiley & Sons, 1979.

Greenwood, William T. *Issues in Business & Society.* 3d ed. Boston: Houghton Mifflin Co., 1976.

Gunness, Robert. "Social Responsibility: The Art of the Possible." *Business and Society Review,* no. 12. (Winter 1974–75), pp. 94–99.

Gyllenhammer, Pehr. "Volvo's Solution to the Blue-Collar Blues." *Business and Society Review/Innovation,* no. 7 (Autumn 1973), pp. 50–53.

Hacker, Andrew, ed. *The Corporation Take-Over.* Garden City, N.Y.: Doubleday & Co., 1964.

————. *The End of the American Era.* New York: Atheneum, 1970.

Hackman, Richard J.; Oldham, Greg; Jansen, Robert; and Purdy, Kenneth. "A New Strategy for Job Enrichment." *California Management Review,* vol. 17, no. 4 (Summer 1975), pp. 57–71.

Haddad, William F., and Pugh, G. Douglas, eds. *Black Economic Development.* Englewood Cliffs, N.J.: Prentice-Hall, 1969.

Hagevik, George H. *Decision Making in Air Pollution Control.* New York: Praeger Publishers, 1970.

Halberstram, David. *The Best and the Brightest.* New York: Random House, 1972.

————. *The Powers That Be.* New York: Alfred A. Knopf, 1979.

Hamilton, Alice. *Exploring the Dangerous Trades.* New York: Harper & Row, Publishers, 1948.

Harrington, Michael. *The Twilight of Capitalism.* New York: Simon and Schuster, 1976.

Harris, Richard. *Freedom Spent.* Boston: Little, Brown & Company, 1976.

Hay, Robert D.; Gray, Edmund D.; and Gates, James E. *Business and Society.* Cincinnati: South-Western Publishing Co., 1976.

Heald, Morrell T. *The Social Responsibilities of Business: Company and Community, 1900–1960.* Cleveland: The Press of Case Western Reserve, 1970.

Heilbroner, Robert L. *The Future of Capitalism.* New York: Macmillan, 1967.

————. "Rhetoric and Reality in the Struggle between Business and the State." *Social Research,* vol. 35, no. 3 (Autumn 1968), pp. 401–25.

————, ed. *In the Name of Profit: Profiles in Corporate Irresponsibility.* Garden City, N.Y.: Doubleday & Co., 1972.

Henry, Harold W. *Pollution Control: Corporate Responses.* New York: AMACOM, 1974.

Hess, Karl. *Dear America.* New York: William Morrow and Co., 1975.

Heyne, Paul T. *Private Keepers of the Public Interest.* New York: McGraw-Hill Book Co., 1968.

Hill, David A., Chaples, Ernest A.; Downey, Matthew, T.; Singell, Larry D.; Solzman, David M.; and Swatez, Gerald M. *The Quality of Life in America: Pollution, Poverty, Power, and Fear.* New York: Holt, Rinehart & Winston, 1973.

Hodgetts, Richard M. *The Business Enterprise: Social Challenge, Social Response.* Philadelphia: W. B. Saunders & Co., 1977.

Holland, Ruth. *Mill Child.* New York: Macmillan, 1970.

Holmes, Sandra L. "Adapting Corporate Structure for Social Responsiveness." *California Management Review,* vol. 21, no. 1 (Fall 1978), p. 47.

Howard, Marshall C. *Legal Aspects of Marketing.* New York: McGraw-Hill Book Co., 1964.

Hughes, Charles L. *Making Unions Unnecessary.* New York: Executive Enterprises Publications Co., 1976.

Hughes, Jonathan L. *The Vital Few: American Economic Progress and Its Protagonists.* Boston: Houghton Mifflin Co., 1966.

International Labour Office. *Multinational Enterprises and Social Policy.* Geneva, 1973.

Jacoby, Neil H. "The Environmental Crisis." *The Center Magazine,* vol. 3, no. 3 (May 1970), pp. 37–55.

————. "The Multinational Corporation." *The Center Magazine,* vol. 3, no. 6 (December 1970), pp. 37–48.

————. *Corporate Power and Social Responsibility.* New York: The Macmillan Co., 1973.

Janger, Allen R., and Schaeffer, Ruth G. *Managing Programs for the Disadvantaged.* New York: The Conference Board, 1970.

Jenkins, David. *Job Power: Blue and White Collar Democracy.* Garden City, N.Y.; Doubleday and Co., Inc., 1973.

Johnson, Harold L. "Socially Responsible Firms: An Empty Box or a Universal Set?" *Journal of Business,* vol. 39 (July 1966), pp. 394–99.

Johnson, Orace. "Corporate Giving: A Note on Profit Maximization and Accounting Disclosure." *Journal of Accounting Research,* vol. 3, no. 1 (Spring 1965), pp. 75–85.

Joseph, James A. "Corporate Philanthropy and the Recession." *Foundation News,* vol. 16, no. 3 (May–June 1975), pp. 32–35.

Josephson, Matthew. *The Robber Barons.* New York: Harcourt, Brace & World, 1962.

Kahn, Herman; Brown, William; and Martel, Leon. *The Next 200 Years: A Scenario for America and the World.* New York: William Morrow & Co., 1976.

Kapp, K. William. *The Social Costs of Private Enterprise.* New York: Schocken Books, 1971.

Kauffman, Carl B. *Man Incorporate: The Individual and His Work in an Organized Society.* New York: Anchor Books, 1969.

Kelley, William T. *New Consumerism: Selected Readings.* Columbus, Ohio: Grid, Inc., 1973.

Kelso, Louis, and Hetter, Patricia. *Two-Factor Theory: The Economics of Reality.* New York: Random House, 1968.

Kendrick, Alexander. *Prime Time: The Life of Edward R. Murrow.* New York: Avon Books, 1969.

Killian, Lewis M. *White Southerners.* New York: Random House, 1970.

Kintner, Earl W. *An Antitrust Primer: A Guide to Antitrust and Trade Regulation Laws for Businessmen.* New York: Macmillan, 1964.

————. *A Primer on the Law of Deceptive Practices.* New York: Macmillan, 1971.

Kirkland, Edward C. *Dream and Thought in the Business Community, 1860–1900.* Ithaca, N.Y.; Cornell University Press, 1956.

————. *Industry Comes of Age: Business, Labor, and Public Policy, 1860–1897.* Vol. 6. *The Economic History of the United States,* edited by Henry David et al. New York: Holt, Rinehart & Winston, 1961.

Klein, Thomas A. *Social Costs & Benefits of Business.* Englewood Cliffs, N.J.: Prentice-Hall, 1977.

Koch, Frank. *The New Corporate Philanthropy: How Society and Business Can Profit.* New York: Plenum Press, 1979.

Kohlmeier, Louis M., Jr. *The Regulators.* New York: Harper & Row. Publishers, 1970.

Kolko, Gabriel. *The Triumph of Conservatism: A Reinterpretation of American History, 1900–1960.* Chicago: Quadrangle Books, 1967.

Knowlton, P. A. *Profit Sharing Patterns.* Evanston, Ill.: Profit Sharing Research Foundation, 1954.

Kreps, Juanita. *Sex in the Marketplace: American Women at Work.* Baltimore: The Johns Hopkins University Press, 1971.

Krooss, Herman E. *American Economic Development.* 2d. ed. Englewood Cliffs, N.J.: Prentice-Hall, 1966.

484   Bibliography

_____. *Executive Opinion: What Business Leaders Said and Thought on Economic Issues, 1920–1960s*. Garden City, N.Y.: Doubleday & Co., 1970.

_____, and Gilbert, Charles. *American Business History*. Englewood Cliffs, N.J.: Prentice-Hall, 1972.

Kugel, Yerachmiel, and Gruenberg, Gladys W. *Ethical Perspectives on Business & Society*. Lexington, Mass.: Lexington Books, 1977.

Larson, John A., ed. *The Regulated Businessman: Business and Government*. New York: Holt, Rinehart & Winston, 1966.

Lasch, Christopher. *The Culture of Narcissism*. New York: W. W. Norton and Company, 1979.

Lasson, Kenneth. *The Workers: Portraits of Nine American Job Holders*. New York: Grossman Publishers, 1971.

Lazer, William, and Kelley, Eugene J. *Social Marketing: Perspectives and Viewpoints*. Homewood, Ill.: Richard D. Irwin, Inc., 1973.

Levitan, Sar A., and Johnston, William B. *Work Is Here to Stay, Alas*. Salt Lake City: Olympus Publishing Co., 1973.

Liebhavsky, H. H. *American Government and Business*. New York: John Wiley & Sons, 1971.

Light, Ivan H. *Ethnic Enterprise in America*. Berkeley, Calif.: University of California Press, 1972.

Linowes, David F. *The Corporate Conscience*. New York: Hawthorn Books, 1974.

Litschert, Robert J., et al. *The Corporate Role & Ethical Behavior: Concepts & Cases*. New York: Van Nos Reinhold Co., 1977.

Lobkowicz, Nicholas. *Marx and the Western World*. Notre Dame, Inc.: University of Notre Dame Press, 1967.

Lodge, George C. *The New American Ideology*. New York: Alfred A. Knopf, 1976.

Lorange, Peter, and Vancil, Richard F. *Strategic Planning Systems*. Englewood Cliffs, N.J.: Prentice-Hall, Inc., 1977.

Lovdal, Michael L.; Bauer, Raymond A.; and Treverton, Nancy H. "Public Responsibility Committees of the Board." *Harvard Business Review*, (May/June 1977), pp. 40–64, 178–81.

Lund, Leonard. *Corporate Organization for Environmental Policymaking*. New York: The Conference Board, 1974.

Lundborg, Louis B. *Future without Shock*. New York: W. W. Norton & Co., Inc., 1974.

Luthans, Fred, and Hodgetts, Richard M. *Social Issues in Business*. 2d ed. New York: Macmillan, 1976.

McCall, David B. "Profit: Spur for Solving Social Ills." *Harvard Business Review*, vol. 51, no. 3 (May–June 1973), pp. 46–56.

McClelland, David. C. *The Achieving Society*. New York: Van Nostrand Reinhold Co., 1961.

McConnell, Grant. *Private Power and American Democracy*. New York: Alfred A. Knopf, Inc., 1966.

Mace, Myles L. *Directors: Myth and Reality*. Boston: Division of Research, Harvard Graduate School of Business Administration, 1971.

McGuire, Joseph F.   *Business and Society.* New York: McGraw-Hill Book Co., 1963.

————.   "The Social Values of Economic Organization." *Review of Social Economy,* vol. 32, no. 1 (April 1974).

————.   "The Social Responsibility of the Corporation." Edwin B. Flippo, ed., *Evolving Concepts in Management.* Chicago: *Proceedings of the Academy of Management Meeting, December, 1964.*

MacIver, R. M.   *The Modern State.* London: Oxford University Press, 1929.

McKie, James W., ed.   *Social Responsibility and the Business Predicament.* Washington, D.C.: The Brookings Institution, 1974.

Magnuson, Warren G., and Carper, Jean.   *The Dark Side of the Marketplace.* Englewood Cliffs, N.J.: Prentice Hall, 1968.

Manne, Henry G., and Wallich, Henry C.   *The Modern Corporation and Social Responsibility.* Washington, D.C.: American Enterprise Institute for Public Policy Research, 1972.

Martyn, Howe.   *Multinational Business Management.* Lexington, Mass.: D. C. Heath & Co., 1970.

Mason, Edward S., ed.   *The Corporation in Modern Society.* Cambridge, Mass.: Harvard University Press, 1959.

Mason, R. Hal.   "Conflicts between Host Countries and the Multinational Enterprise." *California Management Review,* vol. 17, no. 1 (Fall 1974), pp. 5–14.

Mayer, Lawrence A.   "A Large Question about Large Corporations." *Fortune,* vol. 85, no. 5 (May 1972), pp. 185–87.

Medawar, Charles.   *The Social Audit Consumer Handbook: A Guide to the Social Responsibilities of Business to the Consumer.* Atlantic Highlands, N.J.: Humanities Press, Inc., 1978.

Meier, J. B., ed.   *Profit Sharing Manual.* Chicago: Council of Profit Sharing Industries, 1957.

Metz, Robert.   *CBS: Reflections in a Bloodshot Eye.* New York: A Signet Book, 1975.

Metzger, B. L.   *Profit Sharing in Perspective.* 2d ed. Evanston, Ill.: Profit Sharing Research Foundation, 1966.

Meyer, Mitchell, and Fox, Harland.   *Profile of Employee Benefits.* New York: The Conference Board, 1974.

Miller, William, ed.   *Men in Business.* New York: Harper Torchbooks, 1952.

Mills, C. Wright.   *White Collar: The American Middle Classes.* New York: Oxford University Press, 1956.

————.   *The Power Elite.* New York: Oxford University Press, 1957.

Mintz, Morton, and Cohen, Jerry S.   *America, Inc.: Who Owns and Operates the United States?* New York: Dell Publishing Co., Inc., 1972.

Mockler, Robert J.   *Business and Society.* New York: Harper & Row, Publishers, 1975.

Monsen, R. Joseph.   *Modern American Capitalism: Ideologies and Issues.* Boston: Houghton Mifflin Co., 1963.

————.   *Business and the Changing Environment.* New York: McGraw-Hill Book Co., 1973.

Moore, Wilbert E.   *The Professions: Roles and Rules.* New York: Russell Sage Foundation, 1970.

Morison, Elting E.   *From Know-How to Nowhere: The Development of American Technology.* New York: Basic Books, 1974.

Moss, Frank E.   *Initiatives in Corporate Responsibility.* Washington, D.C.: U.S. Government Printing Office, 1972.

Mueller, Robert K.   *New Directions for Directors: Behind the By-Laws.* Lexington, Mass.: Lexington Books, 1978.

Murray, Edward A., Jr.   "The Social Response Process in Commercial Banks: An Empirical Investigation." *Academy of Management Review,* vol. 1, no. 3 (July 1976), pp. 5–15.

Murthy, Svrinivasa, and Salter, Malcolm S.   "Should CEO Pay Be Linked to Results?" *Harvard Business Review,* vol. 53, no. 3 (May–June 1975), pp. 66–73.

Nadel, Mark V.   *The Politics of Consumer Protection.* New York: The Bobbs-Merrill Co., Inc., 1971.

Nader, Ralph.   *Unsafe at Any Speed: The Designed-in Dangers of the American Automobile.* New York: Grossman Publishers, 1972.

Nader, Ralph, Green, Mark J., and Seligman, Joel.   *Constitutionalizing the Corporation: The Case for the Federal Chartering of Giant Corporations.* Washington, D.C.: The Corporate Accountability Research Group, 1976.

————, ————, and ————.   *Taming the Giant Corporation.* New York: W. W. Norton & Co., Inc., 1976.

————, and Green, Mark J., eds.   *Corporate Power in America.* New York: Grossman Publishers, 1973.

National Academy of Engineering.   *Product Quality, Performance, and Cost.* Washington, D.C.: Government Printing Office, 1972.

National Industrial Conference Board.   *Organizing for Effective Public Affairs.* New York, 1969.

————.   *The Consumer Affairs Department: Organization and Function.* New York, 1973.

Nelson, Ralph L.   *Economic Factors in the Growth of Corporation Giving.* New York: National Bureau of Economic Research and Russell Sage Foundation, 1970.

Newcomer, Mabel.   *The Big Business Executive.* New York: Columbia University Press, 1955.

Nicholson, Edward A.; Litschert, Robert; and Anthony, William P.   *Business Responsibility and Social Issues.* Columbus, Ohio: Charles E. Merrill Publishing Co., 1974.

Nicolin, Curt.   *Private Industry in a Public World.* Reading, Mass.: Addison-Wesley Publishing Co., 1977.

Nisbet, Robert.   *Twilight of Authority.* New York: Oxford University Press, 1975.

O'Connor, Rochelle.   *Corporate Contributions in Smaller Companies.* New York: The Conference Board, 1973.

Orr, Leonard H., ed.   "Is Corporate Social Responsibility a Dead Issue?" *Business and Society Review,* no. 25 (Spring 1978), p. 4.

Orren, Karen.   *Corporate Power and Social Change: The Politics of the Life Insurance Industry.* Baltimore, Md.: Johns Hopkins University Press, 1974.

Ostlund, Lyman E.   "Are Middle Managers an Obstacle to Corporate Social Policy Implementation?" *Business and Society Review*, vol. 18, no. 2 (Spring 1978), p. 5.

Palamountain, Joseph C.   *The Politics of Distribution*. Cambridge: Harvard University Press, 1955.

Paluszek, John L.   *Will the Corporation Survive?* Reston, Va.: Reston Publishing Co., Inc., 1977.

Parsons, T.   "An Approach to Psychological Theory in Terms of the Theory of Action." in *Psychology: A Study of Science*. Sigmund Koch, ed., New York: McGraw-Hill Book Co., 1959, vol. 3, pp. 612–711.

Patrick, Kenneth G., and Eells, Richard.   *Education and the Business Dollar: A Study of Corporate Contributions Policy and American Education*. London: Macmillan, 1969.

Perrow, Charles.   *The Radical Attack on Business: A Critical Analysis*. New York: Harcourt Brace Jovanovich, 1972.

Peters, Charles, and Branch, Taylor.   *Blowing the Whistle: Dissent in the Public Interest*. New York: Frederick A. Praeger, 1972.

Peterson, Theodore; Jenson, Jay W.; and Rivers, William L.   *The Mass Media and Modern Society*. New York: Holt, Rinehart and Winston, 1965.

Pfeffer, J.   "Size and Composition of Corporate Board of Directors: The Organization and Its Environment. *Administrative Science Quarterly*, 1972b, 17.

Phatak, Arvind V.   *Evolution of World Enterprises*. New York: American Management Association, 1971.

Phelan, James, and Pozen, Robert.   *The Company State*. New York: Grossman Publishers, 1973.

Pirenne, Henri.   *Economic and Social History of Medieval Europe*. New York: Harcourt, Brace & World, Inc., 1937.

Poor, Riva.   *4 Days, 40 Hours: Reporting on a Revolution in Work and Leisure*. Cambridge, Mass.: Bursk & Poor Publishing, 1970.

Porter, Glenn.   *The Rise of Big Business, 1860–1910*. New York: Thomas Y. Crowell, Inc., 1973.

James E. Post.   *Risk and Response: Management and Social Change in the American Insurance Industry*. Lexington, Mass.: D. C. Heath & Co., 1976.

————.   *Corporate Behavior and Social Change*. Reston, Va.: Reston Publishing Company, Inc., 1978.

Preston, Lee E., and Post, James E.   *Private Management and Public Policy*. Englewood Cliffs, N.J.: Prentice-Hall, 1975.

————; Rey, Francoise; and Dierkes, Meinolf.   "Company Corporate Social Performance: Germany, France, Canada, and the U.S." *California Management Review*, vol. 20, no. 4 (Summer 1978), p. 40.

Profit Sharing Council.   *Guide to Modern Profit Sharing*. Chicago, Ill., 1973.

Purcell, Theodore V., and Cavanagh, Gerald F.   *Blacks in the Industrial World: Issues for the Manager*. New York: The Free Press, 1972.

Rather, Dan, and Herkowitz, Mickey.   *The Camera Never Blinks*. New York: Morrow, 1977.

Reich, Charles A.   *The Greening of America*. New York: Random House, 1970.

Reuschling, Thomas L.   "The Business Institution: A Redefinition of Social Role." *Business and Society*, vol. 9, no. 1 (Autumn 1968), pp. 28–32.

Reynolds, John I. "Improving Business Ethics: The President's Lonely Task." *Business and Society,* vol. 19, no. 1 (Fall 1978), p. 10.

Richman, Barry. "New Paths to Corporate Social Responsibility." *California Management Review,* vol. 15, no. 3 (Spring 1973), pp. 20–36.

Ridgeway, James. *The Politics of Ecology.* New York: E. P. Dutton and Co., Inc., 1970.

Roberts, Keith. "Shareholder Votes: Has Business Won Harvard's Heart?" *Business and Society Review,* no. 20 (Winter 1976–77), pp. 65–67.

Rockefeller, John D., III. *The Second American Revolution: Some Personal Observations.* New York: Harper & Row, Publishers, 1973.

Rose, Arnold M. *The Power Structure: Political Process in American Society.* Fair Lawn, N.J.: Oxford University Press, 1967.

Rose, Sanford. "Multinational Corporations in a Tough New World." *Fortune,* vol. 88, no. 2 (August 1973), pp. 52–56, 134.

Ross, Ralph. *Obligation.* Ann Arbor: The University of Michigan Press, 1970.

Roszak, Theodore. *The Making of a Counter Culture: Reflections on the Technocratic Society and Its Youthful Opposition.* Garden City, N.Y.: Anchor Books, 1969.

Rumelt, Richard P. *Strategy, Structure, and Economic Performance.* Boston: Division of Research, Graduate School of Business Administration, Harvard University, 1974.

Ruml, Beardsley, ed. *The Manual of Corporate Giving.* New York: National Planning Association, 1952.

Sampson, Anthony. *The Sovereign State: The Secret History of I.T.T.* New York: Stein & Day, Publishers, 1973.

―――――. *The Seven Sisters: The Great Oil Companies and the World They Shaped.* New York: The Viking Press, 1975.

Sanford, David. *Who Put the Con in Consumer?* New York: Liveright, 1972.

Sawyer, George. *Business & Society: Managing Corporate Social Impact.* Boston: Houghton Mifflin Co., 1978.

Schlei, Barbara Lindemann, and Grossman, Paul. *Employment Discrimination Law, 1979 Supplement.* Washington, D.C.: Bureau of National Affairs, Inc., 1979.

Schnapper, M. B. *American Labor: A Pictorial Social History.* Washington, D.C.: Public Affairs Press, 1972.

Schrag, Peter. *The End of the American Future.* New York: Simon & Schuster, Inc., 1973.

Schramm, Wilbur, ed. *Mass Communications.* Urbana: University of Illinois Press, 1960.

Schultze, Charles L. "The Public Use of Private Interest." *Harpers,* no. 254 (May 1977), pp. 43–62.

Schumpeter, Joseph A. *Capitalism, Socialism, and Democracy.* New York: Harper and Brothers, 1947.

Selekman, Sylvia K., and Selekman, Benjamin M. *Power and Morality in a Business Society.* New York: McGraw-Hill Book Co., 1956.

Serrin, William. *The Company and the Union: The "Civilized Relationship" of the General Motors Corporation and the United Automobile Workers.* New York: Alfred A. Knopf, 1973.

Sethi, S. Prakash. *Business Corporations and the Black Man: An Analysis of Social Conflict: The Kodak-FIGHT Controversy*. San Francisco: Chandler Publishing Co., 1970.

————. *Japanese Business and Social Conflict: A Comparative Analysis of Response Patterns with American Business*. Cambridge, Mass.: Ballinger Publishing Co., 1975.

————. *Advocacy Advertising and Large Corporations: Social Conflict, Big Business Image, the News Media, and Public Policy*. Lexington, Mass.: D. C. Heath & Co., 1977.

————. *Up Against the Corporate Wall*. 3d ed. Englewood Cliffs, N.J.: Prentice-Hall, 1977.

————, ed. *The Unstable Ground: Corporate Social Policy in a Dynamic Society*. Los Angeles: Melville Publishers, Inc., 1974.

————, and Holton, Richard H. *The Management of the Multinationals: Policies, Operations, and Research*. New York: The Free Press, 1974.

Shaffer, Butler D. "The Social Responsibility of Business: A Flawed Dissent Response." *Business and Society*, vol. 18, no. 2 (Spring 1978), p. 41.

Shapiro, Irving S. "Today's Executive: Private Steward and Public Servant." *Harvard Business Review*, no. 2 (March–April 1978), p. 94.

Shenfield, Barbara. *Company Boards: Their Responsibilities to Shareholders, Employees, and the Community*. London: George Allen & Unwin, 1971.

Sheppard, Harold L., and Herrick, Neal Q. *Where Have All the Robots Gone? Worker Dissatisfaction in the 70s*. New York: The Free Press, 1972.

Shostak, Arthur B., and Gomberg, William, eds. *Blue Collar World: Studies of the American Worker*. Englewood Cliffs, N.J.: Prentice-Hall, 1965.

Silk, Leonard, and Vogel, David. *Ethics and Profits: The Crisis of Confidence in American Business*. New York: Simon and Schuster, 1976.

Simon, William E. *A Time for Truth*. New York: McGraw-Hill Book Co., 1978.

Sloan, Alfred P., Jr. *My Years with General Motors*. Garden City, N.Y.: Doubleday & Co., 1964.

Smith, Adam. *The Wealth of Nations*. New York: The Modern Library, 1937.

Smuts, Robert W. *Women and Work in America*. New York: Schocken Books, 1974.

Sobin, Dennis P. *The Working Poor: Minority Workers in Low-Wage, Low-Skill Jobs*. Port Washington, N.Y.: Kennikat Press, 1973.

Sombart, Werner. *The Jews and Modern Capitalism*. New York: The Free Press, 1951.

Southard, Samuel. *Ethics for Executives*. New York: Thomas Nelson, 1975.

Steade, Richard D. *Business and Society in Transition: Issues and Concepts*. San Francisco: Canfield Press, 1975.

Steiner, George A. *Business and Society*. 2d ed. New York: Random House, 1975.

————. *Strategic Managerial Planning*. New York: Planning Executives Institute, 1977.

————, and Steiner, John, eds. *Issues in Business & Society*. 2d ed. New York: Random House, 1977.

Stobaugh, Robert B., and Associates. *U.S. Multinational Enterprises and the U.S. Economy*. Boston: Harvard Business School, 1972.

Stone, Christopher D. *Where the Law Ends: The Social Control of Corporate Behavior.* New York: Harper and Row, Publishers, 1975.

Sturdivant, Frederick D. *Business and Society: A Managerial Approach.* Rev. ed. Homewood, Ill.: Richard D. Irwin, 1981.

————, ed. *The Ghetto Marketplace.* New York: The Free Press, 1969.

Subcommittee on Labor of the Committee on Labor and Public Welfare, United States Senate. *Compilation of Selected Labor Laws Pertaining to Labor Relations, Part II.* Washington, D.C.: Government Printing Office, 1974.

Sutherland, Edwin H. *White Collar Crime.* New York: Dryden Press, 1949.

Sutton, Francis X.; Harris, Seymour E.; Kaysen, Carl; and Tobin, James. *The American Business Creed.* Cambridge, Mass.: Harvard University Press, 1956.

Swartz, Edward M. *Toys That Don't Care.* Boston: Gambit, Inc., 1971.

Taussig, F. W., and Joslyn, C. S. *American Business Leaders.* New York: Macmillan, 1932.

Tawney, R. H. *Religion and the Rise of Capitalism.* London: Murphy, 1929.

Terkel, Studs. *Working: People Talk about What They Do All Day and How They Feel about What They Do.* New York: Pantheon Books, 1972.

Thomas, Ralph L. *Policies Underlying Corporate Giving.* Englewood Cliffs, N.J.: Prentice-Hall, 1966.

Tillett, Anthony; Kempner, Thomas; and Wills, Gordon, eds. *Management Thinkers.* Baltimore: Penguin Books, Inc., 1970.

Toffler, Alvin. *Future Shock.* New York: Random House, 1970.

Towle, Joseph W., ed. *Ethics and Standards in American Business.* Boston: Houghton Mifflin Co., 1964.

Truman, David. *The Governmental Process.* New York: Alfred A. Knopf, 1951.

Tucker, W. T. *The Social Context of Economic Behavior.* New York: Holt, Rinehart and Winston, 1964.

Tugendhat, Christopher. *The Multinationals.* New York: Random House, 1972.

Turner, James C. *The Chemical Feast: The Nader Report.* New York: Grossman Publishers, 1970.

Turner, Louis. *Multinational Companies and the Third World.* New York: Hill & Wang, 1973.

U.S. Department of Labor. *Growth of Labor Law in the United States.* Washington, D.C.: Government Printing Office, 1967.

U.S. Equal Employment Opportunity Commission. *Affirmative Action and Equal Employment: A Guidebook for Employers.* 2 vols. Washington, D.C.: U.S. Government Printing Office, 1974.

Van Tassel, Alfred J., ed. *Our Environment: The Outlook for 1980.* Lexington, Mass.: D. C. Heath and Co., 1973.

Vaupel, James W., and Curhan, Joan P. *The Making of Multinational Enterprise.* Boston: Division of Research, Graduate School of Business, Harvard University, 1969.

Vernon, Raymond. *Sovereignty at Bay: The Spread of U.S. Enterprise.* New York: Basic Books, 1973.

Vogel, David. "The Corporate Board: Membership and Public Pressure." *Executive*, vol. 3, no. 3 (Spring 1977), pp. 8–11.

_____. *Lobbying the Corporations: Citizen Challenges to Business Authority*. New York: Basic Books, 1978.

Votaw, Dow. *Modern Corporations*. Englewood Cliffs, N.J.: Prentice-Hall, 1965.

_____, and Sethi, S. Prakash. *The Corporate Dilemma: Traditional Values versus Contemporary Problems*. Englewood Cliffs, N.J.: Prentice-Hall, 1973.

Wachtel, Howard M. *Workers' Management and Workers' Wages in Yugoslavia*. Ithaca, N.Y.: Cornell University Press, 1971.

Wade, Michael. *Flexible Working Hours in Practice*. New York: John Wiley and Sons, 1973.

Walton, Clarence C. *Corporate Social Responsibilities*. Belmont, Calif.: Wadsworth Publishing Co., 1967.

_____. *Ethos and the Executive*. Englewood Cliffs, N.J.: Prentice-Hall, 1969.

_____, ed. *Business and Social Progress*. New York: Frederick A. Praeger, 1970.

Walton, Scott, D. *American Business and Its Environment*. New York: Macmillan, 1966.

Warner, W. Lloyd, and Abegglen, James C. *Big Business Leaders in America*. New York: Harper & Brothers, 1955.

Wasson, Chester; Sturdivant, Frederick D.; and McConaughy, David H. *Competition and Human Behavior*. New York: Appleton-Century-Crofts, 1968.

Watson, John H., III. *20 Company-Sponsored Foundations: Programs and Policies*. New York: The Conference Board, 1970.

Wattell, Harold L., ed. *Voluntarism and the Business Community*. Hempstead, N.Y.: Holstra University Yearbook of Business, 1971.

Weber, Max. *The Protestant Ethic and the Spirit of Capitalism*. New York: Scribner, 1963.

Wiebe, Robert H. *Businessmen and Reform: A Study of the Progressive Movement*. Cambridge, Mass.: Harvard University Press, 1962.

_____. *The Search for Order: 1877–1920*. New York: Hill and Wang, Inc., 1967.

Weinstein, James. *The Corporate Ideal in the Liberal State, 1900–1918*. Boston: Beacon Press, 1978.

Weisband, Edward, and Franck, Thomas. *Resignation in Protest: Political and Ethical Choices between Loyalty to Team and Loyalty to Conscience in American Public Life*. New York: Grossman Publishers, 1975.

Welch, Patrick, J. "Social Responsibility, Semantics, and Why We Can't Agree on What We Agree On." *Business and Society*, vol. 18, no. 2 (Spring 1978), p. 38.

Whisenhunt, Donald W. *The Environment and the American Experience: A Historian Looks at the Ecological Crisis*. Port Washington, N.Y.: Kennikat Press, 1974.

White House Conference on the Industrial World Ahead. *A Look at Business in 1990*. Washington, D.C.: U.S. Government Printing Office, 1972.

Wilkins, Mira. *The Emergence of Multinational Enterprise: American Business abroad from the Colonial Era to 1914*. Cambridge, Mass.: Harvard University Press, 1970.

_____. *The Maturing of Multinational Enterprise: American Business Abroad, 1914 to 1970*. Cambridge, Mass.: Harvard University Press, 1973.

Williams, Pierce, and Croxton, Frederick E. *Corporate Contributions to Organized Community Welfare Sources*. New York: National Bureau of Economic Research, Inc., 1930.

Williamson, Oliver E. *Corporate Control and Business Behavior*. Englewood Cliffs, N.J.: Prentice-Hall, 1970.

Wilson, Ian H. *Corporate Environments of the Future*. New York: The President's Association, Special Study no. 61, 1976.

Woods, Barbara, ed. *Eco-Solutions*. Cambridge, Mass.: Schenkman Publishing Co., 1972.

Work in America: Report of a Special Task Force to the Secretary of Health, Education, and Welfare. Cambridge, Mass.: The MIT Press, 1973.

Zeigler, Harmon. *Interest Groups in American Society*. Englewood Cliffs, N.J.: Prentice-Hall, 1964.

Zeitlin, Maurice. "Corporate Ownership and Control: The Large Corporation and the Capitalist Class." *American Journal of Sociology*, vol. 79 (March 1974), pp. 1073–1119.

Index

*This book has been set VIP, in 10 and 9 point
Palatino, leaded 2 points. Part numbers are 24 point
Korinna Bold and part titles are 18 point Korinna
Bold. Case titles are 14 point Korinna. The size of the
type page is 26 by 45½ picas.*